BLACKSTONE'S GUIDE TO

The Mental Health Act 2007

BLACKSTONE'S GUIDE TO

The Mental Health Act 2007

Paul Bowen

OXFORD
UNIVERSITY PRESS

OXFORD

UNIVERSITY PRESS

Great Clarendon Street, Oxford OX2 6DP

Oxford University Press is a department of the University of Oxford.
It furthers the University's objective of excellence in research, scholarship,
and education by publishing worldwide in

Oxford New York

Auckland Cape Town Dar es Salaam Hong Kong Karachi
Kuala Lumpur Madrid Melbourne Mexico City Nairobi
New Delhi Shanghai Taipei Toronto

With offices in

Argentina Austria Brazil Chile Czech Republic France Greece
Guatemala Hungary Italy Japan Poland Portugal Singapore
South Korea Switzerland Thailand Turkey Ukraine Vietnam

Oxford is a registered trade mark of Oxford University Press
in the UK and in certain other countries

Published in the United States
by Oxford University Press Inc., New York

British Library Cataloguing in Publication Data

Data available

Library of Congress Cataloging-in-publication Data

Bowen, Paul, LLB
    Blackstone's guide to the Mental Health Act 2007 / Paul Bowen.
    p. cm. — (Blackstone's guide)
    Includes bibliographical references and index.
    ISBN 978-0-19-921711-3 (pbk. : alk. paper) 1. Mentally ill—Commitment
and detention—England. 2. Mentally ill—Commitment and detention—
Wales. 3. Capacity and disability—England. 4. Capacity and disability—
Wales. 5. Mental health laws—England. 6. Mental health laws—Wales.
I. Title. II. Title: Guide to the Mental Health Act 2007.
    KD737.B69 2007
    344.4204′4—dc22

                                                          2007048034

Typeset by Cepha Imaging Private Ltd, Bangalore, India
Printed in Great Britain
on acid-free paper by
Ashford Colour Press Limited, Gosport, Hampshire

ISBN 978-0-19-921711-3

1 3 5 7 9 10 8 6 4 2

For Mimi, Lily, and Ned

Foreword

Those who practise or sit in the Administrative Court or the Family Division will know the author of this important and invaluable book to be a skilful and tenacious advocate in mental health and mental care cases. Those who use the book—and I hope they will read it and not merely dip into it—will benefit enormously from his detailed knowledge and illuminating analysis of an area of law which is as technically complex as it is socially important.

For those who might wonder how an amending statute can require some 290 pages of explanation, the author explains with engaging frankness in his opening paragraph that the title is a little misleading. The book, as he explains, is really about the Mental Health Act 1983 and the Mental Capacity Act 2005 as they have been amended by the Mental Health Act 2007.

He tells us of the background to the 2007 Act, illuminating both the longer historical perspective and the more recent legislative history. He explains the law both as it was, set out in the original statutes, and as it is (or will be) when the new Act comes into force. He explains how the various statutory regimes—the 1983 Act dealing primarily with the detention for treatment of the mentally ill and the 2005 Act dealing primarily with the care of the mentally incapacitated—inter-relate with the inherent jurisdiction of the Family Division. Human rights, and the impact in particular of Articles 5 and 8 of the Convention for the Protection of Human Rights and Fundamental Freedoms, receive close and welcome attention, as does the decision of the Strasbourg court in *HL v United Kingdom*, the spur—and not before time—to the creation of the regime set out in the new Schedules A1 and 1A to the amended 2005 Act. It is a welcome feature of the analysis that at all stages he considers how the legislation impacts on children, helpfully and appropriately distinguishing for this purpose between those under the age of 16 and those who are 16 or 17.

He debates whether the amendments to the 1983 Act—the redefinition of 'mental disorder' and the replacement of the previous 'treatability' test in particular—will prove to have the undesirable consequences that many feared. Generally speaking he is inclined to be reassuring. Giving food for thought—and no doubt the material for future arguments and judgments—he canvasses the possibility of challenges under the Human Rights Act 1998. Noting that the inherent jurisdiction has continued to develop since it was enshrined in the 2005 Act, and that in consequence the jurisdiction of the Family Division seemingly extends further than the entirely statutory jurisdiction of the Court of Protection, he speculates as to the future development of the two parallel regimes. Not the least of the many invaluable features of the book is the interesting and important final chapter, where he helpfully and lucidly explains the interface between the 2005 Act and the 1983 Act.

Of great practical utility, the two Acts are printed showing both the words deleted and the words added by the 2007 Act, so one can compare at a glance the 'old' and the 'new' text.

Paul Bowen is to be commended and congratulated for the great service he has done us all. I hope and expect that his book will have the success it deserves.

James Munby
6 September 2006

Preface

The Mental Health Act 2007 obtained Royal Assent on 19 July 2007. The reform process began nearly nine years earlier, with the appointment of the Expert Committee under Professor Genevra Richardson in October 1998. One Expert Committee Report, one Green Paper, one White Paper, two Joint Parliamentary Committee reports, three Bills, three reports from the Joint Committee on Human Rights (JCHR), one national campaign, countless research papers, submissions, meetings, rallies, and several Secretaries of State later, has it all been worth it? Many would say it has not. 'A missed opportunity for legislation fit for the 21st century', according to the Mental Health Alliance in its final verdict on the Act, delivered in August 2007. It is hard not to agree.

The 2007 Act is a hotchpotch of provisions amending, rather than replacing (as was originally intended), the Mental Health Act 1983, which still looks dated but now has the added vice of being exponentially more difficult to understand. Key recommendations from the Expert Committee, the JCHR, the Joint Parliamentary Committee, the House of Lords, and stakeholders represented by the Mental Health Alliance which would have given greater prominence to patient autonomy and human rights were not adopted. Any improvements in the final version of the Act were hard won by parliamentarians supported by the tireless campaigners of the Mental Health Alliance.

The 2007 Act also amends the Mental Capacity Act 2005, an elegant piece of legislative architecture which has almost doubled in size with the addition of the decidedly inelegant Schedules A1 and 1A. Conceived as a measure to safeguard the human rights of some of society's most vulnerable people following the cases of *Bournewood* and *HL v United Kingdom*, the 'standard' and 'urgent' authorization procedure in Schedules A1 and 1A instead represents the new triumph of legalism, the provisions so labyrinthine and bureaucratic that those responsible for administering them are likely to take every opportunity to avoid using them.

Still, this is the legislation we have, so we had better get used to it. As I explain in Chapter 1, Part I of the book (Chapters 1 to 7) focuses on the amendments to the 1983 Act. Some analysis of the law as it currently stands has been necessary in order to explain the impact of the changes, but this part of the book is not intended to be a complete analysis of the 1983 Act. Part II (Chapters 8 to 15), on the other hand, is intended to provide an overview of the law relating to personal welfare decision-making on behalf of incapacitated adults and children, as the amendments to the 2005 Act cannot be understood without an explanation of the 2005 Act as it came into force on 1 October 2007 and the common law principles upon which it is based. For reasons of space the Mental Capacity Act Code of Practice is not included but reference is made to its provisions where appropriate. Part II does not deal with the provisions of the 2005 Act governing property and affairs, which are not affected by the 2007 Act.

The 1983 Act and 2005 Act need to be read and understood together, particularly after the amendments of the 2007 Act take effect. Wherever possible in the text I have cross-referred the relevant provisions of the two Acts and sought to explain how they interrelate, particularly in Chapter 15. The two Acts, as amended, are also reproduced as Appendices 1 and 2, with the deleted text and the amended text indicated, so that practitioners may see at a glance how the provisions have changed. These versions are reproduced from those produced by the Department of Health Mental Health Bill team, and my thanks to Richard Rook and his colleagues for producing these and for their permission in reproducing them. The 2007 Act is also reproduced as Appendix 3, *except* those provisions which have amended the 1983 Act or the 2005 Act. I have taken that decision for reasons of space and because those provisions of the 2007 Act are unintelligible in isolation. Where amendments have been made to the text of the 1983 Act or 2005 Act, the relevant amending provision of the 2007 Act is, however, indicated.

It is anticipated that the key parts of the 2007 Act amending the 1983 Act will come into force in October 2008 while the main amendments to the 2005 Act will come into force in April 2009, although some provisions have already been brought into force, for which see para 1.49. On 10 September 2007 the Ministry of Justice published a draft addendum to the Mental Capacity Act Code of Practice on the 'Deprivation of Liberty Safeguards' and draft secondary legislation on the appointment of Schedule A1 assessors and Part 10 representatives for consultation which closes on 2 December 2007. References are made to these as appropriate in Part II. On 25 October 2007 the Department of Health published a new draft Mental Health Act Code of Practice and draft secondary legislation governing the appointment, functions, and qualifications of IMHAs, ACs, and AMHPs. The consultation period closes in 24 January 2008, but the timing of publication is such that I have been able to make only passing reference to these in the text.

Any mistakes, whether in the text of the book or appendices, are my responsibility. Any corrections will be gratefully received.

Paul Bowen
Doughty Street Chambers
p.bowen@doughtystreet.co.uk

October 2007

About the Author

Paul Bowen is a barrister at Doughty Street Chambers in London. He specializes in public law (judicial review) and human rights law, particularly in the areas of health-care, community care, and mental health, with a particular interest in the rights of children and adults with disabilities. Paul has been in many of the leading cases in healthcare and human rights, including *HL v United Kingdom* in the European Court of Human Rights and a number of cases in the House of Lords (*Munjaz*, *R (MH) v Secretary of State for Health*, *Von Brandenburg*, and *Bournewood*). He has been a committee member of the Law Society Mental Health & Disability Committee since 2001 and has been actively involved in the Mental Health Act reform process from the outset, giving evidence on behalf of the Bar Council to the Joint Parliamentary Committee on the Mental Health Bill 2004, and appearing before the House of Commons Committee on the Mental Health Bill 2007. He writes and lectures regularly and is a member of the editorial Advisory Board of the Community Care Law Reports.

Acknowledgments

I should acknowledge and thank, first, Sir James Munby for giving up a good deal of his summer vacation to read a first draft of the book and for his gracious foreword; Anna Edmundson and Sophy Miles, who wrote, respectively, the section on Victims Rights in Chapter 7 and the section on making an application in the Court of Protection in Chapter 14; Helen Kingston for her speedy but careful read-through of a later draft and for her invaluable insights; John Horne, for putting us in touch; Kathryn Pugh and Camilla Parker for their very helpful suggestions on early drafts of Chapters 5 and 6 on how the 2007 Act will affect children; Rowena Daw and Tim Spencer-Lane, who generously shared their considerable experience as Vice-Chair of the Mental Health Alliance and co-Chair of the Alliance's policy group; and Jane Kavanagh, Kathryn Grant, Jodi Towler, and the rest of the team at OUP for all their hard work in bringing the book to fruition.

My thanks also to friends and colleagues with whom I have worked on mental health and mental capacity issues over the last 14 years, particularly Lucy Scott-Moncrieff, who has championed the rights of those with mental disorder for over thirty years, Mary Purcell, Saimo Chahal, and Robert Robinson, to name but a few. Special thanks to those that have provided inspiration, both personal and professional, particularly my parents Hank and Juliet Bowen, my grandmother Susan Ouvry, Michael Nightingale, Graham and Wendy Enderby, Edward Fitzgerald QC, Richard Gordon QC, and my friends and colleagues at Doughty Street Chambers. And to my lovely Mimi, Lily, and Ned, thank you for putting it all into perspective.

Contents—Summary

TABLE OF CASES   xxix

TABLE OF STATUTES   xxxv

TABLE OF SECONDARY LEGISLATION   li

CODES OF PRACTICE   lv

LIST OF TERMS AND ABBREVIATIONS   lvii

PART I: REFORM OF THE MENTAL HEALTH ACT 1983

1. INTRODUCTION   3

2. OVERVIEW OF THE 1983 ACT AND ITS AMENDMENTS   25

3. AMENDMENTS TO THE CRITERIA FOR
   GUARDIANSHIP AND DETENTION UNDER THE
   MENTAL HEALTH ACT 1983   33

4. ADDITIONAL SAFEGUARDS FOR PATIENTS IN
   RELATION TO ADMISSION AND DETENTION   57

5. SUPERVISED COMMUNITY TREATMENT   71

6. MEDICAL TREATMENT FOR MENTAL DISORDER
   UNDER THE 1983 ACT   95

7. OTHER AMENDMENTS   131

PART II: THE MENTAL CAPACITY ACT 2005
AND ITS AMENDMENTS

8. INTRODUCTION AND OVERVIEW   143

9. CARE AND TREATMENT AT COMMON LAW   151

10. CARE AND TREATMENT WITHOUT DETENTION
    UNDER THE MENTAL CAPACITY ACT 2005   165

11. DETENTION FOR CARE AND TREATMENT
    UNDER THE 2005 ACT   195

12. STANDARD AND URGENT AUTHORIZATIONS   215

13. REPRESENTATION OF SCHEDULE A1 DETAINEES   243

14. THE COURT OF PROTECTION, THE PUBLIC GUARDIAN,
    AND COURT OF PROTECTION VISITORS   257

15. THE INTERFACE BETWEEN THE DETENTION
    AND TREATMENT REGIMES AFTER THE 2007 ACT:
    THE 1983 ACT, 2005 ACT, AND COMMON LAW   273

APPENDIX 1. Mental Health Act 1983   295
APPENDIX 2. Mental Capacity Act 2005   441
APPENDIX 3. Mental Health Act 2007   538
APPENDIX 4. The Standard Authorization Procedure Under Schedule A1
            of the 2005 Act   571

INDEX   573

Contents—Detailed

TABLE OF CASES	xxix
TABLE OF STATUTES	xxxv
TABLE OF SECONDARY LEGISLATION	li
CODES OF PRACTICE	lv
LIST OF TERMS AND ABBREVIATIONS	lvii

PART I: REFORM OF THE MENTAL HEALTH ACT 1983

1. INTRODUCTION

A. Structure of the Book	1.01
1. Part I: Reform of the Mental Health Act 1983	1.02
2. Part II: The Mental Capacity Act 2005 and its Amendments	1.03
B. The Background to the 2007 Act	1.04
C. A Brief History of Mental Health Legislation	1.17
1. The Origins of Mental Health Law	1.18
2. Statutory Regulation of Detention Begins	1.20
3. The Lunacy Act 1890 and the Triumph of 'Legalism'	1.23
4. The Pendulum Swings: the Rise of 'Informality' and the 1930 and 1959 Acts	1.26
5. The Development of a Human Rights Discourse: the 1982 and 1983 Acts	1.27
6. Developments Since 1983: the Human Rights Act 1998	1.30
D. The 2007 Act: the Pendulum Swings Again?	1.34
E. Human Rights	1.38
1. The Convention Rights and Other International Standards	1.38
2. The Human Rights Act 1998	1.44
3. The Joint Parliamentary Committee on Human Rights (JCHR)	1.45
4. The Compatibility of the 2007 Act with the Convention Rights	1.48
F. Commencement and Transitional Provisions	1.49
G. Territorial Extent: England and Wales	1.52

2. OVERVIEW OF THE 1983 ACT AND ITS AMENDMENTS

A. Introduction	2.01
B. Informal Admission	2.03
C. Civil and Criminal Powers of Detention	2.04
D. Community Patients	2.06
E. The Nearest Relative	2.08
F. The Definition of Mental Disorder and Exclusions	2.10

G. The Criteria for Guardianship and Detention   2.11

H. Medical Treatment   2.13

I. Discharge of Detained Patients   2.15

J. The Mental Health Review Tribunal   2.17

K. Aftercare   2.20

L. The Code of Practice   2.22

M. The Mental Health Act Commission   2.24

N. The Admission, Detention, and Treatment of Children   2.25

3. AMENDMENTS TO THE CRITERIA FOR GUARDIANSHIP
AND DETENTION UNDER THE MENTAL HEALTH ACT 1983

A. Key Features   3.00

B. Overview of the Current Criteria for Guardianship and Detention   3.01
   1. The Current 'Mental Disorder' Test   3.06
   2. The 'Appropriateness' Test   3.14
   3. The 'Treatability' Test   3.19
   4. The 'Health or Safety' Test   3.22
   5. The 'Self-neglect or Serious Exploitation' Test   3.27

C. The Current Definition of 'Mental Disorder'   3.29
   1. The Four Classifications of Mental Disorder: s 1(2)   3.30
   2. The Legal Significance of Classification   3.31
   3. 'Mental Impairment' and 'Severe Mental Impairment'   3.38
   4. 'Psychopathic Disorder'   3.41
   5. 'Abnormally Aggressive or Seriously Irresponsible Behaviour'   3.44
   6. Exclusions from the Definition of 'Mental Disorder'   3.47

D. The Current 'Treatability' Requirement   3.49
   1. Historical Development of the 'Treatability Test'   3.51
   2. Importation of the Treatability Test into the Tribunal's Test for Discharge   3.53
   3. The Meaning of 'Treatability' and 'Medical Treatment'   3.54
   4. The Impetus for Change   3.57

E. The New Definition of 'Mental Disorder'   3.58
   1. A Wider Definition of Mental Disorder   3.59
   2. The Removal of the Classifications of Mental Disorder   3.61
   3. Repeal of the Exclusion for Promiscuity or Other Immoral Conduct or Sexual
      Deviancy   3.62

F. The New Exception for Persons with 'Learning Disability'   3.63

G. The New 'Appropriate Treatment' Replaces 'Treatability' Test   3.66

H. Definition of 'Appropriate Treatment'   3.71

I. 'Medical Treatment' and the New 'Treatability' Test   3.72

J. Implications of the Amendments   3.75
   1. The New Definition of Mental Disorder and Removal of the
      Classifications of Disorder   3.77

2. Removal of the Exclusions for Sexual Deviancy etc   3.88
3. New Exception for 'Learning Disabled'   3.92
4. The Current and New Tests for 'Treatability' and the New
   'Appropriate Treatment' Test   3.93
5. Further Observations: Global Effect of the Amendments   3.101
6. A Charter for Preventive Detention?   3.105

K. Missed Opportunities: 'Impaired Judgment'   3.109

4. ADDITIONAL SAFEGUARDS FOR PATIENTS IN
   RELATION TO ADMISSION AND DETENTION

A. Key Features   4.00

B. The Code of Practice and the Fundamental Principles   4.01
1. New Duty to 'Have Regard' to the Code   4.02
2. The 'Fundamental Principles'   4.12

C. Amendments to the Nearest Relative Provisions   4.16
1. The Role of the Nearest Relative   4.16
2. Flaws in the Current Law   4.17
3. The Amendments in the 2007 Act   4.20

D. The Mental Health Review Tribunal   4.24
1. Tribunal Reorganization   4.27
2. Hospital Managers' Duties to Refer   4.28
3. Conditionally Discharged Patients on s 45A Hospital and
   Limitation Directions   4.32

E. Independent Mental Health Advocates ('IMHAs')   4.33
1. Appointment of IMHAs for 'Qualifying Patients'   4.34
2. Duties of the 'Responsible Person'   4.37
3. Functions of IMHAs   4.38
4. Withholding of Correspondence with IMHA   4.42

F. Additional Safeguards for the Admission and Detention of Children   4.43
1. Capable Child of 16 or 17 Cannot be Admitted Informally Without Consent   4.44
2. Duty to Place Child in a Suitable Environment   4.45
3. Duty of PCT or Health Authority to Give Information about Specialist
   Facilities for Children   4.50
4. Hospital Managers' Duty to Refer Case to the Tribunal   4.53

G. The Mental Health Act Commission   4.54

5. SUPERVISED COMMUNITY TREATMENT

A. Key Features   5.00

B. Introduction   5.01

C. Existing Forms of Community Treatment Compared   5.07
1. Release on s 17 Leave of Absence   5.08
2. Supervised Discharge   5.12
3. Guardianship   5.19

D. Making a Community Treatment Order: s 17A 5.23
   1. Who May Make a CTO 5.23
   2. When a CTO Must Be Considered 5.25
   3. Who May Be Made the Subject of a CTO 5.26
   4. Who May Not Be Made the Subject of a CTO 5.27
   5. Criteria for Making a CTO: s 17A(5) 5.30

E. Conditions that May Be Imposed on a CTO: s 17B 5.33

F. Effect of SCT: s 17D 5.38

G. Duration, Extension, Expiry, and Discharge 5.42
   1. Duration and Extension: ss 17C and 20A 5.42
   2. Discharge Under s 23 5.45
   3. Discharge by the Tribunal Under s 72 5.47
   4. The Application for Admission for Treatment 'Otherwise Ceases
      to Have Effect' 5.55
   5. Effect of Expiry of CTO: s 20B(1) 5.59

H. Recall of Community Patients 5.60
   1. Criteria for Recall: s 17E 5.60
   2. Effect of Recall: s 17F 5.63

I. Revocation 5.66
   1. Criteria for Revocation: s 17F(4) 5.66
   2. Effect of Revocation: s 17G 5.68

J. Return of Community Patients Absent Without Leave 5.70
   1. Power to Return a Recalled Community Patient to Hospital: s 18 5.70
   2. Provisions Applying to All Recalled Community Patients Who Are AWOL 5.71
   3. Recalled Community Patient AWOL After his Return to Hospital 5.77

K. Aftercare 5.79

L. The Mental Health Act Commission 5.82

M. Human Rights Implications 5.83
   1. Article 5 5.83
   2. Article 8 5.87
   3. SCT Compared with Long-term s 17 Leave 5.89

6. MEDICAL TREATMENT FOR MENTAL DISORDER
UNDER THE 1983 ACT

A. Key Features 6.00

B. Summary of the Existing Legal Framework: Part 4 of the 1983 Act 6.01
   1. The Meaning of 'Medical Treatment' and the 'Treatability Test' 6.02
   2. Section 63: Treatment Provided By or Under the Direction of the
      Responsible Clinician 6.06
   3. Section 57: Irreversible Treatment 6.10
   4. Section 58: Medication and ECT 6.12
   5. Section 62: Emergency Treatment 6.16
   6. Other Provisions of Part 4 6.18

C. Amendments to Part 4   6.21
    1. The New 'Appropriate Treatment' Test   6.21
    2. Extending Clinical Responsibilities to Other Professionals   6.34
    3. Patients to whom Part 4 Applies: New s 56   6.37
    4. Other Amendments   6.38

D. Additional Safeguards for ECT: s 58A   6.42
    1. Summary of the New Safeguards   6.42
    2. Patients with Capacity or Competence   6.44
    3. Patients Lacking Capacity   6.51
    4. Section 62: Urgent Treatment with ECT   6.57

E. Medical Treatment of Community Patients: Part 4A   6.58
    1. Introduction   6.58
    2. Overview of the New Part 4A Procedure   6.64
    3. The Conditions for Administering 'Relevant Treatment': 'Authority to
       Treat' and the 'Certificate Requirement', s 64B(2) and s 64E(2)   6.66
    4. Child Community Patients   6.67
    5. 'Relevant Treatment': s 64A   6.70
    6. 'Authority to Treat'   6.71
    7. 's 58 Type and s 58A Type Treatment' and 'the Certificate Requirement'   6.90

F. Treatment of Recalled Community Patients   6.108
    1. Introduction   6.108
    2. Community Patients who Cannot be Treated Under Part 4A   6.109
    3. Part 4 Applies to Recalled Community Patients: s 56(4)   6.110
    4. Section 62A: Part 4A Certificates Continue to Have Effect After
       Recall or Revocation   6.111

G. The Interface between the 1983 Act and the 2005 Act   6.117

H. Human Rights Implications   6.120
    1. Article 3 Principles   6.120
    2. Article 8 Principles   6.125
    3. Human Rights Implications of the 2007 Amendments   6.133

7. OTHER AMENDMENTS

A. Key Features   7.00

B. Extending Professional Responsibilities   7.01
    1. 'Responsible Clinician' to Replace 'Responsible Medical Officer'   7.03
    2. Medical Recommendations for Detention and Renewals of Detention   7.06
    3. 'Approved Social Worker' Replaced by 'Approved Mental Health Professional'   7.18
    4. Avoiding Conflicts of Interest   7.22

C. Discharge by Hospital Managers Under s 23   7.24

D. Patients Concerned in Criminal Proceedings   7.25
    1. The Removal of Time-limited Restriction Orders   7.27
    2. Extension of Scope of Hospital and Limitation Directions   7.29

E. Offences   7.31

F. Transfer of Patients to and from Scotland etc   7.32

G. Detention in a Place of Safety   7.33

H. Victims' Rights   7.34
   1. Introduction   7.34
   2. 'Victim'   7.35
   3. Current Scope of the 2004 Act   7.36
   4. Amendments Introduced by the 2007 Act   7.38

PART II: THE MENTAL CAPACITY ACT 2005 AND ITS AMENDMENTS

8. INTRODUCTION AND OVERVIEW

A. Introduction   8.01

B. The History of the 2005 Act   8.05
   1. History of Incapacity Legislation   8.05
   2. The Need for Reform Identified   8.10
   3. Government Proposals for Reform and Legislative History of the 2005 Act   8.14

C. Structure of the 2005 Act   8.15

D. *Bournewood*   8.17

E. The 2007 Act and 'Schedule A1'   8.22

F. The Interface between the 1983 Act and the 2005 Act   8.23

9. CARE AND TREATMENT AT COMMON LAW

A. Key Features   9.00

B. Care and Treatment of Adults at Common Law   9.01

C. Bodily Integrity and Autonomy   9.03

D. Capacity and Incapacity at Common Law   9.06

E. Necessity and 'Best Interests'   9.10
   1. The Doctrine of Necessity   9.12
   2. 'Best Interests'   9.13
   3. Best Interests: Some Unresolved Issues   9.16

F. The Nature of the Courts' Jurisdiction at Common Law   9.19
   1. The Demise and the Rise of the High Court's Inherent Jurisdiction   9.19
   2. The Inherent Jurisdiction: Limitations and Unresolved Issues   9.22

G. Children Under 16   9.25
   1. Key Distinctions between Adults and Children Under 16   9.25
   2. Consent and the Right of Autonomy   9.27
   3. The Jurisdiction of the High Court in Relation to Children Under 16   9.31

H. Children Aged 16 and 17   9.36

10. CARE AND TREATMENT WITHOUT DETENTION
    UNDER THE MENTAL CAPACITY ACT 2005
    A. Key Features   10.00
    B. Who the Act Applies To   10.01
    C. Children Aged 16 or 17   10.03
    D. Children Under 16   10.07
    E. The Principles: s 1   10.10
    F. Capacity: ss 2 and 3   10.11
    G. Best Interests: s 4   10.15
    H. The Hierarchy of Substituted Decision-making   10.18
    I. Advance Decisions to Refuse Treatment   10.20
       1. 'Advance Directives' to Refuse Treatment at Common Law   10.20
       2. Advance Decisions to Refuse Treatment Under the 2005 Act   10.21
    J. Lasting Powers of Attorney   10.35
       1. Nature and Effect of a Lasting Power of Attorney   10.35
       2. The Donee's Powers   10.38
       3. Limitations on the Donee's Powers   10.43
       4. Making a Lasting Power of Attorney   10.44
       5. Revocation of an LPA   10.48
       6. Jurisdiction of the Court of Protection in Relation to Lasting
          Powers of Attorney   10.50
    K. Personal Welfare Decisions by the Court of Protection   10.54
       1. The Court's Jurisdiction in Personal Welfare Matters   10.54
       2. Limitations of the Court's Jurisdiction in Personal Welfare Matters 10.56
    L. Court-appointed Deputies   10.57
    M. Acts in Connection with Care and Treatment: s 5   10.59
    N. Life-sustaining etc Treatment   10.61
       1. Special Status for Life-sustaining etc Treatment   10.61
       2. Restrictions on Acts Intended to End Life   10.62
    O. Restraint and the Use of Force   10.66
    P. Deprivations of Liberty   10.69
    Q. Excluded Decisions   10.70
       1. Family Relationships   10.70
       2. Mental Health Matters: Interface between the Treatment Provisions of
          the 2005 Act and the 1983 Act   10.71
       3. Voting   10.74
       4. Medical Research   10.75
    R. Ill-treatment or Neglect   10.76
    S. Independent Mental Capacity Advocates (IMCAs)   10.78
       1. Appointment of IMCAs   10.79
       2. Functions of IMCAs   10.86

T. The Code of Practice Under the 2005 Act   10.89
    1. Lord Chancellor's Duty to Prepare and Issue Codes of Practice   10.89
    2. Duty to Have Regard to the Code of Practice   10.92
    3. Relevance of the Code of Practice in Criminal or Civil Proceedings   10.93

11. DETENTION FOR CARE AND TREATMENT UNDER
    THE 2005 ACT

A. Key Features   11.00
B. Detention at Common Law: 'Bournewood'   11.01
    1. Overview of the Bournewood Case   11.01
    2. The Facts of the Case   11.04
    3. The Judicial Review and Habeas Corpus Proceedings   11.08
    4. The Decision of the House of Lords   11.09
C. *HL v United Kingdom*   11.13
    1. 'Deprivation of Liberty'   11.14
    2. Article 5(1): Not 'in Accordance with a Procedure Prescribed by Law'   11.15
    3. Article 5(4)   11.19
D. 'Deprivation of Liberty'   11.21
    1. The Three Elements of 'Deprivation of Liberty'   11.23
    2. Factors to Consider in Determining whether there is a Deprivation
       of Liberty   11.28
    3. Deprivations of Liberty in Private Care Homes   11.33
E. Detention under the 2005 Act Prior to Amendment   11.35
    1. Detention May Only be Authorized by the Court of Protection under s 16 11.35
    2. Detention Must be Authorized in Advance   11.36
    3. Interface between the Detaining Provisions of the 1983 Act and
       the 2005 Act Before the 2007 Act is in Force   11.37
F. Amendments Introduced by the 2007 Act   11.38
G. Standard and Urgent Authorizations: Sch A1   11.40
    1. Standard Authorizations   11.40
    2. Urgent Authorizations   11.41
H. Detention for Life-saving Treatment: s 4B   11.42
I. The Role of the Court of Protection in Decisions to Detain   11.45
    1. Decisions to Detain Under s 16 of the 2005 Act   11.45
    2. Applications Relating to Standard and Urgent Authorizations Under s 21A 11.47
    3. Other Detention Issues Under s 15   11.48
J. The Detention of Children   11.49
    1. Children Aged 16 or 17   11.50
    2. Children Under 16   11.55
K. s 47 National Assistance Act 1948   11.58

12. STANDARD AND URGENT AUTHORIZATIONS

A. Key Features — 12.00

B. The 'Managing Authority' and 'Supervisory Body' — 12.01
  1. The Managing Authority: Hospitals — 12.03
  2. The Managing Authority: Care Homes — 12.04
  3. The Supervisory Body: Hospitals — 12.05
  4. The Supervisory Body: Care Homes — 12.08
  5. Where the Managing Authority and the Supervisory Body
    are the Same Body — 12.12
  6. Other Conflicts of Interest — 12.13

C. The 'Qualifying Requirements': Part 3 — 12.14
  1. The Age Requirement — 12.15
  2. The Mental Health Requirement — 12.16
  3. The Mental Capacity Requirement — 12.18
  4. The Best Interests Requirement — 12.20
  5. The Eligibility Requirement — 12.25
  6. The 'No Refusals' Requirement — 12.26

D. The Request for a Standard Authorization — 12.29
  1. Procedure for Making a Request for a Standard Authorization — 12.29
  2. Circumstances in which Request for Standard Authorization May be Made — 12.30

E. The Assessment Process: Parts 4 and 9 — 12.41
  1. The Supervisory Body's Duty to Assess whether the Qualifying
    Requirements are Met (Sch A1, para 33) — 12.41
  2. Exception: Previous Assessment — 12.42
  3. Appointment of s 39A IMCA — 12.44
  4. The Assessments and the Assessors — 12.45
  5. Powers and Duties of the Assessors — 12.48
  6. The Mental Health Assessment: Additional Requirements — 12.50
  7. The Best Interests Assessment: Additional Requirements — 12.51
  8. Time Limits for Assessments — 12.56

F. Refusal of the Standard Authorization — 12.58

G. Grant of the Standard Authorization — 12.61

H. Review of the Standard Authorization: Part 8 — 12.62
  1. Duty to Carry Out a Review on Request by an Eligible Person — 12.62
  2. The Grounds for Review — 12.63
  3. Supervisory Body's Duty to Secure Review Assessments — 12.71
  4. Assessments Support Continuing Detention — 12.74
  5. Assessments Do Not Support Continuing Detention — 12.75
  6. Review Process Displaced by a Request for Fresh Standard Authorization — 12.76

I. Termination of the Standard Authorization — 12.78

J. Suspension of the Standard Authorization: Part 6 — 12.79

K. Renewal of the Standard Authorization — 12.81

L. Urgent Authorizations: Part 5   12.82
   1. Conditions for Making an Urgent Authorization   12.82
   2. Period of Urgent Authorization and Extensions   12.85
   3. Appointment of s 39A IMCA   12.87
   4. Formalities   12.88

M. 'Appeals' to the Court of Protection   12.89
   1. Standard Authorizations   12.89
   2. Urgent Authorizations   12.91

N. Human Rights Implications   12.93

13. REPRESENTATION OF SCHEDULE A1 DETAINEES

A. Key Features   13.00

B. s 39A IMCAs   13.01
   1. Appointment of s 39A IMCAs   13.02
   2. Functions of s 39A IMCAs   13.05

C. Part 10 Representatives   13.07
   1. Appointment etc of Representatives   13.09
   2. Functions of Part 10 Representatives   13.15

D. s 39C IMCAs   13.20
   1. Appointment of s 39C IMCAs   13.20
   2. Functions of s 39C IMCAs   13.23

E. s 39D IMCAs   13.24
   1. Appointment of s 39D IMCAs   13.24
   2. Function of s 39D IMCAs   13.28

F. Donees and Deputies   13.29
   1. Appointment of Donees and Deputies   13.30
   2. Functions of Donees and Deputies   13.33

G. Other Persons Nominated by the Detainee as a Consultee   13.35
   1. Appointment of a Nominated Person   13.37
   2. Functions of the Nominated Person   13.38

14. THE COURT OF PROTECTION, THE PUBLIC GUARDIAN, AND COURT OF PROTECTION VISITORS

A. Key Features   14.00

B. The New Court of Protection   14.01

C. Jurisdiction of the Court of Protection   14.02
   1. The Court's General Declaratory Jurisdiction: s 15   14.05
   2. Determining Questions Relating to Advance Decisions: s 26(4)   14.07
   3. Determining Questions Relating to Lasting Powers of Attorney:
      ss 22 and 23   14.08
   4. Court's Power to Make Personal Welfare Decisions: ss 16 and 17   14.09

5. Appointment of Deputies to Make Personal Welfare Decisions:
   s 16, ss 19–20   14.10
6. Determining 'Appeals' Against Urgent and Standard Authorizations: s 21A   14.11
7. Interim Orders and Directions   14.12
8. Restrictions and Limitations on the Court's Jurisdiction   14.14
9. Appeals   14.20

D. Making an Application to the Court of Protection   14.21
   1. Public Funding for Cases in the Court of Protection   14.21
   2. Making an Application in the Court of Protection   14.25
   3. Litigation Friends and Capacity to Conduct Proceedings   14.67

E. The Public Guardian   14.73

F. Court of Protection Visitors   14.75

15. THE INTERFACE BETWEEN THE DETENTION AND TREATMENT REGIMES AFTER THE 2007 ACT: THE 1983 ACT, 2005 ACT, AND COMMON LAW

A. Key Features   15.00

B. Introduction   15.01

C. Detention for Treatment for Mental Disorder   15.02
   1. General Principle: 2005 Act to be Preferred Unless 1983 Act
      Must be Used   15.03
   2. Sch 1A: Persons Ineligible to be Deprived of their Liberty
      under the 2005 Act   15.06
   3. Other Cases   15.25

D. Treatment for Mental Disorder   15.26
   1. The Relevant Treatment Provisions of the 1983 Act and the 2005 Act   15.29
   2. General Principle: 2005 Act May be Used Unless 1983 Act Must be Used   15.31
   3. Complicating Factors   15.32
   4. When Treatment Must be Administered Under the 1983 Act   15.33

E. Detention and Treatment for Physical Disorder   15.47
   1. Treatment for Physical Disorder   15.47
   2. Detention for Treatment for Physical Disorder   15.48

F. Urgent Cases   15.50
   1. Detention for Treatment for Mental Disorder   15.51
   2. Treatment for Mental Disorder Without Detention   15.57

G. Children Aged 16 or 17   15.58
   1. Does the 1983 Act Oust the Common Law Rules Relating to Children?   15.59
   2. Detention for Treatment for Mental Disorder   15.64
   3. Treatment for Mental Disorder   15.67
   4. Detention and Treatment for Physical Disorder   15.72

Contents—Detailed

H. Children Under 16   15.74
   1. Detention for Treatment for Mental Disorder   15.74
   2. Treatment for Mental Disorder   15.75
   3. Detention and Treatment for Physical Disorder   15.76

APPENDIX 1. Mental Health Act 1983   295

APPENDIX 2. Mental Capacity Act 2005   441

APPENDIX 3. Mental Health Act 2007   538

APPENDIX 4. The Standard Authorization Procedure Under Schedule A1
      of the 2005 Act   571

INDEX   573

Table of Cases

References are to Paragraph Numbers

A (Conjoined Twins), Re [2001] 1 Fam 147, CA................................. 10.65

A (Medical Treatment: Male Sterilisation), Re [2000] 1 FCR 193;
[2000] 1 FLR 549 ....9.14, 9.15

A v Harrow Crown Court [2003] EWHC 2020 (Admin); [2003] 1 MHLR 393........ 14.01

A v A Health Authority [2002] EWHC 18 (Fam); [2002] Fam 213.................. 9.22

A v Liverpool City Council [1982] AC 363 .... 9.34

A v United Kingdom (1999) 27 EHRR 611 .... 1.40

A & B v East Sussex (Manual Handling) [2003] EWHC 167 (Admin) 6.131, 10.14

Airedale NHS Trust v Bland [1993] AC 789 ....9.23, 10.65

Airey v Ireland (1979) 2 EHRR 305 .... 1.40

AK (Medical Treatment: Consent), Re [2001] 1 FLR 129 .... 10.20

Assenov v Bulgaria (1997) 28 EHRR 652 .... 1.40

B v Barking, Havering & Brentwood Community Mental Health NHS Trust
[1999] 1 FLR 106 .... 5.89

B v Croydon Health Authority [1995] Fam 133....................... 6.01, 9.11, 15.47

B v Forsey 1988 (SC HL) 28 HL(Sc)............................... 2.01, 11.02, 15.61

Bolam v Friern Hospital Management Committee [1957] 1 WLR 582 .... 9.14

Botta v Italy (1998) 26 EHRR 241 ....1.40, 6.131

C (Adult: Refusal of Medical Treatment), Re [1994] 1 WLR 290.......6.01, 9.08, 9.11, 15.47

C (Detention; Medical Treatment), Re [1997] 2 FLR 180 .... 11.50

Campbell v Secretary of State for the Home Department [1988] AC 120 .... 5.85

E v Channel Four [2005] EWHC 1144 (Fam); [2005] 2 FLR 913 .... 9.21, 14.18, 14.19

Edwards v United Kingdom (2002) 35 EHRR 19 .... 1.40

Enhorn v Sweden (2005) 41 EHRR 30 ....3.104, 12.24

F (Adult: Court's Jurisdiction), Re [2001] Fam 38 .... 8.13, 9.13, 9.21

F (Mental Health Act: Guardianship), Re [2000] 1 FLR 192..................... 3.45

F (Mental Patient: Sterilisation), Re [1990] 2 AC 1 .... 8.10, 9.03, 9.12, 9.14,
9.19, 9.23, 11.11

Gillick v West Norfolk and Wisbech Health Authority [1986] AC 112 .... 6.54, 6.68,
6.72, 9.25, 9.26, 9.28, 9.30, 11.55, 14.72, 15.74

Glass v United Kingdom (2004) 39 EHRR 15............. 6.127, 6.133, 6.134, 9.23, 15.62

Guzzardi v Italy (1980) 3 EHRR 333.. 11.24

Hadfield's Case (1800) 27 St Tr 1281.. 1.20

Hatton v United Kingdom (2003) 37 EHRR 611 .... 1.41

HE v A Hospital NHS Trust [2003] 2 FLR 408...................... 9.23, 10.20, 10.34

Herczegfalvy v Austria (1992) 15 EHRR 437...................... 6.121, 6.128, 6.138

HL v United Kingdom (2004) 40 EHRR 761 . . . . v, 1.03, 1.10, 1.12, 1.33, 1.39, 1.48,
2.03, 3.104, 8.20, 8.21, 8.22, 11.0, 11.12, 11.13–20, 11.21, 11.24, 11.25,
11.28, 11.35, 11.38, 11.51, 11.53, 15.03, 15.65
HM v Switzerland (2002) 38 EHRR 314. . . . . .11.21, 11.24, 11.25, 11.28

JE v DE (1) Surrey CC (2) [2006] EWHC 3459 (Fam); (2007)
10 CCLR 149 . . . . .11.22, 11.25, 11.29, 11.51
Johnson v United Kingdom (1997) 27 EHRR 296 . . . . 5.83
Jordan v United Kingdom (2003) 37 EHRR 2. . . . . 1.40
JT v United Kingdom [2000] 1 FLR 909. . . . . 4.18

Kay v United Kingdom (1998) 40 BMLR 20. . . . . 5.91
Keenan v United Kingdom (2001) 33 EHRR 913 . . . . 1.40

Laskey v United Kingdom (1997) 24 EHRR 39. . . . . 9.05
Lewis v Gibson [2005] EWCA Civ 587 . . . . 3.44
LLBC v TG [2007] EWHC 2640 (Fam) 11.31
A Local Authority (Inquiry: Restraint on Publication),
Re [2004] Fam 96 . . . . 9.21, 14.18, 14.19
A Local Authority v MA [2005] EWHC 2942 (Fam). 9.21, 14.17
A Local Authority v MM [2007] EWHC 2003 (Fam) 9.09, 9.22, 10.11, 10.13, 10.14

Magill v Weeks [2001] UKHL 67 . . . . 12.13
Marckx v Belgium (1979) 2 EHRR 330. . . . . 1.40
Masterman-Lister v Brutton & Co; Masterman-Lister v Jewell [2003] 1 WLR 1511 . . . . . . 9.08
Masterman-Lister v Brutton & Co (Nos 1 and 2) [2002] EWCA Civ 1889;
[2003] EWCA Civ 70; [2003] 1 WLR 1511, CA. 10.14, 14.69
MB (An Adult: Medical Treatment), Re [1997] 2 FCR 541;
[1997] 2 FLR 426, CA. 3.103, 9.08, 9.09, 9.36, 10.11, 11.50, 14.70
MC v Bulgaria (2003) 15 BHRC 627 . . . . 1.40

Neilsen v Denmark (1988) 11 EHRR 175. . . . . .11.21, 11.24, 11.51, 15.65
An NHS Trust v MB [2006] EWHC 507 (Fam); [2006] 2 FLR 319 . . . . 9.25

Oneryildiz v Turkey (2004) ECHR 48939/99 . . . . 1.40
Osman v United Kingdom (2000) 29 EHRR 245 . . . . 1.40

Portsmouth NHS Hospitals Trust v Wyatt [2004] EWHC 2247 (Fam);
[2005] 1 WLR 3995 . . . . 9.25
Practice Note (Declaratory Proceedings: Medical and welfare decisions for adults
who lack capacity) [2002] 1 WLR 325. . . . . 9.23
Pretty v United Kingdom (2002) 35 EHRR 1 . . . . 1.40, 6.126, 10.63

R (A) v Partnerships in Care Ltd [2002] EWHC 529 (Admin);
[2002] 1 WLR 2611 . . . . 11.34
R (Axon) v Secretary of State for Health (Family Planning Association intervening)
[2006] EWHC 37 (Admin); [2006] 1 QB 569 . . . . .9.30, 9.37
R (B) v Ashworth Hospital Authority [2005] UKHL 20; [2005] 2 AC 278; [2006]
1 WLR 810 . . . . 2.01, 3.36, 3.37, 3.42, 3.51, 3.78, 3.79, 3.86, 6.01, 6.121, 15.47

R (B) v Dr S [2005] EWHC 1936 (Admin)..................................9.09
R (B) v Dr S [2006] EWCA Civ 28; [2006] 1 WLR 810............. 1.32, 6.01, 6.04, 6.15,
6.121, 6.124, 15.32
R (Burke) v GMC [2005] EWCA Civ 1003;
[2006] QB 273 ....9.16, 9.17, 9.23, 10.64
R (D) v Secretary of State for the Home Department [2002] EWHC 2805
(Admin); [2003] 1 WLR 1315...1.31
R (D) v Secretary of State for the Home Department [2006]
EWCA Civ 143 ....1.40
R (Daly) v Secretary of State for the Home Department [2001] UKHL 26;
[2001] 2 AC 532 ....6.130, 10.68
R (DR) v Mersey Care NHS Trust [2002] EWHC 1810 (Admin); unreported
7 August 2002 ....5.08, 5.89
R (H) v Mental Health Review Tribunal [2002] EWHC 1522 (Admin);
[2002] QB 1 ....1.31
R (H) v Secretary of State for Health [2005] UKHL 60;
[2006] 1 AC 441 ....4.29, 12.93, 12.94
R (H) v Secretary of State for the Home Department [2003] UKHL 59;
[2004] 2 AC 253 ....5.85
R (KB) v Mental Health Review Tribunal [2003] EWHC 193 (Admin);
[2004] QB 936 ....1.31
R (M) v Secretary of State for Health [2003] EWHC 1094 (Admin);
[2003] 1 MHLR 88...1.31, 4.18
R (Munjaz) v Mersey Care NHS Trust [2003] EWCA Civ 1036;
[2004] QB 395 ....4.04
R (Munjaz) v Mersey Care NHS Trust [2005] UKHL 58; [2006]
2 AC 148 ....1.43, 4.03–11, 10.92
R (P) v Mental Health Review Tribunal [2002] EWCA Civ 697 ....3.44
R (Rayner & Marsh) v Home Secretary & Ors [2007] EWHC 1028 (Admin)............1.31
R (S) v Plymouth City Council [2002] EWCA Civ 388; [2002]
1 WLR 2583 ....4.16, 4.21
R (South West London and St George's Mental Health NHS Trust) v W [2002]
1 MHRL 292...3.98
R (Stennett) v Richmond London Borough Council [2002] UKHL 34;
[2002] 2 AC 1127 ....5.79
R (Wheldon) v Rampton Hospital Authority [2001] 1 MHLR 19.................3.57, 3.98
R (Wilkinson) v Broadmoor [2001] EWCA Civ 1545; [2002] 1 WLR 419.........1.32, 6.15
R (Wooder) v Dr Feggetter [2002] EWCA Civ 554; [2002] 3 WLR 591;
[2003] QB 419 ....1.32, 1.42, 6.132
R v Barking Community Mental Healthcare NHS Trust [1999] 1 FLR 106 ....5.08
R v Birch (1989) 11 Cr App R (S) 202..3.24
R v Bournewood Community and Mental Health NHS Trust ex p L
[1999] AC 458............................1.05, 1.19, 1.33, 1.48, 2.01, 2.03, 8.19,
8.21, 9.07, 11.0, 11.01–12, 15.24
R v Brown [1994] 1 AC 212 ....9.05
R v Canons Park Mental Health Review Tribunal, ex p A
[1995] QB 60 ....3.01, 3.53, 3.57
R v Collins ex p S [1999] Fam 26...2.01
R v Dr Collins ex p Brady [2000] 1 MHLR 17............................15.34, 15.61

R v Drew [2003] UKHL 25; [2003] 1 WLR 1213, HL 3.24
R v Islington London Borough Council, *ex p* Rixon (1996)
   1 CCLR 119 .... 4.08
R v Kirklees Metropolitan Borough Council *ex p* C [1993] 2 FLR 187 .... 4.44, 11.50
R v Managers of the NW London Mental Health Trust *ex p* Stewart
   [1998] QB 628 .... 5.61
R v Mental Health Act Commission *ex p* X (1988) 9 BMLR 77 .... 3.48
R v Mental Health Review Tribunal for South Thames Region *ex p* Smith
   (1999) 47 BMLR 104 .... 3.14
R v Nowhia [1996] 1 Cr App R (S) 7.28
R v Staines (Paula) [2006] EWCA Crim 15 .... 3.24, 7.30
Reid v Secretary of State for Scotland [1999] AC 512 .... 3.01, 3.19, 3.49, 3.53,
              3.54, 3.55, 3.56, 3.57, 3.68, 3.97, 3.105, 6.22, 6.31
Reid v United Kingdom (2003) 37 EHRR 211 .... 3.57, 3.100, 3.104, 11.43
Rex v Coate (1772) Lofft 73 .... 1.19, 11.11
Robb v Home Secretary [1995] Fam 127 .... 9.04

S (A Minor), Re [2005] 1 AC 593 .... 14.19
S (Adult Patient: Sterilisation), Re [2001] Fam 15 .... 9.15
S (FD), Re [2003] 2 FLR 292 .... 9.16, 12.23
S (Hospital Patient: Court's Jurisdiction), Re [1995] Fam 26, DC 9.21, 14.18, 14.19
S (Hospital Patient: Court's Jurisdiction), Re [1996] Fam 1, CA 14.28
St George's Healthcare NHS Trust v S [1999] Fam 26 .... 2.01, 9.04
St Helens BC v PE (1) JW (2) [2006] EWHC 3460 (Fam) 9.21, 14.19
Scott v Wakem (1862) 3 F & F 328 .... 1.19, 11.11
Secretary of State for the Home Department v JJ [2007] UKHL 45 .... 11.21
Sheffield City Council v E [2005] Fam 326 .... 9.22
Sheffield and Horsham v UK (1998) 27 EHRR 163 .... 1.40
Storck v Germany (2005) 43 EHRR 96 .... 1.40, 6.126, 11.21, 11.23,
                         11.25, 11.26, 11.34
Sunderland City Council v PS [2007] EWHC 623 (Fam) 9.23, 11.36, 12.93
Symm v Fraser (1863) 3 F & F 859 .... 1.19, 11.11

T (Adult: Refusal of Treatment), Re [1993] Fam 95 .... 10.20
T, Re [1992] 2 FCR 861 .... 9.08
T v BBC [2007] EWHC 1683 (QB) 14.19
Tarariyeva v Russia, Application no. 4353/03, 14 December 2006 .... 1.40
Thlimmenos v Greece (2000) 31 EHRR 411 .... 1.40, 10.14
TP v United Kingdom (2002) 34 EHRR 2 .... 1.41

Vo v France (2004) ECHR 53924/0; [2004] 2 FCR 577 .... 1.40

W (A Minor) (Medical Treatment: Court's jurisdiction),
   Re [1993] 1 Fam 64 .... 6.60, 9.29, 9.30, 9.32, 9.33, 9.34, 9.37, 10.04
Wilkinson v United Kingdom, Application no 14659/02, (Admissibility)
   28 February 2006 .... 1.43, 6.122, 6.123, 6.124, 6.130
Winterwerp v Netherlands (1979) 2 EHRR 387 .... 3.90, 3.104, 5.84, 5.89,
                          7.09, 7.13, 11.16, 11.17

X & Y v Netherlands (1985) 8 EHRR 235. . . . . 1.40
X City Council v MB; NB and MAB (by his litigation friend the Official Solicitor)
     [2006] EWHC 168 (Fam); [2006] 2 FLR 968. . . . . 9.22
X v United Kingdom (1981) 4 EHRR 181 . . . . 1.28

YL v Birmingham City Council [2007] UKHL 27. . . . . .11.33, 11.34

Z v United Kingdom [2002] 2 FLR 612 . . . . 1.40

Table of Statutes

References are to Paragraph Numbers

Act for the better Care and Maintenance
  of Lunatics being Paupers or
  Criminals in England 1808 . . . . . . .1.21
Air Force Act 1955. . . . . .7.04
Armed Forces Act 2006 . . . . .7.04
Army Act 1955. . . . . .7.04

Care Standards Act 2000
  Part 2 . . . . 12.03, 12.04, 12.48, 10.87
  s 2 . . . . .12.03
  s 3 . . . . .12.04
Children Act 1989 . . . . 9.26, 9.29
  s 1 . . . . .9.25
  s 8 . . . . 9.35, 9.37
  s 9(1) 9.35
  s 25 . . . . 11.50, 11.55
  s 31 . . . . 9.16, 12.23
  s 100(2) 9.32
  s 100(3) 9.32, 9.35
Chronically Sick and Disabled
  Persons Act 1970
  s 2 . . . . 12.02, 12.09
Civil Partnership Act 2004. . . . . .4.19
Crime (Sentences) Act 1997. . . . . .7.29
Criminal Justice Act 2003
  s 154 . . . . .7.31
  s 282 . . . . .7.31
Criminal Lunatics Act 1800 . . . . .1.20
Criminal Procedure (Insanity)
  Act 1964 . . . . 7.04, 7.36
  s 5 . . . . 3.82, 7.30

Data Protection Act 1998
  s 7 . . . . 4.40, 10.88
De Praerogativa Regis. 1.18
Disability Discrimination Act 1995
  Part III. 10.14
  s 1 . . . . .14.22
  s 21 . . . . .10.14
  s 21B 10.14
  s 49A 10.14

Domestic Violence, Crime and Victims
  Act 2004 . . . . 7.0, 7.30, 7.34,
                        7.36, 7.37, 7.38, 7.39
  s 36 . . . . .7.36
  s 39(1) 7.36

Education Act 1996
  s 317 . . . . .4.15
Enduring Powers of Attorney
  Act 1985 .8.04
Equality Act 2006
  s 35 . . . . .4.13

Family Law Reform Act 1969. . . . . .9.36
  s 8 . . . . 10.04, 11.50

Government of Wales Act 1998
  s 27 . . . . .12.06
Government of Wales Act 2006 . . . . . . .4.13

Human Fertilization and Embryology
  Act 1990 .10.70
Human Rights Act 1998 . . . . . . v, 1.07, 1.31,
                        1.39, 1.44, 1.48, 7.11,
                        9.22, 10.15, 14.19, 14.39
  s 3 . . . . 1.44, 15.41
  s 4 . . . . 1.31, 1.44
  s 6 . . . . .1.44, 10.59, 11.34
  s 6(1) 11.33, 11.34
  s 6(3)(b) 11.33
  s 7 . . . . .1.44
  s 8 . . . . .14.39
  s 10 . . . . 1.44, 1.45
  s 19 . . . . .1.44
  ss 72–74. . . . . .1.31
  Sch 1 . . . . .1.44
  Sch 2 . . . . .1.45

Local Authority Social Services
  Act 1970
  s 7 . . . . .10.85

Lunacy Act 1890 . . . . .1.23, 1.24,
1.25, 1.35
Lunatic Asylums Act 1845 . . . . .1.21

Madhouses Act 1774
(14 Geo. III c.49) 1.20
Mental Capacity Act 2005 . . . . v, 1.01,
1.03, 1.07, 1.48, 1.52, 2.02, 2.03, 2.13,
3.111, 4.15, 4.33, 4.39, 5.22, 6.01,
6.42, 6.51, 6.53, 6.56, 6.58, 6.65,
6.72, 6.74, 6.75, 6.79, 6.89, 6.140,
8.02, 8.04, 8.05, 8.06, 8.14, 8.15,
9.01, 9.03, 9.17, 9.39, 10.0, 10.01,
10.05, 10.18, 10.19, 10.69, 10.70,
10.71, 10.73, 10.78, 11.0, 11.21,
11.38, 11.52, 12.59, 12.65, 12.79,
12.94, 13.00, 13.01, 13.09, 14.01,
14.02, 14.03, 14.11, 14.12, 14.16,
14.18, 14.27, 14.69, 14.72, 15.0,
15.01, 15.02, 15.03, 15.04, 15.05,
15.06, 15.10, 15.11, 15.12, 15.14,
15.15, 15.16, 15.17, 15.18, 15.21,
15.22, 15.23, 15.24, 15.25, 15.26,
15.29, 15.30, 15.31, 15.32, 15.33,
15.34, 15.35, 15.36, 15.38, 15.39,
15.40, 15.41, 15.42, 15.43, 15.44,
15.45, 15.46, 15.47, 15.49, 15.52,
15.55, 15.57, 15.58, 15.60, 15.64,
15.66, 15.67, 15.68, 15.69, 15.70,
15.71, 15.75, App 2
s 1 . . . . .4.12, 10.07, 10.10, 10.11,
10.38, 10.55, 10.58, 15.32
s 1(2) 10.04, 10.08, 10.11
s 1(3)–(4) 10.11
s 1(5) 10.15
s 1(6) 10.15, 10.67, 12.24, 12.52
s 2 . . . . 10.07, 10.08, 10.11,
12.18, 15.32
s 2(1) 3.103, 10.11, 10.13,
12.16, 12.18, 14.17
s 2(2) 10.11, 12.18
s 2(3)–(4) 10.11
s 2(5) 6.54, 6.68, 6.72, 6.74,
6.80, 10.07, 10.21, 11.56,
14.72, 15.74, 15.75
s 2(6) 10.07
s 3 . . . . .9.09, 10.07, 10.08, 10.11,
12.18, 14.70, 14.71, 15.32

s 3(1)–(4) 10.11
s 4 . . . . 10.07, 10.38, 10.55,
10.58, 12.51, 15.30, 15.32
s 4(2)–(4) 10.15, 12.52
s 4(5) 10.15, 10.62, 10.64, 10.65
s 4(6) 10.15, 12.52, 15.16
s 4(7) 10.15, 12.52, 13.06, 13.33
s 4(7)(b) 13.06, 13.18, 13.28
s 4(10) 10.61
s 4A 10.69, 11.21, 11.38,
11.42, 15.05, 15.06, 15.48
s 4A(1) 10.43, 10.58, 10.60
s 4A(2)(b) 11.38
s 4A(3)–(5) 11.38
s 4B 10.43, 10.58, 10.60,
10.61, 10.69, 11.0, 11.21, 11.38,
11.42, 11.43, 11.44, 12.84,
15.05, 15.06, 15.50, 15.52,
15.53, 15.55, 15.56
s 4B(1) 15.56
s 4B(5) 11.42
s 5 . . . . .1.03, 6.60, 6.75, 6.118,
8.20, 10.25, 10.59, 10.66, 10.69,
10.72, 10.89, 11.35, 11.52, 15.05,
15.06, 15.30, 15.31, 15.40, 15.41,
15.57, 15.70, 15.72
s 5(1) 10.59
s 5(2) 10.25, 10.59
s 5(5) 8.20
s 6 . . . . .6.60, 15.30, 15.57
s 6(1) 6.76, 10.56, 10.60, 10.66
s 6(3) 6.85
s 6(4) 6.82, 10.66
s 6(5) 10.69, 11.35, 11.38
s 6(6) 10.60
s 6(7) 10.60, 10.61
s 9 . . . . 10.19, 10.44, 15.05,
15.06, 15.30, 15.57
s 9(1) 10.35
s 9(2) 10.44
s 9(2)(c) 6.54, 6.68, 10.03,
10.35, 13.30, 15.70
s 9(3) 10.44
s 9(4)(a)–(b) .10.38
s 10 . . . . .10.19, 10.44, 10.45
s 10(1) 10.45
s 10(3)–(8) 10.45
s 11 . . . . 8.20, 10.19, 15.30, 15.57

Mental Capacity Act 2005 (*cont.*)

s 11(1) 6.76
s 11(4) 6.85, 10.43, 10.56, 10.66
s 11(5) 6.82, 10.66
s 11(6) 8.20, 10.69, 11.35, 11.38
s 11(7) 6.75, 10.33, 10.43
s 11(7)(a) 10.35, 13.30
s 11(7)(b) 10.24, 10.28
s 11(7)(c) 10.38
s 11(8) 10.61
s 11(8)(a) 10.43
s 11(8)(b) 10.38
s 12 . . . . .10.19
s 13 . . . . .10.19
s 13(2) 10.48
s 13(5) 10.49
s 13(6)(a)–(d) 10.48, 10.49
s 13(11) 10.48
s 14 . . . . .10.19
s 14(2) 10.36
s 15 . . . . .11.48, 12.34, 14.04, 14.05,
            14.06, 14.15, 14.18, 14.19
s 15(1)(c) 14.19
s 16 . . . . .8.16, 8.20, 10.19, 10.55,
        10.56, 10.60, 10.69, 11.0, 11.21,
        11.35, 11.37, 11.38, 11.45, 11.52,
        12.34, 12.38, 13.30, 14.04, 14.09,
        14.10, 14.14, 15.05, 15.06, 15.11,
        15.12, 15.13, 15.30, 15.56, 15.57,
            15.65, 15.70, 15.72, 15.73
s 16(1) 10.54, 11.45
s 16(2)(a) 10.54, 11.45, 15.06, 15.12
s 16(2)(b) 10.51, 10.54, 10.57
s 16(3) 10.55
s 16(4)(a) 10.57
s 16(4)(b) 10.58
s 16(5) 14.18
s 16A 10.56, 14.14, 15.05,
            15.07, 15.26, 15.56, 15.65
s 16A(1) 11.45
s 16A(2) 11.45, 15.08
s 17 . . . . 10.19, 10.41, 10.55,
            10.58, 14.04, 14.09, 15.05
s 18(3) 10.07
s 19 . . . . .10.19, 14.04, 14.10
s 19(1) 10.57
s 20 . . . . 8.20, 10.19, 14.04,
            14.10, 15.30, 15.57

s 20(2)(a)–(b) 10.58
s 20(4) 10.58
s 20(5) 10.58, 10.61
s 20(6) 10.58
s 20(7) 6.76, 10.56, 10.58, 10.66
s 20(8) 10.58, 10.66
s 20(9)–(10) 10.58
s 20(11) 6.85, 10.58
s 20(12) 6.82, 10.66
s 20(13) 8.20, 10.69, 11.35, 11.38
s 21A 11.41, 11.47, 11.48,
        12.0, 12.28, 12.34, 12.61, 12.71,
        12.77, 12.78, 12.87, 12.91, 13.06,
        13.17, 13.25, 13.28, 13.33, 14.04,
                14.11, 14.21
s 21A(2) 12.89
s 21A(4) 12.91
s 21A(5)–(6) 12.92
s 22 . . . . 10.47, 10.48, 10.50,
            10.56, 14.04, 14.08
s 22(1) 10.51
s 22(3) 10.50
s 22(3)(b) 10.56
s 22(4) 10.50
s 23 . . . . 10.47, 10.50, 10.56,
                14.04, 14.08
s 23(2) 10.51
s 23(3)(a)–(c) 10.53
s 23(3)(d) 10.36, 10.52
s 24 . . . . .10.19, 10.89, 12.26
s 24(1) 6.54, 6.68, 10.03,
            10.21, 10.22, 15.70
s 24(3)–(5) .10.27
s 25 . . . . 6.79, 10.19, 10.89, 12.26
s 25(1) 10.25
s 25(2) 6.75
s 25(2)(a) 10.27
s 25(2)(b) 10.24, 10.28, 10.43
s 25(2)(c) 10.27
s 25(3) 10.29
s 25(4)(a) 10.29
s 25(5) 10.61
s 25(5)(a)–(b) 10.30
s 25(6) 10.30, 10.61
s 26 . . . . .10.19, 10.89, 12.26
s 26(1) 6.75, 10.22, 10.23, 10.25,
            10.33, 10.56, 10.58, 15.05
s 26(2) 10.25

Mental Capacity Act 2005 (*cont.*)
s 26(4) 10.34, 14.04, 14.07
s 26(5) 10.23, 10.26, 10.31, 10.61
s 27 . . . . 10.43, 10.56, 10.58,
10.60, 10.70
s 28 . . . . 1.03, 10.43, 10.56,
10.58, 10.60, 15.32, 15.34, 15.35,
15.36, 15.38, 15.39, 15.42, 15.43,
15.44, 15.47, 15.60
s 28(1) 6.117, 10.71, 15.31,
15.32, 15.40, 15.57
s 28(1A) 6.56
s 28(1B) 6.75, 6.118, 10.60,
10.72, 15.31, 15.32, 15.40, 15.47,
15.57, 15.60
s 29 . . . . 10.43, 10.56, 10.58, 10.60
ss 30–34 . . . . 10.43, 10.56, 10.58,
10.60, 10.75, 10.89
s 35 . . . . 4.35, 10.79
s 35(6) 10.87, 10.88
s 35(7) 10.79
s 36 . . . . 10.86, 13.05, 13.15,
13.16, 13.23, 13.28
s 36(2) 15.16
s 37 . . . . 10.79, 10.81, 10.82, 13.01
s 37(1) 10.81
s 37(2) 10.82
s 37(4) 10.82
s 37(6) 10.82
s 38 . . . . 10.79, 10.81, 10.83, 13.01
s 38(1) 10.81
s 38(2) 10.83
s 38(2A) 10.83
s 38(3)(b) 10.83
s 38(10) 13.03
s 38A 10.79
s 39 . . . . 10.79, 10.81, 10.83,
13.00, 13.01
s 39(1) 10.81
s 39(2) 10.83
s 39(3) 10.83
s 39(3A) 10.83
s 39(4)(b) 10.83
s 39(7) 13.03
s 39A 1.03, 10.79, 10.81,
10.83, 12.00, 12.32, 12.33, 12.44,
12.49, 12.58, 12.61, 12.85–12.88,
12.91, 13.00, 13.01–13.07, 13.15,

13.18–13.20, 13.28, 13.31,
13.33–13.35, 14.28
s 39A(1)(b) 13.03, 13.35
s 39A(6) 13.03
s 39B 12.0, 12.44, 12.87, 13.02
s 39B(9) 12.32
s 39C 1.03, 10.79, 10.81,
10.83, 12.0, 12.42, 12.49, 13.00,
13.01, 13.13, 13.20–13.23, 13.28,
13.31, 13.33–13.35
s 39C(1)(c) .13.35
s 39C(2)–(3) 13.20
s 39D 1.03, 10.79, 10.81,
12.0, 12.42, 12.49, 12.61, 13.00,
13.01, 13.16, 13.24, 13.26–13.28,
13.31, 13.32, 13.35, 13.36
s 39D(7)–(9) 13.28
s 39D(10) 13.25
s 39E 12.00
s 40 . . . . 10.81, 13.03, 13.20,
13.27, 13.31, 13.33, 13.35
s 40(1)(a) 12.91
s 41 . . . . .10.80
s 42 . . . . .10.91
s 42(1) 10.89, 10.92
s 42(3) 10.92
s 42(5) 10.93
s 43(1)–(2) .10.89
s 43(4) 10.89
s 44 . . . . 6.68, 10.07, 10.76, 10.77
s 45(1) 14.01
s 46 . . . . .14.01
s 46(2)(a)–(c) 14.60
s 47 . . . . 11.60, 14.18
s 47(1) 14.02
s 48 . . . . 9.21, 14.04, 14.12, 14.49
s 49 . . . . 14.13, 14.48, 14.50, 14.75
s 49(2)–(3) .14.13
s 49(6)–(7) .14.50
s 50(1) 11.47, 12.90, 12.91,
13.33, 14.28
s 50(1A) 11.47, 12.90, 12.91,
13.06, 13.17, 14.28
ss 51–52 . . . . .14.01
s 53 . . . . .14.60
s 57 . . . . .14.73
s 58 . . . . .14.73
s 58(1)(d) 14.73, 14.75

Mental Capacity Act 2005 (*cont.*)
s 58(5) 10.88, 14.73
s 59 . . . . .14.74
s 60 . . . . .14.73
s 61 . . . . .14.75
s 62 . . . . 10.62, 10.63
s 64(5) 10.69, 11.21, 11.35,
12.21, 12.31
s 64(6) 11.33
s 67 . . . . .12.94
Sch 1 . . . . .10.44
Part 1 . . . . .10.46
para 1 .10.46
para 2 .10.46
para 3(1) 10.46
Part 2 . . . . .10.47
Sch A1 . . . . v, 1.03, 1.37, 2.02,
2.03, 4.33, 5.27, 8.22, 10.03,
10.23, 10.40, 10.43, 10.58,
10.60, 10.69, 10.79, 10.91,
11.0, 11.21, 11.34, 11.38, 11.40,
11.43, 11.60, 12.0, 12.00, 12.01,
12.02, 12.10, 12.11, 12.12, 12.13,
12.16, 12.26, 12.44, 12.56, 12.65,
12.79, 12.94, 13.00, 13.01, 13.02,
13.06, 13.15, 13.18, 13.24, 13.29,
13.30, 13.31, 13.33, 13.34, 13.35,
14.04, 14.27, 14.28, 15.05, 15.06,
15.08, 15.11, 15.13, 15.22, 15.50,
15.52, 15.54, 15.60, 15.64,
15.73, App 4
Part 4 . . . . .12.73
Part 5 . . . . 12.82, 15.52
Part 6 . . . . 12.65, 12.67, 12.78,
12.79, 12.80, 15.08
Part 8 . . . . 12.00, 12.40, 12.62,
12.65, 12.67, 12.68, 12.78,
12.79, 13.17, 13.25, 13.28
Part 10 . . . . 12.00, 12.52, 12.54,
12.61, 12.62, 12.91, 13.00,
13.03, 13.06, 13.07, 13.08,
13.09, 13.10, 13.11, 13.12,
13.13, 13.14, 13.15, 13.16,
13.17, 13.18, 13.19, 13.20,
13.21, 13.22, 13.23,
13.24, 13.27, 13.28,
13.31, 13.32, 13.33,
13.36, 14.28

para 5(3) 12.66
para 5(6) .6.81
para 6 . . . . 12.21, 12.31
para 12 . . . . 12.45, 12.82
para 12(e) 15.05, 15.07
para 13 . . . . 10.03, 12.15, 12.45,
15.64, 15.73
para 14 . . . . 12.16, 12.45
para 15 . . . . 12.18, 12.45
para 16 . . . . .12.20, 12.45, 12.66
para 17 . . . . 12.25, 12.45, 15.05,
15.07, 15.12, 15.26, 15.54
paras 18–20 . . . . . . 10.23, 10.40, 10.58,
12.26, 12.45, 13.29, 15.05
para 24 . . . . 11.60, 12.11, 12.31,
12.32, 12.76, 12.81,
13.02, 15.54
para 24(2)–(4) 15.54
para 25 . . . . .12.11, 12.39, 13.08
para 27 . . . . .12.38
para 28 . . . . .12.36
para 29 . . . . 12.37, 12.41, 12.76,
12.81, 13.08
para 29(5) 12.37, 12.81
para 30 . . . . .12.11, 12.40,
12.76, 13.08
para 33 . . . . 12.41, 12.43, 12.45,
12.56, 12.73
para 33(5) 12.39, 12.42, 12.77
para 34 . . . . .12.45
paras 35–36 . . . . 12.45, 12.50
para 37 . . . . .12.45
para 38 . . . . 12.45, 12.51
para 39 . . . . .12.45, 12.51, 12.52
para 39(3)(a)–(c) 12.52
para 39(4)–(5) 12.52
para 40 . . . . .12.45, 12.52, 13.33
para 41 . . . . .12.45
paras 42–43 . . . . 12.45, 12.53
para 44 . . . . .12.45, 12.55,
12.58, 12.73
para 44(2) 13.06, 13.19, 13.33
para 45 . . . . .12.45
paras 46–48 . . . . .12.45
para 49 . . . . .12.42, 12.77,
13.18, 13.28
para 49(6) 12.42, 13.18
para 50(1) 12.61

Mental Capacity Act 2005 (*cont.*)

Sch A1 (*cont.*)

para 50(2) 12.36, 12.42,
12.58, 12.86

para 51. . . . . 12.61, 12.78

para 52. . . . . .12.61

para 53. . . . . 12.53, 12.61

paras 54–55 . . . . .12.61

para 57. . . . . .12.61, 13.06,
13.18, 13.33

para 58. . . . . 12.58, 12.86, 13.06,
13.18, 13.33

para 59. . . . . .12.61

para 59(1)–(2) 12.86

para 60. . . . . 12.58, 12.61

para 62(2) 12.61

para 62(3) 12.60, 12.75, 12.78

para 63. . . . . .12.61

para 65(3) 13.17

para 66. . . . . 12.58, 12.61

para 68. . . . . .11.48, 12.11,
12.32, 12.35

para 69. . . . . .11.48, 12.32,
13.02, 13.19

para 69(3)–(5) 12.32

para 69(7) 13.06, 13.33

para 69(8) 12.33, 13.06, 13.33

para 71. . . . . 12.32, 12.41

para 72. . . . . 11.48, 12.33

paras 74–75 . . . . 12.82, 15.52

para 76. . . . . .12.57, 12.82,
13.02, 15.52

para 76(2) 15.54

paras 77–78 . . . . . . .12.82, 12.85, 15.52

paras 79–80 . . . . 12.82, 15.52

para 81. . . . . .12.82, 12.88, 15.52

para 82. . . . . 12.82, 12.88, 13.06,
13.19, 15.52

para 83. . . . . .12.82, 12.87, 15.52

para 84. . . . . .12.57, 12.82,
12.85, 15.52

para 85. . . . . 12.57, 12.82, 12.85,
12.86, 15.52

para 86. . . . . .12.82, 13.06,
13.19, 15.52

para 86(1) 12.85

para 86(3) 12.85

para 87. . . . . 12.82, 15.52

para 88. . . . . .12.82, 12.86, 15.52

para 89. . . . . .12.82, 12.86, 15.52

para 89(4) 12.86

para 90. . . . . 12.82, 12.86, 13.06,
13.19, 15.52

para 91. . . . . .12.65, 12.79, 15.08

para 91(4) 12.65, 12.79

para 92. . . . . .12.65, 12.79,
12.80, 15.08

para 93. . . . . .12.65, 12.79,
12.80, 15.08

para 93(3) 13.17

para 94. . . . . .12.65, 12.79,
12.80, 15.08

para 95 . . . . . 12.65, 12.79, 12.80, 15.08

para 95(3) 13.17

para 96. . . . . 12.65, 12.78, 12.79,
12.80, 15.08

para 96(2) 12.79

para 97. . . . . .12.65, 12.79, 15.08

para 102. . . . . .12.35, 12.62, 13.17

para 103. . . . . .12.62

para 105. . . . . .12.64

para 105(2) 12.67

para 106. . . . . .12.69

para 107. . . . . .12.70

para 108. . . . . .12.71

para 108(1) 13.17

para 109. . . . . .12.71

para 110. . . . . 12.71, 12.77

para 111. . . . . .12.72

para 113(1)–(3) 12.73

para 114. . . . . .12.72

paras 115–116 . . . . .12.74

para 117. . . . . .12.68, 12.75, 12.78

para 118(2) 12.71

para 120(1) 13.17

para 124. . . . . .12.76

para 125(2) 12.03

para 129(3) 12.46

para 129(5) 12.46

para 131. . . . . .12.48

para 132. . . . . 12.49, 12.52, 13.06,
13.18, 13.28, 13.33

para 133. . . . . 12.42, 12.58

para 135. . . . . 13.06, 13.18

para 136. . . . . .13.06, 13.19, 13.33

para 139. . . . . 13.07, 13.21

Mental Capacity Act 2005 (*cont.*)
  Sch A1 (*cont.*)
    para 139(1) 12.61
    para 140. . . . . .13.15
    para 141. . . . . .13.16
    para 143. . . . . 12.54, 13.09
    para 150. . . . . .13.14
    para 159(2) 13.23
    para 160. . . . . .13.23
    para 161(4)–(7) 13.06
    para 175(3) 12.03
    para 176. . . . . .12.03
    para 177. . . . . 12.03, 12.12
    paras 178–179 . . . . .12.04
    para 180. . . . . 12.05, 12.12
    para 181. . . . . .12.07
    para 182. . . . . .12.08
    para 183(1)–(2) 12.10
    para 183(3) 12.11
    para 183(6) 12.11
    para 184. . . . . 12.12, 13.33
    Part 10 . . . . 10.91, 12.0
  Sch 1A . . . . v, 1.03, 8.22, 11.45,
           11.46, 14.14, 15.0, 15.04,
           15.05, 15.06, 15.08, 15.09,
           15.26, 15.33, 15.49, 15.53,
           15.54, 15.56, 15.57, 15.65
    para 2. . . . . .15.09
      case A. 15.05, 15.09, 15.10,
             15.33, 15.34, 15.36
      case B. 15.05, 15.09, 15.12,
           15.14, 15.17, 15.18, 15.23,
           15.33, 15.36, 15.38, 15.45
      case C. 15.05, 15.09, 15.12,
           15.14, 15.17, 15.18, 15.23,
              15.33, 15.39
      case D 12.66, 13.29, 15.05,
           15.09, 15.14, 15.15, 15.17,
              15.23, 15.33
      case E. 12.66, 13.29, 15.05,
           15.09, 15.14, 15.19,
              15.33, 15.45
    para 3. . . . . .15.05, 15.12,
              15.15, 15.16
    para 4. . . . . .15.12
    para 5. . . . . 12.65, 12.66, 12.68,
             12.79, 15.15, 15.19
    para 5(3) 15.19
    para 5(6)–(7) 15.16

    para 8. . . . . .15.10
    para 9. . . . . .15.12
    para 12(1)–(5) 15.21
    paras 13–15 . . . . 15.12, 15.15
    para 16. .15.19
Mental Capacity Bill 2004 . . . . 8.14, 8.20
Mental Deficiency Act 1913. . . . . 1.24,
                    1.25, 8.17
Mental Deficiency Act 1926. . . . . .8.17
Mental Deficiency Act 1939. . . . . .8.17
Mental Health Act 1959. . . . . .1.07, 1.17,
    1.19, 1.26, 1.27, 1.28, 1.33, 1.35,
        3.51, 8.06, 8.07, 8.08, 8.10,
         8.17, 8.18, 8.19, 9.11
  s 5 . . . . 1.26, 1.33, 8.17, 11.02
  s 34(1) 8.07
Mental Health Act 1983. . . . . v, 1.01,
  1.03, 1.05, 1.06, 1.08, 1.13, 1.17, 1.27,
  1.29, 1.31, 1.34, 1.35, 1.48, 1.52,
  2.01, 2.02, 2.25, 2.26, 3.40, 3.51,
  3.52, 3.75, 3.77, 3.79, 3.81, 3.103,
  3.110, 4.0, 4.12, 4.33, 6.03, 6.39,
  6.121, 7.01, 8.01, 8.02, 8.03, 8.05,
  8.09, 8.17, 8.18, 8.22, 9.03, 9.11,
  9.19, 9.25, 10.23, 10.32, 10.69,
  10.73, 10.83, 11.08, 11.09, 11.11,
  12.00, 12.16, 12.25, 12.27, 12.46,
  12.59, 12.65, 12.66, 12.78, 12.79,
  12.93, 14.69, 15.0, 15.01, 15.02,
  15.03, 15.04, 15.05, 15.07, 15.08,
  15.09, 15.10, 15.11, 15.13, 15.14,
  15.19, 15.22, 15.23, 15.24, 15.26,
  15.29, 15.30, 15.31, 15.33, 15.34,
  15.35, 15.41, 15.45, 15.47, 15.50,
  15.51, 15.53, 15.54, 15.56, 15.58,
  15.59, 15.60, 15.61, 15.63, 15.64,
    15.65, 15.66, 15.67, 15.71,
        15.74, App 1
  Part 2 . . . . .2.04, 2.11, 2.15, 3.01,
    5.28, 5.29, 5.61, 7.12, 7.25, 15.61
  Part 3 . . . . .2.04, 2.11, 2.15, 3.01,
    3.23, 4.31, 5.29, 7.06, 7.25, 7.26
  Part 4 . . . . .1.01, 1.02, 1.29, 2.13,
    2.14, 2.24, 3.71, 4.54, 5.0, 5.08,
    5.11, 5.65, 5.69, 6.0, 6.01, 6.05,
    6.25, 6.34, 6.37, 6.58, 6.59, 6.62,
    6.64, 6.70, 6.97, 6.99, 6.107,
    6.110, 6.112, 6.116, 6.117, 6.124,
    6.133, 6.138, 6.140, 7.03, 10.0,

Mental Health Act 1983 (*cont.*)
  Part 4 (*cont.*)
      10.32, 10.43, 10.56, 10.58, 10.60,
      10.71, 10.82, 11.37, 14.15, 15.0,
      15.29, 15.30, 15.31, 15.32, 15.34,
      15.36, 15.38, 15.39, 15.43, 15.46,
      15.47, 15.51, 15.57, 15.60, 15.61,
      15.62, 15.68, 15.71, 15.74, 15.75
  Part 4A 2.14, 2.28, 4.54, 5.0,
      5.10, 5.34, 5.40, 6.0, 6.4, 6.41,
      6.47, 6.49, 6.57–6.65, 6.67, 6.69,
      6.70, 6.73, 6.75, 6.76, 6.86,
      6.89, 6.90, 6.95, 6.97, 6.99,
      6.104–6.109, 6.111–6.116, 6.118,
      6.133, 6.137, 6.138–6.140, 10.0,
      10.08, 10.33, 10.39, 10.43, 10.56,
      10.58, 10.72, 10.82, 14.15, 15.0,
      15.29–15.32, 15.38–15.41, 15.43,
      15.46–15.48, 15.57, 15.60–15.62,
      15.68, 15.71, 15.74, 15.75
  Part 5 . . . . .2.17, 4.24, 4.26
  Part 6 . . . . .7.32
  Part VII 8.04, 8.06, 14.01, 14.03
  s 1 . . . . .12.16
  s 1(2) 2.10, 3.06, 3.07, 3.09,
      3.30, 3.38, 3.39, 3.41, 3.47, 3.59,
      3.61, 3.62, 3.77, 3.103, 8.09
  s 1(2A) 3.63, 3.80, 3.92
  s 1(2B) 3.63, 3.64
  s 1(3) 3.47, 3.48, 3.62
  s 2 . . . . .2.04, 2.08, 3.09, 3.14, 3.15,
      3.22, 3.24, 3.26, 3.64, 3.69,
      3.83, 4.16, 4.28, 4.29, 4.36,
      5.28, 5.61, 7.06, 7.18, 7.22,
      12.66, 15.10, 15.17, 15.19,
      15.21, 15.22, 15.34, 15.51
  s 2(3) 15.21
  s 3 . . . . 2.04, 2.08, 2.20, 3.09, 3.10,
      3.14, 3.19, 3.22, 3.24, 3.26, 3.27,
      3.33, 3.35, 3.49, 3.61, 3.64, 3.66,
      3.79, 3.81, 3.87, 3.93, 3.97, 4.16,
      4.28, 4.36, 5.0, 5.08, 5.13, 5.22,
      5.26, 5.51, 5.79, 7.06, 7.18, 7.22,
      11.07, 12.66, 15.10, 15.17, 15.19,
      15.21, 15.22, 15.34
  s 3(2) 5.66, 5.67, 5.84, 5.91
  s 3(2)(a)(i) 6.03
  s 3(2)(b) 6.03

s 3(2)(c) 15.21
s 3(3) 3.87, 15.21
s 3(4) 3.71, 3.94, 6.25, 6.99
s 4 . . . . .2.04, 3.09, 3.14, 3.15,
      3.64, 3.83, 4.36, 5.28, 5.61, 6.06,
      6.10, 6.37, 6.45, 15.10, 15.17,
      15.32, 15.34, 15.51
s.4(6) 6.81
s 5 . . . . .2.04, 3.09, 3.64, 3.83,
      5.28, 15.32, 15.34, 15.51
s 5(2) 3.17, 4.36, 6.06, 6.10,
      6.37, 6.45, 7.12, 7.13, 11.07
s 5(4) 3.17, 6.06, 6.10,
      6.37, 6.45, 7.12
s 6(1) 5.63
s 6(2) 5.38, 5.68
s 7 . . . . 2.06, 3.15, 3.27, 3.64, 5.07,
      5.19, 7.18, 7.22, 8.02
s 8(1) 5.19, 8.09
s 11 . . . . .7.18
s 11(4) 2.08, 4.16
s 11(6) 3.35, 3.85
s 12 . . . . 7.07, 12.46
s 12(2) 7.06
s 12(2A) 7.07
s 12(3)–(7) 7.23
s 12A 7.22
s 13 . . . . .7.18
s 13(1) 7.21
s 13(1A) 3.87
s 16 . . . . 3.37, 3.61
s 17 . . . . .2.06, 2.07, 4.36, 5.0,
      5.02, 5.03, 5.06, 5.07, 5.08,
      5.10, 5.11, 5.18, 5.22, 5.26,
      5.62, 5.89, 5.91, 5.93, 6.06,
      6.45, 6.59, 6.62, 7.03, 10.71,
      10.83, 15.12, 15.32, 15.36
s 17(1) 5.90
s 17(2A) 2.07, 5.09, 5.11,
      5.18, 5.25, 5.26
s 17(2B) 5.25
s 17(3) 5.65
s 17(4) 5.08, 5.91
s 17(6) 5.23
s 17A 3.64, 3.69, 3.111,
      4.36, 5.10, 5.11, 5.25, 5.44, 6.0,
      6.58, 10.23, 15.12, 15.61
ss 17A–17G .2.07

Mental Health Act 1983 (*cont.*)

s 17A(1) 5.23
s 17A(2) 5.26
s 17A(3) 5.23
s 17A(4) 5.30, 5.90
s 17A(5) 5.30, 5.31, 5.44, 5.90
s 17A(5)(d) 5.32
s 17A(6) 5.32, 5.39, 5.44
s 17B 15.61
s 17B(1) 5.33
s 17B(2) 5.33, 5.35,
5.37, 5.49
s 17B(3) 5.34, 5.37
s 17B(3)(d) 5.60
s 17B(4)–(5) .5.36
s 17B(6) 5.37, 5.60
s 17B(7) 5.37
s 17C 5.42, 15.61
s 17C(c) 5.55
s 17D 15.61
s 17D(1)–(3) .5.38
s 17E 3.63, 5.10, 5.17, 5.23,
5.37, 5.57, 5.60, 5.63, 5.70,
5.92, 6.62, 6.64, 6.105, 6.108,
6.109, 6.110, 6.111, 15.61
s 17E(1) 5.31, 5.47, 5.60
s 17E(2) 5.60
s 17E(3)–(4) .5.61
s 17E(6) 5.63
s 17F 5.42, 5.53, 5.63, 6.64,
6.111, 15.61
s 17F(4) 5.64, 5.66, 5.73, 5.84
s 17F(6) 5.65, 6.110
s 17F(7) 5.64, 5.73, 5.78
s 17F(8) 5.65
s 17F(9)(a) 5.64
s 17G 5.68, 15.61
s 17G(2)–(3) .5.68
s 17G(5) 5.68
s 18 . . . . 5.57, 5.63, 5.70,
5.71, 5.77, 7.18
s 18(2A) 5.63, 5.70
s 18(4) 5.72, 5.73, 5.77
s 18(4)(a) 5.58
s 18(4)(b) 5.71, 5.72
s 18(4B) 5.72
s 19(1)(b) 15.17
s 19A 5.39

s 20 . . . . 3.01, 3.02, 3.04,
3.06, 3.10, 3.11, 3.20, 3.26,
3.50, 3.61, 3.64, 3.82, 3.93,
5.08, 5.38, 5.67, 5.68, 5.89,
7.03, 7.05, 7.08, 7.09
s 20(2)(a)–(b) 5.68
s 20(3) 7.08, 7.10
s 20(4) 3.19, 3.27, 3.28, 3.34,
3.49, 3.67, 5.67, 6.03, 7.08
s 20(4)(c) 5.89
s 20(5A) 5.67, 7.10
s 20(6A) 5.76
s 20A 3.64, 5.34, 5.42, 5.50, 5.72
s 20A(1) 5.42, 5.43
s 20A(3) 5.43, 5.76
s 20A(4) 5.44, 5.74, 5.76
s 20A(5)–(6) .5.44
s 20A(8) 5.44
s 20B(1) 5.59
s 21 . . . . .5.57
s 21(1)–(2) 5.73
s 21(4) 5.78
s 21A 5.57
s 21A(4) 5.74
s 21A(6) 5.75
s 21A(8) 5.75
s 21B 5.72, 5.75
s 21B(2) 5.75
s 21B(4) 5.75
s 21B(4A) 5.75
s 21B(6B) 5.76
s 21B(7A) 5.76
s 22(1)–(5) 5.56
s 22(6) 5.57
s 22(8) 5.57
s 23 . . . . 2.08, 2.15, 2.16,
4.16, 4.22, 5.42, 5.45,
5.46, 5.50, 7.0, 7.03
s 23(1A) 5.46
s 23(2)(c) 5.45
s 23(3) 5.45
s 23(6) 2.16, 7.24
s 25 . . . . . .2.15, 5.45, 5.46, 5.47, 5.50
s 25A 1.7, 1.30, 1.34, 1.50,
2.06, 2.25, 5.02, 5.03, 5.07, 5.12,
5.13, 5.16, 5.24, 7.03, 7.18
s 25A(1)–(2) .5.13
s 25A(4) 5.14

Mental Health Act 1983 (*cont.*)

s 25A(7) 5.13

ss 25B–25C 1.7, 1.30, 1.34,
1.50, 2.06, 2.25, 5.02, 5.03,
5.07, 5.12, 5.16, 5.24

s 25D 1.7, 1.30, 1.34,
1.50, 2.06, 2.25, 5.02, 5.03,
5.07, 5.12, 5.15, 5.16, 5.24

s 25D(3) 5.15

s 25D(4) 5.15

ss 25E–25J 1.7, 1.30, 1.34,
1.50, 2.06, 2.25, 5.02, 5.03,
5.07, 5.12, 5.16, 5.24

s 26 . . . . .1.31, 2.08, 4.16, 4.17, 4.18

s 27 . . . . .2.08, 2.25, 4.16

s 28 . . . . . . .2.08, 2.25, 4.16, 11.37, 14.15

s 29 . . . . .1.31, 2.08, 4.16, 4.17,
4.20, 4.22, 4.29, 7.18

s 29(1) 4.20, 4.22

s 29(1A) 4.22

s 29(2)(za) 4.20

s 29(3)(a) 4.22

s 29(3)(b) 4.22, 4.23

s 29(3)(c)–(d) 4.21, 4.22, 4.23

s 29(3)(e) 4.20, 4.22, 4.23

s 29(4) 4.29

s 30 . . . . 2.08, 4.16, 4.17, 4.22

s 30(1) 4.22

s 30(4) 4.22

s 30(4B) 4.22

s 33 . . . . .2.25

s 33(4) 15.61

s 34 . . . . .5.75

s 34(1) 6.34, 7.03, 7.04

s 35 . . . . .2.04, 3.09, 3.61, 3.64,
3.69, 4.36, 4.50, 5.29, 6.06,
6.10, 6.37, 6.45, 15.10, 15.34

s 35(1) 7.14, 7.16, 7.17

s 35(3)–(5) 7.14, 7.16

s 35(7) 7.15

s 36 . . . . .2.04, 3.09, 3.14, 3.61,
3.64, 3.66, 4.36, 4.50,
5.29, 15.10, 15.34

s 36(2) 6.81

s 37 . . . . .2.04, 2.15, 2.20, 3.09,
3.10, 3.14, 3.19, 3.23, 3.24, 3.26,
3.27, 3.33, 3.35, 3.49, 3.61, 3.64,
3.66, 3.79, 3.82, 3.87, 3.97, 4.50,
5.0, 5.22, 5.26, 5.29, 5.38, 5.68,
5.79, 7.29, 7.30, 15.10

s 37(1) 4.36, 15.34

s 37(2) 3.93

s 37(3) 4.36, 15.34

s 37(4) 4.36, 6.06, 6.10, 6.37,
6.45, 15.32, 15.34

s 37(7) 3.35, 3.85

s 38 . . . . .2.04, 3.61, 3.64, 4.36,
5.29, 15.10, 15.34

s 39(1A)–(1B) 4.50

s 40(1)(b) 5.38, 5.68

s 40(4) 5.26, 5.29, 5.38, 5.68, 7.25

s 41 . . . . .2.04, 2.15, 5.29, 7.0,
7.27, 7.29, 7.30

s 41(3) 7.25

s 42 . . . . .2.06, 2.15, 5.12, 5.61,
6.06, 6.45, 7.27, 15.12, 15.32

s 42(2) 4.36

s 44 . . . . .4.50, 5.29, 15.10

s 44A 2.04

s 45A 2.05, 2.20, 3.09, 3.14,
3.19, 3.24, 3.33, 3.49, 3.61, 3.64,
3.97, 4.32, 4.36, 5.29, 5.79, 7.0,
7.29, 7.30, 15.10, 15.34

s 45A(2) 3.93

s 45A(3)(b) 7.38

s 45A(5) 4.36, 6.37, 6.45,
15.32, 15.34

s 45B 7.29

s 47 . . . . .2.04, 3.09, 3.14, 3.19,
3.23, 3.24, 3.26, 3.33, 3.35,
3.49, 3.61, 3.64, 3.66, 3.79,
3.97, 4.36, 5.29, 5.79, 7.29,
15.10, 15.34

s 47(1) 3.93

s 47(4) 3.35, 3.85

s 48 . . . . .2.04, 2.20, 3.61, 3.64,
3.66, 4.36, 5.29,
5.79, 15.10, 15.34

s 49 . . . . .2.04, 5.29, 7.29

s 50 . . . . 3.63, 3.64

s 51 . . . . .3.63, 3.64, 15.10

s 51(5) 2.04, 3.09, 3.19,
3.33, 4.36, 15.34

s 51(6) 3.14, 3.61, 3.66

ss 52–53 . . . . 3.63, 3.64

s 54(1) 7.06

Mental Health Act 1983 (*cont.*)

s 54A 3.66

s 55(1) 7.03, 7.04

s 56 . . . . 6.10, 6.37, 15.32, 15.43

s 56(1) 4.36, 6.06, 6.10, 6.12,
6.37, 6.70, 6.117, 10.71, 15.31,
15.32, 15.34

s 56(2) 6.10, 6.16, 6.37, 15.51

s 56(3) 5.69, 6.37, 6.45, 6.48,
15.32, 15.34

s 56(3)(c) 15.38

s 56(4) 5.65, 6.37, 6.62, 6.64,
6.110, 15.39

s 56(5) 4.36, 6.37, 6.43, 6.48,
6.56, 15.70, 15.75

s 56(7) 6.56

s 57 . . . . .2.13, 4.36, 6.0, 6.01,
6.04, 6.05, 6.07, 6.10, 6.11,
6.16, 6.17, 6.18, 6.19, 6.23,
6.28, 6.30, 6.35, 6.37, 6.39,
6.40, 6.65, 6.70, 6.104, 6.124,
15.32, 15.34, 15.36, 15.38, 15.42,
15.43, 15.44, 15.45, 15.46

s 57(1)(a)–(b) 6.11

s 57(2) 6.20

s 57(2)(b) 6.04

s 57(3) 6.39, 6.100

s 58 . . . . .1.32, 2.13, 6.0, 6.01,
6.04, 6.05, 6.07, 6.12–15, 6.16,
6.17, 6.18, 6.19, 6.23, 6.28,
6.30, 6.35, 6.37, 6.39, 6.40,
6.42, 6.48, 6.61, 6.64, 6.66,
6.70, 6.84, 6.87, 6.90, 6.91,
6.92, 6.102, 6.104, 6.105,
6.106, 6.107, 6.111, 6.113,
6.124, 6.132, 6.134, 6.140,
15.36, 15.41

s 58(1)(a) 6.91, 6.92

s 58(1)(b) 6.07, 6.93, 6.114

s 58(3) 6.20, 6.98

s 58(3)(b) 6.04, 6.14, 6.20

s 58(4) 6.39, 6.100

s 58A 2.13, 2.27, 4.36, 4.43,
4.54, 6.0, 6.34, 6.35, 6.37, 6.40,
6.45, 6.46, 6.47, 6.48, 6.50, 6.54,
6.55, 6.56, 6.57, 6.61, 6.64, 6.66,
6.84, 6.90, 6.91, 6.93, 6.95, 6.102,
6.106, 6.116, 6.133, 6.140, 10.32,

15.32, 15.35, 15.37, 15.41, 15.62,
15.70, 15.75

s 58A(1)(a) 6.87, 6.95

s 58A(1)(b) 6.87, 6.91, 6.92, 6.95

s 58A(2) 6.43, 6.44, 6.51, 6.53

s 58A(3) 6.43, 6.44, 6.52, 6.98

s 58A(3)(b) 6.116

s 58A(4) 6.41, 6.43, 6.46, 6.98

s 58A(4)(b) 6.116

s 58A(5) 6.41, 6.43, 6.51,
6.53, 6.98

s 58A(5)(c) 10.23, 10.32,
15.32, 15.35

s 58A(5)(c)(ii) 10.39, 10.43, 10.56,
10.58, 14.15

s 58A(6) 6.51

s 58A(7) 6.43, 6.48

s 58A(9) 6.51

s 59 . . . . 6.18, 6.107

s 60 . . . . .6.19, 6.40, 6.104

s 60(1) 6.104

s 60(1A)–(1B) 6.40, 6.104

s 60(1C)–(1D) 6.40, 6.104, 6.112

s 61 . . . . .2.24, 4.54, 6.20, 6.41, 6.107

s 61(1) 6.41

s 61(3) 6.20, 6.107

s 62 . . . . .2.13, 6.01, 6.05, 6.16–17,
6.37, 6.44, 6.46, 6.57, 6.85,
6.104, 6.113, 15.32, 15.57

s 62(1) 6.16, 6.17, 6.19, 6.20

s 62(1A) 6.43, 6.51, 6.87

s 62(1B)–(1C) 6.43

s 62(2) 6.19, 6.20, 6.107

s 62(3) 6.17

s 62A 4.54, 5.69, 6.37,
6.64, 6.101, 6.105, 6.107

s 62A(1)(a) 5.65

s 62A(2) 6.114

s 62A(3) 6.111, 6.116

s 62A(4)(b) 6.115

s 62A(5)(a) 6.111

s 62A(6) 6.113

s 62D 6.101

s 62F 6.101

s 63 . . . . .2.13, 6.01, 6.05–6.09,
6.12, 6.35, 6.37, 6.114, 15.36

s 64(1) 6.34

s 64(1A)–(1B) 6.34

Mental Health Act 1983 (*cont.*)

s 64(3) 3.71, 6.0, 6.24, 6.28,
6.32, 6.99
s 64(3)(b)(i) 6.102
s 64A 6.70
s 64A(1) 6.65
s 64B 6.68, 6.118, 10.60,
10.72, 15.31, 15.40
s 64B(2) 6.64, 6.66
s 64B(2)(b) .6.90
s 64B(3) 6.102
s 64B(3)(b)(ii) 6.102
s 64B(4) 6.92, 6.93, 6.95, 6.114
s 64B(5) 6.92
s 64C 6.68, 6.75, 10.33
s 64C(2)(a) 6.64, 6.71,
6.72, 6.133
s 64C(2)(b) 6.64, 6.68, 6.71,
6.74, 6.83, 10.39, 10.43, 10.56,
10.58, 14.15, 15.41
s 64C(2)(c) 6.77, 6.84
s 64C(3) 6.91, 6.93, 6.95
s 64C(4) 6.64, 6.96
s 64C(5) 6.64, 6.102
s 64D 6.64, 6.68, 6.71, 6.77,
6.79, 6.80, 6.88, 6.106,
6.133, 6.135, 10.33
s 64D(2)–(3) 6.79
s 64D(4) 6.60, 6.79, 6.109, 15.16
s 64D(4)(b) .6.82
s 64D(5) 6.79
s 64D(6) 6.68, 6.79, 6.109,
10.33, 10.39, 10.43,
10.56, 10.58, 14.15
s 64D(7) 6.79
s 64E 6.68
s 64E(1)(b) .6.67
s 64E(2) 6.64, 6.66
s 64E(2)(b) .6.90
s 64E(3) 6.102
s 64E(4) 6.109
s 64E(6) 6.72, 6.133
s 64E(6)(a) 6.64, 6.71
s 64E(6)(b) 6.77, 6.84
s 64E(7) 6.96, 6.102
s 64F 6.64, 6.68, 6.77, 6.80,
6.88, 6.106, 6.133, 6.135
s 64F(4) 6.60, 15.16

s 64F(4)(b) .6.82
s 64G 6.60, 6.64, 6.65, 6.68,
6.71, 6.84, 6.85, 6.88, 6.102,
6.133, 10.33, 15.57
s 64G(2)–(4) 6.85
s 64G(5) 6.85, 6.102
s 64G(6)–(8) 6.87
s 64G(9) 6.86
s 64H 4.54
s 64H(1) 6.107
s 64H(3) 6.64, 6.100
s 64H(4) 6.106, 6.107, 6.115
s 64H(7) 6.107
s 64H(8) 6.115
s 64J 6.81
s 64K 6.79
s 64K(2)–(3) 6.72
s 64K(4)–(5) 6.74
s 65 . . . . .4.27
s 66 . . . . 2.08, 2.18, 4.16,
4.23, 4.25, 4.38
s 66(1)(ca) 5.50
s 66(1)(d) 3.37
s 66(1)(faa) 5.50
s 66(1)(fza) 5.50
s 66(1)(g) 5.45, 5.47, 5.50
s 67 . . . . 2.18, 4.25
s 67(1) 5.54
s 68 . . . . .2.18, 4.25, 4.28, 4.29, 4.31
s 68(1)(c) 5.51, 5.53
s 68(2) 5.51, 5.53
s 68(5) 5.51, 5.53
s 68(6) 4.28, 5.52
s 68(7) 5.53
s 68A 4.30
s 69(1) 6.105
s 70 . . . . 2.18, 4.25
s 71 . . . . 2.18, 4.25
s 71(2) 4.31
s 72 . . . . .2.17, 3.01, 3.03, 3.10,
3.16, 3.19, 3.25, 3.33, 3.49,
3.82, 3.97, 4.22, 4.24, 5.42,
5.45, 5.47, 5.50
s 72(1) 3.68
s 72(1)(a) 3.64
s 72(1)(b) 3.26, 3.27, 3.28, 3.53,
3.64, 3.68, 3.93
s 72(1)(c) 3.64, 3.68, 5.47

Mental Health Act 1983 (*cont.*)

s 72(1)(c)(iii) 5.48
s 72(1A) 5.48
s 72(2) 3.03, 3.68
s 72(3A) 5.24
s 72(4) 3.03, 3.11, 3.20, 3.27,
                            3.50, 3.64
s 72(5) 3.37, 3.61
s 73 . . . . .2.06, 2.17, 3.03, 3.16,
                    3.19, 3.25, 3.33, 3.49, 4.24,
                    4.36, 5.12, 5.24, 5.85, 6.06,
                    6.45, 7.27, 15.12, 15.32
s 73(1) 3.26, 3.53
s 73(2)(b) 5.48
s 73(7) 5.85
s 74 . . . . .2.17, 3.03, 3.16, 3.19,
                    3.25, 3.49, 4.24, 4.36,
                    6.06, 6.45, 7.29
s 75 . . . . 2.18, 4.25
s 75(3) 4.32
ss 80–92 . . . . .7.32
s 94(2) 14.69
s 114 . . . . .7.19
s 114(1) 7.18, 12.47
s 114(2) 7.18
s 114A 7.20
s 115 . . . . .7.18
s 116 . . . . .2.25
s 117 . . . . .1.05, 2.20, 2.21, 4.39,
                    5.12, 5.13, 5.14, 5.15, 5.17,
                    5.18, 5.24, 5.41, 5.79, 5.80,
                    5.81, 5.85, 10.83, 12.02
s 117(2) 2.20, 5.41, 5.79, 5.80
s 118 . . . . 2.22, 4.01, 4.07,
                            4.10, 5.81
s 118(1) 4.08, 4.13, 10.92
s 118(1)(a)–(b) 4.02
s 118(2) 4.08, 4.09
s 118(2A) 4.10, 4.11, 4.13
s 118(2B) 4.13
s 118(2C) 4.15
s 118(2D) 4.02, 10.92
s 120 . . . . .4.54
s 120(1) 4.54
s 121(2) 2.24, 4.54
s 121(2)(b) 6.20
s 121(7) 2.24, 4.54
s 126 . . . . .7.31

s 127 . . . . 7.0, 7.31
s 128 . . . . .7.31
s 130A(1) 4.34
s 130B 4.38
s 130B(1) 4.38
s 130B(3) 4.39
s 130B(4) 4.39, 4.40
s 130B(5) 4.41
s 130B(6) 4.35
s 130C 4.36
s 130C(3)(b) .6.43
s 130C(5) 4.34
s 130D(1)–(5) 4.37
s 131 . . . . .1.26, 1.33, 2.03, 8.17,
                    11.01, 11.02, 15.74
s 131(1) 2.03, 15.05
s 131(2) 2.03, 4.44, 10.05, 11.49,
                    11.52, 15.65, 15.66, 15.74
s 131(3)–(5) 4.44, 10.05,
                    11.52, 15.66, 15.74
s 131A(2) 4.45
s 131A(3) 4.46
s 134 . . . . .2.24, 4.42, 4.54
s 135 . . . . .2.04, 3.09, 3.17, 3.64,
                    3.69, 3.83, 4.36, 6.06, 6.10,
                    6.37, 6.45, 7.18, 15.32, 15.34
s 135(1) 7.33
s 136 . . . . .2.04, 3.09, 3.17, 3.64,
                    3.69, 3.83, 4.36, 5.28, 5.61,
                    6.06, 6.10, 6.37, 6.45, 7.0,
                    7.18, 7.33, 15.32, 15.34, 15.51
s 136(1)–(2) .7.33
s 138 . . . . .7.18
s 140 . . . . .4.51
s 145 . . . . 3.0, 3.00, 3.56, 3.94
s 145(1) 3.54, 3.55, 3.72, 3.94,
                    6.0, 6.02, 6.21, 6.34, 6.70,
                    6.99, 7.04, 7.18
s 145(4) 3.72, 3.73, 3.74, 3.75,
                    3.93, 3.94, 3.95, 3.96, 3.99,
                    6.0, 6.05, 6.22, 6.23, 6.27,
                    6.28, 6.30, 6.31, 6.70, 6.99
s 325 . . . . .15.32
s 562(1A)–(1C) 6.57
Sch 1 . . . . .7.25
  Part 1 . . . . .5.29
    para 1 . . . . .5.26
    para 2A 5.38

Mental Health Act 1983 (*cont.*)
  Sch 1 (*cont.*)
    Part I
      para 2B 5.68
  Sch 2 . . . . .2.17, 4.24, 4.26
    para 3 . . . . .4.27
Mental Health Act 2007 . . . . v, vi, 1.01–1.05,
          1.17, 1.36, 1.37, 1.39, 1.44, 1.48,
          2.03, 2.05, 2.10, 2.12, 2.14,
          2.16, 2.19, 2.21, 2.26, 3.05,
          3.08, 3.13, 3.18, 3.21, 3.26,
          3.29, 3.43, 3.46, 3.74, 3.81,
          3.107, 3.111, 4.01, 4.33, 4.42,
          4.50, 5.21, 5.24, 6.28, 6.34,
          6.37, 6.43, 6.57, 6.62, 6.104,
          7.01, 7.04, 7.07, 7.09, 7.13,
          7.16, 7.26, 7.30, 7.31, 7.32,
          8.01, 8.04, 8.05, 10.0, 10.39,
          10.40, 10.43, 10.55, 10.56,
          10.58, 10.60, 10.61, 10.69,
          10.71, 10.72, 10.79, 10.83,
          11.0, 11.38, 13.01, 14.0, 14.04,
          14.09, 14.11, 14.14, 14.15,
          14.27, 14.28, 15.01–15.04,
          15.28, 15.58, 15.61,
          App 3
  Explanatory Notes
    para 48 . . . . .7.04
    para 124 . . . . .6.111
    para 126 . . . . .6.113
    para 204 . . . . .12.27
    para 216 . . . . .12.52
  s 15 . . . . .7.04
  s 33 . . . . .5.16
  s 36 . . . . .1.50, 5.02, 5.16
  s 45 . . . . .8.22
  s 48 . . . . 7.34, 7.38
  s 51 . . . . .10.58
  s 56 . . . . .1.49, 1.50, 5.16
  s 57 . . . . 1.50, 5.16
  s 58 . . . . .1.52
  Sch 2 . . . . .6.34
  Sch 6 . . . . .7.34, 7.38, 8.22
  Sch 7 . . . . .8.22
  Sch 8 . . . . .8.22
    para 2 . . . . .11.47
  Sch 9
    Part 2, para 12 . . . . .11.60

Sch 10 . . . . .1.51
Mental Health (Amendment)
    Act 1982 . . . . 1.27, 1.29, 3.45,
          8.09, 9.11
Mental Health Bill 2002 . . . . .1.09, 1.10,
          1.46, 4.33, 5.02, 6.136
Mental Health Bill 2004 . . . . .1.11, 1.13,
          3.110, 4.33
Mental Health Bill 2006 . . . . 1.14, 1.46
Mental Health (Care and Treatment)
  (Scotland) Act 2003 . . . . 4.15, 5.01
  s 1 . . . . 4.12, 4.14
  s 1(3)(f) 4.14
  s 57 . . . . .3.110
Mental Health (Patients in the
  Community) Act 1995 . . . . . . 1.30, 5.12
Mental Health (Public Safety and
  Appeals) (Scotland)
  Act 1999 . . . . 3.57, 3.100
Mental Health (Scotland)
  Act 1984 .11.02
Mental Treatment
  Act 1930 . . . . 1.26, 1.35

National Assistance Act 1948 . . . . .10.83
  Part III 12.02
  s 21 . . . . 12.09, 12.10
  s 24 . . . . .12.09
  s 24(5)–(6) .12.10
  s 29 . . . . .12.09
  s 32(3) 12.11
  s 47 . . . . 5.22, 9.11, 11.58, 11.61
  s 47(1) 11.58
National Assistance (Amendment)
  Act 1951
  s 51 . . . . 11.59, 11.61
National Health Service
  Act 1977 .12.06
  s 16D 6.34, 7.04
  Sch 2 . . . . .7.04
National Health Service
  Act 2006 .12.02
  s 7 . . . . .12.06
  s 248 . . . . .4.33
  s 254 . . . . .12.02
  s 275 . . . . .12.03
  Sch 20 . . . . .12.02
National Health Service Acts 12.13

National Health Service and Community
    Care Act 1990
    s 46(3) 5.81, 12.02
    s 47 . . . . .10.83
    s 47(1) 5.81
National Health Service (Wales)
    Act 2006 . . . . 12.02, 12.06
    s 187 . . . . .4.33
    s 206 . . . . .12.03
Navy Discipline Act 1957 . . . . .7.04

Suicide Act 1961
    s 2 . . . . 9.05, 10.62

Vagrancy Act 1714. . . . . .1.20
Vagrancy Act 1744. . . . . .1.20

International legislation
Convention on Human Rights and
    Biomedicine (Biomedicine
    Convention). 1.42
Convention for the Protection of
    Human Rights and Dignity of
    the Human Being with regard
    to the Application of Biology
    and Medicine (Council of
    Europe) 1.42
Convention on the Rights of the
    Child 1.42
European Convention on Human
    Rights. 1.07, 1.43, 5.89,
        10.15, 12.94
    Art 1 . . . . .1.38, 1.40, 6.123
    Art 2 . . . . . .1.32, 1.38, 1.40, 6.121, 10.63
    Art 3 . . . . .1.32, 1.38, 1.40, 6.33,
        6.120, 6.121, 6.124, 6.130,
        6.131, 6.134, 6.136, 6.138,
        9.38, 10.63
    Art 5 . . . . v, 1.10, 1.31, 1.48,
        3.104, 3.112, 4.44, 5.83, 5.84,
        6.128, 7.01, 7.05, 7.17, 8.20, 8.22,
            11.21, 11.26, 11.36, 11.51, 11.53,
            12.93, 12.94, 15.65
    Art 5(1) 1, 1.38, 1.40, 3.90,
        5.83, 5.87, 7.09, 7.11, 7.13, 8.20,
        8.22, 10.69, 11.0, 11.03, 11.18,
        11.23, 11.26, 11.30, 11.33, 11.35,
        11.51, 11.211.15, 12.21, 12.24,
        12.31, 12.59, 12.60, 12.83, 12.93,
            15.65, 15.66
    Art 5(1)(e) 1.38, 3.90, 3.100,
        3.104, 5.84, 7.09, 11.16, 11.61
    Art 5(4) 1.28, 1.31, 1.38, 4.29,
        4.31, 5.24, 5.85, 5.86, 8.22, 11.13,
        11.19, 11.20, 12.93, 12.94
    Art 6 . . . . .1.32, 1.38, 14.69
    Art 8 . . . . .v, 1.31, 1.32, 1.38, 1.40,
        1.41, 1.48, 4.06, 4.18, 4.21, 4.44,
        5.22, 5.87, 5.88, 6.33, 6.131,
        6.132, 6.134, 6.135, 6.136, 6.137,
        6.138, 6.139, 7.39, 9.21, 9.23,
        9.38, 10.14, 10.56, 10.63, 10.68,
            12.83, 15.62, 15.71
    Art 8(1) 5.87, 6.125, 6.126,
            6.128, 6.130
    Art 8(2) 5.87, 6.125, 6.129
    Art 14 . . . . . .1.38, 1.40, 5.24, 5.85, 10.14
    Art 16 . . . . .10.52
International Covenant on Civil and
    Political Rights. 1.42
Statute of the Council of Europe
    Art 15(b) 1.43, 3.100, 4.12
UN Convention on the Rights of
    Persons with Disabilities. 1.42
UN General Assembly Resolution
    46/119 of 17 December 1991 . . . . .1.42
UN Principles for the Protection of
    Persons with Mental Illness and
    for the Improvement of Mental
    Health Care (UN Mental
    Illness Principles) 1.42, 3.112
Principle 16 . . . . .3.110

Table of Secondary Legislation

References are to Paragraph Numbers

Civil Procedure Rules 1998
  (SI 1998/3132) 14.59
  Part 9
    r 9 ....14.25
  Part 21................ 14.67, 14.70
    rr 21.1–21.2.................14.69
  Part 25
    r 25.1.................. 9.21, 14.12
Court of Protection Fees Order 2007
  (SI 2007/1745) 14.30, 14.33
Court of Protection Rules 2007
  (SI 2007/1744) 14.01, 14.13,
          14.25, 14.26, 14.27, 14.60
  Part 7..........................14.40
  Part 8..........................14.30
  Part 9..........................14.33
  Part 10................ 14.49, 14.56
  Part 11.........................14.39
  Part 12.........................14.45
  Part 13.........................14.57
  Part 14.........................14.55
  Part 15.........................14.51
  Part 16.........................14.56
  Part 17............14.67, 14.69, 14.70
  Part 19.........................14.58
  Part 20.........................14.60
  r 3 ....14.48
  r 5 ....14.48
  r 7 .... 14.68, 14.71
  r 25(2) 14.48
  r 25(5) 14.48
  r 42 ....14.41
  r 46(1)–(2)....................14.41
  r 51(1)–(2)....................14.29
  r 51(3) 14.49
  r 54 ....14.30
  r 55 ....14.32
  r 55(b) 14.32
  r 56 ....14.32
  r 57 .... 14.31, 14.42
  r 58 ....14.31

r 60 ....14.32
r 62 ....14.34
r 63 .... 14.30, 14.35
r 64 ....14.37
r 69 ....14.41
r 70 ....14.35
r 72 ....14.42
r 73(4) 14.36
r 74(2) 14.36
r 77(3) 14.49
r 78 ....14.49
r 78(5) 14.49
r 79 ....14.49
r 80 ....14.49
r 81(2) 14.49
r 82 ....14.18
r 82(1) 14.49
r 83 ....14.39
r 84(2) 14.45
r 84(3) 14.45, 14.64
r 84(4) 14.47
r 85 ....14.48
r 89 .... 14.46, 14.49
r 90(2)–(3).....................14.57
r 91 ....14.57
r 91(3) 14.57
r 92 ....14.57
r 97 ....14.55
r 99 ....14.55
r 106 ....14.55
rr 108–114.....................14.55
r 117(3) 14.50
r 117(5)–(6)...................14.50
r 118 ....14.50
r 120 ....14.51
r 123 ....14.52
r 123(2) 14.52
r 123(6) 14.52
r 125(1)(a) 14.53
r 125(6) 14.53
r 126 ....14.52

Civil Procedure Rules 1998
  (SI 1998/3132) (*cont.*)
  r 126(5) 14.53
  r 127 . . . . .14.53
  r 130 . . . . .14.54
  r 132 . . . . .14.56
  r 133 . . . . .14.56
  r 133(4)–(5) 14.56
  rr 134–135 .14.56
  r 140 . . . . .14.67
  r 141 . . . . .14.67, 14.68, 14.71
  rr 142–146 . . . . .14.67
  r 147 . . . . 14.67, 14.68
  rr 148–149 . . . . .14.67
  r 156 . . . . .14.58
  rr 157–158 . . . . .14.58
  r 159 . . . . .14.59
  r 159(2) 14.59
  rr 160–161 . . . . .14.59
  r 164 . . . . .14.59
  r 170(1)(a)–(b) 14.61
  r 171 . . . . .14.64
  r 172 . . . . .14.61
  r 172(5) 14.61
  r 173(1)–(2) .14.63
  rr 175–176 . . . . .14.62
  r 178 . . . . .14.65
  r 179(1)–(2) .14.64
  r 179(3) 14.66
  rr 180–181 . . . . .14.60
Health Authorities (Transfer of
  Functions, Staff Property,
  Rights and Liabilities and
  Abolition) (Wales) Order 2003
  (SI 2003/813) 12.06
Lasting Powers of Attorney, Enduring
  Powers of Attorney and Public
  Guardian Regulations 2007
  (S1 2007/1253) 10.46, 10.47
Local Health Boards (Functions) (Wales)
  Regulations 2003 (SI 2003/150)
  reg 2(2) 12.06
Mental Capacity Act 2005 (IMCA)
  (Expansion of Role) Regulations
  2006 (SI 2006/2883) 10.80, 10.84
  reg 3 . . . . .10.84
  reg 4 . . . . .10.85

  regs 6–7 . . . . .10.86
Mental Capacity Act 2005 (IMCA)
  (General) Regulations 2006
  (SI 2006/1832) 10.79
  regs 3–4 . . . . .10.82
Mental Capacity Act 2005 (IMCA)
  (Wales) Regulations 2007
  (SI 2007/852) 10.79
  reg 4 . . . . .10.82
  regs 6–7 . . . . .10.86
Mental Capacity (Deprivation of
  Liberty: Appointment of
  Relevant Person's
  Representative) Regulations
  2008 (draft) 12.54, 13.09
  reg 5 . . . . .13.10
  regs 6–10 .13.09
  reg 11 . . . . .13.09
  reg 11(2) 13.09
  reg 12 . . . . .13.09
  reg 14 . . . . .13.11
Mental Capacity (Deprivation of
  Liberty: Eligibility, Selection
  of Assessors, Assessments,
  Requests for Standard
  Authorisation and Disputes
  about Ordinary Residence)
  Regulations 2008 (draft)
  reg 2 . . . . .12.47
  reg 4 . . . . .12.46
  regs 5–6 . . . . .12.47
  reg 8 . . . . .12.47
  reg 9(1) 12.56
  reg 9(2) 12.57
  reg 12 . . . . .12.29
  reg 13 . . . . 12.11, 12.29
  regs 14–15 .12.11
Mental Health Act 1983 Approved
  Clinician Directions 2007
  (draft) 6.34, 7.04
Mental Health (Approval of Persons
  to be AMHP) Regulations 2007
  (Draft) 7.19
Mental Health (Hospital, Guardianship
  & Consent to Treatment)
  Regulations 1983
  reg 16 . . . . 6.11, 6.13

Mental Health Regulations 1983
   (SI 1983/893)
   reg 7(3) 5.20
   reg 8(3) 5.20, 15.17
National Assembly for Wales
   (Transfer of Functions) Order
   1999 (SI 1999/672)
   Art 2
   Sch 1 . . . . .4.54
National Health Service (Functions
   of Strategic Health Authorities
   and Primary Care Trusts and
   Administrative Arrangements)
   (England) Regulations 2002
   (SI 2002/2375) 12.06
   reg 3(7) 12.06

Rules of the Supreme Court 1965
   (SI 1965/1776)
   Order 80 . . . . .14.67

European secondary legislation
Recommendation Rec (2004) 10 of
   the Committee of Ministers
   of the Council of Europe 1.43,
                             3.100, 4.12
   Art 17(1) 3.100

Codes of Practice

References are to Paragraph Numbers

Code of Practice (1983 Act)
  (1999 revision) 2.22, 2.23, 4.0,
      4.01, 4.04–4.09, 4.11–4.13, 4.15,
          6.40, 6.82, 6.97, 7.26
  para 15.12 . . . . .9.08
  para 20.8 . . . . .6.59
  para 21 . . . . 4.08, 4.09
  para 65 . . . . .4.05
  para 68 . . . . .4.07
  para 69 . . . . .4.08
Code of Practice (1983 Act)
  (2007 draft) 4.01, 6.82, 6.97, 7.26
para 16.21h 6.96
para 16.22b 6.113
Code of Practice (2005 Act) 1.03,
      10.08, 10.13, 10.15, 10.42, 10.71,
          10.89, 10.90, 10.91, 11.37
  Draft Addendum (2007) 10.91
  para 4.4 . . . . .10.13
  para 5.25 . . . . .10.15
  para 5.41 . . . . .10.15
  para 7.21 . . . . .10.42
  para 12.12 . . . . .10.08
  para 13.22 . . . . .11.37
  Ch 13 . . . . 10.71, 11.37
Code of Practice (2005 Act)
  Deprivation of Liberty
  (draft) 10.91, 11.22, 12.83, 12.84
  Ch 2 . . . . .11.32

para 1.7 . . . . 12.24, 15.03
paras 1.8–1.9 . . . . .15.03
paras 2.8–2.18 . . . . .11.28
para 3.1–3.13 . . . . .12.29
para 3.15 . . . . .12.42
para 3.18 . . . . 12.13, 12.46
para 3.22 . . . . .12.46
para 3.37 . . . . .12.50
paras 3.43–3.58 . . . . .12.51
paras 3.92–3.97 . . . . .12.59
Code of Practice (Draft illustrative
  code Jan 2007) Confidentiality,
  Information Sharing and
  Patient's Access to Records
  Ch 34 . . . . .7.39
Code of Practice (Draft illustrative
  code Jan 2007) Victims
Ch 29.5 . . . . .7.38
para 29.5(C) 7.35

List of Terms and Abbreviatons

1983 Act	the Mental Health Act 1983
2005 Act	the Mental Capacity Act 2005
AC	approved clinician
AMHP	approved mental health professional
ASW	approved social worker
CTO	community treatment order made under the SCT provisions of s 17A of the 1983 Act
Deputy	Court appointed deputy appointed under s 16 of the 2005 Act
Donee	Donee of a Lasting Power of Attorney made under s 9 of the 2005 Act
ECHR	European Convention on Human Rights
ECtHR	European Court of Human Rights
ECT	electro-convulsive therapy
Expert Committee	The Expert Committee, Chaired by Prof. Genevra Richardson, appointed by the government in October 1998 to review mental health legislation
IMCA	independent mental capacity advocate
IMHA	independent mental health advocate
JCHR	Joint Parliamentary Committee on Human Rights
LHB	local health board, the commissioning NHS health body in Wales
LPA	Lasting Power of Attorney made under s 9 of the 2005 Act
MHAC	Mental Health Act Commission
NHS body	National Health Service trust, NHS foundation trust, Local Health Board, Special Health Authority, or Primary Care Trust
Tribunal	Mental Health Review Tribunal
Part 4	Part 4 of the 1983 Act
Part 4A	Part 4A of the 1983 Act
PCT	NHS Primary Care Trust, the commissioning NHS health body in England
RMO	responsible medical officer
SCT	supervised community treatment under s 17A of the 1983 Act
Schedule A1	Schedule A1 of the 2005 Act governing the new deprivation of liberty procedure
SOAD	Second Opinion Appointed Doctor, appointed by the MHAC under Part 4 and 4A of the 1983 Act
Substituted consent	Consent lawfully given by another person such as (for the incapacitated) a donee, deputy, or the Court of Protection; and, for children, a person with parental responsibility or the High Court in its jurisdiction relating to children.

Part I
REFORM OF THE MENTAL HEALTH ACT 1983

1

INTRODUCTION

A. Structure of the Book	1.01
1. Part I: Reform of the Mental Health Act 1983	1.02
2. Part II: The Mental Capacity Act 2005 and its Amendments	1.03
B. The Background to the 2007 Act	1.04
C. A Brief History of Mental Health Legislation	1.17
1. The Origins of Mental Health Law	1.18
2. Statutory Regulation of Detention Begins	1.20
3. The Lunacy Act 1890 and the Triumph of 'Legalism'	1.23
4. The Pendulum Swings: the Rise of 'Informality' and the 1930 and 1959 Acts	1.26
5. The Development of a Human Rights Discourse: the 1982 and 1983 Acts	1.27
6. Developments Since 1983: the Human Rights Act 1998	1.30
D. The 2007 Act: the Pendulum Swings Again?	1.34
E. Human Rights	1.38
1. The Convention Rights and Other International Standards	1.38
2. The Human Rights Act 1998	1.44
3. The Joint Parliamentary Committee on Human Rights (JCHR)	1.45
4. The Compatibility of the 2007 Act with the Convention Rights	1.48
F. Commencement and Transitional Provisions	1.49
G. Territorial Extent: England and Wales	1.52

A. STRUCTURE OF THE BOOK

The title of this book, *Blackstone's Guide to the Mental Health Act 2007*, is a little mis- 1.01
leading, as this is really a book about two other pieces of legislation, the Mental
Health Act 1983 (the 1983 Act) and the Mental Capacity Act 2005 (the 2005 Act),

as they have been amended by the 2007 Act. Accordingly, the book is in two parts: Part I considers the 1983 Act, Part II the 2005 Act. References throughout the book are to the provisions of the 1983 Act and 2005 Act (whether in their original form or as amended, as the context requires), rather than to the provisions as they appear in the 2007 Act. Those amending provisions can, if necessary, be identified from the Appendices to the book, which set out the existing wording of the two Acts, the amended wording and the provision of the 2007 Act which has effected the change. The 2007 Act is not expected to come into force until October 2008 (April 2009 for the amendments to the 2005 Act), so I have sought to explain the law as it applies now and as it will apply once the 2007 Act comes into force.

1. Part I: Reform of the Mental Health Act 1983

1.02 Part I considers the amendments made to the 1983 Act, but does not purport to be a complete account of the 1983 Act and the law made under it. In that sense it is intended primarily to explain the changes effected by the 2007 Act, and should be used as a companion to other books on the subject of the 1983 Act.[1] The Chapters are under the following headings:

- Chapter 1, 'Introduction', looks at the background to the reform of the 2007 Act, a brief history of mental health legislation, human rights issues, commencement, and territorial extent.

- Chapter 2, 'An Overview of the 1983 Act and its Amendments' draws a broad outline of the 1983 Act and the key amendments to its provisions to be made by the 2007 Act.

- Chapter 3, 'Amendments to the Criteria for Guardianship and Detention' looks in detail at the amended definition of 'mental disorder', the removal of the four classifications of mental disorder, the removal of the 'treatability' test, the introduction of a new 'appropriate treatment test', a revised definition of 'medical treatment', and a new 'treatability test', and discusses the implications of the amendments.

- Chapter 4, 'Additional Safeguards for Patients in Relation to Admission and Detention' considers the amendments to the provisions governing the Code of Practice and the new 'fundamental principles', the amendments to the 'nearest relative' provisions, new rights of automatic referral to the Mental Health Review Tribunal, the new Independent Mental Health Advocates (IMHA), additional safeguards for the admission and detention of children, and the extension of the remit of the Mental Health Act Commission.

- Chapter 5, 'Supervised Community Treatment' (SCT), considers the new procedure introduced for the care and control of community patients released from hospital into the community and its implications.

- Chapter 6, 'Medical Treatment Under the 1983 Act', looks at the amendments introduced to Part 4 of the 1983 Act (including new safeguards for the use of ECT)

---

[1] Recommended particularly is Jones, *Mental Health Act Manual* (10th edn, Sweet & Maxwell, 2006).

and new Part 4A, which governs the treatment of patients on SCT, and their implications.

- Chapter 7 'Other Amendments' considers various other amendments introduced by the 2007 Act, in particular those that permit non-medically qualified professionals to take on the functions of the responsible medical officer (now to be the 'responsible clinician').

2. Part II: The Mental Capacity Act 2005 and its Amendments

Part II looks at the 2005 Act *and* the amendments introduced by the 2007 Act, in particular the new procedure for detention of so-called 'Bournewood' patients to be introduced in new Sch A1 and 1A of the 2005 Act. This part of the book is intended to give an overview of decision-making in personal welfare decisions (but not 'property and affairs') under the 2005 Act, both where detention is involved and where there is no detention. The 2005 Act came into force for the first time in its *unamended* form on 1 October 2007. Accordingly, I have tried to explain the law as it applies from 1 October 2007 to April 2009; and from April 2009, when the amendments introduced by the 2007 Act come into force. Part II can be more readily used as a handbook for personal welfare decision-making under the 2005 Act, both as it will apply when it comes into force on 1 October 2007 and as it will apply once the amendments of the 2007 Act come into force. Practitioners should not have an immediate need for recourse to other books on the subject, although space does not permit the Mental Capacity Act Code of Practice to be included (issued in April 2007 but which has yet to be amended to take into account the amendments of the 2007 Act). The Code is available online.[2] Part II is structured as follows:

- Chapter 8, 'Introduction and overview', explains the genesis of the 2005 Act and the amendments to be introduced by the 2007 Act.

- Chapter 9, 'Care and Treatment at Common Law', looks at the common law principles of autonomy, capacity and best interests that underpin the 2005 Act and the development of the doctrine of necessity, and also looks at the treatment of children at common law.

- Chapter 10, 'Care and Treatment Without Detention Under the 2005 Act' considers the 2005 Act in its original conception as it applies to personal welfare decisions and as it came into force on 1 October 2007. It looks at the new mechanisms for substituted decision-making, namely advance decisions refusing treatment, lasting powers of attorney (LPA), the new Court of Protection and court-appointed deputies, and the legal protection under s 5 for other individuals providing care and treatment where no other mechanism for substituted decision-making is in place. It also considers the appointment and functions of new Independent Mental Capacity Advocates (IMCAs).

1.03

---

[2] <http://www.justice.gov.uk/docs/mca-cp.pdf>.

- Chapter 11, 'Detention for Care and Treatment Under the 2005 Act' looks at issues arising out of the detention of incapacitated adults that lead to the introduction of the new Sch A1 and 1A procedure: detention at common law and the *Bournewood* decision, the subsequent judgment of the ECtHR in *HL v United Kingdom*, the government's initial legislative response to the *HL* judgment in the 2005 Act as currently enacted and the introduction of new Sch A1 and 1A by the 2007 Act.

- Chapter 12, 'Standard and Urgent Authorizations' gives detailed consideration to the new procedure for detention introduced by the 2007 Act in Schedule A1 of the 2005 Act.

- Chapter 13, 'Representation of Sch A1 Detainees' considers the appointment and function of new s 39A, s 39C, and s 39D IMCAs and Part 10 Representatives.

- Chapter 14, 'The Court of Protection, The Public Guardian and Court of Protection Visitors' looks at the jurisdiction of the Court of Protection in personal welfare matters, both as the 2005 Act stands and as amended by the 2007 Act, gives a summary of the procedure for making an application under the 2005 Act as it currently stands, and briefly explains the roles of the Public Guardian and Court of Protection Visitors.

- Chapter 15, 'The Interface Between the Detention and Treatment Regimes: the 1983 Act, 2005 Act and Common Law' explains the 'eligibility' requirement in Sch 1A of the 1983 Act which determines when a patient can be detained under the 1983 Act or the 2005 Act; s 28 of the 2005 Act, which determines when a patient can receive treatment under the 2005 Act or the 1983 Act; and grapples with these issues as they relate to the treatment of children.

B. THE BACKGROUND TO THE 2007 ACT

1.04 A history of the process of reform which lead to the 2007 Act is a book in itself. What follows is a brief overview.

1.05 The seeds of the 2007 Act may be said to have been sown by three events, two of them tragic homicides. First, the killing of Jonathan Zito on 17 December 1992 by Christopher Clunis, a paranoid schizophrenic who had ceased taking his medication while in the community, notwithstanding he was at the time under the care of local community mental health services under s 117 of the 1983 Act. Second, the murder of Lynn and Megan Russell on 9 July 1996 by Michael Stone, a convicted offender who suffered from a severe personality disorder and, it was widely believed at the time, had been refused admission to hospital only days before the murders because he was considered an 'untreatable psychopath'.[3] Third, the admission and detention

---

[3] It is now generally accepted that this was not the reason why Michael Stone was not admitted to hospital, and an independent enquiry report—not published until 2006 after objections by Mr Stone were overruled in legal proceedings—found that there had been no material available to the forensic consultant at the time to justify or require him to have considered admission of Mr Stone to hospital at the time of the Russell murders.

in Bournewood Hospital on 22 July 1997 of Mr L, a 48 year old man with severe learning disabilities, as an 'informal' patient and against the wishes of his carers, Mr and Mrs E. In subsequent proceedings for judicial review and habeas corpus the Court of Appeal held that, because he lacked capacity to consent to his admission to hospital, Mr L could only have been lawfully admitted and detained in hospital under the formal provisions of the 1983 Act. Although that decision was later overturned by the House of Lords, the absence of adequate safeguards for such patients had been highlighted and the government promised that amendments would be made to the mental health legislation to provide an alternative to detention under the 1983 Act which nevertheless incorporated sufficient safeguards (the *Bournewood* case[4]).

These three events were the key, if not the only, drivers for three main policy   1.06
objectives that underpinned the government's proposals for the reform of the 1983 Act. First, to make adequate powers of control and treatment available to ensure that patients continued to comply with treatment while in the community. Second, to make it easier to admit and detain so-called 'untreatable psychopaths', notwithstanding the views of their clinicians that no treatment was available which would 'alleviate or prevent a deterioration' of their condition (the 'treatability' test). And, third, to provide adequate safeguards for the detention and treatment of incapable patients like Mr L as an alternative to compulsory admission under the 1983 Act.

This is not to say that these were the only drivers for reform of mental health leg-   1.07
islation. The policy of treating patients with mental disorder in the community, rather than in hospitals, has been an ongoing one since long before the 1959 Act, and the introduction of powers to control and treat patients in the community may be seen as an extension of that process, particularly as the 'aftercare under supervision' provisions introduced by the Mental Health (Patients in the Community) Act 1995 (s 25A to J of the 1983 Act) have not proved a success. The government also wished to use the new legislation as a means of bringing the 1983 Act into line with its obligations under the ECHR and the Human Rights Act 1998, in particular in relation to the provisions governing the 'nearest relative' (see para 4.18). Moreover, the government had already published, in December 1997, a Green Paper on the law relating to the care and treatment of incapacitated individuals,[5] which lead in due course to the 2005 Act. That process is described in Part II.

The process of reform of the 1983 Act began in October 1998 with the appoint-   1.08
ment of an Expert Committee, headed by Prof. Genevra Richardson, (the 'Richardson Committee'), who reported in November 1999.[6] Their terms of reference were, 'to advise on how mental health legislation should be shaped to reflect contemporary patterns of care within a framework which balances the need to protect the rights of

---

[4] *R v Bournewood Community Mental Health NHS Trust ex p L* [1998] AC 458.
[5] *Who Decides?—Making Decisions on Behalf of Mentally Incapacitated Adults*, Cm 3808.
[6] Department of Health, *Report of the Expert Committee: Review of the Mental Health Act 1983*, December 1999.

individual patients and the need to ensure public safety'. A number of the Richardson Committee's recommendations found their way into the subsequent Green Paper on the Reform of the Mental Health Act 1983, also published in November 1999, but several did not. In particular, the government did not adopt the proposal that powers of detention and treatment should be guided by principles of non-discrimination and autonomy, so that individuals with mental disorder should not be detained or treated against their will if they have capacity to refuse the treatment, as in other areas of healthcare. The Richardson Committee's proposal that detention and treatment should also reflect the principle of 'reciprocity', so that where compulsion is employed there should be a concomitant duty on the relevant public bodies to provide appropriate services, was also not taken up. One proposal that did find favour, namely that any long-term detention would have to be authorized in advance by a Mental Health Tribunal, rather than upon review on application by the patient, was later abandoned when the 2004 Bill was withdrawn in March 2006.

1.09 The government published its White Paper, 'Reforming the Mental Health Act', in December 2000 (the 'White Paper'), and a draft Mental Health Bill 2002 was published for consultation in June 2002. The proposals met with considerable opposition, and a report from the Joint Committee on Human Rights[7] identified a number of human rights issues in the draft Bill. The issues raised on consultation included concerns that the definition of mental disorder was now too broad which unduly lowered the threshold for compulsion; that some requirement of 'therapeutic purpose' should be introduced if the 'treatability' test was to be removed; that the proposals for community treatment would substantially increase the use of compulsion; and that proposals for a new Mental Health Tribunal as the gateway to compulsion were impractical and would, in fact, lead to further delays in discharge.

1.10 The government considered the responses, and in September 2004 published a further draft Mental Health Bill (the 2004 Bill).[8] Shortly after the 2004 Bill was published, on 5 October 2004 the ECtHR delivered its long-awaited judgment in *HL v United Kingdom*,[9] the application brought by the unsuccessful appellant in the *Bournewood* case, Mr L. The ECtHR found, materially, that the detention of incapacitated patients such as Mr L under the common law doctrine of necessity did not comply with Article 5 of the ECHR, giving further impetus to the need for reform in this respect.

1.11 A Joint Parliamentary Committee was appointed to scrutinize the 2004 Bill (the Joint Committee). The Joint Committee considered 450 written submissions and heard oral evidence from 124 witnesses, including professionals, carers, and service users, and in March 2005 published a report[10] which, although accepting the need for mental health reform in principle, was critical of the length (307 provisions and 9 Schedules) and drafting of the 2004 Bill, and made over one hundred recommendations for amendments to be made to the Bill. The Joint Committee

---

[7] Joint Parliamentary Committee on Human Rights, report on the Draft Mental Health Bill, 25th Report of Session 2001–2, HL Paper 181, HC Paper 1294, published 11 November 2002.

[8] Cm 6305-I.

[9] [2004] 40 EHRR 761.

[10] Joint Committee on the Mental Health Bill 2004, HL Paper 79-I, HC 95-I Session 2004–5.

were also critical that the Bill placed too much emphasis upon public safety and not enough upon patient rights.

In March 2005 the government produced a consultation paper on its proposals to meet the issues raised by the judgment of the ECtHR in the *HL v United Kingdom* case.[11] **1.12**

In May 2005 a Mental Health Bill was announced as forthcoming legislation in the Queen's Speech. The government's response to the Joint Committee's report was published in July 2005,[12] accepting some but rejecting many of its recommendations. At this stage it was still proposed to introduce a revised Bill during the current Parliamentary Session. In March 2006, however, the government announced that the 2004 Bill and their proposals for a completely new Mental Health Act were to be abandoned, and instead the 1983 Act was to be amended to give effect to the key policy changes outlined above. In particular, an amending Bill would introduce proposals for supervised community treatment, the amendment of the criteria for detention, including the removal of the 'treatability' requirement, and the introduction of a new framework for the detention of incapacitated *Bournewood* patients. **1.13**

The resulting Mental Health Bill 2006 was published and introduced into the House of Lords on 16 November 2006 (HL Bill 1). A statement of compatibility under s 19 HRA was made in relation to the Mental Health Bill 2006 by Lord Warner of Brockley. **1.14**

During the reform process the government proposals, originally set out in its Green Paper in 1999, had triggered the formation of a coalition of interest groups, who came together under the umbrella of the Mental Health Alliance. This coalition eventually comprised 77 organizations including the Royal College of Psychiatrists, the Law Society, Mind (the National Association for Mental Health), Mencap, the Mental Health Foundation, the National Autistic Society, Rethink, the Sainsbury Centre for Mental Health, and YoungMinds. Their concerns centred particularly on the proposals for compulsory treatment in the community, which would extend the scope for compulsion beyond those who required treatment in hospital to a much wider constituency in the community, and the proposals to amend the criteria for detention, which would lower the threshold at which detention would be lawful. The Alliance championed a number of amendments to the Bill during its passage through Parliament, including a new 'therapeutic purpose' test to replace the 'treatability' test; an additional criteria for detention, compulsory treatment and for CTOs that the individual's judgment be 'significantly impaired'; additional conditions for the making of CTOs that would restrict them only to those 'revolving door' patients who had relapsed in the past; statutory rights to advocacy and limitations on the 'informal' admission of 16 and 17 year olds with the consent of a person with 'parental responsibility', among others. **1.15**

---

[11] 'Bournewood' Consultation: The approach to be taken in response to the judgment of the European Court of Human Rights in the 'Bournewood' case, March 2005.

[12] Government response to the report of the Joint Committee on the draft Mental Health Bill 2004, Cm 6624, July 2005.

1.16   The amendments garnered a majority in the House of Lords and considerable support in the House of Commons, and by the end of the process a number of concessions had been obtained, including a new right of advocacy (see para 4.33), restrictions on the informal admission of 16 and 17 year olds (see para 4.44), a new duty on hospital managers to provide an appropriate environment and treatment for children under 18 (see para 4.45), limited restrictions on the imposition of CTOs, and a new 'treatability' test (see para 3.72). Amendments introduced in the House of Lords requiring the judgment to be 'significantly impaired' and which would have restricted the use of CTOs to true 'revolving door' patients were, however, overturned in the Commons (see para 3.109). The Bill completed its passage through Parliament on 4 July 2007 and received Royal Assent on 19 July 2007.

C. A BRIEF HISTORY OF MENTAL HEALTH LEGISLATION[13]

1.17   One reason for reforming the 1983 Act that has been given by the government is that there has not been a proper review of mental health law since 1983; and, moreover, that the 1983 Act was in very large measure an act that amended and updated its predecessor, the 1959 Act. Mental health law therefore requires to be brought up to date. While it is not possible to assess the impact of the 2007 Act at this remove, a few short months after gaining Royal Assent, it is nevertheless possible to put it in the context of that earlier legislation before seeking to draw some, very preliminary, conclusions as to the possible direction in which the law is heading (at para 1.34).

1. The Origins of Mental Health Law

1.18   There has been statutory jurisdiction to control the property and affairs of the mentally disordered since the 14th century. The *De Praerogativa Regis* authorized the Crown to acquire the lands and estates of 'idiots' and 'lunatics'. With respect to the former, whose condition was considered to be life-long, the Crown was entitled to the rents and profits of his estates for life. For those suffering 'lunacy', a condition of unpredictable and often short period, any excess of income over the expenses of maintenance were to be held in trust pending the lunatic's recovery or, in the event of his death, applied 'for the benefit of his soul'.[14]

1.19   This statute related solely to the practical machinery of securing patients' property, but persons of unsound mind and infants could also be placed under the

---

[13] For those seeking a comprehensive history of mental health legislation up to and including the 1983 Act, they are recommended to read Clive Unsworth's *The Politics of Mental Health Legislation* (Oxford University Press, 1987), from which this account is largely drawn. *Mental Health Law* (Sweet & Maxwell, 1996) by Brenda Hoggett (now Baroness Hale of Richmond), is also highly recommended. Phil Fennel's *Treatment without Consent: Law, Psychiatry and the Treatment of Mentally Disordered People since 1845* (Routledge, 1996) gives an excellent account of the history of the treatment of psychiatric disorders and of the measures introduced to control and regulate such treatment.

[14] Clive Unsworth, *The Politics of Mental Health Legislation* (Oxford University Press, 1987) 47.

guardianship of the Crown in its *parens patriae* jurisdiction, which was linked to the Crown' prerogative powers in relation to the estates of such individuals. Decisions could then be taken about his person (including detention) as well as his property. The question of whether the individual was 'incapable of managing his property and affairs' was determined by a Master in Lunacy, with the observance of full Court procedure, sometimes with a jury. If found to be a 'lunatic' then not only his property and affairs, but also the individual's person, was entrusted to a 'committee' (normally an individual) and the care of his property assigned to a 'committee of the estate'.[15] This jurisdiction came in due course to be exercised by the High Court until its revocation following the Mental Health Act 1959, described in paras 8.05– 8.07. In addition to this, rather formal, mechanism for detention, there existed authority at common law a power to detain those who, by reason of mental disorder, were a danger, or potential danger, to themselves or others, in so far as this was shown to be necessary,[16] albeit not for lengthy periods of detention.

2. Statutory Regulation of Detention Begins

Statutory provisions governing the civil commitment of those suffering mental dis- order are of more recent origin. Vagrancy legislation which also mentioned 'wandering lunatics' was introduced in 1714,[17] and the Vagrancy Act 1744 provided that 'persons who by lunacy or otherwise are furiously mad, or are so far disordered in their senses that they may be dangerous to be permitted to go abroad' might, on the order of two or more justices of the peace, be apprehended, 'to be kept safely locked up in some secure place . . . or chained . . . for and during such time only as such lunacy or madness shall continue'. The first legislation relating to mental disorder as such was an Act for regulating Madhouses of 1774,[18] which introduced the requirement that a private 'madhouse' required to be inspected and licensed by Lunacy Commissioners, elected by the Royal College of Physicians, and its owners were liable to a £100 fine for admitting a lunatic without the written order of a medical man. A similar requirement was introduced for 'pauper lunatics' in 1815. Statutory provisions authorizing the detention of the insane in criminal proceedings were introduced at this time, notably the Criminal Lunatics Act 1800, which authorized the detention of those found 'not guilty but insane' in relation to indictable offences. The 1800 Act was introduced to ensure the lawful detention of the defendant in Hadfield's Case (1800) 27 St Tr 1281, who successfully pleaded the defence of insanity to a charge of high treason, arising out of an attempt to assassinate King George III. The development of the criminal procedure governing the trial and detention of

1.20

---

[15] Unsworth (n 14 above) 49.

[16] *Rex v Coate* (1772) Lofft 73, especially at 75, *per* Lord Mansfield CJ; *Scott v Wakem* (1862) 3 F&F 328, 333, *per* Bramwell B; and *Symm v Fraser* (1863) 3 F&F 859, 883, *per* Cockburn CJ; cited by Lord Goff in *Bournewood*, [1999] AC 458, 490.

[17] 12 Anne Stat. 2 c. 23.

[18] 14 Geo. III c. 49.

mentally disordered offenders falls largely outside the scope of this work, however, and is not considered further.

1.21   During the 18th and 19th centuries, for the mentally disordered the rapid urbanization and industrialization of society lead to a 'dramatic escalation in the rate of their consignment to institutions'.[19] Many of these were confined in mixed workhouses, gaols, and houses of correction. The building of public hospitals financed by voluntary public subscription grew during the 18th century, and in 1808 an Act 'for the better Care and Maintenance of Lunatics being Paupers or Criminals in England' empowered local authorities to build institutions for the reception of lunatics at public expense, to end the existing practice of their detention in other types of accommodation which it described as 'highly dangerous and inconvenient'.[20] The Lunatic Asylums Act 1845 made the building of such institutions mandatory.

1.22   In 1807, there were only 2248 people (or 2.26 per 10,000 of population) officially recognized as insane, both in and out of institutions. By 1890, there were 86,167. Ninety per cent of these were paupers and all but a small proportion were acknowledged to be incurable.[21] By way of contrast (and bearing in mind the fivefold increase in population), for the period 2003–4, 14,000 people were detained compulsorily under the 1983 Act as at 31 March 2004, with 45,700 formal admissions during the year 2003–4,[22] including both private and public hospitals. During the same period, there were approximately 155,000 informal admissions to hospitals.[23]

3. The Lunacy Act 1890 and the Triumph of 'Legalism'

1.23   The history of modern mental health legislation begins with the Lunacy Act 1890, when popular public pressure to introduce safeguards against the inappropriate detention of the sane lead to the introduction of much more stringent requirements for admission and detention. Prior to 1890, the detention of 'pauper lunatics' could only be authorized by two justices of the peace upon application by the 'relieving officer' and then later by the 'mental welfare officer'. There were no such requirements for privately paying patients, however, who could be admitted on the application of any person, provided a medical certificate was given in support. Popular consciousness of the vulnerability to abuse of the sane, rather than concern at the conditions of detention of the insane, lead to two demands, in particular: first, the extension of the requirement of the order of a magistrate for detention as a lunatic from pauper to private cases, and second, the abolition or severe restriction of private licensed houses.[24]

---

[19] Unsworth (n 14 above) 60.
[20] Unsworth (n 14 above) 59–60.
[21] Brenda Hoggett, *Mental Health Law* (4th edn, Sweet & Maxwell, 1996), 5–6.
[22] Department of Health Statistical Bulletin 2004/22.
[23] Healthcare Commission, *State of Healthcare Report 2004*, 11.
[24] Unsworth (n 14 above) 81.

The 1890 Act proscribed voluntary admissions to hospital for 'pauper lunatics' 1.24 and introduced the requirement in all cases of involuntary commitment for formal certification by a judicial order, following a petition by relatives or poor law officials and supported by medical evidence. The same requirement was introduced for those admitted under the Mental Deficiency Act 1913, which covered not only the severely incapacitating conditions of idiocy and imbecility, but also the less disabled 'feeble-minded' (who now would be classified under 'mental impairment'). The 1913 Act also authorized, for the first time, the detention of 'moral imbeciles', which comprised 'persons who from an early age display some permanent mental defect coupled with strong vicious or criminal propensities on which punishment has had little or no effect', the forerunner of today's 'psychopathic disorder'.[25]

These formal measures were unpopular with the medical profession and those 1.25 charged with overseeing the legislation, the Lunacy Commission (later the Board of Control). They were seen as unnecessarily 'legalistic' and, because of the stigmatizing effects of certification, doctors shrank from admitting patients under these procedures until, in many cases, it was too late for treatment to have any chance of success. The medical profession was also identifying new forms of mental disorder falling far short of 'madness' or 'lunacy' for which certification and confinement were considered unnecessary, the 'shell-shock' cases of the First World War being among these. Moreover, the demarcation of patients as either 'lunatics' or 'defectives' under the 1890 Act and 1913 Acts, respectively, was reflected in separate institutions for each category; a 'lunatic' could not be confined in a mental handicap institution and vice versa,[26] thus creating an arbitrary barrier to treatment for those falling within both categories.

4. The Pendulum Swings: the Rise of 'Informality' and the 1930 and 1959 Acts

The Mental Treatment Act 1930 marked the first major change, allowing the treat- 1.26 ment of voluntary patients by those who were able to make a written application and a 'temporary status' was introduced for non-volitional patients who required treatment for less than a year. The 1959 Act marked a further break with the legalism of the past, introducing (s 5) the principle that patients should be admitted informally wherever possible, now enshrined in s 131 of the 1983 Act, removing the requirement that certification be approved by two justices and allowing admission on the application of a social worker or nearest relative when supported by two medical recommendations. Judicial oversight was to be provided by a new Mental Health Review Tribunal, which would exercise the function of reviewing a detention already effected rather than providing the authorization in the first place.

---

[25] Unsworth (n 14 above) 153.
[26] Hoggett (n 21 above) 6.

5. The Development of a Human Rights Discourse: the 1982 and 1983 Acts

1.27　If the 1959 Act represents the apogee of 'informality' over 'legalism', the Mental Health (Amendment) Act 1982 (the 1982 Act) and its consolidating statute, the 1983 Act, mark the point at which the pendulum swung back in favour of greater legal controls over the admission and treatment of patients. The 1982 and 1983 Acts introduced a threshold requirement for the use of long-term compulsory powers classified under 'mental impairment' or 'severe mental impairment' (previously 'subnormal' and 'severely subnormal') of 'abnormally aggressive or seriously irresponsible conduct', the introduction of the 'treatability' requirement for those with 'mental impairment' and 'psychopathic disorder', the bolstering of the powers of the nearest relative, the shortening of periods of admission for treatment from one year to six months, the introduction of automatic referrals of patients to the Mental Health Review Tribunal at the end of the period for making an application, conferring power on the Tribunal to order the release of restricted patients, rather than to recommend such release to the Home Secretary, and a dramatic reduction in the powers of the guardian over a person placed in guardianship.

1.28　The Acts' reforming provisions were in considerable part attributable to proposals advanced by Larry Gostin, as Legal and Welfare Rights Officer and later Legal Director of Mind (the National Association for Mental Health) in his book, *A Human Condition*.[27] Larry Gostin was a US lawyer and academic who, inspired by the civil rights movement in the US and its particular application in the field of mental health law,[28] in his role with Mind brought a series of challenges to the Mental Health Act 1959 in the ECtHR. This achieved most notable success in *X v United Kingdom*,[29] which established that absence of a power in the Mental Health Review Tribunal to order the release of a restricted patient violated Article 5(4) ECHR.

1.29　This growing awareness that safeguards were necessary not out of some arid 'legalism' but to protect patients' human rights underlay the other major innovation of the 1982 and 1983 Acts, the introduction—for the first time—of legislative controls over the administration of medical treatment to detained patients. The architects of the 1959 Act had assumed that detention brought with it an implied power to treat; the idea that safeguards were necessary to protect patients from mistaken or unnecessary treatment was hardly raised during the debates that lead to the enactment of the 1959 Act.[30] The arrival of major, often controversial, treatments such as psychosurgery, insulin treatment, electro-convulsive therapy, medication with unpleasant and irreversible side-effects, along with developments in the legal

---

[27] LO Gostin, *A Human Condition: the Mental Health Act 1959* (1975, published by Mind). Professor Gostin is now Associate Dean for Research and Academic Programs at Georgetown University Law centre in the United States.

[28] For an account of this movement, and its outcome, see Paul Appelbaum, *Almost a Revolution: Mental Health Law and the Limits of Change* (Oxford University Press, 1994).

[29] (1981) 4 EHRR 181.

[30] Unsworth (n 14 above) 322.

concepts of consent and autonomy, gave rise to considerable concerns about the unregulated administration of such treatment. Coupled with a new language of human rights with which to articulate those concerns, calls for statutory regulation grew. The result was the safeguards of Part 4 of the 1983 Act, described in detail in Chapter 6.

6. Developments Since 1983: the Human Rights Act 1998

Developments since 1983—other than very recent developments—show no sign of   1.30
the pendulum swinging back the other way. The Mental Health (Patients in the Community) Act 1995, which introduced 'aftercare under supervision' by s 25A to J of the 1983 Act with the aim of providing an effective means of managing and treating patients in the community, has been little used primarily because of its 'legalism' and over-reliance on formality (see paras 5.12–5.18).

The introduction of the Human Rights Act 1998, which came into force in   1.31
October 2000, has continued the trend towards stronger protection of human rights, as a series of decisions by domestic courts have (in some cases) reinforced and entrenched patients' rights. The Courts have made declarations under s 4 of the 1998 Act that provisions of the 1983 Act are incompatible with Article 5 in *R (H) v Mental Health Review Tribunal*[31] (the reverse burden of proof under ss 72 and 73) and in *R (D) v Home Secretary*[32] (in relation to the absence of any right of a transferred post-tariff discretionary lifer to have his case referred to the Parole Board after a recommendation for his discharge by a Tribunal in s 74). In *R (M) v Health Secretary*,[33] a declaration was made that the absence of any means by which a patient can change his nearest relative under ss 26 and 29 of the 1983 Act is incompatible with the patient's rights under Article 8. A series of cases have found that delays in referring and hearing of cases by the Mental Health Review Tribunal are a breach of Article 5(4) for which compensation is payable (*R (KB) v Mental Health Review Tribunal*,[34] *R (Rayner & Marsh) v Home Secretary & Ors*[35]).

In the context of compulsory treatment, in *R (Wilkinson) v Broadmoor*[36] the Court   1.32
of Appeal accepted that a combination of Articles 2, 3, 6, and 8 entitled a patient to a determination by a court of the lawfulness of compulsory treatment in advance of the treatment being given. Moreover, because domestic law created no statutory right to such a hearing, the Administrative Court on judicial review was required to reach its own views on the merits, where the treating doctor was required to prove to a high standard that the treatment was medically necessary. In doing so,

---

[31] [2002] QB 1.
[32] [2003] 1 WLR 1315.
[33] [2003] EWHC 1094 Admin.
[34] [2004] QB 936.
[35] [2007] EWHC 1028 (Admin).
[36] [2002] 1 WLR 419.

if necessary the Court will hear live evidence with cross-examination.[37] *Wilkinson* was followed by the case of *R (Wooder) v Dr Feggetter*,[38] in which the Court of Appeal ruled that, given the fundamental rights engaged by a decision to compulsorily treat an individual (notably Articles 3 and 8), a SOAD is required to give reasons for his decision for endorsing an RMO's treatment plan under s 58.

1.33   Perhaps the most obvious demonstration of the victory of 'legalism' (although I prefer 'human rights') over the 'informality' represented by the 1959 Act is the decision of the ECtHR in *HL v United Kingdom*.[39] In *Bournewood* the House of Lords had expressly affirmed the principle established in s 5 of the 1959 Act and carried through into s 131 of the 1983 Act, that a patient was to receive treatment 'informally' wherever possible, even if (as in Mr L's case) he lacked capacity to consent and, therefore, had not consented to his admission and treatment. If it involved detention, held their Lordships, then the common law doctrine of 'necessity' provided the lawful basis for that treatment, which had been impliedly preserved by s 5 and, thereafter, by s 131. The ECtHR held that to be unlawful; the absence of any 'fair and proper procedures' for determining the length or purpose of the detention meant that the doctrine of 'necessity' did not accord with the Convention notion of 'lawfulness', which carries with it a requirement of adequate legal protections with the aim of avoiding arbitrary or mistaken decision making (described in detail in Chapter 11).

D. THE 2007 ACT: THE PENDULUM SWINGS AGAIN?

1.34   It could be said, with some justification, that the government's proposals throughout the reform process represented a concerted move to swing the pendulum away from the formality and safeguards of the 1983 Act and back towards a less regulated, more 'flexible' procedure for the detention and treatment of those with mental disorder. In particular, (i) the repeal of the aftercare under supervision provisions of s 25A to 25J of the 1983 Act and the introduction of 'supervised community treatment' with lower thresholds for compulsion, and (ii) the amendment of the criteria for detention by removing the four classifications of mental disorder, the requirement for 'abnormally aggressive or seriously irresponsible conduct' for patients suffering personality disorder, and the 'treatability' requirement together represent a less 'legalistic' approach and a consequent weakening of patient safeguards.

1.35   Upon closer inspection, however, it is apparent that these proposals do not represent as big a swing—arguably, any swing—away from the protection of human rights and back to the 'informality' and flexibility of the 1959 Act as at first glance might appear. The debate has, in a sense, moved on. The dichotomy between

---

[37] Although 'if section 58 is properly complied with issues requiring the cross-examination of medical witnesses should not often arise': see *R (B) v Dr S* [2006] 1 WLR 810, para 68.

[38] [2002] 3 WLR 591.

[39] (2004) 40 EHRR 761.

'legalism' and 'informality' or 'medicalism' represented two opposing philosophies which have, to a very great extent, now been reconciled. On the one hand, there were those (the medical profession and the architects of the 1930 and 1959 Acts) who felt that the treatment of mental disorder should be no different from any other form of healthcare, with treatment a matter for doctors' clinical judgment in consultation with the patient. This point of view saw no need for regulation, which was a barrier to treatment and stigmatized those who had no need for compulsion. On the other hand there were those—represented by the architects of the 1890 Act and the reforms that lead to the 1983 Act—who considered that untrammelled medical discretion coupled with unregulated procedures for admission and (later) treatment created a real risk of individuals being arbitrarily detained and treated.

It is clear that the first argument, in favour of informal admission and treatment wherever possible, has to a large extent been won: the proportion of patients who are now detained compared to a hundred or even fifty years ago is immeasurably smaller (see para 1.22).[40] The view is shared by all stakeholders that those with mental disorder should be treated, wherever possible, in the same way as those suffering merely physical disorders. In particular, treatment should be given in the community, rather than in institutions, and those requiring treatment should be treated no differently from those with any other illness or condition, if possible. By the same token, there is now a consensus that, where compulsion is necessary, adequate safeguards to protect human rights and prevent against abuse are necessary. No more compelling evidence of that consensus can be demonstrated than by the Royal College of Psychiatrists' membership of the Mental Health Alliance and its advocacy of criteria for detention based on 'therapeutic purpose' and the additional requirement (which did not find its way into the 2007 Act) that the patient's judgment be 'significantly impaired' before compulsion is authorized. That can only be because the medical profession recognizes that fair and proper legal procedures give legitimacy to doctors' decisions and enhance, rather than undermine, the therapeutic alliance between doctor and patient. 1.36

On analysis the 2007 Act does anything but roll back the law; parts of it, particularly new Sch A1, are so complex and bureaucratic (see para 8.22) that the 2007 Act could be hailed as the new 'triumph of legalism'. It is unlikely that the pendulum will ever swing very much further back towards the 'informality' of the 1959 Act and the primacy it gave to the discretion of doctors over legal procedures. Treatment in the community is now a given; contemporary notions of human rights make it a commonplace that treatment, wherever it is given, should be properly regulated. Where the debate has moved on to (as in so many areas of public life) is the battleground of 'public safety' versus human rights. The traditional allies of 'informality', the medical profession, have defected to the other side; they recognize that proper treatment and human rights march hand in hand. The challenge for them during the reform process, as for the other members of the Mental Health Alliance, has 1.37

---

[40] Hoggett (n 21 above) 8.

been to minimize the authoritarian aspects of the government's proposals while wringing from them as many concessions as possible to increase protection for human rights. In both respects they have been very successful, although that is not to underplay the opportunities missed for improving care and protection for this vulnerable section of society, nor to minimize those aspects of the law that still afford inadequate protection for human rights.

E. HUMAN RIGHTS

1. The Convention Rights and Other International Standards

(a) *The Convention Rights*

1.38 Article 1 of the ECHR provides that 'the High Contracting Parties shall secure to everyone within their jurisdiction the rights and freedoms defined in Section I of the this Convention'. The rights referred to include, so far as material, Article 2 (the right to life), Article 3 (the prohibition against torture and inhuman or degrading treatment), Article 5(1) (the right to liberty), in particular Article 5(1)(e) which permits the detention of persons of 'unsound mind', Article 5(4) (the right to a determination by a 'court' of the lawfulness of detention), Article 6 (the right to a fair trial), Article 8 (the right to respect for private and family life), and Article 14 (the prohibition against discrimination).

1.39 The ECtHR has built up a significant body of case-law relevant to the detention and treatment of persons with mental disorder which has in turn informed the growing body of domestic jurisprudence on the operation of the HRA. Some of the ECtHR's decisions had a direct bearing on the reform process leading to the 2007 Act, in particular its decision in *HL v United Kingdom*.[41] Where relevant these are mentioned in the text (see para 1.48).

(b) *Positive and Negative Obligations*

1.40 The ECtHR has developed the doctrine of 'positive obligations' from the duty in Article 1 of the Convention which obliges contracting States to 'secure to everyone within its jurisdiction the rights and freedoms defined in the Convention'. Positive obligations may be express (as in Article 2), but are often implied, where necessary to give effect to an express obligation, which are primarily negative in nature.[42] 'Negative obligations' prevent the State or its agents violating Convention rights directly. Positive obligations' usually arise so as to require States to take appropriate measures to protect individuals from the acts of third parties (ie non-State agents) which would, if carried out by the State, constitute a Convention violation. They may also arise so as to require States to take measures to protect vulnerable

---

[41] (2004) 40 EHRR 761.

[42] *Marckx v Belgium* (1979) 2 EHRR 330; Clayton & Tomlinson, *The Law of Human Rights'*, (Oxford University Press, 2000) 308–10; Mowbray, *The Development of Positive Obligations under the European Convention on Human Rights* (Hart, 2004) 1–6.

individuals from acts of self-harm[43] or from the consequences of disease[44] or disability.[45] Whether a positive obligation may be said to exist in any given case is a question of balancing the rights of the individual against the interests of the community.[46] 'Positive obligations' have been recognized as arising under several Convention Articles, notably Articles 2, 3, and 8. The Court has now extended the concept of implied positive obligations to Article 5(1): *Storck v Germany*,[47] paras 101–3. The positive obligations that have been developed fall into five categories, although there is considerable overlap between them:

- The primary obligation upon States is to put in place a legislative and administrative framework designed to provide effective deterrence against conduct that would infringe the relevant Convention right.[48]

- The positive obligations under Articles 2 and 3 also require, as a minimum, an effective independent judicial system to be set up so that the cause of death or unlawful treatment may be determined and those responsible made accountable. Where conduct is deliberate this duty will require criminal proceedings to be brought by the State.[49]

- The positive obligation under Article 2 or 3 may also require an official investigation into the death or unlawful treatment, in particular where the State may bear responsibility, but the obligation is not limited solely to cases of killings or ill-treatment by State agents.[50] Any such investigation must be at the instigation of the State[51] and must ensure the victim is involved in the procedure to the extent necessary to safeguard his or her legitimate interests.[52]

- In 'appropriate circumstances', the positive obligation will also require the State to take certain operational measures to protect an individual who is at real and immediate risk of suffering treatment that would infringe his Convention rights.[53]

---

[43] *Keenan v United Kingdom*, (2001) 33 EHRR 913; *R (D) v Home Secretary* [2006] EWCA Civ 143 (suicide attempt not leading to death still triggered Article 2 duty to investigate).

[44] Application no 4353/03, *Tarariyeva v Russia*, 14 December 2006 (Article 2).

[45] *Botta v Italy* (1998) 26 EHRR 241 (Article 8).

[46] *Sheffield and Horsham v UK* (1998) 27 EHRR 163 at 191, para 52.

[47] (2005) 43 EHRR 96.

[48] *A v United Kingdom*, 23 September 1998, ECHR, para 22; *X & Y v Netherlands* (1985) 8 EHRR 235, para 27; *MC v Bulgaria*, Application no 39272/98, 4 December 2003, para 149; *Z v the United Kingdom*, paras 73–5 (Article 3); see also *Airey v Ireland* (1979) 2 EHRR 305, para 32 (Article 8); *Edwards v United Kingdom* (2002) 35 EHRR 19, para 54; *Oneryildiz v Turkey*, paras 89–90; *Osman v United Kingdom*, para 115; Application no 4353/03, *Tarariyeva v Russia*, 14 December 2006, para 74 (Article 2); *Storck v Germany* (2005) 43 EHRR 96 (Article 5).

[49] *X & Y v Netherlands* (1985) 8 EHRR 235, para 27 (Article 3); *Edwards v United Kingdom* (2002) 35 EHRR 19, para 54; *Vo v France*, paras 90–1; *Tarariyeva v Russia*, para 75 (Article 2).

[50] *MC v Bulgaria*, para 151; *Assenov v Bulgaria*, para 102 (Article 3); *R (D) v Home Secretary* [2006] EWCA Civ 143 (suicide attempt not leading to death still triggered Article 2 duty to investigate).

[51] *Edwards v United Kingdom*, (2002) 35 EHRR 19, para 69 (an Article 2 case).

[52] *Jordan v United Kingdom*, (2003) 37 EHRR 2, para 109 (an Article 2 case).

[53] *MC v Bulgaria*, para 152 (Article 3); see also *Osman v United Kingdom*, para 115, *Keenan v United Kingdom*, (2001) 33 EHRR 913, para 90, *Edwards v United Kingdom*, para 54 (Article 2).

- The relevant Convention rights, taken together with the non-discrimination duty in Article 14, also include a positive obligation which is violated when the State, without an objective and reasonable justification, treats differently persons whose situations are the same or *fails* to treat differently persons whose situations are significantly different.[54]

(c) *Implied Procedural Obligations*

1.41　Certain Convention articles, notably Article 8, also contain implied procedural obligations which may also be said to be 'positive obligations'. Thus, for example, there is a requirement to afford a person whose Article 8 rights are affected by a decision an opportunity to be 'involved in the decision-making process, seen as a whole, to a degree sufficient to provide them with the requisite protection of their interests'.[55] To this end, a Court 'may scrutinise the decision-making process to ensure that due weight has been accorded to the interests of the individual'.[56] Thus, a failure to provide an opportunity to make informed representations by failing to disclose relevant material (as in *TP*) or a failure to give reasons for a decision[57] may breach this procedural obligation.

(d) *Other International Standards*

1.42　Also of relevance are international human rights standards which, although non-binding, may nevertheless inform the standards required by the ECHR. These are set out in a number of treaties and other documents, including the International Covenant on Civil and Political Rights (ICCPR), UN Convention on the Rights of Persons with Disabilities (opened for signature on 13 December 2006),[58] the UN Principles for the Protection of Persons with Mental Illness and for the Improvement of Mental Health Care (the UN Mental Illness Principles),[59] the Council of Europe's Convention for the Protection of Human Rights and Dignity of the Human Beings with regard to the Application of Biology and Medicine: Convention on Human Rights and Biomedicine (opened to signature at Oviedo on 4 April 1997) (the Biomedicine Convention).[60] Where children are involved, the standards set out in the Convention on the Rights of the Child (CRC) may be relevant.

(e) *Rec (2004) 10 of the Committee of Ministers of the Council of Europe*

1.43　Of particular relevance in the context of mental health law is 'Recommendation No. Rec(2004)10 of the Committee of Ministers of the Council of Europe to member States concerning the protection of the human rights and dignity of persons with

---

[54] *Thlimmenos v Greece* (2000) 31 EHRR 15, para 44; *Pretty v United Kingdom* (2002) 35 EHRR 1, para 88.
[55] *TP v United Kingdom*, (2002) 34 EHRR 2, para 72.
[56] *Hatton v United Kingdom*, (2003) 37 EHRR 611 para 99, 104.
[57] *R (Wooder) v Dr. Feggetter* [2003] QB 419, paras 44–9.
[58] Signed by 101 countries, including the United Kingdom and the European Union.
[59] Adopted by United Nations General Assembly Resolution 46/119 of 17 December 1991.
[60] Signed by 31 members of the Council of Europe, but not signed by the United Kingdom.

mental disorder', adopted on 22 September 2004 under the terms of Article 15(b) of the Statute of the Council of Europe (Rec (2004)10).[61] This Recommendation was introduced after the Council of Europe conducted a wide-ranging consultation exercise following the publication of its 'White Paper on the protection of the human rights and dignity of people suffering from mental disorder, 3 January, 2000'. Rec(2004)10 creates a number of rights, both procedural and substantive, some of which are already given protection by domestic law and the ECHR, some of which are not. Although the United Kingdom has reserved the right not to apply all of the recommendations, that position may change now that the legislative reform process has been completed.[62] Rec(2004)10 has been referred to by the House of Lords[63] and by the ECtHR[64] in determining the extent of the rights contained in the ECHR, and may be expected to play a part in future human rights litigation in the field of mental health.

2. The Human Rights Act 1998

The ECHR is 'given effect to' in domestic law by the Human Rights Act 1998,   1.44
which came into force on 2 October 2000. The rights are 'given effect' by four mechanisms. First, the HRA confers upon individuals the right to enforce Convention rights directly through the domestic courts. Section 6 provides 'It is unlawful for a public authority to act in a way which is incompatible with a Convention right', unless forced to do so by a provision of primary legislation which cannot be read compatibly with Convention rights. An aggrieved individual may directly rely upon the Convention rights contained in the Schedule to the HRA, whether by bringing proceedings against a public authority or by raising it in other proceedings to which he is a party (s 7). Second, the HRA imposes a strong interpretative obligation upon the Courts to 'read and give effect to' Convention rights in a way which is compatible with the Convention rights (s 3). Third, by s 4 HRA the higher Courts can make a 'declaration of incompatibility' in respect of a provision that cannot be 'read and given effect to' under s 3 in a way that complies with the Convention. s 10 HRA then provides a 'fast-track' mechanism by which the incompatibility may be remedied in Parliament. Fourth, by s 19 the a Minister of the Crown in charge of a bill in either House of Parliament must, before Second Reading of the bill, make a statement to the effect that in his view the provisions of the Bill are compatible with the Convention rights (a 'statement of compatibility') or make a statement to the effect that although he is unable to make a statement of compatibility the

---

[61] Art 15(b) provides: 'In appropriate cases, the conclusions of the Committee may take the form of recommendations to the governments of members, and the Committee may request the governments of members to inform it of the action taken by them with regard to such recommendations.'

[62] See Hansard HC Debs 20 October 2004, column 796W.

[63] *R (Munjaz) v Mersey Care NHS Trust* [2006] 2 AC 148 by Lord Hope, para 88.

[64] *Wilkinson v United Kingdom*, Application no 14659/02, (Admissibility) 28 February 2006, page 12.

government nevertheless wishes the House to proceed with the Bill. There is a growing body of case-law under the HRA as it applies to mental health law. This is not, however, a book about the Human Rights Act and the ECHR or international law, but about the 2007 Act. The relevant ECHR provisions and general principles are now familiar to most practitioners and may be found in other textbooks.[65] A number of the cases are mentioned in para 1.31 above, and where relevant to the 2007 Act they are mentioned in the text of the book (see para 1.48).

3. The Joint Parliamentary Committee on Human Rights (JCHR)

1.45   A further mechanism for securing respect for the Convention rights is the Joint Parliamentary Committee on Human Rights (JCHR). The JCHR is not a creature of the HRA but was established by Parliament to consider (a) matters relating to human rights in the United Kingdom (but excluding consideration of individual cases); (b) proposals for remedial orders, draft remedial orders and remedial orders made under s 10 of and laid under Schedule 2 to the Human Rights Act 1998; and (c) in respect of draft remedial orders and remedial orders, whether the special attention of the House should be drawn to them on any of the grounds specified in Standing Order 73 (Joint Committee on Statutory Instruments).

1.46   The JCHR considered and reported at three stages of the reform process. First, at the time of the Mental Health Bill 2002, with a report dated 11 November 2002 (the First JCHR Report).[66] Second, at the time the Mental Health Bill 2006[67] was introduced to the House of Lords on 16 November, 2006, with a report dated 29 January 2007 (the 2nd JCHR Report).[68] Third, the JCHR considered the Bill following the Commons Committee stage, where most of the amendments made in the House of Lords had been reversed, and produced a report dated 30 May 2007 (the Third JCHR Report).[69]

1.47   The JCHR's conclusions are considered where appropriate within the text. Many of the JCHR's recommendations were taken on board during the process, although not all of them. In those areas where their recommendations have not been accepted, one might expect legal challenges under the HRA to be brought in due course.

---

[65] For a useful overview of the Convention provisions as they relate to mental health, see Karen Reid's *A Practitioner's Guide to the European Convention on Human Rights* (Sweet & Maxwell, 2004) 401–8.

[66] Report of the Joint Committee on Human Rights, 'Draft Mental Health Bill, Twenty-fifth Report of Session 2001–02', HL Paper 181, HC 1294, published 11 November 2002.

[67] HL Bill 34.

[68] Report of the Joint Committee on Human Rights, 'Legislative Scrutiny: Mental Health Bill, Fourth Report of Session 2006–07', HL Paper 40, HC 288, published 4 February 2007.

[69] Report of the Joint Committee on Human Rights, 'Legislative Scrutiny: Seventh Progress Report'. Fifteenth Report of Session 2006–07', HL Paper 112, HC 555, published 30 May 2007.

4. The Compatibility of the 2007 Act with the Convention Rights

There are a number of aspects of the 2007 Act that have human rights implications   1.48
that are likely, in due course, to lead to challenges under the Human Rights Act.
The approach I have adopted is to look at possible human rights issues arising from
the 2007 Act at the appropriate place within the body of the text:

- Chapter 3: Amendments to the Criteria for Guardianship and Detention: see
  para 3.75ff (which considers the implications of the amendments generally, but
  also from an Article 5 perspective)
- Chapter 4: Additional safeguards: see paras 4.31, 4.52
- Chapter 5: Supervised Community Treatment: see para 5.83ff
- Chapter 6: Medical Treatment for Mental Disorder under the 1983 Act: see
  para 6.120ff
- Chapter 7: Other Amendments: see para 7.08ff for issues around renewals of
  detention by non-medically qualified 'responsible clinicians' and para 7.39 for the
  Article 8 implications of sharing confidential medical information with victims of
  crime and their families
- Chapter 9: Care and Treatment at Common Law: the lawfulness of overriding a
  competent or capable child's refusal of treatment: see para 9.39
- Chapter 11: Detention for Care and Treatment under the 2005 Act: treatment of
  Bournewood, HL v United Kingdom, and 'deprivation of liberty'
- Chapter 12: Standard and Urgent Authorizations: paras 12.59, 12.60, 12.93
- Chapter 15: Interface between the Detention and Treatment Regimes: paras 15.30,
  15.41, and 15.62.

F. COMMENCEMENT AND TRANSITIONAL
PROVISIONS

Section 56 provides that the 2007 Act comes into force in accordance with provision   1.49
made by the Secretary of State by order made by statutory instrument. October
2008 is considered to be the likely implementation date for the majority of provisions amending the 1983 Act, although certain provisions may be brought into
force earlier. The key amendment to the 2005 Act (particularily the introduction of
the new 'deprivation of liberty safeguards' in Sch A1) are not expected to be brought
into force until April 2009. Certain provisions have already been brought into force.
The Mental Health Act 2007 (Commencement No 1) Order, SI 2007/2156,
brought s 45 (amending s 23(6) of the 1983 Act, see para 7.24) into force from
1 July 2007. Mental Health Act 2007 (Commencement No 2) Order, SI 2007/2635,
brought into force s 51 (amending s 20(11) of the 2005 Act, see para 10.58, fn 17)
from 1 October 2007. Mental Health Act 2007 (Commencement No 3) Order,

SI 2007/2798, brought into force a number of other provisions from 1 October 2007, namely:

- s 19 (introducing s 114A of the 1983 Act, approval of courses etc for approved mental health professionals; see para 7.20)

- s 20 (amending s 62 of the Care Standards Act 2000)

- s 39 and certain provisions of Sch 5 (amending ss 17, 80D, 81A, 82, 82A, 85(2), and 85A of the 1983 Act in relation to cross-border arrangements; see para 7.32)

- s 40 (amending s 41(1) of the 1983 Act and certain consequential arrangements removing the power of the Crown Court to impose time-limited restriction orders; see para 7.27)

- s 41 (amending s 75(3) of the 1983 Act and certain consequential amendments providing the Mental Heath Review Tribunal with power to revoke a limitation direction for a conditionally discharged s 45A patient; see para 4.32)

- s 42 (amending s 127 of the 1983 Act to increase the penalty for the offence of ill-treatment or wilful neglect from 2 years to 5 years; see para 7.31)

- s 46 (amending s 19(3) and s 145(1) to introduce references to Local Health Boards)

- s 49 (introducing new s 40 of the 2005 Act, and before the further amendments introduced by Sch 9, paras 7(2)–(4); see para 10.81)

From 1 December 2007 Commencement No 3 Order also brings into force s 26 (amending s 26 of the 1983 Act, introducing 'civil partners' to the definition of 'relative' and 'nearest relative'; see para 4.20).

1.50   Section 57 of the 2007 Act provides that an order under s 56 (commencement provision) providing for the commencement of s 36 (which repeals the aftercare under supervision provisions in s 25A–J) may provide, in particular, 'for that section not to apply to or affect a patient who is subject to aftercare under supervision immediately before that commencement, and for the patient to cease to be subject to after-care under supervision, and for his case to be dealt with, in accordance with provision made by the order'. We will therefore have to wait and see whether the s 56 commencement provision preserves existing supervised discharge applications or provides for them to be converted into community treatment orders (CTOs).

1.51   Schedule 10 contains transitional provisions.

G. TERRITORIAL EXTENT: ENGLAND AND WALES

1.52   The 2007 Act applies in England and Wales, as do the Acts it amends (the 1983 and 2005 Acts) (s 58). A number of functions under the 1983 and 2005 Acts exercised by the Secretary of State in England are exercised by the Welsh Ministers in Wales, as set out in the Annex to the Explanatory Notes (not reproduced).

2

OVERVIEW OF THE 1983 ACT AND ITS AMENDMENTS

A.	Introduction	2.01
B.	Informal Admission	2.03
C.	Civil and Criminal Powers of Detention	2.04
D.	Community Patients	2.06
E.	The Nearest Relative	2.08
F.	The Definition of Mental Disorder and Exclusions	2.10
G.	The Criteria for Guardianship and Detention	2.11
H.	Medical Treatment	2.13
I.	Discharge of Detained Patients	2.15
J.	The Mental Health Review Tribunal	2.17
K.	Aftercare	2.20
L.	The Code of Practice	2.22
M.	The Mental Health Act Commission	2.24
N.	The Admission, Detention, and Treatment of Children	2.25

A. INTRODUCTION

The Mental Health Act 1983 (the 1983 Act) provides a comprehensive statutory 2.01 framework for the compulsory detention in hospital and medical treatment of patients suffering from mental disorder.[1] Detention under the 1983 Act is not permitted for any purposes other than treatment for mental disorder or any physical causes or consequences of mental disorder.[2] The 1983 Act displaces any underlying

---

[1] There is a (little used) power to detain in s 47 of the National Assistance Act 1948, discussed at para 11.53.

[2] *R (B) v Ashworth Hospital Authority* [2005] 2 AC 278, para 62; *St George's Healthcare NHS Trust v S; R v Collins ex p S* [1999] Fam 26.

common law principles justifying detention, save in so far as those have been expressly preserved by the 1983 Act.[3]

2.02   The 2007 Act effects a number of amendments to the 1983 Act, outlined below.
Once the 2005 Act comes into force, on 1 October 2007, it will be necessary to understand the interface between the 1983 Act and the 2005 Act (see para 11.37); further
complexities to the relationship will be added once Sch A1 of the 2005 Act, introduced by the 2007 Act, comes into force. This interface is discussed in Chapter 15.

B. INFORMAL ADMISSION

2.03   Compulsory detention under the 1983 Act is a measure of last resort. The vast
majority of patients admitted to psychiatric hospital are so-called 'informal patients',
admitted 'in pursuance of arrangements made in that behalf' under the provisions
of s 131 of the 1983 Act (and see the discussion at para 1.26). Most of these patients
have capacity and consent to their informal admission and treatment. A smaller,
but significant, number lack capacity but, because they do not dissent, are admitted
informally under s 131(1). The lawfulness of this practice was considered in *Bournewood*[4] and the subsequent decision of the ECtHR in *HL v United Kingdom*,[5] and
once the relevant provisions of the 2007 Act come into force will be governed by the
new detention provisions of Sch A1 of the 2005 Act, discussed in Part II of this
book. Section 131 also permits the informal admission of children under common
law powers, which expressly includes children of 16 or 17 with capacity who object
(s 131(2)). The law in this regard is to be amended by the 2007 Act (see para 4.44).

C. CIVIL AND CRIMINAL POWERS OF DETENTION

2.04   For those patients who cannot be admitted 'informally', the 1983 Act provides a
number of powers of detention which fall into three main groups. First, there are the
short-term, emergency powers of detention, namely s 135, s 136, s 4 and s 5. Second,
there are the civil detaining powers, provided for by Part 2 of the 1983 Act, namely
the power to admit for assessment for up to 28 days (s 2) and the longer-term power
to admit for treatment for up to six months, renewable for a further period of
six months and thereafter for a year at a time (s 3). Third, there are a number of
powers to detain in criminal cases (Part 3 of the 1983 Act). These include the powers
of criminal courts to remand an accused to hospital for reports (s 35) or for treatment (s 36) and the power to impose a hospital order (ss 37, 38, and 51(5)), whether
with or without a restriction order under s 41, or a hospital and limitation direction

---

[3] *B v Forsey* 1988 SC (HL) 28, HL(Sc); *R v Bournewood Community Mental Health NHS Trust ex p L* [1999]
AC 458.
[4] *R v Bournewood Community Mental Health NHS Trust ex p L* [1998] AC 458.
[5] (2004) 40 EHRR 761.

(s 45A) upon a person convicted of a criminal offence. The Secretary of State also has administrative powers to transfer serving prisoners (s 47) and other detainees (such as remand prisoners and immigration detainees) (s 48) to psychiatric hospital from prison and other detaining institutions. Again, special restrictions may be placed on such a transferred prisoner under s 49.

The powers of detention are not affected by the 2007 Act, save that the criteria   2.05
for detention are amended (Chapter 3), the grounds for imposing a hospital and limitation direction under s 45A are expanded (paras 7.29) and restriction orders under s 41 can now only be imposed indefinitely (para 7.27).

D. COMMUNITY PATIENTS

The 1983 Act also provides statutory powers for the care and control of patients suf-   2.06
fering from mental disorder in the community, notably by way of guardianship (s 7), aftercare under supervision (s 25A to 25J), the release of patients on s 17 leave and the conditional discharge of restricted patients under s 42 and 73 (see para 5.07ff).

These are amended as follows. Guardianship is unaffected, save in so far as the   2.07
criteria for admission into guardianship are amended (Chapter 3). Aftercare under supervision is repealed, to be replaced by the new provisions for SCT in s 17A to G (Chapter 6). Section 17 is amended so that a patient cannot now be released on s 17 leave for more than 7 days if his responsible clinician has not considered whether he should be released on SCT (s 17(2A)) (see paras 5.35). The conditional discharge of restricted patients is unaffected.

E. THE NEAREST RELATIVE

Section 26–30 of the 1983 Act govern the appointment and removal of the nearest   2.08
relative. The role of the patient's 'nearest relative' under the 1983 Act is a very impor-tant one. The nearest relative may apply for a patient to be detained under s 2 or 3, but may also veto any application for admission under s 3 (s 11(4)) and has power to effect the patient's discharge from detention under s 2 and 3 (s 23) and may in some circumstances apply to the Tribunal on the patient's behalf (s 66).

These provisions are amended to remedy an incompatibility with Convention   2.09
rights: see para 4.16ff.

F. THE DEFINITION OF MENTAL DISORDER AND EXCLUSIONS

A person admitted under one of the compulsory provisions of the 1983 Act must   2.10
be suffering 'mental disorder'. 'Mental disorder' is currently defined in s 1(2) by reference to four classifications: mental impairment, severe mental impairment,

psychopathic disorder, and mental illness, 'and any other disorder or disability of mind'. Certain forms of behaviour, broadly those relating to sexual preferences or conduct and drug and alcohol dependence, are excluded from the definition of mental disorder. Both the definition of mental disorder and the exclusions are significantly amended by the 2007 Act, considered at paras 3.29 and 3.58.

G. THE CRITERIA FOR GUARDIANSHIP AND DETENTION

2.11　The criteria for detention and renewal of detention under the 1983 Act fall, broadly, into five: the 'mental disorder' test, the 'appropriateness' test, the 'treatability' test, the 'safety test', and the 'self-neglect or serious exploitation test', but these differ for each of the various detaining provisions depending upon the length of detention authorized by the particular provision, the classification of mental disorder from which the patient is suffering and between provisions authorizing detention in civil proceedings (Part 2) or criminal proceedings (Part 3). Similar criteria govern a patient's admission into guardianship.

2.12　The 2007 Act amends the criteria for detention by amending the definition of 'mental disorder', removing the 'treatability' requirement and substituting a new requirement that 'appropriate treatment' must be available, but also introduces a new 'treatability' requirement into the definition of 'medical treatment'. These changes, and their implications, are discussed in detail in Chapter 3.

H. MEDICAL TREATMENT

2.13　Part 4 of the 1983 Act provides specific powers to treat patients who, with certain exceptions, are 'liable to be detained' under the 1983 Act (and, in the case of s 57 treatment, any patient, including informal patients) for their mental disorder and any treatment ancillary to that disorder, together with a number of restrictions on treatment and other safeguards intended to protect patients against unnecessary treatment. In contrast to the position at common law and under the 2005 Act, Part 4 authorizes the treatment of patients with capacity who object to their treatment, under s 58 and s 63 and, in emergencies, under s 62. The fact the patient has capacity is a relevant factor that the RMO is to take into account, but it carries no more weight than any other factor: indeed, the fact that treatment requires to be imposed by force, upon a capable or incapacitated patient, is likely to carry more weight. Other, more intrusive treatments are authorized under s 57, but these cannot be imposed without consent. The existing framework for compulsory treatment is considered in Chapter 6, at para 6.01ff.

2.14　Part 4 is amended by the 2007 Act in that additional safeguards have been introduced for ECT in a new provision, s 58A. A new Part of the 1983 Act is introduced, Part 4A, governing the treatment of community patients on SCT. All these amendments are considered in detail in Chapter 6.

I. DISCHARGE OF DETAINED PATIENTS

The provisions governing the discharge of detained patients differ depending upon   2.15
whether a patient is admitted under civil powers in Part 2 or under the criminal
provisions of Part 3. The key power of discharge is s 23, which empowers a patient's
responsible medical officer, the hospital managers or his nearest relative to order the
patient's discharge, subject to the 'barring order' provisions of s 25. For patients
detained under s 37 or its equivalent, the power of discharge may not be exercised
by the nearest relative and, where the special restrictions of s 41 apply, no discharge
may be effected without the consent of the Secretary of State. The Secretary of State
also has power to release restricted patients under s 42.

The provisions of s 23 are amended by the 2007 Act to make provision for the   2.16
discharge of patients from SCT (see para 5.45) and s 23(6) is amended to allow discharge by the hospital managers of a NHS Foundation Trust hospital to be effected
by persons other than non-executive directors (para 7.24).

J. THE MENTAL HEALTH REVIEW TRIBUNAL

The provisions relating to the Tribunal are contained in Part V and Sch 2 of the   2.17
1983 Act. The Mental Health Review Tribunal is under a duty to order the discharge of detained patients under s 72 and s 73, if it is not satisfied that the criteria
for detention are established. For unrestricted patients it has a discretion to discharge in any event. Under s 74 the Tribunal has a power to recommend the
discharge of transferred prisoners and patients on hospital and limitation directions,
but the final decision is taken by the Secretary of State.

The jurisdiction may be exercised on application by the patient or his nearest rela-   2.18
tive under s 66, 70, or 75, upon reference by the Secretary of State under s 67 or 71
or by the hospital managers under s 68.

The provisions governing Tribunals are amended generally in so far as the criteria   2.19
for detention have changed and to take into account the new provisions for supervised community treatment (SCT), considered at paras 5.47ff. Other amendments
effected by the 2007 Act are set out at paras 4.24ff.

K. AFTERCARE

The release of a patient detained under s 3, 37, 45A, 47, or 48 places a duty jointly   2.20
upon his responsible Primary Care Trust and local social services authority to provide him with 'aftercare services' under section 117(2) MHA until such time as
the authority is satisfied he is no longer in need of them. Section 117 gives rise to a
specific, rather than a 'target', duty to provide after-care services to a particular individual person to whom the provision applies. The responsible authorities may not
charge for those services.

2.21   The 2007 Act amends s 117 to include patients on SCT and to provide that the s 117 authorities cannot stop providing such services while the patient is on SCT: see paras 5.79ff.

L. THE CODE OF PRACTICE

2.22   Section 118 places a duty on the Secretary of State (in Wales, upon the National Assembly for Wales) to prepare, and from time to time revise, a code of practice 'for the guidance' of those exercising functions in relation to the admission and treatment of patients under the 1983 Act. The current version was prepared in 1999.

2.23   The Code of Practice is amended to include new 'fundamental principles' and to clarify its status: see paras 4.01ff.

M. THE MENTAL HEALTH ACT COMMISSION

2.24   The Mental Health Act Commission exercises functions delegated to it by the Secretary of State and the National Assembly for Wales under s 121(2) of the 1983 Act in relation to the authorization, by SOADs, of treatment under Part 4, the issuing of notices under s 61 withdrawing SOAD certificates issued under Part 4, the visiting of detained patients and the investigation of complaints under s 120 of the 1983 Act, and the review of decisions to withhold postal packets under s 134 (s 121(7)). These functions have been expanded as discussed at paras 4.54ff.

N. THE ADMISSION, DETENTION, AND TREATMENT OF CHILDREN

2.25   The provisions of the 1983 Act apply also to the detention and treatment of children, with certain modifications:

- Children may be admitted to hospital informally (see paras 4.44, 15.60) and administered treatment without their consent (para 9.25ff), provided the consent of a person with parental responsibility has been given.
- Neither guardianship nor supervised discharge (s 25A–J) apply to children under 16.
- Sections 27 and 28 of the 1983 Act modifies the rules governing the 'nearest relative' for children.
- Section 33 makes special provisions as to wards of court.
- Section 116 imposes certain duties on local authorities to arrange visits to be made in relation to children in care who are admitted to hospital, whether formally or informally.

The 2007 Act has introduced by amendment to the 1983 Act the following, addi-   2.26
tional safeguards relating to the admission and detention of children

- A capable child of 16 or 17 cannot be admitted informally without consent (see
  para 4.44).
- Duty to place child in a suitable environment (see para 4.45).
- Duty of PCT or Health Authority to give information about specialist facilities
  for children (see para 4.50).
- Hospital managers' duty to refer case to the Tribunal (see para 4.28, 4.53).

Additional safeguards have been introduced in relation to treatment of children, as   2.27
follows:

- As with adults, s 58A treatment (ECT) cannot be administered to a detained,
  capable or competent child without both consent and a SOAD certificate;
  incompetent or incapable children can be treated with a SOAD certificate (see
  paras 6.46, 6.53). Note that the new provisions give no role for a person with
  parental responsibility to veto such treatment, which has human rights implications
  (see paras 6.133, 15.62).
- In addition, an informal patient under 18 cannot be given s 58A treatment
  without a SOAD certificate, a safeguard that has not been extended to patients
  over 18 (see para 6.56). Such a patient is also entitled to an IMHA (para 4.36).

The new provisions governing the imposition of SCT (Chapter 5) and treatment   2.28
of such patients under new Part 4A (para 6.67ff) apply to children, by contrast with
the guardianship and aftercare under supervision provisions. Note that the provisions of Part 4A governing the treatment of children on SCT appear to exclude any
role for either those with parental responsibility or the High Court in its jurisdiction
in relation to children either to consent to or refuse treatment. This fundamentally
changes the common law relating to the treatment of children and has human rights
implications: see paras 6.133 and 15.62.

3

AMENDMENTS TO THE CRITERIA FOR GUARDIANSHIP AND DETENTION UNDER THE MENTAL HEALTH ACT 1983

A. Key Features	3.00
B. Overview of the Current Criteria for Guardianship and Detention	3.01
1. The Current 'Mental Disorder' Test	3.06
2. The 'Appropriateness' Test	3.14
3. The 'Treatability' Test	3.19
4. The 'Health or Safety' Test	3.22
5. The 'Self-neglect or Serious Exploitation' Test	3.27
C. The Current Definition of 'Mental Disorder'	3.29
1. The Four Classifications of Mental Disorder: s 1(2)	3.30
2. The Legal Significance of Classification	3.31
3. 'Mental Impairment' and 'Severe Mental Impairment'	3.38
4. 'Psychopathic Disorder'	3.41
5. 'Abnormally Aggressive or Seriously Irresponsible Behaviour'	3.44
6. Exclusions from the Definition of 'Mental Disorder'	3.47
D. The Current 'Treatability' Requirement	3.49
1. Historical Development of the 'Treatability Test'	3.51
2. Importation of the Treatability Test into the Tribunal's Test for Discharge	3.53
3. The Meaning of 'Treatability' and 'Medical Treatment'	3.54
4. The Impetus for Change	3.57
E. The New Definition of 'Mental Disorder'	3.58
1. A Wider Definition of Mental Disorder	3.59
2. The Removal of the Classifications of Mental Disorder	3.61
3. Repeal of the Exclusion for Promiscuity or Other Immoral Conduct or Sexual Deviancy	3.62
F. The New Exception for Persons with 'Learning Disability'	3.63
G. The New 'Appropriate Treatment' Replaces 'Treatability' Test	3.66
H. Definition of 'Appropriate Treatment'	3.71
I. 'Medical Treatment' and the New 'Treatability' Test	3.72

J. Implications of the Amendments   3.75

    1. The New Definition of Mental Disorder and
       Removal of the Classifications of Disorder   3.77
    2. Removal of the Exclusions for Sexual Deviancy etc   3.88
    3. New Exception for 'Learning Disabled'   3.92
    4. The Current and New Tests for 'Treatability' and the
       New 'Appropriate Treatment' Test   3.93
    5. Further Observations: Global Effect of the Amendments   3.101
    6. A Charter for Preventive Detention?   3.105

K. Missed Opportunities: 'Impaired Judgment'   3.109

A. KEY FEATURES

3.00 • A new definition of 'mental disorder', and the removal of the four existing classifications of mental disorder (mental illness, psychopathic disorder, mental impairment, and severe mental impairment).

• Certain categories of behaviour are no longer automatically excluded from the definition of 'mental disorder', namely 'promiscuity or other immoral conduct' and 'sexual deviancy'.

• The exclusion of 'learning disability' from the new definition of mental disorder, save where it is 'associated with abnormally aggressive or seriously irresponsible conduct on his part'.

• A new 'appropriate treatment' test for all forms of mental disorder, replacing the 'treatability' test which previously applied only to 'psychopathic disorder' and 'mental impairment'

• The reintroduction of a revised 'treatability' test by way of a revised definition of 'medical treatment' in s 145

• Discussion of the implications of the amendments and the missed opportunity of introducing an 'impaired judgment' requirement

B. OVERVIEW OF THE CURRENT CRITERIA FOR GUARDIANSHIP AND DETENTION

3.01 The criteria for detention may be conveniently summarized as the 'mental disorder' test, the 'appropriateness' test, the 'treatability' test, the 'health or safety test',[1] and the

---

[1] The terms 'appropriateness test', 'treatability test', and 'safety test' were suggested by Kennedy LJ as a convenient shorthand for the criteria for discharge in s 72: *R v Canons Park Mental Health Review Tribunal, ex p A* [1995] QB 60. In *Reid v Secretary of State for Scotland* [1999] AC 512, Lord Clyde guarded against using these labels too prescriptively, as they 'may operate as a distraction from the proper understanding of the provisions', 539.

'self-neglect or serious exploitation' test.[2] However, these five criteria differ for each of the various detaining provisions depending upon the length of detention authorized by the particular provision, the classification of mental disorder from which the patient is suffering and between those provisions authorizing detention in civil proceedings (Part 2) or criminal proceedings (Part 3).

The criteria also vary as between the powers of admission and those of renewal under s 20. 3.02

These are, however, the criteria that a Mental Health Review Tribunal must be satisfied continue to exist when exercising its jurisdiction under ss 72–4, with the exception of the 'self-neglect or serious exploitation' test. That is a criteria the Tribunal may take into account in deciding whether to exercise its discretion to order a patient's discharge from detention who otherwise meets all the other criteria for detention (s 72(2)), although it does not apply for guardianship applications (s 72(4)). 3.03

Similar criteria apply for guardianship, save the 'treatability' test does not apply on admission to guardianship and the 'appropriateness' and 'health or safety' tests are expressed differently. 3.04

The 2007 Act amends the 'mental disorder' test, repeals the 'treatability' and 'self-neglect or serious exploitation' test and introduces new 'appropriate treatment' and 'treatability' tests, considered in due course. 3.05

1. The Current 'Mental Disorder' Test

'Mental disorder' for the purposes of the 1983 Act is defined in s 1(2). In effect, it comprises four separate criteria relevant to detention, guardianship, renewal under s 20 and discharge by the Tribunal. 3.06

(a) *'Disorder or Disability of Mind'*
The starting point is that the person is suffering a 'disorder or disability of mind' (s 1(2)). 3.07

(b) *The 'Exclusions' Test: Sexual Deviancy etc*
A person does not suffer 'mental disorder' by reason only of promiscuity or other immoral conduct, sexual deviancy, or dependence on alcohol or drugs (see para 3.47), and it follows this is an absolute bar to guardianship or detention under *any* of the provisions of the 1983 Act. The distinction between such conduct and a 'mental disorder' which is caused by or a cause of such conduct (see para 3.48) is not an easy one to apply in practice, however, and it can be lawful to admit a person for assessment in order to determine whether he is suffering a true mental disorder or merely displaying proscribed conduct. 3.08

---

[2] Although this last criteria is relevant only to renewals of detention under s 20 and to the Tribunal's functions under s 72: see para 3.27.

(c) The 'Classifications' Test: the Four Classifications of Disorder

3.09   For the longer-term powers of detention, namely ss 3, 37, 45A, 47, and 51(5), a person can only be detained under one of the four identified classifications of 'mental disorder' (considered at para 3.30). For short-term powers of detention, in particular ss 2, 4, 5, s 135, and 136, it is not necessary to identify a disorder by reference to one of the classifications, it is sufficient to identify a 'disorder or disability of mind' (s 1(2)). Under s 35, it is only necessary that 'there is reason to suspect' the patient is suffering one of the four classifications of disorder. Under s 36 and s 51(5), detention may only be authorized in respect of one of the 'major' disorders, 'mental illness', or 'severe mental impairment'. For s 45A, detention is currently only permitted for those suffering 'psychopathic disorder' (although this is set to change, see para 7.29).

3.10   The 'classifications' test apply to renewals of applications for admission for treatment s 3 and hospital orders under s 37 (s 20) and to the criteria for discharge by the Tribunal in s 72.

3.11   The 'classifications' test also applies to applications for guardianship, renewals of guardianship under s 20 and the Tribunal's functions under s 72(4).

(d) The 'Abnormally Aggressive or Seriously Irresponsible Conduct' Test

3.12   In order to admit to guardianship or detain a patient under the classification of 'mental impairment' or 'severe mental impairment' where those classifications are relevant (see para 3.09), it is necessary that the underlying condition 'is associated with' 'abnormally aggressive or seriously irresponsible conduct'; for 'psychopathic disorder', the underlying condition must 'result in' such conduct (see paras 3.44).

3.13   The 2007 Act affects considerable changes to all these tests, considered in more detail below.

2. The 'Appropriateness' Test

3.14   The patient must be suffering from 'mental disorder' 'of a nature and degree'[3] (the term used in s 2, 3, 4, 36, 37, 45A, 47, and 51(6)) which 'makes it appropriate for him to receive medical treatment in a hospital' (the term used in s 3, 36, 37, 45A, 47, and 51(6)).

3.15   Under the shorter-term powers of detention in s 2 and s 4, the expression used is that the patient's disorder must be of a nature or degree which 'warrants' his detention in hospital for assessment or assessment followed by treatment. For guardianship under s 7 the same term is used: the disorder must be of a nature or degree which 'warrants' his reception into guardianship. Plainly some difference in meaning is intended between 'warrants' and 'makes it appropriate'. Given the context,

---

[3] 'Nature' refers to the particular mental disorder from which the patient is suffering, its chronicity, its prognosis, and the patient's previous response to receiving treatment for disorder. 'Degree' refers to the current manifestation of the patient's disorder: *R v Mental Health Review Tribunal for South Thames Region ex p Smith*, (1999) 47 BMLR 104.

'warrants' suggests a slightly lower threshold for exercising the power than 'makes it appropriate'.

The 'appropriateness' test is applied in renewals under s 20 and by the Tribunal under ss 72, 73, and 74.   3.16

The 'appropriateness' test does not apply to emergency admissions under ss 5(2) or 5(4), 135, or 136.   3.17

The 2007 Act does not amend the 'appropriateness' test.   3.18

3. The 'Treatability' Test

Where the 'classification' of mental disorder must be specified (s 3, 37, 45A, 47, and 51(5)), if the classification is 'mental impairment' or 'psychopathic disorder', a further additional requirement must be established, namely that 'it is likely that treatment in hospital will alleviate or prevent a deterioration of the patient's condition' (the 'treatability' test). The test is also applied to renewals of detention for *all* classifications of disorder (s 20(4)) and by the Tribunal in considering discharge under ss 72, 73, and 74.[4]   3.19

The 'treatability' test does not apply to admission to guardianship nor to the test applied by the Tribunal in guardianship applications under s 72(4).   3.20

The 'treatability test' is considered in more detail, below at paras 3.49. The 'treatability' test is repealed by the 2007 Act and replaced by a new 'appropriate treatment' test. However, a new 'treatability' test is also introduced, this time for all mental disorders: see paras 3.72.   3.21

4. The 'Health or Safety' Test

Detention must be 'necessary either for the patient's own health or safety or to protect others' (the term that appears in s 3). A slightly different formulation appears in s 2, namely that the patient 'ought to be so detained in the interests of his own health or safety or with a view to the protection of others'. For guardianship applications, the test is that 'it is necessary in the interests of the welfare of the patient or for the protection of other persons that the patient should be so received'.   3.22

The test is quite different for detention under the criminal provisions in Part 3. Under s 37 the court must decide that a hospital order is the 'most suitable method of disposing of the case, having regard to the nature of the offence and the character and antecedents of the offender'. Under s 47 the Secretary of State must be of the opinion that transfer is 'expedient', 'having regard to the public interest and all the circumstances'.   3.23

The reason why the tests differ from that in s 3 is that the choices available to the decision-maker are different to those available under ss 37 and 47. In deciding   3.24

---

[4] By virtue of the decision in *Reid v Secretary of State for Scotland* [1999] AC 512, considered below.

whether to recommend or make an application under ss 2 or 3, the recommending doctors and ASW have a choice between detention in hospital or continued freedom in the community, so 'safety' is a key issue. Under s 37 the court is choosing between two different options for detention, prison or hospital, together with various community penalties, as alternatives to freedom in the community, so the exercise is more nuanced. A hospital order may not be 'the most suitable method of disposing of the case' notwithstanding the patient meets the criteria for detention under s 37, for example because the assessment of his continuing risk is such that the additional controls of a life sentence are considered necessary, or there is an element of culpability in the patient's offending. In those circumstances a life sentence or a hospital and limitation direction under s 45A may be more appropriate. The patient can be subsequently transferred to hospital under s 47, at which point the feasibility of providing appropriate treatment in prison is the key issue. Such an approach does not violate the patient's Convention rights.[5]

3.25   The 'health or safety' test is, however, the test that is applied by the Tribunal when deciding whether to order discharge under ss 72 or 73 or to make a recommendation under s 74. In those circumstances, the option is, once again, between detention and freedom, so the safety of the patient and the public becomes the prime consideration.

3.26   The 'health or safety' test in ss 2 and 3, and its analogues in ss 37, 45A, and 47, and as it applies to the power of renewal under s 20 and the Tribunal power of discharge under s 72(1)(b) and s 73(1), is left undisturbed by the 2007 Act.

5. The 'Self-neglect or Serious Exploitation' Test

3.27   A renewal of a s 3 (or 37) detention may also be authorized under s 20(4) where the RMO certifies, as an alternative to being satisfied the 'treatability' test is met, that 'the patient, if discharged, is unlikely to be able to care for himself, to obtain the care which he needs or to guard himself against serious exploitation'. This is not a criteria for admission under any of the powers of detention or guardianship, but it is one of the criteria the Tribunal are obliged to take into account in deciding whether to exercise its discretion to discharge an unrestricted patient where it is nevertheless satisfied that the other criteria for detention are satisfied (s 72(2)(b)), although not in its jurisdiction relating to guardianship (s 72(4)).

3.28   This criterion is also repealed by the 2007 Act, both as it appears in s 20(4) and in s 72(2)(b).

---

[5] *R v Drew* [2003] 1 WLR 1213, HL; see also *R v Staines* [2006] EWCA Crim 15 and *R v Birch* (1989) 11 Cr App R (S) 202, 210.

C. THE CURRENT DEFINITION OF 'MENTAL DISORDER'

Because the current definition of 'mental disorder' is amended by the 2007 Act in a number of respects it is necessary to consider it in more detail. 3.29

1. The Four Classifications of Mental Disorder: s 1(2)

Mental disorder is currently defined in s 1(2) as follows: 'mental disorder means 3.30 mental illness, arrested or incomplete development of mind, psychopathic disorder, and any other disorder or disability of mind and 'mentally disordered' shall be construed accordingly'. There are three categories or classifications of mental disorder: mental illness, psychopathic disorder, and 'arrested or incomplete development of mind', but this last is divided into two sub-categories, 'mental impairment' and 'severe mental impairment', making a total of four classifications. 'Mental illness' is given no further definition, but 'mental impairment', 'severe mental impairment', and 'pyschopathic disorder' are.

2. The Legal Significance of Classification

The different classifications are legally significant in three particular respects. 3.31

(a) *Relevance to 'Abnormally Aggressive or Seriously Irresponsible Conduct*

First, for patients falling within the classification of 'mental impairment', 'severe 3.32 mental impairment' or 'psychopathic disorder', the definitions of each introduce an additional threshold test for detention, namely that the disorder is either 'associated with' or 'results in' 'abnormally aggressive or seriously irresponsible behaviour', considered at para 3.44 below.

(b) *Relevance to 'Treatability'*

Second, patients classified as suffering from 'mental impairment' or 'psychopathic 3.33 disorder' may only be detained under longer term powers (ss 3, 37, 45A, 47, and 51(5)) if an additional requirement is met, namely that treatment is 'likely to alleviate or prevent a deterioration of [the] condition', the so-called 'treatability' test, below, para 3.49. By the same token, a patient who no longer satisfies the 'treatability' test must be released, if necessary by a Tribunal under ss 72 or 73. That requirement does not apply to patients classified under 'severe mental impairment' or 'mental illness'.

Classification has no significance for renewals of detention, however, as s 20(4) 3.34 requires the treatability test to be met for all forms of mental disorder. Nor has it any such significance for guardianship applications.

(c) Requirement for Two Medical Recommendations to Agree on Classification

3.35 Third, a patient may not be compulsorily admitted for treatment under s 3 or made subject to a hospital order under s 37 or a transfer direction under s 47 unless both of the medical recommendations upon which the application is based describe the patient as suffering from the same form of mental disorder (s 11(6), s 37(7), and s 47(4)).

(d) No Relevance to Treatment

3.36 Classification does not, however, have any implications for the treatment that a patient may be administered, once admitted: *R (B) v Ashworth Hospital Authority*.[6]

(e) The power to reclassify: s 16 and s 72(5)

3.37 In view of the legal significance of the patient's classification, the 1983 Act also provides a mechanism for the patient's responsible medical officer to reclassify the patient under s 16, which in turn triggers a right of application to the Mental Health Review Tribunal under s 66(1)(d). The Tribunal also has power to reclassify the patient in the event that it decides not to discharge: s 72(5). The power of reclassification in s 16 does not apply to restricted patients, although the Tribunal's power to reclassify does apply.[7]

3. 'Mental Impairment' and 'Severe Mental Impairment'

3.38 'Mental impairment' means 'a state of arrested or incomplete development of mind (not amounting to severe mental impairment) which includes *significant* impairment of intelligence and social functioning and is associated with abnormally aggressive or seriously irresponsible conduct on the part of the person concerned and 'mentally impaired' shall be construed accordingly' (s 1(2)).

3.39 'Severe mental impairment' means 'a state of arrested or incomplete development of mind which includes *severe* impairment of intelligence and social functioning and is associated with abnormally aggressive or seriously irresponsible conduct on the part of the person concerned and 'severely mentally impaired' shall be construed accordingly' (s 1(2)).

3.40 These categories include that group of individuals suffering from disorders of development, described at the time of the 1983 Act as 'mentally handicapped' and now referred to as 'learning disabled'. The distinction between 'significant' and 'severe' impairment of intelligence etc. may be a difficult matter of clinical judgment, but it is legally significant, because for patients with the less serious disorder the 'treatability' requirement must be met in addition to the other criteria for detention, below paras 3.49ff.

---

[6] [2005] 2 AC 278.
[7] *R (B) v Ashworth Hospital Authority* [2005] 2 AC 278, para 28.

4. 'Psychopathic Disorder'

'Psychopathic disorder' is defined, as follows: 'psychopathic disorder means a per- 3.41
sistent disorder or disability of mind (whether or not including significant impairment of intelligence) which results in abnormally aggressive or seriously irresponsible
conduct on the part of the person concerned' (s 1(2)).

'Psychopathic disorder' is usually seen as a particular type of personality disorder, 3.42
defined in legal terms rather than by reference to any diagnostic category. Disorders
of personality are in theory distinguished from illnesses which overlay the patient's
underlying personality, but in practice the distinction may be hard to draw.[8]

For patients classified with 'psychopathic disorder' there are two additional tests that 3.43
must be met before they can be obtained, the threshold test of 'abnormally aggressive
etc. conduct' test (below para 3.44), and the 'treatability' test, discussed at para 3.49ff
and now removed as a result of the 2007 Act amendments. Whether that means more
such patients can now be detained than before is discussed below, para 3.75ff.

5. 'Abnormally Aggressive or Seriously Irresponsible Behaviour'

Each of 'mental impairment', 'severe mental impairment', and 'psychopathic 3.44
disorder' require the underlying condition to be in some way connected with 'abnormally aggressive or seriously irresponsible behaviour'. 'Mental impairment' and
'severe mental impairment' both require that the condition be 'associated' with such
behaviour, while psychopathic disorder requires the condition to 'result in' such
behaviour. In each case, an assessment must be made not only of the patient's
current presentation but also his past history, in so far as that gives an indication of
the patient's future propensity to engage in the proscribed behaviour.[9]

The expression, when it was first introduced in the Mental Health (Amendment) 3.45
Act 1982 in relation to those with mental impairment, was intended to 'limit the
effect of the . . . Act on mentally handicapped people to those very few people for
whom detention in hospital is essential so that treatment can be provided and for
whom detention in prison should be avoided', and in this context has been given a
'restrictive construction' by the courts.[10]

As will be seen, the test survives the 2007 Act in so far as it relates to this group 3.46
of patients, who are now defined as 'learning disabled', but is removed for patients
with 'psychopathic disorder'.

6. Exclusions from the Definition of 'Mental Disorder'

Section 1(3) of the 1983 Act provides that 'nothing in s 1(2) shall be construed as 3.47
implying that a person may be dealt with under this Act as suffering from mental

---

[8] *R (B) v Ashworth Hospital Authority* [2005] 2 AC 278, para 20.
[9] *Lewis v Gibson* [2005] EWCA Civ 587, para 31; *R (P) v Mental Health Review Tribunal* [2002] EWCA Civ 697.
[10] *Re F (Mental Health Act: Guardianship)* [2000] 1 FLR 192.

disorder, or from any form of mental disorder described in this section, by reason only of promiscuity or other immoral conduct, sexual deviancy or dependence on alcohol or drugs'. This is an absolute bar to detention under any provision of the 1983 Act.

3.48   If, on the other hand, one of the excluded forms of behaviour either causes a mental disorder (such as a drug-induced psychosis), or is a symptom of a mental disorder (for example, paedophilia may be a symptom of an underlying personality disorder), then that mental disorder is not excluded by s 1(3). The patient can then be detained, and receive medical treatment, with the aim of treating that behaviour.[11]

D. THE CURRENT 'TREATABILITY' REQUIREMENT

3.49   The 'treatability' test is one of the criteria for the lawful detention of a patient classified as suffering either 'psychopathic disorder' or 'mental impairment', namely that treatment must be available which is 'likely to alleviate or prevent a deterioration of [the patient's] condition' notably in the provisions authorizing longer term detention, namely s 3, s 37, s 45A, and s 47. The same requirement is one of the criteria for the lawful *renewal* of detention under s 20(4), albeit for *all* classifications of disorder. It is also one of the criteria relevant to discharge by the Tribunal under ss 72, 73, and 74, by virtue of the decision of the House of Lords in *Reid v Secretary of State for Scotland*,[12] considered below.

3.50   'Treatability' is not relevant to guardianship applications nor to the test applied by the Tribunal in deciding whether to end guardianship under s 72(4).

1. Historical Development of the 'Treatability Test'

3.51   The 'treatability' test has its antecedents in the Mental Health Act 1959, which also drew a distinction between the 'major' or more serious forms of mental disorders, namely mental illness and (under the 1959 Act) 'severe subnormality' or (under the 1983 Act) severe mental impairment, and the lesser forms of disorder, namely psychopathic disorder and subnormality or mental impairment. Under the 1959 Act, a patient with one of these lesser forms of disorder could not be admitted for treatment over the age of 21, and had to be discharged no later than the age of 25, unless he was dangerous to himself or others, although he could be made subject to a hospital order or direction at any age if he had committed a criminal offence.[13] Classification was therefore particularly important under the 1959 Act, as it might determine whether a patient could be detained at all.

3.52   By the time the 1983 Act was enacted, the view was taken that some patients with psychopathic disorder or mental impairment could continue to benefit from

---

[11] *R v Mental Health Act Commission ex p X* (1988) 9 BMLR 77, 84.
[12] [1999] AC 512.
[13] *R (B) v Ashworth Hospital Authority* [2005] 2 AC 278, para 25.

treatment over the age of 25, and that the age limits on detention were an arbitrary barrier to treatment for such patients, so they were removed. However, detention was still only justified for as long as it was likely that the available treatment would alleviate or prevent a deterioration of their condition, regardless of safety issues. The 'treatability' test was born.

2. Importation of the Treatability Test into the Tribunal's Test for Discharge

A striking anomaly of the 1983 Act, however, was that the 'treatability' test was not   3.53
expressly provided for as a condition of discharge from detention in s 72(1)(b) and
s 73(1), notwithstanding it was a condition of admission. In *Reid v Secretary of State for Scotland*,[14] the House of Lords had to decide whether a dangerous psychopath had to be released under the Scottish equivalent of s 73(1) if the 'treatability' requirement was no longer met. The House held that the criteria for admission and detention were equivalent, so that a patient detained under the classification of psychopathic disorder was entitled to be released once his condition was no longer 'treatable'. The 'treatability' test was therefore to be read in, by implication, to the criteria for discharge in s 72(1)(b) and s 73(1).

3. The Meaning of 'Treatability' and 'Medical Treatment'

The House of Lords in *Reid* then went on to decide what the 'treatability' require-   3.54
ment meant. They acknowledged that it 'gives effect to the policy that psychopaths should only be detained under compulsory powers in a hospital where there is a good prospect that the treatment which they will receive there will be of benefit'.[15] Nevertheless, the question of whether there was 'treatment' available which was 'likely to alleviate or prevent a deterioration' in the condition could only be answered by reference to the definition of 'medical treatment' in s 145(1).

The definition of medical treatment in s 145(1) includes 'nursing, and also   3.55
includes care, habilitation, and rehabilitation under medical supervision'. The definition is 'a wide one, which is sufficient to include all manner of treatment the purpose of which may extend from cure to containment'. It includes '[m]edication or other psychiatric treatment which is designed to alleviate or to prevent a deterioration of the mental disorder', but 'its scope is wide enough to include other things which are done for either of those two purposes under medical supervision in . . . Hospital. It is also wide enough to include treatment which alleviates or prevents a deterioration of the symptoms of the mental disorder, not the disorder itself which gives rise to them.'[16]

---

[14] [1999] AC 512. The House endorsed the minority judgment of LJ Roch in *R v Canons Park Mental Health Review Tribunal, ex p A* [1995] QB 60, effectively overturning the majority decision that 'treatability' was not a criteria the Tribunal was obliged to take into account under s 72.

[15] [1999] AC 512 *per* Lord Hope at 526.

[16] *Reid v Secretary of State for Scotland* [1999] AC 512, *per* Lord Hope at 529–30.

3.56   Accordingly, the containment of a patient in the structured setting of a psychiatric hospital in an environment which is set up and supervised by the medical
officers, where no other treatment (such as medication or psychological therapy) is
being administered, is *capable* of being 'medical treatment' for the purposes of s 145.
The question of whether that medical treatment is 'likely to alleviate or prevent a
deterioration of his condition' is then 'a practical question which will need to be
resolved in each case on the evidence'. In those acute cases where opinions are
divided as to whether any improvement in the patient's symptoms (for example, a
reduction in violent outbursts) is caused by this 'medical treatment' or is due 'simply
to the fact that he was being confined in secure conditions which prevented
the symptoms of his condition from being manifested' will be 'one of fact for the
[Tribunal] to decide on the facts of each case'.[17]

4. The Impetus for Change

3.57   It may be seen, then, that the 'treatability' test is very widely drawn, so the circumstances in which a patient classified as suffering psychopathic disorder or mental
impairment must be discharged as being 'untreatable' are extremely rare, particularly
as the likelihood of the treatment 'alleviating or preventing a deterioration of the
condition' in the *future* must also be considered.[18] The 'treatability' criteria has nevertheless proved controversial, owing to the perception that it was being used by
doctors to exclude from treatment those they found hard to treat,[19] thereby allowing
dangerous 'psychopaths' to avoid detention and to then kill or seriously harm
innocent members of the public. That perception became linked with certain high
profile homicide cases (see para 1.05). In response to the decision in *Reid* the new
Scottish Parliament introduced the Mental Health (Public Safety and Appeals)
(Scotland) Act 1999, which reversed the decision of the House of Lords by expressly
providing that the 'treatability' test did not apply to decisions of the Sheriff (who
exercised the jurisdiction that in England is exercised by the Tribunal) when exercising his powers of discharge.[20] In England, the removal of the 'treatability' criteria
became one of the major policy initiatives behind the government's decision to
reform the mental health legislation in 1999 (see para 1.04ff).

---

[17] *Reid v Secretary of State for Scotland* [1999] AC 512, *per* Lord Hope at 529–30.
[18] *R v Canons Park Mental Health Review Tribunal, ex p A* [1995] QB 60, *per* Roch LJ, at 81; *R (Wheldon)
v Rampton Hospital* [2001] 1 MHLR 19, para 14.
[19] Richardson Committee Report, 1999, para 5.99.
[20] Reid then challenged the new legislation in the ECtHR as violating Articles 5(1) and 5(4) in *Reid v
United Kingdom* (2003) 37 EHRR 211. That challenge was unsuccessful, see below at para 3.100.

E. THE NEW DEFINITION OF 'MENTAL DISORDER'

Set out below are the relevant amendments; their implications are considered at   3.58
para 3.75ff.

1. A Wider Definition of Mental Disorder

Section 1(2) now provides that 'mental disorder' means any disorder or disability of   3.59
the mind; and 'mentally disordered' shall be construed accordingly.

The test differs from the previous one only in so far as the four classifications of   3.60
mental disorder have now been removed (see para 3.28 above).

2. The Removal of the Classifications of Mental Disorder

The four classifications of disorder have been deleted from the definition of 'mental   3.61
disorder' in s 1(2), although for those suffering from 'learning disability; (currently
classified as 'mental impairment' or 'severe mental impairment'), a new classification
has effectively been introduced, see para 3.63. Those deletions have been carried
through the 1983 Act wherever they had previously appeared, in particular in the
provisions setting out the criteria for detention under ss 3, 35, 36, 37, 38, 45A, 47,
48, 51(6), and from the renewal provisions of s 20. They have also been deleted
from the guardianship provisions. The power of the RMO to reclassify under s 16
and of the Tribunal under s 72(5) are repealed, now being redundant. The implications of this change are discussed at para 3.77.

3. Repeal of the Exclusion for Promiscuity or Other Immoral Conduct or Sexual Deviancy

The new s 1(3) provides that 'Dependence on alcohol or drugs is not considered to   3.62
be a disorder or disability of the mind for the purposes of subsection (2) above'. The
current s 1(3) is to be repealed, so the exclusion for promiscuity or other immoral
conduct or sexual deviancy will be removed. The implications of this repeal are discussed at para 3.88.

F. THE NEW EXCEPTION FOR PERSONS WITH 'LEARNING DISABILITY'

New s 1(2A) provides 'But a person with learning disability shall not be consid-   3.63
ered by reason of that disability to be (a) suffering from mental disorder for the
purposes of the provisions mentioned in subsection (2B) below; or (b) requiring
treatment in hospital for mental disorder for the purposes of ss 17E and 50–3 below,

unless that disability is associated with abnormally aggressive or seriously irresponsible conduct on his part.'

3.64   The provisions mentioned in s 1(2B) are ss 3 (admission for treatment), 7 (guardianship), 17A (CTOs), 20 (renewal of detention), 20A (renewal of CTO), 35 (remand for reports), 36 (remand for treatment), 37 (hospital order), 38 (interim hospital order), 45A (hospital and limitation direction), 47 (transfer direction), 48 (transfer direction for remand prisoners and other detainees), 51 (hospital orders), and 72(1)(b) and (c) and (4) (Tribunal powers of discharge). These powers cannot be exercised unless the individuals condition is 'associated with abnormally aggressive or seriously irresponsible conduct'. Similarly, the references to ss 50–3 mean that a transferred prisoner or other detainee may be returned to prison or other place of detention if their condition is not 'associated etc.'. Accordingly, a person with a learning disability *can* be admitted to hospital *without* their disability being 'associated with abnormally aggressive etc. conduct' under the emergency provisions of s 135, s 136, s 4, and s 5 and for the purposes of an admission for assessment under s 2, and the Tribunal is not obliged to discharge from s 2 under s 72(1)(a) on this basis. Such a patient can also be admitted to guardianship under s 7. On the other hand, to admit a learning disabled patient to SCT under s 17A the 'abnormally aggressive etc.' test must be met.

3.65   The implications of this change are considered at para 3.92.

G. THE NEW 'APPROPRIATE TREATMENT' REPLACES 'TREATABILITY' TEST

3.66   The 'treatability' test (above, para 3.49) in s 3 (admission for treatment), s 37 (hospital orders), s 45A (hospital and limitation directions), and s 47 (transfer directions) is removed, and in its place a new test is to be met, namely that 'appropriate treatment is available' for the patient. This new test applies for all forms of mental disorder, the classifications having been repealed. The same test is added to the criteria in s 36 (remand to hospital for treatment), s 48 (transfer directions for remand prisoners and other detainees), and s 51(6) (hospital orders), which did not previously contain the 'treatability' test.

3.67   The provisions for renewal of detention in s 20(4) are amended in similar fashion, with the 'treatability' test (along with its alternative, the 'self-neglect or serious exploitation' test) repealed and the 'appropriate treatment' test in their place.

3.68   The criteria for discharge in s 72(1)(b) are also amended to include the 'appropriate treatment' test, both for patients who are 'liable to be detained' (s 72(1)(b)) and for community patients on SCT (s 72(1)(c)). The 'treatability' requirement, which had previously been read into s 72(1)(b) as a result of the decision in *Reid v Secretary of State for Scotland*,[21] (see para 3.53) is to be removed by implication from the other

---

[21] [1999] AC 512, *per* Lord Hope at 529–30.

amendments, and is expressly removed in so far as it was a matter the Tribunal was to take into account in exercising its discretion to discharge under s 72(1), by the deletion of s 72(2).

The new 'appropriate treatment' test does not need to be met for patients detained   3.69
under ss 2, 35, 135, or 136. The test does not apply for patients admitted to guardian-ship, but it does apply to community patients released on SCT under new s 17A.

The implications of this change, together with the new 'treatability test' are   3.70
considered at para 3.93.

H. DEFINITION OF 'APPROPRIATE TREATMENT'

The 'appropriate treatment' test is given further meaning by s 3(4), which provides: 3.71
'In this Act, references to appropriate medical treatment, in relation to a person suffering from mental disorder, are references to medical treatment which is appropriate in his case, taking into account the nature and degree of the mental disorder and all other circumstances of his case.'[22] That, in turn, requires consideration to be given to the meaning of 'medical treatment' and the new 'treatability' test.

I. 'MEDICAL TREATMENT' AND THE NEW 'TREATABILITY' TEST

The test for 'medical treatment' in s 145(1) has been amended so it now reads: 'medi-   3.72
cal treatment includes nursing, psychological intervention and specialist mental health habilitation, rehabilitation and care (but see also subsection (4) below)'.

Section 145(4) reads: 'Any reference in this Act to medical treatment, in relation   3.73
to mental disorder, shall be construed as a reference to medical treatment the pur-pose of which is to alleviate, or prevent a worsening of, the disorder or one or more of its symptoms or manifestations.'

The removal of the 'treatability' requirement from the detaining provisions proved   3.74
extremely controversial during the 2007 Act's passage as a Bill through Parliament. The concerted pressure brought by the Mental Health Alliance and opposition groups in Parliament lead to a last minute concession by the government at the Report Stage in the House of Commons, possibly in order to avoid the Bill's rejec-tion by the House of Lords.[23] Section 145(4) is the result of that concession.

---

[22] The same definition is given in relation to treatment for mental disorder under Part 4 in s 64(3), see para 6.24.

[23] The amendment was introduced by a labour back-bencher, Chris Bryant, undoubtedly with some encouragement from the government. For the debate of the amendment see Hansard, HC Debates, 19 June 2007, Col. 1275.

J. IMPLICATIONS OF THE AMENDMENTS

3.75 What are the implications of these amendments? Very real concerns were expressed throughout the reform process by a cross-section of interest groups united under the Mental Health Alliance, from the Royal College of Psychiatrists to patient advocacy groups, that to repeal the classifications of mental disorder, the exclusions for sexual deviancy and the 'treatability' test would make the threshold for detention in hospital unacceptably low, particularly for patients previously classified as suffering from 'psychopathic disorder'. There was concern that the detaining powers in the 1983 Act as amended would be used as an alternative to the criminal justice system to exercise control over undesirable individuals whose conduct was insufficiently serious, or there was inadequate evidence, to lead to a conviction for criminal offences: 'preventive detention' by any other name. This would undermine the reputation of mental health professionals who would perceive themselves, and be perceived, as gaolers rather than doctors, leading to a loss of public confidence in the mental health system. Their powerful arguments, taken up by opposition groups during the Act's passage as a Bill through Parliament, secured a number of important amendments, perhaps the most important of which is the new 'treatability' test in s 145(4).

3.76 What follows is a discussion of the implications of the individual amendments, followed by some observations about the new criteria as a whole.

1. The New Definition of Mental Disorder and Removal of the Classifications of Disorder

3.77 Although the definition of mental disorder as 'any disorder or disability of mind' appeared in s 1(2) prior to amendment, the removal of the four classifications appears to have a very real impact, given their significance to the circumstances in which patients might be detained.

3.78 Before discussing the impact of the changes, it should be pointed out, first, that this amendment reflects a growing perception that the classifications of disorder are not easily to be equated with the underlying clinical diagnosis, which cannot always be neatly placed into one or other classification. The Richardson Committee, in its report of November 1999, recommended the repeal of these classifications, albeit with additional admission criteria (including a capacity based test for admission). As Baroness Hale said in *R (B) v Ashworth Hospital Authority*:[24] 'Psychiatry is not an exact science. Diagnosis is not easy or clear cut. As this and many other cases show, a number of different diagnoses may be reached by the same or different clinicians over the years. As this case also shows, co-morbidity is very common. It is not easy to disentangle which features of the patient's presentation stem from a disease of the

---

[24] [2005] 2 AC 278, para 31.

mind and which stem from his underlying personality traits.' In the same passage, Baroness Hale cited the MHAC, 10th Biennial Report 2001–3, at para 7.31: 'If there is widespread co-morbidity between personality disorders and mental illness irrespective of Mental Health Act classification, then the dichotomy imposed by legal classification is misleading and obscures the multiple problems shared by patients in the two categories'. The classifications of disorder had become a barrier to successful treatment, rather than an effective legal protection.

Second, and in any event, the implications of the changes are not as great as at first sight might appear. As seen, classification is not relevant to the medical treatment that a patient may be given under the 1983 Act, as *R (B) v Ashworth Hospital Authority* made clear (see para 3.37). Of course, the four classifications are relevant to detention in three respects (above, para 3.31ff). First, they introduce the threshold test of 'abnormally aggressive or seriously irresponsible behaviour' for patients other than those with 'mental illness'. Second, they determine which forms of disorder in respect of which the 'treatability' requirement applies. Third, a person may not be detained under ss 3, 37, or 47 if the recommending doctors do not agree on the classification of disorder. In order to determine the significance of the amendments it is necessary to consider them as they affect each of these functions of classification.

3.79

(a) Removal of Abnormally Aggressive etc. Conduct for 'Psychopathic Disorder'

The test of 'abnormally aggressive etc. behaviour' has in fact only been removed in so far as it relates to patients who would currently fall within the classification of 'psychopathic disorder'. For patients currently classified as suffering 'mental impairment' or 'severe mental impairment', a new classification has been introduced, namely 'persons with learning disability' in new s 1(2A), and the 'abnormally aggressive etc. behaviour' test has been retained for such patients (see para 3.63).

3.80

In so far as 'psychopathic disorder' is concerned, it was never clear what the 'abnormally aggressive etc' test added by way of a criteria for detention that the 'health or safety' test did not (ie detention must be 'necessary for health or safety of the patient or the protection of other persons'). A person with a personality disorder which does not result in 'abnormally aggressive etc. behaviour' may now fall within the definition of 'mental disorder', but he is still unlikely to be detained under s 3 because he will not meet the 'health or safety' test, which is left undisturbed by the 2007 Act.

3.81

Although certain powers under the 1983 Act may be satisfied without the 'health or safety' test being met, particularly those provided for in criminal proceedings under s 37, those can only be exercised once it has been shown the individual has committed, or found to have done the act or made the omission in relation to,[25] a criminal offence, which in most cases would constitute 'seriously irresponsible or abnormally aggressive conduct'. In any event, the 'health or safety' test must thereafter be applied

3.82

---

[25] Those accused found unfit to plead or not guilty by reason of insanity, who may then be subject to a hospital order (with or without restrictions) under s 5 Criminal Procedure (Insanity) Act 1964.

at the time of renewal under s 20 (for s 37 patients) and or consideration of the patient's case by a Tribunal under s 72. The net effect of this change is likely to be minimal.

3.83   Classification was never necessary to establish a detention under ss 2, 4, 5, 135, or 136 (above, para 3.09), so this change will have no impact upon such admissions.

(b) *Relevance of Classifications to 'Treatability'*

3.84   The classifications are currently relevant to the applicability of the current 'treatability' test, as patients with 'mental impairment' or 'psychopathic disorder' can only be detained if this additional criteria for detention is met. With the removal of the current 'treatability' requirement and the introduction of a new 'treatability' test for all forms of disorder, classifications have become redundant for this purpose. The implications of the removal of the current, and the introduction of the new, treatability test is considered below (para 3.93).

(c) *Requirement for Both Medical Recommendations to Agree on Classification*

3.85   The third purpose of the current system of classifications of mental disorder is to prevent the admission to hospital or guardianship of patients where the two recommending doctors could not agree on the classification (s 11(6), s 37(7), and s 47(4)). This barrier to detention has now been removed.

3.86   This change clearly constitutes a reduction in legal protection for patients, but it must be seen in the context of Baroness Hale's observations in *B*, above para 3.78. The fact that two psychiatrists cannot agree on the diagnosis in the case of a patient suffering from a complex psychiatric disorder should not be a barrier to his admission for treatment if they are both agreed that the disorder is one that is so serious the patient should be admitted for treatment.

3.87   That is not to say, however, that where the doctors cannot agree on diagnosis the patient may necessarily be detained. Their recommendations must still state the grounds of their opinion as to why the patient meets the 'appropriateness' test, including their diagnosis, and their reasons as to why the patient meets the 'health or safety' test (s 3(3)), and any inconsistency between the two must be taken into account by the AMHP in deciding under s 13(1A) whether an application under s 3 should be made. Similarly, for patients in criminal proceedings, a judge should not make a hospital order under s 37 where there is an inconsistency between the two medical recommendations where there is no rational explanation for that inconsistency. Any application made, or order made, in those circumstances would be susceptible to a challenge by way of judicial review or an appeal to the Court of Appeal (Criminal Division), respectively.

2. Removal of the Exclusions for Sexual Deviancy etc

3.88   Notwithstanding the degree of controversy this amendment gave rise to during the reform process, the removal of these forms of behaviour from the 'exclusions' to the definition of mental disorder is also unlikely to have a significant effect in practice, for three reasons.

First, it was always the case that any such behaviour which either causes, or is caused by, a mental disorder which otherwise meets the criteria will justify the individual's detention and treatment (above, para 3.47), although the distinction between the two is not easy to make in practice. Such patients were detained in the past, and will continue to be detained. 3.89

Second, a person still cannot be detained *solely* by reason of such conduct, as the other criteria for detention continue to require that a person is suffering from a 'mental disorder' which meets the 'appropriateness' and 'necessity tests'. The same analysis will follow from Article 5(1), which requires that a person should not be detained on the grounds of 'unsoundness of mind' under Art 5(1)(e) unless they are suffering a 'true mental disorder'. A person should not be detained simply because his views or behaviour deviate from the norms prevailing in a particular society: *Winterwerp v Netherlands*.[26] Those who could not be detained before probably still cannot be detained. 3.90

Third, clinically, neither promiscuity nor 'other immoral conduct' by itself is regarded as a mental disorder, so the deletion of that exclusion makes no practical difference. Similarly, sexual orientation alone is not regarded as a mental disorder.[27] 3.91

3. New Exception for 'Learning Disabled'

The new exception in s 1(2A) effectively replaces the classifications of 'mental impairment' and 'severe mental impairment' and is directed to the same constituency, albeit under a more contemporary label. The requirement of 'associated with etc.' will have the same meaning as before, above para 3.44. The (somewhat arbitrary) distinction between 'significant' and 'severe' impairment of intelligence etc., which previously determined whether the 'treatability' test applied, has been removed. The new 'treatability' test now applies to all learning disabled patients, by contrast with the current 'treatability' test which applies only to patients classified under 'mental impairment' (para 3.33). 3.92

4. The Current and New Tests for 'Treatability' and the New 'Appropriate Treatment' Test

The question for consideration here is, how does the new 'treatability' test, introduced through the new 'appropriate treatment' test coupled with a revised definition of 'medical treatment' in s 145(4) (above, para 3.71), differ from the current 'treatability' test removed from ss 3, 20, 37(2), 45A(2), 47(1), and s 72(1)(b) (para 3.66)? 3.93

---

[26] (1979) 2 EHRR 387, para 37.
[27] Explanatory Notes to the 2007 Act, para 24.

3.94   It should be noted at the outset that the fact the new 'treatability' test is introduced as a qualification to the definition of 'medical treatment' in s 145, rather than as a separate criteria for detention, is a distinction without a difference. The new 'treatability' test acquires its effect in relation to decisions to detain through the new 'appropriate treatment' test, which *is* a (new) criteria for detention. In determining whether the 'appropriate treatment' test is met ('appropriate treatment is available for him'), it is necessary first to look to s 3(4), which refers to 'medical treatment which is appropriate in his case'. To determine what medical treatment qualifies for that purpose one then goes to the definition of 'medical treatment' in s 145(1) and, then, s 145(4), which qualifies 'medical treatment' as 'medical treatment the purpose of which is to alleviate, or prevent a worsening of, the disorder or one or more of its symptoms or manifestations'. Thus, the 'appropriate treatment' test is not met unless medical treatment is available 'the purpose of which is to alleviate, or prevent a worsening of, the disorder or one or more of its symptoms or manifestations'. If such treatment is not available then detention is not authorized.

3.95   There are, nevertheless, three key differences between the current 'treatability' test and the new.[28] First, s 145(4) expressly includes in the definition of 'medical treatment' treatment which alleviates or prevents a worsening of the 'symptoms or manifestations' of the disorder as well as the disorder itself. Second, it is now sufficient that the 'purpose' of the treatment is to alleviate or prevent a worsening, rather than it having to be 'likely' the treatment would have that effect. Third, the test now applies to *all* forms of disorder, not just psychopathic disorder and mental impairment (which have, in any event, been removed). These are considered in turn.

(a) *Treatment of the 'Symptoms and Manifestations' etc*

3.96   The first of these differences is unlikely to have any material impact, as 'medical treatment' already includes treatment which addresses the 'symptoms or manifestations' of the disorder, following the ruling of the House of Lords in see *Reid v Secretary of State for Scotland*[29] quoted at para 3.55 above. Section 145(4) simply makes this requirement explicit.

(b) *'Purpose' v 'Likely'*

3.97   The second of these differences—that treatment must have the 'purpose' of alleviating or preventing a worsening, rather than that it is 'likely' to have that effect—plainly involves a difference in emphasis and meaning. A doctor making a recommendation for admission for treatment under ss 3, 37, 45A, or 47 need no longer satisfy himself that treatment is *likely* to have a beneficial effect, as long as the proposed treatment has that *purpose*. Similarly, a court deciding whether to make an order under s 37, or a Tribunal deciding whether to discharge a patient under s 72,

---

[28] It is, of course, significant that the new 'treatability' test applies to patients released on SCT under s 17A, but this is not a distinction to be drawn between the current law and the new law as SCT is itself a new innovation.

[29] [1999] AC 512, *per* Lord Hope at 531, Lord Clyde at 542, Lord Hutton at 551.

need only be satisfied to that extent. It will have to be seen how great a difference this leads to in practice.

However, it should be observed that the requirement that treatment be 'likely' to **3.98**
alleviate or prevent a deterioration was never interpreted as meaning 'on the balance of probabilities' that effect would be achieved. The test was held to have been met even when the treatment benefits were decidedly speculative, where it may have been a more accurate reflection of the reality to say that the 'purpose' of the treatment was to alleviate or prevent a deterioration rather than that outcome was 'likely'.[30] The new term may have this advantage, that doctors, Tribunals, and courts will no longer have to contort the term 'likely' into an unnatural meaning in order to justify a dangerous patient's continued detention, provided treatment is available which has a therapeutic purpose.

(c) 'Treatability' Now Applies to All Forms of Mental Disorder

The third difference, that the 'treatability' test is now extended to all forms of mental **3.99**
disorder, marks a profound change. The removal of the 'treatability' test in relation to psychopathic disorder and mental impairment may have been seen as an illiberal measure that has been rightly remedied by s 145(4), but it was always the case that patients classified as suffering 'mental illness' or 'severe mental impairment' did not benefit from the 'treatability' test. That anomaly has now been remedied.

The introduction of a requirement that there be a 'therapeutic purpose' for all **3.100**
forms of mental disorders sets a standard that the Convention does not even (yet) require.[31] Article 5(1)(e), as currently interpreted, does not import any explicit requirement that medical treatment be provided. It permits the detention of a person with a mental disorder if *either* it is necessary to administer 'therapy, medication or other clinical treatment to cure or alleviate his condition' *or* 'where the person needs control and supervision to prevent him, for example, causing harm to himself or other persons': *Reid v United Kingdom*.[32] On the other hand, in this respect the 1983 Act does meet the standard required by Recommendation No Rec (2004)10 of the Committee of Ministers of the Council of Europe,[33] Article 17(1) of which requires any involuntary placement to have a 'therapeutic purpose'. Time will tell whether the ECtHR will read such a requirement into the Convention requirements of Article 5(1)(e).

---

[30] See, for example, *R (Wheldon) v Rampton Hospital Authority* [20001] 1 MHLR 19; *South West London and St George's Mental Health NHS Trust v W* [2002] 1 MHRL 292.

[31] See also the report of the Joint Committee on Human Rights, 'Legislative Scrutiny: Mental Health Bill, Fourth Report of Session 2006–07', HL Paper 40, HC 288, published 4 February 2007: 'In our view, in terms of the Convention, there would appear to be no obstacle to replacing "treatability" with "availability of appropriate treatment" as a condition of detention.'

[32] (2003) 37 EHRR 211, para 51. This was the application brought following the introduction of the Mental Health (Public Safety and Appeals) (Scotland) Act 1999, discussed at para 3.57.

[33] Recommendation No Rec (2004)10 of the Committee of Ministers of the Council of Europe to member States concerning the protection of the human rights and dignity of persons with mental disorder', adopted on 22 September 2004 under the terms of Article 15(b) of the Statute of the Council of Europe.

5. Further Observations: Global Effect of the Amendments

3.101 As I have sought to explain, the impact of the individual amendments to the criteria for detention is unlikely to be as significant as might at first have appeared.

3.102 Moreover, I suggest the cumulative effect of the amendments is not as significant as some have feared. Patients cannot be detained in many circumstances that they could not be detained before, for two reasons.

3.103 First, the test in s 1(2) is not the same as the test of incapacity in s 2(1) of the 2005 Act, namely that a person is unable to make a decision for himself 'because of an impairment of, or a disturbance in the functioning of, the mind or brain'. At one stage it was proposed that the same tests be adopted.[34] Although the two tests are often likely to lead to the same result in practice, that will not always be so.[35] The test under s 1(2) does not encompass all persons who might to lack capacity. Thus, for example, the appellant in *Re MB*[36] had consented to a Caesarian section but refused to have an anaesthetic because of a needle phobia. The High Court, Family Division held that the appellant's needle phobia constituted an 'impairment of her mental functioning which disabled her', as a result of which she was 'temporarily incompetent'. Accordingly, the Court had jurisdiction to make a declaration that it was in her best interests for the treatment to be administered to her, if necessary by force. Such an 'impairment of mental functioning' would not amount to a 'mental disorder' within the meaning of the 1983 Act, not being a 'true mental disorder'. Incapacity does not automatically equate with 'mental disorder', let alone a mental disorder justifying detention under the 1983 Act.

3.104 Second, detention must still comply with the right to liberty in Article 5 and be justified under the exception provided for by Article 5(1)(e). A person will only be considered to be of 'unsound mind' for the purposes of Article 5(1)(e) where it is reliably shown, by objective medical evidence, that he is suffering from a 'true mental disorder'. A person should not be detained simply because his views or behaviour deviate from the norms prevailing in a particular society. That mental disorder must also be of a 'kind or degree' warranting compulsory confinement' (*Winterwerp v Netherlands*,[37] paras 37–9). Detention is a measure of last resort; less severe measures must first be considered and found to be insufficient before it will be justified: *Enhorn v Sweden*.[38] The validity of continued confinement will depend upon the persistence of such a disorder (*Winterwerp*, para 39). These requirements, collectively referred to as the '*Winterwerp* criteria', provide an irreducible minimum legal standard that must be met before detention is justified, regardless of any changes to the domestic law.

---

[34] See Cl 2(6) of the Draft Mental Health Bill 2002, criticized in the 1st JCHR Report, para 29.

[35] The Explanatory Notes to the 2007, para 17, read: 'Disorders or disabilities of the brain are not mental disorders unless (and only to the extent that) they give rise to a disability or disorder of the mind as well'.

[36] [1997] 2 FLR 426.

[37] (1979) 2 EHRR 387; *HL v United Kingdom*, (2004) 40 EHRR 761, para 98.

[38] (2005) 41 EHRR 30, paras 36, 44, 55; *Reid v United Kingdom* (2003) 37 EHRR 211, para 51.

6. A Charter for Preventive Detention?

One may ask, in any event, what difference there can be between the new 'treatabil- 3.105
ity' test and the current test, bearing in mind the very wide interpretation given to
the term 'medical treatment' and the very wide discretion given to medical practitioners and Tribunals in deciding whether treatment 'alleviates or prevents a deterioration' of the patient's condition in *Reid*, above, para 3.56. Are the current criteria
for detention a charter for 'preventive detention'? And if not, are the new criteria for
detention any more likely to lead to that outcome?

The answer to the first question, in this writer's view, is no. Whether treatment is 3.106
medical treatment, and whether it is likely to alleviate or prevent a deterioration of a
patient's mental disorder, is a judgment that is underpinned not only by clinical
considerations, but also by ethical ones. By requiring a doctor to consider whether
treatment is available which is likely to confer benefit on the patient, the (current)
'treatability' test calls on the psychiatrist to apply his profession's ethical standards,
which have at their core the benefit of treatment to the individual patient rather
than to wider interests of public safety. If 'treatment' is doing nothing for the *patient*,
the doctor is obliged, both by law and by his own professional duty, to release him,
or to argue for his release, even if he continues to present a risk to public safety. The
doctor is required to take public safety considerations into account, but not at the
expense of his primary duty to the patient.

The answer to the second question is harder to answer. The new 'appropriate 3.107
treatment' and 'treatability' tests preserve the requirement of benefit to the patient
and, accordingly, the primacy of doctors' professional clinical and ethical duties.
Although it introduces a lower threshold of 'therapeutic purpose' rather than of
'likely benefit', as we have seen the current 'likely benefit' test has been interpreted
generously in favour of the treating doctor, so the amendments to the detention for
criteria should not make it any more likely that those individuals diagnosed with
'personality disorder' who are assessed as 'dangerous' can be preventively detained
than before. Indeed, the threshold for detention may now be *higher* than it was
before, as the test now is that 'appropriate treatment *is available*'; it will not be sufficient to say such treatment may be available in the future. Under the current 'treatability' test, the prospects of treatment that has a beneficial effect becoming available
in the future may also be considered: see para 3.57.

What is more likely to lead to 'preventive detention' is another change wrought 3.108
by the 2007 Act, namely the widening of the role of responsible medical officer
(to be renamed the 'responsible clinician') to other professionals, considered at
para 7.01ff. While, as a matter of law, the 'treatability' test, even in its new incarnation, requires the medical 'treatment' to benefit the individual, not the wider public,
some of these new professionals—for example, forensic psychologists—are as likely
to have trained in a prison setting as a hospital setting, where public safety overrides
the duty to the prisoner. If the new 'treatability' test is to continue to operate as a
legal and ethical barrier to 'preventive detention', it will mean that these new 'responsible clinicians' must themselves put benefit to the patient before considerations of

public safety. Indeed, it should be a requirement of qualification as a 'responsible clinician'.

K. MISSED OPPORTUNITIES: 'IMPAIRED JUDGMENT'

3.109   There was strong support during the reform process for introducing an additional admission criteria that would give increased importance to autonomy, the right of a capable individual to refuse admission and treatment (for which see para 9.03). The Richardson Committee recommended that a new Mental Health Act should be based on the concept that, as far as possible, people with mental disorders should be treated equally with people suffering from physical disorders—in other words, their autonomy and choices should be respected. Based on that principle, the Committee recommended that people with mental disorders should only be treated under compulsion if they lack capacity.[39]

3.110   This proposal was taken up by the Joint Parliamentary Committee on the Mental Health Bill 2004,[40] who recommended the introduction of an additional admission criteria, namely that the individual's ability to make decisions about the provision of treatment be 'significantly impaired' before compulsion would be justified. The test was a compromise between a 'capacity' based test and those, like the 1983 Act, which do not expressly require any consideration to be given to the right of autonomy. This formulation had been adopted by the Scottish Parliament in s 57 of the Mental Health (Care and Treatment) (Scotland) Act 2003, and a test of this kind is contained in the UN Principles for the Protection of Persons with Mental Illness, Principle 16 and recommended by the World Health Organization (WHO) Resource Book on Mental Health, Human Rights and Legislation.

3.111   The House of Lords amended the 2007 Act during its passage as a Bill to introduce the 'significantly impaired judgment' test, both to the admission criteria, the renewal criteria and to the criteria for a CTO in s 17A, but the amendments were reversed on the Bill's return to the Commons at Report Stage. An opportunity has been missed to bring the provisions for compulsion under the 1983 Act into line with more contemporary attitudes towards respect of patient autonomy that are reflected, for example, in the Scottish legislation and the 2005 Act.

3.112   There is nothing in the current jurisprudence on Article 5 ECHR that requires an individual's judgment to be 'impaired', so it cannot be said that the omission of the test necessarily has human rights implications. But there are signs that notions of patient autonomy are gaining ground as a requirement both of detention and treatment, as the UN Principles, the WHO Resource Book and the Scottish legislation demonstrate. It may be that, in due course, Article 5 is interpreted in the same way.

---

[39] Department of Health: *Report of the Expert Committee: Review of the Mental Health Act 1983*, December 1999, para 2.1ff, particularly para 2.7.

[40] Joint Committee on the Mental Health Bill 2004, HL Paper 79-I, HC 95-I Session 2004–5, para 156.

4

ADDITIONAL SAFEGUARDS FOR PATIENTS IN RELATION TO ADMISSION AND DETENTION

A.	Key Features	4.00
B.	The Code of Practice and the Fundamental Principles	4.01
	1. New Duty to 'Have Regard' to the Code	4.02
	2. The 'Fundamental Principles'	4.12
C.	Amendments to the Nearest Relative Provisions	4.16
	1. The Role of the Nearest Relative	4.16
	2. Flaws in the Current Law	4.17
	3. The Amendments in the 2007 Act	4.20
D.	The Mental Health Review Tribunal	4.24
	1. Tribunal Reorganization	4.27
	2. Hospital Managers' Duties to Refer	4.28
	3. Conditionally Discharged Patients on s 45A Hospital and Limitation Directions	4.32
E.	Independent Mental Health Advocates ('IMHAs')	4.33
	1. Appointment of IMHAs for 'Qualifying Patients'	4.34
	2. Duties of the 'Responsible Person'	4.37
	3. Functions of IMHAs	4.38
	4. Withholding of Correspondence with IMHA	4.42
F.	Additional Safeguards for the Admission and Detention of Children	4.43
	1. Capable Child of 16 or 17 Cannot be Admitted Informally Without Consent	4.44
	2. Duty to Place Child in a Suitable Environment	4.45
	3. Duty of PCT or Health Authority to give Information about Specialist Facilities for Children	4.50
	4. Hospital Managers' Duty to Refer Case to the Tribunal	4.53
G.	The Mental Health Act Commission	4.54

A. KEY FEATURES

4.00
- New 'fundamental principles' governing the operation of the 1983 Act set out in the Act, but taking effect through the Code of Practice.
- The status of the Code of Practice as decided in *Munjaz* given statutory effect.
- 'Nearest relative' provisions amended to allow a patient to replace their nearest relative and to allow 'civil partners' to act as nearest relative.
- Improved rights of automatic reference to the Mental Health Review Tribunal ('Tribunal') for all detained patients.
- New right to an Independent Mental Health Advocate (IMHA) for all patients who are liable to be detained, community patients on SCT and other patients where s 57 or s 58A treatment is being discussed.
- Improved safeguards for the admission and detention of children.
- Role of the MHAC expanded to include community patients on SCT.

B. THE CODE OF PRACTICE AND THE FUNDAMENTAL PRINCIPLES

4.01 Section 118 places a duty on the Secretary of State (in Wales, upon the National Assembly for Wales) to prepare, and from time to time revise, a code of practice 'for the guidance' of those exercising functions in relation to the admission and treatment of patients under the 1983 Act. The current version was prepared in 1999, but a revised Code will be published to take account of the amendments effected by the 2007 Act in due course.

1. New Duty to 'Have Regard' to the Code

4.02 New s 118(2D) provides that in performing functions under this Act persons mentioned in s 118(1)(a) or (b) shall 'have regard' to the code.

4.03 The question arises as to whether this provision simply restates the test formulated by the House of Lords in *R (Munjaz) v Mersey Care NHS Trust*[1] or in any way undermines that decision.

4.04 In *Munjaz* the House heard an appeal brought by the Mersey Care NHS Trust, with the support of the Secretary of State for Health, against the ruling of the Court of Appeal to the effect that the Code of Practice 'should be observed by all hospitals unless they have a good reason for departing from it in relation to an individual patient. They may identify good reasons for particular departures in relation to groups of patients who share particular well-defined characteristics, so that if the

---

[1] [2006] 2 AC 148, para 21, 69.

patient falls within that category there will be a good reason for departing from the Code in his case. But they cannot depart from it as a matter of policy and in relation to an arbitrary dividing line which is not properly related to the Code's definition of seclusion and its requirements.'[2]

It was the Secretary of State's case on the appeal, with which Mersey Care NHS   4.05
Trust agreed, that the Court of Appeal had overstated the significance of the Code of Practice, which only required that the relevant professionals 'have regard to' the provisions of the Code (para 65).

The minority (Lord Steyn and Lord Browne-Wilkinson) opposed the appeal,   4.06
upholding the Court of Appeal's ruling that the Code of Practice could not be departed from as a matter of policy. They reached that conclusion by reference, in particular, to the Convention requirement in Article 8 that any interferences with the right to respect for private life (such as those involved in the seclusion of patients) must be 'in accord-ance with the law' (and see para 6.128). In the absence of a statutory framework gov-erning the use of seclusion, the Code of Practice was the only 'law' governing such interferences. The Code should, accordingly, have the force of law, ie it should be binding unless there was a very good reason for departing from it.

The majority (Lords Bingham, Hope, and Scott) did not go so far, and allowed   4.07
the appeal against the Court of Appeal's ruling. However, they did not accept the Secretary of State's submission that s 118 only required that the relevant profession-als 'have regard to' the Code. As Lord Hope said, at para 68, 'Statutory guidance of this kind is less than a direction. *But it is more than something to which those to whom it is addressed must "have regard to".*'

Lord Hope then went on, at para 69: 'The Court of Appeal said . . . that the Code   4.08
is something that those to whom it is addressed are expected to follow unless they have good reason for not doing so.[3] Like my noble and learned friend, Lord Bingham of Cornhill, (para 21) I would go further. They must give cogent reasons if in any respect they decide not to follow it. These reasons must be spelled out clearly, logically and convincingly. I would emphatically reject any suggestion that they have a discretion to depart from the Code as they see fit. Parliament by enacting section 118(1) has made it clear that it expects that the persons to whom the Code is addressed will follow it, unless they can demonstrate that they have a cogent reasons for not doing so. This expectation extends to the Code as a whole, from its state-ment of the guiding principles to all the detail that it gives with regard to admission and to treatment and care in hospital, except for those parts of it which specify forms of medical treatment requiring consent falling within section 118(2) where the treat-ment may not be given at all unless the conditions which it sets out are satisfied.'

In his leading speech, Lord Bingham said at para 21 that 'the guidance should be   4.09
given great weight. It is not instruction, but it is much more than mere advice which an addressee is free to follow or not as it chooses. It is guidance which any hospital

---

[2] [2004] QB 395, 436, para 76.
[3] *R v Islington London Borough Council ex p Rixon* (1996) 1 CCLR 119, 123, *per* Sedley J.

should consider with great care, and from which it should depart only if it has cogent reasons for doing so. Where, which is not this case, the guidance addresses a matter covered by section 118(2), any departure would call for even stronger reasons. In reviewing any challenge to a departure from the Code, the court should scrutinize the reasons given by the hospital for departure with the intensity which the importance and sensitivity of the subject matter requires.'

4.10   On one interpretation, the adoption of the test in s 118(2A) represents a legislative reversal of the test propounded by the House in *Munjaz*, which expressly rejected the Secretary of State's argument that s 118 only required those to whom the Code applied to 'have regard' to it. It is clear from the parliamentary debates, however, that that was not the government's intention. In response to a question during debate on the Bill in the House of Lords on 6 March 2007, Lord Hunt[4] said this: 'The noble Baroness, Lady Barker, asked again about the status of the code and whether the principles can be departed from. The answer is yes, but only where there are cogent reasons for doing so that are demonstrably justifiable. That is consistent with the decision being proposed in relation to *Munjaz*.' The Explanatory Notes to the 2007 Act confirm that to be the case: see para 45.

4.11   Accordingly, s 118(2A) should be interpreted in accordance with the principles set out in the passages cited from *Munjaz*. There may be good reason to depart from the Code—case-law may have superseded a particular provision, or (as in *Munjaz*) the special considerations that apply to the detention and treatment of patients in high security psychiatric hospitals may suffice—but such departures will be rare and the reasons for the departure spelled out clearly, logically, and convincingly.

2. The 'Fundamental Principles'

4.12   A recent development in the drafting of legislation is to set out the fundamental principles upon which it is based on the face of the legislation. Like a Bill of Rights in miniature, they not only create legal duties, but also set the ethical and philosophical underpinning for the provisions that follow. For example, s 1 of the 2005 Act enshrines a number of core principles (see para 10.10). Section 1 of the Mental Health (Care and Treatment) (Scotland) Act 2003 (the 2003 Act) also does so. There was much debate during the reform process as to whether a new Mental Health Act should include, on its face, a statement of the principles which should underpin its operation, or whether it was sufficient to include such principles in a non-binding Code of Practice. Advocates of the first approach pointed to legislation such as the 2005 Act and the 2003 Act, and to international instruments such as Recommendation No Rec (2004)10 of the Committee of Ministers of the Council of Europe,[5] Chapter II of which articulates a number of general principles.

---

4 Minister of State, Department of Health at the material time.
5 Recommendation No Rec (2004)10 of the Committee of Ministers of the Council of Europe to Member States concerning the protection of the human rights and dignity of persons with mental disorder, adopted on 22 September 2004 under the terms of Article 15(b) of the Statute of the Council of Europe.

The government's view, as explained by Lord Hunt in debate on 6 March 2006, was that such principles were better set out in the Code of Practice because of technical difficulties with grafting them onto an existing piece of legislation.[6] The option adopted, in the event, was to set out in the body of the 1983 Act those fundamental principles which should be included in the Code of Practice. Whether this compromise will mean there is any lesser legal protection for these principles is a moot question, but it is hard to escape the impression that they have been accorded less priority than had they been given the status of primary legislative provisions.

Accordingly, new s 118(2A) provides that the Code of Practice, prepared by the Secretary of State under s 118(1),[7] shall include a statement of the principles which the Secretary of State thinks should inform decisions under the 1983 Act. By s 118(2B), in preparing the statement of principles the Secretary of State shall, in particular, ensure that each of the following matters is addressed: 4.13

- respect for patients' past and present wishes and feelings;
- respect for diversity generally including, in particular, diversity of religion, culture, and sexual orientation (within the meaning of section 35 of the Equality Act 2006);
- minimizing restrictions on liberty;
- involvement of patients in planning, developing and delivering care and treatment appropriate to them;
- avoidance of unlawful discrimination;
- effectiveness of treatment;
- views of carers and other interested parties;
- patient wellbeing and safety; and
- public safety.

These broadly reflect the principles set out in s 1 of the Mental Health (Care and Treatment) (Scotland) Act 2003, but a striking omission is (s 1(3)(f) of the 2003 Act) 'the importance of providing the maximum benefit to the patient'. 4.14

Section 118(2C) provides that the Secretary of State shall also have regard to the desirability of ensuring the efficient use of resources, and the equitable distribution of services. No such equivalent provision is contained in the 2005 Act or the 2003 Act. Although the requirement to have regard to the 'efficient use of resources' is not unprecedented,[8] it appears to be intended to qualify the nature and extent of the duties otherwise placed upon the Secretary of State; and, it follows, of those whose 4.15

---

[6] Hansard, HL Debates, 6 March 2007, Col. 118.

[7] The responsibility for preparing and revising the Code of Practice in relation to Wales was transferred to the National Assembly for Wales, but, by virtue of the Government of Wales Act 2006, this function transferred to and is now exercisable by the Welsh Ministers.

[8] See, for example, the duty of local education authorities to provide for the special educational needs of children in a community, foundation, or voluntary school or a maintained nursery school in s 317 of the Education Act 1996.

responsibility it is to follow the Code of Practice. The duty to have regard to the 'equitable distribution of services' is, on the other hand, completely without precedent, but suggests a similar aim of ratcheting down the relevant duties otherwise created.

C. AMENDMENTS TO THE NEAREST RELATIVE PROVISIONS

1. The Role of the Nearest Relative

4.16   Sections 26–30 of the 1983 Act govern the appointment and removal of the nearest relative. The role of the patient's 'nearest relative' under the 1983 Act is a very important one. The nearest relative may apply for a patient to be detained under ss 2 or 3 or admitted into guardianship, may veto any application for admission under s 3 or into guardianship (s 11(4)), and has power to effect the patient's discharge from detention under s 2 and 3 and from guardianship (s 23) and may in some circumstances apply to the Tribunal on the patient's behalf (s 66). The role was described by Hale LJ in *R (S) v Plymouth City Council*[9] in these terms: 'Although the identity of the nearest relative is prescribed by statute, the object of the statute is to identify the person with the closest family relationship to the patient. The powers are given to the nearest relative partly for the protection of the patient and partly for the protection of the family which may otherwise face intolerable burdens in looking after him.'

2. Flaws in the Current Law

4.17   The current provisions relating to the appointment and removal of the nearest relative provisions in s 26 and ss 29–30 are flawed, in two respects.

4.18   First, appointment of the nearest relative under s 26 is automatic, and gives the individual no choice over the appointment of their nearest relative and no mechanism by which the nearest relative can be removed where he is unsuitable or the patient otherwise wishes to replace him. Indeed, for this reason the provisions have already been found to be incompatible with Article 8.[10]

4.19   Second, the provisions for the appointment of the 'nearest relative' do not provide for civil partners under the Civil Partnership Act 2004.

3. The Amendments in the 2007 Act

4.20   The nearest relative provisions have been amended to remedy these flaws, as follows:

- The definition of 'relative' and 'nearest relative' have been amended to include civil partners.

---

[9] [2002] 1 WLR 2583, para 43.
[10] See *JT v United Kingdom* [2000] 1 FLR 909; *R (M) v Secretary of State for Health* [2003] 1 MHLR 88.

- The patient may now make an application under s 29 for the displacement of his nearest relative: s 29(1)(2)(za).
- The grounds upon which the nearest relative may be displaced now include 'that the nearest relative of the patient is otherwise not a suitable person to act as such': s 29(3)(e).

Of course it will be open to others, including an AMHP, to apply under ground 4.21 (3)(e), for example where the nearest relative is objecting to the patient's detention. It is suggested that this ground should not be used to displace a nearest relative who is objecting to the patient's admission or is seeking his discharge where the grounds in (3)(c) and (d) cannot be met. That would run counter to the purpose for which the amendment was made. The relationship of patient and nearest relative is one protected by Article 8[11] and so the same interpretation could be reached by reading the provision restrictively, so as to minimize unwarranted interferences with that right.

Further amendments have also been made to ss 29 and 30: 4.22

- The requirement in s 29(1) that the acting nearest relative be, in the court's opinion, a 'proper person' to act as the nearest relative is substituted by s 29(1A), which requires that the person is, in the court's opinion, a 'suitable' person to act.
- A new right in s 30(1) for the patient to apply to discharge—or vary—an order appointing an acting nearest relative. A nearest relative displaced under the new ground will also be able to apply for such an order, but the nearest relative must first obtain leave of the court.
- The court can currently appoint an acting nearest relative only for a limited period: new 30(4B) will allow the court to make an appointment for an indefinite period where displacement is authorized under s 29(3)(a), (b), or (e).
- By new s 30(4) an order made under s 29(3)(c) or (d) ceases to have effect if the patient is subsequently discharged under ss 23 or 72 or after a period of three months, whichever is the earlier. There is no power to make an indefinite order in these circumstances.

Section 66 has been amended to limit applications to the Tribunal from displaced 4.23 nearest relatives, to those nearest relatives displaced on grounds set out in sections 29(3)(c) or 29(3)(d) of the 1983 Act. A person who has been displaced as the nearest relative because he or she is too ill to act (s 29(3)(b)), or unsuitable to act (s 29(3)(e)), will not have the right to apply to the Tribunal.

D. THE MENTAL HEALTH REVIEW TRIBUNAL

The provisions relating to the Tribunal are contained in Part V and Sch 2 of the 1983 4.24 Act. The Mental Health Review Tribunal is under a duty to order the discharge of detained patients or those subject to guardianship under s 72 and s 73, if it is not

---

[11] *R (S) v Plymouth City Council* [2002] 1 WLR 2583, para 43.

satisfied that the criteria for detention or guardianship are established. For unrestricted patients it has a discretion to discharge in any event. Under s 74 the Tribunal has a power to recommend the discharge of transferred prisoners and patients on hospital and limitation directions, but the final decision is taken by the Secretary of State.

4.25   The jurisdiction may be exercised on application by the patient or his nearest relative under ss 66, 69, 70, or 75, upon reference by the Secretary of State under ss 67 or 71 or by the hospital managers under s 68.

4.26   The provisions relating to the Tribunal in Part V and Sch 2 of the 1983 Act are amended generally in so far as the criteria for detention have changed (see Chapter 3) and to take into account the new provisions for supervised community treatment (SCT) (see para 5.47). In addition the following, specific amendments are made:

1. Tribunal Reorganization

4.27   Section 65 is amended so that a single Tribunal for England replaces the existing multiple regional Tribunals in England with one Tribunal and continues the single Tribunal for Wales. A single President is to be appointed for each Tribunal (Sch 2, para 3). The term 'president' as it is currently used under the 1983 Act to refer to the chair of a Tribunal constituted for particular proceedings will be replaced with 'chairman'.

2. Hospital Managers' Duties to Refer

4.28   New s 68 establishes a duty on the hospital managers to refer to the Tribunal the case of any patient who has been detained under s 3 or transferred from guardianship (as before), detailed under s 2 (new) or made subject to SCT (new) (para 5.51) for more than six months and, thereafter, after 3 years (in the case of a patient under the age of 18, 1 year) (s 68(6)).

4.29   Section 68 now includes a duty to refer the case of a patient admitted for assessment under s 2. Although generally such a patient may be detained for only 28 days, that period is automatically extended where an application to displace a nearest relative is made under s 29 (s 29(4)), and during that extended period there is no right to apply to the Tribunal. This was one of the issues that gave rise to the appeal in *R (H) v Secretary of State for Health*[12] where the House of Lords held that the absence of any right of appeal during this extended s 2 detention did not violate Article 5(4), overturning the decision of the Court of Appeal. Notwithstanding the decision of the House of Lords, this amendment goes some way to remedying the situation by ensuring the patient's case is automatically referred after six months.

4.30   By s 68A the Secretary of State or the Welsh Ministers may reduce those periods by regulations.

---

[12] [2006] 1 AC 441.

As for patients admitted in criminal proceedings under Part 3, the new duty to refer only applies to non-restricted[13] patients, and only requires the hospital managers to refer after a period of 3 years.[14] The Explanatory Notes state that is because such a patient's initial detention has been subject to judicial consideration by the sentencing court and they cannot themselves apply to the MHRT in the first six months period (para 157). While that is correct, it must be borne in mind that a reference under s 68 is a safeguard for those who cannot or choose not to apply. For the first group, there must be some doubt whether a period of three years is sufficient for Article 5(4) purposes.

3. Conditionally Discharged Patients on s 45A Hospital and Limitation Directions

Section 75(3) is amended so that, on the application of a patient who has been conditionally discharged from hospital while subject to a hospital and limitation directions, the Tribunal may direct that the patient's limitation direction is to cease to have effect, in which case the patient's hospital direction will also cease to have effect, and the patient will be absolutely discharged. Hospital and limitation directions may be imposed by the Crown Court in accordance with section 45A of the 1983 Act where the court considers it appropriate to direct the prisoner's detention in hospital for medical treatment as well as passing a prison sentence (see para 7.29). The amendment brings the position of patients subject to limitation directions into line with other restricted patients, in that section 75(3) will now apply to both.

E. INDEPENDENT MENTAL HEALTH ADVOCATES ('IMHAs')

The right to an independent mental health advocate for patients subject to compulsory powers under the 1983 Act was promised in the White Paper and included in both the 2002 and 2004 Bills. The right to an independent mental capacity advocate (IMCA) was introduced by the 2005 Act (10.78) and is expanded by the 2007 Act for Sch A1 detainees (Chapter 13). The National Health Service Act 2006, s 248 and the National Health Service (Wales) Act 2006, s 187, have introduced rights to advocacy for individuals making complaints in relation to health and social care services. The only surprising thing about the introduction of a right to advocacy in the 2007 Act, then, is that the relevant provisions were not tabled by the government until the Commons Report stage, at the last gasp of the 2007 Act's passage through Parliament as a Bill.

4.31

4.32

4.33

---

[13] By s 71(2) the Secretary of State is required to refer the case of a restricted patient whose case has not been considered by a tribunal within the last 3 years.

[14] Except patients placed in guardianship in criminal proceedings who are subsequently transferred to hospital.

1. Appointment of IMHAs for 'Qualifying Patients'

4.34 By s 130A(1), the 'appropriate authority'[15] must make such arrangements as it considers reasonable to enable IMHAs to be available to help 'qualifying patients' and may make regulations as to the appointment of IMHAs.

4.35 Nothing prevents a patient from declining to be provided with help by an IMHA (s 130B(6)). No provision is made for the situation where a patient who lacks capacity declines to be provided with help by an IMHA, but it is suggested that if he does lack capacity then he should not be taken to have made a proper decision to decline and an IMHA should be appointed. By comparison, an incapable patient is entitled to an IMCA under s 35 of the 2005 Act regardless of whether he accepts or declines (see para 10.78ff).

4.36 A patient is a 'qualifying patient' in the following circumstances (s 130C):

- A patient who is 'liable to be detained' under the 1983 Act, other than under ss 4, 5(2) or 135–6. It follows that a patient is entitled to an IMHA if he is 'liable to be detained' under any of s 2, s 3, s 35, s 36, s 37(1), s 37(3), s 37(4), s 38, s 45A, s 45A(5), s 47, s 48 or s 51(5) of the 1983 Act.
- A patient on s 17 leave, as such patients are 'liable to be detained'.
- A restricted patient who has been conditionally discharged under s 42(2), s 73, or s 74, as such patients are 'liable to be detained'.
- A community patient on SCT under s 17A.
- A patient subject to guardianship.
- A patient who is not otherwise a 'qualifying patient' for whom the possibility of being given a form of treatment to which s 57 applies is being discussed. This applies to a patient who is neither 'liable to be detained' nor a community patient on SCT. Section 57 treatment, which is the most hazardous or irreversible of treatments for mental disorder, may not be applied to any patient without the safeguards of s 57 being applied (s 56(1)) (see para 6.10).
- A child (under 18) who is not otherwise a 'qualifying patient' for whom the possibility of being given a form of treatment to which s 58A (ECT) applies is being discussed. This applies to an 'informal' child patient who is neither 'liable to be detained' nor a community patient on SCT. Such patients cannot be given ECT without the safeguards of s 58A (s 56(5)) (see para 6.56).

2. Duties of the 'Responsible Person'

4.37 By s 130D(1) the 'responsible person' in relation to a 'qualifying patient' shall take such steps as are practicable to ensure he understands that help is available to him from an IMHA and how to obtain that help, which includes giving the requisite information both orally and in writing (s 130D(4)). The 'responsible person' will

---

[15] In England the Secretary of State, and in Wales the National Assembly, s 130C(5).

be either the managers of the hospital, the responsible clinician or approved clinician, or the responsible social services authority: see s 130D(2). The duty is triggered at the time the patient becomes subject to the relevant compulsory regime or when the relevant treatment is first discussed: s 130D(3). The same information shall be given to the patient's nearest relative, with some exceptions (s 130D(5)).

3. Functions of IMHAs

Section 130B provides that the 'help' to be provided by an IMHA shall include: 4.38

- help in obtaining information about the provisions of the 1983 Act by virtue of which the patient is a 'qualifying patient'; any conditions or restrictions to which he is subject; what medical treatment is to be given to him or is proposed or discussed, why it is proposed or discussed, the authority under which it is or would be given and the requirements of the 1983 Act which apply in connection with the giving of the treatment to him (s 130B(1));
- help in obtaining information about and understanding his rights which may be exercised under the 1983 Act;
- help, by way of representation or otherwise, in exercising those rights (although the IMHA has no separate right to apply for a Tribunal on the patient's behalf under s 66).

Section 130B(3) provides that for the purpose of discharging these functions the   4.39
IMHA may visit and interview the patient in private, visit and interview any person who is professionally concerned with his medical treatment, require the production of and inspect any records relating to his detention or treatment in any hospital or registered establishment or to any after-care services provided for him under s 117 of the 1983 Act; or require the production of and inspect any records of, or held by, a local social services authority which relate to him. By s 130B(4), an IMHA is only entitled to inspect or have produced to him such records where the patient has capacity to consent, and does consent or, if he lacks capacity, the production or inspection would not conflict with a decision made by a donee or deputy or the Court of Protection (within the meaning of the 2005 Act) and the record holder considers that the records may be relevant to the help to be provided to the IMHA and the production or inspection is appropriate.

Where the patient has capacity to consent, and does consent, the duty of disclo-   4.40
sure on the record holder imposed by s 130B(4) is of the same order as that imposed by s 7 Data Protection Act 1998. Where the patient lacks capacity, however, the duty does not go as far as s 7, in particular by reason of the fact the record holder may withhold any record if it considers it not relevant to the IMHA's functions or that the production or inspection is otherwise 'inappropriate'. If a record holder refuses to disclose documents to an IMHA in these circumstances then a request by P (the 'data access subject') may be made by the patient's donee, a deputy or the Court of Protection under s 7 of the 1998 Act.

4.41   The IMHA shall comply with any reasonable request to visit the patient made by the patient, his nearest relative or an AMHP (s 130B(5)).

4. Withholding of Correspondence with IMHA

4.42   Section 134 of the 1983 Act is amended to ensure that hospital managers cannot withhold correspondence between patients and their advocates.

F. ADDITIONAL SAFEGUARDS FOR THE ADMISSION AND DETENTION OF CHILDREN

4.43   The 2007 Act has introduced by amendment to the 1983 Act the following, additional safeguards relating to the admission and detention of children.[16]

1. Capable Child of 16 or 17 Cannot be Admitted Informally Without Consent

4.44   A child aged 16 or 17 with capacity[17] may (as before) consent to their informal admission to hospital notwithstanding the objection of a person with parental responsibility. A capable child cannot now be admitted informally on the basis of consent given by a person with parental responsibility if the child does not consent (new s 131(2) to (5), introduced by the 2007 Act). This provision replaces the common law rule by which a person with parental responsibility could give consent to treatment (which could be taken to include the admission of a child aged 16 or 17 to a psychiatric hospital for treatment), notwithstanding their refusal of consent (see *Re C (Detention: Medical Treatment)* [1997] 2 FLR 180 and para 11.50). It remains the case that a person with parental responsibility can admit an incapable child of any age to hospital: see para 11.50 and *R v Kirklees MBC ex p C* [1993] 2 FLR 187 (although note the discussion at para 10.05). There must be some question as to whether a person with parental responsibility can consent to treatment on behalf of a capable child once admitted if the child does not consent: see paras 9.37 and 10.05, below.

2. Duty to Place Child in a Suitable Environment

4.45   A new duty is introduced by the 2007 Act in relation to children aged under 18 who are admitted to hospital, whether informally or under compulsion, requiring hospital managers to ensure that the patient's environment is suitable having regard to his age and subject to his needs (new s 131A(2)).

---

[16] Additional safeguards relating to the *treatment* of children under the 1983 Act, in particular the extension of s 58A (ECT) safeguards to informal child patients, are considered in Chapter 6, in particular paras 6.46 and 6.56.

[17] For a discussion of the concept of capacity and competence in relation to children, see para 9.25ff.

In determining how to discharge this duty the hospital managers shall consult a 4.46
person with suitable knowledge of cases involving children (new s 131A(3)).

This amendment was introduced to provide legislative support for the govern- 4.47
ment's policy in the National Service Framework for Children and Maternity
Services, Standard 9, namely that children and young people who require admission
to hospital for mental health care have access to appropriate care in an environment
suited to their age and development.

The duty to ensure that the environment on the ward—for a voluntary or detained 4.48
under 18 year old—is suitable to meet the particular needs of the specific child falls to
the hospital managers, who must consult with a suitably qualified professional. The
duty is not placed on the Primary Care Trust or Local Health Board which has funding
responsibility. This raises the question whether, and to what extent, the hospital managers can raise a lack of resources as a defence to a failure to discharge this duty.

The suitability of the environment will be dictated by a number of factors such as 4.49
the age of the child, the nature of the illness and the duration of the inpatient stay.
For example, a 17 year old in a psychotic crisis admitted for three days would not
need educational services to be available, but would need access to staff trained to
deal with young people. A 16 year old with an eating disorder who was accommodated for six months would need access to education, a unit which could offer family
therapy and might need an environment in which younger siblings could visit.

3. Duty of PCT or Health Authority to Give Information about Specialist Facilities for Children

Where a criminal court is considering making a hospital order under s 37 or a 4.50
remand under ss 35 or 36 or a committal under s 44 of the 1983 Act in relation to
a child under 18, a new power is introduced by the 2007 Act to request information
from a PCT or Local Health Board about the availability of accommodation or
facilities designed so as to be specially suitable for patients who have not attained the
age of 18 years (s 39(1A) and (1B)).

Section 140 has also been amended to place the duty upon PCTs and Local 4.51
Health Boards to provide information to local social services authorities specifying
the hospital or hospitals administered or available to them in which arrangements
are made for the reception or the provision of accommodation or facilities designed
so as to be specially suitable for patients who have not attained the age of 18 years.

These amendments may be expected to encourage PCTs and LHBs to plan and 4.52
commit resources to specialist Children and Adolescent Mental Health services in
order to prevent under 18 year olds from being placed inappropriately on adult
wards, a practice which is vulnerable to human rights challenge.

4. Hospital Managers' Duty to Refer Case to the Tribunal

A child under 18 shall, like any other patient, have his case referred to the Tribunal 4.53
on expiry of the period of six months from the date of admission, but shall also have

a further reference after a period or periods of 1 year since his case was last considered by a Tribunal (s 68(6)) (see also para 4.28).

G. THE MENTAL HEALTH ACT COMMISSION

4.54 The Mental Health Act Commission exercises functions delegated to it by the Secretary of State and the National Assembly for Wales[18] under s 121(2) of the 1983 Act in relation to the authorization, by SOADs, of treatment under Part 4, the issuing of notices under s 61 withdrawing SOAD certificates issued under Part 4, the visiting of detained patients and the investigation of complaints under s 120 of the 1983 Act, and the review of decisions to withhold postal packets under s 134 (s 121(7)). These functions have been expanded as follows:

- The SOAD's functions in relation to the authorization of treatment has been extended to include treatment authorized under Part 4A for community patients on SCT (see para 6.90ff) and for informal child patients under s 58A (see para 6.56ff).

- The MHAC's function in relation to the requirement of (what will be) the responsible clinician to furnish a report to it under s 61 is extended for patients receiving treatment under s 62A and 58A (see para 6.41).

- The MHAC's function in relation to the withdrawal of SOAD certificates issued under Part 4 has been expanded to include those issued under s 58A (para 6.41) and SOAD certificates issued in respect of community patients on SCT (s 64H) (see para 6.107).

- The MHAC's functions in relation to the visiting of patients and the investigation of complaints under s 120 of the 1983 Act have been extended to include community patients on SCT, whether in hospital or any other establishment (s 120(1), as amended).

---

[18] The Secretary of State's functions are delegated to the National Assembly for Wales by SI 1999/672, Art 2, Sch 1.

5

SUPERVISED COMMUNITY TREATMENT

A.	Key Features	5.00
B.	Introduction	5.01
C.	Existing Forms of Community Treatment Compared	5.07
	1. Release on s 17 Leave of Absence	5.08
	2. Supervised Discharge (Repealed)	5.12
	3. Guardianship	5.19
D.	Making a Community Treatment Order: s 17A	5.23
	1. Who May Make a CTO	5.23
	2. When a CTO Must Be Considered	5.25
	3. Who May Be Made the Subject of a CTO	5.26
	4. Who May Not Be Made the Subject of a CTO	5.27
	5. Criteria for Making a CTO: s 17A(5)	5.30
E.	Conditions that May Be Imposed on a CTO: s 17B	5.33
F.	Effect of SCT: s 17D	5.38
G.	Duration, Extension, Expiry, and Discharge	5.42
	1. Duration and Extension: ss 17C and 20A	5.42
	2. Discharge Under s 23	5.45
	3. Discharge by the Tribunal Under s 72	5.47
	4. The Application for Admission for Treatment 'Otherwise Ceases to Have Effect'	5.55
	5. Effect of Expiry of CTO: s 20B(1)	5.59
H.	Recall of Community Patients	5.60
	1. Criteria for Recall: s 17E	5.60
	2. Effect of Recall: s 17F	5.63
I.	Revocation	5.66
	1. Criteria for Revocation: s 17F(4)	5.66
	2. Effect of Revocation: s 17G	5.68
J.	Return of Community Patients Absent Without Leave	5.70
	1. Power to Return a Recalled Community Patient to Hospital: s 18	5.70
	2. Provisions Applying to All Recalled Community Patients Who Are AWOL	5.71
	3. Recalled Community Patient AWOL After his Return to Hospital	5.77

K. Aftercare   5.79
L. The Mental Health Act Commission   5.82
M. Human Rights Implications   5.83
    1. Article 5   5.83
    2. Article 8   5.87
    3. SCT Compared with Long-term s 17 Leave   5.89

A. KEY FEATURES

5.00 • SCT applies to all detained patients, children, and adults.

• SCT only applies to patients detained under s 3 or a hospital order under s 37 or its equivalent.

• SCT may only be imposed on a patient who is already detained.

• A patient may not be released on s 17 leave for more than 7 days unless the responsible clinician has first decided whether SCT is appropriate.

• A detained patient may be released on conditions by his responsible clinician on a community treatment order (CTO) for up to six months, renewable for six months and thereafter for periods of one year at a time.

• The Mental Health Review Tribunal has no power to order a detained patient's release on SCT, although it may make a recommendation for release.

• A patient on SCT may be recalled to hospital for up to 72 hours where treatment may be imposed under Part 4 of the 1983 Act, including the treatment of patients who have capacity

• A CTO may be revoked if the responsible clinician is of the opinion that the criteria for making an application for admission for treatment under s 3 of the 1983 Act are satisfied

• Provisions relating to the duration, expiry, renewal, and return of patients absent without leave are considered in detail

• A new framework for compulsory treatment is introduced by Part 4A for patients on SCT, but this does not authorize the treatment of a patient who has capacity without his consent (considered in Chapter 6).

B. INTRODUCTION

5.01 SCT has been described as 'one of the most controversial proposals' in the 2007 Act,[1] perhaps because it has been perceived as a public protection measure rather than a means of improving the delivery of treatment. Certainly it has been an integral part

---

[1] Kings Fund Briefing, April 2007, 'Supervised Community Treatment'.

of the government's policy for reform of mental health legislation since the appointment of the Expert Committee in 1998, and is widely perceived as introduced in response to public safety concerns arising out of high profile homicide cases (see para 1.06). Moreover, the SCT provisions suffer by comparison with a similar mechanism for community treatment introduced by the Mental Health (Care and Treatment) (Scotland) Act 2003 in terms of the available safeguards against abuse it provides, in particular the requirement under the 2003 Act that community treatment can only be imposed upon someone whose judgment is impaired by reason of mental disorder. An equivalent amendment was introduced into the 2007 Act during its passage through the House of Lords but was reversed on its return to the Commons (see para 3.109). Whether the safeguards in the Scottish legislation Act make a great deal of difference in practice, they have helped to create a consensus in Scotland that the 2003 Act is fair to patients and will restrict inappropriate use of the compulsory powers. In England and Wales no such consensus has been reached.

In its final incarnation SCT is, at least, no more draconian than one of the existing forms of community treatment—s 17 leave—that has been available for many years and is overwhelmingly used by doctors in preference to the provisions for 'after-care under supervision' in ss 25A–J of the 1983 Act which SCT is intended to replace (and which are consequently repealed[2]). It is not an alternative to detaining a patient who otherwise does not qualify for any form of compulsion under the provisions of the 1983 Act. This is a key difference between SCT and the government's original proposals in the Mental Health Bill 2002, which allowed a 'non-resident' treatment order to be imposed upon someone who otherwise could not have been admitted to hospital. By restricting the use of SCT and, at the same time, limiting the circumstances in which s 17 leave may be used as a long-term control measure for patients in the community and by prescribing the circumstances in which a patient may be recalled to hospital, SCT may prove to be less controversial in its operation than expected and, paradoxically, less likely to lead to human rights violations than the existing law (see below, para 5.89). 5.02

SCT represents a mid-point between the practically unregulated mechanism of s 17 leave and the more formal and bureaucratic provisions of 'supervised discharge' in ss 25A–J of the 1983 Act. It introduces a mechanism for recall and compulsory treatment which 'aftercare under supervision' lacked, but which s 17 possesses, but with greater safeguards than the s 17 procedure. While there are concerns that the introduction of SCT will lead to an increase in compulsion, with estimates of the number of CTOs in place of up to 13,000 at any one time, this does not necessarily imply an increase in the total numbers of people under compulsion as these may be patients who would otherwise need to be compulsorily detained in hospital or on s 17 leave of absence. The Kings Fund has analysed evidence from SCT systems from across the world in seeking to determine whether they have lead, on the one hand, to increased use of compulsion generally or, on the other, to better outcomes 5.03

---

[2] s 36 of the 2007 Act.

for patients in terms of greater compliance with medication, reduced rates of hospital admissions, and reduced levels of self-harm and violence. The evidence is inconclusive on both counts. In particular, there is no discernible reduction in the overall rates of homicides by people with mental illness.[3]

5.04   A report commissioned by the Department of Health by Churchill et al., 'International experiences of using community treatment orders', which reviewed the use of CTOs in 74 different jurisdictions, reached a similar conclusion, albeit expressed in rather stronger terms (at p 179):

5.05   'Proponents of CTOs argue that they will lead to a decrease in hospital admissions and that they are less coercive than the hospitalization or imprisonment alternatives . . . There is, so far, no evidence to support this . . . There were no significant differences between groups on any measures of health service utilization, social functioning or satisfaction at one year. CTO recipients were no less likely to be readmitted to hospital, and they were just as likely to comply with medication as those receiving standard care. The numbers of acts of violence and arrests, and the numbers of people who were homeless by one year were also similar in both groups. In fact, none of the nine experimental studies found evidence suggesting that CTOs reduce either hospital readmission or length of stay, or that they improve compliance . . . In summary, this review has found very little evidence of positive effects of CTOs in the areas where they might have been anticipated.'

5.06   Those conclusions do not, of course, support a policy of introducing compulsion to where none has gone before; rather they undermine it. As we shall see, however, compulsion in the community—in the form, particularly, of s 17 leave—has been in existence for many years.

C. EXISTING FORMS OF COMMUNITY TREATMENT COMPARED

5.07   In the case of an unrestricted patient (detained under Part 2 or Part 3) there are currently three different mechanisms by which a person may be supervised in the community:

- leave of absence (including long-term leave of absence) granted by the responsible medical officer under s 17 of the 1983 Act;
- 'aftercare under supervision' under ss 25A–J of the 1983 Act (to be repealed by the 2007 Act);
- guardianship under s 7 of the 1983 Act.

---

[3] Kings Fund Briefing, April 2007, 'Supervised Community Treatment'. See also Churchill et al, 'International experiences of using community treatment orders'.

1. Release on s 17 Leave of Absence

(a) *Criteria, Procedure, and Powers of s 17 Leave of Absence*

By s 17 a patient's responsible medical officer may grant leave of absence to any 5.08
patient who is for the time being liable to be detained in hospital, subject to such
conditions (if any) he considers necessary in the interests of the patient or the protection of other persons. Leave of absence may be long-term and a patient's liability
to detention under section 3 may be renewed under section 20 of the 1983 Act even
while the patient is on leave of absence, provided that a significant element of his
treatment requires treatment at hospital, although not necessarily as an in-patient.[4]
The patient may be recalled to hospital under section 17(4) where it 'appears to the
responsible medical officer that it is necessary to do so in the interests of the patient's
health or safety or for the protection of other persons'. While in the community he
remains subject to Part 4 of the 1983 Act and liable to the compulsory treatment
powers contained there.

Section 17 leave is not amended by the 2007 Act but by s 17(2A) the responsible 5.09
clinician cannot release a patient on leave of absence for more than 7 days without
first considering SCT. Its use as a means of long-term community treatment should
in due course come to an end, which may be seen as a good thing given the human
rights implications of its use for these purposes (see below, para 5.89).

(b) *The Effect of the Amendments of the 2007 Act*

(c) *SCT Compared with s 17 Leave of Absence*

SCT may be distinguished from s 17 leave in the following respects. First, the 5.10
responsible clinician must be satisfied the relevant criteria for SCT are satisfied
before releasing a patient under s 17A (below, para 5.31), whereas s 17 prescribes no
criteria whatsoever. Second, SCT is subject to provisions for expiry, renewal, and
discharge and the patient has a right to apply to the Tribunal to be discharged,
wheareas s 17 contains no such safeguards beyond those that apply to the underlying
application for admission for treatment. Third, the criteria for recall from SCT
under s 17E (below, para 5.60) are more stringent (if not by a significant degree)
than those that apply to s 17 leave of absence. Fourth, a patient on SCT is treated
under the provisions of Part 4A (which do not permit the compulsory treatment of
a competent patient) whereas a patient on leave of absence under s 17 remains 'liable
to be detained' and subject to the provisions of Part 4 of the 1983 Act, which
includes the imposition of compulsory treatment on a competent patient (considered in Chapter 6). Both forms of community treatment have in common the fact
that a *recalled* patient may be subject to compulsory treatment under Part 4 in the
event of a recall (see para 6.108ff).

The government believes that s 17 leave of absence and SCT will serve complemen- 5.11
tary, but different, purposes. 'Essentially, leave is for patients who are not yet ready

---

[4] *B v Barking Community Mental Healthcare NHS Trust* [1999] 1 FLR 106; *R (DR) v Mersey Care NHS Trust* [2002] EWHC 1810 (Admin).

to be discharged from detention. SCT patients, on the other hand, will not be subject to detention but rather to being recalled to hospital, which is not the same thing.'[5] Whether that is a distinction that means very much in practice remains to be seen. What is clear, however, is that, as a result of s 17(2A), many—if not most—of those patients currently on long-term leave of absence under s 17 will now have to be discharged under s 17A.

2. Supervised Discharge

(a) *Criteria, Procedure, and Powers*

5.12 Sections 25A–J of the 1983 Act make provision for 'aftercare under supervision' (hereafter 'supervised discharge') and were introduced by the Mental Health (Patients in the Community) Act 1995, which came into force on 1 April 1996. They apply to unrestricted patients aged 16 or over for whom there would otherwise be no means of placing conditions upon their discharge, by contrast with restricted patients who may be conditionally discharged under ss 42 or 73. The provisions were intended to be applied to patients who need an especially high level of supervision to ensure that they receive the section 117 aftercare services that they need to live in a community context.

5.13 By s 25A, where a patient is liable to be detained in a hospital in pursuance of an application for admission for treatment under s 3 an application may be made for him to be supervised after he leaves hospital 'with a view to securing that he receives the after-care services provided for him under section 117' (a 'supervision application') (s 25A(1)). Once a supervision application has been duly made and accepted by the responsible s 117 PCT (s 25A(7)) and the patient has left hospital, he is 'subject to after-care under supervision' (s 25A(2)).

5.14 A supervision application can be made only on the grounds that the patient '(a) is suffering from mental disorder, being mental illness, severe mental impairment, psychopathic disorder or mental impairment; (b) there would be a substantial risk of serious harm to the health or safety of the patient or the safety of other persons, or of the patient being seriously exploited, if he were not to receive the after-care services to be provided for him under s 117 below after he leaves hospital; and (c) his being subject to after-care under supervision is likely to help to secure that he receives the after-care services to be so provided' (s 25A(4)).

5.15 By s 25D the responsible section 117 after-care bodies can impose certain conditions for the purpose of securing that the patient receives the after-care services provided for him under s 117. The conditions that can be imposed are as to residence, attendance at specified places and times for the purpose of medical treatment, occupation, education or training; and that 'access to the patient be given at any place where the patient is residing to the supervisor, any registered medical practitioner or any approved social worker or to any other person authorized by the supervisor' (s 25D(3)). A patient subject to supervised discharge can be 'taken and conveyed' by

[5] Kings Fund Briefing, *Supervised Community Treatment* (April 2007) 2.

the supervisor or any person authorized by him to any place where the patient is required to reside or to attend for any of these purposes (s 25D(4)).

(b) *The Effect of the Amendments of the 2007 Act*
Sections 25A–J are repealed by the 2007 Act, s 33, on a date to be appointed.[6]   5.16

(c) *SCT Compared with Supervised Discharge*
SCT may be distinguished from supervised discharge as follows. First, with SCT   5.17
there is a power to recall a patient who is non-compliant with medication and then treat them upon recall (below, para 6.108), whereas with supervised discharge it is necessary to formally section a patient before administering compulsory treatment. Second, the criteria for admission to SCT and for supervised discharge differ (compare s 17A(5) with s 25A(4)). Third, there is no requirement with SCT that the s 117 authorities (PCT and local authority) accept the patient, by contrast with supervised discharge. Fourth, it is for the responsible clinician, not the s 117 authorities, to impose the conditions. This has certain advantages in that the responsible clinician can, in effect, force the hand of the s 117 authorities to provide aftercare by discharging a patient on SCT, thereby triggering the s 117 authorities' duties to provide s 117 aftercare. Fifth, there is no power to 'take and convey' a patient who is subject to SCT, unlike with supervised discharge, but that is because the mechanism for returning the patient to hospital is recall under s 17E followed by return under s 18 in the event the patient does not comply with the recall notice (below, para 5.63). Sixth, SCT applies to children under 16, whereas supervised discharge does not.

Although aimed at broadly the same client group as SCT (although SCT also   5.18
applies to patients under 16), the supervised discharge provisions have been perceived by psychiatrists as ineffective when faced with patient non-compliance and they have been relatively little used.[7] The bureaucracy involved in obtaining the consent of the s 117 authorities has doubtless been another barrier to their use. Many patients who would otherwise have been placed under supervised discharge have instead been released on long-term leave of absence under s 17, which lacks many of the patient safeguards of SCT. These patients must in future be discharged on SCT, unless there is good reason not to do so (s 17(2A).

3. Guardianship

(a) *Criteria, Procedure, and Powers*
A guardianship order may be made, for patients aged 16 or over, under s 7 of the   5.19
1983 Act on the grounds that the patient is suffering from a mental disorder of a

---

[6] As regards transitional provisions for those already on supervised discharge, s 57 of the 2007 Act provides that an order under s 56 (the commencement provision) providing for the commencement of s 36 (which repeals ss 25A–J) may provide, in particular, 'for that section not to apply to or affect a patient who is subject to aftercare under supervision immediately before that commencement, and for the patient to cease to be subject to after-care under supervision, and for his case to be dealt with, in accordance with provision made by the order'.

[7] 640 patients were discharged under these provisions in 2004/5: Kings Fund Briefing on Supervised Community Discharge, April 2007.

nature or degree which warrants his reception into guardianship and it is necessary in the interests of the welfare of the patient or for the protection of other persons that he should be so received. The application is made by an approved social worker on the recommendation of two registered medical practitioners certifying that the above-mentioned conditions are complied with. The guardian may be either the local social services authority or any other person accepted by that authority. The guardian exercises the power to require the patient to reside at a place specified by him, to attend at specified places and times for the purpose of medical treatment, occupation, education, or training; and to require access to the patient to be given at any place where the patient is residing to any registered medical practitioner, approved social worker, or other person so specified (s 8(1)).

5.20   A patient who is already detained in hospital may be transferred into the guardianship of a local social services authority under the provisions of section 7(3) Mental Health Regulations 1983, provided authority for the transfer is given by the hospital managers and the transfer has been agreed by the local social services authority which will be responsible if the proposed transfer takes effect. A person so transferred can also be transferred back to hospital: see section 8(3) Mental Health Regulations.

(b) *The Effect of the Amendments of the 2007 Act*

5.21   The guardianship provisions are left unaffected by the 2007 Act, save in relation to the criteria for admission to and discharge from guardianship, considered in Chapter 3.

(c) *SCT Compared with Guardianship*

5.22   The first, key distinction between SCT and guardianship is that the latter may be imposed notwithstanding a patient does not, and never has, met the criteria for admission to hospital under s 3 or s 37. Second, there is no power to impose treatment on a patient subject to guardianship, although there is a procedure for 'transferring' a patient from guardianship to hospital with minimal formality and without the need for any criteria to be satisfied (above, para 5.20). Third, the initiative for making a guardianship application comes from the local authority social services department rather than from a patient's doctor. In practice, guardianship tends to be used as a means of enabling a local authority to exercise a degree of control over vulnerable, often incapacitated, adults living in the community. The other forms of community treatment (s 17 leave, supervised discharge and, now, SCT) are aimed more at ensuring patients—usually with mental illness—continue to take their medication. In terms of their 'client group', guardianship is better compared with s 47 of the National Assistance Act 1948 (see para 11.53) and the inherent jurisdiction in relation to incapacitated patients (now governed by the 2005 Act),, although guardianship is not limited to patients lacking capacity. Fourth, guardianship cannot be imposed on a child under 16, whereas SCT can. This raises issues as to whether the treatment of such children without any statutory role for those with parental authority may violate their Article 8 rights (para 6.133).

D. MAKING A COMMUNITY TREATMENT ORDER: s 17A

1. Who May Make a CTO

Section 17A(1) provides that the responsible clinician may by order in writing discharge   5.23
a detained patient from hospital, subject to his being liable to recall in accordance with
s 17E. An order made under s 17A(1) is referred to as a 'community treatment order'
(s 17A(3)) (CTO) and a patient subject to a CTO is a 'community patient' (s 17(6)).

It is a striking omission from the 2007 Act that the Mental Health Review   5.24
Tribunal has not been given power to order a detained patient's release on SCT,
although it does have power to recommend such a release (s 72(3A)). By contrast,
the Tribunal has power under s 73 to discharge restricted patients on conditions. It
is true that the Tribunal did not have power to release detained patients on supervised discharge under ss 25A–J, but that is more readily understandable given the
legal framework for supervised discharge requires the s 117 authorities to agree to
the order being made. A CTO may be made without the s 117 authorities giving
their consent and it is hard to understand why the Tribunal has not been given the
power to discharge on SCT. There is a good argument that the absence of such a
power is incompatible with Article 5(4) of the Convention, whether alone or taken
together with Art 14 (see below, para 5.85).

2. When a CTO Must Be Considered

By s 17(2A), the responsible clinician may not grant 'longer-term leave of absence'   5.25
to a patient unless he first considers whether the patient should be made the subject
of a CTO under section 17A instead. For these purposes, longer-term leave is any
period of leave lasting at least seven days (s 17(2B)).

3. Who May Be Made the Subject of a CTO

A CTO may only be made in relation to a 'detained patient'. A 'detained patient' is   5.26
a patient who is liable to be detained in a hospital in pursuance of an application for
admission for treatment (s 17A (2)). This includes patients subject to a civil section
3 application for admission for treatment and those subject in criminal proceedings
to a section 37 hospital order or its equivalent (ss 47, 48, 51(5), which takes effect
as an application for admission for treatment (s 40(4)) and to which the SCT provisions are expressly applied by Sch 1, Part 1, para 1, as amended. It also includes
patients on leave of absence under s 17, who remain 'liable to be detained' while on
leave. While there may be a number of patients on s 17 leave who will be placed on
SCT once these provisions come into force, the number should fall off as no new
s 17 leave placements of more than seven days can be made without consideration
first being given to the patient being placed on SCT (s 17(2A)). That said, responsible clinicians may find it useful to begin the resettlement process by a series of

short-term leaves of absence followed by release on SCT, and s 17 leave may still be used for transfers between hospitals before formal transfers are made.

4. Who May Not Be Made the Subject of a CTO

5.27 The following cannot be made the subject of a CTO because they are not 'liable to be detained': a person who is not the subject of any regime under the 1983 Act (which includes an incapacitated individual detained under the provisions of Sch A1 of the 2005 Act) and a patient subject to guardianship.

5.28 The following patients detained under the civil provisions of the 1983 Act (Part II) cannot be made the subject of a CTO because they are not detained under 'an application for admission for treatment' for the purposes of s 17A(2): a patient on an application for admission for assessment under s 2 and a patient detained under any of the emergency provisions of the 1983 Act, namely ss 4, 5, or 136.

5.29 Patients detained under the criminal provisions of the 1983 Act (Part III) other than under a s 37 hospital order or its equiralent cannot be the subject of a CTO. In the case of patients detained under ss 35, 36, 38, 44, or 45A, this is because the civil provisions of Part II do not apply to them in the same way as they do to patients detained under s 37.[8] A restricted patient (on a section 37 order with a restriction under s 41, or a prisoner transferred under ss 47 or 48 on a restriction direction under s 49) cannot be made the subject of a CTO either. That is because only those provisions of Part 2 that are set out in Sch 1 Part II apply to restricted patients, and ss 17A–G are not among them. Restricted patients can, however, be conditionally discharged under s 73 or s 42 which has substantially the same effect as a CTO. The 2007 Act does not amend the conditional discharge regime for restricted patients.

5. Criteria for Making a CTO: s 17A(5)

5.30 The responsible clinician[9] may not make a CTO unless, in his opinion, the 'relevant criteria' are satisfied and an AMHP states in writing that he agrees with that opinion and it is appropriate to make that order (s 17A(4)).

5.31 The relevant criteria[10] are (a) the patient is suffering from mental disorder of a nature or degree which makes it appropriate for him to receive medical treatment; (b) it is necessary for his health or safety or for the protection of other persons that he should receive such treatment; (c) subject to his being liable to be recalled as

---

[8] By virtue of s 40(4) and Sch 1 Part I.

[9] An amendment introduced in the House of Lords at the 3rd reading to the effect that a CTO had to be made or at least approved by a registered medical practitioner was reversed at the Committee Stage in the House of Commons.

[10] Further additional criteria that would have required the patient's judgment to be 'significantly impaired', a necessity to protect others from serious harm and a history of non-compliance with community treatment before a CTO could be imposed were introduced during the 3rd reading in the House of Lords and again reversed at the Committee Stage: see para 3.109.

mentioned in paragraph (d), such treatment can be provided without his continuing to be detained in a hospital; (d) it is necessary that the responsible clinician should be able to exercise the power under section 17E(1) to recall the patient to hospital; and (e) appropriate medical treatment is available for him (s 17A(5)) (for which see para 3.71).

In determining whether the criterion in s 17A(5)(d) is met, the responsible clini- 5.32
cian shall, in particular, consider, having regard to the patient's history of mental disorder and any other relevant factors, what risk there would be of a deterioration of the patient's condition if he were not detained in a hospital (as a result, for example, of his refusing or neglecting to receive the medical treatment he requires for his mental disorder) (s 17A(6)).

E. CONDITIONS THAT MAY BE IMPOSED ON A CTO: s 17B

A community treatment order shall specify conditions to which the patient is to 5.33
be subject while the order remains in force (s 17B(1)). But, subject to s 17B(3), the order may specify conditions only if the responsible clinician, with the agreement of the AMHP, thinks them necessary or appropriate for one or more of the following purposes (a) ensuring that the patient receives medical treatment; (b) preventing risk of harm to the patient's health or safety; (c) protecting other persons (17B(2)).

Section 17B(3) provides that the CTO *must* specify a condition that the patient 5.34
make himself available for examination, both for the purposes of any renewal under 20A and to enable a Part 4A medical treatment certificate to be given in his case (s 17B(3)).

Other conditions that *may* be imposed are not specified, but they could include 5.35
(provided the test in s 17B(2) is satisfied) a condition that the patient reside at a particular place; makes himself available at particular times and places for the purposes of medical treatment; receives medical treatment in accordance with the responsible clinician's directions; or abstains from particular conduct.

The responsible clinician may at any time vary or suspend conditions specified in 5.36
a CTO (s 17B(4) and (5)).

A failure to comply with a condition to attend for examination under s 17B(3) is 5.37
itself a ground for recall (s 17E(2), below at para 5.60). A failure to comply with any other condition may be taken into account by the responsible clinician in determining whether to recall a community patient under s 17E, although the power of recall is not limited to situations where there has been such a failure (s 17B(6)–(7)).

F. EFFECT OF SCT: s 17D

The application for admission for treatment in respect of the patient does not cease 5.38
to have effect by virtue of his becoming a community patient, but while he remains a community patient the authority of the managers to detain him under section

$6(2)^{11}$ is suspended and he is no longer 'liable to be detained' (s 17D(1) and (2)), although he remains liable to be recalled to hospital. The provisions for expiry and renewal of the admission for treatment order in s 20 do not apply to him while he remains a community patient and, accordingly, authority for detention under the application for admission for treatment does not expire for as long as the CTO is in force (s 17D(3)).

5.39   The patient will be the responsibility of the hospital in which he was liable to be detained immediately before the CTO was made (the 'responsible hospital') (s 17A(6)), although responsibility may be transferred to another hospital in accordance with regulations made under s 19A.

5.40   A community patient may no longer be given medical treatment under the provisions of Part 4 but will be subject to the provisions of new Part 4A (considered separately, in Chapter 6).

5.41   A community patient is entitled to aftercare services under s 117 (s 117(2) (see para 5.79).

G. DURATION, EXTENSION, EXPIRY, AND DISCHARGE

1. Duration and Extension: ss 17C and 20A

5.42   A community treatment order remains in force until either (a) the period provided for in s 20A(1) has expired; (b) the patient is discharged under s 23 or by a Tribunal under s 72; (c) the application for admission for treatment in respect of the patient otherwise ceases to have effect; or (d) the order is revoked under section 17F, whichever occurs first (s 17C).

5.43   Section 20A(1) provides that a CTO remains in force for a period of up to 6 months, beginning on the day on which it was made. Thereafter it may be extended for a period of six months. Any further extensions will be for periods of one year at a time (s 20A(3)), subject to any extensions made in relation to recalled community patients who are absent without leave (see below, para 5.71).

5.44   A CTO is extended if, no more than two months before the CTO is due to expire, the responsible clinician examines the patient and furnishes a report to the hospital managers that, in his opinion, the criteria in s 20A(6) and (8) are met (s 20A(4)).[12] The criteria set out in s 20A(6) are in materially the same terms as the criteria for the making of a CTO in s 17A(5) and (6), at para 5.30 above. Before furnishing such a report the responsible clinician must consult with at least one other person who has been professionally involved in the patient's care (s 20A(8)), such as a nurse, AMHP,

---

[11] Or, in the case of a patient detained under s 37, s 40(1)(b) (s 17G(2) as modified by s 40(4) and Sch 1 Part I, para 2A).

[12] An amendment in similar terms to that made to s 17A expanding the criteria for renewing a CTO (see n 9 and n 10 above) and requiring renewal to be made or approved by a doctor was made in the House of Lords but again overturned in the House of Commons at Committee Stage.

psychologist, or another doctor. Where a report is so furnished the hospital managers must inform the patient (s 20A(5)).

2. Discharge Under s 23

By s 23(2)(c) a patient who is subject to a CTO may, by order made in writing,   5.45
be discharged by the responsible clinician, the hospital managers or the patient's
nearest relative.[13] The nearest relative's power of discharge is subject to the provisions
of s 25 (as with a detained patient), which provides that the nearest relative must
give 72 hours' written notice to the hospital managers of his decision to discharge
the CTO. The discharge may be barred by the responsible clinician if he certifies
a report to the managers that the patient, if discharged, would be likely to act in
a manner dangerous to other persons or to himself. In those circumstances the
nearest relative may apply to the Tribunal for the patient's discharge under s 72
(s 66(1)(g)).

By s 23(1A), subject to the provisions of the section and s 25, a community   5.46
patient shall cease to be liable to recall, and the underlying application for admission
for treatment ceases to have effect, if an order in writing discharging him from such
liability is made in accordance with s 23.

3. Discharge by the Tribunal Under s 72

(a) *Jurisdiction: Criteria for Discharge in Respect of Community Patients*
Section 72 has been amended by the 2007 Act to include provision for the discharge   5.47
of patients subject to a CTO. New s 72(1)(c) provides that the tribunal shall direct the
discharge of a community patient if they are not satisfied (i) that he is then suffering
from mental disorder or mental disorder of a nature or degree which makes it appropriate for him to receive medical treatment; or (ii) that it is necessary for his health or
safety or for the protection of other persons that he should receive such treatment; or
(iii) that it is necessary that the responsible clinician should be able to exercise the
power under section 17E(1) to recall the patient to hospital; or (iv) that appropriate
medical treatment is available for him; or (v) in the case of an application under
s 66(1)(g) (namely, an application brought by a nearest relative where a 'barring order'
has been made by the responsible clinician under s 25), that the patient, if discharged,
would be likely to act in a manner dangerous to other persons or to himself.

By s 72(1A), 'in determining whether the criterion in subsection 72(1)(c)(iii) above   5.48
is met, the tribunal shall, in particular, consider, having regard to the patient's history
of mental disorder and any other relevant factors, what risk there would be of a deterioration of the patient's condition if he were to continue not to be detained in a hospital
(as a result, for example, of his refusing or neglecting to receive the medical treatment

---

[13] The Secretary of State may also order discharge under s 23(3).

he requires for his mental disorder)'. This curiously worded provision is explained in the Explanatory Notes, para 149, as follows: 'In determining this point the tribunal must consider the risk that the patient's condition will deteriorate in the community, as a result, for example, of their refusing or neglecting to receive the treatment they need. In considering that risk the tribunal must have regard to the patient's history of mental disorder and any other relevant factors.' Section 72(1A) might have been better worded if it read, ' . . . if he were *no longer liable to be recalled to* hospital', the wording used in s 73(2)(b) setting out the circumstances in which the Tribunal must absolutely discharge a restricted patient, rather than conditionally discharge him.

(b) *Jurisdiction: No Power to Vary or Discharge Conditions of SCT*

5.49   It is another striking omission from the new legislative framework that the Tribunal is given no power to vary or discharge the provisions of a CTO on an application or reference made to it in respect of a patient on SCT. There are likely to be many cases before the Tribunal where the issue is not whether the patient should be on SCT but whether the conditions imposed by the responsible clinician are necessary, in particular having regard to the criteria in s 17B(2) (see para 15.33). While the Tribunal can and should express its views about the necessity of a condition and to make a non-statutory recommendation that it be varied or removed, if that is not complied with by the responsible clinician the only remedy available to the patient will be to bring a claim for judicial review of the offending condition(s). That is an inappropriately complex, expensive and (therefore) inaccessible remedy for many patients in what should be a matter of routine for the Tribunal. It is arguable that the absence of a power to order the variation or removal of the conditions of SCT is susceptible to a human rights challenge (see below, para 5.86).

(c) *Applications and References in Respect of Community Patients*

5.50   A community patient may make an application to the Tribunal for discharge at any time within the six month period of the CTO (s 66(1)(ca)). Thereafter the patient may make an application at any time during the period for which the CTO is extended under s 20A (six months or one year) (s 66(1)(fza) and (faa)). As noted above, the nearest relative may apply to the Tribunal for the patient's discharge under s 72 (s 66(1)(g)) in the event that a discharge order made under s 23 is barred by the responsible clinician under s 25.

5.51   Where no application or reference has been made by or on behalf of a community patient, on expiry of the period of six months from the date on which the patient was originally admitted for treatment the hospital managers must refer the patient's case to the Tribunal (ss 68(1)(c)), 68(2) and 68(5)). Thus a patient admitted to hospital under section 3 who is released on a CTO before the expiry of six months must still have his case referred to the Tribunal under these provisions after six months if no other application or reference has been made.

5.52   The managers must also refer the case of a patient where a period of more than three years (in the case of a patient under the age of 18, 1 year) has elapsed since his case was last considered by a Tribunal (s 68(6)).

Where a community patient's CTO is revoked under s 17F the managers must   5.53
refer the patient's case to the Tribunal as soon as possible after the order is revoked
(s 68(7)). In addition, the requirement of a referral after the expiry of the period of
six months and three years applies equally to such patients as to other detained
patients (ss 68(1)(c)), 68(2), and 68(5)) (see para 4.28).

The Secretary of State may at any time refer the case of a community patient to   5.54
the Tribunal under s 67(1), as amended.

4. The Application for Admission for Treatment 'Otherwise Ceases to Have Effect'

Section 17C(c) provides that the CTO will remain in effect until, materially, 'the   5.55
application for admission for treatment in respect of the patient otherwise ceases to
have effect'. This may happen in two situations.

(a) *Special Provisions as to Patients Sentenced to Imprisonment*

If a community patient is sentenced to a period of imprisonment of more than   5.56
six months, the application for admission for treatment ceases to have effect
(s 22(1)–(3)). However, if a community patient is sentenced to a period of imprisonment of less than six months and during that period a CTO would otherwise
have ceased to be in force, the CTO will be deemed not to expire until the end of
the day upon which he is released from custody (s 22(4)–(5)).

If the patient had been recalled to hospital under s 17E before his sentence   5.57
began he is deemed to have been AWOL and may be returned to hospital under
s 18. The CTO will be extended for a further week under s 21 to enable a report
to be furnished by the responsible clinician further extending the CTO under
s 21A (s 22(6)) (see further, below at para 5.70ff). If the patient had not been
recalled to hospital at the time his sentence began, he may not be returned to
hospital under s 18 although the CTO will still be extended for a further week
under s 21 for the responsible clinician to further extend the CTO under s 21A
(s 22(8)).

(b) *Recalled Patients Who Are Absent Without Leave*

Where a recalled patient is AWOL the period of his CTO may be automati-   5.58
cally extended by up to six months, during which time he may be returned to
hospital (s 18(4), below para 5.71). If he has not been returned to hospital by
the end of that period, however, the CTO will come to an end and the underlying
application for admission for treatment will cease to have effect (s 20B(1)).

5. Effect of Expiry of CTO: s 20B(1)

Upon the expiry of a CTO the community patient is deemed to be discharged abso-   5.59
lutely from liability to recall and the application for admission for treatment ceases
to have effect (s 20B(1)).

H. RECALL OF COMMUNITY PATIENTS

1. Criteria for Recall: s 17E

5.60 The responsible clinician may by notice in writing recall a community patient to hospital if in his opinion (a) the patient requires medical treatment in hospital for his mental disorder; and (b) there would be a risk of harm to the health or safety of the patient or to other persons if the patient were not recalled to hospital for that purpose (s 17E(1)). The responsible clinician may also recall a community patient to hospital if the patient fails to comply with a condition imposed under s 17B(3)(d), namely a condition that the patient makes himself available for examination, for example by a SOAD or for the purposes of renewing the CTO (s 17E(2)). A failure to comply with any other condition may nevertheless be taken into account by the responsible clinician in determining whether to recall a community patient under s 17E (s 17B(6)).

5.61 The patient may be recalled to a different hospital than the one in which he was originally detained (s 17E(3)) and may be recalled even though he is already in hospital at the time (s 17E(4)). This latter provision will usually apply when the patient has been admitted as an informal patient, but there is no reason in principle why he may not have been initially admitted under one of the emergency provisions such as s 136, s 4; s 5, or s 2.[14]

5.62 The criteria for recall compare favourably, in human rights terms, with those for s 17 leave (above, 5.08) and is unlikely to have human rights implications (para 5.83), but revocation (para 5.84) and treatment thereafter (para 6.139) may do so.

2. Effect of Recall: s 17F

5.63 A notice in writing under s 17E recalling a patient to hospital is sufficient authority for the hospital managers to detain the patient (s 17E(6)). A notice under s 17E does not confer a power to 'take and convey' a patient to hospital, by contrast with, for example, s 6(1) which confers upon the applicant, or any person authorized by the applicant, a power to take and convey a patient to hospital who has been made the subject of an application for admission for treatment. However, if the patient does not comply with a recall notice, he may be returned to hospital under s 18 as a patient who is absent without leave (s 18(2A), below, para 5.70). This power may be exercised immediately upon issue of the recall notice if the patient refuses to return to hospital,[15] although the patient will have to be given an opportunity to comply with the notice before he can be returned to hospital under s 18.

---

[14] By analogy with the position with restricted patients who may be admitted under Part II of the 1983 Act rather than being formally recalled under s 42: *R v Managers of the NW London Mental Health Trust ex p Stewart* [1998] QB 628.

[15] Draft Illustrative Memorandum, para 70.

Section 17F(7) provides that a recalled patient may be detained for up to 72   5.64
hours before he must either be released or the CTO revoked under s 17F(4). The
period of 72 hours runs from the time the patient's detention in hospital begins, not
the time that the recall notice is given (s 17F(9)(a)).

During the 72 hour period the patient may be administered treatment for mental   5.65
disorder, if necessary against his will, under the provisions of Part 4 (s 56(4),
s 62A(1)(a)), considered separately at para 6.108. The patient may be transferred to
another hospital (s 17(3)). The responsible clinician may release the patient at any
time, but not after the CTO has been revoked (s 17F(6)). Upon release the CTO
remains in force (s 17F(8)).

I. REVOCATION

1. Criteria for Revocation: s 17F(4)

The responsible clinician may by order in writing revoke the community treatment   5.66
order if, in his opinion, the conditions in s 3(2) are satisfied in respect of the patient;
and an AMHP states in writing that he agrees with that opinion and that it is appropriate to revoke the order (s 17F(4)).

An amendment to the 2007 Act was introduced in the House of Lords, the effect   5.67
of which would have been that a CTO could not be revoked unless a 'medical
practitioner' (ie a doctor) had given a written recommendation certifying that the
conditions in s 3(2) were satisfied. This was intended to meet the situation where the
'responsible clinician' is not a medical practitioner (see para 7.01). This amendment
was overturned on the Bill's return to the House of Commons. A similar amendment made to s 20 of the 1983 Act, relating to the circumstances in which a non-
medically qualified responsible clinician could renew a patient's detention, was also
overturned, but in its place a new s 20(5A) was introduced. This provision requires
that a person who has been professionally concerned with the patient's medical
treatment, who belongs to a profession other than that to which the responsible clinician belongs, states in writing that he agrees that the criteria for renewal in s 20(4)
are satisfied (para 7.10). Curiously, no such provision was introduced in relation to
revocation of CTOs, making the revocation mechanism more vulnerable to a human
rights challenge: see below, para 5.84.

2. Effect of Revocation: s 17G

The effect of revoking the CTO is that the hospital managers once more have   5.68
authority to detain the patient under s 6(2)[16] (s 17G(2)) and the patient is once
again 'liable to be detained' under the 1983 Act (s 17G(3)). The patient is treated as

---

[16] Or, in the case of a patient detained under s 37, s 40(1)(b) (s 17G(2) as modified by s 40(4) and Sch 1
Part I, para 2B).

if subject to the original application for admission for treatment rather than a new application, save that for the purposes of renewal under s 20 the patient is treated as if admitted to hospital in pursuance of the application for admission for treatment on the day on which the order was revoked (s 17G (5)). Accordingly, the initial period of detention will be six months and subsequent periods of extension will be calculated on the basis there have been no previous extensions. The first period of extension will therefore be for six months(s 20(2)(a)), and any further periods of extension will be for one year (s 20(2)(b)).

5.69   A patient who is 'liable to be detained' after the revocation of a CTO will also be subject to the compulsory treatment provisions of Part 4 (s 56(3)), subject to the provisions of s 62A (see para 6.108).

J. RETURN OF COMMUNITY PATIENTS ABSENT WITHOUT LEAVE

1. Power to Return a Recalled Community Patient to Hospital: s 18

5.70   By s 18(2A), where a community patient is at any time absent from a hospital to which he is recalled under section 17E above, he may be taken into custody and returned to the hospital by any AMHP, by any officer on the staff of the hospital, by any constable, or by any person authorized in writing by the responsible clinician or the managers of the hospital. The power to return a community patient to hospital under s 18 does not apply unless a recall notice has been made under s 17E and the patient has refused to comply with it or has subsequently absconded from hospital following his return. In either event, there are time limits after which the community patient cannot be returned to hospital which may, in certain circumstances, be extended. These provisions are the same in both cases, although additional provisions apply for those going AWOL after their return.

2. Provisions Applying to All Recalled Community Patients Who Are AWOL

(a) *Extension of Period of Liability for Recall*

5.71   If a recalled community patient goes AWOL and his CTO is due to expire in less than six months, the CTO is automatically extended for a maximum period of six months from the date he goes AWOL. If the patient is still AWOL after six months or after the end of the period for which the CTO is in force, whichever is the later, he cannot be returned to hospital under s 18 (s 18(4)(b)). He will be deemed to be discharged from liability to recall under the CTO and the underlying application for admission for treatment will cease to have effect (s 20B(1)). However, during this extended period he remains liable to be returned to hospital under s 18.

5.72   In determining for the purposes of s 18(4)(b) whether a CTO is in force, any report furnished by the responsible clinician under ss 20A or 21B shall not be taken to have extended the CTO unless the extension began before the day he went AWOL (s 18(4B)).

If the patient is AWOL in the week before the date upon which the CTO expires   5.73 under s 18(4), but is then returned to hospital under s 18 or returns himself to hospital before that date, the CTO will be extended for a further week after his return to hospital (s 21(1)–(2)). During this one week period the responsible clinician may decide to renew the CTO (see following paragraphs), but the patient would still have to be released after the 72 hour period in s 17F(7) (para 5.64) unless the decision is taken to revoke the CTO under s 17F(4).

(b) Recalled Community Patient AWOL for Less Than 28 Days

If the community patient has been AWOL for less than 28 days the time period   5.74 for furnishing a report under s 20A(4) (extending the CTO for six months or a year) is extended by the same one week period after his return (s 21A(4)). There is no requirement for the responsible clinician to examine the patient afresh before he issues his report, provided he has previously conducted an examination within the previous two months as required by s 20A(4).

(c) Recalled Community Patient AWOL for More Than 28 Days

If, on the other hand, the patient has been AWOL for more than 28 days, the   5.75 responsible clinician[17] must examine the patient upon his return to hospital within one week. If it appears to him that the conditions for renewal of a community treatment order in s 20A(6)(8) are satisfied (above, para 5.44), he shall furnish a report to the hospital managers to that effect (s 21B(2)). If no such report is furnished within the one week period, the community treatment period shall be deemed to expire at the end of that period (s 21B(4)) unless it is revoked in the meantime, in which case the responsible clinician is not obliged to furnish the report under s 21B(2) (s 21B(4A)).

If renewed, the CTO will then be extended for the relevant period provided for   5.76 by s 20A(3) (six months or one year) from the date upon which the CTO would have expired (s 20(6A)). If the patient has been AWOL for so long that the period, so extended, would expire before the date the report was furnished, then it shall be extended for the further period provided for by s 20A(3) (one year) (s 21B(6B)). In either case, if the CTO (as renewed) ceases to be in force within a period of two months of the day upon which the report is furnished, the report may be used for the purposes of s 20A(4) to authorize a further period of extension under s 20A(3) (s 21B(7A)).

---

[17] s 21B refers to the 'appropriate practitioner', defined in s 34 as the 'responsible clinician' for patient subject to a CTO.

3. Recalled Community Patient AWOL After his Return to Hospital

5.77　If the patient absconds after his return to hospital, he may be returned to hospital under s 18 at any time before the time limit provided for by s 18(4) expires (see para 5.71 above). The provisions relating to the furnishing of reports by the responsible clinician to renew a CTO in the event the patient is AWOL for more or less than 28 days also apply (paras 5.74–5.76 above).

5.78　　In addition, if the patient returns to hospital, either voluntarily or under s 18, before the 72 hour time limit in s 17F(7) expires, that period is extended for a further period of 72 hours from the time he is returned to hospital (s 21(4)), after which he must either be released or his CTO revoked. If his return takes place after the expiry of that period then a fresh 72 hour period would begin under s 17F(7).

K. AFTERCARE

5.79　The release of a patient detained under ss 3, 37, 45A, 47, or 48 places a duty jointly upon his responsible Primary Care Trust and local social services authority to provide him with 'aftercare services' under section 117(2) MHA until such time as the authority is satisfied he is no longer in need of them. Section 117 gives rise to a specific, rather than a 'target', duty to provide aftercare services to a particular individual person to whom the provision applies. The responsible authorities may not charge for those services.[18]

5.80　　Section 117(2) has been amended so that the s 117 applies to patients on SCT and it is not open to the authorities to stop providing aftercare services while the patient remains on SCT.

5.81　　Aftercare services under s 117 are 'community care services' for the purposes of s 46(3) National Health Service and Community Care Act 1990 (the 1990 Act) and local authorities, with assistance from the Primary Care Trust, are under a duty to assess the patient's need for aftercare services while in hospital under s 47(1) of the 1990 Act. That duty is an ongoing one while the patient is in the community. A further assessment duty is created by the 'Care Programme Approach' guidance, which require local social services and health authorities to adopt the 'Care Programme Approach'.[19] Both assessment duties will apply to patients on SCT.

---

[18]　*R (Stennett) v Richmond LBC* [2002] 2 AC 1127, para 10.

[19]　See LASSL 90(11)/ HC (90) 23 and LASSL 94(4)/ HSG (94) 27, as expanded upon in the informal guidance 'Building Bridges—A guide to arrangements for the inter-agency working for the care and protection of severely mentally ill people'. See also Chapter 27 of the Code of Practice issued by the Health Secretary under section 118 MHA.

L. THE MENTAL HEALTH ACT COMMISSION

See para 4.54.   5.82

M. HUMAN RIGHTS IMPLICATIONS

1. Article 5

The ECtHR has already accepted the principle that conditions may be placed upon   5.83
the release of a patient back into the community, even if that delays their release,
without violating Article 5(1).[20] The release of a patient on SCT is unlikely to
engage the right to liberty in Article 5, although it might theoretically do so if the
conditions are so stringent as to amount, in practice, to a 'deprivation of liberty'
(for which see the discussion in para 11.21ff), although it is hard to conceive of the
circumstances in which that might arise. By the same token, the recall of a patient is
unlikely to have Article 5 implications as the criteria for recall in s 17E reflect the
Winterwerp criteria (see following paragraph) at least in so far as those criteria are
not required to be met in an emergency. As recall is only authorized for up to 72
hours it would probably come within the definition of an 'emergency'.

There are, however, three aspects of the new legal framework for SCT that may   5.84
be open to a human rights challenge engaging Article 5. First, the provisions governing the *revocation* of a CTO may not comply with Article 5(1)(e) in that a 'responsible clinician' who is *not* also a medically qualified doctor can exercise the power
if, in his opinion, the conditions in s 3(2) of the 1983 Act are satisfied (s 17F(4),
above para 5.67). For a lawful detention under Article 5(1)(e) on the grounds of
'unsound mind' the patient must be reliably shown by 'objective medical expertise'
to be suffering from a mental disorder of a kind or degree warranting compulsory
confinement (the '*Winterwerp*' criteria, after *Winterwerp v Netherlands*[21]). Where
the responsible clinician is not a medically qualified doctor, it is arguable that this
requirement for 'objective medical expertise' is not met. This was one of the
arguments marshalled by those who supported the House of Lords amendments
that would have required the approval of a doctor before a CTO could be revoked,
which were subsequently overturned in the Commons (see above, para 5.67; see also
para 7.08ff).

The second area in which the legislation is liable to challenge lies in the fact that   5.85
the Mental Health Review Tribunal is not given jurisdiction to release a patient on
SCT. This is by contrast, in particular, with the Tribunal's jurisdiction in relation to
restricted patients, in respect of whom it has a power to order discharge on conditions (s 73 of the 1983 Act). The power to impose conditions can be of 'great benefit

---

[20] *Johnson v United Kingdom* (1997) 27 EHRR 296, para 63.
[21] (1979) 2 EHRR 387, paras 39–40.

to patients and the public, and conducive to the Convention object of restricting the curtailment of personal liberty to the maximum, because it enables tribunals to ensure that restricted patients compulsorily detained in hospital represent the hard core of those who suffer from mental illness, are a risk to themselves or others and cannot be effectively treated and supervised otherwise than in hospital' (*Regina (H) v Secretary of State for the Home Department* [2004] 2 AC 253, para 26). In deciding whether to discharge a restricted patient the Tribunal can, and must, have regard to any conditions of discharge it might impose.[22] A patient who continues to require medical treatment which can be given in the community is more likely to be discharged if the Tribunal can impose conditions to ensure he receives that treatment than if it cannot. Moreover, under section 73(7) the Tribunal can defer an order for conditional discharge pending the making of 'suitable arrangements', the effect of which is to trigger an enforceable duty on the section 117 authorities to provide suitable aftercare in order to fulfil those conditions.[23] The unrestricted patient, with no means of enforcing the section 117 authorities' aftercare duty, remains detained because no accommodation is available. There is no objective justification for discriminating against unrestricted patients in this way, and the absence of any jurisdiction to release such patients on SCT may breach Article 5(4), either alone or taken together with Article 14.

5.86   Third, the fact that the Tribunal does not have power to vary or discharge conditions of SCT upon an application or reference made to it may be open to challenge.[24] At present the only options available to the Tribunal on an application or reference by a patient on SCT is to confirm the CTO or discharge it altogether (above, para 5.47). There may be circumstances in which the Tribunal considers the conditions of the SCT to be unnecessary. If those conditions are so intrusive as to amount to a 'deprivation of liberty' then Article 5(4) would require the patient to have speedy access to a 'court' to determine the lawfulness of that deprivation of liberty, which (in those circumstances) would require the 'court' to be able to discharge the offending conditions. It may be, however, that the Article 5(4) requirement in those circumstances would be met by the availability of an application for judicial review in the Administrative Court. That will offer little assistance in those cases—which are likely to be plentiful—where the real issue before the Tribunal is the suitability of the conditions imposed on SCT rather than whether it should be in place at all.

2. Article 8

5.87   The imposition of conditions on release, including liability to recall to hospital, constitutes an interference with the right to respect for private and family life under

---

[22] *Campbell v Home Secretary* [1988] AC 120, 127E.

[23] *R (H) v Home Secretary* [2004] 2 AC 253, para 29.

[24] This is an issue raised by the JCHR in their 2nd Report, para 58.

Article 8(1), requiring justification under Article 8(2). To be lawful, any interference with the right in Article 8(1) must pursue one of the aims listed in Article 8(2) and be a necessary and proportionate means of achieving that aim. Moreover, any such interference must be 'in accordance with the law', which means much the same as the requirement in Article 5(1) that any detention be 'in accordance with a procedure prescribed by law'. To satisfy this requirement, national law must be sufficiently accessible and foreseeable to satisfy the principle of legal certainty and must provide adequate guarantees against arbitrary and mistaken interferences (see para 6.128).

The release of a patient on SCT almost certainly does not, of itself, constitute an unlawful interference with his Article 8 rights if the new provisions are lawfully applied. SCT plainly pursues a legitimate objective, namely 'the protection of health'. The provisions for the imposition of SCT are sufficiently accessible and foreseeable and provide adequate guarantees against abuse and are therefore 'in accordance with the law'.[25] **5.88**

3. SCT Compared with Long-term s 17 Leave

Indeed, SCT is probably less likely to violate the Convention than does the long-term use of section 17 leave, which is currently the form of 'community treatment' most commonly used by psychiatrists to ensure patient compliance with medication. Section 17 has been used as a form of 'conditional discharge', particularly since the Court of Appeal's decision in *B v Barking, Havering & Brentwood Community Mental Health NHS Trust*[26] to the effect that a patient may have his detention renewed under section 20 while on long-term leave of absence. The Court held that the words in s 20(4)(c) MHA 'that [treatment] cannot be provided unless he continues to be detained' mean 'unless he continues to be *liable to be* detained' and not 'actually detained', so that a patient's detention may be renewed even though he does not have any need for in-patient treatment, provided it was envisaged the patient would receive 'medical treatment in hospital'. In *R (DR) v Mersey Care NHS Trust*[27] Wilson J held that leave of absence *itself* constituted 'medical treatment in hospital'. Convenient as this may be for treating psychiatrists, the procedure for placing a patient on s 17 leave has Convention implications, certainly by comparison with SCT. **5.89**

First, there are no criteria for the placing of conditions on a patient's leave of absence under s 17(1) beyond the requirement the responsible medical officer (in future, the responsible clinician) considers them 'necessary in the interests of the patient or for the protection of other persons'. Arguably, the criteria are too vague to meet the requirement in Article 8 that any interference be 'in accordance with the law' (see para 6.128). By contrast, to release a patient on SCT the responsible clinician must certify that the criteria in s 17A(5) are met (above, para 5.31), and an **5.90**

---

[25] Although note the 2nd JCHR Report, para 51.
[26] [1999] 1 FLR 106.
[27] Unreported, 7 August 2002.

AMHP must state in writing that he agrees with that opinion and that it is appropriate to make the order (s 17A(4)).

5.91   Second, a patient on long-term leave of absence may have his leave revoked and be recalled to hospital under section 17(4) where it 'appears to the responsible medical officer that it is necessary to do so in the interests' of the patient's health or safety or for the protection of other persons'. That is not the same as being satisfied the criteria for admission under s 3(2) are made out, and potentially allows the recall of a patient in circumstances where the *Winterwerp* criteria are not satisfied. In *Kay v United Kingdom*[28] the ECtHR made it clear that a conditionally discharged patient cannot be recalled to hospital unless there is up to date medical evidence demonstrating 'unsoundness of mind' in accordance with the *Winterwerp* criteria; the same principle applies to patients on leave of absence. The writer is not aware of any challenge to the use of s 17 that raises this argument.

5.92   Under SCT, on the other hand, a patient may not be recalled under s 17E unless the responsible clinician is of the opinion 'the patient requires medical treatment in hospital for his mental disorder' and 'there would be a risk of harm to the health or safety of the patient or to other persons if the patient were not recalled to hospital for that purpose' (para 5.60), which is unlikely to have Convention implications for the reasons given at para 5.83.

5.93   In these respects, SCT raises less human rights implications than s 17 leave, although it may be liable to challenge for the reasons given at para 5.84.

---

[28] (1998) 40 BMLR 20; see also *R (MM) v Home Secretary* [2007] EWCA Civ 687.

6

MEDICAL TREATMENT FOR MENTAL DISORDER UNDER THE 1983 ACT

A. Key Features	6.00
B. Summary of the Existing Legal Framework: Part 4 of the 1983 Act	6.01
1. The Meaning of 'Medical Treatment' and the 'Treatability Test'	6.02
2. Section 63: Treatment Provided By or Under the Direction of the Responsible Clinician	6.06
3. Section 57: Irreversible Treatment	6.10
4. Section 58: Medication and ECT	6.12
5. Section 62: Emergency Treatment	6.16
6. Other Provisions of Part 4	6.18
C. Amendments to Part 4	6.21
1. The New 'Appripriate Treatment' Test	6.21
2. Extending Clinical Responsibilities to Other Professionals	6.34
3. Patients to Whom Part 4 Applies: New s 56	6.37
4. Other Amendments	6.38
D. Additional Safeguards for ECT: s 58A	6.42
1. Summary of the New Safeguards	6.42
2. Patients with Capacity or Competence	6.44
3. Patients Lacking Capacity	6.51
4. Section 62: Urgent Treatment with ECT	6.57
E. Medical Treatment of Community Patients: Part 4A	6.58
1. Introduction	6.58
2. Overview of the New Part 4A Procedure	6.64
3. The Conditions for Administering 'Relevant Treatment': 'Authority to Treat' and the 'Certificate Requirement', s 64B(2) and s 64E(2)	6.66
4. Child Community Patients	6.67
5. 'Relevant Treatment': s 64A	6.70
6. 'Authority to Treat'	6.71
7. 's 58 Type and s 58A Type Treatment' and 'the Certificate Requirement'	6.90

	F.	Treatment of Recalled Community Patients	6.108
		1. Introduction	6.108
		2. Community Patients who Cannot be Treated Under Part 4A	6.109
		3. Part 4 Applies to Recalled Community Patients: s 56(4)	6.110
		4. Section 6 2A: Part 4A Certificates Continue to Have Effect After Recall or Revocation	6.111
	G.	The Interface between the 1983 Act and the 2005 Act	6.117
	H.	Human Rights Implications	6.120
		1. Article 3 Principles	6.120
		2. Article 8 Principles	6.125
		3. Human Rights Implications of the 2007 Amendments	6.133

A. KEY FEATURES

6.00 • The 2007 Act has introduced a number of amendments to the provisions governing treatment under the 1983 Act. Part 4 has been extensively amended and Part 4A introduced to govern the circumstances in which treatment may be given to 'community patients' subject to community treatment orders (CTO) imposed under the new s 17A (supervised community treatment or SCT).

• The key features of the amendments to Part 4 are as follows:

• A new definition of 'medical treatment' in s 145(1) and new 'treatability' requirement in s 145(4).

• The removal of the current 'treatability' test in ss 57 and 58.

• A new 'appropriate treatment' test for the SOAD to apply under ss 57 and 58 in s 64(3).

• Treatment may now be given by or under the direction of a non-medically qualified 'responsible clinician'.

• s 57 safeguards extended to short-term detainees and conditionally discharged restricted patients.

• Additional safeguards introduced in s 58A for electro-convulsive therapy (ECT): first, ECT may no longer be administered without the consent of a patient with capacity or, in the case of an incapacitated patient, if it conflicts with an advance decision or a decision of a donee, deputy, or the Court of Protection in accordance with the 2005 Act; second, the circumstances in which ECT may be administered as an emergency measure are limited; third, the safeguards are extended to informal child patients (those under 18).

• The key features of the new Part 4A procedure are set out at para 6.64ff.

B. SUMMARY OF THE EXISTING LEGAL FRAMEWORK: PART 4 OF THE 1983 ACT

Part 4 of the 1983 Act provides specific powers to treat patients who, with certain   6.01
exceptions considered at para 6.06, are 'liable to be detained' under the 1983 Act
(and, in the case of s 57 treatment, any patient,[1] including informal patients) for
their mental disorder and any treatment ancillary to that disorder. Part 4 does not
authorize the administration of treatment for any other form of disorder.[2] Part 4 also
provides a number of patient safeguards, requiring additional conditions to be met
and authority from an independent registered medical practitioner appointed by the
MHAC (the SOAD) before certain forms of treatment may be given. Part 4 therefore has both coercive and protective functions. In contrast to the position at
common law and under the 2005 Act, Part 4 authorizes the treatment of patients
with capacity who object to their treatment, under s 58 and s 63 and, in emergencies, under s 62. The fact the patient has capacity is a relevant factor that the RMO
is to take into account, but it carries no more weight than any other factor: indeed,
the fact that treatment requires to be imposed by force, upon a capable or incapacitated patient, is likely to carry more weight.[3] Other, more intrusive treatments are
authorized under s 57, but these cannot be imposed without consent.

1. The Meaning of 'Medical Treatment' and the 'Treatability Test'

(a) *'Medical Treatment': s 145(1)*
Section 145(1) states that '"medical treatment" includes nursing, and also includes   6.02
care, habilitation and rehabilitation under medical supervision'. The definition is 'a
wide one': see para 3.35.

(b) *The 'Treatability Test': Treatment which is Likely to Alleviate or Prevent a
Deterioration of the Patient's Condition*
The 'treatability' test under the 1983 Act prior to amendment applies in two,   6.03
material contexts. First, it is one of the criteria for the lawful *detention* of a patient
classified as suffering either 'psychopathic disorder' or 'mental impairment', namely
that treatment must be available which is 'likely to alleviate or prevent a deterioration of [the patient's] condition' (notably in s 3(2)(b) and s 37(2)(a)(i)). The same
requirement is one of the criteria for the lawful *renewal* of detention under s 20(4),

---

[1] With some exceptions, see para 6.10.
[2] *R (B) v Ashworth Hospital Authority* [2005] 2 AC 278, para 62; *B v Croydon Health Authority* [1995] Fam 133; *Re C (Adult: Refusal of Medical Treatment)* [1994] 1 WLR 290.
[3] *R (B) v Dr S* [2006] 1 WLR 810, paras 49–50. The human rights implications of compulsory treatment are considered at para 6.120.

albeit for *all* classifications of disorder. The significance of the test in the context of detention, and its more controversial status, is considered at paras 3.49ff.

6.04   Second, and of relevance to this chapter, the 'treatability' requirement is also a pre-requisite for lawful *treatment*, at least for treatment falling within s 57 or 58. Both provisions require that before a SOAD authorizes treatment he must certify in writing that, 'having regard to the likelihood of the treatment alleviating or preventing a deterioration of the patient's condition, the treatment should be given' (s 57(2)(b) and 58(3)(b)). Here, the 'treatability' criteria has given rise to less controversy, but in an important judgment in *R (B) v Dr S*,[4] the Court of Appeal held that the 'treatability' test is not the only test that the SOAD must address in determining whether treatment should be authorized under ss 57 or 58: he must also consider whether the treatment is in the patient's 'best interests', the determination of which question 'will depend on wider considerations than the simple question of the efficacy of the treatment', such as 'whether an alternative and less invasive treatment will achieve the same result' and the 'distress that will be caused to the patient if the treatment has to be imposed by force'.

6.05   The judgment has two important consequences. First, it follows that where treatment is given under any provision of Part 4 the patient's wider 'best interests' must be considered in deciding whether to give the treatment, both by the treating professional and the SOAD. Second, even where the relevant provisions do not incorporate the 'treatability' test, such as in ss 62 or 63, the 'best interests' test still applies which requires the RMO or any other treating professional to consider (among other things) the prospects of the treatment alleviating or preventing a deterioration in the patient's condition. Third, it means that the removal of the 'treatability' test from ss 57 and 58 (albeit with its partial reintroduction in s 145(4)) by the 2007 Act is less significant than it might otherwise have been (see paras 6.21ff below).

2. Section 63: Treatment Provided By or Under the Direction of the Responsible Clinician

6.06   Section 63 applies to patients who are 'liable to be detained' under the 1983 Act except those detained under ss 4, 5(2) or (4), 35, 135, 136, or 37(4) and those restricted patients who have been conditionally discharged under s 42, s 73 or s 74 and not recalled to hospital (s 56(1)). Because patients on s 17 leave of absence are 'liable to be detained', s 63 also applies to such patients.

6.07   Section 63 authorizes the patient's responsible medical officer (RMO), or some other person acting under his direction, to impose treatment without capable consent, except where the treatment falls within one of the categories specified in, or provided for by regulations made under, s 57 or 58. In particular, s 63 authorizes the administration of medication during the first three months of a patient's detention;

---

4 [2006] 1 WLR 810, para 62.

thereafter, s 58(1)(b) requires that further treatment can only be administered with the approval of a SOAD.

As noted above, s 63 does not expressly require the RMO or other treating profes-   6.08
sional to have regard to the likelihood of treatment alleviating or preventing a deterioration of the patient's condition, but because the patient's 'best interests' must be
considered before treatment is given it follows that the prospects of the treatment
having either of those effects must be considered (see above, para 6.04).

The human rights implications of treatment under s 63 is considered at para 6.137,   6.09
below.

3. Section 57: Irreversible Treatment

Section 57 applies to patients who are 'liable to be detained', with the exceptions con-   6.10
tained in s 56(1) (patients detained under ss 4, 5(2) or (4), 35, 135, 136, or 37(4) and
conditionally discharged restricted patients), but by s 56(2) also applies to patients who
are not liable to be detained. The effect of these provisions is that all patients, *except*
those detained under the short-term detaining provisions in ss 4, 5(2) or (4), 35, 135,
136, or 37(4) and conditionally discharged restricted patients, benefit from the safeguards of s 57. The rather anomalous exclusion of these categories of detained patients
is remedied by the replacement s 56 introduced by the 2007 Act, see para 6.37.

Section 57 governs the imposition of particularly invasive or irreversible forms of   6.11
medical treatment for mental disorder. Section 57(1)(a) specifies one form of mental
treatment, namely any surgical operation for destroying brain tissue or for destroying the functioning of brain tissue, but s 57(1)(b) refers to 'any other forms of treatment as may be specified by regulations made by the Secretary of State'. To date, the
only form of treatment so specified is 'the surgical implantation of hormones for the
purposes of reducing male sex drive'.[5] Before such treatment may be given, the provision requires *both* capable consent and a SOAD's certificate to the effect that,
having regard to the likelihood of the treatment alleviating or preventing a deterioration of the patient's conditions, the treatment should be given (the 'treatability'
criteria: see the discussion at para 6.03 above). Before granting a certificate the
SOAD must consult two other persons who have been professionally concerned
with the patient's treatment.

4. Section 58: Medication and ECT

Section 58 applies to the same group of patients as s 63 (s 56(1)): see above, para 6.06.   6.12

Section 58 governs the administration of two forms of treatment: first, 'such forms   6.13
of treatment as may be specified . . . by regulations made by the Secretary of State', of
which the only form of treatment so specified is electro-convulsive therapy (ECT);[6]

---

[5] Reg 16 of the Mental Health (Hospital, Guardianship & Consent to Treatment) Regulations 1983. This
procedure is no longer used: Explanatory Notes to the 2007 Act, para 86.

[6] Reg 16 of the Mental Health (Hospital, Guardianship & Consent to Treatment) Regulations 1983.

and, second, 'the administration of medicine to a patient by any means at any time during a period for which he is liable to be detained as a patient to whom this Part of this Act applies if three months or more have elapsed since the first occasion in that period when medicine was administered to him by any means for his mental disorder'. The three month period runs not from the beginning of the period of detention but from the first occasion upon which medication was administered.

6.14 Section 58 permits the administration of medication notwithstanding the absence of a patient's capable consent, but introduces the safeguard that the treatment must be approved by a SOAD, who must consult with two other persons who have been professionally involved in the patient's medical treatment before giving a certificate. Section 58(3)(b) provides that the prescribed treatment may be imposed where the SOAD 'has certified in writing that the patient *is not capable of understanding* the nature, purpose and likely effects of that treatment *or has not consented to it* but that, having regard to the likelihood of its alleviating or preventing a deterioration of his condition, the treatment should be given' (the 'treatability' criteria: see the discussion at para 6.03 above). The SOAD must therefore distinguish between, on the one hand, patients who are incapable (whether consenting or dissenting) and, on the other, patients who are capable but non-consenting. At common law the decision of the latter would have to be respected, but under the regime provided for by section 58 treatment may be imposed upon both a capable patient who refuses it and an incapable patient who refuses or assents to it (para 6.01).

6.15 In making his decision the SOAD must form his own independent judgment that the treatment should be given,[7] and before doing so he must be satisfied that the treatment is in the patient's 'best interests', which includes factors wider than the alleviation or prevention of deterioration of the disorder or its symptoms, such as whether an alternative but less invasive treatment will achieve the same result and the distress that the patient will suffer if the treatment is administered by force[8] (see above, para 6.04).

5. Section 62: Emergency Treatment

6.16 Section 62 governs the administration of emergency treatment that would otherwise fall within s 57 or s 58.

6.17 Section 62(1) provides that s 57 and 58 do not apply to any treatment (a) which is immediately necessary to save the patient's life; or (b) which (not being irreversible) is immediately necessary to prevent a serious deterioration of his condition; or

---

[7] *R (Wilkinson) v Broadmoor* [2002] 1 WLR 419, *per* Simon Browne LJ at paras 32–3.
[8] *R (B) v Dr SS* [2006] 1 WLR 810, para 62 *per* Lord Phillips CJ.

(c) which (not being irreversible or hazardous) is immediately necessary to alleviate-serious suffering by the patient; or (d) which (not being irreversible or hazardous) is immediately necessary and represents the minimum interference necessary to prevent the patient from behaving violently or being a danger to himself or to others. Treatment is 'irreversible' if it has unfavourable irreversible physical or psychological consequences and 'hazardous' if it entails significant physical hazard (s 62(3)).

6. Other Provisions of Part 4

(a) *s 59 Plans of Treatment*

By s 59 any consent or certificate under ss 57 or 58 may relate to a plan of treatment under which the patient is to be given one or more of the forms of treatment to which that section applies.   6.18

(b) *s 60 Withdrawal of Consent*

A patient who has consented to any treatment or plan of treatment under s 57 or 58 may withdraw his consent at any time, except for emergency treatment under s 62(1) or where the RMO considers that discontinuance of the treatment would cause serious suffering to the patient (s 62(2)).   6.19

(c) *s 61 Review of Treatment*

Where a patient is given treatment in accordance with s 57(2) (irreversible treatment) or s 58(3)(b) (treatment where no capable consent is given), the RMO must provide a report on the treatment to the Mental Health Act Commission on the next occasion the patient's detention is renewed or at any other time when required to do so by the MHAC (ss 61 and 121(2)(b)). By s 61(3) the MHAC may at any time give notice that a certificate issued under ss 57(2) or 58(3)(b) shall not apply after a specified date, and no further treatment may thereafter be given under the certificate other than emergency treatment under s 62(1) or if the RMO considers discontinuance would cause serious suffering to the patient (s 62(2)).   6.20

C. AMENDMENTS TO PART 4

1. The New 'Appripriate Treatment' Test

(a) *Removal of the Current 'Treatability' Criteria in ss 57 and 58*

Sections 57 and 58 have both been amended so that the test the SOAD is required to apply in determining whether treatment should be authorized no longer reads '. . . that, having regard to the likelihood of the treatment alleviating or preventing a deterioration of the patient's condition, the treatment should be given' (above, para 6.04), but instead reads '. . . that it is appropriate for the treatment to be given'.   6.21

However, that test must be read in the light of the definition of 'appropriate treatment' in s 64(3) and the new 'treatability test' in s 145(4), below.

(b) *New 'Appropriate Treatment' Test in s 64(3)*

6.22 Section 64(3) provides 'For the purposes of this Part of this Act, it is appropriate for treatment to be given to a patient if the treatment is appropriate in his case, taking into account the nature and degree of the mental disorder from which he is suffering and all other circumstances of his case.'

6.23 This is the test that applies for the purposes of treatment in Part 4, but is in identical terms to the 'appropriate treatment' test introduced in relation to detention in s 3(4), which is expressed to apply to the whole Act: see para 3.71.

6.24 In determining whether treatment is 'appropriate', it is necessary to consider the new 'medical treatment' test.

(c) *New Test for 'Medical Treatment': s 145(1)'*

6.25 Section 145(1) has been amended so it now reads: ' "medical treatment" includes nursing, psychological intervention and specialist mental health habilitation, rehabilitation and care (but see also subsection (4) below).'

6.26 This definition must also be read in the light of new s 145(4)

(d) *The New 'Treatability' Criteria: s 145(4)*

6.27 Section 145(4) reads, 'Any reference in this Act to medical treatment, in relation to mental disorder, shall be construed as a reference to medical treatment the purpose of which is to alleviate, or prevent a worsening of, the disorder or one or more of its symptoms or manifestations'. The significance of these amendments is discussed below.

(e) *Discussion*

6.28 The removal of the 'treatability' criteria as it applied both to detention[9] and to treatment under s 57 and s 58, taken with the new 'appropriate treatment' test in s 64(3) proved extremely controversial during the 2007 Act's passage as a Bill through Parliament, leading to a last minute concession by the government at the Report Stage in the House of Commons, in response to concerted pressure from pressure groups and in order to avoid the Bill's rejection by the House of Lords (see para 3.74). Section 145(4) was the result of that concession.

6.29 Pressure had also been brought to bear by the JCHR, which had recommended that the 'appropriateness' test, as it related to treatment, should include a requirement that treatment be a 'medical necessity' in order to comply with Convention rights (and see para 6.121).[10]

---

[9] The removal of the 'treatability' criteria was most controversial as it related to the lawful *detention* of patients with psychopathic disorder or mental impairment: see the discussion at paras 3.49–3.57, 3.66–3.74, 3.93–3.108.

[10] 2nd JCHR Report, paras 59–65.

I would suggest that the individual and cumulative impact of these changes is rel- 6.30
atively insignificant, for four reasons.

First, the new definition of 'medical treatment' to include treatment the effect of 6.31
which is to treat the 'symptoms or manifestations' of the disorder is entirely neutral
in effect, as these are matters to which the SOAD or RMO are currently required to
have regard to under the current 'treatability' test:[11] see *Reid v Secretary of State for
Scotland*[12] quoted at para 3.54 above. Section 145(4) simply makes this requirement
explicit.

Second, the new 'appropriate treatment' test, when taken with the new 'treatability' requirement in s 145(4), has very much the same meaning as the current treatability test in ss 57 and 58

Third, the SOAD must still form his own independent judgment (para 6.14) that 6.32
the treatment should be given, and before doing so he must still be satisfied that the
treatment is in the patient's 'best interests'. 'Best interests' involves consideration of
factors including, but going beyond, whether the treatment will or may alleviate or
prevent a deterioration of the condition or its symptoms: see above, para 6.04.
Indeed, the need to take into consideration such wider issues is now made explicit
by new s 64(3), which requires the relevant professional to take into account 'the
nature and degree of the mental disorder from which he is suffering and all other
circumstances of his case'.

Fourth, treatment—in particular, treatment that overrides an individual's compe- 6.33
tent refusal or which requires force—may only be justified under either Article 3 or 8
where it is a 'medical necessity' (see paras 6.121, 6.130). Treatment that does not
meet that test will not be 'appropriate'. The human rights implications of the amendments are considered below, at para 6.120ff.

2. Extending Clinical Responsibilities to Other Professionals

The relevant provisions of Part 4 have all been amended to replace references to the 6.34
'responsible medical officer' with 'the responsible clinician',[13] to reflect the very
significant policy change effected by the 2007 Act that non-medically qualified
mental health professionals will now be able to supervise the treatment of mental
patients (considered in detail at para 7.01ff). The 'responsible clinician' is defined in
s 64(1)[14] as 'the approved clinician with overall responsibility for the case of the
patient in question', while 'approved clinician' is defined in s 145(1) as 'a person
approved by the Secretary of State (in relation to England) or by the Welsh Ministers
(in relation to Wales) to act as an approved clinician for the purposes of this Act'.

---

[11] For a discussion of the implications of the 'treatability' test as it relates to detention, see para 3.74ff
[12] [1999] AC 512, *per* Lord Hope at 531, Lord Clyde at 542, Lord Hutton at 551.
[13] References have also been introduced to the 'approved clinician in charge of a patient's treatment'. These
apply to treatment which may be given to patients who are not 'liable to be detained', namely under s 57 and
s 58A (see s 64(1A) and (1B)).
[14] See also the definition in s 34(1).

As discussed in para 7.03, draft Directions[15] to be issued by the Secretary of State under ss 7 and 8 of the National Health Service Act 2006 will authorize a range of mental health professionals to be an 'approved clinician', including psychologists, nurses, occupational therapists, and social workers, provided they meet the relevant competencies set out in Schedule 2.[16]

6.35   No amendments have been made to the qualifications required of the SOAD, so sections 57 and 58 (and s 58A) treatment will continue to be authorized only by a medical practitioner. However, medical treatment falling within s 63, which includes medication for the first three months, may be administered (although not prescribed) by or under the supervision of a mental health professional who is not medically qualified ('the approved clinician in change of the treatment'). Moreover, once a SOAD certificate has been given under ss 57, 58, or 58A, the administration of the medical treatment may thereafter be administered by or at the direction of a non-medically qualified professional. This will include the administration of medication to those who are competent to refuse the treatment, by the use of reasonable force if necessary.

6.36   The administration of treatment in these circumstances could have human rights implications, considered at para 6.138, below.

3. Patients to whom Part 4 Applies: New s 56

6.37   The 2007 Act has repealed the current s 56 and replaced it with a new provision in very similar terms, but with some important amendments. First, s 57 and (in so far as relevant to s 57 treatment) s 62 now apply to *all* patients (s 56(1), instead of s 56(2)), including those detained under ss 4, 5(2) or (4), 35, 135, 136, or 37(4) and conditionally discharged restricted patients who were previously excluded (see para 6.10). Second, ss 58, 63 and 62 continue to apply, and ss 58A now applies, to patients who are 'liable to be detained', with the same exceptions as before but with the addition of s 45A(5) (during period of conveyance and detention in a place of safety pending admission to hospital) (s 56(3)). Third, new s 56(4) applies the Part 4 regime to recalled community patients, subject to the modifications in s 62A (considered in detail below, para 6.58). Fourth, new s 56(5) applies the safeguards in s 58A to informal child patients (see para 6.56 below).

4. Other Amendments

6.38   The following, further amendments to Part 4 are also made.

(a) *The Consultation Duty in s 57 and 58*

6.39   The consultation duty in s 57(3) and 58(4), has been amended so that of the two persons professionally concerned with the patient's treatment the SOAD must consult, neither may be the responsible clinician or the person in charge of the

---

[15] These are in draft form at present: draft Mental Health Act 1983 Approved Clinician Directions 2008.
[16] See also the Explanatory Notes to the 2007 Act, para 48.

treatment in question. This amendment has been necessary to reflect the fact the responsible clinician or person in charge of the treatment may not be a registered medical practitioner. Under the 1983 Act before amendment neither of the two consultees can be a registered medical practitioner, which excludes the RMO from taking that role. Of course the SOAD will still have to discuss the case with the responsible clinician in the same way as before he discussed it with the RMO.

(b) *Withdrawal of Consent under s 60*

Section 60 has been amended so as to provide that, where the patient has consented to treatment under s 57, s 58 (or s 58A) and later ceases to be capable of understanding its nature, purpose and likely effects, he shall be treated as having withdrawn his consent to the treatment (s 60(1A) and (1B)). Similarly, where treatment has been authorized for a patient who is not capable of understanding the nature etc. of the treatment in question and he later becomes capable, the certificate shall cease to apply to the treatment (s 60(1C) and (1D)). No provision is currently made for either of these situations in the 1983 Act or the Code of Practice.

6.40

(c) *Duty to Furnish Report under s 61*

Section 61 has been amended so as to require the responsible clinician, upon renewal of the patient's detention, to furnish a report on the patient's treatment to the MHAC where treatment has been authorized under s 58A(4) (ECT treatment of a child) or s 58A(5) (ECT for patients lacking capacity). The same duty has been introduced for community patients on SCT who are recalled and treated under an existing Part 4A certificate at the time of any subsequent renewal of the CTO (s 61(1)).

6.41

D. ADDITIONAL SAFEGUARDS FOR ECT: s 58A

1. Summary of the New Safeguards

Electro-convulsive therapy (ECT) is a controversial psychiatric treatment in which seizures are induced with electricity. Its use is currently regulated by s 58, which requires the approval of a SOAD before it can be administered (above, para 6.12). However, the treatment can be imposed upon a competent patient against his wishes (although clinically that would be very rare), and the protection of s 58 does not extend to those who are not 'liable to be detained' under the 1983 Act, such as informal patients and certain excluded categories of detained patient (see para 6.06). They may therefore be given such treatment under the common law and, from 1 October 2007, under the 2005 Act.

6.42

The 2007 Act introduces a range of new restrictions and safeguards on the administration of ECT and 'such other forms of treatment as may be specified . . . by regulations', but as yet no such other forms of treatment have been specified. Accordingly,

6.43

the following commentary focuses only upon ECT. In summary, the new safeguards provide as follows:

- A detained patient over the age of 18 with capacity can only be administered ECT where he consents and where a SOAD has certified in writing that he is capable of consenting, *except* in an emergency (s 58A(2) and (3)) (para 6.44)

- A detained patient under the age of 18 with capacity can only be administered ECT where he has consented to it, a SOAD has certified in writing that he is capable of consenting to it *and* that it is appropriate for the treatment to be given, *except* in an emergency (s 58A(4)) (para 6.46)

- A patient (whether over or under 18) who lacks capacity can only be administered ECT where a SOAD has certified in writing that he lacks capacity *and* that it is appropriate for the treatment to be given *and*, in the case of an adult, the treatment does not conflict with an advance decision which the SOAD is satisfied is valid and applicable or a decision made by a donee of deputy of the Court of Protection, *except* in an emergency (s 58(5)) (para 6.51)

- ECT may be administered in an emergency only where it is immediately necessary to save the patient's life or prevent a serious deterioration in his condition (s 62(1A) to (1C)) (para 6.57)

- The s 58A safeguards for detained patients under 18 also apply to informal patients under the age of 18 (s 56(5) and 58A(7)), who are also entitled to an IMHA whenever the possibility of ECT is discussed with an approved clinician (s 130C(3)(b)) (para 6.56)

2. Patients with Capacity or Competence

(a) *Patients with Capacity Over the Age of 18*

6.44 Other than in an emergency under s 62, ECT may not be given to a patient who has attained the age of 18 years unless he has capacity to consent, he has consented to the treatment in question and either the approved clinician in charge of it or a SOAD has certified in writing that the patient is capable of understanding the nature, purpose and likely effects of the treatment and has consented to it (s 58A(2) and (3)). There is no requirement for the approved clinician or SOAD to certify that it is appropriate for the treatment to be given, by contrast with the position for patients under the age of 18. This raises an interesting question as to whether the SOAD can or should issue a certificate if he does not consider treatment is appropriate; it is suggested he cannot and should not.

6.45 These provisions apply only to adult patients who are 'liable to be detained' under the 1983 Act except those detained under ss 4, 5(2) or (4), 35, 135, 136, or 37(4) or 45A(5) and those restricted patients who have been conditionally discharged under ss 42 or 73, or 74 and not recalled to hospital (s 56(3)). Because patients on s 17 leave of absence are 'liable to be detained', s 58A also applies to such patients. The administration of ECT to community patients on SCT is regulated by Part 4A (para 6.90ff). For the excluded category of detained patients, other community patients and informal patients, ECT may be administered under the 2005 Act: this raises potential Article 8 issues (see para 6.140).

(b) Patients with Capacity Under the Age of 18

Other than in an emergency under s 62, s 58A treatment may not be given to a patient under the age of 18 who has capacity unless he has consented to the treatment and a SOAD (not being the approved clinician in charge of the treatment in question) has certified in writing that the patient is capable of understanding the nature, purpose, and likely effects of the treatment, and that it is appropriate for the treatment to be given (s 58A(4)). This last requirement is an additional one that does not apply to patients over the age of 18 (see above, para 6.44).   6.46

It is to be noted that the term used for children to whom s 58A applies is 'capacity', not 'competence', by contrast with the provisions of Part 4A. 'Competence' is only relevant as it relates to children under the age of 16 (see para 9.28). Because s 58A refers to children under the age of 18, the term 'capacity' has been used. In so far as s 58A applies to children under the age of 16, however, the SOAD will also have to consider whether they are *Gillick* competent.   6.47

The safeguards in s 58A apply both to those children who are 'liable to be detained' under the 1983 Act and (by contrast with adults) to the excluded categories in s 56(3) and to those who are given treatment informally, in whatever setting (s 56(5)). For these informal patients, the effect of s 58 is to apply the safeguards it contains to such patients; it does not of itself confer authority to administer the treatment (s 58A(7)). That authority is derived from the competent (under 16) or capable (16 or 17) patient's consent. The position for incapacitated child patients is considered at para 6.56 below.   6.48

The administration of ECT to community patients on SCT under the age of 18 is governed by Part 4A (para 6.90ff).   6.49

Section 58A does not appear to allow either a person with parental responsibility or the High Court exercising its wardship or inherent jurisdiction to veto a treatment decision to which a competent or capable child has consented and a SOAD has issued a certificate. This issue is considered at para 15.61 and the human rights implications are set out at 6.133.   6.50

3. Patients Lacking Capacity

(c) Patients Lacking Capacity Over the Age of 18

Other than in an emergency under s 62(1A), ECT may not be given to a patient over the age of 18 who lacks capacity unless a SOAD (not being the responsible clinician or the approved clinician in charge of the treatment in question) has certified in writing that the patient is not capable of understanding the nature, purpose and likely effects of the treatment but that it is appropriate for the treatment to be   6.51

given and that giving him the treatment would not conflict with an advance decision which the SOAD is satisfied is valid and applicable or a decision made by a
donee or deputy of the Court of Protection within the meaning of the Mental
Capacity Act 2005[17] (s 58A(2), (5), and (9)). Before giving a certificate under s 58A(5)
the SOAD must consult two other persons who have been professionally concerned
with the patient's treatment, one of whom shall be a nurse and the other shall be
neither a nurse nor a registered medical practitioner (a social worker, for example),
but neither shall be the responsible clinician or the approved clinician in charge of
the treatment in question (s 58A(6)).

6.52   These provisions apply to the same categories of patients as s 58A(3) (ECT for
capable adult patients), for which see para 6.45.

(d) *Patients Who Lack Capacity Under the Age of 18*

6.53   ECT may not be administered to a patient under the age of 18 who lacks capacity
unless a SOAD (not being the responsible clinician or the approved clinician in
charge of the treatment in question) has certified in writing that the patient is not
capable of understanding the nature, purpose and likely effects of the treatment, but
that it is appropriate for the treatment to be given and that giving him the treatment
would not conflict with an advance decision which the SOAD is satisfied is valid
and applicable or a decision made by a donee of deputy of the Court of Protection
within the meaning of the Mental Capacity Act 2005 (s 58A(2) and 58A(5)).

6.54   The relevant provisions in s 58A apply equally to adults as to children, but two
points should be borne in mind. First, where children under 16 are concerned, the
question of whether the patients is 'capable of understanding the nature, purpose
and likely effects of the treatment' must also be determined by reference to the test
for *Gillick* competence (para 9.28). Second, the references to advance decisions,
decisions of donees or deputies and the Court of Protection are irrelevant for child
patients under 16 (to whom the relevant provisions of the 2005 Act do not apply
(s 2(5) of the 2005 Act)), and for 16–17 year olds only the reference to decisions of
a deputy and the Court of Protection have any relevance, as a child under 18 cannot
make an advance decision (s 24(1) of the 2005 Act) or lasting power of attorney
(s 9(2)(c) of the 2005 Act) (see paras 10.03, 10.07).

6.55   As with capable patients, s 58A gives no role for a person with parental responsibility to veto the treatment of an incompetent or incapable child. This is a curious
anomaly, bearing in mind that for incapable adult patients s 58A treatment cannot
be given if a donee or deputy objects or if it conflicts with an advance decision which
is valid and applicable. This issue is discussed at para 15.61 and its human rights
implications are considered at para 6.133.

6.56   The safeguards in s 58A apply both to those children who are 'liable to be detained'
under the 1983 Act and to those who are informally admitted to hospital who are not
community patients (s 56(5)). Again, for informal patients the effect of s 58A is to

---

[17] As these terms are explained in Chapter 10.

apply the safeguards it contains rather than to confer authority to treat (s 56(7)), which for incapacitated child patients aged 16–17 will be derived from the 2005 Act[18] or, if the child is under 16, from parental consent or from a decision of the Court in its wardship or inherent jurisdiction (see para 9.25ff). If that authority is given, s 58A introduces additional safeguards that must be complied with. The SOAD's certificate will not of itself authorize the treatment in the absence of such authority.

4. Section 62: Urgent Treatment with ECT

The 2007 Act also amends s 62 to limit the circumstances in which emergency treat- 6.57
ment may be given under s 58A to two, namely where it is immediately necessary to save the patient's life or to prevent a serious deterioration in his condition (s 62(1A)). Provision is also made for regulations to be made restricting the administration of other forms of treatment (s 62(1B) and (1C)). These limitations have also been reflected in the provisions governing the administration of ECT to patients on SCT under Part 4A, below para 6.87.

E. MEDICAL TREATMENT OF COMMUNITY
PATIENTS: PART 4A

1. Introduction

New Part 4A provides a comprehensive treatment regime for community patients on 6.58
'supervised community treatment' under s 17A (SCT), both adults and children. Unlike Part 4, part 4A does not permit the imposition of compulsory treatment on patients who have capacity or competence, nor does it permit treatment which conflicts with an advance decision which is valid and applicable or with a decision of a donee, deputy or the Court of Protection. Part 4A does not authorize the imposition of treatment in any circumstances that it cannot be administered to community patients not falling within Part 4A, whether under the doctrine of necessity or (from 1 October 2007) under the 2005 Act or, for children, under the common law rules relating to children (see para 9.25ff). For example, an incapacitated patient in the community who is receiving treatment informally, or who is subject to guardianship or conditional discharge, can be given treatment—if necessary by force—under the 2005 Act in precisely the same circumstances as under Part 4A, but without any of the attendant safeguards.

Again by way of contrast with Part 4A, community patients on s 17 leave are 6.59
subject to the Part 4 regime, which permits treatment notwithstanding it conflicts with a capable refusal or an advance decision or other substituted decision-making mechanism (see para 6.01). Although the Code of Practice to the 1983 Act, para 20.8, provides in such circumstances that 'consideration should be given to

---

[18] The MCA is expressly not excluded from operating in these circumstances: see s 28(1A) of the 2005 Act, see para 15.70.

recalling the patient to hospital' rather than exercise the coercive powers of Part 4, the point is that there is *power* to impose such treatment under Part 4, whereas there is no such power under part 4A, even in emergencies.

6.60   In fact, Part 4A prohibits treatment which could otherwise be lawfully administered to patients to whom Part 4A does not apply. Three examples may be given.

- A competent child patient on SCT cannot be given treatment which he refuses. At common law, a competent child may be administered treatment without consent if a person with parental responsibility consents,[19] although see the discussion at paras 9.29, 9.38 below.

- Neither an adult nor a child community patient may be given treatment under Part 4A, other than treatment which is 'immediately necessary', in the absence of consent or substituted consent if they object and force is necessary to administer the treatment (s 64D(4) and 64F(4)) (para 6.77). Under the 2005 Act, on the other hand, treatment may be administered under s 5 notwithstanding P's objections, even if reasonable force is necessary under s 6 (para 10.66).

- Although force may be used to administer emergency treatment to an incapacitated patient who objects, any force used must be necessary to prevent harm to the patient and a proportionate response to the likelihood of the patient's suffering harm (the same requirement in s 6 of the 2005 Act), *and* the treatment must be 'immediately necessary' (s 64G) (para 6.83ff). This last condition does not apply to treatment administered under the 2005 Act (see para 10.66).

6.61   For these reasons, Part 4A is not so much a *coercive* mechanism as a *protective* mechanism, in that it requires the treatment of community patients on SCT to be properly regulated and applies the safeguards of the SOAD certificate procedure to 's 58 and 58A type' treatments.[20]

6.62   Where Part 4A has 'teeth' is in the power of recall to hospital for up to 72 hours under s 17E coupled with the new s 56(4), which applies the compulsory regime of Part 4 to recalled patients, discussed at paras 6.108 below. However, even in this instance the 2007 Act does not represent an erosion of rights guaranteed by the 1983 Act. Under the 1983 Act, as currently formulated, a patient on long-term s 17 leave can either be administered Part 4 treatment while in the community or can be recalled by his responsible medical officer with the minimum of formality and then administered treatment without his consent under Part 4.

6.63   That is not to say, however, that the fact Part 4A goes no further than what the law already permits does not raise human rights issues. There are a number of such issues, many of which were identified by the JCHR during the reform process and not all of which have been addressed: see para 6.133ff.

---

[19] *Re W (A Minor)(Medical Treatment: Court's jurisdiction)* [1993] 1 Fam 64.
[20] See the discussion at para 15.41 as to whether authority to treat under Part 4A in fact comes from Part 4A or some other source of legal authority.

2. Overview of the New Part 4A Procedure

(a) *Key Features of the Part 4A Procedure*
New Part 4A has the following key features: 6.64

- Part 4A applies to all patients, both adults and children, although different provisions apply to 'adult community patients' (adults and children of 16 and 17) and to 'child community patients' (children under 16).

- Part 4A authorizes the administration of 'relevant treatment' to patients on SCT ('community patients'), provided there is 'authority to treat' and, if it is section 58 or 58A type treatment, the 'certificate requirement' is met (s 64B(2) (adult community patients) and s 64E(2) (child community patients) (below, para 6.66).

- 'authority to treat' may be given in one of four situations: first, a capable adult patient (s 64C(2)(a)) or competent child patient (s 64E(6)(a)) consents to the treatment; second, in the case of an incapacitated adult patient, where substituted consent is given (ie by a donee, deputy, or the Court of Protection) (s 64C(2)(b)); third, where no consent or substituted consent has been given, if the requirements of s 64D (adults) or 64F (children under 16) are met; and, fourth, where no consent or substituted consent has been given or the requirements of s 64D or 64F are not met, where treatment is 'immediately necessary' in accordance with s 64G (below, para 6.71).

- Where ss 58 or 58A type treatment is concerned, the 'certificate requirement' is met if the SOAD issues a certificate in accordance with s 64C(4) and after consultation in accordance with s 64H(3) (below, para 6.90).

- The 'certificate requirement' does not apply where the treatment is 'immediately necessary' (s 64C(5) (where consent or substituted consent has been given) and s 64G (where no consent or substituted consent has been given)) (below, para 6.102).

- Where a community patient is recalled under s 17E or revoked under s 17F, s 56(4) authorizes the treatment of such patients under Part 4 (below, para 6.110) and s 62A preserves the effect of SOAD certificates issued under Part 4A (below, para 6.111).

(b) *What Part 4A Does Not Authorize*
Part 4A does *not* authorize: 6.65

- the administration of treatment to which s 57 applies (s 64A(1)) (para 6.70).

- the administration of treatment to a capable adult community patient or a competent child who refuses treatment. Capable or competent patients can never be treated without their consent under Part 4A, even in an emergency (para 6.83).

- the administration of treatment to an incapacitated adult patient that conflicts with a valid advance decision or decision of a donee, deputy or the Court of Protection, *except* where the treatment is 'immediately necessary' and the criteria in s 64G are met.

- the administration of treatment to an incapacitated adult patient or child patient who objects to that treatment, *except* where substituted consent (by a donee, deputy or the Court of Protection) is given under the 2005 Act or where the treatment is 'immediately necessary' and the criteria in s 64G are met.
- the administration of treatment for physical disorders, which is regulated by the 2005 Act (for adults) or, materially, the common law rules (for children under 16) (para 9.25ff).

3. The Conditions for Administering 'Relevant Treatment': 'Authority to Treat' and the 'Certificate Requirement', s 64B(2) and s 64E(2)

6.66   By s 64B(2) (adult patients) and 64E(2) (child patients under the age of 16) 'relevant treatment' may not be given to a patient unless there is 'authority to give it to him' (considered at para 6.71ff) and, where it is 'section 58 type or 58A type treatment', unless 'the certificate requirement is met' (considered at para 6.90ff).

4. Child Community Patients

6.67   Part 4A makes separate provision for 'adult community patients' and 'child community patients'. The latter are defined as those under the age of 16 (s 64E(1)(b)); thus 'adult community patients' are those over the age of 16.

6.68   A similar structure is created for the treatment of both adult and child community patients, but with certain crucial distinctions.

- First, as the relevant provisions of 2005 Act do not apply to children under the age of 16 (s 2(5) of the 2005 Act[21]), there is no mention made in the provisions relevant to child community patients (s 64E, 64F, and 64G) of advance decisions or the giving of substituted consent by a donee of a LPA, deputy or the Court of Protection.
- Second, the provisions governing the treatment of adults (s 64B, 64C, and 64D) also govern the treatment of children aged 16 and 17. Where those provisions refer to advance decisions or decisions of a donee, deputy or the Court of Protection (s 64C(2)(b), s 64D(6)), they are relevant only as they refer to decisions of a deputy or the Court of Protection. A child aged 16 and 17 cannot make an advance decision (s 24(1)) or a LPA (s 9(2)(c)) (see para 10.07).
- Third, the provisions relevant to child community patients (s 64E, 64F, and 64G) use the term 'competence' rather than 'capacity'. 'Competence' is not defined but refers to a child under 16 who is so-called *Gillick* competent,[22] namely one who has sufficient understanding and intelligence to enable him to understand the nature and implications of the proposed treatment. Under the age of 16 a child is presumed to lack competence, and must establish that they have such understanding in relation to proposed treatment to be considered *Gillick* competent (see further, paras 9.28).

---

[21] (See para 10.03).
[22] After the House of Lords decision in *Gillick v West Norfolk and Wisbech Health Authority* [1986] AC 112.

What is not clear is what role parental consent and decisions of the High Court   6.69
in its wardship or inherent jurisdiction play in relation to treatment under Part 4A.
This question is considered at para 15.61 and the human rights implications are
considered at 6.133.

5. 'Relevant Treatment': s 64A

'Relevant treatment' is defined as 'medical treatment for the mental disorder   6.70
from which the patient is suffering', which is not 'a form of treatment to which section 57 applies' (s 64A). That is not to say that s 57 treatment cannot be given to
community patients; s 57 applies to any patient (s 56(1)), including community
patients, but the source of authority to administer such treatment is Part 4, not Part
4A (paras 6.10, 6.37). 'Relevant treatment' includes 's 58 type treatment' (including
medication after three months) and 's 58A type treatment' (including ECT) (see below,
para 6.90). 'Medical treatment' has the meaning given in s 145(1), subject to the
qualification in s 145(4), considered at para 6.21ff above.

6. 'Authority to Treat'

'Authority to treat' may be given in one of four situations: first, a capable adult   6.71
patient (s 64C(2)(a)) or competent child patient (s 64E(6)(a)) consents to the treatment; second, in the case of an incapacitated adult patient, where substituted consent is given (ie by a donee, deputy or the Court of Protection) (s 64C(2) (b)); third,
where no consent or substituted consent has been given, if the requirements of
s 64D (adults) or 64F (children under 16) are met; and, fourth, where no consent
or substituted consent has been given, where treatment is 'immediately necessary' in
accordance with s 64G.

(a) *Treatment Given With Consent of a Capable Adult or a Competent Child*
Section 64C(2)(a) provides that there is 'authority' to give treatment to an adult   6.72
patient who has capacity and has given a valid consent to treatment (s 64C(2)(a)).
For child patients who are 'competent' to consent, s 64E(6) makes similar provision.
'Capacity' has the meaning given by the 2005 Act (s 64K(2) and (3)), which is
considered in detail at para 10.11. 'Competence' has the meaning given at common
law in *Gillick* (see paras 9.28).

There appears to be no scope under Part 4A for a person with parental responsi-   6.73
bility to veto the imposition of such treatment if the child is competent: see paras
15.61and 6.133.

(b) *Treatment Given to Incapacitated Adult Patient With Substituted Consent*
For adult patients (those over 16), there is 'authority to treat' where the patient   6.74
lacks capacity and substituted consent has been given on his behalf by his donee,
deputy or the Court of Protection (s 64C(2)(b)), as those terms are defined in the
2005 Act (s 64K(4) and (5)). Treatment cannot be given to a child under 16 in

these circumstances because the relevant provisions of the 2005 Act does not apply to those under 16 (s 2(5) of the 2005 Act); moreover, for 'adult' patients aged 16 and 17 only the references to decisions of a deputy or the Court of Protection have any relevance (see paras 10.03, 10.07).

6.75   The administration of treatment to an incapacitated community patient remains subject to the provisions of the 2005 Act, notwithstanding it is delivered under Part 4A.[23] This has two, material, consequences. First, treatment may not be given under s 64C with the consent of a donee, deputy or Court of Protection if it conflicts with a valid and applicable advance decision (s 11(7) and s 26(1) of the 2005 Act (para 10.23)), unless the donee is acting under a lasting power of attorney created after the advance decision was made which conferred authority on the donee to give or refuse consent to the treatment to which the advance decisions relates (s 25(2) of the 2005 Act: see further, para 10.24). Similarly, treatment may not be given with the consent of a deputy or the Court of Protection if it conflicts with a valid refusal of treatment by a donee (see para 10.56,10.58).

6.76   Moreover, second, where valid consent has been given by a donee, deputy, or the Court of Protection, Part 4A treatment may be given against the objections of the patient, even if reasonable force ('an act intended to restrain P') is required, provided the requirements of ss 6(1), 11(1), or 20(7) of the 2005 Act are met, for which see para 10.66.

(c) *Treatment Given to Incapacitated Adult or Incompetent Child Patient where there is no Consent or Substituted Consent and which is not 'Immediately Necessary': ss 64D and 64F*

6.77 Where consent or substituted consent has not been given, there is 'authority to treat' if the conditions in s 64D (for adult patients) and 64F (child patients) are met (s 64C(2)(c) and s 64E(6)(b)). The following features are to be noted:

• Treatment may not be given if the patient objects and force is necessary to administer it.

• In the case of an adult over 18, treatment may not be given if it conflicts with an advance decision which is valid and applicable or the decision of a donee, deputy or the Court of Protection.

• In the case of a child aged 16 or 17, treatment may not be given if it conflicts with the decision of a deputy or the Court of Protection.

• In the case of a child of any age, treatment can (apparently) be given notwithstanding the objection of a person with parental responsibility (see para 6.79).

6.78   Treatment may be administered under s 64D (adult patient) in the following circumstances:

• First, the person giving the treatment takes reasonable steps to establish whether the patient lacks capacity to consent to the treatment (the 'first condition') (s 64D(2))

---

[23] Only s 5 of the 2005 Act is excluded from operating in relation to patients receiving treatment under Part 4A: s 28(1B) of the 2005 Act. See further, para 15.39.

- Second, he reasonably believes P lacks capacity ('the second condition') (s 64D(3))
- Third, he has no reason to believe that P objects or, if he does, it is not necessary to use force to give the treatment ('the third condition') (s 64D(4))
- Fourth, the treatment is given by or under the direction of the approved clinician ('the fourth condition') (s 64D(5)); and
- Fifth, the treatment does not conflict with an advance decision which is valid and applicable or a decision made by a donee, deputy or the Court of Protection under the 2005 Act (the 'fifth condition') (s 64D(6), s 64K). A valid advance decision is one that accords with s 25 of the 2005 Act (s 64D(7)). For 'adult' patients aged 16 and 17 only the references to decisions of a deputy or the Court of Protection have any relevance (see para 6.68))

The provisions of s 64F (child patient under 16) are in identical terms to those in 6.79 s 64D, *except* that there is no exclusion if the treatment conflicts with an advance decision or decisions made by a donee, deputy or the Court of Protection, because the relevant provisions of the 2005 Act do not apply to children under the age of 16 (s 2(5)). It is not clear whether the objection of a person with parental responsibility or of the High Court in its wardship or inherent jurisdiction have the same effect: see the discussion at para 15.61. For the potential human rights implications, see para 6.133.

In determining whether the patient 'objects' for the purposes of s 64D(4) or 6.80 64F(4), a person shall consider all the circumstances so far as they are reasonably ascertainable, including the patient's behaviour, wishes, feelings, views, beliefs, and values, although circumstances from the past shall be considered only so far as it is still appropriate to consider them (s 64J).[24]

There is no statutory definition given for what is meant by 'force' in s 64D(4)(b) 6.81 and 64F(4)(b), but in the draft Code of Practice it is referred to as 'the application of physical force to whatever extent to the patient'. 'Force' may therefore be distinguished from the threat of force. In the 2005 Act, the term used is 'restraint', which is defined as the use *or threat* of reasonable force or the restriction of P's liberty of movement, whether or not P resists (ss 6(4), 11(5), and 20(12)). It would appear, by implication, that threats of force and restrictions on P's liberty of movement are permitted to administer treatment under these provisions, notwithstanding P's objections. This is an issue that has concerned the Royal College of Psychiatrists and the Children's Commissioner, who point out that the use of threats to recall a patient could be used to compel compliance with medication, which is particularly inappropriate for children who do not have the protection afforded by a donee or an advance decision.[25] For the human rights implications this raises, see para 6.135.

As we have seen, if an incapacitated adult community patient does object where 6.82 force is necessary to give the treatment he can still be treated if substituted consent

---

[24] These reflect the matters that must be taken into account under the 2005 Act: see s 4(6), s 36(2), and Sch A1 para 5(6).

[25] 3rd JCHR Report, para 1.21.

is given by a donee, deputy, or the Court of Protection under s 64C(2)(b) (above, para 6.74): for children of 16 or 17, if given by a deputy or the Court of Protection. The same does not apply for child community patients under 16. They must either be recalled or an application made under the authority of the Court in its inherent jurisdiction or its wardship jurisdiction (see further, para 9.31ff). It appears consent could not be given by a person with parental responsibility in these circumstances (see paras 15.61, 6.133).

(d) *Treatment which is 'Immediately Necessary': s 64G*

6.83   Section 64G is titled 'Emergency treatment for patients lacking capacity or competence', and it confers 'authority to treat' an incapacitated adult community patient (s 64C(2)(c)) or incompetent child community patient (s 64E(6)(b)), including the use of s 58 and 58A type treatment, notwithstanding the patient's objections or the fact that the treatment conflicts with the decision of a donee, deputy or the Court of Protection. Where the treatment is s 58 or s 58A type treatment, s 64G also authorizes the administration of treatment notwithstanding the 'certificate requirement' is not met (see further, para 6.102). Section 64G does not authorize the treatment of capable or competent patients who are refusing treatment, however.

6.84   The conditions of s 64G are as follows:

- first, the person giving treatment reasonably believes P lacks capacity ('the first condition') (s 64G(2))

- second, the treatment 'is immediately necessary' ('the second condition') (s 64G(3))

- third, 'if it is necessary to use force', 'the treatment needs to be given in order to prevent harm to the patient and the use of such force is a proportionate response to the likelihood of the patient's suffering harm, and to the seriousness of that harm' ('the third condition') (s 64G(4)).[26]

6.85   Except where s 58A type treatment is involved, treatment is 'immediately necessary' if (s 64G(5))[27]

- it is immediately necessary to save the patient's life; or

- it is immediately necessary to prevent a serious deterioration of the patient's condition and is not irreversible; or

- it is immediately necessary to alleviate serious suffering and is not irreversible or hazardous; or

- is immediately necessary, represents the minimum interference necessary to prevent the patient from behaving violently or being a danger to himself or others and is not irreversible or hazardous.

---

[26] This is the same limitation on the use of restraint under the 2005 Act ('an act intended to restrain P'): see s 6(3), s 11(4), and s 20(11).

[27] These are the same criteria for the administration of emergency treatment under Part 4, s 62.

Treatment is 'irreversible' if 'it has unfavourable irreversible physical or psycho-   6.86
logical consequences' and 'hazardous' if 'it entails significant physical hazard' (the
test in s 62(3), imported into Part 4A by s 64G(9)).

Where the treatment is s 58A type treatment under s 58A(1)(a) (ie ECT), treat-   6.87
ment is immediately necessary only if it is immediately necessary to save the patient's
life or to prevent a serious deterioration of the patient's condition and is not irreversible (s 64G(6)). Where the treatment is s 58A type treatment under s 58A(1)(b)
(none yet specified), it is immediately necessary in such circumstances as may be
specified in regulations (s 64G(7) and (8)). The same limitations have been introduced on the administration of ECT to patients treated under Part 4, s 62(1A)
(above, para 6.57).

Section 64G differs from s 64D (adult patients), and 64F (children) in five   6.88
respects. First, as regards adult patients, treatment may be administered under s 64G
notwithstanding that it conflicts with a valid advance decision or decision of a donee
deputy or the Court of Protection. Second, as regards both adult and child patients,
force may used if it is necessary to give the treatment. Third, there is no requirement
that 'the person giving the treatment takes reasonable steps to establish whether the
patient lacks capacity to consent to the treatment'. Fourth, in the case of 's 58 or
s 58A type treatment', no SOAD certificate is required. Fifth, there is no requirement that the treatment be given by or under the direction of the approved clinician
in charge of the treatment.

The Royal College of Psychiatrists, the Children's Commissioner, and the JCHR   6.89
have all raised concerns about the administration of emergency treatment in these
circumstances, particularly on children who may actively resist, and the JCHR has
called for further guidance on the circumstances in which this treatment may be
used.[28] The issue has particular resonance for child patients because they do not
enjoy the protections of the 2005 Act (or, for 16 to 17 year olds, only very limited
protection, see paras 10.03 and 10.07) and Part 4A apparently excludes a person
with parental responsibility from objecting to treatment on the child's behalf
(para 15.61). This is an issue that has human rights implications, see para 6.133.

7. 's 58 Type and s 58A Type Treatment' and 'the Certificate Requirement'

The second requirement that must be met before 'relevant treatment' may be   6.90
administered to an adult or child community patient under Part 4A is that, where
it is 's 58 type or s 58A type treatment', the 'certificate requirement' has been met
(ss 64B(2)(b) and 64E(2)(b)).

(a) s 58 Type Treatment'

Treatment is 's 58 type treatment' if, at the time when it is given, s 58 would have   6.91
applied to it had the patient been a detained patient at the time (s 64C(3)). This

---

[28] 3rd JCHR Report, para 1.25.

provision therefore refers to the administration of treatment, first, under s 58(1)(a), which regulates 'such forms of treatment as may be specified . . . by regulations made by the Secretary of State'. However, the only form of treatment that was previously specified under s 58(1)(a) was ECT, which is now governed by s 58A. Accordingly, at present no treatment is specified under s 58(1)(a). The only 's 58 type treatment' is treatment regulated by s 58(1)(b), namely 'the administration of medicine . . . at any time during a period for which he is liable to be detained as a patient to whom this Part of this Act applies if three months or more have elapsed since the first occasion in that period when medicine was administered to him' (above, para 6.12).

6.92   Also relevant is s 64B(4), which provides that the certificate requirement does not apply to 's 58 type treatment' administered to the patient 'at any time during the period of one month beginning with the day on which the community order is made', although this time extension does not apply to treatment that may be administered under s 58(1)(a) (s 64B(5)).[29] Accordingly, it only applies to medication administered under s 58(1)(b).

6.93   In determining when it is necessary for the responsible clinician to apply for a certificate for s 58A type treatment (medication) in the case of a community patient, Section 64C(3), s 64B(4), and s 58(1)(b) must be read together. The answer is not always straightforward, but some suggested answers are given in the following examples.

- *Example 1:* The patient already has a certificate under Part 4. No new Part 4A certificate need be obtained for the first month after the making of the CTO (by virtue of s 64B(4))

- *Example 2:* The patient has been receiving medication for a period of just under three months prior to his release on SCT, so no Part 4 certificate is necessary before his release. No new part 4A certificate need then be obtained until one month after the making of the CTO by virtue of s 64B(4), notwithstanding by then the patient will have been receiving s 58 type treatment for just under four months without a certificate.

- *Example 3:* The patient has been receiving medication for one month prior to his release on SCT. No Part 4A certificate need be obtained until two months after the making of the CTO by virtue of s 64C(3) read with s 58(1)(b), since by then three months or more will have elapsed since the first occasion in that period when medicine was administered to him. Section 64B(4) does not affect the calculation in such a case.

6.94   The three month time period has been raised by the JCHR as having potential human rights implications,[30] so where a patient receives treatment for up to four months under these provisions that argument acquires greater force: see para 6.137ff.

---

[29] As noted in para 6.13, at present no treatment is specified under s 58(1)(a).
[30] 2nd JCHR Report, para 66; 3rd JCHR Report, para 1.15.

(b) *s 58A Type Treatment: ECT*

Section 64C3 provides that treatment is 's 58A type treatment' if, at the time when   6.95
it is given, s 58A would have applied to it had the patient been a detained patient at
the time. We are concerned, particularly, with s 58A(1)(a), electro-convulsive therapy (ECT). Although s 58A(1)(b) refers to 'such other forms of treatment as may be
specified by the appropriate national authority', no such other forms of treatment
have yet been specified. The requirement for a certificate under Part 4A arises immediately upon release on SCT; there is no one month period of grace akin to that for
s 58 type treatment under s 64B(4).

(c) *When the 'Certificate Requirement' is Met*

The 'certificate requirement' is met for both adult and child patients if a certificate   6.96
has been issued by a SOAD under s 64C(4) (adults), or 64E(7) (children)[31] certifying that it is appropriate for the treatment to be given and, if conditions are specified, those conditions are satisfied. A condition may, for example, specify that the
treatment should only be given for as long as the patient is consenting to it.[32]

It is not clear whether an existing Part 4 SOAD certificate takes effect as a Part 4A   6.97
certificate once the patient is released on SCT, although the draft Code of Practice
suggests that it does (para 16.22a).

There is no requirement for the SOAD to certify that the patient is or is not capa-   6.98
ble of understanding the nature, purpose and likely effects of the treatment, by contrast with ss 58(3) and 58A(3) to (5). Nor is there any requirement to certify that the
treatment does not conflict with a valid advance decision or a decision made by a
donee, deputy or the Court of Protection, by contrast with s 58A(4). These are both
matters that a SOAD would be required to consider in the patient's 'best interests',
however (para 6.04).

In determining whether it is 'appropriate for treatment to be given' the SOAD   6.99
must apply the new 'appropriate treatment' test. Although the test as it applies in
Part 4 by virtue of s 64(3) is expressed only to apply to treatment given under that
Part (above, para 6.24), the same test is provided for by s 3(4) which is expressed to
apply to the whole of the 1983 Act, which includes Part 4A. The SOAD will apply
the definition of 'medical treatment' in s 145(1), as amended, and the new 'treatability' test in s 145(4) (above, para 6.27). As with certificates issued under Part 4, it will
be necessary for the SOAD to form his own independent judgment that the treatment should be given, and before doing so he must be satisfied that the treatment is
in the patient's 'best interests': see above, paras 6.04, 6.15. To ensure that treatment
that is imposed against the patient's will complies with Convention rights, he must
also consider whether it is a medical necessity: see paras 6.121, 6.131.

Before issuing the certificate the SOAD must consult two other persons who have   6.100
been professionally involved with the patient's medical treatment (not including the

---

[31] s 64C(4) is imported into the framework for child patients by s 64E(7).
[32] Draft Illustrative Code of Practice, para 16.21h.

responsible clinician), at least one of whom is not a registered medical practitioner (s 64H(3)[33]).

6.101   The SOAD certificate need be given only once; there is no requirement for it to be renewed either after a period of time or if there is a relevant change of circumstances, including the patient's recall to hospital and the revocation of his CTO (see s 62A). (See below, paras 6.104 and 6.111).

(d) Treatment which is 'Immediately Necessary': when the 'Certificate Requirement' Does Not Apply

6.102   The 'certificate requirement' does not apply to s 58 or s 58A type treatment which is 'immediately necessary' (s 64B(3)). If the source of the authority to treat is the capable adult patient's consent or, for an incapacitated adult patient, the substituted consent of a donee, deputy or the Court of Protection (s 64B(3)(b)(ii)), treatment is 'immediately necessary' if it satisfies the test in s 64C(5). If the source of the authority to treat is s 64G (s 64(B)(3)(i)), treatment is 'immediately necessary' if it satisfies the test in s 64G(5). The tests in s 64C(5) and 64G(5) are in identical terms, including the qualifications that apply in relation to s 58A type treatment (see above, para 6.87). For children under 16, the equivalent provisions are s 64E(3) and (7), which imports the 'immediately necessary' test in s 64C(5) for child patients.

6.103   Further guidance is necessary as to when these emergency treatment provisions are to be used, particularly for children: see the 3rd JCHR Report, para 1.25 (see para 6.89).

(e) Withdrawal of Consent and Patients Regaining Capacity

6.104   Part 4A contains no equivalent provision to s 60 in Part 4, which provides that a patient is free to withdraw his consent to treatment under s 57 or 58 at any time (s 60(1), above para 6.19). Section 60 further provides, by amendments introduced by the 2007 Act, that where a patient treated under Part 4 ceases to be capable of understanding the nature, purpose and likely effects of treatment, he is treated as having withdrawn his consent (s 60(1A) and (1B)). Where an incapacitated patient later recovers capacity, the certificate shall cease to apply to the treatment (s 60(1C) and (1D)). Thereafter treatment cannot be given without a fresh certificate, other than in an emergency under s 62 (para 6.40).

6.105   In most situations the absence in Part 4A of an equivalent to s 60(1) or s 60(1A) to (1D) should not be problematic. Treatment under Part 4A can no longer be given if a capable or competent patient withdraws his consent. Where a certificate has been issued in relation to an incapacitated patient who later recovers capacity, there is no requirement to seek a fresh certificate, but if the patient then refuses treatment there will be no authority to treat, so treatment will have to end. However, if he is then recalled to hospital under s 17E, s 58 type treatment may still be given to him under the authority of that certificate if it expressly states that it should apply in

---

[33] See ss 58(4) and 57(3) for the equivalent provision under Part 4.

those circumstances, by virtue of s 62A, see para 6.111. This has human rights implications: para 6.139.

Where a patient who has consented to s 58 or s 58A type treatment loses capacity 6.106 there is nothing in Part 4A that requires a fresh certificate to be obtained. Provided there is still authority to treat (either by substituted consent or under s 64D or s 64F), the existing certificate would appear to continue to have effect. Given there is no time limit on a SOAD certificate this must be a matter of concern and may have human rights implications. In these circumstances it might be appropriate for the patient's IMHA to notify the MHAC, which could give notice under s 64H(4) terminating the certificate and requiring a new certificate to be obtained.

(f) *Other Requirements: Plans of Treatment, the Role of the MHAC etc*
Similar requirements govern the SOAD procedure under Part 4A as apply for those 6.107 issued under Part 4 (above, paras 6.18–6.20). The certificate may relate to a plan of treatment under which the patient is to be given one or more forms of s 58 type treatment, whether within a specified period or otherwise (s 64H(1)[34]). The Mental Health Act Commission may at any time give notice directing that a Part 4A certificate shall not apply to treatment given to a patient after a date specified in the notice (s 64H(4)[35]), at which point the approved clinician in charge of the treatment will have to restart the process for obtaining a certificate, unless he considers that discontinuance of treatment would cause serious suffering to the patient (s 64H(7)[36]). On the other hand, there is no requirement akin to s 61 for the responsible clinician to furnish a report to the MHAC when the CTO is renewed, unless the patient has been recalled and treated under s 62A (above, para 6.41).

F. TREATMENT OF RECALLED COMMUNITY PATIENTS

1. Introduction

Another key policy objective behind the government's proposals for reform of the 6.108 mental health legislation was to introduce a form of supervised community treatment that would permit compulsory treatment to be imposed upon community patients without the need formally to readmit them: see the discussion in Chapter 1. The solution eventually adopted by the government was to introduce the SCT procedure, together with a relatively light-touch treatment mechanism under Part 4A, but with power to recall a patient under s 17E for up to 72 hours, whereupon the mechanism for compulsory treatment under Part 4 could be brought to bear.

---

[34] See s 59 for the equivalent provision under Part 4.
[35] See s 61(3) for the equivalent provision under Part 4.
[36] See s 62(2) for the equivalent provision under Part 4.

2. Community Patients who Cannot be Treated Under Part 4A

6.109 Certain community patients cannot be treated in the community under Part 4A (above, para 6.65). First, a community patient who has capacity (or, in the case of a child, is competent) to refuse treatment, and does refuse treatment can never be treated without their consent under Part 4A, even in an emergency. Such a patient can only be treated against his wishes if he is recalled under s 17E. Second, where a child (s 64E(4)) or adult (s 64D(4)) community patient lacks capacity and the patient objects and force is necessary to give the treatment and, in the case of an adult, substituted consent has not been given by a donee, deputy or the Court of Protection. Third, in the case of an incapacitated adult patient, the treatment conflicts with a valid advance decision or a decision of a donee, deputy or the Court of Protection (s 64D(6)). Patients who fall into these last two categories cannot be treated under Part 4A unless the treatment is 'immediately necessary'. For treatment which is not 'immediately necessary' these patients will need to be recalled under s 17E if the criteria are met.

3. Part 4 Applies to Recalled Community Patients: s 56(4)

6.110 A community patient who is recalled to hospital under s 17E may then be treated under the compulsory treatment provisions of Part 4 (s 56(4)). Detention under 17E—and therefore treatment under Part 4—is authorized for up to 72 hours, whereupon the patient must either be released or his CTO revoked (s 17F(6)).

4. Section 62A: Part 4A Certificates Continue to Have Effect After Recall or Revocation

(a) *s 58 Type Treatment*

6.111 Where a community patient is recalled under s 17E or his CTO revoked under s 17F, a valid SOAD certificate authorizing 's 58 type treatment' (medication) issued under Part 4A will continue to have effect (s 62A(3)), provided the certificate expressly provides that it is to apply 'in that case', namely in the event that the patient is recalled or his CTO revoked (s 62A(5)(a)).[37] That includes the administration of medication to a capable patient who was previously compliant who has been recalled because he is now refusing treatment, for example having regained capacity. It is suggested that the certificate would have to specify not only that treatment could be given upon recall, but also that it may be given notwithstanding the patient's capable objections.

6.112 Nevertheless, treatment in these circumstances does raise a number of difficult issues. That is particularly so in the case of a patient who regains capacity and objects to treatment. As we have seen (above, para 6.104), there is no equivalent under Part 4A to s 60(1C) and (1D) which provide that, if an incapable patient receiving Part 4 treatment later recovers capacity, the SOAD certificate ceases to have effect. Under Part 4A, the certificate will continue to have effect. This is problematic. The SOAD will have examined the patient at a time when the patient lacked capacity.

---

[37] Explanatory Notes to the 2007 Act, para 124.

How can he certify that treatment should be appropriately given to a patient once he regains capacity, given that the regaining of capacity is a big change in circumstances and may not happen until years later? It is suggested that any SOAD's certificate that authorizes treatment in these circumstances—and any treatment actually given in these circumstances—could potentially be open to challenge on human rights grounds, see para 6.139.

If the Part 4A certificate does not specify that s 58 type treatment may be given in the event of recall, that treatment can still be administered if the approved clinician in charge of the treatment considers that the discontinuance of the treatment would cause serious suffering to the patient (s 62A(6))[38] or if it is 'immediately necessary' within the meaning of s 62.   6.113

If no Part 4A SOAD certificate is in place, s 62A(2) provides that 'for the purposes of s 58(1)(b) above, the patient is to be treated as if he had remained liable to be detained since the making of the community treatment order'. This means the patient was first administered recall or revocation does not commence a further three month period during which treatment may be given under s 63 without a certificate under s 58(1)(b). This will also mean that the one month period during which the 'certificate requirement' following the making of the CTO (s 64B(4)) does not apply. The operative date for calculating the three month period in s 58(1)(b) is still the first occasion upon which the patient was administered medication, whether that was while detained or on SCT.   6.114

If a notice has been issued by the MHAC under s 64H(4) discontinuing a Part 4A certificate and the approved clinician considers that it would cause the patient serious suffering to stop the treatment under s 64H(8) then treatment can also continue under that certificate in the event of a recall or revocation (s 62A(4(b)) (above, para 6.107).   6.115

(b) s 58A Type Treatment

A Part 4A certificate authorizing s 58A type treatment (ECT) will also authorize the administration of treatment upon recall if there is 'authority to treat' within the meaning of Part 4A and the certificate requirement is met (s 62A(3). It will not authorize the treatment of a capable patient who is refusing treatment because there is no 'authority to treat' a capable patient who refuses ECT under Part 4A, and ECT cannot be administered to such a patient under Part 4 (ss 58A(3)(b), 58A(4)(b)) (para 6.44).   6.116

G. THE INTERFACE BETWEEN THE 1983 ACT AND THE 2005 ACT

s 28(1) of the 2005 Act provides that nothing in the 2005 Act authorizes anyone to give a patient medical treatment for mental disorder, or to consent to a patient being given medical treatment for mental disorder, if at the time his treatment is regulated by Part 4 of the 1983 Act, which regulates the medical treatment for mental disorder   6.117

---

[38] Explanatory Notes to the 2007 Act, para 126; Draft Illustrative Code of Practice, para 16.22b.

of patients who are 'liable to be detained' in hospital under the 1983 Act (s 56(1)), including patients who are actually detained. This is the only relevant provision governing the interface between the 1983 Act and 2005 Act between 1 October 2007, when the 2005 Act comes into force, and October 2008, the anticipated date for entry into force of the 2007 Act, and which is relatively straightforward: see para 10.71.

6.118   Matters become more complicated after the 2007 Act comes into force. In relation to the treatment of community patients on SCT, s 28(1B) of the 2005 Act provides that treatment falling within s 64B of the 1983 (treatment of incapacitated adult patients over the age of 16) may not be administered under s 5 of the 2005 Act, which effectively prevents the administration of treatment to incapacitated patients on SCT unless it is authorized by a donee, deputy or the Court of Protection and subject to the safeguards in Part 4A.

6.119   The interface between the treatment provisions of the 1983 Act and the 2005 Act after the 2007 Act comes into force is complicated, particularly as it relates to children, and is discussed in detail in Chapter 15, with the interface between the relevant treatment provisions considered at para 15.26ff.

H. HUMAN RIGHTS IMPLICATIONS

1. Article 3 Principles

6.120   Article 3 provides, 'No one shall be subjected to torture or to inhuman or degrading treatment or punishment', which imports both negative and positive obligations (see para 1.40).

(a) *Negative Obligation: No Violation if Treatment is Life-saving or a 'Medical Necessity'*

6.121   The compulsory treatment of a capable or incapable patient, will not violate Article 3 if it is necessary as a life-saving measure or it is a 'medical necessity', notwithstanding it otherwise reaches the necessary level of severity to engage Article 3 (*Herczegfalvy v Austria*,[39] para 83; *Nevmerzhitsky v Ukraine*, para 94; *R (B) v Dr S*,[40] para 47; *R(B) v Ashworth*,[41] para 31). That is because in either situation there is a conflict between an individual's right to physical integrity under Article 3 and the State's positive obligation to protect life under Article 2, 'a conflict which is not solved by the Convention itself' (*Nevmerzhitsky*, para 93). Accordingly, it is for contracting States to resolve the conflict themselves under their own domestic law. Necessarily that means that different States may reach different conclusions and within individual States the balance may be struck differently in different situations. Thus, at common law, the United Kingdom has struck the balance between the sanctity of life (Article 2) and the right of physical integrity (Article 3) in favour of the latter, so that a capable patient has an

---

[39] (1992) 15 EHRR 437.
[40] [2006] 1 WLR 810, para 62.
[41] [2006] 1 WLR 810, para 62.

absolute right to refuse medical treatment, whatever the consequences for him personally (see para 9.04). On the other hand, the 1983 Act has struck the balance in favour of Article 2 (protecting the health and safety of the patient and protecting others) rather than Article 3, so that treatment may be imposed upon a capable patient notwithstanding his objections. Both can be lawful for Convention purposes.

'Medical necessity', is not limited to life-saving treatment, but can also cover   6.122
treatment, such as anti-psychotic medication, imposed as part of a therapeutic regime (*Wilkinson v United Kingdom*[42]). 'Medical necessity' is determined from the point of view of established principles of medicine. The decision as to what therapeutic methods are necessary is principally one for the national medical authorities: those authorities have a certain margin of appreciation in this respect since it is in the first place for them to evaluate the evidence in a particular case (*Wilkinson v United Kingdom*, p 20).

(b) *Positive Obligation: Safeguards in Part 4*

The duty in Article 1 of the Convention to 'secure to everyone within its jurisdiction   6.123
the rights and freedoms defined in the Convention', taken together with Article 3, requires States to take measures designed to ensure that individuals within their jurisdiction are not subjected to ill-treatment, including ill-treatment administered by private individuals (see para 1.40). There is a particular need for States to take such measures in the context of psychiatric hospitals, where patients are typically in a position of inferiority and helplessness (*Wilkinson v United Kingdom*, p 21).

The measures contained in Part 4 of the 1983 Act, in particular the requirement   6.124
for authorization by a SOAD under ss 57 and 58, are in principle sufficient to discharge that obligation. There is no requirement that treatment is authorized in advance by a court (*Wilkinson*, p 22). However, where there is prima facie evidence that proposed medical treatment will give rise to a violation of Article 3, then it will be necessary to determine that issue in advance of the treatment being given, if necessary by hearing oral evidence with cross-examination. If, however, the real issue is whether the patient is suffering mental disorder at all then that is an issue that should be determined by the Tribunal (*R (B) v Dr S*[43]).

2. Article 8 Principles

Article 8(1) provides, so far as is material, 'Everyone has the right to respect for his   6.125
private and family life.' Article 8(2) then continues, 'There shall be no interference by a public authority with the exercise of this right except such as is in accordance with the law and is necessary in a democratic society in the interests of national security . . . for the protection of health . . . or for the protection of the rights and freedoms of others.'

---

[42] Application no 14659/02, Admissibility Decision, 28 February 2006.
[43] [2006] 1 WLR 810, para 62.

(a) *'Private and Family Life'*

6.126 The concept of 'private life' includes both the physical and psychological integrity of a person. Even a minor interference with the physical integrity of an individual is an interference with the right to respect for private life under Article 8(1), if it is carried out against the individual's will (*Storck v Germany*,[44] para 168). That is so whether the individual has capacity or not. Capacity is nevertheless a relevant consideration; the notion of autonomy and the right to self-determination are important principles underpinning the interpretation of the guarantees in Article 8(1) (*Pretty v United Kingdom*,[45] para 61).

6.127 Medical treatment of a child will also engage the family right of a person with parental responsibility to give or refuse consent to that treatment: *Glass v United Kingdom*.[46]

(b) *In Accordance with the Law*

6.128 Any interference with the right in Article 8(1) must be 'in accordance with the law'. This imports similar notions of 'lawfulness' to the requirement in Article 5 that any deprivation of liberty be 'in accordance with a procedure prescribed by law' (see paras 11.15). Both expressions require, as a starting point, that the impugned measure should have some basis in national law. However, the expressions also denote a *quality* or *standard* which the domestic law must meet. First, the law must be accessible to the person concerned ('accessibility'). This will usually be met if the law is published, but it will depend upon the context whether this requirement is met. Second, the person concerned must be able (if necessary with appropriate legal advice) to foresee the circumstances in and conditions upon which a public author-ity is empowered to exercise the power concerned, although the degree of precision required will depend upon the particular subject matter ('foreseeability'). Third (and closely connected with the notion of 'foreseeability'), domestic law must con-tain 'adequate legal protections and "fair and proper procedures" to ensure to indi-viduals the minimum degree of protection to which citizens are entitled under the rule of law in a democratic society' ('the aim of avoiding arbitrariness') (*Herczegfalvy v Austria*,[47] paras 88–92). In the field of psychiatric detention the European Court of Human Rights has held that there is a greater need for precision because 'the per-sons concerned are frequently at the mercy of the medical authorities' *Herczegfalvy v Austria*, para 91.

6.129 The last requirement—ensuring to individuals the minimum degree of protection to which citizens are entitled under the rule of law in a democratic society ('the aim of avoiding arbitrariness')—is also reflected in the requirement in Article 8(2) that an interference must be 'necessary in a democratic society'.

---

[44] (2005) 43 EHRR 96.
[45] (2002) 35 EHRR 1.
[46] (2004) 39 EHRR 15.
[47] (1992) 15 EHRR 437, paras 88–92.

(c) *Negative Obligation: No Violation if 'Necessary in a Democratic Society'*

Compulsory treatment, including treatment of a capable patient, may be a lawful   6.130
interference with Article 8(1) if it pursues the legitimate objective of protecting
health, is rationally connected to that legitimate objective and the means used to
impair the right or freedom are no more than is necessary to accomplish the objective (ie proportionate).[48] To this extent, the test is indistinguishable from that under
Article 3: in both cases treatment is lawful if it is a 'medical necessity'. We have seen,
above, that patient autonomy is protected under Article 8. What is not clear, however, is the weight which should be attached to the fact that a patient has capacity.
In *Wilkinson v United Kingdom* the ECtHR found no violation of Article 8 because
the applicant 'had not demonstrated that the hospital authorities were not entitled
to regard him as lacking the capacity to consent to the treatment in question.' That
begs the question what their conclusion would have been had they concluded the
applicant did have capacity to refuse the treatment. At the domestic level, the Courts
have so far rejected any argument that Article 8 requires respect to be given to a
capable treatment refusal; the patient's capacity is no more than a relevant consideration to take into account (see para 6.01). There may yet be further human rights
challenges around this issue: see below, para 6.136.

(d) *Positive Obligations*

Article 8, like Article 3, also contains implied 'positive obligations', which may   6.131
require the State to adopt measures designed to secure respect for private life (*Botta v
Italy*;[49] *A & B v East Sussex (Manual Handling)*[50]) (see para 1.40).

(e) *Procedural Safeguards*

Article 8 also imports a requirement that procedural safeguards be provided for in   6.132
domestic law to prevent arbitrary or mistaken interferences with the Convention
right (see para 1.41). So, for example, in *R (Wooder) v Dr Feggetter*,[51] the Court of
Appeal ruled that, given the fundamental rights engaged by a decision to compulsorily treat an individual, a SOAD is required to give the patient an opportunity to
make representations and thereafter to give reasons for his decision for endorsing an
RMO's treatment plan under section 58.

3. Human Rights Implications of the 2007 Amendments

(a) *Treatment of Child in the Face of Objection by a Parent*

Where a child is either subject to Part 4 or Part 4A, there appears to be no scope for   6.133
a parent to veto treatment that the child consents to under s 58A (ECT) (see para 6.50)

---

[48] Paraphrased from the classic statement of proportionality by Lord Steyn in *R (Daly) v Home Secretary*
[2001] 2 AC 532, para 27. See also *Wilkinson v United Kingdom*, page 25; see also the 2nd JCHR Report, para 65).
[49] (1998) 26 EHRR 241.
[50] [2003] EWHC 167 (Admin) paras 75, 93*, 99, 102, 113, 114.
[51] [2002] 3 WLR 591.

or administered with the child's consent under s 64C(2)(a) (over 16) or s 64E(6) (under 16) (para 6.73). Of more concern, where a child is incompetent or incapacitated, a person with parental responsibility cannot refuse treatment to be administered under s 58A (para 6.54), ss 64D, or 64F (treatment not requiring 'force' to which patient does not object) (paras 6.79, 6.82) or treatment administered in an 'emergency' under s 64G (para 6.89) (and see the analysis at para 15.61ff). This is to be contrasted with the position with adults: all of these provisions (apart form s 64G) prohibit the treatment of an incapacitated adult where it is inconsistent with a valid advance decision or the decision of a donee or deputy. It is arguable that to impose treatment upon an incompetent or incapacitated child in the face of objections by a person with parental responsibility could violate the right to family life in Article 8, considering *Glass v United Kingdom* (see paras 6.133 and 15.61). This issue is raised by the JCHR in its 3rd Report, para 1.22. This problem is compounded by the absence of any statutory test of 'competence'.

(b) *Force-feeding*

6.134 Force-feeding is not a treatment falling within s 58 and there is no requirement for a SOAD. This issue is raised by the JCHR in its 2nd Report, para 69. It is arguable that force-feeding involves such an invasive method of treatment that not to have in place the safeguard of a SOAD gives rise to an Article 8 breach: such an interference is not 'in accordance with the law' (para 6.128) and/or it breaches the State's positive obligations to adopt measures to respect private life (para 1.40). It may even breach Article 3. The case of *Nevmerzhitsky* involved force-feeding, and although the circumstances of the case were particularly unpleasant (to the extent the ECtHR was satisfied they amounted to 'torture') the lower threshold, of 'inhuman and degrading treatment', can be reached by force-feeding without the same degree of intrusiveness.

(c) *Definition of 'Force' in ss 64D and 64F*

6.135 Treatment may be imposed upon an objecting patient who lacks capacity or competence if it does not involve 'force' (paras 6.81). That might nevertheless permit treatment to be administered using threats of force. This raises very acute issues, particularly in relation to children: see the 3rd JCHR Report, paras 1.21 and 1.25. It is strongly arguable that to secure a vulnerable individual's acquiescence to invasive treatment through threats of force would violate Article 8. 'Force' should be given an interpretation that is as compatible as possible with Convention rights to mean both actual force and threats of force.

(d) *Respect for Autonomy*

6.136 The JCHR in its 1st Report, on the Mental Health Bill 2002, expressed doubt as to whether it was lawful to override a capable patient's refusal of consent. As seen, Articles 3 and 8 permit compulsory treatment, even of a capable patient, where it is necessary to save life or it is a 'medical necessity' (para 6.21). What is not yet clear is what weight is to be given to the fact the patient has capacity; a weightier factor is likely to be that force is required in order to administer the treatment (para 6.01).

However, treatment imposed upon a patient who is objecting which also has other features that have Convention implications (such as those in paras 6.137–6.139, below) will be more likely to lead to a violation if the patient has capacity, particularly if force is used.

(e) *Three Month Time Period for Medication Without SOAD*

The JCHR raised the issue in both its 2nd (para 66) and 3rd Reports (para 1.15) 6.137
that three months is too long a period without the opportunity for review and supervision by a SOAD of the responsible clinician's decision to impose the treatment, and questioned whether this might breach the state's positive obligation under Article 8 to provide effective supervision and review of treatment. The argument gains further weight in the context of Part 4A patients who can, in theory, wait up to four months before there is an obligation to obtain a SOAD certificate (see para 6.94).

(f) *Medical Treatment by a Non-medically Qualified Responsible Clinician*

It is now possible for a responsible clinician who is not medically-qualified to treat 6.138
and oversee the treatment of patients under Part 4 and 4A, although the requirement that a SOAD be medically qualified is retained (para 6.34). This raises issues under Article 8 if treatment is authorized by a person who is not medically qualified. It could also raise Article 3 issues if the treatment was sufficiently invasive. The principle established in *Herczegfalvy* that treatment which is a medical necessity 'according to the principles of established medicine' is not in principle a breach of Article 3 (para 6.121) suggests that such treatment may breach Article 3 if it is not in accordance with those principles: a similar conclusion could be reached under Article 8 (para 6.130). As the JCHR pointed out in its 2nd Report, para 26 and its 3rd Report, para 1.8, there are certain minimum standards of medical training (some of which are required by EU law) some of which may not be met by clinicians approved for the purposes of the 1983 Act. This may be addressed by introducing adequate standards for approval as an 'approved clinician'.

(g) *Treatment of Recalled Community Patients on SCT*

The treatment of a recalled community patient, if necessary without his consent, 6.139
under a SOAD certificate issued under Part 4A raises human rights issues under Article 8, particularly where the certificate was issued at a time when the patient lacked capacity and he has since regained it, and is now objecting (see para 6.112). The circumstances in which a certificate can be used in those circumstances will probably have to be narrowly construed in order to ensure Convention compliance.

(h) *Treatment of Patients With ECT and Medication Without Part 4 or 4A Safeguards*

For that group of patients who do not fall within Part 4 or 4A for the purposes of 6.140
s 58 treatment (paras 6.12, 6.58) or s 58A treatment (paras 6.145, 6.58), treatment may be given either with their consent or, if the patient lacks capacity, under the 2005 Act without the safeguard of a SOAD certificate. As seen, the protection of the SOAD procedure has been extended to informal child patients (those under 18) for

s 58A treatment. It is striking that ECT and medication can continue to be given to patients who lack capacity, and medication can continue to be given to children, without a SOAD certificate. This issue is raised by the JCHR in its 2nd Report, at paras 93–101. It would probably be difficult to establish that the absence of these safeguards is, of itself, incompatible with the State's positive obligation to protect vulnerable patients; the margin of discretion allowed the State will be a wide one. Nevertheless, in any individual case where such treatment is given, the lack of safeguards will make it more likely that there has been a Convention violation.

7
OTHER AMENDMENTS

A.	Key Features	7.00
B.	Extending Professional Responsibilities	7.01
	1. 'Responsible Clinician' to Replace 'Responsible Medical Officer'	7.03
	2. Medical Recommendations for Detention and Renewals of Detention	7.06
	3. 'Approved Social Worker' Replaced by 'Approved Mental Health Professional'	7.18
	4. Avoiding Conflicts of Interest	7.22
C.	Discharge by Hospital Managers Under s 23	7.24
D.	Patients Concerned in Criminal Proceedings	7.25
	1. The Removal of Time-limited Restriction Orders	7.27
	2. Extension of Scope of Hospital and Limitation Directions	7.29
E.	Offences	7.31
F.	Transfer of Patients to and from Scotland etc	7.32
G.	Detention in a Place of Safety	7.33
H.	Victims' Rights	7.34
	1. Introduction	7.34
	2. 'Victim'	7.35
	3. Current Scope of the 2004 Act	7.36
	4. Amendments Introduced by the 2007 Act	7.38

A. KEY FEATURES

- The range of professionals who may exercise the functions currently excercised by registered medical practitioners and ASWs under the 1983 Act is widened. **7.00**

- Discharge under s 23 by hospital managers of NHS Foundation Trust hospitals is no longer restricted to 'non-executive directors'.

- Patients in criminal proceedings: time-limited restriction orders under s 41 are abolished and s 45A hospital and limitation directions are extended to include patients with any mental disorder.

- Increase in penalty for the offence of ill-treatment in s 127 from 2–5 years.
- New provisions governing transfers between Scotland etc.
- New power under s 136 to transfer patients from one place of safety to another.
- Extending victims' rights under the Domestic Violence, Crime and Victims Act 2004 to include victims of crime where the offender has been subject to a mental health disposal without restrictions.

B. EXTENDING PROFESSIONAL RESPONSIBILITIES

7.01 Another key policy objective behind the 2007 Act has been to extend the range of professionals who may exercise statutory functions in relation to detention and treatment under the 1983 Act. The 2007 Act amends the 1983 Act so that certain functions previously exercised by the 'responsible medical officer' (RMO) and the Approved Social Worker (ASW) may now be exercised by members of other professional bodies, who will now be called the 'responsible clinician' and 'approved mental health professional' (AMHP), respectively. Medical recommendations for the initial detention must still be made by qualified doctors, although renewals of detention may be authorized by a non-medically qualified 'responsible clinician', which raises potential issues under Article 5.

7.02 These amendments as they relate to medical treatment are considered at para 6.34ff.

1. 'Responsible Clinician' to Replace 'Responsible Medical Officer'

7.03 A patient, once admitted, comes under the care of a 'responsible medical officer' (RMO), defined in ss 34(1) and 55(1) as 'the registered medical practitioner in charge of the treatment of the patient'. The RMO exercises a number of key functions in relation to leave of absence (s 17), renewal (s 20), discharge (s 23), and treatment (Part 4) of a detained patient. For patients on guardianship, the RMO is the 'medical officer authorized by the local social services authority to act as the responsible medical officer' (s 34(1)). For patients on supervised discharge under s 25A, the term used is 'the community responsible medical officer'. What they all have in common is that the role is statutorily required to be performed by a qualified medical doctor.

7.04 Under the 2007 Act, all references to the RMO are to be replaced by references to the 'responsible clinician'.[1] The 'responsible clinician' is defined in amended s 34(1)[2] as, in relation to a patient liable to be detained under s 2 or s 3, 'the approved

---

[1] Section 15 of the 2007 Act makes consequential amendments to the Army Act 1955, the Air Force Act 1955, the Naval Discipline Act 1957, the Criminal Procedure (Insanity) Act 1964, and the Armed Forces Act 2006 to replace the term 'responsible medical officer' with the term 'responsible clinician', where it is mentioned in those Acts.

[2] See also the definition in s 64(1).

clinician with overall responsibility for the case of the patient in question',[3] and in relation to a patient subject to guardianship, the 'approved clinician authorized by the responsible local social services authority to act as the responsible clinician'. 'Approved clinician' is defined in s 145(1) as 'a person approved by the Secretary of State (in relation to England) or by the Welsh Ministers (in relation to Wales) to act as an approved clinician for the purposes of this Act'. Draft Directions[4] to be issued by the Secretary of State under ss 7 and 8 of the National Health Service Act 2006 will authorize a range of mental health professionals to be an 'approved clinician', including psychologists, nurses, occupational therapists and social workers, provided they meet the relevant competencies set out in Schedule 2.[5]

The 'responsible clinician' will now exercise the functions previously the respon-   7.05
sibility of the RMO, together with the new functions created in relation to SCT. The significance of this change in relation to the administration of medical treatment is considered at paras 6.138, while the Article 5 implications this gives rise to with renewals of detention under s 20 and other authorizations for detention are considered at para 7.08 below.

2. Medical Recommendations for Detention and Renewals of Detention

(a) *Medical Recommendations in Support of Initial Detention*

At present any medical recommendation in support of an application under s 2 or 3   7.06
or an order under Part 3 authorizing detention in criminal proceedings, or any guardianship application, must be provided by a registered medical practitioner. For longer-term admissions and guardianship applications, where two recommendations are necessary, at least one of the registered medical practitioners must be 'approved for the purposes of this section by the Secretary of State as having special experience in the diagnosis or treatment of mental disorder' (s 12(2)). Similar provision is made in relation to orders made in criminal proceedings by s 54(1).

The 2007 Act does not affect this requirement: all medical recommendations   7.07
in support of detention must continue to be by registered medical practitioners. The 2007 Act does introduce s 12(2A) so that an 'approved clinician' who is also a registered medical practitioner may be approved under s 12, but a non-medically qualified 'approved clinician' cannot be so approved.

(b) *Renewals of Detention under s 20*

Any renewal of detention under s 20 must currently be authorized by a registered   7.08
medical practitioner, the RMO, by furnishing a report to the hospital managers in accordance with s 20(3) if 'it appears to him' that the conditions in s 20(4) are satisfied, namely that 'the patient is suffering from mental illness, severe mental impairment, psychopathic disorder or mental impairment, and his mental disorder

---

[3] Section 55(1) contains similar provision in relation to patients under Part 3.

[4] Draft Mental Health Act 1983 Approved Clinician Directions 2008.

[5] See also the Explanatory Notes to the 2007 Act, para 48.

is of a nature or degree which makes it appropriate for him to receive medical treatment in a hospital; and such treatment is likely to alleviate or prevent a deterioration of his condition; and it is necessary for the health or safety of the patient or for the protection of other persons that he should receive such treatment and that it cannot be provided unless he continues to be detained'.

7.09   The 2007 Act substitutes the medically qualified RMO with the potentially non-medically qualified 'responsible clinician', who now exercises the function of renewal under s 20. This caused considerable concern during the course of the Act's passage as a Bill through Parliament, given its Article 5(1) implications. A lawful detention under Article 5(1)(e) requires not only that the *Winterwerp* criteria (above, para 3.104) are met at the time of the original admission, but also at any subsequent renewal. That will include the requirement that the criteria be established by 'objective medical expertise' both at the time of the original admission and at the time of any renewal.

7.10   These concerns lead to another last minute amendment, this time during the Bill's final consideration by the House of Lords on ping pong. Section 20(5A) provides: 'But the responsible clinician may not furnish a report under subsection (3) above unless a person (a) who has been professionally concerned with the patient's medical treatment; but (b) who belongs to a profession other than that to which the responsible clinician belongs, states in writing that he agrees that the conditions set out in subsection (4) above are satisfied.'

7.11   Accordingly, if the responsible clinician is *not* a registered medical practitioner, he must consult another person who has been professionally concerned with the patient's treatment, which may (not must) be a qualified medical practitioner. It is suggested that any renewal of detention by a non-medically qualified responsible clinician where the other professional consulted is also not medically qualified will be vulnerable to a challenge under the Human Rights Act 1998, although whether there has been a violation of Article 5(1) will depend very much upon the individual qualifications and experience of the responsible clinician and the consultee. This issue is raised by the JCHR in its 2nd Report, para 26, and its 3rd Reports, para 1.7 and 1.14.

(c) Doctor's Holding Power in s 5(2)

7.12   Under s 5(2) the registered medical practitioner in charge of the treatment of an informal patient may authorize the patient's detention for 72 hours upon furnishing a report to the hospital managers that 'an application ought to be made under [Part 2] for the admission of the patient to hospital'. This is by contrast with the nurse's holding power in s 5(4), who may authorize the detention of an informal patient for up to 6 hours where it is not practicable to secure the immediate attendance of a doctor for the purposes of s 5(2).

7.13   The 2007 Act amends s 5(2) so the doctor's holding power may now be exercised by an 'approved clinician'. As we have seen, the 'approved clinician' need not necessarily be a qualified medical practitioner. Where authorization is given by someone who is not medically qualified there is unlikely to be an Article 5(1) violation, as the *Winterwerp* criteria (above, para 3.104), including the requirement of 'objective *medical* expertise' do not apply with such force in cases of emergency.

(d) *Reports for Remands to Hospital under s 35*

By s 35(1) a criminal court may remand an accused to hospital for the purposes of a   7.14
report on his medical condition provided (s 35(3)) the court is satisfied, on the written or oral evidence of a registered medical practitioner, that there is reason to suspect that the accused person is suffering from one of the four classifications of
disorder. By s 35(4) the court shall not remand an accused person under s 35(1)
unless it is satisfied, on the written or oral evidence of a registered medical practitioner who would be responsible for making that report or of some other person
representing the hospital managers, that a bed will be av ailable within 7 days. By
s 35(5) where an order under s 35(1) has been given the court may further remand
the accused person if it appears to the court, on the written or oral evidence of the
registered medical practitioner responsible for making the report, that a further
remand is necessary for completing the assessment.

A remand may not be for more than 28 days at a time, and the total period of   7.15
remand may not exceed 12 weeks (s 35(7)).

The 2007 Act amends ss 35(4) and 35(5) to substitute 'approved clinician' for   7.16
'registered medical practitioner'. Section 35(3) is not, however, affected. The effect
is as follows. An order may not be made under s 35(1) in the first instance without
written or oral evidence from a doctor that the criteria in s 35(3) are made out. The
eventual report itself may, however, be prepared by a non-medically qualified
'approved clinician', who may give evidence to the court under s 35(4) to satisfy the
court that a bed is available and s 35(5) where further remands are necessary.

It follows there will be no Article 5 implications of a remand under s 35(1) given   7.17
the requirement for a qualified doctor to authorize the initial remand and the
maximum period of remand of 12 weeks.

3. 'Approved Social Worker' Replaced by 'Approved Mental Health Professional'

The Approved Social Worker (ASW) has as his primary function the making of   7.18
applications for admission for assessment and treatment under ss 2 and 3 of the
1983 Act and applications for guardianship under s 7 in accordance with the duties
imposed by ss 11 and 13, although has a number of other functions under ss 18,
25A, 29, 115, 135 136, and 138. The ASW is appointed by the local social services
authority under s 114(1) and is defined in s 145(1) as 'an officer of a local social
services authority appointed to act as an approved social worker for the purposes of
this Act'. Section 114(2) requires that to be appointed under s 114(1), a social
worker must be approved by the local authority as having 'appropriate competence
in dealing with persons who are suffering from mental disorder.

All the references to ASWs have now been replaced with references to AMHPs, who   7.19
will now exercise the functions of the ASW. Section 114, which replaces the
old s 114, provides that the local social services authority will appoint an AMHP if satisfied that he has appropriate competence in dealing with persons who are suffering from
mental disorder, in accordance with regulations by the 'appropriate national authority',
namely the Secretary of State (in relation to England) or by the Welsh Ministers (in

relation to Wales). Draft Regulations[6] provide that a range of professionals, including nurses, occupational therapists and chartered psychologists may be approved to act as an AMHP in accordance with the conditions and competencies set out in the Schedule.

7.20   New s 114A is introduced into the 1983 Act in relation to the approval of courses for AMHPs. This allows the General Social Care Council and the Care Council for Wales, which are the statutory bodies set up to regulate the social work profession, to approve courses for the training of English and Welsh AMHPs respectively, regardless of the trainees' profession.

7.21   Amendments are also made to s 13(1), the effect of which is to provide for local authority social services authorities to continue to have a role in ensuring that there is an adequate AMHP service, whether they choose to run the AMHP service themselves or enter into agreements with other social services authorities and/or NHS bodies.

4. Avoiding Conflicts of Interest

7.22   New s 12A of the 1983 Act introduces a power to enable regulations to be made by the Secretary of State in respect of England and the Welsh Ministers in respect of Wales setting out when, because of a potential conflict of interest, an AMHP may not make an application for admission to hospital or guardianship under section 2, 3, or 7 of th e 1983 Act, or a medical practitioner may not provide a medical recommendation accompanying such an application.

7.23   The power replaces the provisions of section 12(3) to (7) of the 1983 Act, which set out when a medical practitioner may not provide a medical recommendation in support of an application, because of their position either in relation to the applicant, the patient or the other practitioner providing a medical recommendation.

C. DISCHARGE BY HOSPITAL MANAGERS UNDER s 23

7.24   The power of hospital managers of an NHS Foundation Trust to discharge a patient under s 23 has been amended so that it is no longer necessary for three non-executive directors to sit on the panel (s 23(6)). The power may now be exercised by there people 'authorized by the board of the trust in that behalf' who are neither an executive director nor an employee of the trust. The amending provision of the 2007 Act, s 45, was the first to be brought into force, from 24 July 2007.

D. PATIENTS CONCERNED IN CRIMINAL PROCEEDINGS

7.25   The provisions relating to patients concerned in criminal proceedings are governed by Part 3 of the 1983 Act, albeit much of Part 2 of the Act applies to patients subject

---

[6] The Mental Health (Approval of Persons to be AMHP) Regulations 2008 (Draft).

to the provisions of Part 3, with suitable modifications, by virtue of s 40(4), s 41(3), and Sch 1.

The provisions of Part 3 have been amended in line with the general amendments 7.26 already discussed, namely the amendments to the criteria for detention (Chapter 3), the new principles in the Code of Practice (Chapter 4) and the extension of professional responsibilities (above, para 7.01). Part 3 patients will also have the benefit of the new safeguards introduced in relation to children and IMHAs (Chapter 4). Beyond these general amendments, the framework of Part 3 is left unaffected by the 2007 Act, save in two particular respects; the removal of time-limited restriction orders, and the extension of the 'hospital and limitation direction' provisions to all patients suffering mental disorder.

1. The Removal of Time-limited Restriction Orders

Section 41 of the 1983 Act is amended to remove the power of the Crown Court to 7.27 make restriction orders for a limited period. As a result, restriction orders imposed by the Court will remain in force until they are discharged by the Secretary of State under s 42 or the Tribunal under s 73.

Time limited restriction orders have always been rare, as the Courts have adopted 7.28 the course of making unlimited orders unless there is medical evidence to demonstrate that the patient can be cured within a particular period.[7] The net effect of this change is therefore likely to be very limited.

2. Extension of Scope of Hospital and Limitation Directions

Hospital and limitation directions were introduced by the Crime (Sentences) Act 7.29 1997, which introduced s 45A and s 45B into the 1983 Act. They empower the Crown Court, when imposing a prison sentence, to also make a direction that the offender be admitted to hospital for treatment (a hospital direction), together with a direction that the offender be subject to the special restrictions set out in s 41 (a limitation direction). The effect is that, by contrast with a patient who is made subject to a restriction order under ss 37 and 41, if the criteria for detention under the 1983 Act are no longer made out he may be returned to prison, rather than released. In this respect a ss 45A patient is treated very much like a transferred prisoner under ss 47 and 49, and has the same rights of access to a Tribunal under s 74.

Section 45A is currently only available for patients classified as suffering from 7.30 'psychopathic disorder'. The amendments to s 45A effected by the 2007 Act have the effect of extending its scope to all patients, a course of action which was recommended by the Court of Appeal in *R v Staines (Paula)*.[8] One may expect an increase in the use of s 45A in the light of these amendments and the recommendations in

---

[7] eg *R v Nowhia* [1996] 1 Cr App R (S).
[8] [2006] EWCA Crim 15.

Staines as an alternative to s 37/41 restriction orders where the court wishes to leave open the option of returning the patient to prison in the event the patient is not benefiting from treatment (and see the discussion at para 3.24).[9]

E. OFFENCES

7.31 The maximum penalty for imprisonment on conviction on indictment for the offence of ill treatment of patients in s 127 of the 1983 Act is currently 2 years; under the 2007 Act it is increased to 5 years. The maximum penalty on imprisonment on summary conviction for the same offence will increase from six months to one year on the commencement of ss 154 and 282 of the Criminal Justice Act 2003. The maximum penalties on summary conviction for the offences at ss 126 (forgery, false statements etc) and 128 (assisting patients to absent themselves without leave etc) of the 1983 Act will also increase on the commencement of those provisions of the 2003 Act.

F. TRANSFER OF PATIENTS TO AND FROM SCOTLAND ETC

7.32 The 1983 Act, Part 6 (ss 80–92) makes provision for the transfer of patients to and from Scotland, Northern Ireland, the Channel Islands and the Isle of Man. These are amended by the 2007 Act to make it possible to transfer patients subject to 'non-resident treatment' outside England and Wales (currently this will only apply to patients in Scotland) to SCT in England and Wales and vice versa.

G. DETENTION IN A PLACE OF SAFETY

7.33 Section 136 of the 1983 Act has been amended to allow a person who is removed to a place of safety under s 135(1) or s 136(1) and then detained for the purpose of assessment under s 136(2) to now be transferred to another place of safety within the overall period of 72 hours authorized by the section. This clarifies an uncertainty that previously existed as to the extent of the power.

H. VICTIMS' RIGHTS

1. Introduction

7.34 Section 48 and Schedule 6 of the 2007 Act amend provisions in the Domestic Violence, Crime and Victims Act 2004 (the '2004 Act'), extending the rights of victims of

---

[9] Although s 45A orders cannot be made in relation to a person found unfit to plead or not guilty by reason of insanity: s 5 Criminal Procedure (Insanity) Act 1964, as amended by the Domestic Violence, Crime and Victims Act 2004.

mentally disordered offenders or those found unfit to plead or not guilty by reason of insanity to include cases where a mental health disposal is made without restrictions. The amendments in the 2007 Act were introduced by the Government following campaigning by victims' groups for routine sharing of information about risk presented by mentally disordered offenders between different agencies and with victims.

2. 'Victim'

The concept of 'victim' includes the person who appears to the local probation   7.35
board to be, or to act for, the victim of certain criminal offences. This includes a victim's family in a case where the offence has resulted in the victim's death or incapacity, and in other cases where the victim's age or personal circumstances make it sensible to approach a family member in the first place.[10]

3. Current Scope of the 2004 Act

The 2004 Act was intended to strengthen the rights of victims generally and it   7.36
contains specific provisions relating to the victims of violent and sexual offences committed by mentally disordered offenders. From 1 July 2005, victims have been entitled to receive information and make representations where (a) a person is convicted of a violent or sexual offence; (b) receives a hospital order or a hospital direction, or is transferred from prison to hospital under a transfer direction; and (c) is made subject to special restrictions, respectively a restriction order, a limitation direction or a restriction direction (s 39(1)). Section 36 applies where patients have been found unfit to plead and to have committed the act or found not guilty by reason of insanity, under the Criminal Procedure (Insanity) Act 1964 (as amended by the 2004 Act) in respect of a violent or sexual offence and then made subject to a hospital order with restrictions. If the criteria are met, the victim has rights: to elect to receive information about the patient's discharge from hospital and any conditions imposed; and to make representations about whether the patient should be subject to any conditions in the event of his discharge.

The 2004 Act places statutory duties on certain authorities to provide informa-   7.37
tion to a 'victim' including:

- The local probation board. It must inform the victim whether the patient is to be subject to any conditions if discharged; provide details of conditions relating to contact with the victim or his/her family; notify the victim of the date when a restriction order ceases to have effect; and provide such information 'as the board considers appropriate' in all the circumstances of the case. In practice Victim Liaison Officers will discharge these duties on each board's behalf.
- The Home Secretary. Where she is considering a discharge, she must inform the probation board whether the patient is to be discharged; if so, whether it is a conditional

---

[10] See para 29.5(C), Draft Illustrative Code of Practice, January 2007.

or absolute discharge; and if it is a conditional discharge, what those conditions are. The Home Secretary must inform the board if discharge conditions are varied or the patient is recalled to hospital; and of the date any restriction order is lifted.

- The Mental Health Review Tribunal. Where a patient has applied themselves, or their case is referred by the Home Secretary, the Tribunal must inform the probation board if the patient is to be discharged; if so, whether it is a conditional or absolute discharge; and if it is a conditional discharge, what the conditions are. The board must also be informed of any variation of conditions and the date any restriction order is lifted.[11]

4. Amendments Introduced by the 2007 Act

7.38 Section 48 of the 2007 Act inserts new provisions in the 2004 Act to extend victims' rights to receive information and make representations about mentally disordered offenders who have been convicted of a criminal offence of a sexual or violent nature, but who are not made subject to restrictions by way of a restriction order under s 41 or a limitation direction under s 45A(3)(b). Schedule 6 of the 2007 Act sets out the duties and the procedures in detail.[12]

7.39   The Government has agreed to consult on a Code of Practice[13] dealing with public bodies' sharing of information about mentally disordered offenders yet has stressed '*patients have a right to confidentiality, but the public have a right to know that systems and services are in place to support people with a mental disorder*'.[14] A crucial issue arises: although some information sharing may be necessary for public protection, information should only be shared with individuals or public authorities when it is necessary to do so. The 2004 Act requires disclosure of information relating to discharge and conditions of discharge but particular care needs to be taken when considering sharing this as it can come extremely close to providing details about the patient's medical condition or treatment in a way that raises concerns about patient confidentiality and Article 8 rights under the Convention. To protect the interests of patients, the finalized Code will need to oblige decision-makers to consider the effect on the patient's mental state and risks of negative reprisals for him as a result of sharing information with victims.

---

[11] See also MHRT guidance on victims' rights of access to tribunal hearings, July 2005 and March 2007 available from <http://www.mhrt.org.uk>, which outlines procedure for cases covered by the 2004 Act and those that are not.

[12] See also Chapter 29.5 of *Victims*, Draft Illustrative Code of Practice, January 2007.

[13] In the interim, see Chapter 34 of *Confidentiality, Information Sharing and Patient's Access to Records*, Draft Illustrative Code of Practice, January 2007.

[14] Rosie Winterton MP, Minister of State for Health Services, Hansard HC Deb, 18 June 2007, Col 1118.

Part II
THE MENTAL CAPACITY ACT 2005 AND ITS AMENDMENTS

8

INTRODUCTION AND OVERVIEW

A.	Introduction	8.01
B.	The History of the 2005 Act	8.05
	1. History of Incapacity Legislation	8.05
	2. The Need for Reform Identified	8.10
	3. Government Proposals for Reform and Legislative History of the 2005 Act	8.14
C.	Structure of the 2005 Act	8.15
D.	*Bournewood*	8.17
E.	The 2007 Act and 'Schedule A1'	8.22
F.	The Interface between the 1983 Act and the 2005 Act	8.23

A. INTRODUCTION

Mental health law requires provision to be made, broadly, for three groups of **8.01** individuals. First, there are those who by reason of mental disorder present such a risk to themselves or to others that detention is necessary to provide them with the treatment they need. Successive pieces of legislation have provided the legal framework for the care and treatment of this group, as described in Chapter One, and the 1983 Act provides the current framework, with the amendments introduced by the 2007 Act as explained in Part I of this book.

Second, there are those who suffer long-term, debilitating conditions such as **8.02** severe learning disability who have always been incapable of making decisions for themselves. They do not usually require detention but do need a framework in place by which decisions about their property and affairs, where they will live, what medical treatment they should receive and with whom they may have contact can be taken, which will also safeguard doctors and other carers from civil or criminal liability for any steps taken in order to care for or treat the individual. Where their condition puts them at risk to themselves or others then detention under the 1983 Act may be warranted. If it does not, then the framework of guardianship under s 7 of the 1983 Act may be called for. However, for reasons explained below, guardianship does not provide a complete statutory code for the care of this group, in particular it does not confer jurisdiction on the guardian to make decisions about medical treatment. Moreover, guardianship does not authorize the detention of such individuals when circumstances require it, but where the formal processes of detention under the 1983 Act are not required. Until the 2005 Act comes into force, the gaps in the framework of law for this group have been filled by judges developing common law principles on a case-by-case basis.

8.03   Third, there are those who, by accident or disease or some other event, lose capacity to make decisions for themselves, whether temporarily or over the long term. As with the second group, a framework of law is necessary to enable decisions to be taken on the individual's behalf in relation to their property and affairs and personal welfare, including medical treatment and (where necessary) detention for the purposes of receiving that treatment where the formal processes of the 1983 Act are not called for. For this group, a further legal mechanism is necessary to enable the individual to make decisions about their property and affairs or their personal welfare while they have capacity that will be respected in the event that they lose capacity. The need for such a mechanism is particularly acute in those highly contentious cases involving refusals of treatment the effect of which will be the death of the patient ('end of life' decisions). Such decisions are only likely to become more common as the population ages. As with the second group, there has (until now) been no systematic legal framework covering decision-making for this third group, with the gaps being filled by the common law. These developments in the common law are discussed in detail in Chapter 9.

8.04   The 2005 Act makes provision for the second and third groups, assuming jurisdiction over personal welfare decision-making on behalf of such patients and codifying much of the common law principles that had developed to fill the gaps in the law. The 2005 Act also assumes jurisdiction over patients' property and affairs, in doing so replacing the provisions of Part VII of the 1983 Act and the Enduring Powers of Attorneys Act 1985, which fall outside the scope of this work.. Where the 2005 Act is deficient is in relation to the framework for *detention* of patients in the second and third groups, where detention under the 1983 Act is either unavailable or inappropriate. It is to meet this need that amendments to the 2005 Act have been introduced by the 2007 Act, as explained at para 8.17ff.

B. THE HISTORY OF THE 2005 ACT

1. History of Incapacity Legislation

8.05   Before considering the provisions of the 2005 Act governing personal welfare decisions, and why the 2005 Act is now being amended by the 2007 Act, it is necessary to consider the history of the law as it relates to such decision-making. The roots of the 2005 Act lie in the same early history of mental health legislation as the 1983 Act, described in Chapter 1 at para 1.18ff. Since at least the 14th century, those of 'unsound mind' could be cared for under the *parens patriae* jurisdiction of the Crown, later assigned by Royal Warrant to the Lord Chancellor and the judges of the High Court who had jurisdiction to make decisions on behalf of such individuals in relation both to their property and affairs and personal matters. The jurisdiction was indistinguishable from the High Court's wardship jurisdiction in relation to children.

In 1957 the Percy Commission,[1] upon whose recommendations the 1959 Act were based, proposed that this jurisdiction should be placed on a statutory footing, through two mechanisms. A new Court of Protection was to be created with jurisdiction over the property and affairs of those who were incapable, by reason of mental disorder, of managing their property and affairs. This mechanism in due course became Part VII of the 1983 Act and, now, is catered for by the 2005 Act.   **8.06**

The second mechanism the Percy Commission proposed was guardianship, which would enable decisions to be made about the personal welfare of those vulnerable individuals who did not need detention but could not care for themselves, or be cared for, without some formal structure in place. Such a mechanism was necessary if the 1959 Act was to meet its objective of reducing the need for those with mental disorder to be detained, described at para 1.26 above. The guardianship provisions introduced by the 1959 Act conferred upon the guardian the powers of a father over a child under 14 (s 34(1)), although the jurisdiction was not based on capacity or lack of it. As seen at para 9.25, the common law powers of a person with parental responsibility include power to consent or refuse consent on behalf of an incompetent child and to override a competent child's refusal of treatment. To that extent the powers of the guardian were co-extensive with the Court's *parens patriae* jurisdiction and were intended to replace that jurisdiction in its entirety, and on 1 November 1960 the Royal Warrant conferring the *parens patriae* jurisdiction upon the Lord Chancellor and the judges of the High Court was revoked.   **8.07**

I have described in Chapter 1 how during the 1970's a new human rights discourse about mental health law came to the fore (para 1.27), and the guardianship provisions of the 1959 were not immune to these developments. The guardianship powers, which were usually exercised by a local authority, came to be regarded as 'very wide, and somewhat ill-defined, and out of keeping, in their paternalistic approach, with modern attitudes to the care of the mentally disordered'.[2] It was recommended that they be cut back, 'limited to restricting the liberty of the individual only to the extent necessary to ensure that various forms of medical treatment, social support, training or occupation are undertaken'.[3]   **8.08**

---

[1] *Report of the Royal Commission on the Law Relating to Mental Illness and Mental Deficiency 1954–1957* (1957) (Cmnd 169).

[2] 1981 White Paper, Reform of Mental Health Legislation (1981) (Cmnd 8405) 16, ch 4, para 43.

[3] 'Review of the White Paper 1959', Cmnd 7230, §4.17; see also 1981 White Paper, Reform of Mental Health Legislation (1981) (Cmnd 8405) paras 43–5.

8.09   To that end, two restrictions on the guardianship powers were introduced in the Mental Health (Amendment) Act 1982 and later consolidated in the 1983 Act. First, to obtain a guardianship order in relation to a mentally handicapped person (suffering from 'mental impairment', rather than 'subnormality'), the patient's condition had to be 'associated with abnormally aggressive or seriously irresponsible conduct' (s 1(2) of the 1983 Act). The second restriction introduced by the 1982 Act was to limit the extent of the powers of a guardian to those now set out in s 8(1) of the 1983 Act, namely to direct the individual to reside at a particular place, to attend any place at any time for the purposes of medical treatment, occupation, education or training; and to direct that access be given to the RMO or a social worker. Those powers do not give the guardian authority to consent to medical treatment or to impose other restrictions, such as contact with others.

2. The Need for Reform Identified

8.10   It was not until 1989 that the gap left in the law as a result of these changes was 'discovered', when the Court of Appeal and later the House of Lords were faced with the dilemma of how to authorize an operation to sterilize a young woman with severe learning disabilities, F, in circumstances where all agreed it was in her best interests: *Re F (Mental Patient: Sterilisation)* [1990] 2 AC 1. The Court no longer exercised a *parens patriae* jurisdiction with respect to adult persons of unsound mind, as this had been removed following the coming into force of the 1959 Act. Moreover, following the reduction in the powers of the guardian in the 1983 Act, a guardian no longer had power to give consent on an adult patient's behalf.

8.11   The solution the courts adopted was to 'rediscover' its inherent jurisdiction to make declarations, in advance, that a particular course of action (if pursued) would not amount to a tortious or criminal act because the common law defence of necessity would be available. Chapter 9 picks up the narrative at para 9.19, and explains how the jurisdiction has come to be developed over the ensuing years.

8.12   Notwithstanding that the courts have been able to develop their newly rediscovered jurisdiction to meet the challenges they have been presented with, calls for the statutory regulation of decision-making on behalf of incapable adults have grown. A Select Committee on Medical Ethics (1993–94) HL 21-II called for Parliament to give more specific definition as to what were the relevant factors in determining 'best interests'. In the early 1990's the Law Commission produced a series of Consultation Papers (Nos 128–30) entitled 'Mentally Incapacitated Adults and Decision-Making', culminating in its Report, 'Mental Incapacity', Law Com No 231, published in February 1995, together with a draft Incapacity Bill (upon which the 2005 Act was, in due course, based). The introduction to the Report, at para 1.1, reads as follows: '1.1 This report is concerned with the ways in which decisions may lawfully be made on behalf of those who are unable to make decisions for themselves . . . It is widely recognized that, in this area, the law as it now stands is unsystematic and full of glaring gaps. It does not rest on clear or modern foundations of principle. It has failed to keep up with social and demographic changes. It has also failed to keep up with developments in our understanding of the rights and needs of those with mental disability.'

The calls for reform have included those from the judiciary themselves. As the President of the Family Division, Dame Butler-Sloss, said in *Re F (Adult: Court's Jurisdiction)* [2001] Fam 38, at 50: 'The assumption of jurisdiction by the High Court on a case by case basis does not, however, detract from the obvious need expressed by the Law Commission and by the government for a well structured and clearly defined framework of protection of vulnerable, mentally incapacitated adults, particularly since the whole essence of declarations under the inherent jurisdiction is to meet a recognized individual problem and not to provide general guidance for mentally incapacitated adults. Until Parliament puts in place that defined framework, the High Court will still be required to help out where there is no other practicable alternative.' 8.13

3. Government Proposals for Reform and Legislative History of the 2005 Act

In December 1997 the Government published a Green Paper on the law relating to the care and treatment of incapacitated individuals.[4] The Lord Chancellor's announcement to the House of Lords on 10 December 1997 stated: 'The law is confusing and fragmented. Many carers in particular are expected to make decisions on behalf of incapacitated adults without a clear idea as to the legal authority for those decisions. Everybody will know of a friend or relative whose lives are affected by the current state of the law.' In October 1999 the Lord Chancellor published the Government's proposals, 'Making Decisions' (Cm 4465), in the light of the 4000 responses it received. A Draft Mental Incapacity Bill was published in June 2003. The Bill was scrutinized by a Joint Scrutiny Committee of both Houses of Parliament who received over 1200 written submissions and heard oral evidence from 61 witnesses. It reported in November 2003 and also published the evidence it received. The Department for Constitutional Affairs published its response in February 2004 and published a revised Mental Capacity Bill which was introduced into the House of Commons on 17 June 2004. In November 2004, the Joint Committee on Human Rights published their views on the Mental Capacity Bill[5] and the Department for Constitutional Affairs published their response in January 2005. The 2005 Act received Royal Assent on 7 April 2005 and came into force on 1 October 2007. 8.14

C. STRUCTURE OF THE 2005 ACT

The 2005 Act, in its original conception, provides a framework for decision-making required for the care and treatment of the second and third groups described at 8.15

---

[4] *Who Decides?—Making Decisions on Behalf of Mentally Incapacitated Adults*, Cm 3808.
[5] JCHR Report, *'Scrutiny of Bills: Final Progress Report'* Twenty-third Report of Session 2003–04, HL Paper 210, HC 1282.

para 8.02. The 2005 Act enshrines the common law principle that a capable adult may consent or reject any treatment, regardless of the outcome (the principle of autonomy or self-determination) and extends it, by enabling adults to make decisions in advance of losing capacity that will have legal effect in that event. A capable adult can now make an advance decision about his personal welfare which must be respected by a decision-maker or a Court in the event that he loses capacity, and may for the first time execute a 'lasting power of attorney' (LPA), appointing a donee to make decisions on his behalf concerning his personal welfare once he loses capacity. It also provides a hierarchy of substituted decision-making based on principles of autonomy, capacity and 'best interests' and creates a new court, the Court of Protection, which assumes the jurisdiction of the old Court of Protection in relation to property and affairs (not covered by this book) and acquires the inherent common law jurisdiction of the High Court in relation to personal welfare decisions. The ambit of the 2005 Act in relation to care and treatment decisions is described in detail in Chapter 10, and the Court of Protection is considered in Chapter 14.

8.16   The framework provided by the 2005 Act in its current form is, however, primarily concerned with the care and treatment of those who lack capacity. It does not provide any mechanism for the *detention* of the incapacitated, other than by an order of the Court of Protection under s 16, for reasons now explained.

D. BOURNEWOOD

8.17   Among the reforms introduced by the 1959 Act was to repeal the Mental Deficiency Act 1913 and its successors, the 1926 and 1939, under which those severely incapacitated individuals ('idiots', 'imbeciles', and the 'feeble-minded', now described under the less stigmatizing label of 'learning disabled') were detained. The 1959 Act introduced a more informal framework, based on the principle that patients should be admitted to hospital informally wherever possible (see para 1.26 above). Among those who the Percy Commission recommended could be cared for 'informally' and without the need for compulsion were the 'large number, probably the great majority, of the patients at present cared for in mental deficiency hospitals, most of whom are childlike and prepared to accept whatever arrangements are made for them. There is no more need to have power to detain these patients in hospital than in their own homes or any other place which they have no wish to leave. We strongly recommend that the principle of treatment without certification should be extended to them.'[6]

8.18   In light of that recommendation, s 5 of the 1959 Act was introduced. Those incapacitated adult patients who would previously have been detained under the Mental Deficiency Acts were to be admitted informally, provided they did not object to

---

[6] *Report of the Royal Commission on the Law Relating to Mental Illness and Mental Deficiency 1954–1957* (1957) (Cmnd 169), paras 289–291.

their detention. This practice continued under the 1983 Act, which carried forward the principle of 'informality' in s 5 of the 1959 Act through its successor provision, s 131 of the 1983 Act.

This, however, left the care and treatment, and the detention, of such incapaci-   8.19
tated individuals completely unregulated and without any of the safeguards provided for by the 1959 Act and, subsequently, the 1983 Act. In successive reports the newly created Mental Health Act Commission highlighted the problem of so-called 'de facto' detained patients, for whom the Commission exercised no statutory responsibility to keep their care under review (see, for example, the Commission's First Biennial Report, 1983–85, para 8.10). It was not until 1997 and the case of *Bournewood*, however, that this issue came to a head, described in detail in Chapter 11. The resulting decision of the House of Lords (*R v Bournewood Community Mental Health NHS Trust ex p L* [1998] AC 458), while endorsing the lawfulness of this practice (pressing once more into service the doctrine of 'necessity'), nevertheless highlighted the need for greater safeguards for this vulnerable group (see para 11.11), and the government promised to take this issue under consideration in its reform of mental capacity law that had begun in 1997 with the publication of the 'Who decides?' Green Paper.

Mr L took his case to the ECtHR, however, which handed down its judgment in   8.20
October 2004, *HL v United Kingdom*.[7] The ECtHR's decision is considered in detail at para 11.13ff but, in summary, it held that L had been 'deprived of his liberty' within the meaning of Article 5(1) while he had been an informal patient and, moreover, his detention had been unlawful in so far as the common law doctrine of necessity failed to provide sufficient safeguards against arbitrary detention to meet the Article 5 requirement that detention must be 'in accordance with a procedure prescribed by law'. The Government's immediate response to *HL* was to make certain amendments to the Mental Capacity Bill, restricting the circumstances in which a person could be 'deprived of his liberty' to orders by the new Court of Protection, pending consideration of what mechanism should be introduced to regulate deprivations of liberty of the kind outlawed by *HL* (see para 11.21). Thus the 2005 Act, when first passed, provided that an incapacitated person ('P') could not be deprived of his liberty other than by an order of the Court under s 16 in relation to a matter concerning P's personal welfare. Any deprivation of liberty by a person purporting to act in P's best interest in relation to P's care and treatment under s 5, by a donee of a lasting power of attorney ('donee') under s 11 or by a deputy appointed by the Court under s 20 were expressly prohibited.[8]

In the meantime the Government considered what steps were necessary to bring   8.21
the law into line with its Convention obligations. It issued interim guidance to NHS bodies and local authorities on steps that could be taken to minimize the risk of detention. In March 2005 the government produced a consultation paper on its

---

[7] (2004) 40 EHRR 761.
[8] s 5(5), 11(6), and 20(13), respectively.

proposals to meet the issues raised by the judgment of the ECtHR in the *HL v United Kingdom* case.[9]

E. THE 2007 ACT AND 'SCHEDULE A1'

8.22 The government's proposals for introducing additional safeguards for what became known as '*Bournewood*' patients went through several different incarnations as various drafts of the Mental Health Bill were introduced, consulted on and then amended or withdrawn, a process described in Chapter 1. The structure that eventually found favour is that which is to be introduced in Sch A1 and 1A of the 2005 Act, described in detail in Chapters 11 and 12. Many were (and remain) of the view that a relatively light touch scheme would have been sufficient, for example by amending the Guardianship provisions of the Mental Health Act 1983 or by modest amendments to the existing framework of the 2005 Act. In the event, the mechanism adopted by the government in Schedules A1 and 1A of the 2005 Act[10] is anything but 'light touch': it is long (Schedule A1 contains 13 Parts and 186 paragraphs), complex, overly bureaucratic and, ironically, may still not comply with the requirements of Articles 5(1) and 5(4). The Joint Committee on Human Rights were so concerned by its complexity as to raise the possibility that it may not satisfy the Article 5 requirement that the law be sufficiently accessible and foreseeable to meet the requisite standard of 'lawfulness' set by the Convention: an irony indeed, given the impetus for these changes was the ECtHR's finding in *HL* that the existing law was incompatible with Article 5. The new procedure is described in Chapters 11 and 12, and the procedure for the extension of IMCA's and other representatives is described in Chapter 13.

F. THE INTERFACE BETWEEN THE 1983 ACT AND THE 2005 ACT

8.23 The amendments introduced by the 2007 Act, both to the 1983 Act and the 2005 Act, will lead to excruciating difficulties for those charged with responsibility for deciding both which detention regime and which treatment regime is appropriate for a person suffering from mental disorder. This complexity becomes increased exponentially for children. I have tried, in Chapter 15, to explain how the various regimes are intended to work together. It is likely to be some time before those who will have to use the legislation will be able to understand its complexities.

---

[9] 'Bournewood' Consultation: The approach to be taken in response to the judgment of the European Court of Human Rights in the 'Bournewood' case, March 2005.

[10] Introduced by s 45 and Sch 6–8 of the Mental Health Act 2007.

9

CARE AND TREATMENT AT COMMON LAW

A.	Key Features	9.00
B.	Care and Treatment of Adults at Common Law	9.01
C.	Bodily Integrity and Autonomy	9.03
D.	Capacity and Incapacity at Common Law	9.06
E.	Necessity and 'Best Interests'	9.10
	1. The Doctrine of Necessity	9.12
	2. 'Best Interests'	9.13
	3. Best Interests: Some Unresolved Issues	9.16
F.	The Nature of the Courts' Jurisdiction at Common Law	9.19
	1. The Demise and the Rise of the High Court's Inherent Jurisdiction	9.19
	2. The Inherent Jurisdiction: Limitations and Unresolved Issues	9.22
G.	Children Under 16	9.25
	1. Key Distinctions between Adults and Children Under 16	9.25
	2. Consent and the Right of Autonomy	9.27
	3. The Jurisdiction of the High Court in Relation to Children Under 16	9.31
H.	Children Aged 16 and 17	9.36

A. KEY FEATURES

- The common law right of bodily integrity means that care and medical treatment 9.00
  of an individual may be an unlawful assault and battery in the absence of lawful
  justification, which may derive from consent, from statute or from the common
  law doctrine of necessity.

- The common law right of autonomy or self-determination means an adult with
  capacity may consent to care and medical treatment, and may also refuse such
  treatment, whatever the consequences, and an adult is presumed to have capacity
  unless the contrary is shown.

- Under the common law doctrine of necessity, care or treatment may be administered to an incapacitated adult, including the use of reasonable force, provided it is in his 'best interests'.

- The High Court may in its inherent jurisdiction declare in advance that the care or treatment of an incapacitated adult is lawful.

- Different principles apply for children under 16 and for children aged 16 and 17.

B. CARE AND TREATMENT OF ADULTS AT COMMON LAW

9.01 Before considering the provisions of the 2005 Act it is necessary first to understand the common law rights of bodily integrity and of autonomy and the principles of capacity (including the presumption of capacity) and best interests as they apply to adults (those over 18) which, with some exceptions, the 2005 Act effectively codifies. These common law principles are left undisturbed by the 2005 Act and will continue to apply where the 2005 Act does not.

9.02 The principles are similar but require separate consideration for children under 16 and those aged 16 and 17.

C. BODILY INTEGRITY AND AUTONOMY

9.03 Underlying both the common law and the 2005 Act are the rights of bodily integrity and autonomy from which the other principles spring. The right to integrity of the person is the right not to have one's person interfered with beyond 'the normal vicissitudes of everyday life' without lawful justification. Care and medical treatment are an interference with the right to integrity of the person and may constitute an unlawful assault and battery in the absence of some lawful justification.[1] Lawful justification may derive, materially, from a capable individual's consent; in the case of an incapacitated person, from the common law doctrine of necessity and, from 1 October 2007, the 2005 Act; and, in either case, from statute, notably the Mental Health Act 1983. The position as regards children is considered at para 9.25ff, below.

9.04 The right of autonomy or self-determination denotes the right of an individual of 'sound mind' to make choices about, materially for our purposes, his body, which are respected by others and by the law. A capable person may consent to care or treatment, making the treatment lawful. Similarly, a capable person's refusal to consent to care or treatment must be respected, however drastic the consequences for

---

[1] *Re F* [1990] 2 AC 1, 73–4.

the individual concerned, including death[2] or (in the case of a pregnant woman) the death of an unborn child.[3]

At common law the right of autonomy is subject only to two exceptions: first, a capable person may be restrained in order to protect others from harm. Second, a capable person may not consent to treatment which involves their death or the infliction of really serious harm. Indeed, to cause a consenting person's death still constitutes the offence of murder and to assist a person's suicide is a criminal offence, contrary to s 2 of the Suicide Act 1961, while the infliction of really serious harm on a consenting individual, at least in the context of sado-masochistic sexual practices, will constitute a criminal offence of causing grievous bodily harm.[4] Those exceptions apart, where he has capacity, 'over himself, over his own body and mind, the individual is sovereign'.[5]   9.05

D. CAPACITY AND INCAPACITY AT COMMON LAW

The common law recognizes the right of autonomy only where a person has capacity to make the choice he purports to make. 'Capacity' denotes the ability of an individual to exercise legal rights or to undertake legal duties. A person may lack capacity, for example, to exercise the right to vote, to marry, to engage in sexual intercourse, to enter into a contract, to consent to treatment or to decide with whom he or she will associate or where he or she will live. Lack of capacity may be temporary or permanent, and may derive from the fact the individual is unconscious or suffers from a mental disorder, or is a child (for which see para 9.25ff).   9.06

Capacity is, then, the key to the existence of the right of autonomy or self-determination, and to the exercise of certain rights, including that of bodily integrity.[6]   9.07

At common law there is a presumption in favour of capacity for those aged 18 or more: it is for the person asserting that P lacks capacity to prove it, on the balance of probabilities.[7] Capacity represents a continuum; a person may have capacity to make some decisions, but not others. A person need only have such capacity as is 'commensurate with the gravity of the decision he purported to make'.[8] The question of capacity is always issue specific[9] and may also be time specific—a person's capacity may improve or deteriorate over time. The question of whether a patient lacks capacity is therefore not a simple one. A person suffering mental disorder may   9.08

---

[2] *Robb v Home Secretary* [1995] Fam 127.

[3] *St George's Healthcare NHS Trust v S* [1999] Fam 26, 47.

[4] *R v Brown* [1994] 1 AC 212; *Laskey v United Kingdom* (1997) 24 EHRR 39.

[5] JS Mill, *On Liberty* (1859).

[6] Note particularly the speech of Lord Steyn in *R v Bournewood Community and Mental Health NHS Trust ex p L* [1990] AC 458, 493A–494B.

[7] *Re MB (An Adult: Medical Treatment)* [1997] 2 FCR 541, 549D–E.

[8] *per* Lord Donaldson in *Re T* [1992] 2 FCR 861, at 874; cited with approval in *Re MB* [1997] 2 FCR 541, CA, at 549G–H.

[9] *Masterman-Lister v Brutton & Co, Masterman-Lister v Jewell* [2003] 1 WLR 1511.

still have capacity to consent to—and to refuse— medical treatment (Mental Health Act Code of Practice, para 15.12). Moreover, a detained patient is not necessarily incapable of giving consent to treatment: ibid, para 16.4.[10]

9.09   A person lacks capacity if some impairment or disturbance of mental functioning renders the person unable to make a decision whether to consent or to refuse treatment. That inability will occur when (a) the patient is unable to comprehend and retain the information which is material to the decision, especially as to the likely consequences of having or not having the treatment in question; (b) the patient is unable to use the information and weigh it in the balance as part of the process of arriving at the decision (the *Re MB* test),[11] which may be because the patient does not believe the treatment information being given to him, by reason of that impairment or disturbance of mental functioning.[12] The test of capacity is formulated slightly differently as it relates to decisions to marry or to engage in sexual intercourse, because historically these decisions have been closely connected with other branches of the law (in the one case the matrimonial law and in the other the criminal law). That does not mean the test in *Re MB* is irrelevant in either context: it is simply that such a refined analysis is probably not necessary where the issue is as simple as the question whether someone has the capacity to marry or the capacity to consent to sexual relations.[13] The test for whether a person has capacity to litigate is also expressed in slightly different terms: see para 14.67. Again, however, that does not mean the *Re MB* test is irrelevant. These tests are, at least on one level of abstraction, indistinguishable from each other and the new statutory test of capacity in s 3 of the 2005 Act. All are based upon the same 'general theory of what is meant by "understanding" a problem and having the capacity to decide what to do about it' (*per* Munby J in *A Local Authority v MM*,[14] paras 71–3).

E. NECESSITY AND 'BEST INTERESTS'

9.10   Incapacity does not take away an individual's underlying rights to their property, their confidentiality, their bodily integrity or their right of association, it only affects the extent to which the law respects an individual's choices in the exercise of those rights. Any interference with those underlying rights must still be justified, otherwise it will be unlawful. Consent is a lawful justification for any such intervention, but incapacity vitiates consent.

9.11   Statute can authorize the necessary decisions to be made, but following the coming into force of the Mental Health Act 1959, which swept away the existing *parens patriae* jurisdiction of the Courts to make decisions on behalf of the mentally

---

[10] See also *Re C* [1994] 1 WLR 290 (patient detained in Broadmoor had capacity to refuse to allow his gangrenous leg to be amputated)).

[11] *Re MB (An Adult: Medical Treatment)* [1997] 2 FCR 541, CA, at 553H–554B *per* Butler-Sloss LJ.

[12] *R(B) v Dr SR* [2005] EWHC 1936 (Admin), para 38.

[13] *Local Authority v MM* [2007] EWHC 2003 (Fam), *per* Munby J at paras 83–7.

[14] [2007] EWHC 2003 (Fam), paras 71–3.

incompetent, and the reduction in the powers the guardian enjoyed under the 1959 Act as a result of the Mental Health (Amendment) Act 1983 (see para 8.05ff), the only statutory framework for the compulsory detention and treatment of the incapacitated has been the Mental Health Act 1983, other than the little used s 47 National Assistance Act 1948 (see para 11.58).[15] The 1983 Act does not authorize the treatment of incapacitated adults for their mental disorder if they do not require detention and it does not authorize any treatment for physical disorder,[16] although acts necessary to treat the physical symptoms or consequences of an underlying mental disorder are permitted.[17] Until the 2005 Act comes into force in October 2007, there is no statutory authority to give treatment other than under the 1983 Act. The common law doctrine of necessity has instead been developed to fill the gap.

1. The Doctrine of Necessity

The common law doctrine of necessity is of ancient origin, developed by the courts   9.12
to provide a common law defence to justifiable action which was, nevertheless, unlawful in the absence of consent. The requirements of the principle are simply that (1) there must be 'a necessity to act when it is not practicable to communicate with the assisted person' (in the present context, due to incapacity) and (2) 'that the action taken must be such as a reasonable person would in all the circumstances take, acting in the best interests of the assisted person'.[18] The need to 'rediscover' the doctrine in the context of medical treatment of the incapacitated arose in the case of *Re F (Mental Patient: Sterilisation)* in 1989, for the reasons described in Chapter 8 and at para 9.19 below.

2. 'Best Interests'

The concept of 'best interests' was initially developed in relation to proposed medi-   9.13
cal treatment for incapacitated individuals, such as the sterilization of long-term incapacitated patients and the treatment of non-consenting individuals by way of naso-gastric feeding, blood transfusions, caesarian births, and the like. More recently the Courts have considered what is in the 'best interests' of incapacitated individuals in the context of less specific, longer term decisions such as whether they may be lawfully detained (*Bournewood*, considered at para 11.01), where and with whom the individual is to live and with whom they are to associate, notably in the Court of Appeal decision of *Re F (Adult Patient)*.[19] These developments in the jurisdiction are considered further, at para 9.19 below.

---

[15] The Mental Health Act 1959 contained no provisions authorizing compulsory treatment, and lacked any legal safeguards against its misuse: see Chapter 1, above and also Phil Fennel, 'Treatment without consent', Routledge, 1996, Chapter 11.

[16] *Re C (Adult: Refusal of Medical Treatment)* [1994] 1 WLR 290.

[17] *B v Croydon HA* [1995] Fam 133.

[18] *Re F (Mental Patient: Sterilisation)* [1990] 2 AC 1, 75 H *per* Lord Goff of Chieveley.

[19] [2001] Fam 38.

9.14   Whether treatment was in a patient's 'best interests' was initially considered to be a purely clinical decision, to be judged by the common law 'negligence' standard in *Bolam v Friern Hospital Management Committee* [1957] 1 WLR 582.[20] This test came under much criticism,[21] but the Court of Appeal subsequently held in *Re A (Medical Treatment: Male Sterilisation)*[22] that the narrow *Bolam* approach to 'best interests' is not the correct one. A doctor making decisions about the future treatment of incapacitated patients owes a duty not to act negligently, but he is also under 'a second duty, . . . he must act in the best interests of a mentally incapacitated patient'.

9.15   While this development raises a number of questions—for example, does a breach of the 'best interests' duty which is not negligent give rise to any cause of action in damages—the Courts now adopt the approach that, in deciding what is best for the disabled patient, the judge must have regard to the patient's welfare as the paramount consideration. That embraces issues 'far wider than the medical', including emotional and social considerations. Indeed, 'it would be undesirable and probably impossible to set bounds to what is relevant to a welfare determination'.[23] The evaluation of best interests is akin to a welfare appraisal, which should involve drawing up a balance sheet, setting the actual and potential gains of a proposed course of action against the actual and potential losses if that proposed course of action is not adopted. It is 'only if the account is in relatively significant credit will the judge conclude that the application is likely to advance the best interests of the claimant'.[24]

3. Best Interests: Some Unresolved Issues

9.16   Several issues remain to be resolved. First, there is still no definition of 'best interests', as such. It may be that any such definition may not be very useful: 'the concept of 'best interests' depends very much on the context in which it is used'[25] and upon a close examination of the facts of the individual case. Certain principles have been developed, however. In cases involving life-threatening conditions, there is a very strong presumption in favour of giving life-saving treatment.[26] In the context of a decision whether to remove P from his family to a hospital or care home, the starting point of the assessment should be the normal assumption that mentally incapacitated adults will be better off if they live with a family rather than in an institution,

---

[20] *Re F* [1990] 2 AC 1, 78B–E.

[21] The Select Committee on Medical Ethics (1993–4) HL 21-II called for Parliament to give more specific definition as to what are the relevant factors in determining 'best interests'. The Law Commission attempted to do so in 1995 with its draft Incapacity Bill, prepared together with its report on Mental Incapacity, Law Com. 231, which formed the basis of the 2005 Act.

[22] [2000] 1 FCR 193, 200–1.

[23] *Re S (Adult Patient: Sterilisation)* [2001] Fam 15, 30E, *per* Thorpe LJ.

[24] *Re A (Male Sterilisation)* [2000] 1 FLR 549, *per* Thorpe LJ, 560E.

[25] *R (Burke) v GMC* [2006] QB 273, para 29.

[26] *R (Burke) v GMC* [2006] QB 273, para 61.

although there is no threshold requirement to establish before a public authority can intervene such as a risk of significant harm equivalent to s 31 of the Children Act 1989.[27] Other situations may require different approaches.

Second, there is some question over whether the test of 'best interests' is a subjec- 9.17 tive one, by reference to what P would consider to be in his best interests if he had capacity to make the decision, or an objective test, by reference to the opinions of those who are caring for him. At common law the Court of Appeal in *R (Burke) v General Medical Council* ruled that the test is an objective one.[28] The 2005 Act, on the other hand, appears to require a more subjective approach, based on what P would consider to be in his best interests: this is considered further, below, para 10.15.

Third, does 'best interests' mean the 'best of all possible alternatives' or the best of 9.18 the available alternatives? This has considerable significance in cases involving the removal of disabled individuals from their home and family because a local author- ity or NHS body refuses to provide the necessary community care or healthcare support to enable them to live at home. In these circumstances it is not clear whether the Court can declare that P's best interests are served by remaining at home, with appropriate support, if the public authorities charged with the responsibility for providing that support refuse to do so: see also para 9.22, below.

F. THE NATURE OF THE COURTS' JURISDICTION AT COMMON LAW

1. The Demise and the Rise of the High Court's Inherent Jurisdiction

Prior to 1959 the High Court exercised a *parens patriae* jurisdiction over incapaci- 9.19 tated adults that was indistinguishable from the wardship jurisdiction in relation to children. Chapter 8 explains how that jurisdiction came to be revoked in 1959 to be replaced by guardianship, and how the very wide powers of the guardian came to be restricted by the time of the 1983 Act. The gap that this left in the law relating to the care of incapacitated adults was 'discovered' in 1989 when the Court of Appeal and later the House of Lords were faced with the dilemma of how to authorize an operation to sterilize a young woman with severe learning disabilities, F, in circum- stances where all agreed it was in her best interests: *Re F (Mental Patient: Sterilisation)* [1990] 2 AC 1. The solution the courts adopted was to 'rediscover' its inherent juris- diction to make declarations, in advance, that a particular course of action (if pursued) would not amount to a tortious or criminal act because the common law defence of necessity would be available.

In that original conception the jurisdiction was very limited. There was no 9.20 power to enforce a declaration made in those terms as it did no more than declare a

---

[27] *Re S (FD)* [2003] 2 FLR 292, para 48.
[28] *R (Burke) v GMC* [2006] QB 273, para 29.

particular course of action would be lawful; it did not say that another course of action would be unlawful and had no coercive effect, unlike an injunction. A question arose as to whether there was any jurisdiction to grant interim declarations: if there was not, the jurisdiction would be unworkable in emergency cases where an urgent answer was required from the court. A further question arose as to whether the jurisdiction could be exercised in other contexts than the medical, where the immediate factual scenario in which the patient would be treated was relatively predictable, such as the regulation of contact and residence where the factual scenario was less predictable and more likely to change during the lifetime of any declaration. Would a declaration continue to have its protective effect if circumstances changed?

9.21 The first of these questions was answered by the introduction of authority to make interim declarations in CPR 25.1.[29] The second was answered in *Re F (Adult Patient)*,[30] when the Court of Appeal held that the jurisdiction did extend to the making of declarations in wider social welfare contexts to protect vulnerable incapacitated adults from abuse, by relying (among others) on the State's positive duty under Article 8 of the Convention to protect vulnerable adults. The jurisdiction has since developed still further, so that the courts now exercise a jurisdiction in relation to incompetent adults which is for all practical purposes indistinguishable from its well-established *parens patriae* or wardship jurisdiction in relation to children,[31] including the restraint of publications and the making of injunctions.[32] Necessity is no longer the touchstone for the jurisdiction.[33] The jurisdiction has even been exercised where it has not yet been established that the individual lacks capacity, 'while proper inquiries are made' and while the court ascertains whether or not an adult is in fact in such a condition as to justify the court's intervention.[34] Moreover, the jurisdiction may be exercised in respect of a person who is incapacitated not by reason of an impairment of mind or brain but because of coercion or some other undue influence.[35]

2. The Inherent Jurisdiction: Limitations and Unresolved Issues

9.22 Certain limitations remain. First, the Court cannot make orders in private law 'best interests' proceedings the effect of which is to bind a public authority in relation to

---

[29] Although there was still no statutory authority for the making of an interim declaration; this has now been remedied by s 48 of the 2005 Act.

[30] [2001] Fam 38.

[31] *E v Channel Four* [2005] 2 FLR 913, para 55.

[32] *Re S (Hospital Patient)* [1996] Fam 26, 36 *per* Hale J; *In re A Local Authority (Inquiry: Restraint on Publication)* [2004] Fam 96, para 102 *per* Butler-Sloss LJ, *E v Channel Four* [2005] 2 FLR 913, para 55.

[33] *St Helens BC v PE (1) JW (2)* [2006] EWHC 3460 (Fam).

[34] *In re S (Hospital Patient: Court's Jurisdiction)* [1995] Fam 26 *per* Hale J (as she then was) esp at 33, 36; *A Local Authority v MA* [2005] EWHC 2942 (Fam), para 47.

[35] *A Local Authority v MA* [2005] EWHC 2942 (Fam).

the exercise of its public law functions.[36] Even if the Court can make a decision that it is in P's best interests, for example, to be cared for at home, it cannot make an order compelling a local authority or PCT to provide such care. Such orders can only be made in judicial review or in proceedings brought under the Human Rights Act 1998. Second, there are limitations on the matters the court may adjudicate upon. For example, the Court cannot declare that it is in P's best interests to marry (although it can declare that P has, or lacks, capacity to do so),[37] nor to engage in sexual relations (although can, once again, declare that P has, or lacks, capacity do so[38]).

A further issue, yet to be conclusively answered, is whether there are any cases   9.23
which must as a matter of *law* be authorized in advance by the Court, or whether it is only ever a matter of good practice for a doctor or hospital authority to seek a declaration in advance of carrying out treatment on, or withholding or withdrawing treatment from, an incapacitated individual. In *Airedale NHS Trust v Bland*[39] several law lords observed that in cases involving the termination of treatment for those in a permanent vegetative state, an application should be brought for a declaration 'at least for the time being and until a body of experience and practice has been built up which might obviate the need for application in every case'.[40] In cases involving decisions (including advance decisions) requiring the withholding or withdrawal of life-sustaining treatment[41] and in cases involving non-therapeutic sterilization,[42] similar 'good practice' guidance has been given, but there is no obligation in law to make any such application.[43] The sole exceptions are, first, where a doctor seeks to overturn the decision of a child's parent who objects to the giving or withdrawal of treatment, in which case there may be a duty under Article 8 to make a prior application to the Court before giving or withdrawing that treatment.[44] Second, a recent domestic law decision, *Sunderland City Council v PS*[45] suggests that decisions giving rise to a deprivation of liberty also require a Court hearing *in advance* of the decision to detain (see also para 11.36).

This will be an area for reconsideration when the 2005 Act comes into force   9.24
(and see paras 10.34 and 10.55).

---

[36] *A v A Health Authority* [2002] Fam 213.

[37] *Sheffield City Council v E* [2005] Fam 326, at paras 95–102.

[38] *X City Council v MB, NB and MAB (by his litigation friend the Official Solicitor)* [2006] EWHC 168 (Fam), [2006] 2 FLR 968; *A Local Authority v MM* [2007] EWHC 2003 (Fam).

[39] [1993] AC 789.

[40] Lord Keith at [1993] AC 789, 859.

[41] In *HE v A Hospital NHS Trust* [2003] 2 FLR 408, paras 53–4, Munby J observed that where doctors or hospital authorities entertained any doubt about the validity of a treatment refusal they should, in the public interest, not hesitate to seek the assistance of the courts and should not leave this to the patient's family.

[42] *Re F* [1990] 2 AC 1, see also Practice Note (Declaratory Proceedings: Medical and welfare decisions for adults who lack capacity), 1 May 2002 paras 3, (reported at [2002] 1 WLR 325).

[43] *R (Burke) v GMC* [2006] QB 273, paras 79–80.

[44] *Glass v United Kingdom* (2004) 39 EHRR 15.

[45] [2007] EWHC 623 (Fam).

G. CHILDREN UNDER 16

1. Key Distinctions between Adults and Children Under 16

9.25 As with adults, at common law any medical treatment of a child is an unlawful assault or battery, and any detention a false imprisonment (considered at para 11.49), in the absence of some lawful justification for it. Lawful justification may derive from the consent of a *Gillick*[46] competent child; from the common law doctrine of necessity; and from the Mental Health Act 1983. Moreover, the determination of whether treatment should be given is the 'best interests' test, in the much the same way as it applies to adults, underpinned by the statutory welfare test in s 1 of the Children Act 1989.[47]

9.26 There are two key distinctions at common law:

- The law relating to consent and the right of autonomy is very different both for children under 16 and for children aged 16 and 17.
- The jurisdiction of the High Court to authorize treatment differs for children. The High Court's inherent jurisdiction in relation to adults only applies to those who lack capacity. For children, by contrast, the High Court may authorize treatment, including treatment of a *Gillick* competent child, in its wardship or inherent jurisdiction or under the Children Act 1989.

2. Consent and the Right of Autonomy

9.27 The law of consent in relation to children under 16 has the following special features.

(a) 'Competence' and the Presumption of 'Incompetence'

9.28 For children under 16 there is no presumption of capacity, instead there is a presumption of 'incompetence'. To give a valid consent to treatment it must be established that a child has sufficient understanding and intelligence to enable him to understand the nature and implications of the proposed treatment (*Gillick* competence, after the decision of the House of Lords in *Gillick v West Norfolk and Wisbech Health Authority*[48]).

(b) Parental Rights and the Right of Autonomy

9.29 At common law, a competent child under 16 does not enjoy the right of self-determination or autonomy (discussed at paras 9.03) to the same extent as an adult. A child's parent or a person with parental responsibility (such as a local authority in whose care a child has been placed under the Children Act 1989) or the High Court (below) may give or refuse consent to medical treatment on the child's behalf, whether the child is competent or not. A parental consent to medical treatment will

---

[46] After the House of Lords decision in *Gillick v West Norfolk and Wisbech Health Authority* [1986] AC 112.

[47] *Portsmouth NHS Hospitals Trust v Wyatt* [2005] 1 WLR 3995, para 87; *An NHS Trust v MB* [2006] 2 FLR 319, para 16.

[48] [1986] AC 112.

override a competent child's refusal of consent,[49] although the circumstances in which that may lawfully happen as a child grows in maturity will dwindle, bearing in mind that parental responsibility only exists for the benefit of the child and is justified only in so far as it enables the parent to perform his duties towards the child.[50]

A competent child may, however, give a valid consent to treatment, which over-   9.30
rides a parental refusal of consent.[51]

3. The Jurisdiction of the High Court in Relation to Children Under 16

There are several options for engaging the jurisdiction of the High Court in deci-   9.31
sions concerning the treatment of children. What follows is a brief summary.

(a) *The High Court's Wardship Jurisdiction*
The High Court in its wardship jurisdiction may make treatment decisions on   9.32
behalf of children under the age of 18, although in doing so the High Court is effectively exercising its inherent jurisdiction in relation to such children (considered
below): wardship provides the machinery through which the inherent jurisdiction is
exercised.[52] The wardship jurisdiction may not be exercised when the child is the
subject of a care order under the Children Act 1989 (s 100(2) of the Children Act
1989). The proper application in such a case is to seek the leave of the High Court
under s 100(3) of the 1989 Act to exercise its inherent jurisdiction.[53]

(b) *The High Court's Inherent* 'Parens Patriae' *Jurisdiction*
The High Court in its inherent *parens patriae* jurisdiction may make treatment deci-   9.33
sions on behalf of all children, whether competent or otherwise, and may override
treatment consents and refusals made by a child or person with parental responsibility, if it considers it to be in the child's 'best interests'.[54]

The inherent jurisdiction may be exercised whether the child is a ward of court   9.34
or not.[55] The jurisdiction is theoretically without limit, although it cannot be exercised so as to compel a public authority to exercise its public law functions.[56] This
jurisdiction encompasses but is wider than the Court's inherent jurisdiction in relation to adults; in particular, it may be exercised in relation to competent children.

---

[49] *Re W (A Minor)(Medical Treatment: Court's jurisdiction)* [1993] 1 Fam 64, 78D–F.
[50] *R (Axon) v Secretary of State for Health (Family Planning Association intervening)* [2006] 1 QB 569, paras 129–130.
[51] *Gillick v West Norfolk and Wisbech Health Authority* [1986] AC 112, *Re W (A Minor)(Medical Treatment: Court's jurisdiction)* [1993] 1 Fam 64.
[52] *Re W (A Minor)(Medical Treatment: Court's jurisdiction)* [1993] 1 Fam 64, 85A.
[53] Ibid, [1993] 1 Fam 64, 73F, 84H.
[54] Ibid, [1993] 1 Fam 64, 83G–H.
[55] Ibid, [1993] 1 Fam 64, 73F.
[56] Ibid, [1993] 1 Fam 64, 85C; *A v Liverpool City Council* [1982] AC 363.

(c) *Courts' Jurisdiction to Make 'Specific Issue' Orders under s 8 Children Act 1989*

9.35   The courts have jurisdiction under s 8 of the Children Act 1989 to make a 'specific issue order' for the purpose of determining a specific question which has arisen, or which may arise, in connection with any aspect of parental responsibility for a child, which may include any question as to the child's medical treatment. This jurisdiction may not be exercised where the child is the subject of a care order under the 1989 Act (s 9(1)); the appropriate application is to seek leave under s 100(3) to invoke the High Court's inherent jurisdiction.

H. CHILDREN AGED 16 AND 17

9.36   The principles outlined at para 9.25ff in relation to children under 16 also apply to children aged 16 or 17, but with the following modifications. Key among these is the statutory presumption of capacity in s 8 of the Family Law Reform Act 1969. Although at common law the presumption of incompetence applies to all children, once a child reaches the age of 16, s 8 of the 1969 Act creates a rebuttable presumption that he is capable of giving a valid consent to 'any surgical, medical or dental treatment'. In determining whether a child lacks capacity the same test is applied as for adults, namely that in *Re MB*, considered at para 9.06ff.

9.37   Section 8 has certain limitations, however.

- First, 'any surgical, medical or dental treatment' does not include (for example) the donation of organs or the giving of blood.[57]

- Second, s 8 only has the effect of allowing a capable child aged 16 or 17 to give a valid consent to treatment. A capable child who refuses to consent to treatment may still be given treatment with the consent of a person with parental responsibility or of the High Court in its jurisdiction relating to children; in this respect, a child of 16 or 17 is in the same position as a child under 16 (above para 9.29), although a refusal of consent is nevertheless a very important consideration in making clinical judgments and for parents and the court in deciding whether themselves to give consent: *Re W (A Minor)(Medical Treatment: Court's Jurisdiction).*[58]

9.38   There are powerful arguments that to override a competent child's refusal of treatment in a given case would violate his right to respect for private life under Article 8 (for which see para 6.121). That is not to say, however, that the continuation in existence of the right of a person with parental responsibility, or the power of the High Court, to override a capable child's decision in an appropriate case is a breach of Article 8. The right of autonomy is not absolute, even for capable adults, at least as far as the Convention is concerned. The Convention permits a capable adult's

---

[57] Ibid, [1993] 1 Fam 64, 78F.

[58] Ibid, [1993] 1 Fam 64, 83G–H, 84A–B (Lord Donaldson MR); 86B, 87G–H (Balcombe LJ); see also *R (Axon) v Secretary of State for Health (Family Planning Association intervening)* [2006] 1 QB 569, paras 129–130.

refusal of treatment—even treatment, including force-feeding, which reaches the necessary threshold of severity for the purposes of Article 3—to be overturned where that is considered a 'medical necessity' (see para 6.121).

As we will see in the next chapter, the 2005 Act applies to children of 16 or 17 as it does to adults, with some exceptions (para 10.03ff). An interesting question arises whether the 2005 Act has displaced the common law rules and s 8 needs to be reconsidered, particularly in light of the statutory presumption of capacity in s 1(2) of the 2005 Act. This is considered at para 10.04ff. 9.39

10

CARE AND TREATMENT WITHOUT DETENTION UNDER THE MENTAL CAPACITY ACT 2005

A.	Key Features	10.00
B.	Who the Act Applies To	10.01
C.	Children Aged 16 or 17	10.03
D.	Children Under 16	10.07
E.	The Principles: s 1	10.10
F.	Capacity: ss 2 and 3	10.11
G.	Best Interests: s 4	10.15
H.	The Hierarchy of Substituted Decision-making	10.18
I.	Advance Decisions to Refuse Treatment	10.20
	1. 'Advance Directives' to Refuse Treatment at Common Law	10.20
	2. Advance Decisions to Refuse Treatment Under the 2005 Act	10.21
J.	Lasting Powers of Attorney	10.35
	1. Nature and Effect of a Lasting Power of Attorney	10.35
	2. The Donee's Powers	10.38
	3. Limitations on the Donee's Powers	10.43
	4. Making a Lasting Power of Attorney	10.44
	5. Revocation of an LPA	10.48
	6. Jurisdiction of the Court of Protection in Relation to Lasting Powers of Attorney	10.50
K.	Personal Welfare Decisions by the Court of Protection	10.54
	1. The Court's Jurisdiction in Personal Welfare Matters	10.54
	2. Limitations of the Court's Jurisdiction in Personal Welfare Matters	10.56
L.	Court-appointed Deputies	10.57
M.	Acts in Connection with Care and Treatment: s 5	10.59
N.	Life-sustaining etc Treatment	10.61
	1. Special Status for Life-sustaining etc Treatment	10.61
	2. Restrictions on Acts Intended to End Life	10.62
O.	Restraint and the Use of Force	10.66

P.	Deprivations of Liberty	10.69
Q.	Excluded Decisions	10.70
	1. Family Relationships	10.70
	2. Mental Health Matters: Interface between the	
	Treatment Provisions of the 2005 Act and the 1983 Act	10.71
	3. Voting	10.74
	4. Medical Research	10.75
R.	Ill-treatment or Neglect	10.76
S.	Independent Mental Capacity Advocates (IMCAs)	10.78
	1. Appointment of IMCAs	10.79
	2. Functions of IMCAs	10.86
T.	The Code of Practice Under the 2005 Act	10.89
	1. Lord Chancellor's Duty to Prepare and Issue	
	Codes of Practice	10.89
	2. Duty to Have Regard to the Code of Practice	10.92
	3. Relevance of the Code of Practice in Criminal or	
	Civil Proceedings	10.93

A. KEY FEATURES

10.00
- The 2005 Act creates a statutory framework for the making, materially, of personal welfare decisions on behalf of incapacitated adults, including care and treatment.

- The 2005 Act also applies to children aged 16 or 17, with some modifications, and certain provisions apply to children under 16.

- The 2005 Act effectively codifies the common law rights of bodily integrity and autonomy and the principles of capacity and best interests, although existing common law principles continue to operate where the 2005 Act does not apply.

- The 2005 Act creates a new hierarchy of mechanisms for substituted decision-making for incapacitated individuals, in descending order: advance decisions refusing treatment; decisions of donees of lasting powers of attorney (LPAs); personal welfare decisions of the Court of Protection; decisions of court-appointed deputies; and decisions made by individuals providing care and treatment where no other mechanism for substituted decision-making is in place.

- Special provision is made for life-saving treatment, treatment requiring restraint and the use of force, deprivations of liberty, mental health treatment of patients falling within Part 4 or 4A of the 1983 Act, certain excluded decisions (marriage, adoption etc.), medical research and the criminal offence of ill-treatment or neglect of an incapacitated individual.

- The right to an Independent Mental Capacity Advocates (IMCA) for certain categories of care and treatment is introduced.

- In so far as the 2005 Act governs personal welfare decisions not involving detention, it is not materially affected by the 2007 Act.

B. WHO THE ACT APPLIES TO

The 2005 Act applies to any incapacitated individual, P, aged 16 or over and intro- 10.01
duces a new framework for substituted decision-making both as regards personal
welfare matters and property and affairs.

The Act applies to children under 16 and children aged 16 or 17 with the modifi- 10.02
cations considered below.

C. CHILDREN AGED 16 OR 17

The common law rules relating to the treatment of children prior to the 2005 Act 10.03
coming into force are considered at para 9.25ff above. The 2005 Act applies to children aged 16 or 17 as much as it applies to adults, with the following modifications:[1]

- A child aged 16 or 17 may not make a lasting power of attorney (s 9(2)(c)).

- A child aged 16 or 17 may not make an advance decision refusing medical
  treatment (s 24(1)).

It would follow that for 16 or 17 year olds, the statutory presumption of capacity 10.04
in s 8 of the Family Law Reform Act 1969 needs to be reconsidered in the light of
the statutory presumption of capacity in s 1(2) of the 2005 Act, which has none of
the limitations of s 8 (see para 9.37). A capable child of 16 or 17 should now also be
able to give a valid consent to all matters including (for example) the donation of
organs or the giving of blood, which was held not to fall within the meaning of 'any
surgical, medical or dental treatment' in *Re W (A Minor)(Medical Treatment: Court's
jurisdiction)*.[2]

It may also be the case that the common law, in particular the rule that a capable 10.05
child's decision may be overridden by a person with parental responsibility or the
High Court in its jurisdiction in relation to children, has now been displaced by the
comprehensive statutory regime of the 2005 Act. A capable 16 or 17 year old might
now enjoy the right of autonomy in the same way as an adult. However, it would
appear to be implicit from new s 131(2) to (5) of the 1983 Act (introduced by the
2007 Act) (above para 4.44) that the power of a person with parental responsibility
to give consent on behalf of a capable 16 or 17 year old has *not* been displaced by
the 2005 Act: if it had been, these provisions would be unnecessary. By the same
token, there must be some question as to whether the provisions of the 2005 Act
displace the common law right of a parent to give or refuse consent on behalf of an

---

[1] A child aged 16 or 17 may not be made subject to the urgent or standard authorization procedure in
Sch A1 (Sch A1, para 13). This is considered in the Chapter on detention under the 2005 Act, see paras 12.15,
15.61.

[2] [1993] 1 Fam 64, 78F.

incapable child, although if they have not been displaced in relation to capable children it is unlikely that they have been in relation to incapable children. These points will nevertheless require resolution.

10.06   See also paras 4.44, 9.36, 11.50ff, 15.58ff.

D. CHILDREN UNDER 16

10.07   Section 2(5) provides that 'No power which a person, D, may exercise under the Act in relation to a person who lacks capacity or where D reasonably thinks that a person lacks capacity is exercisable in relation to a person under 16'.[3] This effectively excludes all the provisions in the 2005 Act authorizing the taking of decisions on behalf of children under 16 in personal welfare matters. It does not exclude the principles in s 1, the test of capacity in s 2 and 3 or the 'best interests' test in s 4, nor does it exclude the criminal offence in s 44 (ill-treatment or neglect). The effect is that the existing common law rules governing the treatment of children (considered in para 9.25ff) continue to apply, with certain exceptions.

10.08   First, to the extent the 2005 Act does apply it would logically follow that the common law presumption that a child under 16 is 'incompetent' to consent to medical treatment has been reversed by s 1(2) of the 2005 Act. Second, it would follow that the statutory concept and meaning of 'capacity' in ss 2 and 3 of the 2005 Act has replaced that of 'competence'. This is plainly not what the government thinks it means, however: see the 2005 Act Code of Practice, para 12.12. Moreover, the concept of 'competence' is expressly preserved in relation to the treatment of children under 16 on SCT under Part 4A of the 1983 Act, introduced by the 2007 Act. This point will also require resolution.

10.09   Please refer also to paras 4.44, 11.49ff, 15.58ff.

E. THE PRINCIPLES: s 1

10.10   Section 1 sets out five principles that apply for the purposes of the 2005 Act:

- A person must be assumed to have capacity unless it is established that he lacks capacity.
- A person is not to be treated as unable to make a decision unless all practicable steps to help him to do so have been taken without success.
- A person is not to be treated as unable to make a decision merely because he makes an unwise decision.
- An act done, or decision made, under this Act for or on behalf of a person who lacks capacity must be done, or made, in his best interests.

---

[3] s 2(6) provides that s 2(5) is subject to s 18(3) in relation to the powers of the Court of Protection in relation to property and affairs.

- Before the act is done, or the decision is made, regard must be had to whether the purpose for which it is needed can be as effectively achieved in a way that is less restrictive of the person's rights and freedom of action.

F. CAPACITY: ss 2 AND 3

Sections 1–3 of the 2005 Act describe the circumstances in which an individual, P, 10.11 may be found to lack capacity, and may be summarized as follows:

- P is assumed to have capacity unless it is established, on the balance of probabilities, that he lacks capacity (s 1(2) and s 2(4)). This reflects the position at common law (above, para 9.08), subject to the observations made in relation to children at paras 10.04 and 10.08.

- P lacks capacity in relation to a matter if he is unable to make a decision for himself in relation to the matter because of an impairment of, or a disturbance in the functioning of, the mind or brain (s 2(1)), whether temporary or permanent (s 2(2)). This is the common law test propounded in *Re MB* (above, para 9.08) and therefore includes such conditions as needle phobia which may temporarily deprive a person of capacity to refuse life-saving medical treatment.

- P is unable to make a decision for himself if he is unable (a) to understand the information relevant to the decision, including information about the reasonably foreseeable consequences of deciding one way or another or of failing to make the decision, (b) to retain that information, (c) to use or weigh that information as part of the process of making the decision, or (d) to communicate his decision (whether by talking, using sign language or any other means) (s 3(1) and 3(4)). This broadly reflects the common law test (above, para 9.08), including a requirement that P be able to communicate his decision. There is no mention, however, that P might be deprived of capacity if he does not *believe* the treatment information he is given by reason of mental disorder (above, para 9.08), although I have little doubt that this requirement will be read into the requirement of 'understanding' or 'using' that information: indeed, this is the conclusion reached by Munby J in *A Local Authority v MM* [2007] EWHC 2003 (Fam), at para 81.

- P is not to be taken to lack capacity by reason only of the fact (a) the decision is an unwise one (s 1(4)), (b) because of his age or appearance or any condition of his, or an aspect of his behaviour, which might lead others to make unjustified assumptions about his capacity (s 2(3)), or (c) the fact that he is able to retain the information relevant to a decision for a short period only (s 3(3)).

- P is not to be taken to lack capacity unless all practicable steps to help him have been taken without success (s 1(3)) and is not to be taken as unable to understand the information relevant to a decision if he is able to understand an explanation of it given to him in a way that is appropriate to the circumstances (using simple language, visual aids or any other means) (s 3(2)).

10.12   These provisions effectively codify the existing common law rules in relation to capacity, discussed above, with certain added components. The following short observations may be made.

10.13   First, although not expressly stated as such, it is clear that P need only have such capacity as is commensurate with the gravity of the decision to be taken, as any assessment of capacity is expressly by reference to 'a matter' (s 2(1)). The position therefore remains as at common law (above para 9.09) that P may have capacity to make some decisions, but not others: see also the 2005 Act Code of Practice, para 4.4 and *A Local Authority v MM* [2007] EWHC 2003 (Fam), paras 64–75.

10.14   Second, the statutory test specifically proscribes any discriminatory assumptions being made about a person's capacity (or lack of it) by reason of their age, appearance, condition, or behaviour and requires that decisions depriving P of capacity are not taken unless all practicable steps have been taken to help him, including the use of communication aids. These non-discrimination requirements do not feature in the common law case-law in relation to capacity,[4] although they can be derived from other legal principles such as the non-discrimination duty in Article 14 of the Convention,[5] the positive obligations under Article 8 to take measures to enable a disabled person to participate in decisions about his life[6] and the requirement upon a service provider (which would include, say, a hospital) not to discriminate in the provision of goods and services under Part III Disability Discrimination Act 1995 (the 1995 Act), which includes the duty to make 'reasonable adjustments' under s 21, and the specific and general non-discrimination duties upon public authorities in s 21B and s 49A of the 1995 Act. Nevertheless, the express requirements in the 2005 Act are important and welcome.

G. BEST INTERESTS: s 4

10.15   Section 1(5) of the 2005 Act states that an act done, or decision made, under the Act for or on behalf of a person who lacks capacity must be done, or made, in his best interests. The Act does not seek to define 'best interests', but (as at common law) it clearly encompasses matters way beyond the purely medical, as section 4(2) requires the person making the determination of best interests (D) to

---

[4] There is some reference in the case law on capacity to litigate that a person must be able to make a decision with appropriate advice, *Masterman-Lister v Brutton & Co (Nos 1 and 2)* [2003] 1 WLR 1511, which may be taken to apply to all decisions, not simply decisions relating to litigation: see *A Local Authority v MM* [2007] EWHC 2003 (Fam), paras 71–2.

[5] It may be a breach of article 14 not to recognize differences and to make appropriate adjustments to compensate for a person's disability: see *Thlimmenos v Greece* (2001) 31 EHRR 411. These principles are reinforced by the provisions of the UN Convention on the rights of Persons with Disabilities, opened for signature on 30 March 2007 (see <http://www.un.org/disabilities/convention/>).

[6] See para 1.04 and *A & B v East Sussex (Manual Handling)* [2003] EWHC 167 (Admin) paras 75, 93*, 99, 102, 113, 114.

'consider all the relevant circumstances'. Section 4(2) also enjoins D to take a number of steps, namely:

- To consider whether it is likely that P will at some time have capacity in relation to the matter in question and, if it appears likely that he will, when that is likely to be (s 4(3)). The Act does not say what D should do if he decides P will have capacity in future, but the only logical inference is that D should, if possible, wait until such time as P does have capacity to enable him to make the decision for himself (and as the 2005 Act Code of Practice makes clear at para 5.25).

- So far as reasonably practicable, to permit and encourage the person to participate, or to improve his ability to participate, as fully as possible in any act done for him and any decision affecting him (s 4(4)).

- To consider, so far as is reasonably ascertainable, (a) P's past and present wishes and feelings (and, in particular, any relevant written statement made by him when he had capacity), (b) the beliefs and values that would be likely to influence his decision if he had capacity, and (c) the other factors that he would be likely to consider if he were able to do so (s 4(6)). This suggests that the 'best interests' decision is not a purely objective one, but a subjective one, seeking to reflect what P would wish if he had capacity to take the decision himself, by contrast with the common law position (above, para 9.17).[7]

- To take into account, if it is practicable and appropriate to consult them, the views of (a) anyone named by the person as someone to be consulted on the matter in question or on matters of that kind, (b) anyone engaged in caring for the person or interested in his welfare, (c) any donee of a lasting power of attorney granted by the person, and (d) any deputy appointed for the person by the court, as to what would be in the person's best interests and, in particular, as to the matters mentioned in s 4(6) (s 4(7)). This consultation duty again reinforces the notion that the 'best interests' decision should, so far as possible, reflect what P would have chosen for himself.

- Before the act is done, or the decision is made, to have regard to whether the purpose for which it is needed can be as effectively achieved in a way that is less restrictive of the person's rights and freedom of action (s 1(6)). This is, in effect, a 'proportionality' requirement, mandated in any event by the Convention and the Human Rights Act 1998 (and see para 6.131).

- Where the determination relates to life-sustaining treatment he must not, in considering whether the treatment is in the best interests of the person concerned, be motivated by a desire to bring about his death (s 4(5)). This is considered further below, at para 10.61.

These steps are based on the proposals made by the Law Commission in its 1995 report on Mental Incapacity.[8]   10.16

The Act does not provide a complete answer to the issues highlighted at para 9.16 above. 'Best interests' still has no definition; it appears that 'best interests' is a   10.17

---

[7] See also the Code of Practice, para 5.41.
[8] Law Commission *Mental Incapacity* (Law Com No 231, 1995) paras 3.26–3.27.

subjective, rather than objective, decision; and what is 'best' may mean either the best of all possible alternatives or just of the available alternatives. Case-law alone will resolve these issues.

H. THE HIERARCHY OF SUBSTITUTED DECISION-MAKING

10.18　The 2005 Act creates a hierarchy of five, separate substitute decision-making mechanisms by which care and treatment of an incapacitated individual, P (not including detention, for which see Chapter 11) may be rendered lawful. The hierarchy reflects the over-arching principle of the Act that the wishes of the individual and his right of autonomy are to be respected to the greatest extent possible, even once he has lost capacity. These will be considered in descending order in the hierarchy.

10.19　First, the Act codifies the binding legal effect at common law of 'advance decisions', decisions refusing treatment and made by P before he lost capacity, which by law must be complied with after, and notwithstanding, he loses capacity (ss 24–6). An advance decision that is valid and applicable will trump all other decision-making mechanisms (with two exceptions, see below, paras 10.23 and 10.24). Second, the Act empowers competent adults, for the first time, to make 'lasting powers of attorney' (LPAs) in relation to personal welfare decisions, by which a competent adult may appoint a person (a 'donee') to take decisions about their personal welfare in the event that they lose capacity, including the giving or refusing of consent to treatment (ss 9–14). A valid decision of a donee of an LPA will trump all other decision-making processes except an advance decision refusing treatment (subject to the exceptions considered at paras 10.23 and 10.24). Third, the Court of Protection may, on an application, by order make decisions on P's behalf in relation to his personal welfare (ss 16 or 17). The Court of Protection may not make decisions that conflict with a valid advance decision or the valid decision of a donee, although it can determine the validity of any such decision. Fourth, the Court of Protection may instead appoint a deputy to make decisions on P's behalf (ss 16, 19–20). A deputy may not take a decision which conflicts with a valid advance decision or decision of a donee. Fifth, and last, where no other decision-making mechanism is in place, a person (D) may do 'an act in connection with the care or treatment' of P without incurring any liability if he does so in the reasonable belief that it is in P's best interests. D may not, however, do an act which conflicts with a valid decision of a donee or deputy, nor with any advance decision that is valid and applicable, other than in emergency life-saving situations pending the decision of a court.

I. ADVANCE DECISIONS TO REFUSE TREATMENT

1. 'Advance Directives' to Refuse Treatment at Common Law

10.20　Consistent with the right of autonomy, at common law a competent adult patient's anticipatory refusal of consent (a 'living will' or 'advance directive') remains binding and effective notwithstanding that the patient has subsequently lost capacity. There are no formal requirements for an advance directive, which may be made orally or in writing, nor are there any age limits as to who may make an advance directive (by contrast with the position under the 2005 Act). However, once it is established that P lacks capacity, the presumption in favour of life requires that the existence and continuing validity of an advance directive in relation to the decision in question must be established by clear and convincing evidence if it is to be given effect.[9]

2. Advance Decisions to Refuse Treatment Under the 2005 Act

(a) Nature, Effect, and Limitations of Advance Decisions

The 2005 Act codifies the common law principle that a competent patient may make binding treatment decisions which must be respected after he loses capacity, at least so far as adults are concerned. Children under 16 are excluded from the relevant provisions of the Act by s 2(5) and those between 16 or 17 cannot make advance decisions under the 2005 Act (s 24(1)).   10.21

Section 24(1) defines 'advance decision' as 'a decision made by a person ('P'), after he has reached 18 and when he has capacity to do so, that if (a) at a later time and in such circumstances as he may specify, a specified treatment is proposed to be carried out or continued by a person providing health care for him, and (b) at that time he lacks capacity to consent to the carrying out or continuation of the treatment, the specified treatment is not to be carried out or continued'. Section 26(1) then provides that 'if P has made an advance decision which is (a) valid and (b) applicable to a treatment, the decision has effect as if he had made it, and had had capacity to make it, at the time when the question arises whether the treatment should be carried out or continued'.   10.22

An advance decision which is valid and applicable therefore takes precedence over all other decision-making mechanisms under the 2005 Act once its maker has lost capacity. It is treated as if it were a decision made by a competent individual (s 26(1)) and must, accordingly, be respected by all other decision-makers, including any court-appointed deputy and the Court of Protection, although nothing in an apparent advance decision stops a person providing life-sustaining treatment or doing any act he reasonably believes to be necessary to prevent a serious deterioration in P's condition while a decision as respects any relevant issue is sought from the court (s 26(5)) (the first of the exceptions referred to at para 10.19: see further, para 10.26). Once the 2007 Act comes into force, an advance decision will also operate: 10.23

- to veto P's detention under Sch A1 of the 2005 Act (see paras 18–20 of Sch A1, para 12.26 below), although (like a capable refusal) it cannot prevent P's detention under the 1983 Act;

- to veto the administration of ECT for a patient 'liable to be detained' under the 1983 Act, (s 58A(5)(c) of the 1983 Act, see para 10.32 below);

---

[9] *HE v A Hospital NHS Trust* [2003] 2 FLR 408; *Re T (Adult: Refusal of Treatment)* [1993] Fam 95; *Re AK (Medical Treatment: Consent)* [2001] 1 FLR 129.

- to veto treatment that could otherwise be administered to a patient released on supervised community discharge (SCT) under s 17A, (see para 10.33 below).

10.24   The donee of a LPA may not make a decision which conflicts with an advance decision (s 11(7)(b)), unless it is one created after the advance decision was made and conferred authority on the donee to give or refuse consent to the treatment to which the advance decision relates (s 25(2)(b)). This is the second exception referred to at para 10.19: see further, para 10.28.

10.25   As regards a person, D, who does (or proposes to do) an 'act in connection with care or treatment' under s 5, the effect of an advance decision is provided for by ss 25(1) and ss 26(1) and (2). These rather tortuous provisions may be translated as follows. A person (D) who proposes to do an 'act in connection with care and treatment' to P in the reasonable belief that P lacks capacity and that it will be in P's best interests for that act to be done does not incur any tortious or criminal liability in respect of that act (s 5(2)), *unless* it conflicts with an advance decision that he is satisfied exists and which is 'valid' and 'applicable' (s 25(1) and s 26(1)). If D goes ahead with the treatment in those circumstances he will have no defence to a civil action for trespass and battery. On the other hand, if D respects an advance decision he reasonably believes exists which is valid and applicable to the treatment in question, he will not incur any liability for the consequences of withholding or withdrawing the treatment (s 26(2)), whatever the consequences, including P's death or serious disability.

10.26   If there is any question as to the validity or applicability of an advance decision, D may provide life-sustaining treatment or do any act he reasonably believes to be necessary to prevent a serious deterioration in P's condition while a decision is sought from the court (s 26(5)). Where P's death or serious disability is the likely outcome of respecting the advance decision D may be well-advised to seek the court's guidance in any event, particularly if there is any dispute among family members as to whether treatment should be given (see para 10.34 and para 9.23).

(b) *'Valid'*

10.27   An advance decision is not 'valid' if P has withdrawn the decision at a time when he had capacity to do so or has done anything else clearly inconsistent with the advance decision remaining his fixed decision (s 25(2)(a) and (c)). A decision may be withdrawn or altered at any time when P has capacity to do so (s 24(3)), whether in writing or otherwise (s 24(4) and (5)). If P withdraws the advance decision after he has lost capacity that may be something 'clearly inconsistent with the advance decision remaining his fixed decision'.

10.28   An advance decision is also not valid if it conflicts with a LPA created after the advance decision was made and which conferred authority on the donee to give or refuse consent to the treatment to which the advance decision relates (s 25(2)(b)). This is the only circumstance in which an advance decision which is otherwise valid and applicable to the treatment in question can be overridden by a donee under an LPA (s 11(7)(b)).

(c) 'Applicable to the Treatment in Question'

The advance decision is not 'applicable to the treatment in question' in any of the   10.29
following situations. First, and unsurprisingly, if at the material time P has capacity
to give or refuse consent to it (s 25(3)). Second, if that treatment is not the treatment
specified in the advance decision (s 25(4)(a)). Third, if any circumstances specified
in the advance decision are absent (s 25(4)(a)). Fourth, if there are reasonable
grounds for believing that circumstances exist which P did not anticipate at the time
of the advance decision and which would have affected his decision had he anticipated them (s 25(4)(a)). Additional requirements apply in relation to life-sustaining
treatment (below).

(d) Life-sustaining Treatment etc

In the case of life-sustaining treatment, an advance decision will not be 'applicable   10.30
to the treatment' unless two further conditions are met. First, the decision is verified
by a statement by P to the effect that it is to apply to that treatment even if life is at
risk (s 25(5)(a). Second, the decision and statement must be in writing, signed by P
or by another person in P's presence and by P's direction, the signature is made or
acknowledged by P in the presence of a witness, and the witness signs it, or acknowledges his signature, in P's presence (s 25(5)(b) and 25(6)).

As already noted, nothing in an apparently valid advance decision stops a person   10.31
providing life-sustaining treatment or doing any act he reasonably believes to be
necessary to prevent a serious deterioration in P's condition while a decision as
respects any relevant issue is sought from the court (s 26(5)) (see also 10.61).

(e) Treatment Falling Within the Mental Health Act 1983

An advance decision will generally have no effect in relation to treatment adminis-   10.32
tered to a patient who is 'liable to be detained' under the 1983 Act, as treatment may
be imposed upon such patients under Part 4 of the Act notwithstanding the patient's
consent or lack of it. An exception to this is treatment falling within new s 58A of
the 1983 Act, namely ECT, which cannot now be administered (other than in an
emergency under s 62(1A)) unless a SOAD has certified, among other matters, that
the treatment does not conflict with an advance decision which the SOAD is satisfied is valid and applicable (s 58A(5)(c) of the 1983 Act) (see para 6.51). For other
forms of treatment, an advance decision will be a matter that should be taken into
account and given proper weight, in the same way as a competent refusal of treatment (see para 6.01).

Treatment may not be administered to a community patient on SCT under new   10.33
Part 4A of the 1983 Act if it conflicts with an advance decision which is valid and
applicable, other than emergency treatment under s 64G of the 1983 Act. This
applies equally whether the purported source of 'authority to treat' is s 64D (by
virtue of s 64D(6)) or s 64C (treatment with the consent of a donee or deputy or the
Court of Protection), because such substituted consent is subject to any contrary
advance decision which is valid and applicable (ss 11(7) and 26(1) of the 2005 Act)
(see paras 6.75 and 6.78).

(f) Resolving Disputes About Advance Decisions

10.34 The Court may make a declaration as to whether an advance decision is valid or applicable to treatment (s 26(4)), and doctors and hospital authorities may be well-advised to seek the Court's guidance where there is any question about the validity or applicability of an advance decision, as at common law,[10] although there is no *requirement* under the 2005 Act that an application be made (see para 9.23).

J. LASTING POWERS OF ATTORNEY

1. Nature and Effect of a Lasting Power of Attorney

10.35 A lasting power of attorney is a power of attorney by which the donor, P, confers on the donee or donees authority to make decisions about matters concerning his personal welfare or his property and affairs[11] (s 9(1)). An LPA in personal welfare decisions can only be made when P is over the age of 18 and has capacity to execute it (s 9(2)(c)) but does not come into effect until after the document has been registered with the Public Guardian and P loses, or the donee reasonably believes that P has lost, capacity in relation to the matter in question[12] (s 11(7)(a)).

10.36 A donee who acts in purported exercise of the power conferred by the LPA in good faith will not incur any liability (s 14(2)) and may, in any event, be relieved of any liability he does incur by the Court of Protection under s 23(3)(d).

10.37 LPAs in relation to personal welfare decisions are a wholly new creation of the 2005 Act and represent (along with the provisions governing the Court of Protection and court-appointed deputies) a fundamental departure from the common law position that no person can give or refuse consent on behalf of another adult (see para 9.11).

2. The Donee's Powers

10.38 The donee of a valid LPA may give or refuse consent to any act in connection with care or treatment, including the carrying out or continuation of treatment by a person providing health care for P (s 11(7)(c)), subject to any conditions or restrictions contained in the LPA (s 9(4)(b) and 11(8)(b)) and in accordance with s 1 (principles) and s 4 (best interests) (s 9(4)(a)).

10.39 A donee will also have certain functions under the 1983 Act once the 2007 Act comes into force. A donee may *refuse* (but not give) consent to P being given ECT when detained under the 1983 Act under s 58A(5)(c)(ii) (para 6.51) and may give

---

[10] In *HE v A Hospital NHS Trust* [2003] 2 FLR 408, paras 53–4, Munby J observed that where doctors or hospital authorities entertained any doubt about the validity of a treatment refusal they should, in the public interest, not hesitate to seek the assistance of the courts and should not leave this to the patient's family.

[11] We are concerned here only with those made in relation to personal welfare.

[12] This is by contrast with lasting powers of attorney in relation to property and affairs, which may be expressed to apply whether P has capacity or not.

(s 64C(2)(b)) or refuse (s 64D(6)) consent to other medical treatment under new Part 4A of the 1983 Act, where P is a community patient on SCT, see paras 6.74 and 6.77.

When the 2007 Act comes into force the donee will also exercise a number of important functions in relation to the making and review of standard authorizations for detention under Sch A1. A 'standard authorization' cannot be made if a donee refuses (Sch A1, paras 18–20, below para 12.26). Moreover, the donee may give consent to P's detention under Sch A1 where P would otherwise be 'ineligible' for detention (see paras 15.15 and 15.23). A donee may also have a number of functions as P's representative under Sch A1, considered at para 13.29ff. 10.40

Matters concerning P's 'personal welfare' that the donee has authority to make decisions about are not specified in the Act but will include those in respect of which the Court of Protection may make orders under s 17 (subject to the limitations referred to at paras 10.40 above), namely: 10.41

- deciding where P is to live;
- deciding what contact, if any, P is to have with any specified persons;
- making an order prohibiting a named person from having contact with P;
- giving or refusing consent to the carrying out or continuation of a treatment by a person providing health care for P;
- giving a direction that a person responsible for P's health care allow a different person to take over that responsibility.

Additional matters might include the following (see the 2005 Act Code of Practice, para 7.21) 10.42

- the donor's day-to-day care, including diet and dress;
- assessments for and provision of community care services;
- whether the donor should take part in social activities, leisure activities, education, or training;
- the donor's personal correspondence and papers;
- rights of access to personal information about the donor;
- complaints about the donor's care or treatment.

3. Limitations on the Donee's Powers

The donee's powers are subject to the following limitations: 10.43

- The donee may give or refuse consent to the carrying out of life-sustaining treatment only where the LPA contains express provision to that effect (s 11(8)(a)).
- The donee's authority is subject to any advance decision that is valid and applicable to the treatment in question (s 11(7)), unless the LPA was made after the advance decision and conferred authority on the donee to give or refuse consent to the treatment to which the advance decision relates (s 25(2)(b)).

- The donee may only use, or authorize the use, of restraint (reasonable force or a restriction on P's liberty of movement) if three conditions are met: first, P lacks (or the donee reasonably believes P lacks) capacity in relation to the matter in question; second, the donee reasonably believes that it is necessary to do the act in order to prevent harm to P; and, third, the act is a proportionate response to the likelihood of P's suffering harm and the seriousness of that harm (s 11(4)). This is considered in more detail at para 10.66 below.

- A donee of an LPA may not detain, or authorize the detention, of P (para 10.69). After the 2007 Act comes into force, he will only be able to authorize detention in accordance with the provisions of either (a) Sch A1, by virtue of new s 4A(1)) (above, para 10.40); or (b) s 4B (deprivation of liberty necessary for life-sustaining treatment, see para 11.45 below).

- A donee may not give, or authorize to be given, to P treatment for mental disorder that is regulated by Part 4 of the 1983 Act (s 28) (see para 10.71 and Chapter 15). Once the 2007 Act comes into force, the donee may *refuse* (but not give) consent to P being given ECT when detained under the 1983 Act under s 58A(5)(c)(ii) (see para 6.51) and may give (s 64C(2)(b)) or refuse (s 64D(6)) consent to other medical treatment under new Part 4A of the 1983 Act, where P is a community patient on SCT: see paras 6.74 and 6.77 and Chapter 15.

- A donee may not make any of the decisions set out in s 27 on P's behalf (marriage, sexual relations etc; see para 10.70).

- A donee may not cast a vote on behalf of P (s 29).

- A donee may not give consent for P to be subject to medical research unless the conditions in s 30 to s 34 are satisfied (para 10.75).

4. Making a Lasting Power of Attorney

10.44 An LPA may only be made by a competent adult over the age of 18, must comply with the provisions of s 10 and must be made and registered in accordance with Sch 1 of the 2005 Act (s 9(2)). An instrument which purports to create a LPA which does not comply with s 9, 10, or Sch 1 confers no authority (s 9(3)).

10.45 Section 10 provides, materially, that the donee must be over the age of 18 (s 10(1)); makes provision for when two or more persons are appointed as donees, including whether powers are to be exercised jointly, severally, or jointly and severally (s 10(3)–(7)); and states that a donee cannot appoint a substitute or successor, although the LPA itself may appoint a replacement donee or donees (s 10(8)).

10.46 The formalities for making a LPA are set out in Sch 1, Part 1 and are, in summary, as follows:

- the LPA must be a written document set out in the statutory form prescribed by regulations[13] (Sch 1, Part 1, para 1), although Sch 1 Part 1 para 3(1) does enable

---

[13] Lasting Powers of Attorney, Enduring Powers of Attorney and Public Guardian Regulations, SI 2007/1253. A copy of the form can be obtained online at <http://www.guardianship.gov.uk/downloads/LPA_PW_1007.pdf>).

the Court of Protection to treat a LPA as valid even if it is not in the prescribed form if the Court is satisfied 'that the persons executing the instrument intended it to create a lasting power of attorney';

- the document must include prescribed information about the nature and effect of the LPA (as set out in the regulations);
- the donor must sign a statement saying that they have read the prescribed information (or somebody has read it to them) and that they want the LPA to apply when they no longer have capacity (Sch 1, Part 1, para 2);
- the document must name people (not any of the donees) who should be told about an application to register the LPA, or it should say that there is no-one they wish to be told (Sch 1, Part 1, para 2);
- each donee must sign a statement saying that they have read the prescribed information and that they understand their duties—in particular the duty to act in the donor's best interests (Sch 1, Part 1, para 2);
- the document must include a certificate completed by an independent third party, confirming that in their opinion, the donor understands the LPA's purpose, nobody used fraud or undue pressure to trick or force the donor into making the LPA and there is nothing to stop the LPA being created (Sch 1, Part 1, para 2).

10.47 The formalities for registering a LPA with the Public Guardian are set out in Sch 1, Part 2 and in regulations,[14] but are not considered here in detail. The LPA may be registered either before P loses capacity or afterwards. Any dispute concerning whether the LPA is in the proper form or should be registered may be referred to the Court of Protection for determination under ss 22 or 23 (see below, para 10.50).

5. Revocation of an LPA

10.48 A LPA relating to personal matters may be revoked in one of the following ways:

- The donor revokes the LPA at any time when he has capacity to do so (s 13(2)).
- The Court of Protection revokes the LPA in accordance with s 22.
- The donee disclaims his appointment in accordance with regulations (s 13(6)(a)).
- The death of the donee (s 13(6)(b).
- The dissolution or annulment of a marriage or civil partnership between the donor and the donee, unless the instrument provides otherwise (s 13(6)(c) and 13(11)).
- The donee's lack of capacity (s 13(6)(d)).

10.49 Where there is more than one donee one of the events in s 13(6)(a) to (d) will terminate the donee's appointment but will not revoke the LPA (s 13(5)) if the LPA authorizes the donees to act jointly and severally.

---

[14] Lasting Powers of Attorney, Enduring Powers of Attorney and Public Guardian Regulations, SI 2007/1253.

6. Jurisdiction of the Court of Protection in Relation to Lasting Powers of Attorney

10.50 The Court may determine any question as to the validity (s 22) or the operation (s 23) of a LPA. As to the validity of an LPA, the Court may revoke an LPA or direct that it is not to be registered if satisfied it was induced by fraud or undue pressure or if the donee has behaved, is behaving or proposes to behave in a way that contravenes, or would contravene, his authority or is not, or would not be, in P's best interests (s 22(3) to (4)).

10.51 Once an LPA is executed or registered the Court may determine any question as to its meaning or effect (s 22(1)). In particular, the Court may give directions with respect to the decisions that the donee has authority to make and which P lacks capacity to make and give any consent or authorization to act which the donee would have to obtain from P if P had capacity to give it (s 23(2)). This last power appears, on the face of it, to give the Court power to extend the donee's authority under a LPA, for example to permit the donee to give or refuse consent in circumstances other than those provided for by the LPA. That would enable the Court to extend the range of a LPA rather than make a personal welfare decision itself or appoint a deputy to do so under s 16(2)(b), but this does not appear to be the purpose for which the provision was introduced.[15]

10.52 By s 23(3)(d) the Court may relieve the donee wholly or partly from any liability which he has or may have incurred on account of a breach of his duties as donee. This is a curious provision, and there must be some question as to its extent. If the donee has acted unlawfully and P or another has suffered loss as a result it is unlikely that this power can be exercised without risking a violation of P's or the other person's Article 6 rights.

10.53 The court may also give directions as to the supply of reports, accounts, records, information and documents by the donee and as to his remuneration or expenses (s 23(3)(a) to (c)).

K. PERSONAL WELFARE DECISIONS BY THE COURT OF PROTECTION

1. The Court's Jurisdiction in Personal Welfare Matters

10.54 The Court of Protection not only has power to determine the validity, applicability, and operation of advance decisions and LPAs, but may also, by making an order, make decisions on an incapacitated individual, P's, behalf in relation to matters concerning P's personal welfare (s 16(1) and 16(2)(a)) or appoint a deputy to make

---

[15] See Hansard, HL Debates 27 Jan 2005, Col 1426–7, Baroness Ashton of Upholland explained the provision as enabling the Court to give consent on behalf of P in circumstances where the donee has a conflict of interest, for example when the donee is buying P's property and cannot act both as vendor and purchaser.

decisions on P's behalf (s 16(2)(b)). The appointment and function of deputies is considered at para 10.57 below.

The court may, in particular, make decisions in relation to P's personal welfare as set out in s 17 (above, para 10.42), including the giving or refusing of consent to treatment, subject to the limitations set out below. The Court may also make decisions which involve depriving P of his liberty under s 16 (see para 11.48); indeed, until the 2007 Act comes into force, the only means of lawfully detaining P under the 2005 Act is by a Court order (para 11.52). In making any such decisions the Court is bound by s 1 (principles) and s 4 (best interests) (s 16(3)). There is nothing in the Act, however, that stipulates when an application *must* be made under s 16: see the discussion in para 9.23. **10.55**

2. Limitations of the Court's Jurisdiction in Personal Welfare Matters

The Court's power to make decisions on behalf of P is subject to the following limitations: **10.56**

- The Court is not expressly subject to the same limitations as a donee or deputy in relation to the use of restraint (the use of force or the placing of any restrictions upon P's liberty) as in s 6(1), s 11(4), and s 20(7). There can be little doubt, however, that the Court cannot make any order authorizing the restraint of P unless satisfied of the same conditions, namely that P lacks capacity or the judge reasonably believes him to lack capacity, the judge reasonably believes it necessary to do the act to prevent harm to P and the act is a proportionate response to the likelihood of P's suffering harm and the seriousness of that harm. Such a reading would be necessary in order to comply with Article 8 of the Convention.

- Although no provision expressly states as such, the Court may not make any decision that is inconsistent with an advance decision which is valid and applicable, because an advance decision takes effect as if made by a competent person (s 26(1)) which the Court cannot override.

- Similarly, although not expressly provided for, the Court may not make any decision which is inconsistent with a valid decision of a donee of a LPA. The powers of the Court in relation to decisions of donees are limited to determining the validity or operation of an LPA, including giving directions as to the decisions that the donee has authority to make (ss 22–3, see above para 10.50). There is no specific provision by which the decision of the Court may take precedence over that of the LPA; it follows, by implication, that the Court does not have that power. The Court can, however, revoke a LPA if satisfied the donee is not acting in P's best interests (s 22(3)(b)).

- While the Court has jurisdiction to make decisions detaining P under s 16, once the 2007 Act comes into force, the Court may not detain P if he is 'ineligible' to be deprived of his liberty (s 16A). This is considered at para 11.48 and Chapter 15.

- The Court may not give, or authorize to be given, to P treatment for mental disorder that is regulated by Part 4 of the 1983 Act (s 28) (see para 10.71). Once the 2007 Act comes into force, the Court may *refuse* (but not give) consent to P being given ECT when detained under the 1983 Act under s 58A(5)(c)(ii) (para 6.51) The Court will also be able to give (s 64C(2)(b)) or refuse (s 64D(6)) consent to other medical treatment under new Part 4A of the 1983 Act, where P is a community patient on SCT: see paras 6.74 and 6.77 and Chapter 15.

- The Court may not make any of the decisions set out in s 27 on P's behalf (marriage, sexual relations etc; see para 10.70).

- The Court may not cast a vote on behalf of P (s 29).

- The Court may not give consent for P to be subject to medical research unless the conditions in s 30 to s 34 are satisfied (para 10.75).

L. COURT-APPOINTED DEPUTIES

10.57 As already noted, the Court of Protection may either make decisions itself in relation to P's personal welfare or it may appoint a deputy to make decisions on P's behalf (s 16(2)(b)), although a decision of the court is to be preferred to the appointment of a deputy (s 16(4)(a)). The Court may not appoint a deputy who is under the age of 18 (s 19(1)).

10.58 The court may confer upon a deputy any powers it considers necessary or expedient, which may include power to take all or any of the decisions referred to in s 17, which must be exercised in accordance with the provisions of s 1 (principles) and s 4 (best interests) (s 20(6)). However, the powers conferred on a deputy should be as limited in scope and duration as is reasonably practicable in the circumstances (s 16(4)(b)).[16] A deputy may not:

- prohibit a named person from having contact with P (s 20(2)(a));

- direct a person responsible for P's health care to allow a different person to take over that responsibility (s 20(2)(b));

- make any decision which is inconsistent with a valid decision made by the donee of a LPA (s 20(4));

- refuse consent to the carrying out or continuation of life-sustaining treatment in relation to P (s 20(5));

- make any decision which is inconsistent with an advance decision which is valid and applicable (s 26(1));

---

[16] When the 2007 Act comes into force a deputy will also exercise a number of important functions in relation to the making and review of standard authorizations for detention under Sch A1. A 'standard authorization' cannot be made if a donee refuses (Sch A1, paras 18–20, below paras 12.26). Moreover, a deputy may give consent to P's detention under Sch A1 where P would otherwise be 'ineligible' for detention (see paras 15.15 and 15.23). A deputy may also exercise a number of functions as P's representative under Sch A1, considered at para 13.29ff.

- restrain P, unless authority to do so is expressly conferred upon him to do so by the Court and the following conditions are met: first, P lacks (or is reasonably believed to lack) capacity in relation to the matter in question; second, it is reasonably believed that it is necessary to do the act in order to prevent harm to P; and, third, the act is a proportionate response to the likelihood of P's suffering harm and the seriousness of that harm (see para 10.66) (s 20(7) to (11)[17]);

- detain, or authorize the detention, of P (para 10.69). After the 2007 Act comes into force, he will only be able to authorize detention in accordance with the provisions of (a) Sch A1, by virtue of s 4A(1)) (above, para 10.40); or (b) s 4B (deprivation of liberty necessary for life-sustaining treatment, see para 11.45 below);

- give, or authorize to be given, to P treatment for mental disorder that is regulated by Part 4 of the 1983 Act (s 28) (see para 10.71). Once the 2007 Act comes into force, the deputy may *refuse* (but not give) consent to P being given ECT when detained under the 1983 Act under s 58A(5)(c)(ii) (para 6.51) and may give (s 64C(2)(b)) or refuse (s 64D(6)) consent to other medical treatment under new Part 4A of the 1983 Act, where P is a community patient on SCT: see paras 6.74 and 6.77 and Chapter 15;

- make any of the excluded decisions set out in s 27 on P's behalf (marriage, sexual relations etc; see para 10.70);

- cast a vote on behalf of P (s 29);

- give consent for P to be subject to medical research unless the conditions in s 30 to s 34 are satisfied (para 10.75).

M. ACTS IN CONNECTION WITH CARE AND TREATMENT: s 5

Section 5 effectively codifies the common law doctrine of necessity by providing a defence to any criminal or tortious suit to any person, D, who does any 'act in connection with the care or treatment' of another person, P, if before doing the act, D takes reasonable steps to establish whether P lacks capacity in relation to the matter in question, and when doing the act, D reasonably believes that P lacks capacity in relation to the matter, and that it will be in P's best interests for the act to be done (s 5(1) and 5(2)). Section 5 does not exclude any liability for loss or damage arising from D's negligence and, although not specified, any liability of any public authority for loss or damage arising from an act made unlawful by s 6 of the Human Rights Act 1998.

10.59

---

[17] The requirement in s 20(11) currently reads that the act is a 'proportionate response to (a) the likelihood of P's suffering harm; *or* (b) the seriousness of that harm'. This is a drafting error which is corrected by s 51 of the 2007 Act, so 'or' now reads 'and'.

10.60   D may not, however:

- use restraint (reasonable force or a restriction on P's liberty of movement) unless three conditions are met: first, P lacks (or the donee reasonably believes P lacks) capacity in relation to the matter in question; second, D reasonably believes that it is necessary to do the act in order to prevent harm to P; and, third, the act is a proportionate response to the likelihood of P's suffering harm and the seriousness of that harm (s 6(1)) (see para 10.66);

- do any act which conflicts with a valid decision by a donee or deputy (s 6(6)), although that does not stop D from providing life-sustaining treatment, or doing any act which he reasonably believes to be necessary to prevent a serious deterioration in P's condition, while a decision as respects any relevant issue is sought from the court (s 6(7)) (see para 10.61);

- deprive P of his liberty (see further 10.69). Once the 2007 Act is in force, detention is only permitted in accordance with the provisions of Sch A1 or a court order under s 16 (s 4A(1)) or s 4B, considered at 10.69 and Chapter 11;

- make any of the decisions set out in s 27 on P's behalf (marriage, sexual relations etc: see para 10.70);

- give, or authorize to be given, to P treatment for mental disorder that is regulated by Part 4 of the 1983 Act (s 28) (see para 10.71);

- once the 2007 Act is in force, give, or authorize to be given, to P treatment for mental disorder falling within s 64B (treatment of community patients on SCT) (s 28(1B)) (see para 10.72);

- cast a vote on behalf of P (s 29);

- give consent for P to be subject to medical research unless the conditions in s 30 to s 34 are satisfied (see para 10.75)

N. LIFE-SUSTAINING ETC TREATMENT

1. Special Status for Life-sustaining etc Treatment

10.61   A number of provisions of the 2005 Act give special status to treatment which is life-sustaining[18] or necessary to prevent a serious deterioration in P's condition, which reflect the presumption that operates at common law in favour of the preservation of life (above, para 9.16). These provisions may be summarized as follows:

- A person may provide treatment which is life-sustaining or necessary to prevent a serious deterioration in P's condition notwithstanding it conflicts with an

---

[18] Section 4(10) provides that 'Life-sustaining treatment' means treatment which in the view of a person providing health care for the person concerned is necessary to sustain life.

apparently valid advance decision (s 26(5)) or the decision of a donee or deputy (s 6(7)) while a decision as respects any relevant issue is sought from the court.

- An advance decision is not applicable to life-sustaining treatment unless the additional requirements of s 25(5) and (6) are satisfied (see para 10.30).

- A donee may not refuse life-sustaining treatment unless the LPA contains express provision to that effect (s 11(8)) (see para 10.43).

- A deputy may not refuse life-sustaining treatment at all (s 20(5)) (see para 10.58).

- Once the 2007 Act comes into force, a person may detain P for the purpose of giving treatment which is life-sustaining or to do a 'vital act', defined as an act which the person doing it reasonably believes to be necessary to prevent a serious deterioration in P's condition, while a decision as respects any relevant issue is sought from the court (s 4B) (considered at para 11.45).

2. Restrictions on Acts Intended to End Life

In addition to these limitations on the circumstances in which life-sustaining treat- 10.62 ment may be withheld or withdrawn, the 2005 Act contains two further provisions introduced to meet some of the objections raised during its passage through Parliament that the Act would undermine the current prohibition against euthanasia and assisted suicide. Accordingly, s 4(5) provides that '[i]n determining P's best interests, a person may not be motivated by a desire to bring about P's death' and s 62 states 'For the avoidance of doubt, it is hereby declared that nothing in this Act is to be taken to affect the law relating to murder or manslaughter or the operation of section 2 of the Suicide Act 1961 (assisting suicide)'.

There is a discussion of the limitations of the right of autonomy at common law 10.63 at para 9.05, above. This is not the place for a detailed examination of the lawfulness of the current ban on the law against assisted suicide, which has in any event been upheld by the ECtHR as not violating Article 2 or 3 and as being a lawful and proportionate interference with the right to respect for private life under Article 8 in *Pretty v United Kingdom*.[19] Suffice to say, s 62 makes it clear the 2005 Act does not change the position. Nor is this the place to reflect upon the paradox of the fact that a court may end the life of an incapacitated individual on the basis of an assessment that their life has become intolerable (see next paragraph), but a capable person cannot obtain assistance to end their own life when they decide for themselves it has become intolerable.

Section 4(5) requires closer consideration. There is no doubt that, in some circum- 10.64 stances, it is not in P's 'best interests' for life-sustaining treatment to continue and it has been held to be lawful to withhold or withdraw life-sustaining treatment in those circumstances. 'The courts have accepted that where life involves an extreme degree of pain, discomfort or indignity to a patient, who is sentient but not

---

[19] (2002) 35 EHRR 1.

competent and who has manifested no wish to be kept alive, these circumstances may absolve the doctors of the positive duty to keep the patient alive. Equally the courts have recognized that there may be no duty to keep alive a patient who is in a persistent vegetative state.'[20] To withdraw life-sustaining treatment from a person in those circumstances plainly *is* motivated by a desire to bring about P's death. It was certainly the government's intention when introducing the provision that the law as it then stood was not changed by s 4(5),[21] but how can that line of cases be squared with s 4(5)?

10.65   The answer may lie in the principle of 'double-effect'. This principle permits a doctor, for example, to give pain-relieving drugs to a patient, knowing that they will hasten the patient's death, without committing a criminal offence, provided the primary purpose of giving that treatment is to relieve pain.[22] The same might be said where life-sustaining treatment is to be withheld or withdrawn if the purpose is bring to an end P's intolerable suffering; although the *consequence* is to bring about P's death, the *motivation* is to end P's suffering. This is a supremely contentious area, and we may expect this issue to be litigated before too long.

O. RESTRAINT AND THE USE OF FORCE

10.66   The use of restraint—defined as the use or threat of reasonable force or the restriction of P's liberty of movement, whether or not P resists (s 6(4), 11(5), and 20(12))—may be authorized or imposed by a donee, deputy or a person, D, doing an 'act in connection with care and treatment' under s 5, only if three conditions are met. The first is that P lacks (or is reasonably believed to lack) capacity in relation to the matter in question. The second is that it is reasonably believed that it is necessary to do the act in order to prevent harm to P. The third condition is that the act is a proportionate response to the likelihood of P's suffering harm and the seriousness of that harm (ss 6(1), 11(4), and 20(7)). In the case of a deputy, there is the additional requirement that the order appointing him must expressly provide that he has authority to make such decisions (s 20(8)).

10.67   These conditions reinforce the principle in s 1(6), that where an act is done, or a decision is made, regard must be had to whether the purpose for which it is needed can be as effectively achieved in a way that is less restrictive of the person's rights and freedom of action (s 1(6)).

10.68   The same principles may in turn be derived from the Convention principle of proportionality, which requires that any interference with a qualified Convention right (such as, materially, Article 8) should pursue a legitimate objective, be rationally

---

[21] See Hansard, HC Debates, 15 March 2005, Col 1293, to the effect that 4(5) 'does not change the law as it stands at the moment'.

[20] R *(Burke) v GMC* [2006] QB 273, para 33.

[22] See eg *Airedale NHS Trust v Bland* [1993] AC 789 at 867; *Re A (Conjoined Twins)* [2001] 1 Fam 147 at 199.

connected to that legitimate objective and the means used to impair the right or freedom should be no more than is necessary to accomplish the objective.[23]

P. DEPRIVATIONS OF LIBERTY

Detention for care and treatment at common law and under the 2005 Act, both as 10.69 it is currently enacted and as it will be amended by the 2007 Act, is considered in Chapters 11 and 12. In summary, the 2005 Act, as currently enacted, prohibits any person (D) acting under s 5 or any donee or deputy from depriving P of his liberty (s 6(5), s 11(6), and s 20(13)) (see para 11.35). Section 64(5) of the 2005 Act states that 'deprivation of liberty' has the same meaning in the Act as in Article 5(1) of the Convention (para 11.21). Detention may only lawfully be authorized under the 2005 Act where the Court authorizes it under s 16. The 2007 Act has amended the 2005 Act, introducing s 4A and 4B and repealing s 6(5), s 11(6), and s 20(13). Section 4A will prohibit will detention other than in three situations: an order of the Court under s 16; for life-saving or other emergencies (s 4B), and under the new Sch A1 procedure (see 11.36). The complex interface between the 2005 Act and the 1983 Act after the 2007 Act comes into force is considered in Chapter 15. Pending the coming into force of the 2007 Act, however, detention under the 2005 Act can only be authorized by a court under s 16 (para 11.35).

Q. EXCLUDED DECISIONS

1. Family Relationships

Nothing in the 2005 Act permits a decision on any of the following matters to be 10.70 made on behalf of a person consenting to marriage or a civil partnership; consenting to have sexual relations; consenting to a decree of divorce or a dissolution order; consenting to a child being placed for adoption or to the making of an adoption order; discharging parental responsibilities in matters not relating to a child's property; and giving a consent under the Human Fertilization and Embryology Act 1990 (s 27). That does not preclude the Court making declarations as to whether a person has, or does not have, capacity to make any of those decisions, as at common law (see para 9.22).

2. Mental Health Matters: Interface between the Treatment Provisions of the 2005 Act and the 1983 Act

s 28(1) of the 2005 Act provides that nothing in the 2005 Act authorizes anyone to 10.71 give a patient medical treatment for mental disorder, or to consent to a patient being given medical treatment for mental disorder, if at the time his treatment is regulated

---

[23] Paraphrased from the classic statement of proportionality by Lord Steyn in *R (Daly) v Home Secretary* [2001] 2 AC 532, para 27.

by Part 4 of the 1983 Act, which regulates the medical treatment for mental disorder of patients who are 'liable to be detained' in hospital under the 1983 Act (s 56(1)), including patients who are actually detained and those who are on s 17 leave of absence. This is the only provision governing the interface between the 1983 Act and the 2005 Act until the 2007 Act comes into force and is relatively straightforward. Any patient who falls within Part 4 (see above, para 6.06) cannot be given treatment for mental disorder under the 2005 Act. For further guidance on the relationship between the 1983 Act and the 2005 Act before the 2007 Act comes into force, see Chapter 13 of the 2005 Act Code of Practice.

10.72   Matters become very much more complicated after the 2007 Act comes into force, which introduces new Part 4A governing the treatment of community patients on SCT. New s 28(1B) of the 2005 Act provides that treatment falling within s 64B of the 1983 Act (treatment of incapacitated adult patients on SCT) may not be administered under s 5 of the 2005 Act, which prevents the administration of treatment to incapacitated patients on SCT by a person, D, purporting to act in P's best interests under s 5. It does not exclude treatment decisions authorized by a donee, deputy or the Court of Protection.

10.73   The interface between the 2005 Act and the 1983 Act after the 2007 Act comes into force is so complicated it has the whole of Chapter 15 to itself; treatment for mental disorder is considered at para 15.26ff.

3. Voting

10.74   Nothing in the Act permits a decision on voting at an election (or referendum) to be made for any person. As with family relationships (above, para 10.70), there appears to be no reason in principle why the Court cannot make a declaration that a person has, or lacks, capacity to vote, although it is difficult to envisage the circumstances in which such a declaration would be sought.

4. Medical Research

10.75   Section 30 to s 34 permit research to be carried out on patients lacking capacity, but subject to a number of safeguards. The detail of these provisions lies outside the scope of this book.

R. ILL-TREATMENT OR NEGLECT

10.76   Any person who has the care of an incapacitated individual, P, or his donee or deputy, is guilty of a criminal offence if he ill-treats or wilfully neglects P. Any such person will be liable on summary conviction for a term not exceeding 12 months or a fine not exceeding the statutory maximum or both and, on conviction on indictment, to imprisonment for a term not exceeding 5 years or a fine or both (s 44).

10.77   Section 44 also applies to children under 16.

S. INDEPENDENT MENTAL CAPACITY ADVOCATES (IMCAs)

A welcome innovation in the 2005 Act is to introduce a statutory right to an 'independent mental capacity advocate' or IMCA for incapacitated individuals in circumstances where an NHS body or local authority proposes to take steps in relation to the care and treatment of P that might involve significant interferences with P's rights, whether to bodily integrity or to respect for their home and their private and family life.   10.78

1. Appointment of IMCAs

By s 35, the 'appropriate authority'[24] must make such arrangements as it considers reasonable to enable IMCAs to be available to represent and support those to whom s 37, s 38 and s 39 relate and may make regulations as to the appointment of IMCAs.[25] An IMCA must be appointed where an NHS body is proposing to provide 'serious medical treatment' to P (s 37).or if an NHS body or local authority is proposing to provide P with accommodation (s 38 and 39). This right has now been extended by the 2007 Act which has introduced sections 39A, 39C, and 39D, which require the appointment of an IMCA for detainees subject to Schedule A1, considered in Chapter 13.[26]   10.79

By s 41 the appropriate authority may also make regulations expanding the role of IMCAs and the Secretary of State has done so in England, expanding the circumstances in which an IMCA is to be appointed to include reviews of arrangements of accommodation and adult protection cases (below, para 10.84).[27]   10.80

(a) *No Duty to Appoint IMCA Where There is a More Appropriate Consultee*

The duty to appoint an IMCA arises only where the responsible authority is satisfied that there is no person, other than one engaged in providing care or treatment for P in a professional capacity or for remuneration, whom it would be appropriate for it to consult in determining what is in P's best interests (s 37(1), 38(1), and 39(1)). If any of the following is available to be consulted, the duty to appoint an IMCA under any of s 37, 38, or 39,[28] does not arise: any person nominated by P to be   10.81

---

[24] In England, the Secretary of State, and in Wales the National Assembly, s 35(7).

[25] The Mental Capacity Act 2005 (IMCA) (General) Regulations 2006, SI 2006/1832 (for England); The Mental Capacity Act 2005 (IMCA) (Wales) Regulations 2007, SI 2007/852 (for Wales) (both in force from 1 October 2007).

[26] Sections 38 and 39 have been accordingly amended by the MHA 2007 to make it clear that they do not apply where an IMCA must be appointed under sections 39A or 39C.

[27] The Mental Capacity Act 2005 (IMCA) (Expansion of Role) Regulations 2006, SI 2006/2883 (in force from 1 April 2007).

[28] And, when the 2007 Act is in force, s 39A, 39C or 39D.

[29] Section 40 has been amended by the 2007 Act to delete references to donees of enduring powers of attorney and to include references to s 39A, 39C, and 39D IMCAs.

consulted in matters affecting his interests, the donee of a lasting power of attorney or a deputy appointed by the Court (s 40[29]). Note s 40 has been amended by the 2007 Act to delete references to donees of enduring powers of attorney and to include references to s 39A, 39C, and 39D IMCAs (see below, para 13.03).

10.82 (b) *s 37 IMCAs: Provision of Serious Medical Treatment by NHS Body*
Section 37 requires a NHS body[30] to instruct an IMCA to represent P wherever it is proposing that P be provided with 'serious medical treatment', other than where treatment needs to be provided as a matter of urgency (s 37(4) or it is treatment for mental disorder regulated by Part 4 or 4A of the 1983 Act (s 37(2)). 'Serious medical treatment' means 'treatment which involves providing, withdrawing or withholding treatment in circumstances where (a) in a case where a single treatment is being proposed, there is a fine balance between its benefits to the patient and the burdens and risks it is likely to entail for him, (b) in a case where there is a choice of treatments, a decision as to which one to use is finely balanced, or (c) what is proposed would be likely to involve serious consequences for the patient'.[31]

10.83 (c) *s 38 & 39 IMCAs: Provision of Accommodation by NHS Body or Local Authority*
Sections 38 and 39, respectively, apply if an NHS body or local authority proposes to make arrangements for P to be accommodated in a hospital or care home for more than 28 days (in the case of a hospital) or more than 8 weeks (in the case of a care home). The duty does not arise where the placement needs to be made as a matter of urgency (ss 38(3)(b) and 39(4)(b)) or where P is accommodated as a result of an obligation imposed on him under the 1983 Act (s 38(2) and 39(3)). This last exception will include a person detained under the 1983 Act or anyone residing in a hospital or care home as a condition of s 17 leave of absence, supervised community discharge, conditional discharge, or on guardianship. Such patients are instead entitled to an IMHA (see para 4.33). In the case of accommodation provided by a local authority, the duty is triggered only where accommodation is provided under the National Assistance Act 1948 or s 117 of the 1983 Act as a result of a decision following an assessment under section 47 National Health Service and Community Care Act 1990 (s 39(2)). A further exception to the duty in ss 38 and 39 is introduced by the 2007 Act, namely if a 39A or 39C IMCA must be appointed instead (s 38(2A) and 39 (3A)) (see Chapter 13).

---

[30] In England an NHS body is a Strategic Health Authority, NHS Foundation Trust, Primary Care Trust, NHS Trust or Care Trust: Mental Capacity Act 2005 (IMCA) (General) Regulations 2006, Reg 3; in Wales an NHS body is a Local Health Board, an NHS trust all or partly in Wales or a Special Health Authority performing functions only or mainly in Wales.
[31] s 37(6) and Mental Capacity Act 2005 (IMCA) (General) Regulations 2006, Reg 4 (England); Mental Capacity Act 2005 (IMCA) (Wales) Regulations 2007, Reg 4.

(d) *Reg 3 IMCA: Review of Arrangements as to Accommodation*

Reg 3 of the IMCA (Expansion of Role) Regulations[32] extends the duty to appoint **10.84** an IMCA where an NHS body or local authority has been providing accommodation of the kind referred to for a continuous period of at least 12 weeks and a review of the arrangements is proposed or in progress, whether under a care plan or otherwise.

(e) *Reg 4 IMCAs: Adult Protection Cases*

Reg 4 of the IMCA (Expansion of Role) Regulations provides that an IMCA is to be **10.85** appointed when an NHS body or local authority proposes to take, or has taken, protective measures in relation to P following receipt of an allegation that P is being or has been abused or is an abuser, or in accordance with guidance issued under s 7 Local Authority Social Services Act 1970.[33]

2. Functions of IMCAs

Section 36 MCA provides that the 'appropriate authority' may make regulations to **10.86** make provision for the functions of IMCAs, to include providing support so that P may participate as fully as possible in any relevant decision, obtaining and evaluating relevant information, ascertaining what P's wishes and feelings would be likely to be and the beliefs and values that would be likely to influence P if he had capacity, ascertaining what alternative courses of action are available in relation to P and obtaining a further medical opinion where treatment is proposed and the IMCA thinks one should be obtained. Regulations have now been made conferring those functions.[34] An IMCA so appointed has the same right to challenge any decision made in relation to any matter as he would have if he were a person other than an IMCA engaged in caring for P or interested in his welfare.[35]

For the purposes of enabling him to carry out his functions, an IMCA may inter- **10.87** view P in private and may, at all reasonable times, examine and take copies of any health record, any record of, or held by, a local authority compiled in connection with a social services function, and any record held by a person registered under Part 2 of the Care Standards Act 2000 (namely the person who 'carries on or manages' any independent hospital or care home), which the person holding the record considers may be relevant to the IMCA's investigation (s 35(6)).

The duty of disclosure on the record holder imposed by s 35(6) does not go as far **10.88** as the duty of disclosure imposed by s 7 Data Protection Act 1998, in particular by reason of the fact the record holder may withhold any record it does not consider to

---

[32] Mental Capacity Act 2005 (IMCA) (Expansion of Role) Regulations 2006.
[33] See Department of Health Guidance, 'No secrets: Guidance on developing and implementing multi-agency policies and procedures to protect vulnerable adults from abuse'.
[34] Mental Capacity Act 2005 (IMCA) (General) Regulations 2006, Reg 6 (England); Mental Capacity Act 2005 (IMCA) (Wales) Regulations 2007, Reg 6.
[35] Ibid, Reg 7 in both England and Wales.

be 'relevant' to the IMCA's investigation. If a record holder does refuse to disclose documents to an IMCA then a request by P (the 'data access subject') should be made under s 7 of the 1998 Act. If P lacks capacity to make that request it should presumably be possible for it to be made by his donee, a deputy, or the Court of Protection. An alternative might be to request the Public Guardian to make a request for the documents under s 58(5) of the 2005 Act; his right of access is to all documents 'so far as the record relates to P'.

T. THE CODE OF PRACTICE UNDER THE 2005 ACT

1. Lord Chancellor's Duty to Prepare and Issue Codes of Practice

10.89 By s 42(1) of the 2005 Act the Lord Chancellor must prepare and issue one or more Codes of Practice for the guidance of (a) persons assessing whether a person has capacity in relation to any matter, (b) persons acting in connection with the care or treatment of another person under s 5, (c) donees of lasting powers of attorney, (d) deputies appointed by the court, (e) persons carrying out research in reliance on any provision made by or under the Act (and otherwise with respect to sections 30–34) and (f) IMCAs. The Code of Practice must also be made with respect to the provisions of ss 24–6 (advance decisions and apparent advance decisions) and such other matters concerned with the 2005 Act as the Lord Chancellor thinks fit. Before issuing any Code the Lord Chancellor must consult the National Assembly for Wales and any other person he considers appropriate (s 43(1)) and must lay a copy of the Code before both Houses of Parliament for a 40 day period (s 43(2) and (4)). He must then arrange for any code to be published in such a way as he considers appropriate for bringing it to the attention of persons likely to be concerned with its provisions.

10.90 A Code of Practice has been issued under the 2005 Act (the '2005 Act Code of Practice') which came into force on 1 April 2007, a copy of which is available online.[36]

10.91 Section 42 is amended by the 2007 Act so as to require the Lord Chancellor also to issue a Code of Practice for the guidance of persons exercising functions under Schedule A1 and representatives appointed under Part 10 of Schedule A1. At the time of writing a draft addendum to the Code of Practice has been issued for consultation.[37]

2. Duty to Have Regard to the Code of Practice

10.92 Section 42(3) provides that it is the duty of a person to 'have regard to' any relevant code if he is acting in relation to a person who lacks capacity and is exercising one of

---

[36] <http://www.justice.gov.uk/docs/mca-cp.pdf>.

[37] 'Mental Capacity Act 2005 – Deprivation of Liberty Safeguards. Draft addendum to the Mental Capacity Act 2005 Act Code of Practice'. The draft addendum was issued for consultation on 10 September 2007; the consultation closes on 2 December 2007: <http://www.justice.gov.uk/publications/cp2307.htm>.

the functions referred to in s 42(1). This is the same duty imposed by new s 118(2D) of the 1983 Act in relation to the Code of Practice issued under s 118(1), and it follows will take effect in the manner provided for by *R (Munjaz) v Mersey Care NHS Trust*,[38] described in para 4.02ff.

3. Relevance of the Code of Practice in Criminal or Civil Proceedings

By s 42(5), if it appears to a court or tribunal conducting any criminal or civil proceedings that a provision of a code or a failure to comply with a code is relevant to a question arising in the proceedings, the provision or failure must be taken into account in deciding the question.

10.93

---

[38] [2006] 2 AC 148, para 21, 69.

11

DETENTION FOR CARE AND TREATMENT UNDER THE 2005 ACT

A. Key Features	11.00
B. Detention at Common Law: 'Bournewood'	11.01
1. Overview of the Bournewood Case	11.01
2. The Facts of the Case	11.04
3. The Judicial Review and Habeas Corpus Proceedings	11.08
4. The Decision of the House of Lords	11.09
C. *HL v United Kingdom*	11.13
1. 'Deprivation of Liberty'	11.14
2. Article 5(1): Not 'in Accordance with a Procedure Prescribed by Law'	11.15
3. Article 5(4)	11.19
D. 'Deprivation of Liberty'	11.21
1. The Three Elements of 'Deprivation of Liberty'	11.23
2. Factors to Consider in Determining whether there is a Deprivation of Liberty	11.28
3. Deprivations of Liberty in Private Care Homes	11.33
E. Detention under the 2005 Act Prior to Amendment	11.35
1. Detention May Only be Authorized by the Court of Protection under s 16	11.35
2. Detention Must be Authorized in Advance	11.36
3. Interface between the Detaining Provisions of the 1983 Act and the 2005 Act Before the 2007 Act is in Force	11.37
F. Amendments Introduced by the 2007 Act	11.38
G. Standard and Urgent Authorizations: Sch A1	11.40
1. Standard Authorizations	11.40
2. Urgent Authorizations	11.41
H. Detention for Life-saving Treatment: s 4B	11.42
I. The Role of the Court of Protection in Decisions to Detain	11.45
1. Decisions to Detain Under s 16 of the 2005 Act	11.45

	2. Applications Relating to Standard and Urgent Authorizations Under s 21A	11.47
	3. Other Detention Issues Under s 15	11.48
J.	The Detention of Children	11.49
	1. Children Aged 16 or 17	11.50
	2. Children Under 16	11.55
K.	s 47 National Assistance Act 1948	11.58

A. KEY FEATURES

11.00 • The House of Lords in *Bournewood*[1] established, first, that an informal admission to hospital of an incapacitated individual, P, did not (and will rarely) amount to a detention at common law; moreover, that where such an admission did constitute a 'detention', it was justified and lawful under the common law doctrine of necessity.

• On appeal, the ECtHR in *HL v United Kingdom*[2] found, first, that admission to hospital in the circumstances in *Bournewood* did amount to a 'deprivation of liberty' within the meaning of Article 5(1) requiring lawful justification; moreover, that a 'deprivation of liberty' under the common law doctrine of necessity was not lawful for the purposes of Article 5(1).

• The 2005 Act, as originally enacted in response to *HL v United Kingdom*, prohibits a 'deprivation of liberty', whether in a hospital or care home and whether funded publicly or privately, by any other means than by order of the Court of Protection under s 16.

• The 2007 Act amends the 2005 Act to introduce further detaining mechanisms to make such detention lawful, namely the 'standard' and 'urgent' authorization procedure of Sch A1 and the urgent detention procedure under s 4B.

• The detention of children aged 16 and 17 and under 16 considered.

B. DETENTION AT COMMON LAW: 'BOURNEWOOD'

1. Overview of the Bournewood Case

11.01 Prior to the House of Lords decision in *R v Bournewood Community Mental Health NHS Trust ex p L* [1998] AC 458 (*Bournewood*), concern had been expressed for a number of years about the status of so-called 'de facto' detainees in psychiatric hospitals: those incapacitated patients admitted to hospital informally under s 131

---

[1] *R v Bournewood Community Mental Health NHS Trust ex p L* [1998] AC 458.
[2] (2004) 40 EHRR 761.

of the 1983 Act, rather than under its compulsory provisions (and attendant safeguards), because they did not object to their admission (see para 8.17ff). The question of law that this gave rise to was, could a person who lacked capacity to give a valid consent to treatment be admitted and detained in hospital without being formally 'sectioned' under the 1983 Act and, if so, what was the legal basis for their detention and treatment? The opportunity for the courts to resolve this issue came on 22 July 1997 when Mr L, a 48 year old man with severe learning disabilities, was admitted to Bournewood Hospital as an 'informal' patient and against the wishes of his carers, Mr and Mrs E. In subsequent proceedings for judicial review and habeas corpus the Court of Appeal held that, because he lacked capacity to consent to his admission to hospital, Mr L could only have been lawfully admitted and detained in hospital under the formal provisions of the 1983 Act.

The hospital appealed to the House of Lords, who allowed the appeal. The House 11.02
held, first, that Mr L had not been 'detained' in hospital, so that there was no need to establish any legal basis for his admission. Second, and in any event, the House held that s 5 of the Mental Health Act 1959, the predecessor to s 131 of the 1983 Act, had expressly retained available alternatives to detention under the Act, including the common law doctrine of 'necessity' under which an incapacitated patient could be detained.[3]

The case that Mr L subsequently took to the ECtHR challenged both aspects 11.03
of the ruling: first, as to whether Mr L had, in fact, been 'deprived of his liberty' within the meaning of Article 5(1); and, second, whether that deprivation of liberty under the common law doctrine of necessity had been lawful for the purposes of Article 5(1). The ECtHR found for Mr L on both counts.

2. The Facts of the Case

Mr L was born in 1949 and at the time of the events leading to the litigation he 11.04
was 48. He has suffered from autism since birth and cannot speak, although to those who know him well he is able to communicate his needs and feelings in other ways. His needs are complex and he requires 24 hour care. Since the age of 13 Mr L had lived in institutional care at Bournewood Hospital. In March 1994, aged 45, Mr L moved to live with Mr & Mrs E at their home under a scheme called 'Lifeways' by which long stay mentally disordered patients were provided with accommodation and care in the community. Mr L's discharge was initially on a trial basis. He was not formally discharged from Bournewood Hospital and the hospital remained responsible for his care and treatment. During the day Mr L attended a day-care centre run by the local authority.

---

[3] The House distinguished its earlier decision of *B v Forsey*, 1988 SC(HL) 28, HL(Sc) in which they had held that the detention of a patient under common law powers outside the scope of the Mental Health (Scotland) Act 1984 had been unlawful, the comprehensive statutory framework having impliedly removed any common law authority to detain.

11.05   On 22 July 1997 Mr L was at the day-care centre when he became particularly agitated. He was taken to the accident and emergency unit at Bournewood hospital where he was assessed as being in need of in-patient treatment. He was recorded as making no attempt to leave. Having consulted, Dr P and Dr M considered that the best interests of Mr L required his admission for in-patient treatment. Dr M did consider his committal under the 1983 Act but concluded that that was not necessary as Mr L was compliant and did not resist admission. Mr L was therefore admitted as an 'informal patient'.

11.06   The decision was also taken to prevent the E's from visiting Mr L because of the doctors' concerns Mr L might expect to come home with them and would become agitated if he had to remain in hospital. In the event Mr and Mrs E were not able to see Mr L until November 1997, four months later.

11.07   Mr L remained admitted as an 'informal' patient in the IBU of the hospital until 29 October 1997. During that time he was not free to leave; had he attempted to do so he would have been stopped. There was some dispute about whether the doors to the IBU were locked, but he was deprived of the only means available to him of leaving by reason of the fact Mr and Mrs. E could not visit him and take him home. On 29 October 1997 he was formally admitted to hospital under s 5(2) of the 1983 Act (following the success of the appeal in the judicial review and habeas corpus proceedings, below) and subsequently under a s 3 application for admission for treatment. An application was then made to the Mental Health Review Tribunal but before it could convene the hospital discharged Mr L back to the care of Mr and Mrs E on 5 December 1997, where he remains to this day.

3. The Judicial Review and Habeas Corpus Proceedings

11.08   Mr and Mrs E issued joined judicial review and habeas corpus proceedings challenging the lawfulness of the detention on 25 September 1997. At first instance the claims failed but on 29 October 1997 the Court of Appeal ruled that Mr L's detention had been unlawful, whereupon the hospital moved to have him admitted under the provisions of the 1983 Act. The hospital appealed, with the support of the government.

4. The Decision of the House of Lords

11.09   The decision of the Court of Appeal had caused a very strong reaction. Two strands of opinion emerged. On the one hand, there were those who felt that to detain such individuals, often when their family members had no objection to their placement, was unnecessary and stigmatizing. On the other side of the debate were those who felt that the judgment had extended valuable rights to a vulnerable group who had been ignored for too long. Undoubtedly the House were influenced by evidence that the numbers of incapacitated individuals in care homes and hospitals across England and Wales who would have to be detained under the 1983 Act would effectively treble as a result of the decision of the Court of Appeal.

On 25 June 1998 the House of Lords allowed the hospital's appeal, on two bases.   11.10
First, by a 3 to 2 majority, the House held that Mr L had not been 'detained'. Lord
Steyn (supported by Lord Nolan) gave a powerfully dissenting judgment on this
issue, concluding that: 'The suggestion that [the applicant] was free to go is a fairy
tale . . . In my view [the applicant] was detained because the health care professionals
intentionally assumed control over him to such a degree as to amount to complete
deprivation of his liberty.' As we shall see, Lord Steyn's analysis was in due course
preferred by the ECtHR.

The second basis of the judgment was that, if Mr L had been detained, his deten-   11.11
tion had been justified under the common law doctrine of necessity, applying *Re F*[4]
(considered in Chapter 9, above) and a series of 18th and 19th century cases that
supported the proposition that the common law permitted the detention of those
who were a danger, or potential danger, to themselves or others, in so far as this was
shown to be necessary.[5] On this ground the House was unanimous, but Lord Steyn
made it clear that it was not a result he welcomed, and concluded his judgment with
the following observations which presaged the subsequent decision of the ECtHR:

The general effect of the decision of the House is to leave compliant incapacitated patients without the safeguards enshrined in the Act of 1983. This is an unfortunate result. The Mental Health
Act Commission has expressed concern about such informal patients in successive reports. And in
a helpful written submission the Commission has again voiced those concerns and explained in
detail the beneficial effects of the ruling of the Court of Appeal. The common law principle of
necessity is a useful concept, but it contains none of the safeguards of the Act of 1983. It places
effective and unqualified control in the hands of the hospital psychiatrist and other health care
professionals. It is, of course, true that such professionals owe a duty of care to patients and that
they will almost invariably act in what they consider to be the best interests of the patient. But
neither habeas corpus not judicial review are sufficient safeguards against misjudgments and
professional lapses in the case of compliant incapacitated patients. Given that such patients are
diagnostically indistinguishable from compulsory patients, there is no reason to withhold the specific and effective protections of the Act of 1983 from a large class of vulnerable mentally incapacitated individuals. Their moral right to be treated with dignity requires nothing less. The only
comfort is that counsel for the Secretary of State has assured the House that reform of the law is
under active consideration.

While it was true, as the Secretary of State submitted, that reform of the law relat-   11.12
ing to the care and treatment of incapacitated adults was under active consideration
at that time (the government had published its Green Paper on mental capacity in
December 1997[6]), it was only following the subsequent Strasbourg decision in *HL v
United Kingdom* that the extent of the reforms that would need to be introduced
became clear.

---

  [4] [1990] 2 AC 1.

  [5] *Rex v Coate* (1772) Lofft 73, especially at 75, *per* Lord Mansfield CJ; *Scott v Wakem* (1862) 3 F & F 328,
333, *per* Bramwell B; and *Symm v Fraser* (1863) 3 F & F 859, 883, *per* Cockburn CJ.

  [6] 'Who Decides? Making Decisions on Behalf of Mentally Incapacitated Adults', Cm 3808, Dec 1997.

C. *HL V UNITED KINGDOM*

11.13 Mr L lodged his application to the ECtHR in December 1998. A hearing took place in the Human Rights Building, Strasbourg, on 27 May 2003. Judgment was handed down on 5 October 2004,[7] the ECtHR finding unanimously that Mr L had been deprived of his liberty within the meaning of Article 5(1); that the deprivation of liberty had not been 'in accordance with a procedure prescribed by law' and was therefore contrary to Article 5(1); and, in any event, Mr L had not had access to a 'court' with jurisdiction to determine the lawfulness of his detention, contrary to Article 5(4).

1. 'Deprivation of Liberty'

11.14 The ECtHR found unanimously that Mr L had been deprived of his liberty. It found that 'the key factor in the present case to be that the health care professionals treating and managing the applicant exercised complete and effective control over his care and movements from the moment he presented acute behavioural problems on 22 July 1997 to the date he was compulsorily detained on 29 October 1997' and that 'it is clear . . . that the applicant's contact with his carers was directed and controlled by the hospital, his carers visiting him for the first time after his admission on 2 November 1997. Accordingly, the concrete situation was that the applicant was under continuous supervision and control and was not free to leave' (para 91). This aspect of the ruling is considered under the heading 'Deprivation of Liberty' at para 11.21, below.

2. Article 5(1): Not 'in Accordance with a Procedure Prescribed by Law'

11.15 It was argued on Mr L's behalf that at the relevant time the concepts of 'best interests' and 'necessity' were imprecise and unforeseeable and, accordingly, Mr L's detention had not been lawful, because it was not 'in accordance with a procedure prescribed by law' as that term is understood in Convention terms.

11.16 At paras 114–15 of its judgment the Court outlined the key components of the Convention concept of 'lawfulness' and 'in accordance with a procedure prescribed by law'. First, the lawfulness of detention must be lawful as a matter of domestic law. Second, and given the importance of personal liberty, the relevant national law must meet the standard of 'lawfulness' set by the Convention, which requires that all law be sufficiently precise to allow the citizen—if need be, with appropriate advice—to foresee, to a degree that is reasonable in the circumstances, the consequences which a given action might entail. Third, given the essential objective of Article 5(1) is to prevent individuals being deprived of their liberty in an arbitrary fashion, this objective, and the broader condition that detention be 'in accordance with a

---

[7] *HL v United Kingdom* (2004) 40 EHRR 761.

procedure prescribed by law', require the existence in domestic law of adequate legal protections and 'fair and proper procedures'. Fourth, in the context of a detention under Article 5(1)(e) on the grounds of 'unsound mind', the *Winterwerp*[8] criteria had to be met (for which, see para 3.104).

The ECtHR went on to consider whether Mr L's detention had been lawful. They considered, first, the question whether the common law doctrine of necessity   11.17
was sufficient to encompass the *Winterwerp* criteria, and were satisfied that it did (para 116). Indeed, they were satisfied that those criteria had been met on the facts, (para 101). Next, they considered whether the doctrine of necessity was sufficiently well-developed in 1997 to have satisfied the test of 'foreseeability' (para 117–19). However the court did not feel the need to reach a conclusion on this question, because it was satisfied that the further element of 'lawfulness', the aim of avoiding arbitrariness through adequate legal protections and 'fair and proper procedures', had not been satisfied (para 119). The ECtHR noted the following features of the common law doctrine of necessity in the particular context of detention which demonstrated how the law fell short of this particular requirement (para 120):

- The lack of any fixed procedural rules by which the admission and detention of compliant incapacitated persons is conducted.

- The lack of any formalized admission procedures which indicate who can propose admission, for what reasons and on the basis of what kind of medical and other assessments and conclusions.

- There is no requirement to fix the exact purpose of admission (for example, for assessment or for treatment) and, consistently, no limits in terms of time, treatment, or care attach to that admission.

- There is no specific provision requiring a continuing clinical assessment of the persistence of a disorder warranting detention.

- There is no representative of a patient who could make certain objections and applications on his or her behalf akin to that available to those detained under the 1983 Act, which would be of equal importance for patients who are legally incapacitated and have extremely limited communication abilities.

The ECtHR went on 'As a result of the lack of procedural regulation and limits, the Court observes that the hospital's health care professionals assumed full control   11.18
of the liberty and treatment of a vulnerable incapacitated individual solely on the basis of their own clinical assessments completed as and when they considered fit: as Lord Steyn remarked, this left "effective and unqualified control" in their hands. While the Court does not question the good faith of those professionals or that they acted in what they considered to be the applicant's best interests, the very purpose of procedural safeguards is to protect individuals against any "misjudgments and professional lapses"' (para 121). This absence of procedural safeguards failed to

---

[8] *Winterwerp v Netherlands* (1979–80) 2 EHRR 387, para 39.

protect against arbitrary deprivations of liberty on grounds of necessity, and, accordingly, there had been a violation of Article 5(1) (para 124).

3. Article 5(4)

11.19 The ECtHR went on to find that Mr L's right to a determination of the lawfulness of his detention under Article 5(4) had also been violated, because the standard of review in operation at the time in judicial review and habeas corpus proceedings ('Super-Wednesbury') did not provide a review that was wide enough to bear on those conditions which are essential for the lawful detention of a person, in this case, on the ground of unsoundness of mind, in particular because it did not allow a determination of the *merits* of the question as to whether the mental disorder persisted (para 137).

11.20 Other issues arise under Article 5(4) with the new legal framework (see below, para 12.89), but this is not one of them: in 'best interests' proceedings before the High Court and in proposed proceedings before the Court of Protection the court will decide the issue of whether P should be detained on the *merits*, rather than by a *review* of the lawfulness of those who have made the decision to detain. Where the decision to detain is challenged in any other context, however (such as on judicial review or a habeas corpus application) then this requirement for a *merits* review will be of particular relevance.

D. 'DEPRIVATION OF LIBERTY' 0

11.21 The question of whether P has been 'deprived of his liberty' is critical to the question of when lawful authority must be obtained to avoid a violation of Article 5(1). With the coming into force of the 2005 Act, it determines when authority must be obtained from the Court of Protection under s 16 (see para 11.35 below), as 'deprivation of liberty' under the 2005 Act has the meaning given to it by Article 5(1) ((s 6(5),11(6), and 20(13)). Once the 2007 amendments come into force, it will determine when and whether new s 4A of the 2005 Act is engaged, which prohibits a 'deprivation of liberty' within the meaning of Article 5(1) (new s 64(5)) other than in three situations: first, where the Court has made an order under s 16; second, where the Sch A1 procedure is used; and, third where it is authorized in emergencies under s 4B (see further, para 11.38). The question of whether a person has been deprived of his liberty for the purposes of Article 5(1), particularly a person admitted to a hospital or care home ostensibly for their own benefit, is not straightforward, however, as the facts of a series of cases decided by the ECtHR in Strasbourg demonstrate: *Neilsen v Denmark*,[9] *HM v Switzerland*,[10] *HL v United Kingdom,* and *Storck v Germany.*[11] The determination is intensely fact-sensitive and the dividing line between a deprivation of liberty and a 'mere' restriction on movement is not

---

[9] (1988) 11 EHRR 175.
[10] (2002) 38 EHRR 314.
[11] (2005) 43 EHRR 96.

easy to determine. For example, in *JJ v Secretary of State for the Home Department* [2007] UKHL 45, the House of Lords held that a control order under the Prevention of Terrorism Act 2005 imposing a curfew of 18 hours gave rise to a deprivation of liberty, but (according to Lord Brown) a curfew of 16 hours would not. It is therefore proposed only to outline the relevant principles here.

11.22

The relevant authorities were reviewed by Munby J in *JE v DE (1) Surrey CC (2)*,[12] to which readers are referred for a full discussion of the relevant case-law. Draft guidance as to what constitutes a deprivation of liberty is contained in the draft Addendum to the Mental Capacity Act Code of Practice,[13] hereafter the 'Draft Deprivation of Liberty Code of Practice'.

1. The Three Elements of 'Deprivation of Liberty'

11.23

There are three elements relevant to the question of whether in the case of an adult there has been a 'deprivation' of liberty engaging the State's obligation under Article 5(1):[14]

- an *objective* element of a person's confinement in a particular restricted space for a not negligible length of time (*Storck v Germany*, para 74);

- a *subjective* element, namely that the person has not validly consented to the confinement in question (*Storck v Germany*, at para 74);

- the deprivation of liberty must be one for which the State is responsible (*Storck v Germany*, para 89).

(a) *The Objective Element*

11.24

As regards the *objective* element:

- The starting point must be the concrete situation of the individual concerned and account must be taken of a whole range of criteria such as the type, duration, effects and manner of implementation of the measure in question. The distinction between a deprivation of and a restriction upon liberty is merely one of degree or intensity and not one of nature or substance: *Guzzardi v Italy*,[15] para 92, *Nielsen v Denmark*, para 67, *HM v Switzerland*, para 42, *HL v United Kingdom*, para 89, and *Storck v Germany*, para 42.

- The key factor is whether the person is, or is not, free to leave. This may be tested by determining whether those treating and managing the person exercise complete and effective control over the person's care and movements (*HL v United Kingdom*, para 91).

---

[12] (2007) 10 CCLR 149.

[13] 'Mental Capacity Act 2005—Deprivation of Liberty Safeguards. Draft addendum to the Mental Capacity Act 2005 Act Code of Practice'. The draft addendum was issued for consultation on 10 September 2007; the consultation closes on 2 December 2007: <http://www.justice.gov.uk/publications/cp2307.htm>.

[14] Different considerations may apply in the case of a child where a parent or other person with parental authority has, in the proper exercise of that authority, authorized the child's placement and thereby given a substituted consent.

[15] (1980) 3 EHRR 333.

- Whether the person is in a ward which is 'locked' or 'lockable' is relevant but not determinative (*HL v United Kingdom*, para 92).

(b) *The Subjective Element*

11.25 As regards the *subjective* element, there is no deprivation of liberty if a person gives a valid consent to their confinement. In this respect the Strasbourg jurisprudence differs from domestic law, in which the presence or absence of consent goes to the question of whether a detention is lawful, rather than to whether there is a detention in the first place. Either way the same result is achieved:

- A person may give a valid consent to their confinement only if they have capacity to do so (*Storck v Germany*, at paras 76 and 77). This reflects the position at common law.

- Express refusal of consent by a person who has capacity will be determinative of this aspect of 'deprivation of liberty' (*Storck v Germany*, at para 77). The same cannot be said of a person who lacks capacity, although his objections to remaining where he is will be a factor that strongly indicates a deprivation of liberty, as in *JE v DE*.

- Where a person has capacity, consent to their confinement may be inferred from the fact that the person does not object (*HL v United Kingdom*, para 93 and *Storck v Germany*, at para 77 explaining *HM v Switzerland*[16] at para 46), but no such conclusion may be drawn in the case of a patient lacking capacity to consent (*HL v United Kingdom* at para 90).

- The fact that the person may have given himself up to be taken into detention does not mean that he has consented to his detention, whether he has capacity (*Storck v Germany*, para 75) or not (*HL v United Kingdom*, para 90). The right to liberty is too important in a democratic society for a person to lose the benefit of the Convention protection for the single reason that he may have given himself up to be taken into detention.

(c) *Whether Detention is Imputable to the State*

11.26 As regards the third element, where the deprivation of liberty is effected by a private individual or institution, it is necessary to show that it is imputable to the State ie the State is responsible. This may happen in one of three ways (*Storck v Germany*, para 89):

- Firstly, by the direct involvement of public authorities in the person's detention. If the detention takes place in a hospital or care home that is run by a public authority then that is the most obvious way in which the State will become directly involved. However, even where the place of detention is privately owned the State may be, or become, directly involved in the detention. In *Storck*, for example, the applicant was detained in a private psychiatric hospital but on at least one occasion, after she had escaped, she had been captured by the police and returned to the hospital.

---

[16] (2002) 38 EHRR 314.

That was considered to be sufficient to engage the State's responsibility for the detention.

- Secondly, the State can violate Article 5(1) in that its courts, in domestic proceedings brought by a detainee, fails to interpret the provisions of civil law relating to a claim in the spirit of Article 5.
- Thirdly, the State could violate its positive obligations to protect the detainee against interferences with his liberty carried out by private persons.

This subject is returned to below, at para 11.34.   11.27

2. Factors to Consider in Determining whether there is a Deprivation of Liberty

Not every incapacitated individual who is admitted to hospital or a care home is   11.28
automatically deprived of their liberty upon admission. However, an incapacitated person confined in a hospital or care home for anything more than a few days who is prevented from leaving, whether for their own safety or otherwise, probably is being deprived of their liberty. The key factor is that they are not 'free to leave' (the objective element) and they have not given valid consent to their confinement because of their lack of capacity (the subjective element). Only if the individual has capacity to consent can their lack of objection be taken as consent (*HM*, see above para 11.25). Other relevant factors indicating a 'deprivation of liberty' (at least, the objective element) include where the person has no, or very limited, choice about their life within the care home or hospital; where the person is prevented from maintaining contact with the world outside the care home or hospital (as in *HL v United Kingdom*); and where restraint is used upon admission or to administer care or treatment.[17] 'Restraint' in this context would include chemical restraint, where a patient is given sedating medication (as in *HL v United Kingdom*).

To establish a deprivation of liberty it is not necessary for P to raise an objection   11.29
to his confinement, although (as *JE v DE* demonstrates) that factor reinforces the conclusion he is being deprived of his liberty. Nor is it necessary for the regime *within* the hospital or care home to be a restrictive one (locked doors, the use of seclusion or medication to control patients). Nor, indeed, is it necessary for P be prevented from having access to his family or carers (although it may be a factor indicating a deprivation of liberty): indeed, P's family or carers may be happy with the arrangement, but if P is not 'free to leave' there may still be a deprivation of liberty.

On the other hand, there will probably be no deprivation of liberty within the   11.30
meaning of Article 5(1) in the following circumstances:

- P is living at home being cared for by family members who prevent him from wandering out the door on his own, and he cannot leave the house unless accompanied by a family member. There is no relevant 'deprivation of liberty', because the detention (even if the 'objective element' is satisfied) cannot be imputed to the State (see the third element, above para 11.26). The State may *become*

---

[17] Draft Deprivation of Liberty Code of Practice, paras 2.8–2.18.

responsible, however: for example, if P is being abused or neglected in the family home and is not permitted access to the outside world, and a local social services authority is aware of his situation but takes no action to remedy it.

- P is in a care home or hospital setting for a relatively short period of time of a day or two, perhaps a period of respite care before being returned home. This is unlikely to be a deprivation of liberty, because the period of confinement is 'negligible' (above, para 11.23).

11.31 More difficult, for example, is where P is a long-term care home resident who is not permitted to leave on his own, for his own personal safety, but he is supported in accessing the community on a regular basis, either by his family or professional carers; there are no limitations on where he may go and who he may see (albeit accompanied by family member or carer); he is free to move about within the institution; and P is not objecting to his placement. This may, or may not, be a deprivation of liberty, but will probably not be (see *LLBV v TG* [2007] EWHC 264C (Fam)).

11.32 The Draft Deprivation of Liberty Code of Practice, Chapter 2, gives further guidance as to the circumstances in which a deprivation of liberty may arise, but there will undoubtedly be further litigation around this issue.

3. Deprivations of Liberty in Private Care Homes

11.33 The 2005 Act, as unamended, prohibits any 'deprivation of liberty' within the meaning of Article 5(1) other than by the Court of Protection under s 16 (s 6(5), 11(6), and 20(13)) (below, para 11.35). The prohibition does not expressly include detentions in private hospitals and care homes. It is only with the amendments introduced by the 2007 Act that the Prohibition on deprivation of liberty in the 2005 Act is explicitly applied to placements in care homes and hospitals that are both privately and publicly funded (new s 64(6)). This raises the question, first, whether placements in private hospitals and care homes are governed by the 2005 Act as it came into force on 1 October 2007 and before the 2007 Act comes into force. It is suggested that the 2005 Act does include such placements. The 2005 Act codifies the common law doctrine of necessity which applies equally to private individuals as to public authorities. Any deprivation of liberty in a private care home or hospital after 1 October 2007 must be authorized under s 16 of the 2005 Act.

11.34 A second question arises, namely whether a deprivation of liberty in a private care home or hospital that does not comply with the 2005 Act will also be unlawful and give rise to a claim under the Human Rights Act 1998. In *YL v Brimingham City Council*,[18] the House of Lords held that a private care home provider is not a 'public authority' for the purposes of s 6(1) of the Human Rights Act 1998 because it does not carry out 'functions of a public nature' for the purposes of s 6(3)(b). This would appear to preclude a Human Right Act claim where detention takes place in a private care home. However, the exercise of coercive powers can constitute 'functions of a public nature' sufficient to make the detaining institution a 'public authority' for the

---

[18] [2007] UKHL 27.

purposes of s 6 of the Human Right Act, [19] as the House of Lords in *YL v Brimingham City Council* acknowledged.[20] A similar approach is taken under Article 5 in determining whether a deprivation of liberty is 'imputable to the State'—that is to say, it is one for which the State may be held responsible (*Storck v Germany*, para 89, above, para 11.26). The deprivation of liberty may be 'imputable' to the State in a number of ways, in particular if the individual is detained under coercive powers conferred by the State. From 1 October 2007 such coercive powers are introduced under the 2005 Act, s 16, and once the 2007 Act comes into force Sch A 1 introduces further detaining powers, which apply to both private and publicly funded placements. It is likely that a detention that is effected under such powers is imputable to the State for Article 5 purposes and constitutes 'functions of a public nature' for the purposes of s 6(3)(b). It is strongly arguable, moreover, that a private care home that *failed* to obtain authority to detain under the 2005 Act will still be liable for a claim for breach of Article 5 under the Human Rights Act, although the point is not without difficulty.

E. DETENTION UNDER THE 2005 ACT PRIOR TO AMENDMENT

1. Detention May Only be Authorized by the Court of Protection under s 16

As discussed at para 8.17ff above, the initial response of the government to the decision of the ECtHR in *HL v United Kingdom* was to introduce amendments to the Mental Capacity Bill, which was then passing through Parliament, restricting the circumstances in which deprivation of liberty would be authorized. As a consequence the 2005 Act, as currently enacted, prohibits any person (D) acting under s 5 or a donee or deputy from depriving P of his liberty (s 6(5), s 11(6), and s 20(13)), notwithstanding detention is considered to be in P's 'best interests', where 'deprivation of liberty' has the same meaning in the 2005 Act as in Article 5(1) of the Convention (s 6(5), s 11(6), and s 20(13)). From 1 October 2007 these provisions of the 2005 Act will be in force. The amendments effected by the 2007 Act will probably come into force in April 2009. In the meantime, *any* deprivation of liberty of an incapacitated adult under the 2005 Act must, and can only, be authorized by the Court of Protection under s 16. 11.35

2. Detention Must be Authorized in Advance

Moreover, authorization must be obtained from the Court of Protection under s 16 *before* the detention begins. In *Sunderland City Council v PS* [21] Munby J reached the same conclusion in respect of decisions taken under the doctrine of necessity in order to comply with Article 5, and the same principle must apply once the 2005 Act comes into force: see also the discussion at 12.93ff. 11.36

---

[19] *R (A) v Partnerships in Care Ltd* [2002] 1 WLR 2610, 2619.
[20] [2007] UKHL 27, paras 28 (Lord Scott), (Baroness Hale), 121 (Lord Mance), 166 (Lord Neuberger).
[21] [2007] EWHC 623 (Fam).

3. Interface between the Detaining Provisions of the 1983 Act and the 2005 Act Before the 2007 Act is in Force

11.37 The 2005 Act contains no provision analogous to s 28 (which precludes treatment being administered under the 2005 Act which falls within the provisions of Part 4 of the 1983 Act, see para 10.71) to determine when the detaining provisions of the 2005 Act can be used in preference to those of the 1983 Act. As will be seen in Chapter 15, once the 2007 Act comes into force a complex set of provisions will determine which of the detaining regimes takes precedence. Until that time, however, as a rule of thumb, only if P requires detention for treatment for physical disorder must the 2005 Act be used, with the detention to be authorized by the Court under s 16. Where P requires detention in hospital for treatment for mental disorder, the detention may be authorized under either the 2005 Act or the 1983 Act. The safest approach will probably be to use the 1983 Act. The 2005 Act Code of Practice, Chapter 13, is titled 'What is the relationship between the Mental Capacity Act and the Mental Health Act 1983'. Para 13.12 of the Code provides that it might be necessary to consider using the 1983 Act rather than the 2005 Act if:

- it is not possible to give the person the care or treatment they need without carrying out an action that might deprive them of their liberty

- the person needs treatment that cannot be given under the MCA (for example, because the person has made a valid and applicable advance decision to refuse all or part of that treatment)

- the person may need to be restrained in a way that is not allowed under the MCA

- it is not possible to assess or treat the person safely or effectively without treatment being compulsory (perhaps because the person is expected to regain capacity to consent, but might then refuse to give consent)

- the person lacks capacity to decide on some elements of the treatment but has capacity to refuse a vital part of it—and they have done so, or

- there is some other reason why the person might not get treatment they need, and they or somebody else might suffer harm as a result.

F. AMENDMENTS INTRODUCED BY THE 2007 ACT

11.38 The prohibition on detention in the 2005 Act outlined above was the immediate legislative response to *HL v United Kingdom*. After a period of time for reflection and consultation, the government unveiled its proposals for the detention of an incapacitated individual, P, which it chose to introduce by amendment to the 2005 Act, which are now to be found in the 2007 Act. The procedure introduced by the 2007 Act sees the repeal of s 6(5), s 11(6), and s 20(13) and the introduction of new s 4A of the 2005 Act, which prohibits any deprivation of liberty other than in three situations: first, as before, where an order of the Court of Protection has been made under s 16 of the 2005 Act relating to a matter concerning P's personal welfare (s 4A(3) and

208

(4)); second, where detention is necessary to give P life-sustaining treatment or to do any 'vital act' pending a decision of the Court of Protection (s 4A(2)(b) and s 4B); and, third, where the detention has been authorized under Sch A1 (s 4A(5)). It is the procedure provided for by Sch A1 that represents the Government's solution to the dilemma posed by *HL v United Kingdom* (and see para 8.22). Deprivation of liberty still has meaning given to it in Article 5(1) (new s 64(5)), and the prohibition on deprivation of liberty other than in the circumstances provided for in s 4A applies to placements in care homes and hospitals that are both privately and publicly funded (new s 64(6)).

Detention under the 2005 Act, both as originally enacted and as amended, does not entitle a hospital or care home to do anything other than detain for the purpose of the authorization. The giving of care and treatment will still be governed by the relevant provisions of the 1983 Act or of the 2005 Act, considered in Chapters 6 and 10. The interface between the detaining provisions of the two Acts once the 2007 Act comes into force is much more complex than currently (considered at para 11.37, above) and is considered in detail in Chapter 15.

11.39

G. STANDARD AND URGENT AUTHORIZATIONS: Sch A1

1. Standard Authorizations

Schedule A1 provides authority for the deprivation of liberty of incapacitated individuals over the age of 18 by means of two mechanisms, 'standard authorizations' and 'urgent authorizations'. 'Standard authorizations' sanction detention for up to 1 year. The court of Protection has jurisidiction to determine applications concerning standard authorizations under s 21A (see para 12.89). The procedure for a standard authorization is considered in Chapter 12 and is summarized under 'Key Features' at the beginning of that chapter.

11.40

2. Urgent Authorizations

'Urgent authorizations' authorizing detention for up to 7 days may be given by the managing authority, pending the completion of the 'standard authorization' procedure where P's need to be detained is so urgent that it should begin before a standard authorization has been granted. In some circumstances the period may be extended to 14 days. The Court of Protection also has jurisdiction under s 21A to determine issues arising out of the making of urgent authorizations (para 12.91). Urgent authorizations are considered in detail at para 12.82ff.

11.41

H. DETENTION FOR LIFE-SAVING TREATMENT: s 4B

New s 4B provides that a person (D) is authorized to deprive P of his liberty while a decision as respects any relevant issue is sought from the court. Three conditions

11.42

must be met: first, that there is a question about whether D is authorized to deprive P of his liberty under s 4A; second, that the deprivation of liberty is wholly or partly for the purpose of, or consists wholly of, giving P life-sustaining treatment, or doing any vital act; and, third, that the deprivation of liberty is necessary in order to give the life-sustaining treatment, or do the vital act. A 'vital act' is any act which the person doing it reasonably believes to be necessary to prevent a serious deterioration in P's condition (s 4B(5)).

11.43   The criteria for detention under s 4B are strict—stricter than under the urgent authorization procedure in Sch A1—in that detention must be necessary to administer treatment to save life or prevent a serious deterioration in P's condition *and* an application must have been made, or must shortly be made, to the Court of Protection. But there is no indication, in the Act at least, as to when the s 4B procedure should be used rather than the urgent authorization procedure. Section 4B is presumably intended to permit P's detention for the purpose of administering emergency treatment for physical, rather than mental, disorder, although there is no reason in principle why it should necessarily be limited for that purpose. Indeed, there is no reason in principle why a person cannot be admitted under the 'urgent authorization' procedure in Sch A1 for the purposes of administering treatment for physical, rather than mental, disorder. Certainly there is no requirement that detention under Article 5(1)(e) on the grounds of 'unsound mind' must be for the purposes of medical treatment for mental, rather than physical, disorder, although see para 3.100.[22]

11.44   The question of whether the s 4B procedure may be used in respect of a P who is otherwise 'ineligible' to be detained under the 2005 Act is considered at para 15.50ff.

I. THE ROLE OF THE COURT OF PROTECTION IN DECISIONS TO DETAIN

1. Decisions to Detain Under s 16 of the 2005 Act

11.45   Under the 2005 Act in its unamended form, the Court of Protection may, by making an order, make decisions on behalf of P in relation to matters concerning P's personal welfare (s 16(1) and 16(2)(a)) (see para 10.54ff). This includes the making of decisions the effect of which is to deprive P of liberty (paras 10.69, 11.35–11.37). Once the 2007 Act comes into force, the Court may not make an order for detention if P is 'ineligible' for detention within the meaning of Sch 1A (s 16A(1)) (considered in detail in Chapter 15, especially paras 15.02–15.25). Moreov er, if a provision of a welfare order under s 16 authorizes P to be deprived of his liberty and he subsequently becomes 'ineligible', the provision ceases to have effect for as long as the person remains ineligible (s 16A(2)) (see para 15.08).

---

[22] Indeed, there is some question as to whether any treatment need be given: detention may be justified on public safety grounds *Reid v United Kingdom* (2003) 37 EHRR 211, para 51. This is discussed in para 3.100.

The Court of Protection's jurisdiction to detain also applies to children aged 16   11.46
or 17 (see below, para 11.49), who also may not be detained if 'ineligible' within the
meaning of Sch 1A (see para 15.58ff). The Court of Protection has no jurisdiction
to make orders for detention in relation to children under 16, in respect of whom
the common law provisions will apply (below, para 11.55).

2. Applications Relating to Standard and Urgent Authorizations Under s 21A

Neither the standard or urgent authorization procedure requires the approval of the   11.47
new Court of Protection, although the Court has jurisdiction under new s 21A,[23]
upon application by P, his donee, deputy, or representative,[24] to determine any question relating to whether the criteria for either an urgent or standard authorization
are met, the period of detention authorized and the conditions upon which it is
made. This jurisdiction is considered at para 12.89.

3. Other Detention Issues Under s 15

Issues relating to detention may come before the Court of Protection in other con-   11.48
texts. For example, where a request is made by an 'eligible person' to the supervisory
body to decide whether or not there is an unauthorized deprivation of liberty (Sch
A1, para 68), the supervisory body is obliged to appoint an assessor to decide that
issue under para 69. If the assessor decides that P is not being deprived of his liberty
under para 72 of Sch A1, the Court of Protection has no jurisdiction to review
that decision under s 21A if the 'eligible person' wishes to take the matter further,
but could determine the matter in its general declaratory jurisdiction under s 15
(see para 12.32).

J. THE DETENTION OF CHILDREN

The detention of children other than under the provisions of the 1983 Act is, in the   11.49
main, governed by the same common law rules concerning the treatment of children, discussed in para 9.25ff. For the informal admission of children under
s 131(2) of the 1983 Act, and the additional safeguards on such informal admission
introduced by the 2007 Act, see paras 4.43–4.44. What follows is a discussion of
common law rules and the provisions of the 2005 Act which apply to the *detention*
of children. The interface between the detention and treatment provisions of the
2005 Act, the 1983 Act, and the common law rules after the 2007 Act comes into
force are considered in more detail in Chapter 15, particularly para 15.58ff.

---

[23] Introduced by para 2 of Sch 8 MHA 2007.
[24] No permission is required to bring an application: s 50(1) and (1A).

1. Children Aged 16 or 17

(a) *Detention at Common Law*

11.50 At common law a child of 16 or 17 is presumed to have capacity to consent to medical treatment, including detention for treatment, by virtue of s 8 of the Family Law Reform Act 1969 (above, para 9.36). The test for whether such a child has capacity to consent to treatment, including detention for treatment, is the same as for adults, namely that in *Re MB*, above at para 9.06ff. An incapable child may be detained for treatment with the consent of a person with parental responsibility or by the High Court in its jurisdiction relating to children (see *R v Kirklees MBC ex p C* [1993] 2 FLR 187). A capable child of 16 or 17 can be administered treatment with the consent of a person with parental responsibility or the High Court in its jurisdiction relating to children, which includes detention: *Re C (Detention: Medical Treatment)*,[25] subject to the provisions of s 25 of the Children Act 1989 (restrictions on the use of secure accommodation for children). However, a refusal of consent is an important consideration (see above, para 9.38).

11.51 The detention of a capable or incapable child of 16 or 17 by a person with parental responsibility raises issues under Article 5, considering *HL v United Kingdom*. (above, para 11.15).[26]

(b) *The Position under the 2005 Act Prior to the Amendments of the 2007 Act*

11.52 The 2005 Act applies to children of 16 or 17, with certain modifications (see para 10.03ff). There must, now, be some question as to whether a capable child may still be detained under the authority of a person with parental responsibility or by the High Court (para 10.05). However, it would appear to be implicit from new s 131(2) to (5) of the 1983 Act (introduced by the 2007 Act) (above para 4.44), which will prohibit the informal admission of a capable child of 16 or 17 on the authority of a person with parental responsibility, that the power of a person with parental responsibility to give consent on behalf of a capable 16 or 17 year old has not been displaced. If it had been, these provisions would be unnecessary. This issue will require early resolution. As regards an incapable child, there must be some question also as to whether the 2005 Act displaces the common law rules relating to the giving of consent by a person with parental responsibility. If those rules have not been displaced in relation to capable children, however, it is unlikely that they have been in relation to incapable children (above, para 10.05). If the common law rules have been displaced it would have some significance for decisions to detain, which under the 2005 Act may only be authorized by the Court of Protection under s 16 (above, para 11.35). If a parent's common law right to give consent on behalf of an incapable child has been displaced, he or she will ordinarily be in the position of a person 'acting

---

[25] [1997] 2 FLR 180.

[26] (2004) 40 EHRR 761. In *Neilsen v Denmark* (1988) 11 EHRR 175 the ECtHR upheld the right of a parent to admit a competent child to hospital, finding that it did not give rise to a 'deprivation of liberty' for the purposes of Art 5(1). There must be some doubt as to whether this decision would now be followed in the light of the analysis in *JE v DE* (2007) 10 CCLR 149.

in connection with care or treatment' under s 5, and detention cannot be authorized under s 5 (para 11.35). This point will also require resolution in due course.

The detention of a capable or incapable child of 16 or 17 by a person with paren- 11.53
tal responsibility raises issues under Article 5, considering *HL v United Kingdom* (above, para 11.51).

(c) *The Position under the 2005 Act Following the Coming Into Force of the 2007 Act*
A capable 16 or 17-year-old can no longer be admitted to hospital without his con- 11.54
sent on the authority of a person with parental responsibility (new s 131(2) to (5)) (see para 4.44). The interface of the detaining regimes of the 1983 Act, the 2005 Act, and the common law is considered in more detail in Chapter 15 at para 15.58ff.

2. Children Under 16

(a) *Detention at Common Law*
At common law there is a presumption that a child under 16 is 'incompetent'. To give 11.55
a valid consent to treatment, including detention for treatment, it must be established that a child has sufficient understanding and intelligence to enable him to understand the nature and implications of the proposed treatment (*Gillick* competence, after the decision of the House of Lords in *Gillick v West Norfolk and Wisbech Health Authority*[27]). Treatment decisions, including detention for treatment, will generally be made by a person with parental responsibility or by the High Court in its jurisdiction relating to children, which may authorize the treatment for treatment of both incompetent and *Gillick* competent children under 16 (above, para 9.29). This includes detention for treatment, as for children over 16 (above, para 11.50ff), subject to the provisions of s 25 of the Children Act 1989 (restrictions on the use of secure accommodation for children).

(b) *The Position under the 2005 Act Prior to the Amendments of the 2007 Act*
The position should not change once the 2005 Act comes into force, as s 2(5) of the 11.56
2005 Act excludes application of the provisions authorizing the taking of decisions on behalf of children under 16 in personal welfare matters, which will include decisions to detain (above, para 10.07). The common law rules relating to children under 16 continue to apply.

(c) *The Position under the 2005 Act Following the Coming Into Force of the 2007 Act*
See para 15.74. 11.57

K. s 47 NATIONAL ASSISTANCE ACT 1948

Section 47 of the National Assistance Act 1948 provides power to admit to hospital 11.58
or other types of residential care 'persons who are suffering from grave chronic disease

---

[27] [1986] AC 112.

or, being aged, infirm or physically incapacitated, are living in unsanitary conditions, and are unable to devote to themselves, and are not receiving from other persons, proper care and attention' (s 47(1)). The procedure is commenced on the application of the local authority to the magistrates' court, supported by a report from the 'community physician' certifying the grounds exist. Seven days' notice of the application must be given to the person who it is proposed to be removed, and the order may only be made after the court has heard oral evidence of the allegations in the certificate and it is satisfied of this and that is expedient to make the order. Once made, the order authorizes detention for up to three months, renewable for further periods of three months.

11.59   An emergency power to remove is provided by s 51 of the National Assistance (Amendment) Act 1951, which may be exercised by a single justice authorizing detention for up to three weeks.

11.60   Section 47 is amended by the 2007 Act, Sch 9, Part 2, para 12, so as to disapply the provision in any case where either an order has been made by the Court of Protection authorizing the managing authority of a hospital or care home to provide P with proper care and attention, or an authorization under Schedule A1 is in force or the managing authority is under a duty to request an authorization by virtue of Sch A1, para 24.

11.61   It is not clear how often either the s 47 or s 51 procedure is now used, and there are clear human rights implications of removing a person who is not of 'unsound mind' within the meaning of Article 5(1)(e) and who is not incapacitated. Article 5(1)(e) authorizes the detention of persons 'for the prevention of the spreading of infectious diseases, of persons of unsound mind, alcoholics or drug addicts or vagrants'; it does not authorize the detention of persons in need of care and attention on physical grounds.

12

STANDARD AND URGENT
AUTHORIZATIONS

A. Key Features	12.00
B. The 'Managing Authority' and 'Supervisory Body'	12.01
1. The Managing Authority: Hospitals	12.03
2. The Managing Authority: Care Homes	12.04
3. The Supervisory Body: Hospitals	12.05
4. The Supervisory Body: Care Homes	12.08
5. Where the Managing Authority and the Supervisory Body are the Same Body	12.12
6. Other Conflicts of Interest	12.13
C. The 'Qualifying Requirements': Part 3	12.14
1. The Age Requirement	12.15
2. The Mental Health Requirement	12.16
3. The Mental Capacity Requirement	12.18
4. The Best Interests Requirement	12.20
5. The Eligibility Requirement	12.25
6. The 'No Refusals' Requirement	12.26
D. The Request for a Standard Authorization	12.29
1. Procedure for Making a Request for a Standard Authorization	12.29
2. Circumstances in which Request for Standard Authorization May be Made	12.30
E. The Assessment Process: Parts 4 and 9	12.41
1. The Supervisory Body's Duty to Assess whether the Qualifying Requirements are Met (Sch A1, para 33)	12.41
2. Exception: Previous Assessment	12.42
3. Appointment of s 39A IMCA	12.44
4. The Assessments and the Assessors	12.45
5. Powers and Duties of the Assessors	12.48
6. The Mental Health Assessment: Additional Requirements	12.50
7. The Best Interests Assessment: Additional Requirements	12.51
8. Time Limits for Assessments	12.56
F. Refusal of the Standard Authorization	12.58
G. Grant of the Standard Authorization	12.61

H. Review of the Standard Authorization: Part 8   12.62
   1. Duty to Carry Out a Review on Request by
      an Eligible Person   12.62
   2. The Grounds for Review   12.63
   3. Supervisory Body's Duty to Secure Review Assessments   12.71
   4. Assessments Support Continuing Detention   12.74
   5. Assessments Do Not Support Continuing Detention   12.75
   6. Review Process Displaced by a Request for Fresh
      Standard Authorization   12.76

I. Termination of the Standard Authorization   12.78

J. Suspension of the Standard Authorization: Part 6   12.79

K. Renewal of the Standard Authorization   12.81

L. Urgent Authorizations: Part 5   12.82
   1. Conditions for Making an Urgent Authorization   12.82
   2. Period of Urgent Authorization and Extensions   12.85
   3. Appointment of s 39A IMCA   12.87
   4. Formalities   12.88

M. 'Appeals' to the Court of Protection   12.89
   1. Standard Authorizations   12.89
   2. Urgent Authorizations   12.91

N. Human Rights Implications   12.93

A. KEY FEATURES

12.00   • The 'standard authorization' procedure usually begins with a request by the managing authority, generally the managers of the hospital or care home in which P is, or may be, deprived of his liberty, to the 'supervisory body', usually the PCT, LHB or local authority.

• The supervisory body carries out an assessment of whether P meets the 'qualifying requirements' for detention. The 'qualifying requirements' are, in summary, that P is over 18; is suffering from a 'mental disorder'; lacks capacity to decide whether to be accommodated; it must be in P's best interests to be detained; P is not more appropriately detained under the 1983 Act (the 'eligibility requirement'); and the detention is not inconsistent with a valid advance decision or the decision of a donee or deputy.

• If the assessments conclude that the criteria are met, the supervisory body must grant the authorization, for up to one year and upon such conditions as it considers necessary.

• The standard authorization may be renewed for further periods of up to one year and may be reviewed at any time under Part 8.

- P is to be represented at all times while subject to Sch A1. If he is unbefriended, s 39A to 39E introduce statutory rights to an independent mental capacity advocate (IMCA) (considered in Chapter 13).

- Once a standard authorization is in place the supervisory body must appoint a Part 10 'representative' to act on P's behalf (also considered in Chapter 13).

- P, his representative or an IMCA may apply for a review of a standard authorization under Part 10 of Sch A1 and may apply to the Court of Protection to exercise its jurisdiction under s 21A in relation to any matter concerning a standard authorization.

- 'Urgent authorizations' authorizing detention for up to 7 days may be given by the managing authority, pending the completion of the 'standard authorization' procedure where P's need to be detained is so urgent that it should begin before a standard authorization has been granted. In some circumstances the period may be extended to 14 days. The Court of Protection also has jurisdiction under s 21A to determine issues arising out of the making of urgent authorizations.

- The flowchart in Appendix 4 describes the process of making a standard authorization.

B. THE 'MANAGING AUTHORITY' AND 'SUPERVISORY BODY'

Under the scheme provided for by Schedule A1, the 'managing authority' has respon-   12.01
sibility for making a request for a standard authorization in relation to a relevant person ('P') and the 'supervisory body' has the responsibility of assessing whether P meets the criteria for granting the standard authorization. Identifying who is the relevant managing authority is unlikely to cause too much difficulty as it will generally be the body or individual responsible for running the relevant hospital or care home.

A more difficult task may arise when determining the relevant supervisory body,   12.02
however. Schedule A1 provides for the supervisory body to be identified by the same mechanism by which the body with responsibility for providing P with health care services under the NHS Acts[1] (PCT or Local Health Board) and community care services (local authority) under relevant legislation[2] is identified. As budgetary pressures increase, disputes arise more regularly between NHS bodies and local authorities for different areas as to whether an individual is their responsibility or not. These can often take many months to resolve, on occasion requiring court proceedings. Where such disputes arise in the case of an individual otherwise falling within Schedule A1, it is likely that the identity of the relevant 'supervisory body' will not be possible to determine while that dispute is resolved, although draft regulations have been issued that should meet this problem (see para 12.11). Moreover, making the body responsible for funding P's placement the same body responsible for determining whether

---

[1] The National Health Service Act 2006 and the National Health Service (Wales) Act 2006.

[2] Primarily under Part III National Assistance Act 1948 but also under s 2 Chronically Sick and Disabled Persons Ac 1970, ss 254 & Sch 20 NHS Act 2006, and s 117 Mental Health Act 1983: see s 46(3) National Health Service and Community Care Act 1990.

P should be detained there creates considerable scope for conflicts of interest (see below, para 12.13). Difficult issues may also arise where P is in a care home but her care package is funded by an NHS body as NHS continuing care: the supervisory body will be the local authority but the care commissioners will be the relevant NHS body.

1. The Managing Authority: Hospitals

12.03 The term 'managing authority' is defined in Sch A1, paras 176–7. For NHS Hospitals,[3] if the hospital is vested in the appropriate national authority (the Secretary of State or the National Assembly for Wales) or is owned by the local authority but used as a hospital by the appropriate national authority, the managing authority is the Primary Care Trust (PCT), Special Health Authority or Local Health Board responsible for the administration of the hospital. If the hospital is vested in a PCT, NHS Trust, NHS Foundation trust or Local Health Board, the 'managing authority' is that Trust or Board. For independent hospitals,[4] the 'managing authority' is the person registered, or required to be registered, under Part 2 of the Care Standards Act 2000 (CSA 2000),[5] that is to say the person who 'carries on or manages' the hospital.

2. The Managing Authority: Care Homes

12.04 For care homes,[6] 'managing authority' is defined in Sch A1, paras 178–9. The 'managing authority' is the person registered, or required to be registered, under Part 2 of the CSA 2000, namely the person who 'carries on or manages' the care home.

3. The Supervisory Body: Hospitals

12.05 Where the relevant hospital is in England, if a PCT commissions the relevant care or treatment, the PCT is the supervisory body. If the National Assembly for Wales or a Local Health Board commission the relevant care or treatment, the National Assembly is the supervisory body, notwithstanding the hospital is situated in England. In any other case, the supervisory body is the PCT for the area in which the relevant hospital is situated.[7]

12.06 Commissioning responsibility in England is determined by reference to directions made by the Secretary of State under s 7 NHS Act 2006 and, in Wales, by the National Assembly for Wales under the NHS (Wales) Act 2006. Under the regulations currently in force[8] Primary Care Trusts (PCTs), are responsible for providing healthcare services to those individuals registered with a GP practice in their

---

[3] As defined by s 275 NHSA 2006 and s 206 of the NHS (Wales) Act 2006; Sch A1, para 125(2).

[4] As defined by s 2 of the Care Standard Act 2000; Sch A1, para 175(3).

[5] Sch A1, para 177.

[6] As defined by s 3 of the CSA 2000; Sch A1, para 178.

[7] Sch A1, para 180.

[8] National Health Service (Functions of Strategic Health Authorities and Primary Care Trusts and Administration Arrangements) (England) Regulations 2002, 2002/2375 (the NHS Functions Regs) (made under the NHS Act 1977). The Department of Health has also issued guidance to PCTs entitled, 'Establishing

catchment area and, if they are not so registered, to those who are 'usually resident' in that area.[9] In Wales, Local Health Boards[10] are responsible for the provision of healthcare services to 'persons usually resident in the area for which the Local Health Board is established'.[11]

Where the relevant hospital is in Wales, the National Assembly for Wales are the supervisory body, but if a Primary Care Trust commissions the relevant care or treatment, that Trust is the supervisory body.[12]

12.07

4. The Supervisory Body: Care Homes

The supervisory body is the local authority for the area in which the relevant person is 'ordinarily resident', but if the relevant person is not ordinarily resident in the area of a local authority, the supervisory body is the local authority for the area in which the care home is situated.[13]

12.08

'Ordinary residence' has an autonomous meaning, developed to determine the responsibility of a local authority for providing residential accommodation to individuals in its catchment area under ss 21 and 24 National Assistance Act 1948 (NAA 1948) and other community care services under s 29 NAA 1948 and s 2 Chronically Sick and Disabled Persons Act 1970 (CSDPA). The term 'ordinarily resident' refers to a person's residence which 'he has adopted voluntarily and for settled purposes as part of the regular order of his life for the time being, whether of short or of long duration'.[14] 'Voluntarily' implies, moreover, that the person has capacity to make that choice.

12.09

Two statutory exceptions to the ordinary residence rule are provided for by s 24(5) and (6) NAA 1948, which are expressly adopted in Schedule A1 for the purposes of determining the identity of the 'supervisory body'.[15] Section 24(5) provides that where a person is provided with residential accommodation under s 21 NAA in the area of another local authority, he continues to be 'ordinarily resident' in the area in which he was ordinarily resident immediately before the residential accommodation was provided for him. Section 24(6) states that, where a person is admitted to an NHS hospital, he remains ordinarily resident in the area in which he was ordinarily resident immediately before he was admitted to hospital.

12.10

---

the Responsible Commissioner' (the Responsible Commissioner Guidance). The current version was issued in September 2007.

[9] Reg 3(7) of the NHS Functions Regs.

[10] By s 27 Government of Wales Act 1998 the services then provided by Health Authorities (which included functions under the NHS Act 1977 delegated from the Secretary of State for Health under the Regulations) were, from 31 March 2003 (SI 2003/813), transferred to Local Health Boards (save in relation to certain exceptions, including medium secure forensic psychiatric services).

[11] Reg 2(2) of the Local Health Boards (Functions) (Wales) Regulations 2003, SI 2003/150 (The Welsh Regulations).

[12] Sch A1, para 181.

[13] Sch A1, para 182.

[14] *Shah v Barnet* [1983] 2 AC 209, 343.

[15] Sch A1, para 183(1)–(2).

12.11   Any question of ordinary residence is to be determined by the Secretary of State or by the National Assembly for Wales.[16] This reflects the existing mechanism for resolving 'ordinary residence' disputes under s 32(3) NAA 1948. Judicial review proceedings are sometimes the only means of resolving such disputes, however, particularly where very expensive care packages are involved. Regulations may make provision about arrangements that are to have effect before, upon or after the determination of any question as to the ordinary residence of a person.[17] Draft regulations provide that where a request is made to a local authority (local authority A) from a care home under Sch A1, para 24, 25, or 30 for a standard authorization (see para 12.29ff) or from an eligible person to decide whether there is an unauthorized deprivation of liberty in a care home under Sch A1, para 68 (below para 12.32), and local authority A wishes to dispute that it is the supervisory body, any question as to the ordinary residence of the relevant person is to be determined by the Secretary of State. In the meantime, local authority A must act as 'supervisory body', unless another local authority (local authority B) agrees to act as the supervisory body.[18] These provisions should avoid the situation of an individual otherwise coming within Schedule A1 being left in limbo.

5. Where the Managing Authority and the Supervisory Body are the Same Body

12.12   It may be seen that the 'managing authority' and 'supervisory body' are likely to be the same body where P is detained in an NHS Hospital.[19] Schedule A1 provides that the fact that a single body are acting as both managing authority and supervisory body does not prevent them from carrying out functions under this Schedule in each capacity, subject to any modifications contained in regulations made for this purpose.[20] Draft regulations provide that where the managing authority and supervisory body are the same, the supervisory body may not select a person who is employed to work for the body to carry out a best interests assessment.[21]

6. Other Conflicts of Interest

12.13   There may or may not be a conflict of interest where the managing authority and the supervisory body are the same body. But conflicts of interest are bound to arise where the supervisory body is also responsible for providing P with a package of care under relevant community care legislation or under the NHS Acts. P may wish to be cared for at home, rather than in hospital or in a care home. The supervisory

---

[16] Sch A1, para 183(3).

[17] Sch A1, para 183(6).

[18] Draft Mental Capacity (Deprivation of Liberty: Eligibility, Selection of Assessors, Assessments, Requests for Standard Authorizations and Disputes about Ordinary Residence) Regulations 2008, Regs 13–15.

[19] Sch A1, paras 177 and 180.

[20] Sch A1, para 184.

[21] Draft Mental Capacity (Deprivation of Liberty: Eligibility, Selection of Assessors, Assessments, Requests for Standard Authorizations and Disputes about Ordinary Residence) Regulations 2008, Reg 8(3).

body may refuse to fund such a care package in the exercise of its functions under community care legislation or the NHS Acts, on the grounds more cost effective treatment can be provided in a hospital or a care home. The hospital or care home then seek the supervisory body's authorization for P's detention. The supervisory body then has a conflict: it has already decided that P should be cared for (and therefore detained) in the hospital or care home, so how can it then decide whether that detention is authorized under Sch A1? A fair-minded and impartial observer may well conclude that there was a real possibility the supervisory body would be biased in favour of detention, rendering the decision unlawful.[22] It may be argued that this concern will be met by the requirement that the assessment must be undertaken by independent assessors (see paras 12.46–12.47, below and the Draft Deprivation of Liberty Code of Practice, para 3.18).

C. THE 'QUALIFYING REQUIREMENTS': PART 3

The managing authority's duty to request a standard authorization, and the supervisory body's duty to grant a standard authorization, are determined by whether they consider the 'qualifying requirements' for detention to be made out in P's case. There are six qualifying requirements, which are considered in turn.   12.14

1. The Age Requirement

The relevant person ('P') meets the age requirement if he has reached 18.[23] The detention of incapacitated children is considered at para 11.49ff.   12.15

2. The Mental Health Requirement

P must be suffering from a mental disorder within the meaning of the Mental Health Act 1983, but disregarding any exclusion for persons with learning disability.[24] P will meet this requirement if he suffers from 'any disorder or disability of the mind'.[25] Learning disabled individuals may therefore be detained under Sch A1 even if they do not present with 'abnormally aggressive or seriously irresponsible behaviour', by contrast with the position under the 1983 Act (see para 3.63ff). Note the test for mental disorder under the 1983 Act is not the same test as the incapacity test under s 2(1) of the 2005 Act. While it will often be the case that if the 'mental capacity requirement' is satisfied then the 'mental health requirement' will also be met, that will not always be the case (see para 3.103).   12.16

---

[22] See eg *Magill v Weeks* [2001] UKHL 67.
[23] Sch A1, para 13.
[24] Sch A1, para 14.
[25] s 1 Mental Health Act 1983. The new definition of mental disorder and the exclusions for learning disability are discussed elsewhere, in Chapter 3.

12.17   One further complicating factor is that different assessors may be responsible for the 'mental health assessment' and the 'mental capacity assessment' (see below, para 12.46), raising the spectre of different conclusions by different professionals on what, in most (if not all) cases, will be the same question of substance.

3. The Mental Capacity Requirement

12.18   P will satisfy this requirement if he lacks capacity in relation to the question whether or not he should be accommodated in the relevant hospital or care home for the purpose of being given the relevant care or treatment.[26] The question of whether he lacks capacity will be determined by reference to ss 2 and 3 of the 2005 Act (para 10.11). Thus, P lacks capacity in relation to a matter if 'at the material time he is unable to make a decision for himself in relation to the matter because of an impairment of, or a disturbance in the functioning of, the mind or brain', whether permanent or temporary.[27] He will be unable to make a decision for himself if he is unable '(a) to understand the information relevant to the decision, (b) to retain that information, (c) to use or weigh that information as part of the process of making the decision, or (d) to communicate his decision (whether by talking, using sign language, or any other means)'.[28]

12.19   These concepts are discussed separately, in Chapter 10.

4. The Best Interests Requirement

12.20   To meet this requirement, four conditions must be met: first, P is, or is to be, a 'detained resident'; second, it is in P's best interests for him to be a detained resident; third, it is necessary for him to be a detained resident in order to prevent him suffering harm; and, fourth, detention is a proportionate response to the likelihood of him suffering harm and the seriousness of that harm (Sch A1, para 16).

12.21   A 'detained resident' is defined by Sch A1, para 6 as 'a person detained in a hospital or care home — for the purpose of being given care or treatment — in circumstances which amount to deprivation of the person's liberty'. 'Deprivation of liberty' has the same meaning as in Article 5(1) ECHR (s 64(5) of the 2005 Act), which is considered in detail at paras 11.21.

12.22   The concept of 'best interests' has been discussed in Chapter 10, but is considered below at para 12.52 in relation to the 'best interests' assessment.

12.23   In the context of assessing whether to detain P in hospital or care home, however, the starting point of the assessment should be the normal assumption that P will be better off if they live with a family rather than in an institution—however benign and enlightened the institution may be, and however well integrated into the community. A P who has been looked after within their family will be better off if they

---

[26] Sch A1, para 15.
[27] s 2(1) and (2) of the 2005 Act.
[28] s 3 of the 2005 Act.

continue to be looked after within the family rather than by the State, although there is no threshold requirement to establish before a public authority can intervene to remove a P from his home such as a risk of significant harm equivalent to s 31 of the Children Act 1989.[29] The longer P has been cared for by the family, the more carefully must any proposals for intervention be scrutinized and the more cautious the decision-maker should be before accepting too readily the assertion that the State can do better than the family.[30]

The requirement that detention is necessary to prevent harm to P and is a proportionate response given the likelihood of his suffering harm and the seriousness of that harm means that the 'best interests' requirement is one of *necessity* rather than *desirability*. Detention is a measure of last resort: see also the Draft Deprivation of Liberty Code of Practice, para 1.7. The same conclusion may be derived from s 1(6) of the 2005 Act and the principles governing Article 5(1), which requires that detention be used only once less severe measures have first been considered and found to be insufficient.[31] Thus it will be relevant to examine what steps have been taken, for example, to care for P in his family home, with appropriate community care and healthcare support. 12.24

5. The Eligibility Requirement

P is eligible unless ineligible by virtue of Schedule 1A.[32] This is considered in more detail, at Chapter 15, but in short P will be ineligible for detention under Sch A1 if he is or ought to be detained under the Mental Health Act 1983 or he his subject to a compulsory regime under the 1983 Act and his detention under Sch A1 would be incompatible with some requirement imposed under that regime. 12.25

6. The 'No Refusals' Requirement

P cannot be detained under Sch A1 if a valid refusal to his detention or treatment has been made (Sch A1, paras 18–20). A 'refusal' for these purposes is any valid advance decision made under ss 24–6 of the 2005 Act or a valid decision of a donee of a LPA or deputy appointed by the Court of Protection refusing that treatment. Advance decisions and decisions of donees and deputies are considered at paras 10.20, 10.35. 12.26

The purpose of this provision is to treat people in this situation as if they had capacity to consent but are refusing to be admitted or stay in hospital or are not consenting to the treatment for mental disorder they are to be given there. In such cases, 12.27

---

[29] *Re S (FD)* [2003] 2 FLR 292, para 48.
[30] Ibid para 49.
[31] *Enhorn v Sweden* (2005) 41 EHRR 30 at 36, 44, 55.
[32] Sch A1, para 17.

they would either have to be detained under the 1983 Act, or another way of treatment would have to be found.[33]

12.28 An objection by P or by his family or carers is not sufficient to meet the 'no refusals requirement', although they would be able to challenge any standard authorization by applying to the Court of Protection under s 21A.

D. THE REQUEST FOR A STANDARD AUTHORIZATION

1. Procedure for Making a Request for a Standard Authorization

12.29 The standard authorization procedure generally begins with a request by the managing authority to the supervisory body, which triggers the supervisory body's duty to assess whether the 'qualifying requirements' are met in P's case (below, para 12.41). The request must be made in the prescribed form (when available) and contain the information required by regulations.[34] Where possible, authorization should be obtained in advance of the deprivation of liberty; if this is not possible, the managing authority must itself grant an urgent authorization and then obtain standard authorization within 7 calendar days. see para 12.82ff, below.[35]

2. Circumstances in which Request for Standard Authorization May be Made

12.30 A request for a standard authorization may, and in some cases must, be made in the following circumstances.

(a) *No Authorization in Place: Duty to Make a Request (Sch A1, para 24)*

12.31 Where no authorization is yet in place, the managing authority *must* make a request where it appears to the managing authority, first, that the relevant person ('P') is, or is about to be, accommodated in the relevant hospital or care home; second, P is, or is likely within the next 28 days to become, a 'detained resident'; and, third, P meets, or is likely to meet within the next 28 days, all the qualifying requirements (Sch A1, para 24). As we have seen, a 'detained resident' is one who is detained in a hospital or care home in circumstances which amount to a 'deprivation of liberty' (Sch A1, para 6), which has the same meaning as in Article 5(1) (s 64(5)). The 'qualifying requirements' are considered at para 12.14 above.

(b) *No Authorization in Place: Third Party Request for Authorization (Sch A1, para 68)*

12.32 A third party (an 'eligible person') may ask the managing authority to make a request for a standard authorization if it appears to the 'eligible person' that P is deprived of

---

[33] Explanatory Notes to Mental Health Act 2007, para 204.

[34] Currently provided for in Regs 12 and 13 of the draft Mental Capacity (Deprivation of Liberty: Eligibility, Selection of Assessors, Assessments, Requests for Standard Authorizations and Disputes about Ordinary Residence) Regulations 2008.

[35] And see the Draft Deprivation of Liberty Code of Practice, paras 3.1–3.13.

his liberty without authorization. The managing authority must then consider whether it 'appears' to them that the criteria triggering their duty to make a request under Sch A1, para 24 are met. If the managing authority refuses the 'eligible person's request, he or she may then request the supervisory body to decide whether P is being detained without authorization (Sch A1, para 68). This triggers the supervisory body's duty to appoint an assessor (Sch A1, para 69[36]) and a s 39A IMCA to represent P if he is otherwise unrepresented.[37] If the assessor determines P is being detained without authorization it has the same effect as if a request had been made by the managing authority, and an assessment of whether the 'eligibility requirements' are met must then take place.[38]

If the assessor determines that P is not being detained, or that he is being detained 12.33 but the detention is already authorized, he must notify the 'eligible person' who made the request, P, the managing authority and any s 39A IMCA[39] and that will be the end of the matter.

There is no specific right for an 'eligible person' to then challenge either finding 12.34 in the Court of Protection—the jurisdiction in s 21A applies only where an urgent or standard authorization is in force—but the Court would have jurisdiction to determine the question whether P was being 'deprived of his liberty' under its general declaratory jurisdiction in s 15 and, if it found he was, could either order his detention under s 16 or make some other order (see para 11.48).

An 'eligible person' is defined, for the purposes of para 68 of Sch A1, as 'any 12.35 person other than the managing authority of the relevant hospital or care home'. Thus any person interested in P's welfare may make the request under para 68. This is not to be confused with the 'eligible person' who may request the supervisory body to carry out a review of a standard authorization under para 102 of Sch A1 (below, para 12.62), which is defined as meaning either the relevant person (P), his representative or the managing authority.

(c) *Previous Refusal of Standard Authorization: Duty to make Request where Change of Circumstances (Sch A1, para 28)*

If the managing authority has previously requested a standard authorization which 12.36 has been refused by the supervisory body[40] because one or other of the qualifying requirements is not met, a fresh request must be made if it appears to the managing authority that there has been a change in P's case and, because of that change, the supervisory body are likely to give a standard authorization if requested.[41]

---

[36] The duty does not arise if it appears to the supervisory body that the request is frivolous or vexatious or the question has already been decided and there has been no change of circumstances which would merit the question being decided again: Sch A1, para 69(3) to (5).

[37] Section 39B(9) of the 2005 Act.

[38] Sch A1, para 71.

[39] Sch A1, para 72, 69(8).

[40] Under Sch A1, para 50(2).

[41] Sch A1, para 28.

(d) *Existing Standard Authorization or Court Order: Duty to make Request when Due to Expire (Sch A1, para 29)*

12.37 Where a standard authorization is already in place, the managing authority must make a request for a further authorization once the existing standard authorization is due to expire.[42] No specific timescale is provided for; the managing authority is obliged to make the request if, in its view, it would be 'unreasonable to delay making the request until a time nearer the expiry of the existing authority'.[43]

12.38 Where detention is already authorised by an order of the court under s 16 of the 2005 Act, the managing authority must make a request for a standard authorization when it is due to expire,[44] again only once the managing authority considers it would be 'unreasonable' to delay any longer.

(e) *Existing Standard Authorization: Duty to make Request where Change in Place of Detention (Sch A1, para 25)*

12.39 Where a standard authorization is in place and P is transferred to a new care home or hospital, and becomes a detained resident in this new care home or hospital, the new managing authority must make a request for a fresh authorization.[45] This will not necessarily mean the supervisory body will have to carry out fresh assessments as to whether the qualifying requirements are met. If the supervisory body has in its possession an assessment completed within the last 12 months and there is no reason to believe the assessment may no longer be accurate, no fresh assessment is necessary.[46] This is considered at para 12.42, below.

(f) *Existing Standard Authorization is Being Reviewed (Sch A1, para 30)*

12.40 Last, the managing authority may make a request for a fresh authorization when a review of the existing authorization has been requested, or is being conducted, in accordance with Sch A1, Part 8.[47] Reviews are considered at paras 12.62, below.

E. THE ASSESSMENT PROCESS: PARTS 4 AND 9

1. The Supervisory Body's Duty to Assess whether the Qualifying Requirements are Met (Sch A1, para 33)

12.41 With one exception, where a request for a standard authorization is made to it by the managing authority or, following a request from a third party, P has been found to be deprived of his liberty under Sch A1, para 71 (para 12.32), the supervisory body is under a duty to secure that P is assessed to determine whether each of the

---

[42] Sch A1, para 29.
[43] Sch A1, para 29(5).
[44] Sch A1, para 27.
[45] Sch A1, para 25.
[46] Sch A1, para 33(5).
[47] Sch A1, para 30.

'qualifying requirements' authorizing a deprivation of liberty are met in his case (Sch A1, para 33).

2. Exception: Previous Assessment

The exception to this duty is where the supervisory body has in its possession an   12.42
equivalent assessment, in writing, that has been carried out within the preceding 12 months and the supervisory body is satisfied there is no reason why the assessment may no longer be accurate. In these circumstances the supervisory body need not secure a further assessment in relation to the particular qualifying requirement or requirements covered by those assessments,[48] although if it proposes to rely upon an earlier best interests assessment the supervisory body must first consult P's representative or s 39C or s 39D IMCA.[49] If those assessments conclude the particular qualifying requirement is not met, then that is the end of the matter: the supervisory body need not secure any further assessments[50] and it must refuse the request for authorization.[51] Great care should be taken in deciding whether to use an equivalent assessment and this should not be done routinely.[52]

If, on the other hand, the assessment or assessments conclude the particular quali-   12.43
fying requirement is met, the assessment will stand as one of the assessments required to be carried out under Sch A1, para 33, and the supervisory body will have to secure that further assessments are carried out in relation to the other qualifying requirements.

3. Appointment of s 39A IMCA

A s 39A IMCA must be appointed where a person becomes subject to Sch A1 and   12.44
there is no appropriate person (other than one engaged in providing care or treatment in a professional capacity or for remuneration) to consult in determining P's best interests. A person becomes 'subject to Sch A1' where, among others, a request for a standard authorization has been made by the managing authority (s 39B). The appointment and functions of the IMCA are discussed in detail in paras Chapter 13.

4. The Assessments and the Assessors

The supervisory body must secure that assessments are made in relation to each   12.45
of the 'qualifying requirements' (Sch A1, para 33); thus, there must be an 'age assessment' (para 34), a 'mental health assessment' (paras 35–6), a 'mental capacity

---

[48] Sch A1, para 33(5) and 49.
[49] Sch A1, para 49(6).
[50] Sch A1, para 133.
[51] Sch A1, para 50(2).
[52] The Draft Deprivation of Liberty Code of Practice, para 3.15.

assessment' (para 37), a 'best interests assessment' (paras 38–45), an 'eligibility assessment' (paras 46–7) and a 'no refusals assessment' (para 48). In each case the assessment must determine whether or not the relevant 'qualifying requirement' is met, Sch A1, paras 12–20 (above, para 12.14).

12.46   To this end the supervisory body must appoint a person to carry out each of the assessments, in accordance with Regulations.[53] The same person may be appointed to carry out each of the assessments, *except* that the mental health assessment and the best interests assessment must be carried out by different people (Sch A1, para 129(5)). Draft regulations made under Sch A1, para 129(3) provide that a person is eligible to carry out a mental health assessment if they are approved under s 12 Mental Health Act 1983 or are a registered medical practitioner who a supervisory body is satisfied has special experience in the diagnosis and treatment of mental disorder.[54]

12.47   The draft regulations also provide that a best interests assessment may be carried out by an 'approved mental health professional', a registered social worker, nurse, occupational therapist or chartered psychologist.[55] The draft regulations also provide that the best interests assessor may not be a person who is involved in the care, or making decisions about the care, of the relevant person or employed by the care home or hospital in which P is detained,[56] so as to minimize the risk of conflicts of interest (see above, para 12.13). A mental capacity assessment may be carried out by a person who is eligible to conduct either a mental health assessment or a best interests assessment.[57]

5. Powers and Duties of the Assessors

12.48   An assessor may at all reasonable times examine and take copies of any health record, any record held by a local authority compiled in accordance with a social services function and any record held by a person registered under Part 2 Care Standards Act 2000 which the assessor considers may be relevant to the assessment which is being carried out.[58]

12.49   The assessor must take into account any information given, or submissions made, by P's representative or any s 39A, 39C, or 39D IMCA (Sch A1, para 132).

---

[53] Sch A1, para 129(3). The Draft Deprivation of Liberty Code of Practice, para 3.18, provides that it will be unusual for there to be six separate assessors. Steps should be taken to minimize the burden on the person being assessed. There is no reason why assessments cannot cover more than the particular qualification requirement, for example if an assessment under the 1983 Act or a community care assessment is to be made, then it should be combined if possible (ibid, para 3.22).

[54] Draft Mental Capacity (Deprivation of Liberty: Eligibility, Selection of Assessors, Assessments, Requests for Standard Authorizations and Disputes about Ordinary Residence) Regulations 2008, Reg 4.

[55] Ibid, Reg 5 'approved mental health professional' means a person approved under s 114(1) Mental Health Act 1983 to act as an AMHP for the purposes of that Act (ibid, Reg 2).

[56] Ibid, Reg 8.

[57] Ibid, Reg 6.

[58] Sch A1, para 131.

6. The Mental Health Assessment: Additional Requirements

The mental health assessor is required to consider not only whether P meets the   12.50
mental health requirement, but also to consider how P's mental health is likely to be
affected by his being a detained resident and to notify the best interests assessor of
his conclusions.[59] The supervisory body should, where possible, appoint a doctor
who already knows P and is involved in his care, which may reduce any distress that
might otherwise be caused.[60]

7. The Best Interests Assessment: Additional Requirements

Sch A1, paras 38 and 39 provide for some of the steps that the assessor must take in   12.51
carrying out the best interests assessment, but he is also subject to the more general
duties under the 2005 Act, in particular under s 4 (para 10.15).[61]

The steps that the best interests assessor is required to take in carrying out his   12.52
assessment are as follows (although it is not entirely clear whether his test is a subjective one, seeking to ascertain what P's wishes would be, or an objective one: see the
discussion at paras 9.17 and 10.15, above):

- First, he must consider whether it is likely that P will at some time have capacity
  in relation to the matter in question and, if it appears likely that he will, when that
  is likely to be (s 4(3)).

- Second, he must support P in participating in the decision-making process as far
  as reasonably practicable (s 4(4)).

- Third, he must seek to determine what P's wishes would have been in relation to
  the decision in question by reference to his past and present wishes and feelings,
  his beliefs and values and other factors P would be likely to consider if he were able
  to do so (s 4(6)). This would have to include considering whether P has made any
  relevant advance decision: if so, and detention would be in conflict with an
  advance decision which is valid and applicable, the 'no refusals' requirement would
  not be met and the assessment procedure would end (see para 12.26).

- Fourth, he must consult the managing authority;[62] must take into account, if it is
  practicable and appropriate to consult them, the views of anyone named by P as
  someone to be consulted, P's carer, donee, deputy (by s 4(7));[63] and must take into
  account any information given, or submissions made, by any IMCA or Part 10
  representative.[64] Again, if P has a donee who makes a valid objection to detention,
  the 'no refusals' requirement is not met and the assessment will come to an end
  (para 12.26).

---

[59] Sch A1, paras 35–6.
[60] Draft Deprivation of Liberty Code of Practice, para 3.37.
[61] See also paras 3.43–3.58 of the Draft Deprivation of Liberty Code of Practice.
[62] Sch A1, para 39.
[63] See the Explanatory Notes to the 2007 Act, para 216.
[64] Sch A1, paras 40 and 132.

- Fifth, he must have regard to whether P's needs can be as effectively met in a way that is less restrictive of his rights and freedom of action (s 1(6)) (and see para 12.23 above).

- Sixth, he must take into account all the relevant circumstances (s 4(2)). In particular he must have regard to the conclusions of the mental health assessor, including his views as to the impact detention will have upon P's mental health,[65] and he must have regard to any community care or NHS continuing care needs assessment and care plan prepared by the supervisory body (PCT or local authority).[66]

12.53   If the best interests assessor concludes that the best interests requirement is met in P's case, he must state the maximum authorization period (such maximum period which in the assessor's opinion would be appropriate, not exceeding one year)[67] and make recommendations for any conditions to which the standard authorization should be subject.[68]

12.54   Draft Regulations made under Sch A1, para 143[69] provide that the best interests assessor must also assess whether P has capacity to select his own representative for the purposes of Sch A1, Part 10 and make the necessary recommendations for the appointment of such representative, considered in Chapter 13.

12.55   If the best interests assessor concludes that P is a detained resident but the best interests requirement is not met, he must include a statement in his written assessment that there is an unauthorized deprivation of liberty.[70] In those circumstances the managing authority and the care commissioner (likely to be the supervisory body) will need to consider how the care plan could be changed to avoid a deprivation of liberty. If P is not yet a resident in the care home or hospital, the revised care plan may not involve admission to that facility.[71] A package of care supporting P at home is likely to be the alternative.

8. Time Limits for Assessments

12.56   Sch A1 does not specify the period within which the assessments must be completed, but the draft Regulations made under Sch A1, para 33 provide that all assessments required for a standard authorization must be completed within 21 days

---

[65] Sch A1, para 39(3)(a).
[66] Sch A1, paras 39(3)(b)–(c), 39(4)–(5).
[67] Sch A1, para 42. Regulations may provide for a shorter period than 1 year to apply in relation to some or all standard authorizations: para 42.
[68] Sch A1, paras 43 and 53.
[69] Draft Mental Capacity (Deprivation of Liberty: Appointment of Relevant Person's Representative) Regulations 2008.
[70] Sch A1, para 44.
[71] Draft Deprivation of Liberty Code of Practice, para 3.95.

from the date the supervisory body receives a request for such an authorization from a managing authority.[72]

Where a supervisory body receives a request for a standard authorization and the managing authority has given an urgent authorization under Sch A1, para 76 (para 12.82), all assessments must be completed during the period the urgent authorization is in force.[73] Urgent authorizations are given by the managing authority pending completion of a request for a standard authorization, where the need for immediate detention demands it, for a period of up to 7 days. This period may be extended by the supervisory body at the request of the managing authority for up to 7 days where there are 'exceptional reasons why it has not yet been possible for the request [for standard authorization] to be disposed of'.[74] In those circumstances, the timescale for completing the assessments is extended by a further 7 days.

F. REFUSAL OF THE STANDARD AUTHORIZATION

Where any of the assessments conclude that one or other of the 'qualifying requirements' are not met, the assessment process comes to an end (Sch A1, para 133) and the supervisory body cannot grant a standard authorization (Sch A1, para 50(2)). If the best interests assessor has concluded that the best interests requirement is not met and that P is being detained without authorization, he must state as much in his written assessment.[75] The supervisory body must as soon as reasonably practicable give notice of the fact it has refused the request to the relevant person, his representative, any s 39A IMCA, the managing authority of the relevant hospital or care home and every interested person consulted by the best interests assessor,[76] whereupon the request is considered 'disposed of'.[77] The supervisory body must keep a written record of any requests they have been prohibited from giving.[78]

The Act is silent, however, as to the consequences of a refusal of authorization. It may be that the reason no standard authorization has been given is because the 'no refusals requirement' or the 'eligibility requirement' are not met, in which case the most likely outcome is that P will become subject to the regime of the 1983 Act. If the conclusion is that P is not suffering from mental disorder, or the view is taken that he has capacity, or the best interests assessor concludes it is not in his best interests to be detained in the relevant hospital or care home, a real dilemma may arise. In most cases, P will already be a detained resident in the relevant hospital or care home and will not be able to simply walk out once authority for his detention is

12.57

12.58

12.59

---

[72] Draft Mental Capacity (Deprivation of Liberty: Eligibility, Selection of Assessors, Assessments, Requests for Standard Authorizations and Disputes about Ordinary Residence) Regulations 2008, Reg 9(1).
[73] Ibid, Reg 9(2).
[74] Sch A1, paras 84–5.
[75] Sch A1, para 44.
[76] Sch A1, para 58.
[77] Sch A1, para 66.
[78] Sch A1, para 60.

refused by the supervisory authority. Even if P is able to leave, he may need community care or other support to enable him to return home which the supervisory body may have refused to provide in the exercise of its community care or healthcare functions. If the responsible authority (NHS body or local authority) refuses to provide those services an application for judicial review will be necessary. P's continuing detention in these circumstances will have Article 5(1) implications. The Draft Deprivation of Liberty Code of Practice makes clear that in these circumstances an unauthorised deprivation of liberty must not be permitted to continue, if necessary by the supervisory body (or care commissioner, if different) revising P's care plan (paras 3.92–3.97).

12.60   Where the supervisory body refuses to grant a request for a standard authorization where there is an existing authorization, the refusal has no effect upon the validity of the existing authorization which will continue in force.[79] This is a curious provision; if the qualifying requirements are no longer met then authority for detention should cease immediately, or at least within a reasonable period thereafter to enable alternative arrangements for P to be made: contrast the position after a review concludes that detention is not justified (para 12.75). For the detention to continue in force may again have Article 5(1) implications.

G. GRANT OF THE STANDARD AUTHORIZATION

12.61   The supervisory body must give a standard authorization if all assessments are positive and they have written copies of all those assessments (Sch A1, para 50(1)). The following steps must then be taken:

- The supervisory body must decide the period during which the standard authorization is to be in force, which must not exceed 1 year (Sch A1, para 51), and may provide for it to come into force at a time after it is given (Sch A1, para 52). Where the standard authorization is a renewal of an existing authorization, the existing authorization terminates at the time when the new authorization comes into force (Sch A1, para 62(2)). A standard authorization comes into force when it is given or at such later time as may be provided for (Sch A1, para 63).

- The supervisory body must decide the conditions upon which standard authorization is to be made, having regard to the recommendations made in the best interests assessment about such conditions, whereupon the managing authority is obliged to ensure that those conditions are complied with (Sch A1, para 53).

- The standard authorization must be in writing and must state the name of the relevant person, the name of the relevant hospital or care home, the period during which the authorization is to be in force, the purpose for which it is given, any conditions and the reason why each qualifying requirement is met (Sch A1, paras 54–5).

---

[79] Sch A1, para 62(3).

- The supervisory body must as soon as practicable give a copy of the standard authorization to each of the relevant person, his representative, any s 39A IMCA, the managing authority of the relevant care home and every interested person consulted by the best interests assessor (Sch A1, para 57), whereupon the request is considered 'disposed of' (Sch A1, para 66).

- The managing authority must take such steps as are practicable, including giving information both orally and in writing, to ensure that P understands the effect of the authorization, his right to make an application to the Court to exercise its jurisdiction under s 21A, the right under Part 8 to request a review, the right to have, and how to have, a section 39D IMCA appointed. The same information must be given to P's representative (Sch A1, para 59).

- The supervisory body must keep a written record of the standard authorizations they have given (including all the information required to be contained in an authorization by virtue of para 55) (Sch A1, para 60).

- The supervisory body must appoint a person to be P's representative under Part 10 as soon as practicable after a standard authorization is given (Sch A1, para 139(1)). The appointment and functions of the Part 10 representative are considered in detail in Chapter 13.

H. REVIEW OF THE STANDARD AUTHORIZATION: PART 8

1. Duty to Carry Out a Review on Request by an Eligible Person

When a standard authorization is in force, the supervisory body may carry out a review at any time, and must do so when requested to do so by an 'eligible person', namely P, his Part 10 representative or the managing authority (Sch A1, para 102). An eligible person may request a review at any time and the managing authority must make such a request if one or more of the qualifying requirements appears to them to be 'reviewable' (Sch A1 para 103). 12.62

2. The Grounds for Review

A qualifying requirement is 'reviewable' if P ceases to meet one of the qualifying requirements ('the non-qualification ground'), the reason why P meets one of the qualifying requirements has changed ('the change of reason ground') or some change in P's case makes it appropriate to vary the conditions of the authorization ('the change of condition ground'). 12.63

(a) The 'Non-qualification Ground'
The 'non-qualification ground' is met if P ceases to meet any of the 'qualifying requirements' (Sch A1, para 105), although special rules apply so far as the 'eligibility' requirement is concerned. 12.64

12.65   The 'eligibility' requirement is considered in detail in Chapter 15, but, in summary, P is 'ineligible' to be detained under the 2005 Act if he is or ought to be detained under the Mental Health Act 1983 or subject to a compulsory regime under the 1983 Act and his detention under Sch A1 would be incompatible with some requirement imposed under that regime. Where P becomes 'ineligible' during the term of a standard authorization, Part 6 (Sch A1, paras 91–7) provides that the standard authorization is suspended for 28 days and thereafter terminated if P continues to be 'ineligible' (see para 12.79). An exception to that rule is where P is 'ineligible' by virtue of para 5 of Sch 1A, in which case the appropriate step is for a review to take place under Part 8 (Sch A1, Part 6, para 91(4)).

12.66   Part 8 then provides (Sch A1, para 105(2)) that a standard authorization is reviewable in the same circumstances. Para 5 of Sch 1A applies to patients on guardianship or who are 'within the scope' of the 1983 Act (that is to say, they qualify for compulsory admission under s 2 or s 3 of the 1983 Act) (Cases 'D' and 'E' in Sch 1A, para 2). Such patients are considered to be 'ineligible' for detention under the 2005 Act if, materially, the proposed course of action under the 2005 Act would authorize P to be a 'mental patient' (a person accommodated in a hospital for the purposes of being given medical treatment for mental disorder)[80] (the 'first condition'), P objects to being a mental patient or to being given some or all of the mental health treatment (the 'second condition'), and no valid consent has been given by a donee or deputy (the 'third condition') (Sch 1A, para 5).

12.67   It follows (although one has to look to Part 6 rather than Part 8 for this conclusion) that if the standard authorization is reviewable because P is 'ineligible' for any other reason, then it is suspended (then terminated) in accordance with Part 6 rather than reviewed under Part 8.

12.68   It may be that the reason why a standard authorization is not immediately suspended in the circumstances described in Sch 1A, para 5 is because the Part 8 review process offers an opportunity for one of the assessors to persuade P to withdraw his objection or to secure a valid consent from a donee or deputy, so that P will no longer be 'ineligible'. If at the end of the review process P is still 'ineligible' on this ground then the supervisory body must terminate the standard authorization under Sch A1, para 117 (below, para 12.75).

(b) *The 'Change of Reason Ground'*

12.69   A standard authorization is reviewable on the 'change of reason ground' if the reason why P meets one of the qualifying requirements is not the reason stated in the standard authorization (Sch A1, para 106). It applies to all the 'qualifying requirements' except the age requirement, for obvious reasons (people, sadly, do not get younger).

---

[80] Definition of 'mental patient' in Sch 1A, para 16 and referred to in Sch 1A, para 5(3).

(c) *The 'Variation of Conditions' Ground*

The 'variation of conditions' ground only applies to the 'best interests' requirement, 12.70
which is reviewable where there has been a change in P's case and, because of
that change, it would be appropriate to vary the conditions to which the standard
authorization is subject (Sch A1, para 107).

3. Supervisory Body's Duty to Secure Review Assessments

Where the supervisory body are to carry out a review of the standard authori- 12.71
zation, they must first give notice to P, his representative and to the managing
authority (Sch A1, para 108), and must then decide which, if any, of the qualifying
requirements appear to be reviewable (Sch A1, para 109). If the supervisory
body decides that none of the qualifying requirements appear to be reviewable
it need take no further action (Sch A1, para 110); that is the end of the review
(Sch A1, para 118(2)). It appears the supervisory body can take this decision without carrying out any assessments. In those circumstances, the only remedy available
to P or his representative will be to make an application to the Court of Protection
under s 21A.

If one or more qualifying requirements appear to be reviewable the super- 12.72
visory body must secure that a separate review assessment is carried out in relation
to each qualifying requirement, subject to one exception. The supervisory body
is not obliged to carry out a 'best interests' review assessment if the best interests requirement is only reviewable on the 'change of conditions' ground and
the change in the relevant person's care is not significant, having regard to the
nature of the change and the period it is likely to last (Sch A1, para 111). The supervisory body may then change the conditions without conducting a fresh assessment
(para 114).

The assessment process is then essentially the same as that which takes place 12.73
before a standard authorization is made. The assessor(s) appointed by the supervisory body must comply with the same duties in Part 4 (Sch A1, para 113(1),
see above at para 12.45ff), except the best interests assessor is not obliged to include
a statement that there is an unauthorised deprivation of liberty under Sch A1,
para 44, and rather than make recommendations about what conditions should
apply under Sch A1, para 33 he must make recommendations as to how the conditions are to be varied (Sch A1, para 113(2) and (3)).

4. Assessments Support Continuing Detention

Where the assessments are in favour of continuing detention the supervisory author- 12.74
ity must go on to consider whether the standard authorization needs to be varied
on the change of reason ground or the variation of conditions ground (Sch A1,
paras 115–16). There does not, however, appear to be any scope for the supervisory
authority to set a new date for the expiry of the standard authorization, even if all
the qualifying criteria have been assessed as met. The standard authorization will still

expire when it was originally due to expire, unless a fresh request for an authorization is made by the managing authority.

5. Assessments Do Not Support Continuing Detention

12.75   If any of the review assessments are negative the supervisory body must terminate the standard authorization with immediate effect (Sch A1, para 117). This is by contrast with the position where a request for a fresh authorization leads to the conclusion that one of the qualifying requirements are not met, in which case the existing standard authorization remains in force (Sch A1, para 62(3)) (para 12.60).

6. Review Process Displaced by a Request for Fresh Standard Authorization

12.76   Instead of requesting a review the managing authority may make a request for a fresh standard authorization (Sch A1, para 30), in which case the review process either does not begin or, if already begun, goes no further (Sch A1, para 124). The managing authority may make such a request either because it chooses to do so under Sch A1, para 30 or is bound to do so under Sch A1, para 24 taken with para 29 because the existing authorization is due to expire (para 12.37).

12.77   There does not appear to be any particular advantage, to any party, of the review route as opposed to a request for a fresh authorization, save as regards the effect of a negative assessment: in the case of a review, a negative assessment leads to immediate termination of the authorization, whereas a negative assessment following a request for a fresh assessment does not bring the existing authorization to an end. Other than that, there is little to choose between them. In both cases the supervisory authority can decide not to commission any further assessments. On a review, it may decide that none of the qualifying requirements appear to be reviewable (Sch A1, para 110), bringing the process to an end. When presented with a request for a fresh authorization, it may rely upon the assessments it already possesses and decide that there is no reason why they may no longer be accurate (Sch A1, para 33(5) and 49). In either event, if P or his representative, donee or deputy object the remedy will be to make an application to the Court of Protection to exercise its jurisdiction under s 21A.

I. TERMINATION OF THE STANDARD AUTHORIZATION

12.78   The standard authorization may come to an end in one of a number of ways. First, if not renewed, it will automatically come to an end at the expiry of the term prescribed by the supervisory body at the time the standard authorization was granted under Sch A1, para 51. Second, if during the course of a review under Part 8 one of the review assessments concludes that one of the qualifying criteria are not met, the supervisory body must terminate the standard authorization with immediate effect (Sch A1, para 117).[81] Third, if, at the end of the 28-day period of suspension under Part 6 (below), P continues to be ineligible (for example, because he is still detained under the 1983 Act), the standard authorization ceases to have effect (Sch A1, para 96). Fourth, if on an application to the Court of Protection under s 21A the standard authorization is discharged.

J. SUSPENSION OF THE STANDARD AUTHORIZATION: PART 6

Part 6 (paras 91–7) applies when a standard authorization is in force but the managing authority are satisfied that the relevant person has ceased to meet the 'eligibility requirement'. The 'eligibility requirement' and the interface between detention under the 2005 Act the 1983 Act is considered separately in Chapter 15, but in short P will not meet the 'eligibility requirement' if he is or ought to be detained under the Mental Health Act 1983 or he is subject to a compulsory regime under the 1983 Act and his detention under Sch A1 would be incompatible with some requirement imposed under that regime. If P becomes 'ineligible' during the term of a standard authorization, Part 6 (Sch A1, paras 91–7) provides that the standard authorization is suspended for 28 days and thereafter terminated if P continues to be 'ineligible' (Sch A1, para 96(2)). An exception to that rule is where P is 'ineligible' by virtue of para 5 of Sch 1A, in which case the appropriate step is for a review to take place under Part 8 (Sch A1, para 91(4)) (see para 12.65 above).   12.79

Where Part 6 applies the managing authority must give the supervisory body notice (Sch A1, para 92) whereupon the standard authorization is suspended for 28 days from the day when notice is given (Sch A1, para 93, 96). If during that period the managing authority are satisfied P meets the eligibility requirement again it must give notice to that effect to the supervisory body (Sch A1, para 94), whereupon the standard authorization ceases to be suspended (Sch A1, para 95). If no such notice is served by the end of the 28 day period the standard authorization ceases to have effect (Sch A1, para 96).   12.80

K. RENEWAL OF THE STANDARD AUTHORIZATION

As discussed above, at para 12.37, where a standard authorization is in place the managing authority is under a duty to make request for a further authorization once the existing standard authorization is due to expire (Sch A1, paras 24 and 29). The request must be made if it would be 'unreasonable to delay making the request until a time nearer the expiry of the existing authority' (Sch A1, para 29(5)). The request   12.81

---

[81] But note the anomaly where a request for a fresh authorization leads to the conclusion that one of the qualifying requirements are not met, in which case the existing standard authorization remains in force (para 62(3)).

triggers the process already described: para 12.41ff. If no request is made, the standard authorization will terminate at the end of the period authorized.

L. URGENT AUTHORIZATIONS: PART 5

1. Conditions for Making an Urgent Authorization

12.82　The procedure for making an 'urgent authorization' is governed by Part 5 of Sch A1, at paras 74–90. By Sch A1, para 76, the managing authority must give an urgent authorization when it is required to make, or has made, a request for a standard authorization and P's need to be detained is so urgent it is appropriate for the detention to begin before the request is made or disposed of. The circumstances in which the managing authority must make a request for a standard authorization are considered in paras 12.29. In particular, the managing authority is required to make a request for a standard authorization where it appears to it that all the 'qualifying requirements' in Sch A1, para 12 are, or shortly will be, met. So if the managing authority has good reason to suppose that all the qualifying requirements are *not* met, it cannot apply for an urgent authorization.

12.83　No elaboration is given as to when P's need to be detained is 'so urgent it is appropriate for the detention to begin before the request is made or disposed of', and the draft Deprivation of Liberty Code of Practice adds little more guidance, noting that 'Urgent authorizations should normally only be used in response to sudden unforeseen needs'. An earlier draft of the Code of Practice suggested that the procedure might be used in order to remove a person living at home, with relatives, into a hospital to enable 'a more accurate assessment to take place'.[82] Those circumstances, it is suggested, do not give rise to such a degree of urgency as to justify detention and the consequent anguish and suffering of removing P from his home and family. It is illuminating that this example has been removed from the more recent draft Code. To use the procedure in such a case may violate Article 5(1), 8, or both. The only circumstances which should justify the urgent procedure would be if P is in imminent danger of harm, whether self-imposed, due to neglect, or self-neglect, or due to the deliberate actions of others. In any other situation an order of the Court of Protection should be sought in advance of any action being taken.

12.84　This conclusion is reinforced by comparing the urgent authorization procedure with that provided by s 4B for detaining a person for 'life-sustaining treatment' or to do a 'vital act'. The s 4B procedure will only apply where an application is about to be, or has already been, made to the Court of Protection and it is necessary to take steps to save life or prevent a serious deterioration in P's health. Against that background, it cannot have been intended that the 'urgent authorization' procedure

---

[82] Paras 114–15 of the Draft Illustrative Code of Practice, published by the Department of Health on 22 December 2006, available at: <http://www.dh.gov.uk/en/Publicationsandstatistics/Publications/PublicationsPolicyAndGuidance/DH_064603>.

can be used, where no application has been made or need be made to the Court of Protection, without, at the very least, a requirement that detention is necessary to prevent P from suffering imminent harm.

2. Period of Urgent Authorization and Extensions

The managing authority must decide the period during which the authorization is   12.85
in force, which may not exceed 7 days (Sch A1, para 78). No new urgent authorization may be given but the managing authority may request the supervisory body to
extend the duration (Sch A1, para 77). The supervisory body may extend the urgent
authorization for a maximum period of 7 days, provided a request for a standard
authorization has been made, there are 'exceptional reasons' why it has not yet been
possible for the request to be disposed of and it is essential for the existing detention
to continue until the request is disposed of (Sch A1, paras 84–5). If the supervisory
body refuse the request for an extension they must notify the managing authority
with their reasons (Sch A1, para 86(1). The managing authority must give a copy of
that notice to the P and any s 39A IMCA (Sch A1, para 86(3)).

An urgent authorization comes into force when it is given, and ceases to be in   12.86
force at the end of the maximum period stated in the authorization, subject to
any extension under Sch A1, para 85, or when a standard authorization comes into
force under Sch A1, para 50(1) (Sch A1, paras 88–9). If a request for a standard
authorization is refused under Sch A1, paras 50(2), the urgent authorization ceases
to be in force when the managing authority receives notice under Sch A1, para 58
(Sch A1, para 89(4)). The supervisory body is required to give notice that the
authorization has ceased to be in force to the relevant person and any s 39A IMCA
(Sch A1, para 90).

3. Appointment of s 39A IMCA

When an urgent authorization is made the managing authority must notify the   12.87
supervisory body which must appoint a s 39A IMCA to represent P if no other
more appropriate consultee is available (s 39B). The managing authority must take
such steps as are practicable to ensure that the relevant person understands the effect
of the authorization and the right under s 21A to make an application to the court
(Sch A1, para 83) (see Chapter 13).

4. Formalities

The urgent authorization must be in writing and state the name of the relevant   12.88
person, the name of the relevant hospital or care home, the period during which
the authorization is to be in force and the purpose for which the authorization
is given (Sch A1, para 81). The managing authority must keep a written record of
why they have given the urgent authorization and, as soon as practicable, must give

a copy of the authorization to the relevant person and any s 39A IMCA (Sch A1, para 82).

M. 'APPEALS' TO THE COURT OF PROTECTION

1. Standard Authorizations

12.89   Section 21A(2) provides that, where a standard authorization has been given, the Court of Protection may determine any question relating to any of the following matters: (a) whether the relevant person meets one or more of the qualifying requirements; (b) the period during which the standard authorization is to be in force; (c) the purpose for which the standard authorization is given; (d) the conditions subject to which the standard authorization is given. On any such application the Court of Protection may make an order varying or terminating the standard authorization, or directing the supervisory body to vary or terminate it.

12.90   An application may be made, without the need for permission, by P, a person with parental responsibility (if aged under 18), the donor or donee of a LPA to which the application relates, a deputy or other person appointed by the Court (s 50(1)) or the relevant person's 'representative' (s 50(1A). For any other applicant permission will be required (para 14.28).

2. Urgent Authorizations

12.91   Where an urgent authorization has been given, the Court may determine any question relating to whether the urgent authorization should have been given, the period during which the urgent authorization is to be in force or the purpose for which the urgent authorization is given (s 21A(4)). Permission to apply is not required if the application is brought by P, his donor, or deputy (s 50(1)). The position is not entirely clear in so far as the s 39A IMCA is concerned. Section 50(1A) provides that permission is not required for an application to the court under s 21A 'by the relevant person's representative'. Where P is subject to the urgent authorization procedure he does not have a Part 10 representative; his 'representative' is the s 39A IMCA. It is suggested that 'representative' in s 50(1A) should be given this broader meaning so as to include applications brought by the s 39A IMCA or, for that matter, any person who has been nominated by P as a person to be consulted in matters affecting his interests (s 40(1)(a)).

12.92   The Court may make an order varying or terminating the urgent authorization, or directing the managing authority of the relevant hospital or care home to vary or terminate the urgent authorization (s 21A(5)). The court may also make an order about a person's liability for any act done in connection with the standard or urgent authorization before its variation or termination, including to exclude a person from liability (s 21A(5) and (6)).

N. HUMAN RIGHTS IMPLICATIONS

There is no mechanism by which a detained P's case *must* be referred to the Court   12.93
of Protection once a standard authorization is in place; it is left entirely to P or his
representative to decide whether to make an application. If neither P nor his representative, or any other person, makes an application to the Court of Protection then
he may be deprived of his liberty for months, possibly years, without any Article
5(4) determination by a court as to whether the deprivation of liberty is warranted
under Article 5(1). There is conflicting authority as to whether this state of affairs is
a violation of Article 5. In *R (H) v Secretary of State for Health* [83] the House of Lords
held that Article 5(4) did not require that an incapacitated adult detained under the
1983 Act have her case automatically referred to the Mental Health Review Tribunal,
provided every 'sensible effort [is] made to enable the patient to exercise that right if
there is reason to think that she would wish to do so' (para 23). On the other hand,
in *Sunderland CC v PS*,[84] Munby J held that where it is proposed to detain an incapacitated adult, in order to comply with Article 5 the detention must be authorised
by the court on application made by the local authority and *before* the detention
commences (para 23). Plainly if Article 5 requires consideration by a court *before*
detention, then any mechanism which does not require *any* consideration by a court
must be incompatible.

But even if Article 5(4) does not require a hearing before the detention begins, it   12.94
is likely that it does require a hearing shortly thereafter if there is any reason to
believe P wishes to challenge it (*R (H) v Secretary of State for Health*, above) or, it is
suggested, if it cannot be determined whether P wishes to challenge his detention
or not. While the House of Lords in *R (H)* found there was no right to an automatic referral to a Mental Health Review Tribunal for an incapacitated individual,
the case involved a very different legal framework to that under the 2005 Act. There
were a number of mechanisms by which the patient's case could come to be considered by a Tribunal, among which was the Secretary of State's power to make a reference under s 67. As regards this latter power, Baroness Hale held that 'the Secretary
of State is under a duty to act compatibly with the patient's Convention rights
and would be well advised to make such a reference as soon as the position is drawn
to her attention' (para 30). A managing authority or supervisory body that is detaining, or authorizing the detention, of an incapacitated individual is surely in the
same position as the Secretary of State if no application is brought in the Court of
Protection by P or his representative: they must make an application themselves.
Otherwise the statutory framework created by Sch A1 does not comply with
Article 5.

---

[83] [2006] 1 AC 441.
[84] [2007] EWHC 623 (Fam).

13

REPRESENTATION OF SCHEDULE A1 DETAINEES

A.	Key Features	13.00
B.	s 39A IMCAs	13.01
	1. Appointment of s 39A IMCAs	13.02
	2. Functions of s 39A IMCAs	13.05
C.	Part 10 Representatives	13.07
	1. Appointment etc of Representatives	13.09
	2. Functions of Part 10 Representatives	13.15
D.	s 39C IMCAs	13.20
	1. Appointment of s 39C IMCAs	13.20
	2. Functions of s 39C IMCAs	13.23
E.	s 39D IMCAs	13.24
	1. Appointment of s 39D IMCAs	13.24
	2. Function of s 39D IMCAs	13.28
F.	Donees and Deputies	13.29
	1. Appointment of Donees and Deputies	13.30
	2. Functions of Donees and Deputies	13.33
G.	Other Persons Nominated by the Detainee as a Consultee	13.35
	1. Appointment of a Nominated Person	13.37
	2. Functions of the Nominated Person	13.38

A. KEY FEATURES

- The 2005 Act, in particular Schedule A1, contains a number of measures designed **13.00** to ensure that a Sch A1 detainee is not left without an advocate or other representative at any time while a request for standard authorization is being considered or once an authorization has been given.

- During the standard or urgent authorization process, the supervisory body is obliged, if no other appropriate person is available to consult in determining P's best interests, to appoint an independent mental capacity advocate (IMCA) under s 39A of the 2005 Act (a 's 39 IMCA').

- Once a standard authorization is in place the supervisory body is under a duty to appoint a 'representative' under Sch A1, Part 10 to represent P's interests for as long as the authorization is in force.

- A s 39D IMCA must be appointed if P's Part 10 representative is unpaid and P's rights are not being adequately protected.

- A s 39C IMCA must be appointed if P's Part 10 representative ceases to act for him, pending the appointment of a new representative.

- The Schedule A1 procedure does not transplant the functions of donees of lasting powers of attorney ('donees') or Court-appointed deputies ('deputies'), who continue to exercise their respective functions and also have a number of additional functions under Sch A1.

- Moreover, where there is a donee, deputy or some other person nominated by P to be consulted in matters affecting his interests there is no duty on the supervisory body to appoint a s 39A or s 39C IMCA. This Chapter also considers how the s 39A and s 39C IMCA functions are exercised by the donee, deputy, or other nominated person in these circumstances.

B. s 39A IMCAS

13.01 One of the welcome innovations of the 2005 Act was to introduce a statutory right to an 'independent mental capacity advocate' or IMCA for incapacitated individuals in circumstances where an NHS body or local authority proposed to take steps that might involve significant interferences with P's rights, whether to bodily integrity or to respect for their home and their private and family life. Thus an IMCA must be appointed under s 37 of the 2005 Act where an NHS body is proposing to provide 'serious medical treatment' to P. An IMCA must also be appointed, under ss 38 and 39 of the 2005 Act, if an NHS body or local authority is proposing to provide P with accommodation, even if P's placement in a hospital or care home does not amount to a deprivation of liberty, and in certain other situations, considered in detail at para 10.78ff. The duty to provide an IMCA applies where there is no other person—other than someone acting in a professional capacity—whom it would be more appropriate to consult in determining P's best interests. This right has now been extended, by ss 39A, 39C, and 39D to detainees who become subject to Schedule A1.[1]

1. Appointment of s 39A IMCAs

13.02 Section 39A of the 2005 Act obliges a supervisory body to appoint a s 39A IMCA to represent a relevant person, P, who becomes 'subject to Schedule A1'. There are

---

[1] Sections 38 and 39 have been accordingly amended by the MHA 2007 to make it clear that they do not apply where an IMCA must be appointed under s 39A or 39C.

three circumstances in which this may occur: first, where an urgent authorization has been given by a managing authority under Sch A1, para 76; second, a request for a standard authorization has been made by the managing authority under, materially, Sch A1, para 24; and, third, where the supervisory body has appointed an assessor to determine whether P is a detained resident following a third party request for a standard authorization under Sch A1, para 69 (s 39B).

The supervisory body's duty to appoint a s 39A IMCA is triggered once the managing authority notifies the supervisory body that P is subject to Schedule A1 and that there is no appropriate person (other than one engaged in providing care or treatment in a professional capacity or for remuneration) to consult in determining P's best interests (s 39A(1)(b)). The following persons are considered a more appropriate person to represent P's interests: any person nominated by P to be consulted in matters affecting his interests, the donee of a lasting power of attorney or a deputy appointed by the Court (s 40). Where an existing standard authorization is in place, P's representative appointed under Sch A1, Part 10 will also be a more 'appropriate person' to consult, as such a person is not to be taken as 'engaged in providing care or treatment in a professional capacity or for remuneration'.[2]   13.03

In the absence of any such person, however, the supervisory body must appoint a s 39A IMCA.   13.04

2. Functions of s 39A IMCAs

The functions of IMCAs in the generality of cases are set out in s 36 of the 2005 Act, considered at paras 10.86.   13.05

The s 39A IMCA has the following, additional functions under Sch A1:   13.06

- To be consulted. The s 39A IMCA may give information or make submissions to assessors, which assessors must take into account in carrying out their assessments (Sch A1, para 132). Although Sch A1, para 132 does not impose an express duty on the best interests assessor to consult a s 39A IMCA, such a duty may be implied from that provision and, in any event, the general duty to consult in s 4(7) applies. By s 4(7)(b), a person seeking to determine P's best interests (which would include a 'best interests' assessor under Sch A1) must consult anyone 'engaged in caring for the person or interested in his welfare', which would include a s 39A IMCA.

- To receive copies of documents required to be served under Schedule A1, namely (i) any urgent authorization from the managing authority;[3] (ii) any notice from the supervisory body declining to extend the duration of an urgent authorization;[4] (iii) any copy of a notice from the supervisory body that an urgent authorization has ceased to be in force;[5] (iv) any standard authorization assessments that the

---

[2] Section 39A(6); see also s 38(10) and 39(7) for similar provisions.
[3] Sch A1, para 82.
[4] Sch A1, para 86.
[5] Sch A1, para 90.

supervisory body are given,[6] (v) any standard authorization, if granted, from the supervisory body.[7]

- To be notified by the supervisory body in the event that (i) the supervisory body are unable to give a standard authorization because all the standard authorization assessments did not come to a positive conclusion;[8] (ii) a best interests assessor concludes, in accordance with Sch A1, para 44(2), that P is being deprived of his liberty without authorization;[9] (iii) the supervisory body are requested by a third party to assess whether P is being deprived of his liberty.[10]

- To apply to the Court of Protection to exercise its jurisdiction under s 21A in connection with a matter relating to the giving or refusal of a standard or urgent authorization.[11] Section 50(1A) provides that permission is not required for an application to be made to the Court under s 21A by 'the relevant person's representative'. It is not clear whether this includes a s 39A IMCA but it is suggested that 'representative' should be given a broad interpretation to include a s 39A IMCA rather than a narrow meaning limited to the person appointed as a representative under Part 10 (see para 12.91).

C. PART 10 REPRESENTATIVES

13.07   Part 10 of Sch A1 provides for the appointment and functions of the relevant person's Part 10 representative. The supervisory body must appoint a person to be the relevant person's Part 10 representative as soon as practicable after a standard authorization is given or if a vacancy arises while a standard authorization is in force.[12] Thus P will not have a Part 10 representative until a standard authorization has been made in his case; before then, his interests will be protected by the 39A IMCA or, if none has been appointed because another person can more appropriately represent P's interests, by that person.

13.08   However, where a standard authorization is in force P will already have a Part 10 representative in place. Accordingly, if a request for a fresh authorization is made by the managing authority (because the existing authorization is due to expire,[13] there is a change in the place of detention[14] or a review of the existing authorization is being conducted under Part 8[15]), the functions otherwise exercised by the s 39A IMCA will be exercised by the Part 10 representative. It is therefore necessary to

---

[6] Sch A1, para 135.
[7] Sch A1, para 57.
[8] Sch A1, para 58.
[9] Sch A1, para 136.
[10] Sch A1, para 69(7)–(8).
[11] Sch A1, para 161(4)–(7).
[12] Sch A1, para 139.
[13] Sch A1, para 29.
[14] Sch A1, para 25.
[15] Sch A1, para 30.

consider the functions of the Part 10 representative both during the term of a standard authorization and when a fresh authorization is sought.

1. Appointment etc of Representatives

The appointment, monitoring, suspension, termination, and payment of Part 10 representatives is provided for in Part 10 of Schedule A1 and regulations made thereunder. In keeping with the overall ethos of the 2005 Act, Sch A1, para 143 provides that P should select his own Part 10 representative where he has capacity to do so, in default of which his donee, a deputy, a best interests assessor or the supervisory body may do so, in accordance with regulations made thereunder. Draft regulations have been made[16] which provide that the best interests assessor, when conducting the 'best interests assessment', must determine whether P has capacity to choose his own Part 10 representative.[17] If P has capacity he may select a family member, friend, or carer.[18] If P lacks capacity a donee or deputy, whose scope of authority permits it, may select a family member, friend, or carer.[19] In either case, if the family member, friend, or carer is eligible to be a Part 10 representative, the best interests assessor must recommend his or her appointment to the supervisory body.[20] If P or his donee or deputy do not wish to make, or cannot make, a selection, the best interests assessor may select a family member, friend, or carer and recommend his or her appointment to the supervisory body.[21] However the recommendation is made, the supervisory body is bound to accept it.[22] If no recommendation is made then the supervisory body may select and appoint a Part 10 representative to perform the role in a professional capacity.[23] Only a Part 10 representative appointed by the supervisory body in a professional capacity may be paid for carrying out their functions.[24]   **13.09**

To be 'eligible' to act as a Part 10 representative a person must be 18 years of age or over, willing and able to act, not prevented by ill-health from carrying out the role and have no conflict of interest, in particular neither they nor any close relative may have a financial interest in the care home or hospital in which P is detained.[25]   **13.10**

The Part 10 representative will be appointed for the period of the standard authorization issued. A person ceases to be a Part 10 representative at the end of that period or in the meantime if they inform the supervisory body that they are no   **13.11**

---

[16] Draft Mental Capacity (Deprivation of Liberty: Appointment of Relevant Person's Representative) Regulations 2008.
[17] Ibid Reg 6.
[18] Ibid Reg 7.
[19] Ibid Reg 8.
[20] Ibid Reg 9.
[21] Ibid Reg 10.
[22] Ibid Reg 12.
[23] Ibid Reg 11.
[24] Ibid Reg 11(2).
[25] Ibid Reg 5.

longer willing to act or if P (where he has made the original selection) or his donee or deputy (where they have made the original selection) inform the supervisory body that they object to that person continuing to be a Part 10 representative. The supervisory body may also terminate the appointment if it is satisfied the Part 10 representative is not maintaining sufficient contact with P in order to support and represent them or because they are no longer eligible to act in that capacity.[26]

13.12   There does not appear to be any provision for removing a Part 10 representative where he or she is not exercising their functions in P's best interests. Nor does there appear to be any means by which the Court of Protection may appoint or remove a Part 10 representative directly, although it may do so indirectly by appointing a deputy who may request the supervisory body to terminate the Part 10 representative's appointment.

13.13   Where the appointment of a Part 10 representative has been terminated, the supervisory body may be obliged to appoint a s 39C IMCA: see below, para 13.20.

13.14   Sch A1 Part 10 also provides that regulations may make provision about the circumstances in which functions exercisable by P's Part 10 representative may be suspended and thereafter revived,[27] but no such regulations had been made at the time of writing.

2. Functions of Part 10 Representatives

13.15   Schedule A1 does not have a similar provision to s 36 of the 2005 Act (functions of IMCAs) setting out the general functions of the Part 10 representative, but the supervisory body must not select a Part 10 representative unless satisfied that the individual would, if appointed, 'maintain contact, represent and support the relevant person in matters relating to or connected with Schedule A1'.[28]These may be taken to be the general functions of the Part 10 representative.

13.16   In practice, the functions of the Part 10 representative will, in many cases, be identical to those exercised by the s 39A IMCA and the s 39D IMCA as provided for in regulations under s 36 (see above, para 10.86), with one key distinction. A s 39A IMCA will only be appointed if no more appropriate person is available to represent P's interests, such as a donee, deputy, or other person P has chosen. On the other hand, the appointment of a Part 10 representative, and its functions, are in addition to those of a donee or deputy.[29] So while the s 39A IMCA will, necessarily, be the only person available to represent P's interests, the Part 10 representative must be appointed in addition to any donee or deputy. In practice, of course, they can (and often will be) the same person. But, at least in theory, a separate Part 10 representative may be appointed alongside a donee or deputy.

---

[26] Ibid Reg 14.
[27] Sch A1, para 150.
[28] Sch A1, para 140.
[29] Sch A1, para 141.

During the term of a standard authorization, the Part 10 representative has the   13.17
following specific functions:

- To apply to the Court of Protection to exercise its jurisdiction under s 21A in connection with any matter relating to the giving or refusal of a standard or urgent authorization. Section 50(1A) provides permission is not required for an application made under s 21A by 'the relevant person's representative'.

- To request a review of a standard authorization under Part 8.[30]

- To be notified by the supervisory body in the event that (i) a standard authorization ceases to be in force;[31] (ii) a standard authorization has been suspended where the 'eligibility requirement' is no longer met[32] or, having been suspended, is no longer suspended on that ground;[33] (iii) a review of a standard authorization is to be carried out under Part 8[34] or one has been completed.[35]

When a fresh request for a standard authorization has been made, the Part 10   13.18
representative discharges many, if not all, of the functions of the s 39A IMCA on a
first request for a standard authorization. Those functions are:

- To be consulted. As with the s 39A IMCA, the Part 10 representative may give information or make submissions to assessors, which assessors must take into account in carrying out their assessments (Sch A1, para 132). Although para 132 does not impose an express duty on an assessor to consult a Part 10 representative, such a duty may be implied from that provision and, in any event, the general duty to consult in s 4(7)(b) will apply. The Part 10 representative is also to be consulted where the supervisory body proposes to rely upon an existing best interests assessment rather than arranging for a fresh assessment under Sch A1, para 49.[36]

- To receive copies of documents required to be served under Schedule A1, namely (i) any standard authorization assessments that the supervisory body are given,[37] (ii) any standard authorization, if granted, from the supervisory body;[38] And (iii) (as interested party who has been consulted) notification from the supervisory body that they are unable to give a standard authorization because all the Sch A1 assessments did not come to a positive conclusion (Sch A1, para 58).

---

[30] Sch A1, para 102.
[31] Sch A1, para 65(3).
[32] Sch A1, para 93(3).
[33] Sch A1, para 95(3).
[34] Sch A1, para 108(1).
[35] Sch A1, para 120(1).
[36] Sch A1, para 49(6).
[37] Sch A1, para 135.
[38] Sch A1, para 57.

13.19   Certain functions of the s 39A IMCA are *not* exercised by the Part 10 representative, because they relate to a first standard authorization when a Part 10 representative will not yet have been appointed.[39]

D. s 39C IMCAS

1. Appointment of s 39C IMCAs

13.20 A s 39C IMCA must be appointed when a relevant person ('P') is subject to Schedule A1, the appointment of P's Part 10 representative ends and there is no other appropriate person (other than one engaged in providing care or treatment in a professional capacity or for remuneration) to consult in determining P's best interests. In those circumstances the managing authority must notify the supervisory body accordingly, which must then make the appointment ((s 39C(2) & (3)). Thus, as with s 39A IMCAs, there is no requirement to appoint a s 39C IMCA if P already has a donee, deputy or other person nominated by P to be consulted in matters relating to his best interests (s 40). A new Part 10 representative will be appointed in due course (see above, para 13.07), but in the meantime P's interests are protected by their donee, deputy, or other consultee.

13.21   A s 39C IMCA will only ever be appointed once a standard authorization is already in place, as their function is to replace a Part 10 representative whose appointment has been terminated, and a Part 10 representative will only have been appointed once a standard authorization has been made: see above, para Sch A1, para 139.

13.22   A s 39C IMCA's appointment comes to an end once a new Part 10 representative has been appointed in accordance with regulations.

2. Functions of s 39C IMCAs

13.23 A s 39C IMCA has the same general functions as any other IMCA, as set out in s 36 and in regulations made thereunder (see above, para 10.86). The specific functions that they exercise will be the same as those exercised by the Part 10 representative as set out at para 13.17 above.[40] Those functions are exercised until a new Part 10 representative is appointed in accordance with regulations. Once a new Part 10 representative has been appointed there is no requirement for any of the functions

---

[39] Namely to receive copies of documents required to be served under Sch A1, (i) any urgent authorization from the managing authority (Sch A1, para 82); (ii) any notice from the supervisory body declining to extend the duration of an urgent authorization (Sch A1, para 86); (iii) any copy of a notice from the supervisory body that an urgent authorization has ceased to be in force (Sch A1, para 90); and to be notified by the supervisory body in the event that (i) a best interests assessor concludes, in accordance with Sch A1, para 44(2), that P is being deprived of his liberty without authorization (Sch A1, para 136); (ii) the supervisory body are requested by a third party to assess whether P is being deprived of his liberty (Sch A1, para 69).

[40] Sch A1, para 159(2): 'In the application of the relevant provisions, references to the relevant person's representative are to be read as references to the s 39C IMCA.'

exercised by the s 39C IMCA to be exercised again by, or towards, the new Part 10 representative.[41]

E. s 39D IMCAS

1. Appointment of s 39D IMCAs

The supervisory body must instruct a s 39D IMCA to represent P where an authori-   13.24
zation under Sch A1 is in force in relation to P, P has a Part 10 representative 'R' appointed under Part 10, R is not being paid under regulations made under Part 10 for acting as P's Part 10 representative, and either (a) P or R make a request to the supervisory body to instruct an IMCA, or (b) the supervisory body have reason to believe that, without the help of an IMCA, P and R would be unable to exercise one or both of the 'relevant rights', or have each failed to exercise a relevant right when it would have been reasonable to exercise it, or that P and R are each unlikely to exercise a relevant right when it would be reasonable to exercise it.

The 'relevant rights' are the right to apply to the Court to exercise its jurisdiction   13.25
under s 21A and the right of review under Part 8 (s 39D(10)).

If the supervisory body has already appointed a s 39D IMCA at the request of   13.26
R or because they had reason to believe the matters at (b) in para 13.24 above, they must appoint a further s 39D IMCA if P so requests.

Section 40 provides that the duty to appoint an IMCA, including a s 39D IMCA,   13.27
does not apply where there is a donee, deputy, or other person nominated by P as a person to be consulted on matters to which the duty relates. It is possible, however, that where there is such a person they have also been appointed to act as P's unpaid Part 10 representative, R. If the criteria in s 39D for an appointment of a paid s 39D IMCA are met, then it is suggested a s 39D IMCA should still be appointed, notwithstanding the fact that R is a donee or deputy or other nominated person.

2. Function of s 39D IMCAs

The functions of s 39D IMCAs are set out in s 39D(7) to (9), although they will   13.28
have the same general functions as any other IMCA, as set out in s 36 and in regulations made thereunder (see para 10.86). Their role may be distinguished from that of s 39A and s 39C IMCAs, however, in that their primary function is to support P and his Part 10 representative, R, in discharging R's functions, rather than discharging those functions themselves.

- A s 39D IMCA is required to take such steps as are practicable to help P and R to understand the effect of the authorization; the purpose of the authorization; the duration of the authorization; any conditions to which the authorization is subject;

---

[41] Sch A1, para 160.

the reasons why each assessor who carried out an assessment in connection with the request for the authorization, or in connection with a review of the authorization, decided that P met the qualifying requirement in question; the relevant rights; how to exercise the relevant rights.

• The s 39D IMCA is required to take such steps as are practicable to help P or R to exercise the relevant rights (the right to apply to court under s 21A or to exercise the right of review under Part 8), if it appears to the advocate that P or R wishes to exercise either of those rights.

• If the s 39D IMCA helps P or R to exercise the right of review, the s 39D IMCA may make submissions to the supervisory body on the question of whether a qualifying requirement is reviewable.

• Consultation. The s 39D IMCA may give information, or make submissions, to any assessor carrying out a review assessment. (Sch A1, para 132). Although para 132 does not impose an express duty on an assessor to consult a s 39D IMCA, such a duty may be implied from that provision and, in any event, the general duty to consult in s 4(7)(b) will apply. The s 39D IMCA is also to be consulted where the supervisory body proposes to rely upon an existing best interests assessment rather than arranging for a fresh assessment under Sch A1, para 49.

F. DONEES AND DEPUTIES

13.29 The appointment and functions of donees of lasting powers of attorney ('donees') and Court-appointed deputies ('deputies') is considered in Chapter 10. They exercise the functions under Sch A1 of either giving or refusing consent to treatment (paras 10.38 and 10.57, above)), refusing Sch A1 detention in the first place (Sch A1, paras 18–20, see para 12.26), and consenting to Sch A1 detention for a P who would otherwise be 'ineligible' ('Case D', para 15.15 below and 'Case E', para 15.23 below). This section is concerned with their specific functions as they relate to their role as representative for P while detained under Schedule A1.

1. Appointment of Donees and Deputies

13.30 A donee will have been appointed before the relevant person, P, has lost capacity (s 9(2)(c)), but cannot exercise his functions—at least in relation to personal welfare decisions—until after P has lost capacity (s 11(7)(a)). A deputy will have been appointed by the Court of Protection only after a finding that P has lost capacity in relation to a matter or matters (s 16). A donee's appointment will always have been made before P becomes subject to Schedule A1, but a deputy may have been appointed after P becomes so subject.

13.31 As we have seen, where a donee or deputy is in place there is no duty to appoint a s 39A IMCA, a s 39C IMCA, or a s 39D IMCA (s 40). The donee or deputy is considered a more appropriate person to represent P's interests and to be consulted in relation to decisions affecting him than a professional advocate. In these circumstances, the donee or deputy has a significant role to play in safeguarding P's interests. Where, on the other hand, a standard authorization is already in place, a Part 10 representative must be appointed under Part 10 notwithstanding the existence of a donee or deputy (above, para 13.16). In those circumstances the functions of the donee or deputy under the Schedule will be less important, as the Part 10 representative will discharge the representative functions under Sch A1 on P's behalf. The Part 10 representative may, of course, be the same individual as the donee or deputy.

As discussed at paras 13.27 above, where P has a donee or deputy who is also acting as their Part 10 representative, and the conditions of s 39D are otherwise met, it is suggested that a s 39D IMCA should still be appointed.   13.32

2. Functions of Donees and Deputies

The functions exercised by the donee or deputy under the Schedule A1 procedure closely match those of the s 39A and 39C IMCAs, with certain important exceptions.   13.33

- To be consulted. Although Sch A1 para 132 (assessor's duty to take into account information or submissions from P's Part 10 representative, s 39A IMCA or s 39C IMCA) does not apply to donees or deputies, by s 4(7), P's donee or deputy is one of the individuals that a person seeking to determine P's best interests (which would include a 'best interests' assessor under Sch A1) must consult. Moreover donees and deputies are listed among the 'interested persons' that the best interests assessor may consult for the purposes of his assessment under Sch A1, para 40 (Sch A1, para 184).
- To receive copies of documents required to be served under Schedule A1. The position in this respect is not straightforward, however. The only specific requirement that a donee or deputy should be served with relevant documents is Sch A1, para 57, which requires that any standard authorization, if granted, from the supervisory body be served on any 'interested party consulted by the best interests assessor', which includes (Sch A1, para 184) a donee or deputy. Other documents that must be served on the s 39A IMCA are not required to be served on the donee or deputy (for which see para 13.06 above). However, as each of these must also be served on the relevant person, P, presumably it is expected that copies will make their way to the donee or deputy. This causes no problems when a standard authorization is already in place and a Part 10 representative is in post, as the relevant s 39A IMCA functions are exercised by the Part 10 representative (see above). It may conceivably cause problems where a first authorization is being sought (so no Part 10 representative is in place) or when the appointment of the Part 10 representative has been terminated, and no s 39C IMCA has been appointed, in each case because of s 40 (see para 13.31).
- To be notified by the supervisory body (again because of the donee and deputy's status as an 'interested party' under Sch A1, para 184) in the event that (i) the

supervisory body are unable to give a standard authorization because all the assessments did not come to a positive conclusion;[42] (ii) a best interests assessor concludes, in accordance with Sch A1, para 44(2), that P is being deprived of his liberty without authorization.[43] There is, however, no requirement on the supervisory body to notify the donee or deputy in the event it is requested by a third party to assess whether P is being deprived of his liberty, by contrast with a s 39A IMCA.[44]

• To apply to the Court of Protection to exercise its jurisdiction under s 21A in connection with a matter relating to the giving or refusal of a standard or urgent authorization. By s 50(1) no permission is required for an application to the court for the exercise of its powers under the Act by a donee or deputy.

13.34   Thus, apart from their role in relation to the giving and refusing of consent under Schedule A1 and their general functions under the 2005 Act, a donee or deputy's functions are largely the same as those of the s 39A and 39C IMCA.

G. OTHER PERSONS NOMINATED BY THE DETAINEE AS A CONSULTEE

13.35   The supervisory body's duty to appoint a s 39A, 39C, or 39D IMCA arises only if there is no appropriate person (other than one engaged in providing care or treatment in a professional capacity or for remuneration) to consult in determining P's best interests (s 39A(1)(b) and s 39C(1)(c)). By s 40 MCA, no IMCA need be appointed under, materially, s 39A, 39C, or 39D if there is a donee, deputy or 'a person nominated by P (in whatever manner) as a person to be consulted in matters affecting his interests'. The previous section considered, among others, how the s 39A and 39C functions under Sch A1 are exercised by a donee or deputy; this section considers how those functions are to be exercised by 'a person nominated by P' as his consultee.

13.36   As discussed at paras 13.27ff above, where P has a 'nominated person' who is also acting as their Part 10 representative, and the conditions of s 39D are otherwise met, it is suggested that a s 39D IMCA should still be appointed.

1. Appointment of a Nominated Person

13.37   A person may be nominated 'in whatever manner', so it will not be necessary for the appointment to have been made in writing or with any other formalities, although it will be necessary for the supervisory body to be satisfied that the appointment was indeed made and that P had capacity at the time that he made it.

---

[42] Sch A1, para 58.
[43] Sch A1, para 136.
[44] Sch A1, para 69(7)–(8).

2. Functions of the Nominated Person

Where P has nominated a person to be consulted in matters affecting his interests 13.38
there is no requirement for the supervisory body to appoint a s 39A, 39C, or s 39D
IMCA, by virtue of s 40. In practice those functions will be discharged by the nominated person. As will be seen, however, Schedule A1 makes no provision for any of
the s 39A or s 39C functions to be discharged by the nominated person:

- To be consulted. By s 4(7)(a), 'anyone named by [P] as someone to be consulted
  on the matter in question' is one of the individuals that a person seeking to
  determine P's best interests must consult, although Sch A1 para 132 (assessor's
  duty to take into account information or submissions from P's Part 10
  representative, s 39A IMCA, or s 39C IMCA) does not apply to such persons, who
  are not listed among the individuals that the best interests assessor may consult for
  the purposes of his assessment under Sch A1, para 40 (Sch A1, para 184).

- None of the functions of the s 39A or 39C IMCAs in relation to receiving copies
  of documents and notification under Schedule A1 apply to a person nominated
  by P as his consultee. Although these functions must all be exercised in relation to
  P himself (see above), that may not always be sufficient. The problem will not
  arise where a Part 10 representative is in post, as the notice and notification
  functions are discharged by that individual.

- To apply to the Court of Protection to exercise its jurisdiction under s 21A in
  connection with a matter relating to the giving or refusal of a standard or urgent
  authorization. By s 50(1A) no permission is required for an application to the
  court for the exercise of its powers under the Act 'by the relevant person's
  representative'. This provision, it is suggested, should be broadly construed so as
  to include any representative exercising functions under Sch A1, whether a person
  nominated by P to be consulted in matters relating to his interests, a s 39A or 39C
  IMCA or a Part 10 representative (see paras 12.91 and 14.28).

14

THE COURT OF PROTECTION, THE PUBLIC GUARDIAN, AND COURT OF PROTECTION VISITORS

A. Key Features	14.00
B. The New Court of Protection	14.01
C. Jurisdiction of the Court of Protection	14.02
1. The Court's General Declaratory Jurisdiction: s 15	14.05
2. Determining Questions Relating to Advance Decisions: s 26(4)	14.07
3. Determining Questions Relating to Lasting Powers of Attorney: ss 22 and 23	14.08
4. Court's Power to Make Personal Welfare Decisions: ss 16 and 17	14.09
5. Appointment of Deputies to Make Personal Welfare Decisions: s 16, ss 19–20	14.10
6. Determining 'Appeals' Against Urgent and Standard Authorizations: s 21A	14.11
7. Interim Orders and Directions	14.12
8. Restrictions and Limitations on the Court's Jurisdiction	14.14
9. Appeals	14.20
D. Making an Application to the Court of Protection	14.21
1. Public Funding for Cases in the Court of Protection	14.21
2. Making an Application in the Court of Protection	14.25
3. Litigation Friends and Capacity to Conduct Proceedings	14.67
E. The Public Guardian	14.73
F. Court of Protection Visitors	14.75

A. KEY FEATURES

- From 1 October 2007 a new Court of Protection, with the same status as the High Court, assumed the jurisdiction of the old court in relation to P's property and affairs and a new jurisdiction in relation to P's personal welfare matters.   14.00

- The 2007 Act amends and expands the jurisdiction of the Court of Protection in relation, in particular, to detention issues.
- Overview of the procedure for funding and making an application to the Court of Protection.
- The Public Guardian and Court of Protection Visitors briefly explained.

. B. THE NEW COURT OF PROTECTION

14.01 Section 45(1) of the 2005 Act establishes a new Court of Protection, designated a 'superior court of record' which gives it the same status as the High Court in that its decisions cannot be judicially reviewed and its orders are valid unless and until set aside on appeal.[1] The Court replaces the existing Court of Protection, which is an office of the Supreme Court, in relation to the management of incapacitated adults' property and affairs (formerly exercised under Part VII of the 1983 Act, now repealed by the 2005 Act) and acquires a new jurisdiction to determine issues concerning the personal welfare of incapacitated adults. The Court will have a central registry and additional registries in the regions. The jurisdiction may be exercised by judges nominated under s 46 who may be the President of the Family Division, the Vice-Chancellor, a High Court judge, a circuit judge or a district judge. Applications are to be determined in accordance with rules and practice directions made under s 51 and s 52. Rules have now been made under s 51 (The Court of Protection Rules 2007 (the Rules)).[2] The new Court of Protection came into being when the 2005 Act came into force, on 1 October 2007.

C. JURISDICTION OF THE COURT OF PROTECTION

14.02 Although a 'superior court of record', as a creature of statute the Court of Protection only has the jurisdiction specifically conferred upon it by the 2005 Act. This means that it has no inherent jurisdiction, but for the fact that by s 47(1) 'the Court has in connection with its jurisdiction the same powers, rights, privileges and authority as the High Court'. Thus, in addition to having the same powers as the High Court (for example) to compel the attendance of witnesses, enforcement of its orders and the punishment of contempts, it appears that the Court of Protection will also be able to exercise the High Court's inherent jurisdiction in relation to incapacitated adults. Although the intention of the legislation was to codify the inherent jurisdiction, it is not abolished by the 2005 Act, and it will be necessary to invoke the inherent jurisdiction in those cases where it is wider than the statutory jurisdiction (see below, para 14.17).

---

[1] *A v Harrow Crown Court* [2003] 1 MHLR 393.
[2] SI 2007/1744. Copies can be obtained at: <http://www.uk-legislation.hmso.gov.uk/si/si200717.htm>.

The newly formed Court of Protection assumes the jurisdiction of the old court   14.03
in relation to matters concerning P's property and affairs, although that jurisdiction
is now conferred by the 2005 Act, which repeals Part VII of the 1983 Act. That
jurisdiction falls outside the scope of this work.

The Court of Protection acquires jurisdiction, for the first time, to adjudicate   14.04
upon matters concerning P's personal welfare. The jurisdiction falls into seven areas,
although there is a good deal of overlap between them. First, it has a general declaratory jurisdiction in relation to incapacitated adults that broadly codifies the existing
inherent jurisdiction of the High Court in relation to incapacitated adults, with
some possible exceptions (s 15). Second, the Court may determine any question
relating to the creation, meaning and effect of lasting powers of attorney and give
directions in relation thereto (LPAs) (s 22 and s 23). Third, the Court may make
declarations as to the existence, validity, and applicability of advance decisions
(s 26(4)). Fourth, the Court has jurisdiction to make decisions on P's behalf in
relation to a matter or matters concerning his personal welfare, including detention
(s 16 and s 17). Fifth, the Court may appoint a deputy to make decisions on P's
behalf in relation to such matters (s 16, 19, and 20). Sixth, by s 21A the Court exercises a specific jurisdiction to determine matters arising out of the making of standard and urgent authorizations under Sch A1 (although not until the amendments
effected by the 2007 Act come into force). Seventh, the Court may make interim
orders and give directions pending the determination of any application to it (s 48).

1. The Court's General Declaratory Jurisdiction: s 15

By s 15 of the 2005 Act, the court may make declarations as to whether a person has   14.05
or lacks capacity to make a decision specified in the declaration, or upon such matters as are specified in the declaration, and as to the lawfulness or otherwise of any
act done, or yet to be done, in relation to that person. An 'act' includes an omission
and a course of conduct.

This provision effectively codifies the inherent jurisdiction of the High Court to   14.06
make declarations as to the 'best interests' of incapacitated adults (above, Chapter 9),
at least as that jurisdiction was understood to be at the time of the Law Commission's
draft Incapacity Bill in 1995,[3] upon which s 15 is modelled. There is some question
as to whether the jurisdiction under s 15 is quite as extensive as the inherent jurisdiction has been developed more recently, however. This is considered at para 14.17
below.

2. Determining Questions Relating to Advance Decisions: s 26(4)

The Court may make a declaration as to whether an advance decision is valid or   14.07
applicable to treatment (s 26(4)), for which see paras 9.23 and 10.34.

---

[3] Law Commission *Mental Incapacity* (Law Com No 231, 1995) Annex A.

3. Determining Questions Relating to Lasting Powers of Attorney: ss 22 and 33

14.08 Section 22 and s 23 apply where P has executed, or purported to execute, an instrument with a view to creating a LPA or an instrument has been registered as a LPA: see para 10.50.

4. Court's Power to Make Personal Welfare Decisions: ss 16 and 17

14.09 The Court's power to make personal welfare decisions in cases where detention is not involved is considered at para 10.54ff. Section 16 also empowers the Court to make decisions depriving P of his liberty, considered at paras 11.45. Until the 2007 Act comes into force, the only means by which P may be deprived of his liberty is by an order of the Court under s 16 (para 11.35ff).

5. Appointment of Deputies to Make Personal Welfare Decisions: s 16, ss 19–20

14.10 The power to appoint deputies to make personal welfare decisions is considered at para 10.57ff.

6. Determining 'Appeals' Against Urgent and Standard Authorizations: s 21A

14.11 The Court's power to determine issues arising out of the making of a standard or urgent authorization under s 21A is considered at paras 12.89 (standard authorizations) and 12.90 (urgent authorizations), respectively. This jurisdiction will not be exercisable until the amendments to the 2005 Act effected by the 2007 Act come into force.

7. Interim Orders and Directions

14.12 Section 48, which is headed 'Interim Orders and directions', provides that the Court may, pending the determination of an application to it, make an order or give directions in respect of any matter if there is reason to believe that P lacks capacity in relation to the matter, the matter is one to which its powers under this Act extend, and it is in P's best interests to make the order, or give the directions, without delay (s 48). This provides statutory authority, for the first time, for the power to make interim declarations set out in CPR 25.1 (above, para 9.21) and for the Court to act where it has not yet been established that P lacks capacity. The High Court had already developed power to make orders and give directions while 'proper enquiries' were made under its inherent jurisdiction (see para 9.21).

14.13 The general power to give directions is supplemented by the specific power in s 49 to call for reports. The Court may direct the Public Guardian, a Court of Protection Visitor (s 49(2), a local authority or an NHS body to arrange for a report to be made by one of its officers or employees or by such other person as the authority or the NHS body considers appropriate (s 49(3)). There is also power in the

Rules enabling reports to be commissioned from independent doctors and social workers, as is currently the practice in the High Court (below, para 14.51).

8. Restrictions and Limitations on the Court's Jurisdiction

(a) *Deprivations of Liberty*

For the position before the 2007 Act comes into force, see paras 10.69, 11.35. After the 2007 Act comes into force the Court may not make an order for detention under s 16 if P is 'ineligible' within the meaning of Sch 1A (s 16A): see para 11.45 and Chapter 15, especially paras 15.02–15.25.   14.14

(b) *Treatment for Mental Disorder: s 28*

The Court may not give, or authorize to be given, to P treatment for mental disorder that is regulated by Part 4 of the 1983 Act (s 28) (see paras 10.71 and 15.26ff). Once the 2007 Act comes into force, the Court may *refuse* (but not give) consent to P being given ECT when detained under the 1983 Act under s 58A(5)(c)(ii) (para 6.51) and may give (s 64C(2)(b)) or refuse (s 64D(6)) consent to other medical treatment under new Part 4A of the 1983 Act, where P is a community patient on SCT: see paras 6.74 and 6.77 and Chapter 15.   14.15

(c) *Other Limitations*

The limitations on the Court of Protection in relation to the exercise of its jurisdiction in personal welfare decisions is considered at paras 10.56. The following further observations may be made.   14.16

While the jurisdiction conferred by the 2005 Act is clearly wider than the High Court's inherent jurisdiction in relation to incapacitated adults in some respects (for example, in matters concerning LPAs, which previously did not exist), in other respects the jurisdiction may not be as wide. For example, first, it is not clear if the Court's jurisdiction may be exercised in relation to those who are deprived of capacity for reasons other than their mental functioning. The jurisdiction is exercisable in relation to adults who lack capacity, which is defined in s 2(1) as a person who is unable to make a decision for himself in relation to the matter because of 'an impairment of, or a disturbance in the functioning of, the mind or brain' (s 2(1)). This would appear to exclude those who are incapacitated for some other reason, such as coercion or other undue influence, in respect of whom the inherent jurisdiction may be exercised (para 9.21).[4]   14.17

Second, although the High Court has now developed the inherent jurisdiction to include the power to grant injunctions,[5] it is not clear if the Court of Protection has a power to grant injunctions under the 2005 Act. There does not appear to be a power to do so under s 15, although there may be power to do so under s 16(5).   14.18

---

[4] For which see *A Local Authority v MA* [2005] EWHC 2942 (Fam).
[5] *Re S (Hospital Patient)* [1995] Fam 26, 36 *per* Hale J; *In re A Local Authority (Inquiry: Restraint on Publication)* [2004] Fam 96, para 102 *per* Butler-Sloss LJ, *E v Channel Four* [2005] 2 FLR 913, para 55.

It may be that s 47 of the 2005 Act will operate to confer power to make injunctions in these circumstances, and in any event the Rules do provide for the making of injunctions (rule 82).

14.19   Third, there must also be a question whether s 15 authorizes the Court to make declarations as to P's wider best interests or whether it is limited to the (traditional) jurisdiction to declare in advance that a course of action will be lawful by application of the doctrine of necessity. We have seen how the inherent jurisdiction has developed beyond the confines of the doctrine of necessity[6] (above, para 9.21), as a result of which it is no longer necessary for declarations to be couched in terms that 'it is lawful as being in P's best interests that . . .': it is enough for the Court to simply declare that 'it is in P's best interests that . . .'.[7] But s 15(1)(c) specifically links the making of declarations to 'the lawfulness of any act done, or yet to be done', rather than to what is in P's best interests: necessity appears to still be the touchstone of the jurisdiction. As already noted, s 15 was drafted by the Law Commission in 1995, at a time when the inherent jurisdiction was not understood to go any further than authorizing the court to declare in advance that a course of action would be lawful because the doctrine of necessity would provide a defence to any tortious or criminal claim. If the jurisdiction is limited in this way it may be necessary for the Court of Protection to invoke the inherent jurisdiction, although beyond the instance already given of a person incapacitated by something other than an impairment etc. of the mind or brain, it is difficult to envisage what those circumstances might be. Possibly it might include the jurisdiction in relation to the restraint of publications, but that jurisdiction is now exercised under the Human Rights Act 1998.[8]

9. Appeals

14.20   See below, para 14.60.

D. MAKING AN APPLICATION TO THE COURT OF PROTECTION

1. Public Funding for Cases in the Court of Protection

14.21   The Legal Services Commission (LSC) can fund advice (Legal Help and Help at Court) and Legal Representation in certain cases before the Court of Protection. Public funding at all levels depends upon an applicant satisfying the financial eligibility tests set by the LSC. The Ministry of Justice has indicated this requirement will be waived in cases arising from standard or urgent authorizations under s 21A.

---

[6] *Re S (Hospital Patient)* [1995] Fam 26, 36 *per* Hale J; *In re A Local Authority (Inquiry: Restraint on Publication)* [2004] Fam 96, para 102 *per* Butler-Sloss LJ, *E v Channel Four* [2005] 2 FLR 913, para 55; *St. Helens BC v PE (1) JW (2)* [2006] EWHC 3460 (Fam).

[7] *St Helens BC v PE (1) JW (2)* [2006] EWHC 3460 (Fam).

[8] *Re S (A Minor)* [2005] 1 AC 593, para 23; *T v BBC* [2007] EWHC 1683 (QB), para 7.

Legal help is available in relation to making LPAs and advance decisions when the maker is aged 70 or over or disabled within the meaning of s 1 Disability Discrimination Act 1995. 14.22

Legal representation is available in cases concerning P's life, liberty, physical safety, medical including psychological treatment, capacity to marry, capacity to enter into sexual relations, and right to family life. Furthermore the court must have ordered, or be likely to order, an oral hearing at which it will be necessary for the applicant to be represented. The LSC will consider discharging a public funding certificate should the court decide that a hearing is not necessary (see Funding criteria 28.3.7). 14.23

All applications for legal representation must be made to the LSC's Mental Health Units. Guidance on funding can be found on the LSC's website at <http://www.legalservice.gov.uk>. 14.24

2. Making an Application in the Court of Protection

The procedure is governed by the Court of Protection Rules 2007 (the Rules).[9] In cases not expressly provided for by the Rules, or practice directions made under the Rules, the Civil Procedure Rules 1998 apply (rule 9). Practice directions and forms have been published on the Public Guardianship website: <http://www.guardianship.gov.uk/uk>. 14.25

The Rules are in 23 Parts with 202 provisions, so what follows is necessarily no more than a brief summary of the key provisions. 14.26

The Rules only apply to applications made under the 2005 Act as it came into force on 1 October 2007, both in relation to personal welfare matters and relating to P's property and affairs. The Rules do not yet make provision for applications relating to the new detention procedure under Sch A1 introduced by the 2007 Act. Amendments will need to be made in due course when those provisions come into force, probably in April 2009. 14.27

(a) *Who May Apply and the Requirement of Permission*

There is no statutory restriction on who may make an application, and the Court will probably apply the same rule as in applications made under the inherent jurisdiction, namely that any person with a genuine and legitimate interest in obtaining a decision may apply.[10] However, permission from the Court is required for an application made by anyone other than P, anyone with parental responsibility (if aged under 18), the donor or donee of a LPA to which the application relates, a deputy or other person appointed by the Court (s 50(1)). When the amendments effected by the 2007 Act come into force, permission will not be required for applications by the relevant person's 'representative' under Sch A1 (s 50(1A)). There is 14.28

---

⁹ SI 2007/1744. Copies can be obtained at: <http://www.uk-legislation.hmso.gov.uk/si/si200717.htm>.
¹⁰ *Re S (Hospital Patient)* [1996] Fam 1.

some question as to whether this will include P's s 39A IMCA where a challenge is to be made to an urgent authorization, at which time no Part 10 representative is in place (see para 12.91) or a person nominated by P to be consulted in matters affecting his interests (para 13.38).

14.29   Permission is not required for an application by the Official Solicitor or Public Guardian (rule 51(1)), nor in cases listed in rule 51(2) (certain applications concerning P's property and affairs, LPAs or EPAs). In all other cases permission must be obtained.

(b) Obtaining Permission (Part 8)

14.30 Rule 54 describes how to apply for permission. The applicant must file a permission form with any information or documents which may be specified in a practice direction; a draft of the application form he seeks to have issued and an assessment of capacity form where required by a practice direction. Rule 63 explains what the application form must contain (see para 14.35, below). A fee of £400 is payable.[11]

14.31   Rule 57 details the requirements for acknowledging a permission application. A person who fails to comply with these provisions may not take part in the permission hearing without leave (rule 58) (see para 14.42).

14.32   The court can grant the application for permission, in whole or part, or subject to conditions, without a hearing and may give directions (rule 55). The court may also refuse the application without a hearing (rule 55(b)) in which case that decision may be appealed (rule 60). Alternatively the court can fix a permission hearing. It will notify the applicant and other persons it thinks fit and will send those people the documents filed with the permission form and a form for acknowledging notification (rule 56).

(c) Making the Application (Part 9)

14.33 If permission is granted, or if permission is not required, the applicant must make an application in accordance with Part 9 of the Rules. A fee of £400 is payable. In cases where a fee was payable in order to seek permission no further fee is due.[12]

14.34   The general rule is that proceedings are started when the court issues an application form at the request of the applicant (rule 62).

14.35   The application form must (a) state the matter which the applicant wants the court to decide; (b) state the order which the applicant is seeking; (c) name (i) the applicant; (ii) P; (iii) as a respondent, any person (other than P) whom the applicant reasonably believes to have an interest which means that he ought to be heard in relation to the application (as opposed to being notified of it in accordance with rule 70); and (iv) any person whom the applicant intends to notify in accordance with rule 70; and (d) if the applicant is applying in a representative capacity, state what that capacity is (rule 63).

---

[11] Court of Protection Fees Order SI 2007/1745 contains details of fees and exemptions.
[12] Court of Protection Fees Order SI 2007/1745.

P is not to be named as a respondent unless the court orders otherwise (rule 73(4)), but by rule 74(2) P is bound by orders or directions in the same way that a party is bound. 14.36

When an applicant files his application form with the court, he must also file (a) in accordance with the relevant practice direction, any evidence upon which he intends to rely (although see para 14.51 for limitations on expert evidence); (b) if permission was required to make the application, a copy of the court's order granting permission; (c) an assessment of capacity form, where this is required by the relevant practice direction; (d) any other documents referred to in the application form; and (e) such other information and material as may be set out in a practice direction (rule 64). 14.37

The Court will then issue the application which the applicant must serve on anyone named as a respondent within 21 days. 14.38

(d) Human Rights (Part 11)

A party relying on or seeking a remedy under the Human Rights Act 1998 must provide the court with details of the alleged infringement and the remedy sought (which must be taken to include compensation under s 8). The court cannot make a declaration of incompatibility unless 21 days notice has been given to the Crown (rule 83). 14.39

(e) Notification to be given to P (Part 7)

Part 7 sets out the requirements for notifying P of the issue or withdrawal of an application form as well as other circumstances where P must be notified. 14.40

P must be notified once an application has been issued (rule 42 and 69), but there is no requirement that he be notified of an application for permission. P must be provided with the information personally, in a manner appropriate to P's circumstances, for example using simple language or visual aids (rule 46(1) and (2)). 14.41

(f) Responding to an Application for Permission and an Application

Rule 57 explains how to respond to an application for permission and Rule 72 explains how to respond after an application has been issued and served where permission has been granted or is not required. The following requirements apply in both cases. 14.42

A person who is served with or notified of an application form and who wishes to take part in proceedings must file an acknowledgment of service or notification, together with a witness statement containing any evidence establishing his interest in the proceedings and, if he seeks a different order, any evidence upon which he intends to rely for that purpose, not more than 21 days after the application form was served or notification of the application was given. The court will serve the acknowledgment of service or notification on the applicant and on any other person who has filed such an acknowledgment. 14.43

14.44   The acknowledgment of service or notification must (a) state whether the person consents to the application; (b) state whether he opposes the application and, if so, set out the grounds for doing so; (c) state whether he seeks a different order from that set out in the application form and, if so, set out what that order is; (d) indicate whether he wishes to be joined as a party; (e) state his interest in the proceedings. The acknowledgment or notification must contain an address for service and be signed by him or his legal representative.

(g) *Dealing with the Application (Part 12)*

14.45   Rule 84(2) allows the Court to deal with the application or any part of it without a hearing. Rule 84(3) sets out the factors which the court must consider when deciding whether it is necessary to hold a hearing.

14.46   Rule 89 allows P, or any party to the proceedings, or any other person affected by an order which has been made either without a hearing or without notice, to apply to the court for reconsideration of the order within 21 days of the order being served, or such other period as the Court directs.

14.47   If the court decides a hearing of an application is necessary it will notify the parties and state whether the hearing is for directions only or to dispose of the application (rule 84(4)).

(h) *Directions and Case Management*

14.48   The court may give directions at any time, with or without a hearing, of its own initiative as well as on the application of a party (rule 85). The court can make any directions it sees fit, including ordering s 49 reports, joining P as a party and appointing a litigation friend, deciding whether to hold all or part of the hearing in public, and deciding which type of judge should hear the case. Rule 5 provides that the court will further the overriding objective of dealing with a case justly (rule 3) by 'actively managing' cases. Rule 25(2) lists the Court's general powers of case management which the Court may exercise even if no party has sought that order (rule 25(5)).

(i) *Interim Applications (Part 10)*

14.49   Jurisdiction to make interim applications is provided for by s 48 of the 2005 Act (above, para 14.12). Permission is not needed to make these applications (rule 51(3)). The person seeking the order must file an application notice and evidence he relies on unless he has already filed it (rule 78). The notice must state the order or direction sought and the brief grounds (rule 79). The provisions as to service appear at rule 80 and rule 81(2). The remedies available, which include injunctions, are listed at rule 82 (1). The Court can grant an interim remedy before an application form has been issued if the matter is urgent or if it is necessary to do so in the interests of justice (rule 77(3)). The court can dispense with the requirement for an application notice but the evidence in support must state why notice has not been given (rule 78(5). A person against whom an order is made without notice can use rule 89 to ask the court to reconsider the order.

(j) s 49 Reports

The Court has power to order reports under s 49 of the 2005 Act (para 14.13). 14.50
Rule 117 (3) describes the steps to be taken by a person ordered to prepare a s 49
report. Rule 117(5) allows the report writer to examine and take copies of any document in the Court records. The court retains the power to exclude certain documents (rule 117(6)). Section 49(7) allows the Public Guardian or Court of Protection
Visitor who prepares a s 49 report to examine and take copies of P's health and social
care records. The Court can direct an oral or written report (s 49(6)). The Court can
permit parties to put written questions to the person making the Section 49 report
(rule 118).

(k) Experts (Part 15)

The only expert evidence that can be filed without the Court's permission is evi- 14.51
dence filed with the permission form or application form, and then a party may only
rely upon it to the extent the Court allows. The expert evidence so filed is limited to
evidence that P lacks decision-making capacity in respect of the matter which the
application concerns, or evidence as to P's best interests, or evidence that is required
by any rule or practice direction (rule 120).

In all other cases a party wishing to obtain expert evidence must apply for a direction 14.52
(rule 123). He must identify the expert's field and if practicable the individual expert he
wishes to instruct. He must provide any other material information about the expert
and a draft letter of instruction (rule 123(2). The Court can limit the amount of the
expert's costs which that party may recover from any other party (rule 123(6)). The
court can give directions as to what an expert's report can cover (rule 126).

Expert evidence can be obtained from an expert instructed by one party or from 14.53
a single joint expert. If one party alone instructs an expert, the letter of instruction
is not privileged (rule 126(5)); other parties can put written questions to the expert
(rule 125(1)(a)), and if the expert does not answer the Court may order that the
party who instructed the expert cannot rely upon the evidence of the expert or
recover the costs from the other party (rule 125(6)). Any party may rely on the
evidence obtained by the expert of another party (rule 127).

Rule 130 allows the Court to direct that evidence on a particular issue is given by 14.54
one expert only.

(l) Evidence (Part 14)

This part covers the use of written evidence (rule 97), serving statements (rule 99), 14.55
issuing witness summonses (rule 106) and depositions (rules 108–14).

(m) Disclosure (Part 16)

The court can order a party to give general or specific disclosure on the court's own 14.56
initiative or the application of another party (rule 133). A party's duty to disclose documents is limited to those which are or have been in his control (rule 133(4)). 'Control'
is defined in rule 133(5). A party discloses a document by stating that it exists or has
existed (rule 132). The procedure for general or specific disclosure appears at rule 134.

Disclosure is an ongoing duty until the proceedings are concluded (rule 135). A party to whom a document is disclosed has the right to inspect it unless that document is no longer in the control of the party who disclosed it or that party has the right or duty to withhold inspection of it. A part 10 application (above, para 14.49) can be made to resolve a dispute as to whether a party can withhold inspection of a document.

(n) *Hearings (Part 13)*

14.57 Hearings will generally be in private (defined at rule 90(2)). The court may allow any person or class of person to attend a private hearing or part of it. The court can exclude any person or class of person from all or part of a private hearing (rule 90(3)). The court can allow information about proceedings or the texts of judgments or orders to be published (rule 91) and can impose restrictions on publishing the identity of the parties, P (whether or not a party), a witness or any other person (rule 91(3)). The court may order all or part of a hearing to be held in public (rule 92). Where the Court has held a hearing and made a final order, declaration or decision, a further fee of £500 is payable.

(o) *Costs (Part 19)*

14.58 In cases concerning P's personal welfare the general rule is that there will be no order as to the costs of the proceedings or that part of the proceedings that concern P's personal welfare (rule 157). Where proceedings concern P's property and affairs, the general rule is that the costs of the proceedings or that part of the proceedings P's property and affairs will be paid by P or charged to his estate (rule 156). When the proceedings concern both, the Court will attempt to apportion the costs as between the two issues (rule 158).

14.59 The court may depart from the above rules if the circumstances justify this (rule 159). In exercising this power, the Court will regard to all the circumstances, including the conduct of the parties (rule 159(2)). The provisions of the CPR apply with modifications set out in rule 160. Provisions as to assessment are at rules 161 and 164.

(p) *Appeals (Part 20)*

14.60 By s 53 a right of appeal lies to the Court of Appeal from any decision of the Court, although the Court of Protection Rules may provide that where a decision is taken by a district judge or a circuit judge, the right of appeal may lie to a higher judge of the court (a circuit judge or High Court judge, respectively) rather than to the Court of Appeal. Rules 180–1 provide as follows:

- Where the original decision was taken by a district judge, an appeal will lie to a circuit judge, but any further appeal will be to the Court of Appeal.
- Where the original decision was taken by a circuit judge, an appeal will lie to a judge nominated under s 46(2)(a) to (c), namely the President of the Family Division, the Vice-Chancellor or a High Court judge, and thereafter to the Court of Appeal.
- Any appeal against a decision made by the President of the Family Division, the Vice Chancellor or a High Court judge lies to the Court of Appeal only.

With the exception of an appeal against an order for committal to prison, permission to appeal is always required (rule 172). Permission can be requested from the judge of the Court from whose decision the appeal is brought (the 'first instance judge' (rule 170(1)(b)) or from an 'appeal judge' namely the judge of the Court to whom the appeal was made (rule 170(1)(a)). If the first instance judge refuses permission it can be sought from the appeal judge (rule 172(5)). 14.61

A person seeking permission to appeal from an appeal judge must file an appellant's notice. The procedure to be followed by both the Appellant and Respondent is set out in Rule 175 and 176. A fee of £400 is payable. 14.62

The court will only grant permission to appeal where it considers that the appeal has a real prospect of success or there is some other compelling reason why the appeal should be heard (rule 173(1)). An order giving permission can limit the issues that are to be heard and can be subject to conditions (rule 173(2)). 14.63

An appeal will be limited to a review of the original decision unless a practice direction provides otherwise or the appeal judge considers that a re-hearing would be in the interests of justice (rule 179(1)). Unless he orders otherwise, the appeal judge will not receive oral evidence or any evidence that was not before the first instance judge (rule 179(2)). The appeal may be determined with or without a hearing (rule 171) and in deciding whether to hold a hearing the court must consider the matters listed in rule 84(3). 14.64

An appeal judge has all the powers of the first instance judge whose decision is being appealed (rule 178). 14.65

Rule 179(3) provides that an appeal judge will allow an appeal where the decision of the first instance judge was wrong or unjust, because of a serious procedural or other irregularity in the proceedings before the first instance judge. 14.66

3. Litigation Friends and Capacity to Conduct Proceedings

(a) *Litigation Friends: Part 17 of the Rules*
CPR 21 (formerly RSC Ord 80) governs the appointment of litigation friends 14.67 for those who lack capacity to litigate in civil proceedings, and has been extensively amended with effect from 1 October 2007 to give effect to the 2005 Act. Also Part 17 (rules 140–9) of the new Court of Protection Rules 2007 as effect in relation to proceedings commenced in the new Court of Protection. Part 17 contains its own framework for determining when a litigation friend is to be appointed, but the test for when a person has capacity to litigate is the same as under new CPR 21: namely, whether P has capacity to conduct the proceedings. The case law under 'old' CPR 21 (and its predecessor, Ord 80) is still relevant and is considered, below.

(b) *Capacity to Conduct the Proceedings: Adults*
By rule 141 a litigation friend must be appointed for an adult person who is a party 14.68 to proceedings who lacks, or is alleged to lack, capacity in relation to any matter that is subject of an application to the court (P) or who lacks capacity to conduct

the proceedings (a 'protected party', as defined in rule 7). Rule 141 is subject to rule 147, which provides that where a person ceases to lack capacity to conduct proceedings the court may by order bring the appointment of the litigation friend to an end.

14.69   The touchstone for whether a litigation friend must act under Part 17 is therefore whether the party to proceedings has 'capacity to conduct proceedings'. This is the same test as in 'new' CPR 21, but differs from the test in 'old' CPR 21.2, which provided that a 'patient' must have a litigation friend to conduct proceedings on his behalf. A 'patient' was defined in CPR 21.1 as 'a person who by reason of mental disorder within the meaning of the Mental Health Act 1983 is incapable of managing and administering his property and affairs'. This phrase was taken from s 94(2) of the 1983 Act, which sets out the circumstances in which the Court of Protection may assume responsibility for the property and affairs of a person with mental disorder (and which, from 1 October 2007, has been repealed by the 2005 Act). The test was considered by the Court of Appeal *Masterman-Lister v Brutton and Co (Nos 1 and 2)* [2003] 1 WLR 1511. The Court recognized that to deprive a person of litigation capacity is not a step to be taken lightly, as it may potentially violate the individual's right of access to a court at common law and under Article 6 (ibid, para 17). The question of whether a person is 'incapable of managing and administering his property and affairs' is not to be determined by reference to their capacity, without professional advice, to take investment decisions in relation to large sums of money—few people have such capacity. Rather, the question is issue specific: does the person have sufficient insight and understanding to conduct litigation, with appropriate advice, as to which 'the mental abilities required include the ability to recognize a problem, obtain and receive, understand and retain relevant information, including advice; the ability to weigh the information (including that derived from advice) in the balance in reaching a decision, and the ability to communicate that decision', (ibid, para 26 *per* Kennedy LJ).

14.70   Thus the test under both Part 17 and new CPR 21 is, in effect, the same as under the 'old' CPR 21, namely whether P has capacity to conduct the relevant proceedings. In determining that question the same approach should be adopted, which (at least on one level of abstraction) is indistinguishable from the common law formulation of capacity to consent to medical treatment in *Re MB* and the statutory test of capacity in s 3 of the 2005 Act (above, para 9.09).

(b) *Capacity to Conduct Proceedings: Children*

14.71   In the case of a 'child' (namely a child under 18, see rule 7), rule 141 requires a litigation friend to be appointed unless the court makes an order permitting the child to conduct proceedings without a litigation friend. The circumstances in which the court can or should make such an order are not defined, but the same general principles must apply as to adults: does the child have capacity to conduct proceedings? For children over the age of 16, this will be determined by the statutory test for capacity in s 3 of the 2005 Act, and the approach outlined at paras 14.69–14.70 in relation to adults should apply.

For children under the age of 16 there may be some circumstances in which the Court will be asked to determine issues under the 2005 Act, notwithstanding the limitations of s 2(5) (see para 10.07). If and in so far as the Court does exercise any jurisdiction in relation to children under 16, the question of whether they have capacity to conduct proceedings will be determined by analogy with the test in *Gillick*, see para 9.28. 14.72

E. THE PUBLIC GUARDIAN

A new office of the Public Guardian is established by s 57 of the 2005 Act with the functions set out in s 58; primarily, to establish and maintain a register of LPAs and orders appointing deputies, and to supervise donees and deputies. To this end the Public Guardian may, among other things, direct a Court of Protection Visitor to visit any donee or deputy or the person granting the LPA or for whom the deputy is appointed, P, and to make a report to him on such matters as he may direct (s 58(1)(d)) and may examine and take copies of any of P's health and social care records (s 58(5)). By s 49(2) the Court of Protection may require a report to be made to it by the Public Guardian. Section 60 requires the Public Guardian to make an annual report to the Lord Chancellor about the discharge of his functions. 14.73

Section 59 provides for the establishment of the Public Guardian Board, whose function is to scrutinize and review the way in which the Public Guardian discharges his functions. 14.74

F. COURT OF PROTECTION VISITORS

A Court of Protection Visitor is a person nominated by the Lord Chancellor under s 61 to a panel of Special or General Visitors to carry out visits and produce independent reports as directed by the Court of Protection (s 49) or the Public Guardian (s 58(1)(d)). A Special Visitor must be a registered medical practitioner, or appears to the Lord Chancellor to have other suitable qualifications, with special knowledge and experience in cases of impairment of or disturbance in the functioning of the mind or brain. 14.75

15

THE INTERFACE BETWEEN THE DETENTION AND TREATMENT REGIMES AFTER THE 2007 ACT: THE 1983 ACT, 2005 ACT, AND COMMON LAW

A.	Key Features	15.00
B.	Introduction	15.01
C.	Detention for Treatment for Mental Disorder	15.02
	1. General Principle: 2005 Act to be Preferred Unless 1983 Act Must be Used	15.03
	2. Sch 1A: Persons Ineligible to be Deprived of their Liberty under the 2005 Act	15.06
	3. Other Cases	15.25
D.	Treatment for Mental Disorder	15.26
	1. The Relevant Treatment Provisions of the 1983 Act and the 2005 Act	15.29
	2. General Principle: 2005 Act May be Used Unless 1983 Act Must be Used	15.31
	3. Complicating Factors	15.32
	4. When Treatment Must be Administered under the 1983 Act	15.33
E.	Detention and Treatment for Physical Disorder	15.47
	1. Treatment for Physical Disorder	15.47
	2. Detention for Treatment for Physical Disorder	15.48
F.	Urgent Cases	15.50
	1. Detention for Treatment for Mental Disorder	15.51
	2. Treatment for Mental Disorder Without Detention	15.57
G.	Children Aged 16 or 17	15.58
	1. Does the 1983 Act Oust the Common Law Rules Relating to Children?	15.59
	2. Detention for Treatment for Mental Disorder	15.64
	3. Treatment for Mental Disorder	15.67
	4. Detention and Treatment for Physical Disorder	15.72

H. Children Under 16   15.74
  1. Detention for Treatment for Mental Disorder   15.74
  2. Treatment for Mental Disorder   15.75
  3. Detention and Treatment for Physical Disorder   15.76

A. KEY FEATURES

15.00 • As a general principle, the informality of the 2005 Act is to be preferred to the formality of the 1983 Act, unless the 1983 Act *must* be used. The application of this principle in practice is not straightforward, however.

• *Detention for treatment for mental disorder.* The interface between the detaining provisions of the two Acts is based upon a number of principles which are, to a certain extent, in conflict: (i) detention is a measure of last resort; (ii) patient autonomy is to be respected, if possible; (iii) where detention is necessary, the informality of the 2005 Act is to be preferred to the formality of the 1983 Act; (iv) appropriate safeguards are necessary in order that human rights are respected; (v) where treatment can only be given safely under the 1983 Act, it must take precedence. The complexity of the interface between the two regimes is a consequence, in part, of the conflicts between these principles.

• P may be detained for treatment for mental disorder under the 2005 Act, as amended. However, P cannot be detained under the 2005 Act if either (a) P has made a valid refusal to detention or (b) if he comes within Sch 1A of the 2005 Act, in which case he is 'ineligible' for detention under the 2005 Act and the 1983 Act takes precedence. This also applies in urgent cases.

• *Treatment for mental disorder.* P may be given treatment for mental disorder under the 2005 Act. However, where P is subject to one of the treatment regimes of the 1983 Act (Part 4 or 4A), the 1983 Act *must* be used.

• *Detention and treatment for physical disorder* will always be regulated by the 2005 Act.

• *Children of 16 and 17 and children under 16.* In each case consideration must be given to the interrelationship of the 2005 Act and the 1983 Act with the common law rules relating to the detention and treatment of children.

B. INTRODUCTION

15.01 A patient detained or otherwise subject to compulsion under the 1983 Act ('patient') does not necessarily lack capacity; many (if not most) have the capacity to make decisions for themselves. By the same token, an incapacitated individual ('P') does not necessarily require treatment for mental disorder under the provisions of the 1983 Act; for most this can be provided under the 2005 Act. There is a group of patients who potentially fall within both categories, however. An incapacitated individual, P, may require hospital treatment for mental disorder as an in-patient. A patient detained under the 1983 Act may lose capacity and require treatment for physical disorder. A community patient subject to the provisions of the 1983 Act (whether on leave of absence, conditional discharge, guardianship, or a community treatment order) may require treatment for both mental and physical disorders. As a general principle, the informality of the 2005 Act is to be preferred to the formality of the 1983 Act, unless the 1983 Act *must* be used. That principle is not that easy to apply in practice, however: particularly in the case of children. This Chapter looks at the provisions which determine the circumstances in which P is to be detained or treated under the 1983 Act or the 2005 Act after the 2007 Act comes into force, under the following headings: detention for treatment for mental disorder; treatment for mental disorder; detention and treatment for physical disorder; urgent cases; children aged 16 or 17; and children under 16.

C. DETENTION FOR TREATMENT FOR MENTAL DISORDER

This section considers the interface between the detaining provisions of the 1983 Act and the 2005 Act *after* the amendments effected by the 2007 Act come into force. For the position *before* the 2007 Act comes into force, see para 11.35ff. 15.02

1. General Principle: 2005 Act to be Preferred Unless 1983 Act Must be Used

(a) *The Principles in Play*

The hierarchy of decision-making involving detention under the 1983 and 2005 Acts following the amendments of the 2007 Act broadly reflects the following principles. First, detention is a measure of last resort and should not be imposed under any regime if there is a less restrictive alternative available and then only for the shortest period necessary.[1] Second, P's right of autonomy should be respected as much as possible. Third, where detention is necessary, it should if possible be effected under the informal provisions of the 2005 Act, with the compulsory framework of the 1983 Act as a measure of last resort. Fourth, detention under the 2005 Act should be subject to appropriate safeguards, to comply with the human rights obligations identified in *HL*. Fifth, where P can only receive the treatment he requires by detention under the 1983 Act, then the 1983 Act takes precedence. 15.03

These principles are, to a certain extent, in conflict. For example, respecting an individual's right of autonomy is obviously inconsistent with detaining him. The 1983 and 2005 Acts, as amended by the 2007 Act, effect a compromise by prohibiting detention under the 2005 Act where a valid refusal to detention is made, but permitting detention under the 1983 Act if that is the only safe way to ensure P receives the treatment he requires. Similarly, there is a conflict between informality, 15.04

---

[1] See also Draft Deprivation of Liberty Code of Practice, paras 1.7–1.9.

on the one hand, and patient safeguards (or human rights), on the other (as discussed in Chapter 1). The 1983 and 2005 Acts, as amended by the 2007 Act, offer a choice between the relatively informal detention mechanism of Sch A1 (which has fewer safeguards) and the more formal detention mechanism of the 1983 Act (which contains greater patient safeguards). The complexity of the interface between the two regimes is driven, in part, by the conflicts between the principles upon which their provisions are based.

(b) *The Principles in Practice: Interface Between the 1983 Act and 2005 Act*

15.05 Thus, the interface between the detaining provisions of the 2005 Act and the 1983 Act is as follows:

(1) An incapable adult, P, requiring admission to a psychiatric hospital for medical treatment may still be admitted as an informal patient under s 131(1) if his admission does not amount to a deprivation of liberty.

(2) If P is being, or is to be, 'deprived of his liberty' in a psychiatric hospital, his detention may nevertheless be authorized under the provisions of the 2005 Act, as amended, rather than under the 1983 Act, subject to the following:

(a) Detention under the 2005 Act is only permitted by order of the Court of Protection under s 16, in an emergency under s 4B or subject to the safeguards of the standard or urgent authorization procedure of Sch A1 (s 4A). Detention is not permitted under the unregulated provisions of s 5 (acts in connection with care or treatment), s 9 (decisions of donees), or s 16 (decisions of deputies) (see paras 11.38).

(b) Detention is not permitted under the 2005 Act if P has made an advance decision that is valid and applicable refusing detention in hospital for mental disorder, or a donee or deputy have made such a refusal. In those circumstances the Court of Protection is bound by the advance decision (s 26(1)) or the decision of the donee (but not of a deputy) (see para 10.56), and the Sch A1 procedure may not be used because in those circumstances the 'no refusals' requirement is not met (Sch A1, paras 18–20) (see para 12.26). P may still be detained under the 1983 Act, however.

(c) Detention is not authorized under the 2005 Act if the 1983 Act *must* be used by virtue of Sch 1A, in which case P is 'ineligible' to be detained under the 2005 Act. He cannot then be detained by the Court of Protection (s 16A) nor can he be detained on a standard authorization under Sch A1 (Sch A1, paras 12(e) and 17). But the informality of the 2005 Act is still to be preferred, if possible. Thus, P may still be admitted, and detained, under the 2005 Act even though otherwise falling within Case D (guardianship) or E ('within the scope' of the 1983 Act) of Sch 1A if he does not object or his donee or deputy consents to his detention under the 2005 Act (below, paras 15.15 and 15.19).

(3) Only if P has made a valid objection to detention under the 2005 Act or is otherwise 'ineligible' for detention under the 2005 Act and there is no other way

that P can safely be administered medical treatment for mental disorder should ✗
the 1983 Act be used. In those circumstances, however, *only* the 1983 Act may
be used.

2. Sch 1A: Persons Ineligible to be Deprived of their Liberty under the 2005 Act

As we have seen (para 11.38), s 4A of the 2005 Act prohibits any form of detention 15.06
under the 2005 Act, with three exceptions: first, when the detention is made by an
order of the Court of Protection in relation to P's personal welfare under s 16(2)(a);
second, when the detention is authorized under Schedule A1 (standard and urgent
authorizations); and, third, when detention is necessary for life-saving or other
emergency treatment under s 4B. Detention is therefore not permitted under s 5
('acts in connection with care or treatment'), s 9 (by a donee of an LPA), or s 16
(by a court-appointed deputy).

The 1983 Act is then given pre-eminence as a detaining mechanism by s 16A and 15.07
paras 12(e) and 17 of Sch A1 of the 2005 Act, which respectively prohibit any order
being made by a Court, or a standard authorization being made, if P is 'ineligible to
be deprived of his liberty by this Act'.

P is 'ineligible' if he falls within Cases A to E of new Sch 1A of the 2005 15.08
Act, below. Moreover, P may become 'ineligible' during the term of a standard
authorization or a Court welfare order, the effect of which is that the standard
authorization or Court order is suspended: in the case of a standard authorization,
for a period of 28 days, whereupon it is terminated if P remains ineligible (Part 6 of
Sch A1, paras 91–7) (see para 12.79); and, in the case of a court order, indefinitely
(s 16A(2)).

The 2005 Act defines five categories of ineligible person (Cases A–E). These are 15.09
set out in a table in Sch 1A, para 2 of the 2005 Act, with definitions given in the rest
of that Schedule.

(a) *Case A: Patients Detained under the Mental Health Act 1983*

P is ineligible for detention under the 2005 Act if subject to the 'hospital treat- 15.10
ment regime' *and* detained under the 1983 Act (Case A in the Table, at para 2).
P is subject to the 'hospital treatment regime' if subject to a 'hospital treatment
obligation' under the relevant enactment (the 1983 Act ss 2, 4, 3, 35, 36, 37, 38, 44,
45A, 47, 48, 51) or any other enactment which has the same effect (Sch 1A,
para 8).

The interface between the two Acts for this category of patient is relatively 15.11
straightforward. P cannot be detained for treatment for mental disorder both under
the 1983 Act and under the 2005 Act, whether as the result of a Court order made
under s 16 or an urgent or standard authorization under Sch A1. Even if P requires
medical treatment for a physical disorder he will be ineligible for *detention* under the
2005 Act for that purpose, although as regards any *treatment* for that physical disorder the 2005 Act applies.

(b) *Cases B and C: Patients on Leave of Absence, Conditional Discharge, or on Community Treatment Order*

15.12   A P who is subject to the 'hospital treatment regime' (above, para 15.10) but not detained (ie on leave of absence under section 17 or conditional discharge under ss 42 or 73 of the 1983 Act) (Case B) or who is subject to the 'community treatment regime' (a community treatment order under section 17A or its equivalent[2] (CTO)) (Case C) will be 'ineligible' for detention under the 2005 Act if either:

- the proposed course of action under the 2005 Act (the 'authorised course of action')[3] is 'not in accordance with a requirement which the relevant regime imposes', such as a condition of a patient's leave of absence under s 17, of his conditional discharge under ss 42 or 73 or of a CTO under s 17A of the 1983 Act, including any requirement as to residence (Sch 1A, para 3); or

- the proposed care or treatment to be administered under the 2005 Act (the 'relevant care or treatment')[4] 'consists in whole or in part of medical treatment for mental disorder in a hospital' (Sch 1A, para 4).

15.13   For these categories of P, an order for detention cannot be made by a Court under section 16, or a standard authorization made under Sch A1. If detention is necessary, P will have to be recalled to hospital under the provisions of the 1983 Act.

15.14   Note the contrast between a P in Case B & C, on the one hand, and Case D (guardianship) and Case E ('within the scope' of the 1983 Act), on the other. A P in Case D or E can still be eligible for detention under the 2005 Act, notwithstanding the proposed course of action involves treatment for mental disorder as a hospital in-patient, if P does not object or his donee or deputy has made a valid consent. P in Case B or C, on the other hand, will be ineligible for such treatment regardless of whether he objects or someone on his behalf consents to the treatment: the 1983 Act is the only available route to detention.

(c) *Case D: Patients Subject to Guardianship*

15.15   A P who is subject to the guardianship regime (Case D) will be ineligible if the proposed course of action under the 2005 Act (the 'authorised course of action')[5] is either:

- not in accordance with a requirement imposed by the guardianship order, including any requirement as to where P is to reside (Sch 1A, para 3), or

- would authorize P to be a 'mental patient' (a person accommodated in a hospital for the purposes of being given medical treatment for mental disorder)[6] (the 'first

---

[2] Sch 1A, para 9.

[3] Defined in Sch 1A, paras 13–15: 'authorised course of action' means, in the case of a decision by the court under s 16, any course of action amounting to deprivation of liberty which the order under section 16(2)(a) authorizes if the proposed provision were included in the order; and, in the case of a decision under Sch A1, para 17, the accommodation of the relevant person in the relevant hospital or care home for the purpose of being given the relevant care or treatment, if the standard authorization were given.

[4] Defined in Sch 1A, paras 13–15.

[5] Sch 1A, paras 13–15, see n 3.

[6] Definition of 'mental patient' in Sch 1A, para 16 and referred to in Sch 1A, para 5(3).

condition'), P objects to being a mental patient or to being given some or all of the mental health treatment (the 'second condition'), and no valid consent has been given by a donee or deputy (the 'third condition') (Sch 1A, para 5).

In determining whether P 'objects' for the purposes of para 3, regard must be had to all the circumstances so far as they are reasonably ascertainable, including the patient's behaviour, wishes and feelings, views, beliefs, and values, although circumstances from the past shall be considered only so far as it is still appropriate to consider them (para 5(6) and (7)).[7] Any objection made by P is, necessarily, one that he lacks capacity to make, but nevertheless has legal effect. An objection by a family member or carer will not have the same effect, unless they are the donee of a LPA or a court-appointed deputy, although their views will be relevant in determining whether P objects. Of course, if P has made a valid advance decision objecting to his detention, or a donee or deputy objects to his admission, then he cannot be detained under the 2005 Act (above, para 15.05). 15.16

For a P in Case D the position is essentially the same as for other community patients (Cases B & C), in that P is 'ineligible' if his detention would conflict with a requirement imposed by the guardianship order. The difference is that if P does not object or his donee or deputy consents he can still be detained under the 2005 Act, notwithstanding the proposed course of action involves treatment for mental disorder as a hospital in-patient. If P does object and no substituted consent is given he is then 'ineligible', and will either continue to receive treatment in the community or be transferred from guardianship to hospital[8] or admitted under s 2, 3, or 4 of the 1983 Act, depending on the urgency. 15.17

As with the other community patients in Cases B and C above, guardianship does not make P ineligible for detention under the 2005 Act if he requires treatment in hospital for a *physical* disorder. 15.18

(d) *Case E: Patients Falling 'Within the Scope' of the Mental Health Act 1983*

A P who is 'within the scope of' s 2 or s 3 of the 1983 Act' (Case E) is ineligible if the proposed course of action (the 'authorised course of action') would authorize P to be a 'mental patient' (a person accommodated in a hospital for the purposes of being given medical treatment for mental disorder)[9] (the 'first condition'), P objects to being a mental patient or to being given some or all of the mental health treatment (the 'second condition'), and no valid consent has been given by a donee or deputy (the 'third condition') (Sch 1A, para 5). 15.19

In determining whether P 'objects', the criteria referred to in para 15.16 must be taken into account. 15.20

---

[7] These reflect the matters that must be taken into account under see s 4(6) and s 36(2) of the 2005 Act, and s 64D(4) and s 64F(4) of the 1983 Act.

[8] Under s 19(1)(b) of the 1983 Act and Reg 8(3) of the Mental Health Regulations 1983, SI 1983/893.

[9] Definition of 'mental patient' in Sch 1A, para 16 and referred to in Sch 1A, para 5(3).

15.21　　P is 'within the scope' of s 2 or s 3 of the 1983 Act if 'an application in respect of P could be made under section 2 or 3 of the Mental Health Act and P could be detained in a hospital in pursuance of such an application, were one made' (Sch 1A, para 12(1)). In making that assessment it is to be assumed, first, that the necessary medical recommendations under s 2(3) or s 3(3) have been given as required and, second, (as regards the requirement in s 3(2)(c) that 'treatment cannot be provided unless he is detained under' s 3), that such treatment cannot be provided under the 2005 Act (Sch 1A, para 12(2)–(5)).

15.22　　This provision requires a judgment to be made that P meets the criteria for detention under ss 2 or 3 of the 1983 Act, but without the benefit of any medical recommendation. There is scope here for P to fall between two stools, if the assessor under the 2005 Act concludes that P is not 'eligible' because he should be detained under the 1983 Act and then, subsequently, the medical recommendations do not support detention under the 1983 Act. In that case, P would then become 'eligible' for detention under the 2005 Act. In practice, this issue is most likely to arise where P is being assessed under the Sch A1 procedure. In such a case the 'best interests' assessor (para 12.51) and the mental health assessor (para 12.50) should both consider whether P meets the criteria for detention under ss 2 or 3 of the 1983 Act. If they both conclude he meets the criteria for detention, the best interests assessor should be able to make the application, with the mental health assessor signing one of the medical recommendations. A second medical recommendation would need to be obtained.

15.23　　As with a P in Case D (guardianship), the fact P falls within the scope of the 1983 Act does not preclude his detention for treatment under the 2005 Act if he does not object or his donee or deputy gives a valid consent. Similarly, as with Cases B, C, and D, there is no bar to P being detained under the 2005 Act for treatment for a physical disorder.

15.24　　The exception for patients who do not object allows the admission to hospital under the 2005 Act of the so-called '*Bournewood*' patient (above, para 11.01): the 'non-dissenting' P who requires treatment in a psychiatric hospital who, if he were dissenting, would otherwise need to be detained under the 1983 Act, although it is a moot question whether the patient in the Bournewood case, Mr L, could today be said to have been not 'objecting' applying the test referred to in para 15.16 above.

3. Other Cases

15.25　In all other cases, P's detention for care and treatment for mental disorder will be authorized under the 2005 Act, subject to the provisions relating to children.

D. TREATMENT FOR MENTAL DISORDER

15.26　The previous section was concerned with detention for treatment for mental disorder, which is governed by the 'ineligibility' provisions of s 16A, Sch A1, para 17 and

Sch 1A. This section considers treatment for mental disorder where detention is not in issue, either because P is already detained under the 1983 Act or 2005 Act or because he does not require detention.

The following principles govern the treatment of adults. The position of children is considered separately, below. 15.27

This section addresses the position *after* the amendments effected by the 2007 Act come into force. For the position before the 2007 Act comes into force, see para 10.71. 15.28

1. The Relevant Treatment Provisions of the 1983 Act and the 2005 Act

Treatment under the 1983 Act may be administered either under Part 4 (for patients who are 'liable to be detained') or new Part 4A (for community patients on SCT). Detailed consideration is given to these provisions in Chapter 6. 15.29

The circumstances in which treatment may be given under the 2005 Act are considered in Chapter 10, but, in summary, treatment may be administered in one of four ways. First, under s 5, as an 'act in connection with care or treatment' of an incapacitated adult that is in his 'best interests' as defined in s 4. Second, with the authority of P's donee under a lasting power of attorney (s 9). Third, with the authority of a deputy appointed by the Court of Protection (s 16) and, fourth, under an order made by the Court of Protection (s 16). Such treatment may be administered using reasonable force, providing the provisions of s 6, s 11, or s 20 relating to the use of 'restraint' are complied with. The key distinctions between the two Acts, for present purposes, are these. First, that treatment may be given under Part 4 (but not Part 4A) of the 1983 Act to a capable patient who is refusing treatment (see para 6.01); under the 2005 Act, treatment may only be given to those who lack capacity. Second, under the 1983 Act certain forms of treatment (medication after 3 months (s 58(1)(b)) and ECT (s 58A)) can only be administered with certain safeguards, in particular the need for approval by an independent second opinion appointed doctor (SOAD). Where the same treatment may be administered under the 2005 Act, these safeguards do not apply. This may have human rights implications: see para 6.140. 15.30

2. General Principle: 2005 Act May be Used Unless 1983 Act Must be Used

The general principle is that treatment for mental disorder may be administered under the 2005 Act, unless it is treatment regulated by Part 4 or Part 4A. Thus: 15.31

- s 28(1) of the 2005 Act provides that nothing in the 2005 Act authorizes anyone to give a patient medical treatment for mental disorder, or to consent to a patient being given medical treatment for mental disorder, if at the time his treatment is regulated by Part 4 of the 1983 Act, which regulates the medical treatment for mental disorder of patients who are 'liable to be detained' in hospital under the 1983 Act (s 56(1)), including patients who are actually detained (see para 10.71).

- In relation to the treatment of community patients on SCT, s 28(1B) of the 2005 Act provides that treatment falling within s 64B of the 1983 (treatment of incapacitated adult patients over the age of 16) may not be administered under s 5 of the 2005 Act. The effect of this provision is not so straightforward: see para 15.40.

3. Complicating Factors

15.32 Matters then become more complicated:

- Although not explicitly stated, treatment administered under Part 4 or 4A of the 1983 Act must still comply with the general principles set out in ss 1–4 of the 2005 Act, in particular the presumption of capacity and the principle of 'best interests'.[10] These general principles are not displaced by s 28(1) or 28(1B).
- Some detained patients are specifically excluded from Part 4, namely those admitted under the short-term, emergency procedures of s 4, s 5, s 325, s 135, s 136, s 37(4), and s 45A(5) (see s 56(3)). For those that lack capacity, their treatment is governed by the 2005 Act, raising human rights issues (see para 6.140).
- Those who are 'liable to be detained' for the purposes of s 56 of the 1983 Act includes some patients receiving treatment in the community, namely those on s 17 leave. Accordingly, their treatment remains governed by Part 4 and no treatment for mental disorder may be given, or authorized to be given, to such patients under the 2005 Act by virtue of s 28(1).
- Part 4 covers all patients, whether detained, informally admitted or in the community, in relation to those forms of particularly invasive medical treatment governed by s 57 of the 1983 Act (s 56(1)). Such treatment cannot be given, or authorized to be given, under the 2005 Act, again by virtue of s 28(1). As treatment under s 57 requires consent then such treatment can never be administered to an incapacitated P, other than in an emergency in accordance with s 62.
- For patients falling within Part 4, new s 58A has introduced certain aspects of the 2005 Act in relation to treatment to which it applies (currently only ECT) (see para 6.42ff). For a patient lacking capacity, such treatment may not be given if it conflicts with an advance decision which is valid and applicable or with the decision of a donee or deputy or the Court of Protection (s 58A(5)(c)). However, where treatment is administered under s 58A, the source of authority for detention is the 1983 Act, not the 2005 Act.
- For patients falling within Part 4A (see para 6.58ff), certain aspects of the 2005 Act are introduced. Part 4A treatment cannot be given if it conflicts with an advance decision which is valid and applicable or with a decision of a donee, deputy or the Court of Protection. By the same token, treatment can be administered under Part 4A with the consent of a donee, deputy or the Court of

---

[10] These principles must already be applied to treatment administered under Part 4 as they have been developed at common law (*R (B) v Dr S* [2006] 1 WLR 810, para 62: para 6.04 above).

Protection. However, the source of authority is *probably* Part 4A, rather than the 2005 Act (although see the discussion at para 15.41, below).

- Neither Part 4 nor Part 4A govern the treatment of other community patients, namely patients on conditional discharge under ss 42 or 73 (who are specifically excluded from Part 4 by s 56(3)) and patients on guardianship (who are not 'liable to be detained' for the purposes of s 56(1)). Section 28 does not apply and this group of patients can be treated under the 2005 Act if they lack capacity, raising human rights issues (see para 6.140).

4. When Treatment Must be Administered Under the 1983 Act

It is convenient to consider, first, the interrelationship of the treatment régimes of the 1983 Act and the 2005 Act in relation to each of the five categories of patient (Cases A to E) identified in Sch 1A of the 2005 Act. This is for convenience only, as Sch 1A is relevant only in determining which *detention* regime is appropriate, not which *treatment* regime is appropriate in the absence of detention. 15.33

(a) *Case A: Patients Detained Under the Mental Health Act 1983*

By s 28 of the 2005 Act no person may give, or consent to a patient being given, medical treatment for mental disorder at a time when his treatment is regulated by Part 4 of the 1983 Act. Those who are 'liable to be detained' under the 1983 Act (s 56(1)) are covered by Part 4, which includes (but is not limited to) patients who are in fact detained, except those detained under the short-term, emergency provisions of s 4, s 5, s 35, s 135, s 136, s 37(4), and s 45A(5) (see new s 56(3), para 6.37. Thus the 2005 Act cannot be used to administer medical treatment for *mental* disorder to an incapacitated patient detained under any of s 2, s 3, s 36, s 37(1), s 37(3), s 38, s 45A, s 47, s 48, or s 51(5) of the 1983 Act.[11] Those incapacitated patients detained under the short-term, emergency provisions referred to can only be treated under the 2005 Act (except s 57 treatment), and without the attendant safeguards of Part 4 (see para 6.140).

New s 58A has introduced certain aspects of the 2005 Act in relation to certain categories of treatment, currently limited to ECT (see para 6.42ff). For an incapacitated patient, such treatment may not be given if it conflicts with an advance decision which is valid and applicable or with the decision of a donee or deputy or the Court of Protection (s 58A(5)(c)). However, the 1983 Act remains the governing statute and authority to give s 58A treatment derives from the 1983 Act, not the 2005 Act: s 28 of the 2005 Act applies. 15.35

---

[11] The common law doctrine of necessity, and the High Court's inherent jurisdiction in relation to incapacitated adults (both of which survive notwithstanding the introduction of the 2005 Act), are almost certainly also displaced by the comprehensive statutory framework of Part 4 (*R v Dr Collins ex p Brady*, [2000] 1 MHLR 17) and because otherwise the purpose of s 28 would be frustrated.

(b) *Case B(i): Patients on Leave of Absence*

15.36 A P on leave of absence under s 17 of the 1983 Act remains 'liable to be detained' under the Act and therefore falls within Part 4 of the 1983 Act. Accordingly, as with Case A, s 28 of the 2005 Act prohibits the administration of treatment for mental disorder under the 2005 Act. If medical treatment for mental disorder is to be administered to a P on s 17 leave in the community it is administered under the provisions of Part 4, generally under s 63 and, where they apply, s 57 and s 58 with its attendant safeguards (and note para 6.59).

15.37 For s 58A treatment, the position will be as for detained patients: see above, paras 15.35.

(c) *Case B(ii): Patients on Conditional Discharge*

15.38 A restricted patient on conditional discharge is expressly excluded from the provisions of Part 4 (s 56(3)(c)). Accordingly, the administration of treatment for mental disorder under the 2005 Act to an incapacitated patient on conditional discharge is not excluded by s 28 of the 2005 Act. While treatment cannot be administered to the patient without his consent for as long as he has capacity, if he loses capacity he may be treated under the 2005 Act, but without any of the safeguards in Part 4 or Part 4A (see para 6.140), save in so far as treatment under s 57 is concerned.

(d) *Case C: Patients on Community Treatment Orders (SCT)*

15.39 Part 4A of the 1983 Act creates a new regime for the treatment of community patients subject to CTOs, considered in detail in Chapter 6. Part 4A does not authorize treatment in any circumstances that the 2005 Act does not: compulsory treatment of a capable, refusing patient is not authorized in any circumstances, and treatment of an incapacitated, objecting patient is not permitted without substituted consent, except in an emergency (para 6.58ff). Note that a recalled patient on SCT is treated under Part 4 of the 1983 Act (new s 56(4), above para 6.110) so treatment under the 2005 Act is then excluded by s 28 of the 2005 Act.

15.40 Section 28(1) of the 2005 Act does not apply to treatment which is regulated by Part 4A of the 1983 Act, but by s 28(1B) treatment falling within s 64B may not be administered under s 5 of the 2005 Act (acts in connection with care and treatment). Section 64B regulates treatment to incapacitated adult patients (those over the age of 16), which is effectively *all* treatment that could be administered to an incapacitated patient under Part 4A or the 2005 Act, because the 2005 Act does not apply to children under 16. The exclusion of s 5 of the 2005 Act means that treatment falling with Part 4A may be administered under the 2005 Act if it is authorized by a donee, deputy or by the Court of Protection.

15.41 This raises a difficult question. If treatment falling with Part 4A is authorized by a donee, deputy or the Court of Protection (as it may be under s 64C(2)(b), above para 6.74), is it administered under the 1983 Act or the 2005 Act? And if the treatment is authorized under the 2005 Act, rather than the 1983 Act, does treatment that is so authorized also have to comply with the provisions of Part 4A, in particular the 'certificate requirement' of authorization by the SOAD for s 58 and s 58A type treatment? While as a matter of strict construction it appears treatment may be given to a community patient on SCT both under the 2005 Act (subject to the exclusion in s 28(1B) in relation to s 5 of the 2005 Act) and under Part 4A, plainly what is intended is that a patient on SCT should not be administered treatment for mental disorder other than in accordance with the safeguards of Part 4A. Authority for the administration of the treatment may derive from either source, but the safeguards of Part 4A must be applied. If it were necessary the same construction would result from applying s 3 of the Human Rights Act 1998.

Section 57 also applies to patients on SCT so s 28 excludes the use of the 2005 Act for such treatment. 15.42

(e) *Case D: Patients Subject to Guardianship*

Patients subject to guardianship do not come within Part 4A and, because they are not 'liable to be detained' for the purposes of s 56 of the 1983 Act, they do not fall within the compulsory treatment provisions of Part 4. Section 28 does not apply and treatment may therefore be authorized under the 2005 Act (other than treatment falling within s 57), and without the attendant safeguards of Part 4 or 4A (see para 6.140). 15.43

Section 57 also applies to such patients so s 28 excludes the use of the 2005 Act for such treatment. 15.44

(f) *Case E: Patients 'Within the Scope' of the 1983 Act*

This category has little relevance as regards the appropriate treatment regime as P falling into this category should quickly be admitted to hospital under the 1983 Act, whereupon he falls within Case A, above. Nevertheless, treatment of such a P before he is so admitted will be governed by the 2005 Act, except treatment falling within s 57 of the 1983 Act. 15.45

(g) *Other Cases*

For any other adult P treatment will be administered under the 2005 Act and without the safeguards of Part 4 and 4A, other than treatment falling within s 57 of the 1983 Act. 15.46

E. DETENTION AND TREATMENT FOR PHYSICAL DISORDER

1. Treatment for Physical Disorder

Treatment for *physical* disorder is straightforward. Any adult P who requires treatment for a physical disorder is to be treated under the 2005 Act, even if detained or otherwise subject to compulsion under the 1983 Act. The 1983 Act provides no authority to treat a patient for a physical disorder, unless it is a symptom or underlying cause of the mental disorder.[12] Treatment for physical disorder of a patient 15.47

---

[12] *R (B) v Ashworth Hospital Authority* [2005] 2 AC 278, para 62; *B v Croydon Health Authority* [1995] Fam 133; *Re C (Adult: Refusal of Medical Treatment)* [1994] 1 WLR 290.

detained under the 1983 Act is not excluded by s 28 or 28(1B) of the 2005 Act as such treatment is not regulated by either Part 4 or 4A of the 1983 Act.

2. Detention for Treatment for Physical Disorder

15.48   Sometimes it will be necessary to detain P in order to administer treatment for a physical disorder, and s 4A of the 2005 Act applies (above, para 11.38).

15.49   P cannot be 'ineligible' for detention under the 2005 Act within the meaning of Sch 1A where the purpose of detention is to provide treatment for a *physical* disorder.

F. URGENT CASES

15.50   The situation governing emergency treatment under section 4B and urgent authorizations under Sch A1 and their relationship with the urgent detention and community treatment provisions under the 1983 Act requires separate consideration.

1. Detention for Treatment for Mental Disorder

15.51   Under the 1983 Act there are a number of mechanisms by which detention may be authorized on an emergency basis, such as s 2, s 4, s 5, and s 136 (although treatment may not be imposed under Part 4 for patients detained under ss 4, 5, or 136 (s 56(2)).

15.52   Under the 2005 Act, two mechanisms for urgent detention are provided; first, the urgent authorization procedure in Sch A1, Part 5 paras 74–90; and, second, the procedure in s 4B where detention is necessary for the purpose of giving life-saving treatment or doing any 'vital act' in s 4B pending resolution of the issue before the Court of Protection.

15.53   While it is not entirely clear which procedure is to be adopted as between each of them (considered at paras 11.46), there is no doubt that both the 'urgent authorization' and the s 4B procedures are subordinate to the detention procedures under the 1983 Act for a patient who is 'ineligible' for detention within the meaning of Sch 1A, for the following reasons.

(a) *The 'Urgent Authorization' Procedure in Sch A1 of the 2005 Act*

15.54   The choice of 'urgent authorization' or detention under the 1983 is governed by the 'eligibility' provisions of Sch 1A in very much the same way as for standard authorizations, above para 15.02. A patient who would be 'ineligible' for detention under the 'standard authorization' procedure in Sch A1 of the 2005 Act will also be 'ineligible' for the purposes of the 'urgent authorization' procedure. That is because one of the conditions for making an 'urgent authorization' is that the ' managing authority' are required to make a request under, materially, para 24 of Sch A1 (para 76(2)), and they will only be required to make such a request if it appears to them that P is, or is about to, meet all of the 'qualifying requirements' (para 24(2)–(4)).

One of those qualifying requirements is the 'eligibility requirement' in para 17 of Sch A1. Thus, if it appears to the managing authority that P is 'ineligible' within the meaning of Sch 1A they cannot make an urgent authorization. The urgent mechanisms of the 1983 Act must be used.

(b) *Life-saving etc Treatment: s 4B of the 2005 Act*

Section 4B provides that a person (D) may deprive P of his liberty while a decision 15.55
as respects any relevant issue is sought from the court, provided some question requires resolution as to whether D is authorized to deprive P of his liberty and which is for the purpose of giving, and is necessary in order to give, life-sustaining treatment or to do some vital act (see para 11.45). Section 4B does not provide that the treatment to be provided is for physical rather than mental disorder, but that is plainly the primary purpose of s 4B. The question arises, can it also be used to detain a person who is otherwise 'ineligible' for detention under the 2005 Act to give treatment for mental disorder which is either life-saving or some other 'vital act'?

In the writer's view, detention cannot be authorized under s 4B for the purposes 15.56
of administering treatment for mental disorder if the patient is otherwise 'ineligible' within the meaning of Sch 1A. That is because in those circumstances the Court of Protection would be prohibited from making an order for detention for treatment for mental disorder under s 16 if the patient is 'ineligible' (s 16A, above para 15.07), so there would be no 'relevant issue' for the court to determine within the meaning of s 4B(1). The emergency mechanisms for detaining and treating under the 1983 Act must be utilized.

2. Treatment for Mental Disorder Without Detention

Para 15.26ff above looked at the circumstances in which the 2005 Act may be used 15.57
(if at all) to administer treatment for mental disorder to incapacitated patients who are otherwise 'ineligible' for detention for treatment within the meaning of Sch 1A. The position will be no different for emergency treatment. Section 28(1) and 28(1B) of the 2005 Act will exclude the operation of the 2005 Act for those categories of patient falling within Part 4 and Part 4A, considered above. The urgent treatment provisions of Part 4 (s 62) and Part 4A (s 64G) will be used (treatment which is 'immediately necessary'). Where Part 4 or Part 4A do not have to be used then treatment may be administered in an emergency under s 5 of s 2005 or, if a donee or deputy gives consent, under ss 9 or 16, if necessary by using restraint or reasonable force, providing the provisions of s 6, s 11, or s 20 are complied with (and note para 10.61).

G. CHILDREN AGED 16 OR 17

We are concerned here with the interrelationship of the 1983 Act and the 2005 Act 15.58
with the common law rules relating to children after the 2007 Act comes into force: the position prior to the 2007 Act coming into force is considered at para 10.03ff

and 11.49ff. As with incapacitated adults, the 2005 Act may be used to detain and treat incapacitated children of 16 or 17 unless the 1983 Act must be used. For children of 16 and 17 it is necessary, however, to take account of two further complicating factors first, the modifications to the 2005 Act as it applies to children (above, para 10.03); and, second, the effect of the common law rules relating to the detention (above paras 11.49–11.55) and treatment (above, para 9.25ff) of children. Before considering the available alternatives to detention and treatment under the various regimes, it is necessary to consider whether the common law rules have any part to play where the 1983 Act would otherwise apply.

1. Does the 1983 Act Oust the Common Law Rules Relating to Children?

15.59   As we have seen, at common law a person with parental responsibility may consent to treatment, including detention, on behalf of a child, whether capable or not. The High Court also has jurisdiction both to consent to and refuse treatment on behalf of such a child in its jurisdiction relating to children. The question for consideration is this: where a child is detained under the 1983 Act, or placed upon a CTO, does the 1983 Act oust the common law rules, both in relation to detention and treatment?

15.60   As we have seen, the detaining provisions of the 2005 Act are excluded by the 'eligibility' provisions in Sch 1A, and the treatment provisions excluded by ss 28 and 28(1B) of the 2005 Act where the treatment falls within Part 4 or 4A of the 1983 Act. There are no equivalent provisions in the 1983 Act which expressly disapply the common law rules relating to the treatment of children, however, but have these rules been impliedly displaced by the 1983 Act?

15.61   In my view, the answer is 'probably'. The arguments that suggest the 1983 Act has ousted the common law rules are as follows:

- First, general principles of public law would suggest that the common law is displaced by a complete statutory code for detention and treatment such as the one found in the 1983 Act.[13]

- Second, the conclusion follows by implication from s 33(4) of the 1983 Act, as amended by the 2007 Act. This provides that 'where a [CTO] has been made in respect of a minor who is a ward of court, the provisions of this Part of this Act relating to community patients have effect in relation to the minor subject to any order which the court makes in the exercise of its wardship jurisdiction; but this does not apply as regards any period when the minor is recalled to hospital under section 17E above'. This provision expressly preserves the primacy of the High Court in its wardship jurisdiction in relation to some decisions taken in relation to a child on a CTO who is a ward of court, but not all such decisions: only those that relate to 'this Part of this Act' (namely Part 2), and expressly not those taken once

---

[13] *B v Forsey*, 1988 SC(HL) 28, HL(Sc); *R v Dr Collins ex p Brady*, [2000] 1 MHLR 17.

the child is recalled under s 17E. Part 2 includes ss 17A–G, so, for example, decisions by the High Court in its wardship jurisdiction will prevail over any condition placed on a CTO by the responsible clinician. Section 33(4) does not include the treatment provisions of Part 4A, however. This would mean, by implication, that the High Court's jurisdiction is displaced in relation to treatment decisions which fall within s 4A. Moreover, the High Court's jurisdiction is expressly excluded once the child is recalled to hospital under s 17E, so it will have no role in relation to treatment decisions under Part 4 after recall. It also follows by implication from s 33(4) that the common law rules relating to children—both the exercise of the rights of those with parental responsibility and the jurisdiction of the High Court in relation to children—are displaced except in so far as they are expressly retained by s 33(4). Accordingly, where a child has been detained or is subject to a CTO, neither those with parental responsibility nor the High Court have any role to play in relation to detention or treatment decisions other than where s 33(4) applies.

On the other hand, the following arguments would suggest that the common law rules have not been ousted.

- The High Court's inherent jurisdiction in relation to children is, in theory,   15.62
  unlimited (see para 9.34). It cannot be ousted without clear statutory wording.

- To exclude a person with parental responsibility from having any role in treatment decisions gives rise to a number of anomalies in relation to the treatment of children under Part 4 (particularly s 58A) and Part 4A (see para 6.133). Treatment falling within s 58A (ECT) may not be given to an adult if it conflicts with an advance decision or the decision of a donee or deputy; a child's parent, on the other hand, cannot veto such treatment for their child (see paras 6.50, 6.55). Similarly, under Part 4A, a donee or deputy can consent or refuse treatment on behalf of an incapacitated adult, but a child's parent has no such right (paras 6.69, 6.73, 6.82). This may have significant human rights implications (see para 6.133). In *Glass v United Kingdom*,[14] the ECtHR held that the administration of treatment to a child in the face of a parent's objections and without a court order violated Article 8.

For the purposes of the discussion that follows it is assumed that the common law   15.63
rules are ousted where the 1983 Act applies.

2. Detention for Treatment for Mental Disorder

(a) *Children of 16 or 17 Who Lack Capacity*

A child of 16 or 17 who lacks capacity who requires in-patient treatment for mental   15.64
disorder may be detained under the 2005 Act unless he must be detained under the 1983 Act, for the same reasons as an adult (above, para 15.05). He cannot, however,

---

[14] (2004) 39 EHRR 15.

be detained under the urgent or standard authorization procedure in Sch A1 of the 2005 Act, which only apply to those over 18 (Sch A1, para 13).

15.65   Alternatives to detention under the 1983 Act are as follows:

- He can be admitted to hospital by order of the Court of Protection under s 16 of the 2005 Act, including an order that he be detained, but not if he is 'ineligible' within the meaning of Sch 1A (s 16A) (for which see above, para 15.08ff).

- He can be detained by order of the High Court in its jurisdiction in relation to children (para 11.50), but not if treatment can only safely be given under the 1983 Act. The common law rules are ousted by the 1983 Act (above, para 15.59).

- He can be admitted informally under s 131(2) with the consent of a person with parental responsibility, by contrast with a child who has capacity (para 4.44). However, if such admission gave rise to a deprivation of liberty it would raise Article 5 issues, considering *HL v United Kingdom*.[15] In that case detention by Court order or under the 1983 Act is to be preferred. However, if treatment can only safely be delivered under the 1983 Act, informal admission with the consent of a person with parental responsibility is not available: the common law rules are ousted by the 1983 Act (para 15.59).

(b) *Children of 16 or 17 With Capacity*

15.66   A child of 16 or 17 with capacity who requires in-patient treatment for mental disorder cannot be detained under the 2005 Act, which applies only to individuals who lack capacity. He may be detained under the 1983 Act, but the following are alternatives to detention under the 1983 Act:

- If he consents he may be admitted to, and detained in, hospital informally under s 131(2) of the 1983 Act, as before.

- If he refuses to be admitted he may no longer be admitted informally with the consent of a person with parental responsibility: s 131(2)–(5) of the 1983 Act (see para 4.44 above). In that case it will be necessary to detain him under the 1983 Act.

- If he refuses admission he can probably be admitted and detained by order of the High Court in its jurisdiction in relation to children (above, paras 9.38, 11.50). However, if treatment can only safely be given under the 1983 Act it (probably) must be used, as the 1983 Act ousts the common law rules relating to children (above, para 15.59).

---

[15] (2004) 40 EHRR 761. In *Neilsen v Denmark* (1988) 11 EHRR 175 the ECtHR upheld the right of a parent to admit a competent child to hospital, finding that it did not give rise to a 'deprivation of liberty' for the purposes of Art 5(1). There must be some doubt as to whether this decision would now be followed.

3. Treatment for Mental Disorder

(a) *Children of 16 or 17 Who Lack Capacity*

As with adults, treatment for mental disorder may be given to a child of 16 or 17   15.67
under the 2005 Act if he lacks capacity, unless it must be given under the 1983 Act,
applying the principles outlined above at para 15.26ff. That is subject to the following qualifications.

When treatment falls within Part 4 or 4A of the 1983 Act, both the 2005 Act and   15.68
the common law rules relating to children are displaced: see para 15.59 above.

Where treatment can be given under the 2005 Act, it can probably also be   15.69
administered under the common law rules relating to children, subject to the question of whether those rules have been displaced or modified by the 2005 Act (above,
para 10.05).

When the treatment can be given both under the 2005 Act and under the   15.70
common law rules relating to treatment, the following should be borne in mind:

- Children of 16 or 17 fall within the 2005 Act, but the provisions relating to
  advance decisions (s 24(1)) and lasting powers of attorney (s 9(2)(c)) do not apply.
  The available routes to treatment under the 2005 Act are s 5 (acts in connection
  with care or treatment), by a court appointed deputy or by order of the Court of
  Protection under s 16.

- Under the common law rules, treatment can be given either by a person with
  parental responsibility or by the High Court. There will be no material difference
  between treatment administered to an incapable child with the consent of a parent
  under the common law rules or under s 5 of the 2005 Act; the distinction relates
  to children who have capacity, for whom treatment may be given under the
  common law rules notwithstanding their objection (below, para 15.71).

- Additional safeguards under s 58A (ECT) of the 1983 Act apply to children under
  18 who are neither 'liable to be detained' under the 1983 Act (s 56(5)) nor on a
  CTO (see paras 6.48, 6.56). Thus, where such treatment is administered under the
  2005 Act, or under the common law rules, the safeguards of s 58A still apply.

(b) *Children of 16 or 17 Who Have Capacity*

The 2005 Act has no part to play for any person who has capacity. Treatment   15.71
may be given under the common law rules relating to children unless it must be
given under the 1983 Act under Part 4 or 4A of the 1983 Act. Treatment not
falling within Part 4 or 4A can be given with the consent of a person with parental
responsibility, or the High Court, notwithstanding a capable child's refusal of treatment. That may raise issues under Article 8 (see para 9.39).

4. Detention and Treatment for Physical Disorder

For children aged 16 or 17, treatment for physical disorder, including admission to   15.72
hospital, may be authorized by the common law rules relating to children (para 9.25),

under s 5 of the 2005 Act or by the Court of Protection under s 16 of the 2005 Act, subject to the discussion at para 10.05.

15.73   Hospital admission may include detention where it is authorized by the High Court in its jurisdiction in relation to children (para 11.49ff), or by the Court of Protection under s 16 of the 2005 Act, which is not displaced by 'ineligibility' if the purpose of detention is treatment for physical disorder. Detention cannot be authorized under the urgent or standard authorization procedure in Sch A1 of the 2005 Act, which only applies to those over 18 (Sch A1, para 13).

H. CHILDREN UNDER 16

1. Detention for Treatment for Mental Disorder

15.74   The common law rules relating to the treatment of children under 16 are considered at para 9.25ff above, and those relating to the detention of such children at para 11.55ff. The material provisions of the 2005 Act do not apply at all to a child under the age of 16 (s 2(5)) (para 10.07). The common law rules relating to the detention of treatment apply, except where treatment is regulated by Part 4 or 4A of the 1983 Act, in which case the common law rules are ousted (above, para 15.59). The following alternatives to detention under the 1983 Act apply for all child patients under 16:

- A child under 16 who is *Gillick* competent to give a valid consent to treatment and who does consent may, if hospital admission is required, be admitted as an informal patient under s 131 of the 1983 Act, as before.

- A child under 16 may also be admitted informally under s 131 with the consent of a person with parental responsibility; in the case of a *Gillick* competent child, notwithstanding their refusal. The new provisions of s 131(2) to (5) (see para 4.44) do not apply to children under 16.

- A child under 16, whether competent or not, may also be admitted to hospital, and detained if necessary, by order of the High Court in its jurisdiction relating to children, notwithstanding the child's objections or those of a person with parental responsibility (above, para 11.55). However, if treatment can only safely be given under the 1983 Act it (probably) must be used, as the 1983 Act ousts the common law rules relating to children (above, para 15.59).

2. Treatment for Mental Disorder

15.75   Children under 16 cannot be treated, or have their treatment authorized, under the 2005 Act (s 2(5)). The common law rules relating to the treatment of children apply, subject to the following modifications:

- Treatment falling within Part 4 or 4A must be given under the 1983 Act: the common law rules are displaced (para 15.59, above)

- Additional safeguards under s 58A (ECT) of the 1983 Act apply to children under 18 who are neither 'liable to be detained' under the 1983 Act (s 56(5)) nor on a CTO (see paras 6.48, 6.56). Thus, where such treatment is administered under the 2005 Act, or under the common law rules, the safeguards of s 58A still apply.

3. Detention and Treatment for Physical Disorder

The common law rules relating to the treatment (para 9.25ff) and detention (para 11.55) of children apply.   15.76

APPENDIX 1

Mental Health Act 1983

AS IT IS TO BE AMENDED BY THE MENTAL HEALTH ACT 2007

KEY

Material to be deleted by the 2007 Act is in italics, eg *omitted material looks like this.*
Material to be added by the 2007 Act is in square brackets, eg [added material looks like this].

ANNOTATIONS

At the end of each section (or paragraph of a Schedule) the relevant provision of the 2007 Act is in italics, square brackets, and also in smaller type.

MENTAL HEALTH ACT 1983

CHAPTER 20

CONTENTS

PART 1
APPLICATION OF THE ACT

1   Application of Act: 'mental disorder'

PART 2
COMPULSORY ADMISSION TO HOSPITAL AND GUARDIANSHIP

Procedure for hospital admission

2   Admission for assessment
3   Admission for treatment
4   Admission for assessment in cases of emergency
5   Application in respect of patient already in hospital
6   Effect of application for admission

Guardianship

  7 Application for guardianship
  8 Effect of guardianship application, etc
  9 Regulations as to guardianship
 10 Transfer of guardianship in case of death, incapacity, etc of guardian

General provisions as to applications and recommendations

 11 General provisions as to applications
 12 General provisions as to medical recommendations
[12A] [Conflicts of interest]
 13 Duty of *approved social workers* [approved mental health professionals] to make applications for admission or guardianship
 14 Social reports
 15 Rectification of applications and recommendations
 16 Reclassification of patients

Position of patients subject to detention or guardianship

 17 Leave of absence from hospital
[17A] [Community treatment orders]
[17B] [Conditions]
[17C] [Duration of community treatment order]
[17D] [Effect of community treatment order]
[17E] [Power to recall to hospital]
[17F] [Powers in respect of recalled patients]
[17G] [Effect of revoking community treatment order]
 18 Return and readmission of patients absent without leave
 19 Regulations as to transfer of patients
[19A] [Regulations as to assignment of responsibility for community patients]

Duration of detention or guardianship [authority] and discharge

 20 Duration of authority
[20A] [Community treatment period]
[20B] [Effect of expiry of community treatment order]
 21 Special provisions as to patients absent without leave
21A Patients who are taken into custody or return within 28 days
21B Patients who are taken into custody or return after more than 28 days
 22 Special provisions as to patients sentenced to imprisonment, etc
[22] [Special provisions as to patients sentenced to imprisonment, etc]
 23 Discharge of patients
 24 Visiting and examination of patients
 25 Restrictions on discharge by nearest relative

After-care under supervision

25A Application for supervision
25B Making of supervision application
25C Supervision applications: supplementary
25D Requirements to secure receipt of after-care under supervision
25E Review of after-care under supervision etc
25F Reclassification of patient subject to after-care under supervision
25G Duration and renewal of after-care under supervision
25H Ending of after-care under supervision
25I Special provisions as to patients sentenced to imprisonment etc
25J Patients moving from Scotland to England and Wales

Functions of relatives of patients

26 Definition of 'relative' and 'nearest relative'
27 Children and young persons in care
28 Nearest relative of minor under guardianship, etc
29 Appointment by court of acting nearest relative
30 Discharge and variation of orders under s 29

Supplemental

31 Procedure on applications to county court
32 Regulations for purposes of Part II
33 Special provisions as to wards of court
34 Interpretation of Part II

PART 3

PATIENTS CONCERNED IN CRIMINAL PROCEEDINGS
OR UNDER SENTENCE

Remands to hospital

35 Remand to hospital for report on accused's mental condition
36 Remand of accused person to hospital for treatment

Hospital and guardianship orders

37 Powers of courts to order hospital admission or guardianship
38 Interim hospital orders
39 Information as to hospitals
39A Information to facilitate guardianship orders
40 Effect of hospital orders, guardianship orders and interim hospital orders

Restriction orders

41 Power of higher courts to restrict discharge from hospital
42 Powers of Secretary of State in respect of patients subject to restriction orders
43 Power of magistrates' courts to commit for restriction order
44 Committal to hospital under s 43
45 Appeals from magistrates' courts

Hospital and limitation directions

45A Power of higher courts to direct hospital admission
45B Effect of hospital and limitation directions

Transfer to hospital of prisoners, etc

47 Removal to hospital of persons serving sentences of imprisonment, etc
48 Removal to hospital of other prisoners
49 Restriction on discharge of prisoners removed to hospital
50 Further provisions as to prisoners under sentence
51 Further provisions as to detained persons
52 Further provisions as to persons remanded by magistrates' courts
53 Further provisions as to civil prisoners and persons detained under the Immigration Acts

Supplemental

54 Requirements as to medical evidence
54A Reduction of period for making hospital orders
55 Interpretation of Part III

PART 4
CONSENT TO TREATMENT

56 *Patients to whom Part IV applies*
[56] [Patients to whom Part 4 applies]
57 Treatment requiring consent and a second opinion
58 Treatment requiring consent or a second opinion
[58A] [Electro-convulsive therapy, etc]
59 Plans of treatment
60 Withdrawal of consent
61 Review of treatment
62 Urgent treatment
[62A] [Treatment on recall of community patient or revocation of order]
63 Treatment not requiring consent
64 Supplementary provisions for Part IV

[PART 4A
TREATMENT OF COMMUNITY PATIENTS NOT RECALLED TO HOSPITAL]

[64A]   [Meaning of 'relevant treatment']
[64B]   [Adult community patients]
[64C]   [Section 64B: supplemental]
[64D]   [Adult community patients lacking capacity]
[64E]   [Child community patients]
[64F]   [Child community patients lacking capacity]
[64G]   [Emergency treatment for patients lacking capacity or competence]
[64H]   [Certificates: supplementary provisions]
[64I]   [Liability for negligence]
[64J]   [Factors to be considered in determining whether patient objects to treatment]
[64K]   [Interpretation of Part 4A]

PART 5
MENTAL HEALTH REVIEW TRIBUNALS

Constitution etc

65   Mental Health Review Tribunals

Applications and references concerning Part II patients

66   Applications to tribunals
67   References to tribunals by Secretary of State concerning Part II patients
68   *Duty of managers of hospitals to refer cases to tribunal*
[68]   [Duty of managers of hospitals to refer cases to tribunal]
[68A]   [Power to reduce periods under section 68]

Applications and references concerning Part III patients

69   Applications to tribunals concerning patients subject to hospital and guardianship orders
70   Applications to tribunals concerning restricted patients
71   References by Secretary of State concerning restricted patients

Discharge of patients

72   Powers of tribunals
73   Power to discharge restricted patients
74   Restricted patients subject to restriction directions
75   Applications and references concerning conditionally discharged restricted patients

General

76 Visiting and examination of patients
77 General provisions concerning tribunal applications
78 Procedure of tribunals
79 Interpretation of Part V

PART 6
REMOVAL AND RETURN OF PATIENTS WITHIN THE UNITED KINGDOM

Removal to [and from] Scotland

80 Removal of patients to Scotland
[80ZA] [Transfer of responsibility for community patients to Scotland]
80A Transfer of responsibility for [conditionally discharged] patients to Scotland
[80B] [Removal of detained patients from Scotland]
[80C] [Removal of patients subject to compulsion in the community from Scotland]
[80D] [Transfer of conditionally discharged patients from Scotland]

Removal to and from Northern Ireland

81 Removal of patients to Northern Ireland
[81ZA] [Removal of community patients to Northern Ireland]
81A Transfer of responsibility for patients to Northern Ireland
82 Removal to England and Wales of patients from Northern Ireland
82A Transfer of responsibility for [conditionally discharged] patients to England and Wales from Northern Ireland

Removal to and from Channel Islands and Isle of Man

83 Removal of patients to Channel Islands or Isle of Man
[83ZA] [Removal or transfer of community patients to Channel Islands or Isle of Man]
83A Transfer of responsibility for [conditionally discharged] patients to Channel Islands or Isle of Man
84 Removal to England and Wales of offenders found insane in Channel Islands and Isle of Man
85 Patients removed from Channel Islands or Isle of Man
[85ZA] [Responsibility for community patients transferred from Channel Islands or Isle of Man]
85A Responsibility for [conditionally discharged] patients transferred from Channel Islands or Isle of Man

Removal of aliens

86 Removal of alien patients

Return of patients absent without leave

87 Patients absent from hospitals in Northern Ireland
88 Patients absent from hospitals in England and Wales
89 Patients absent from hospitals in the Channel Islands or Isle of Man

General

90 Regulations for purposes of Part VI
91 General provisions as to patients removed from England and Wales
92 Interpretation of Part VI

PART 7
MANAGEMENT OF PROPERTY AND AFFAIRS OF PATIENTS

[Repealed by Mental Capacity Act 2005]

PART 8
MISCELLANEOUS FUNCTIONS OF LOCAL AUTHORITIES
AND THE SECRETARY OF STATE

Approved social workers

114 *Appointment of approved social workers*

[Approved mental health professionals]

[114]   [Approval by local social services authority]
[114A] [Approval of courses etc for approved mental health professionals]
115 *Powers of entry and inspection*
[115]   [Powers of entry and inspection]

Visiting patients

116 Welfare of certain hospital patients

After-care

117 After-care

Functions of the Secretary of State

118 Code of practice
119 Practitioners approved for Part IV and s 118
120 General protection of detained patients
121 Mental Health Act Commission
122 Provision of pocket money for in-patients in hospital
123 Transfers to and from special hospitals

PART 9
OFFENCES

126 Forgery, false statements, etc
127 Ill-treatment of patients
128 Assisting patients to absent themselves without leave, etc
129 Obstruction
130 Prosecutions by local authorities

PART 10
MISCELLANEOUS AND SUPPLEMENTARY

Miscellaneous provisions

[130A] [Independent mental health advocates]
[130B] [Arrangements under section 130A]
[130C] [Section 130A: supplemental]
[130D] [Duty to give information about independent mental health advocates]
   131 Informal admission of patients
[131A] [Accommodation, etc for children]
   132 Duty of managers of hospitals to give information to detained patients
[132A] [Duty of managers of hospitals to give information to community patients]
   133 Duty of managers of hospitals to inform nearest relatives of discharge
   134 Correspondence of patients
   135 Warrant to search for and remove patients
   136 Mentally disordered persons found in public places
   137 Provisions as to custody, conveyance and detention
   138 Retaking of patients escaping from custody
   139 Protection for acts done in pursuance of this Act
   140 Notification of hospitals having arrangements for *reception of urgent* [special] cases
   141 Members of Parliament suffering from mental illness
[142A] [Regulations as to approvals in relation to England and Wales]
[142B] [Delegation of powers of managers of NHS foundation trusts]

Supplemental

143 General provisions as to regulations, orders and rules
144 Power to amend local Acts

145 Interpretation
146 Application to Scotland
147 Application to Northern Ireland
148 Consequential and transitional provisions and repeals
149 Short title, commencement and application to Scilly Isles

Schedules

Schedule 1 Application of Certain Provisions to Patients Subject to Hospital and Guardianship
    Part I Patients not subject to special restrictions
    Part II Patients subject to special restrictions

Schedule 2 Mental Health Review Tribunals

Schedule 5 Transitional and Saving Provision

MENTAL HEALTH ACT 1983
1983 CHAPTER 20

An Act to consolidate the law relating to mentally disordered persons. [9th May 1983]

BE IT ENACTED by the Queen's most Excellent Majesty, by and with the advice and consent of the Lords Spiritual and Temporal, and Commons, in this present Parliament assembled, and by the authority of the same, as follows:–

PART I
APPLICATION OF ACT

1 Application of Act: 'mental disorder'

(1) The provisions of this Act shall have effect with respect to the reception, care and treatment of mentally disordered patients, the management of their property and other related matters.

(2) In this Act—

'mental disorder' means mental illness, arrested or incomplete development of mind, psychopathic disorder and any other disorder or disability of mind and 'mentally disordered' shall be construed accordingly;

['mental disorder' means any disorder or disability of the mind; and

'mentally disordered' shall be construed accordingly;]

'severe mental impairment' means a state of arrested or incomplete development of mind which includes severe impairment of intelligence and social functioning and is associated with abnormally aggressive or seriously irresponsible conduct on the part of the person concerned and 'severely mentally impaired' shall be construed accordingly;

'mental impairment' means a state of arrested or incomplete development of mind (not amounting to severe mental impairment) which includes significant impairment of intelligence and social functioning and is associated with abnormally aggressive or seriously irresponsible conduct on the part of the person concerned and 'mentally impaired' shall be construed accordingly;

'psychopathic disorder' means a persistent disorder or disability of mind (whether or not including significant impairment of intelligence) which results in abnormally aggressive or seriously irresponsible conduct on the part of the person concerned;

and other expressions shall have the meanings assigned to them in section 145 below.

[(2A) But a person with learning disability shall not be considered by reason of that disability to be—

(a) suffering from mental disorder for the purposes of the provisions mentioned in subsection (2B) below; or

(b) requiring treatment in hospital for mental disorder for the purposes of sections 17E and 50 to 53 below,

unless that disability is associated with abnormally aggressive or seriously irresponsible conduct on his part.

(2B) The provisions are—

(a) sections 3, 7, 17A, 20 and 20A below;

(b) sections 35 to 38, 45A, 47, 48 and 51 below; and

(c) section 72(1)(b) and (c) and (4) below.]

(3) Nothing in subsection (2) above shall be construed as implying that a person may be dealt with under this Act as suffering from mental disorder, or from any form of mental disorder described in this section, by reason only of promiscuity or other immoral conduct, sexual deviancy or dependence on alcohol or drugs.

[(3) Dependence on alcohol or drugs is not considered to be a disorder or disability of the mind for the purposes of subsection (2) above.

(4) In subsection (2A) above, 'learning disability' means a state of arrested or incomplete development of the mind which includes significant impairment of intelligence and social functioning.]

[*Definition of 'mental disorder' substituted by section 1(2) of the 2007 Act. Definitions of 'severe mental impairment', 'mental impairment' and 'psychopathic disorder' omitted by section 1(3)(a) to (c) respectively. Subsections (2A) & (2B) inserted by section 2(2). Subsection (3) substituted by section 3. Subsection (4) inserted by section 2(3).*]

PART II
COMPULSORY ADMISSION TO HOSPITAL AND GUARDIANSHIP

Procedure for hospital admission

2 Admission for assessment

(1) A patient may be admitted to a hospital and detained there for the period allowed by subsection (4) below in pursuance of an application (in this Act referred to as 'an application for admission for assessment') made in accordance with subsections (2) and (3) below.

(2) An application for admission for assessment may be made in respect of a patient on the grounds that—

(a) he is suffering from mental disorder of a nature or degree which warrants the detention of the patient in a hospital for assessment (or for assessment followed by medical treatment) for at least a limited period; and

(b) he ought to be so detained in the interests of his own health or safety or with a view to the protection of other persons.

(3) An application for admission for assessment shall be founded on the written recommendations in the prescribed form of two registered medical practitioners, including in each case a statement that in the opinion of the practitioner the conditions set out in subsection (2) above are complied with.

(4) Subject to the provisions of section 29(4) below, a patient admitted to hospital in pursuance of an application for admission for assessment may be detained for a period not exceeding 28 days beginning with the day on which he is admitted, but shall not be detained after the expiration of that period unless before it has expired he has become liable to be detained by virtue of a subsequent application, order or direction under the following provisions of this Act.

3 Admission for treatment

(1) A patient may be admitted to a hospital and detained there for the period allowed by the following provisions of this Act in pursuance of an application (in this Act referred to as 'an application for admission for treatment') made in accordance with this section.

(2) An application for admission for treatment may be made in respect of a patient on the grounds that—

(a) he is suffering from *mental illness, severe mental impairment, psychopathic disorder or mental impairment and his mental disorder is* [mental disorder] of a nature or degree which makes it appropriate for him to receive medical treatment in a hospital; and

(b) *in the case of psychopathic disorder or mental impairment, such treatment is likely to alleviate or prevent a deterioration of his condition; and*

(c) it is necessary for the health or safety of the patient or for the protection of other persons that he should receive such treatment and it cannot be provided unless he is detained under this section[; and

(d) appropriate medical treatment is available for him].

(3) An application for admission for treatment shall be founded on the written recommendations in the prescribed form of two registered medical practitioners, including in each case a statement that in the opinion of the practitioner the conditions set out in subsection (2) above are complied with; and each such recommendation shall include—

(a) such particulars as may be prescribed of the grounds for that opinion so far as it relates to the conditions set out in paragraphs (a) and *(b)* [(d)] of that subsection; and

(b) a statement of the reasons for that opinion so far as it relates to the conditions set out in paragraph (c) of that subsection, specifying whether other methods of dealing with the patient are available and, if so, why they are not appropriate.

[(4) In this Act, references to appropriate medical treatment, in relation to a person suffering from mental disorder, are references to medical treatment which is appropriate in his case, taking into account the nature and degree of the mental disorder and all other circumstances of his case.]

[*Words in subsection (2)(a) substituted by paragraph 2 of Schedule 1 to the 2007 Act. Subsection 2(b) (and following 'and') omitted, subsection (2)(d) inserted and words in subsection (3)(a) substituted by section 4(2). Subsection (4) inserted by section 4(3).*]

4 Admission for assessment in cases of emergency

(1) In any case of urgent necessity, an application for admission for assessment may be made in respect of a patient in accordance with the following provisions of this section, and any application so made is in this Act referred to as 'an emergency application'.

(2) An emergency application may be made either by an *approved social worker* [approved mental health professional] or by the nearest relative of the patient; and every such application shall

include a statement that it is of urgent necessity for the patient to be admitted and detained under section 2 above, and that compliance with the provisions of this Part of this Act relating to applications under that section would involve undesirable delay.

(3) An emergency application shall be sufficient in the first instance if founded on one of the medical recommendations required by section 2 above, given, if practicable, by a practitioner who has previous acquaintance with the patient and otherwise complying with the requirements of section 12 below so far as applicable to a single recommendation, and verifying the statement referred to in subsection (2) above.

(4) An emergency application shall cease to have effect on the expiration of a period of 72 hours from the time when the patient is admitted to the hospital unless—

    (a) the second medical recommendation required by section 2 above is given and received by the managers within that period; and

    (b) that recommendation and the recommendation referred to in subsection (3) above together comply with all the requirements of section 12 below (other than the requirement as to the time of signature of the second recommendation).

(5) In relation to an emergency application, section 11 below shall have effect as if in subsection (5) of that section for the words 'the period of 14 days ending with the date of the application' there were substituted the words 'the previous 24 hours'.

[*Words in subsection (2) substituted by paragraph 2(a) of Schedule 2 to the 2007 Act.*]

5 Application in respect of patient already in hospital

(1) An application for the admission of a patient to a hospital may be made under this Part of this Act notwithstanding that the patient is already an in-patient in that hospital or, in the case of an application for admission for treatment, that the patient is for the time being liable to be detained in the hospital in pursuance of an application for admission for assessment; and where an application is so made the patient shall be treated for the purposes of this Part of this Act as if he had been admitted to the hospital at the time when that application was received by the managers.

(2) If, in the case of a patient who is an in-patient in a hospital, it appears to the registered medical practitioner [or approved clinician] in charge of the treatment of the patient that an application ought to be made under this Part of this Act for the admission of the patient to hospital, he may furnish to the managers a report in writing to that effect; and in any such case the patient may be detained in the hospital for a period of 72 hours from the time when the report is so furnished.

(3) *The registered medical practitioner in charge of the treatment of a patient in a hospital may nominate one (but not more than one) other registered medical practitioner on the staff of that hospital to act for him under subsection (2) above in his absence.*

[(3) The registered medical practitioner or approved clinician in charge of the treatment of a patient in a hospital may nominate one (but not more than one) person to act for him under subsection (2) above in his absence.

(3A) For the purposes of subsection (3) above—

    (a) the registered medical practitioner may nominate another registered medical practitioner, or an approved clinician, on the staff of the hospital; and

    (b) the approved clinician may nominate another approved clinician, or a registered medical practitioner, on the staff of the hospital.]

(4) If, in the case of a patient who is receiving treatment for mental disorder as an in-patient in a hospital, it appears to a nurse of the prescribed class—

(a) that the patient is suffering from mental disorder to such a degree that it is necessary for his health or safety or for the protection of others for him to be immediately restrained from leaving the hospital; and

(b) that it is not practicable to secure the immediate attendance of a practitioner [or clinician] for the purpose of furnishing a report under subsection (2) above,

the nurse may record that fact in writing; and in that event the patient may be detained in the hospital for a period of six hours from the time when that fact is so recorded or until the earlier arrival at the place where the patient is detained of a practitioner [or clinician] having power to furnish a report under that subsection.

(5) A record made under subsection (4) above shall be delivered by the nurse (or by a person authorised by the nurse in that behalf) to the managers of the hospital as soon as possible after it is made; and where a record is made under that subsection the period mentioned in subsection (2) above shall begin at the time when it is made.

(6) The reference in subsection (1) above to an in-patient does not include an in-patient who is liable to be detained in pursuance of an application under this Part of this Act [or a community patient] and the references in subsections (2) and (4) above do not include an in-patient who is liable to be detained in a hospital under this Part of this Act [or a community patient].

(7) In subsection (4) above 'prescribed' means prescribed by an order made by the Secretary of State.

[*Words in subsection (2) and (4) inserted by section 9(2)(a) & (c) of the 2007 Act respectively. Subsections (3) and (3A) substituted for current subsection (3) by section 9(2)(b). Words inserted in subsection (6) by paragraph 2 of Schedule 3.*]

6 Effect of application for admission

(1) An application for the admission of a patient to a hospital under this Part of this Act, duly completed in accordance with the provisions of this Part of this Act, shall be sufficient authority for the applicant, or any person authorised by the applicant, to take the patient and convey him to the hospital at any time within the following period, that is to say—

(a) in the case of an application other than an emergency application, the period of 14 days beginning with the date on which the patient was last examined by a registered medical practitioner before giving a medical recommendation for the purposes of the application;

(b) in the case of an emergency application, the period of 24 hours beginning at the time when the patient was examined by the practitioner giving the medical recommendation which is referred to in section 4(3) above, or at the time when the application is made, whichever is the earlier.

(2) Where a patient is admitted within the said period to the hospital specified in such an application as is mentioned in subsection (1) above, or, being within that hospital, is treated by virtue of section 5 above as if he had been so admitted, the application shall be sufficient authority for the managers to detain the patient in the hospital in accordance with the provisions of this Act.

(3) Any application for the admission of a patient under this Part of this Act which appears to be duly made and to be founded on the necessary medical recommendations may be acted upon without further proof of the signature or qualification of the person by whom the application or any such medical recommendation is made or given or of any matter of fact or opinion stated in it.

(4) Where a patient is admitted to a hospital in pursuance of an application for admission for treatment, any previous application under this Part of this Act by virtue of which he was liable to be detained in a hospital or subject to guardianship shall cease to have effect.

Guardianship

7 Application for guardianship

(1) A patient who has attained the age of 16 years may be received into guardianship, for the period allowed by the following provisions of this Act, in pursuance of an application (in this Act referred to as 'a guardianship application') made in accordance with this section.

(2) A guardianship application may be made in respect of a patient on the grounds that—

(a) he is suffering from mental disorder, *being mental illness, severe mental impairment, psychopathic disorder or mental impairment and his mental disorder is* of a nature or degree which warrants his reception into guardianship under this section;

(b) it is necessary in the interests of the welfare of the patient or for the protection of other persons that the patient should be so received.

(3) A guardianship application shall be founded on the written recommendations in the prescribed form of two registered medical practitioners, including in each case a statement that in the opinion of the practitioner the conditions set out in subsection (2) above are complied with; and each such recommendation shall include—

(a) such particulars as may be prescribed of the grounds for that opinion so far as it relates to the conditions set out in paragraph (a) of that subsection; and

(b) a statement of the reasons for that opinion so far as it relates to the conditions set out in paragraph (b) of that subsection.

(4) A guardianship application shall state the age of the patient or, if his exact age is not known to the applicant, shall state (if it be the fact) that the patient is believed to have attained the age of 16 years.

(5) The person named as guardian in a guardianship application may be either a local social services authority or any other person (including the applicant himself); but a guardianship application in which a person other than a local social services authority is named as guardian shall be of no effect unless it is accepted on behalf of that person by the local social services authority for the area in which he resides, and shall be accompanied by a statement in writing by that person that he is willing to act as guardian.

[Words in subsection (2)(a) omitted by paragraph 3 of Schedule 1 to the 2007 Act.]

8 Effect of guardianship application, etc

(1) Where a guardianship application, duly made under the provisions of this Part of this Act and forwarded to the local social services authority within the period allowed by subsection (2) below is accepted by that authority, the application shall, subject to regulations made by the Secretary of State, confer on the authority or person named in the application as guardian, to the exclusion of any other person—

(a) the power to require the patient to reside at a place specified by the authority or person named as guardian;

(b) the power to require the patient to attend at places and times so specified for the purpose of medical treatment, occupation, education or training;

(c) the power to require access to the patient to be given, at any place where the patient is residing, to any registered medical practitioner, *approved social worker* [approved mental health professional] or other person so specified.

(2) The period within which a guardianship application is required for the purposes of this section to be forwarded to the local social services authority is the period of 14 days beginning with the date on which the patient was last examined by a registered medical practitioner before giving a medical recommendation for the purposes of the application.

(3) A guardianship application which appears to be duly made and to be founded on the necessary medical recommendations may be acted upon without further proof of the signature or qualification of the person by whom the application or any such medical recommendation is made or given, or of any matter of fact or opinion stated in the application.

(4) If within the period of 14 days beginning with the day on which a guardianship application has been accepted by the local social services authority the application, or any medical recommendation given for the purposes of the application, is found to be in any respect incorrect or defective, the application or recommendation may, within that period and with the consent of that authority, be amended by the person by whom it was signed; and upon such amendment being made the application or recommendation shall have effect and shall be deemed to have had effect as if it had been originally made as so amended.

(5) Where a patient is received into guardianship in pursuance of a guardianship application, any previous application under this Part of this Act by virtue of which he was subject to guardianship or liable to be detained in a hospital shall cease to have effect.

[*Words in subsection (1)(c) substituted by paragraph 2(b) of Schedule 2 to the 2007 Act.*]

9 Regulations as to guardianship

(1) Subject to the provisions of this Part of this Act, the Secretary of State may make regulations—
  (a) for regulating the exercise by the guardians of patients received into guardianship under this Part of this Act of their powers as such; and
  (b) for imposing on such guardians, and upon local social services authorities in the case of patients under the guardianship of persons other than local social services authorities, such duties as he considers necessary or expedient in the interests of the patients.

(2) Regulations under this section may in particular make provision for requiring the patients to be visited, on such occasions or at such intervals as may be prescribed by the regulations, on behalf of such local social services authorities as may be so prescribed, and shall provide for the appointment, in the case of every patient subject to the guardianship of a person other than a local social services authority, of a registered medical practitioner to act as the nominated medical attendant of the patient.

10 Transfer of guardianship in case of death, incapacity, etc of guardian

(1) If any person (other than a local social services authority) who is the guardian of a patient received into guardianship under this Part of this Act—
  (a) dies; or
  (b) gives notice in writing to the local social services authority that he desires to relinquish the functions of guardian,
the guardianship of the patient shall thereupon vest in the local social services authority, but without prejudice to any power to transfer the patient into the guardianship of another person in pursuance of regulations under section 19 below.

(2) If any such person, not having given notice under subsection (1)(b) above, is incapacitated by illness or any other cause from performing the functions of guardian of the patient, those functions may, during his incapacity, be performed on his behalf by the local social services authority or by any other person approved for the purposes by that authority.

(3) If it appears to the county court, upon application made by an *approved social worker* [approved mental health professional acting on behalf of the local social services authority], that any person other than a local social services authority having the guardianship of a patient received into guardianship under this Part of this Act has performed his functions negligently or in a manner contrary to the interests of the welfare of the patient, the court may order that the guardianship of the patient be transferred to the local social services authority or to any other person approved for the purpose by that authority.

(4) Where the guardianship of a patient is transferred to a local social services authority or other person by or under this section, subsection (2)(c) of section 19 below shall apply as if the patient had been transferred into the guardianship of that authority or person in pursuance of regulations under that section.

[(5) In this section 'the local social services authority', in relation to a person (other than a local social services authority) who is the guardian of a patient, means the local social services authority for the area in which that person resides (or resided immediately before his death).]

[*Words in subsection (3) substituted by paragraph 3(2) of Schedule 2 to the 2007 Act. Subsection (5) inserted by paragraph 3(3) of Schedule 2.*]

General provisions as to applications and recommendations

11 General provisions as to applications

(1) Subject to the provisions of this section, an application for admission for assessment, an application for admission for treatment and a guardianship application may be made either by the nearest relative of the patient or by an *approved social worker* [approved mental health professional]; and every such application shall specify the qualification of the applicant to make the application.

[(1A) No application mentioned in subsection (1) above shall be made by an approved mental health professional if the circumstances are such that there would be a potential conflict of interest for the purposes of regulations under section 12A below.]

(2) Every application for admission shall be addressed to the managers of the hospital to which admission is sought and every guardianship application shall be forwarded to the local social services authority named in the application as guardian, or, as the case may be, to the local social services authority for the area in which the person so named resides.

(3) Before or within a reasonable time after an application for the admission of a patient for assessment is made by an *approved social worker, that social worker* [approved mental health professional, that professional] shall take such steps as are practicable to inform the person (if any) appearing to be the nearest relative of the patient that the application is to be or has been made and of the power of the nearest relative under section 23(2)(a) below.

(4) *Neither an application for admission for treatment nor a guardianship application shall be made by an approved social worker if the nearest relative of the patient has notified that social worker, or the local social services authority by whom that social worker is appointed, that he objects to the application being made and, without prejudice to the foregoing provision, no such application shall be made by such a social worker except after consultation with the person (if any) appearing to be the nearest relative of the patient unless it appears to that social worker that in the circumstances such consultation is not reasonably practicable or would involve unreasonable delay.*

[(4) An approved mental health professional may not make an application for admission for treatment or a guardianship application in respect of a patient in either of the following cases—

    (a) the nearest relative of the patient has notified that professional, or the local social services authority on whose behalf the professional is acting, that he objects to the application being made; or

    (b) that professional has not consulted the person (if any) appearing to be the nearest relative of the patient, but the requirement to consult that person does not apply if it appears to the professional that in the circumstances such consultation is not reasonably practicable or would involve unreasonable delay.]

(5) None of the applications mentioned in subsection (1) above shall be made by any person in respect of a patient unless that person has personally seen the patient within the period of 14 days ending with the date of the application.

(6) An application for admission for treatment or a guardianship application, and any recommendation given for the purposes of such an application, may describe the patient as suffering from more than one of the following forms of mental disorder, namely mental illness, severe mental impairment, psychopathic disorder or mental impairment; but the application shall be of no effect unless the patient is described in each of the recommendations as suffering from the same form of mental disorder, whether or not he is also described in either of those recommendations as suffering from another form.

(7) Each of the applications mentioned in subsection (1) above shall be sufficient if the recommendations on which it is founded are given either as separate recommendations, each signed by a registered medical practitioner, or as a joint recommendation signed by two such practitioners.

[*Words in subsection (1) and (3) and whole of subsection (4) substituted by paragraphs 4(2) to (4) respectively of Schedule 2 to the 2007 Act. Subsection (1A) inserted by section 22(2). Subsection (6) omitted by Part 1 of Schedule 11.*]

12 General provisions as to medical recommendations

(1) The recommendations required for the purposes of an application for the admission of a patient under this Part of this Act [or a guardianship application] (in this Act referred to as 'medical recommendations') shall be signed on or before the date of the application, and shall be given by practitioners who have personally examined the patient either together or separately, but where they have examined the patient separately not more than five days must have elapsed between the days on which the separate examinations took place.

(2) Of the medical recommendations given for the purposes of any such application, one shall be given by a practitioner approved for the purposes of this section by the Secretary of State as having special experience in the diagnosis or treatment of mental disorder; and unless that practitioner has previous acquaintance with the patient, the other such recommendation shall, if practicable, be given by a registered medical practitioner who has such previous acquaintance.

[(2A) A registered medical practitioner who is an approved clinician shall be treated as also approved for the purposes of this section under subsection (2) above as having special experience as mentioned there.]

(3) Subject to subsection (4) below, where the application is for the admission of the patient to a hospital which is not a registered establishment, one (but not more than one) of the medical recommendations may be given by a practitioner on the staff of that hospital, except where the patient is proposed to be accommodated under section 21(4) or 44(6) of the National Health Service Act 2006, paragraph 15 of Schedule 2 to, or paragraph 11 of Schedule 6 to, that Act, or paragraph 15 of Schedule 2 to, or paragraph 11 of Schedule 5 to, the National Health Service

(Wales) Act 2006 (which relate to accommodation for private patients) or otherwise to be accommodated, by virtue of an undertaking to pay in respect of the accommodation, in a hospital vested in an NHS foundation trust.

(4) *Subsection (3) above shall not preclude both the medical recommendations being given by practitioners on the staff of the hospital in question if—*

    (a) *compliance with that subsection would result in delay involving serious risk to the health or safety of the patient; and*

    (b) *one of the practitioners giving the recommendations works at the hospital for less than half of the time which he is bound by contract to devote to work in the health service; and*

    (c) *where one of those practitioners is a consultant, the other does not work (whether at the hospital or elsewhere) in a grade in which he is under that consultant's directions.*

(5) *A medical recommendation for the purposes of an application for the admission of a patient under this Part of this Act shall not be given by—*

    (a) *the applicant;*

    (b) *a partner of the applicant or of a practitioner by whom another medical recommendation is given for the purposes of the same application;*

    (c) *a person employed as an assistant by the applicant or by any such practitioner;*

    (d) *a person who receives or has an interest in the receipt of any payments made on account of the maintenance of the patient; or*

    (e) *except as provided by subsection (3) or (4) above, a practitioner on the staff of the hospital to which the patient is to be admitted,*

or by the husband, wife, civil partner, father, father-in-law, mother, mother-in-law, son, son-in-law, daughter, daughter-in-law, brother, brother-in-law, sister or sister-in-law of the patient, or of any person mentioned in paragraphs (a) to (e) above, or of a practitioner by whom another medical recommendation is given for the purposes of the same application.

(6) *A general practitioner who is employed part-time in a hospital shall not for the purposes of this section be regarded as a practitioner on its staff.*

(7) *Subsections (1), (2) and (5) above shall apply to applications for guardianship as they apply to applications for admission but with the substitution for paragraph (e) of subsection (5) above of the following paragraph—*

'(e) the person named as guardian in the application.'

[(3) No medical recommendation shall be given for the purposes of an application mentioned in subsection (1) above if the circumstances are such that there would be a potential conflict of interest for the purposes of regulations under section 12A below.]

[*Words inserted in subsection (1) by Section 22(3). Subsection (2A) inserted by section 16. New subsection (3) substituted for subsections (3) to (7) by section 23(4).*]

[12A Conflicts of interest]

[(1) The appropriate national authority may make regulations as to the circumstances in which there would be a potential conflict of interest such that—

    (a) an approved mental health professional shall not make an application mentioned in section 11(1) above;

    (b) a registered medical practitioner shall not give a recommendation for the purposes of an application mentioned in section 12(1) above.

(2) Regulations under subsection (1) above may make—

    (a) provision for the prohibitions in paragraphs (a) and (b) of that subsection to be subject to specified exceptions;

    (b) different provision for different cases; and

(c) transitional, consequential, incidental or supplemental provision.

(3) In subsection (1) above, 'the appropriate national authority' means—

    (a) in relation to applications in which admission is sought to a hospital in England or to guardianship applications in respect of which the area of the relevant local social services authority is in England, the Secretary of State;

    (b) in relation to applications in which admission is sought to a hospital in Wales or to guardianship applications in respect of which the area of the relevant local social services authority is in Wales, the Welsh Ministers.

(4) References in this section to the relevant local social services authority, in relation to a guardianship application, are references to the local social services authority named in the application as guardian or (as the case may be) the local social services authority for the area in which the person so named resides.]

[*Section 12A inserted by section 22(5) of the 2007 Act.*]

13 Duty of *approved social workers* [approved mental health professionals] to make applications for admission or guardianship

(1) It shall be the duty of an approved social worker to make an application for admission to hospital or a guardianship application in respect of a patient within the area of the local social services authority by which that officer is appointed in any case where he is satisfied that such an application ought to be made and is of the opinion, having regard to any wishes expressed by relatives of the patient or any other relevant circumstances, that it is necessary or proper for the application to be made by him.

[(1) If a local social services authority have reason to think that an application for admission to hospital or a guardianship application may need to be made in respect of a patient within their area, they shall make arrangements for an approved mental health professional to consider the patient's case on their behalf.

(1A) If that professional is—

    (a) satisfied that such an application ought to be made in respect of the patient; and

    (b) of the opinion, having regard to any wishes expressed by relatives of the patient or any other relevant circumstances, that it is necessary or proper for the application to be made by him,

he shall make the application.

(1B) Subsection (1C) below applies where—

    (a) a local social services authority makes arrangements under subsection (1) above in respect of a patient;

    (b) an application for admission for assessment is made under subsection (1A) above in respect of the patient;

    (c) while the patient is liable to be detained in pursuance of that application, the authority have reason to think that an application for admission for treatment may need to be made in respect of the patient; and

    (d) the patient is not within the area of the authority.]

(1C) Where this subsection applies, subsection (1) above shall be construed as requiring the authority to make arrangements under that subsection in place of the authority mentioned there].

(2) Before making an application for the admission of a patient to hospital an *approved social worker* [approved mental health professional] shall interview the patient in a suitable manner and satisfy himself that detention in a hospital is in all the circumstances of the case the most

appropriate way of providing the care and medical treatment of which the patient stands in need.

(3) *An application under this section by an approved social worker may be made outside the area of the local social services authority by which he is appointed.*

[(3) An application under subsection (1A) above may be made outside the area of the local social services authority on whose behalf the approved mental health professional is considering the patient's case.]

(4) It shall be the duty of a local social services authority, if so required by the nearest relative of a patient residing in their area, to *direct an approved social worker as soon as practicable to take the patient's case into consideration under subsection (1) above* [make arrangements under subsection (1) above for an approved mental health professional to consider the patient's case] with a view to making an application for his admission to hospital; and if in any such case *that approved social worker* [that professional] decides not to make an application he shall inform the nearest relative of his reasons in writing.

(5) Nothing in this section shall be construed as authorising or requiring an application to be made by an *approved social worker* [approved mental health professional] in contravention of the provisions of section 11(4) above [or of regulations under section 12A above], or as restricting the power of [a local social services authority to make arrangements with an approved mental health professional to consider a patient's case or of] an *approved social worker* [approved mental health professional] to make any application under this Act.

[*Title of section amended by paragraph 5(1) of Schedule 2 to the 2007 Act; subsections (1) to (1C) substituted for current subsection (1) by paragraph 5(2) of that Schedule; words in subsection (2) substituted by paragraph 5(3); subsection (3) substituted in whole by paragraph 5(4); the two sets of words substituted in subsection (4) by paragraphs 5(5)(a) & (b) respectively; 'Approved metal health practitioner' substituted in both places in subsection (5) by paragraph 5(6)(a); and words beginning 'a local social services authority' inserted in that subsection by paragraph 5(6)(b). Words 'or of regulations under section 12A above' inserted in the same subsection (5) by section 22(6).*]

14 Social reports

Where a patient is admitted to a hospital in pursuance of an application (other than an emergency application) made under this Part of this Act by his nearest relative, the managers of the hospital shall as soon as practicable give notice of that fact to the local social services authority for the area in which the patient resided immediately before his admission; and that authority shall as soon as practicable arrange for *a social worker* [an approved mental health professional] to interview the patient and provide the managers with a report on his social circumstances.

[*Words substituted by paragraph 6 of Schedule 2 to the 2007 Act.*]

15 Rectification of applications and recommendations

(1) If within the period of 14 days beginning with the day on which a patient has been admitted to a hospital in pursuance of an application for admission for assessment or for treatment the application, or any medical recommendation given for the purposes of the application, is found to be in any respect incorrect or defective, the application or recommendation may, within that period and with the consent of the managers of the hospital, be amended by the person by whom it was signed; and upon such amendment being made the application or recommendation shall have effect and shall be deemed to have had effect as if it had been originally made as so amended.

(2) Without prejudice to subsection (1) above, if within the period mentioned in that subsection it appears to the managers of the hospital that one of the two medical recommendations on which an application for the admission of a patient is founded is insufficient to warrant the detention of the patient in pursuance of the application, they may, within that period, give notice in writing to that effect to the applicant; and where any such notice is given in respect of a medical recommendation, that recommendation shall be disregarded, but the application shall be, and shall be deemed always to have been, sufficient if—

(a) a fresh medical recommendation complying with the relevant provisions of this Part of this Act (other than the provisions relating to the time of signature and the interval between examinations) is furnished to the managers within that period; and

(b) that recommendation, and the other recommendation on which the application is founded, together comply with those provisions.

(3) Where the medical recommendations upon which an application for admission is founded are, taken together, insufficient to warrant the detention of the patient in pursuance of the application, a notice under subsection (2) above may be given in respect of either of those recommendations; *but this subsection shall not apply in a case where the application is of no effect by virtue of section 11(6) above.*

(4) Nothing in this section shall be construed as authorising the giving of notice in respect of an application made as an emergency application, or the detention of a patient admitted in pursuance of such an application, after the period of 72 hours referred to in section 4(4) above, unless the conditions set out in paragraphs (a) and (b) of that section are complied with or would be complied with apart from any error or defect to which this section applies.

[*Words in subsection (3) repealed by Part 1 of Schedule 11 to the 2007 Act.*]

16 *Reclassification of patients*

(1) If in the case of a patient who is for the time being detained in a hospital in pursuance of an application for admission for treatment, or subject to guardianship in pursuance of a guardianship application, it appears to the appropriate medical officer that the patient is suffering from a form of mental disorder other than the form or forms specified in the application, he may furnish to the managers of the hospital, or to the guardian, as the case may be, a report to that effect; and where a report is so furnished, the application shall have effect as if that other form of mental disorder were specified in it.

(2) Where a report under subsection (1) above in respect of a patient detained in a hospital is to the effect that he is suffering from psychopathic disorder or mental impairment but not from mental illness or severe mental impairment the appropriate medical officer shall include in the report a statement of his opinion whether further medical treatment in hospital is likely to alleviate or prevent a deterioration of the patient's condition; and if he states that in his opinion such treatment is not likely to have that effect the authority of the managers to detain the patient shall cease.

(3) Before furnishing a report under subsection (1) above the appropriate medical officer shall consult one or more other persons who have been professionally concerned with the patient's medical treatment.

(4) Where a report is furnished under this section in respect of a patient, the managers or guardian shall cause the patient and the nearest relative to be informed.

(5) In this section 'appropriate medical officer' means—

(a) in the case of a patient who is subject to the guardianship of a person other than a local social services authority, the nominated medical attendant of the patient; and

(b) *in any other case, the responsible medical officer.*

[*Section repealed by Part 1 of Schedule 11 to the 2007 Act.*]

17 Leave of absence from hospital

(1) The *responsible medical officer* [responsible clinician] may grant to any patient who is for the time being liable to be detained in a hospital under this Part of this Act leave to be absent from the hospital subject to such conditions (if any) as *that officer* [that clinician] considers necessary in the interests of the patient or for the protection of other persons.

(2) Leave of absence may be granted to a patient under this section either indefinitely or on specified occasions or for any specified period; and where leave is so granted for a specified period, that period may be extended by further leave granted in the absence of the patient.

[(2A) But longer-term leave may not be granted to a patient unless the responsible clinician first considers whether the patient should be dealt with under section 17A instead.

(2B) For these purposes, longer-term leave is granted to a patient if—

    (a) leave of absence is granted to him under this section either indefinitely or for a specified period of more than seven consecutive days; or

    (b) a specified period is extended under this section such that the total period for which leave of absence will have been granted to him under this section exceeds seven consecutive days.]

(3) Where it appears to the *responsible medical officer* [responsible clinician] that it is necessary so to do in the interests of the patient or for the protection of other persons, he may, upon granting leave of absence under this section, direct that the patient remain in custody during his absence; and where leave of absence is so granted the patient may be kept in the custody of any officer on the staff of the hospital, or of any other person authorised in writing by the managers of the hospital or, if the patient is required in accordance with conditions imposed on the grant of leave of absence to reside in another hospital, of any officer on the staff of that other hospital.

(4) In any case where a patient is absent from a hospital in pursuance of leave of absence granted under this section, and it appears to the *responsible medical officer* [responsible clinician] that it is necessary so to do in the interests of the patient's health or safety or for the protection of other persons, *that officer* [that clinician] may, subject to subsection (5) below, by notice in writing given to the patient or to the person for the time being in charge of the patient, revoke the leave of absence and recall the patient to the hospital.

(5) A patient to whom leave of absence is granted under this section shall not be recalled under subsection (4) above after he has ceased to be liable to be detained under this Part of this Act.

[(6) Subsection (7) below applies to a person who is granted leave by or by virtue of a provision—

    (a) in force in Scotland, Northern Ireland, any of the Channel Islands or the Isle of Man; and

    (b) corresponding to subsection (1) above.

(7) For the purpose of giving effect to a direction or condition imposed by virtue of a provision corresponding to subsection (3) above, the person may be conveyed to a place in, or kept in custody or detained at a place of safety in, England and Wales by a person authorised in that behalf by the direction or condition.]

[*Words in subsections (1), (3) and (4) substituted by section 9(3)(a) to (c) respectively of the 2007 Act. Subsections (2A) & (2B) inserted by section 33(2). Subsections (6) & (7) inserted by section 39(1).*]

[17A Community treatment orders]

[(1) The responsible clinician may by order in writing discharge a detained patient from hospital subject to his being liable to recall in accordance with section 17E below.

(2) A detained patient is a patient who is liable to be detained in a hospital in pursuance of an application for admission for treatment.

(3) An order under subsection (1) above is referred to in this Act as a 'community treatment order'.

(4) The responsible clinician may not make a community treatment order unless—
   (a) in his opinion, the relevant criteria are met; and
   (b) an approved mental health professional states in writing—
      (i) that he agrees with that opinion; and
      (ii) that it is appropriate to make the order.

(5) The relevant criteria are—
   (a) the patient is suffering from mental disorder of a nature or degree which makes it appropriate for him to receive medical treatment;
   (b) it is necessary for his health or safety or for the protection of other persons that he should receive such treatment;
   (c) subject to his being liable to be recalled as mentioned in paragraph (d) below, such treatment can be provided without his continuing to be detained in a hospital;
   (d) it is necessary that the responsible clinician should be able to exercise the power under section 17E(1) below to recall the patient to hospital;
   (e) appropriate medical treatment is available for him.

(6) In determining whether the criterion in subsection (5)(d) above is met, the responsible clinician shall, in particular, consider, having regard to the patient's history of mental disorder and any other relevant factors, what risk there would be of a deterioration of the patient's condition if he were not detained in a hospital (as a result, for example, of his refusing or neglecting to receive the medical treatment he requires for his mental disorder).

(7) In this Act—
   'community patient' means a patient in respect of whom a community treatment order is in force;
   'the community treatment order', in relation to such a patient, means the community treatment order in force in respect of him; and
   'the responsible hospital', in relation to such a patient, means the hospital in which he was liable to be detained immediately before the community treatment order was made, subject to section 19A below.]

[*Section 17A inserted by section 32(2) of the 2007 Act.*]

[17B Conditions]

[(1) A community treatment order shall specify conditions to which the patient is to be subject while the order remains in force.

(2) But, subject to subsection (3) below, the order may specify conditions only if the responsible clinician, with the agreement of the approved mental health professional mentioned in section 17A(4)(b) above, thinks them necessary or appropriate for one or more of the following purposes—
   (a) ensuring that the patient receives medical treatment;
   (b) preventing risk of harm to the patient's health or safety;
   (c) protecting other persons.

(3) The order shall specify—
   (a) a condition that the patient make himself available for examination under section 20A below; and
   (b) a condition that, if it is proposed to give a certificate under Part 4A of this Act in his case, he make himself available for examination so as to enable the certificate to be given.

(4) The responsible clinician may from time to time by order in writing vary the conditions specified in a community treatment order.

(5) He may also suspend any conditions specified in a community treatment order.

(6) If a community patient fails to comply with a condition specified in the community treatment order by virtue of subsection (2) above, that fact may be taken into account for the purposes of exercising the power of recall under section 17E (1) below.

(7) But nothing in this section restricts the exercise of that power to cases where there is such a failure.]

[*Section 17BA inserted by section 32(2) of the 2007 Act.*]

[17C Duration of community treatment order]

[A community treatment order shall remain in force until—
   (a) the period mentioned in section 20A(1) below (as extended under any provision of this Act) expires, but this is subject to sections 21 and 22 below;
   (b) the patient is discharged in pursuance of an order under section 23 below or a direction under section 72 below;
   (c) the application for admission for treatment in respect of the patient otherwise ceases to have effect; or
   (d) the order is revoked under section 17F below,
whichever occurs first.]

[*Section 17C inserted by section 32(2) of the 2007 Act.*]

[17D Effect of community treatment order]

[(1) The application for admission for treatment in respect of a patient shall not cease to have effect by virtue of his becoming a community patient.

(2) But while he remains a community patient—
   (a) the authority of the managers to detain him under section 6(2) above in pursuance of that application shall be suspended; and
   (b) reference (however expressed) in this or any other Act, or in any subordinate legislation (within the meaning of the Interpretation Act 1978), to patients liable to be detained, or detained, under this Act shall not include him.

(3) And section 20 below shall not apply to him while he remains a community patient.

(4) Accordingly, authority for his detention shall not expire during any period in which that authority is suspended by virtue of subsection (2)(a) above.]

[*Section 17D inserted by section 32(2) of the 2007 Act.*]

[17E Power to recall to hospital]

[(1) The responsible clinician may recall a community patient to hospital if in his opinion—
   (a) the patient requires medical treatment in hospital for his mental disorder; and
   (b) there would be a risk of harm to the health or safety of the patient or to other persons if the patient were not recalled to hospital for that purpose.

(2) The responsible clinician may also recall a community patient to hospital if the patient fails to comply with a condition specified under section 17B(3) above.

(3) The hospital to which a patient is recalled need not be the responsible hospital.

(4) Nothing in this section prevents a patient from being recalled to a hospital even though he is already in the hospital at the time when the power of recall is exercised; references to recalling him shall be construed accordingly.

(5) The power of recall under subsections (1) and (2) above shall be exercisable by notice in writing to the patient.

(6) A notice under this section recalling a patient to hospital shall be sufficient authority for the managers of that hospital to detain the patient there in accordance with the provisions of this Act.]

[*Section 17E inserted by section 32(2) of the 2007 Act.*]

[17F Powers in respect of recalled patients]

[(1) This section applies to a community patient who is detained in a hospital by virtue of a notice recalling him there under section 17E above.

(2) The patient may be transferred to another hospital in such circumstances and subject to such conditions as may be prescribed in regulations made by the Secretary of State (if the hospital in which the patient is detained is in England) or the Welsh Ministers (if that hospital is in Wales).

(3) If he is so transferred to another hospital, he shall be treated for the purposes of this section (and section 17E above) as if the notice under that section were a notice recalling him to that other hospital and as if he had been detained there from the time when his detention in hospital by virtue of the notice first began.

(4) The responsible clinician may by order in writing revoke the community treatment order if—
    (a) in his opinion the conditions mentioned in section 3(2) above are satisfied in respect of the patient; and
    (b) an approved mental health professional states in writing—
        (i) that he agrees with that opinion; and
        (ii) that it is appropriate to revoke the order.

(5) The responsible clinician may at any time release the patient, but not after the community treatment order has been revoked.

(6) If the patient has not been released, nor the community treatment order revoked, by the end of the period of 72 hours, he shall then be released.

(7) But a patient who is released under this section remains subject to the community treatment order.

(8) In this section—
    (a) 'the period of 72 hours' means the period of 72 hours beginning with the time when the patient's detention in hospital by virtue of the notice under section 17E above begins; and
    (b) references to being released shall be construed as references to being released from that detention (and accordingly from being recalled to hospital).]

[*Section 17F inserted by section 32(2) of the 2007 Act.*]

[17G Effect of revoking community treatment order]

[(1) This section applies if a community treatment order is revoked under section 17F above in respect of a patient.

(2) Section 6(2) above shall have effect as if the patient had never been discharged from hospital by virtue of the community treatment order.

(3) The provisions of this or any other Act relating to patients liable to be detained (or detained) in pursuance of an application for admission for treatment shall apply to the patient as they did before the community treatment order was made, unless otherwise provided.

(4) If, when the order is revoked, the patient is being detained in a hospital other than the responsible hospital, the provisions of this Part of this Act shall have effect as if—

    (a) the application for admission for treatment in respect of him were an application for admission to that other hospital; and

    (b) he had been admitted to that other hospital at the time when he was originally admitted in pursuance of the application.

(5) But, in any case, section 20 below shall have effect as if the patient had been admitted to hospital in pursuance of the application for admission for treatment on the day on which the order is revoked.]

[Section 17G inserted by section 32(2) of the 2007 Act.]

18 Return and readmission of patients absent without leave

(1) Where a patient who is for the time being liable to be detained under this Part of this Act in a hospital—

    (a) absents himself from the hospital without leave granted under section 17 above; or

    (b) fails to return to the hospital on any occasion on which, or at the expiration of any period for which, leave of absence was granted to him under that section, or upon being recalled under that section; or

    (c) absents himself without permission from any place where he is required to reside in accordance with conditions imposed on the grant of leave of absence under that section, he may, subject to the provisions of this section, be taken into custody and returned to the hospital or place by any *approved social worker* [approved mental health professional], by any officer on the staff of the hospital, by any constable, or by any person authorised in writing by the managers of the hospital.

(2) Where the place referred to in paragraph (c) of subsection (1) above is a hospital other than the one in which the patient is for the time being liable to be detained, the references in that subsection to an officer on the staff of the hospital and the managers of the hospital shall respectively include references to an officer on the staff of the first-mentioned hospital and the managers of that hospital.

[(2A) Where a community patient is at any time absent from a hospital to which he is recalled under section 17E above, he may, subject to the provisions of this section, be taken into custody and returned to the hospital by any approved mental health professional, by any officer on the staff of the hospital, by any constable, or by any person authorised in writing by the responsible clinician or the managers of the hospital.]

(3) Where a patient who is for the time being subject to guardianship under this Part of this Act absents himself without the leave of the guardian from the place at which he is required by the guardian to reside, he may, subject to the provisions of this section, be taken into custody and returned to that place by any officer on the staff of a local social services authority, by any constable, or by any person authorised in writing by the guardian or a local social services authority.

(4) A patient shall not be taken into custody under this section after the later of—

    (a) the end of the period of six months beginning with the first day of his absence without leave; and

(b) the end of the period for which (apart from section 21 below) he is liable to be detained or subject to guardianship [or, in the case of a community patient, the community treatment order is in force]

and, in determining for the purposes of paragraph (b) above or any other provision of this Act whether a person who is or has been absent without leave is at any time liable to be detained or subject to guardianship, a report furnished under section 20 or 21B below before the first day of his absence without leave shall not be taken to have renewed the authority for his detention or guardianship unless the period of renewal began before that day;

[(4A) In determining for the purposes of subsection (4)(b) above or any other provision of this Act whether a person who is or has been absent without leave is at any time liable to be detained or subject to guardianship, a report furnished under section 20 or 21B below before the first day of his absence without leave shall not be taken to have renewed the authority for his detention or guardianship unless the period of renewal began before that day.

(4B) Similarly, in determining for those purposes whether a community treatment order is at any time in force in respect of a person who is or has been absent without leave, a report furnished under section 20A or 21B below before the first day of his absence without leave shall not be taken to have extended the community treatment period unless the extension began before that day.]

(5) A patient shall not be taken into custody under this section if the period for which he is liable to be detained is that specified in section 2(4), 4(4) or 5(2) or (4) above and that period has expired.

(6) In this Act 'absent without leave' means absent from any hospital or other place and liable to be taken into custody and returned under this section, and related expressions shall be construed accordingly.

[(7) In relation to a patient who has yet to comply with a requirement imposed by virtue of this Act to be in a hospital or place, references in this Act to his liability to be returned to the hospital or place shall include his liability to be taken to that hospital or place; and related expressions shall be construed accordingly.]

[*Words in subsection (1) substituted by paragraph 7(a) of Schedule 2 to the 2007 Act; subsection (2A) inserted by paragraph 3(2) of Schedule 3; words inserted and omitted in subsection (4) by paragraph 3(3)(a)&(b) respectively of that Schedule; subsections (4A) & (4B) inserted by paragraph 3(4); subsection (7) inserted by paragraph 3(5).*]

19 Regulations as to transfer of patients

(1) In such circumstances and subject to such conditions as may be prescribed by regulations made by the Secretary of State—

(a) a patient who is for the time being liable to be detained in a hospital by virtue of an application under this Part of this Act may be transferred to another hospital or into the guardianship of a local social services authority or of any person approved by such an authority;

(b) a patient who is for the time being subject to the guardianship of a local social services authority or other person by virtue of an application under this Part of this Act may be transferred into the guardianship of another local social services authority or person, or be transferred to a hospital.

(2) Where a patient is transferred in pursuance of regulations under this section, the provisions of this Part of this Act (including this subsection) shall apply to him as follows, that is to say—

(a) in the case of a patient who is liable to be detained in a hospital by virtue of an application for admission for assessment or for treatment and is transferred to another hospital, as if the application were an application for admission to that other hospital and as if the patient had been admitted to that other hospital at the time when he was originally admitted in pursuance of the application;

(b) in the case of a patient who is liable to be detained in a hospital by virtue of such an application and is transferred into guardianship, as if the application were a guardianship application duly accepted at the said time;

(c) in the case of a patient who is subject to guardianship by virtue of a guardianship application and is transferred into the guardianship of another authority or person, as if the application were for his reception into the guardianship of that authority or person and had been accepted at the time when it was originally accepted;

(d) in the case of a patient who is subject to guardianship by virtue of a guardianship application and is transferred to a hospital, as if the guardianship application were an application for admission to that hospital for treatment and as if the patient had been admitted to the hospital at the time when the application was originally accepted.

(3) Without prejudice to subsections (1) and (2) above, any patient who is for the time being liable to be detained under this Part of this Act in a hospital vested in the Secretary of State for the purposes of his functions under the National Health Service Act 2006, in a hospital vested in the Welsh Ministers for the purposes of their functions under the National Health Service (Wales) Act 2006, in any accommodation used under either of those Acts, by the managers of such a hospital or in a hospital vested in a National Health Service trust, NHS foundation trust[, Local Health Board] or Primary Care Trust, may at any time be removed to any other such hospital or accommodation which is managed by the managers of, or is vested in the National Health Service trust, NHS foundation trust[, Local Health Board] or Primary Care Trust for, the first-mentioned hospital; and paragraph (a) of subsection (2) above shall apply in relation to a patient so removed as it applies in relation to a patient transferred in pursuance of regulations made under this section.

(4) Regulations made under this section may make provision for regulating the conveyance to their destination of patients authorised to be transferred or removed in pursuance of the regulations or under subsection (3) above.

[*Words in subsection (3) inserted by section 46(2) of the 2007 Act.*]

[19A Regulations as to assignment of responsibility for community patients]

[(1) Responsibility for a community patient may be assigned to another hospital in such circumstances and subject to such conditions as may be prescribed by regulations made by the Secretary of State (if the responsible hospital is in England) or the Welsh Ministers (if that hospital is in Wales).

(2) If responsibility for a community patient is assigned to another hospital—

(a) the application for admission for treatment in respect of the patient shall have effect (subject to section 17D above) as if it had always specified that other hospital;

(b) the patient shall be treated as if he had been admitted to that other hospital at the time when he was originally admitted in pursuance of the application (and as if he had subsequently been discharged under section 17A above from there); and

(c) that other hospital shall become 'the responsible hospital' in relation to the patient for the purposes of this Act.]

[*Section 19A inserted by paragraph 4 of Schedule 3 to the 2007 Act.*]

Duration of detention or guardianship *[authority] and discharge*

20 Duration of authority

(1) Subject to the following provisions of this Part of this Act, a patient admitted to hospital in pursuance of an application for admission for treatment, and a patient placed under guardianship in pursuance of a guardianship application, may be detained in a hospital or kept under guardianship for a period not exceeding six months beginning with the day on which he was so admitted, or the day on which the guardianship application was accepted, as the case may be, but shall not be so detained or kept for any longer period unless the authority for his detention or guardianship is renewed under this section.

(2) Authority for the detention or guardianship of a patient may, unless the patient has previously been discharged [under section 23 below], be renewed—

    (a) from the expiration of the period referred to in subsection (1) above, for a further period of six months;

    (b) from the expiration of any period of renewal under paragraph (a) above, for a further period of one year, and so on for periods of one year at a time.

(3) Within the period of two months ending on the day on which a patient who is liable to be detained in pursuance of an application for admission for treatment would cease under this section to be so liable in default of the renewal of the authority for his detention, it shall be the duty of the *responsible medical officer* [responsible clinician]—

    (a) to examine the patient; and

    (b) furnish to the managers of the hospital where the patient is detained a report to that effect in the prescribed form;

and where such a report is furnished in respect of a patient the managers shall, unless they discharge the patient [under section 23 below], cause him to be informed.

(4) The conditions referred to in subsection (3) above are that—

    (a) the patient is suffering from *mental illness, severe mental impairment, psychopathic disorder or mental impairment, and his mental disorder is* [mental disorder] of a nature or degree which makes it appropriate for him to receive medical treatment in a hospital; and

    (b) such treatment is likely to alleviate or prevent a deterioration of his condition; and

    (c) it is necessary for the health or safety of the patient or for the protection of other persons that he should receive such treatment and that it cannot be provided unless he continues to be detained; [and

    (d) appropriate medical treatment is available for him.]

but, in the case of mental illness or severe mental impairment, it shall be an alternative to the condition specified in paragraph (b) above that the patient, if discharged, is unlikely to be able to care for himself, to obtain the care which he needs or to guard himself against serious exploitation.

(5) Before furnishing a report under subsection (3) above the *responsible medical officer* [responsible clinician] shall consult one or more other persons who have been professionally concerned with the patient's medical treatment

[(5A) But the responsible clinician may not furnish a report under subsection (3) above unless a person—

    (a) who has been professionally concerned with the patient's medical treatment; but

    (b) who belongs to a profession other than that to which the responsible clinician belongs,

states in writing that he agrees that the conditions set out in subsection (4) above are satisfied.]

(6) Within the period of two months ending with the day on which a patient who is subject to guardianship under this Part of this Act would cease under this section to be so liable in

default of the renewal of the authority for his guardianship, it shall be the duty of the *appropriate medical officer* [appropriate practitioner]—

(a) to examine the patient; and

(b) if it appears to him that the conditions set out in subsection (7) below are satisfied, to furnish to the guardian and, where the guardian is a person other than a local social services authority, to the responsible local social services authority a report to that effect in the prescribed form;

and where such a report is furnished in respect of a patient, the local social services authority shall, unless they discharge the patient [under section 23 below], cause him to be informed.

(7) The conditions referred to in subsection (6) above are that—

(a) the patient is suffering from *mental illness, severe mental impairment, psychopathic disorder or mental impairment, and his mental disorder is* [mental disorder] of a nature or degree which warrants his reception into guardianship; and

(b) it is necessary in the interests of the welfare of the patient or for the protection of other persons that the patient should remain under guardianship.

(8) Where a report is duly furnished under subsection (3) or (6) above, the authority for the detention or guardianship of the patient shall be thereby renewed for the period prescribed in that case by subsection (2) above.

(9) *Where the form of mental disorder specified in a report furnished under subsection (3) or (6) above is a form of disorder other than that specified in the application for admission for treatment or, as the case may be, in the guardianship application, that application shall have effect as if that other form of mental disorder were specified in it; and where on any occasion a report specifying such a form of mental disorder is furnished under either of those subsections the appropriate medical officer need not on that occasion furnish a report under section 16 above.*

(10) In this section 'appropriate medical officer' has the same meaning as in section 16(5) above.

[*Cross heading above section amended by section 32(3) of the 2007 Act. Words 'under section 23 below' inserted into subsections (2) and (3) & (6) by paragraph 5(a) and (b) respectively of Schedule 3; 'responsible clinician' substituted for 'responsible medical officer' in subsection (3) by section 9(4)(a); words substituted in subsection (4)(a) and (7)(a) by paragraphs 4(a) and (b) respectively of Schedule 1; subsection (4)(b) (and following 'and') omitted by section 4(4)(a); subsection (4)(d) (and the word 'and' before it) inserted by section 4(4)(b); words from 'but, in the case of mental illness' to the end of subsection (4) omitted by section 4(4)(c); words substituted in subsection (5) by section 9(4)(a); subsection (5A) inserted by section 9(4)(b); 'appropriate practitioner' substituted for 'appropriate medical officer' in subsection (6) by section 9(4)(c). Subsection (9) repealed by Part 1 of Schedule 11. Subsection (10) omitted by section 9(4)(c).*]

[20A Community treatment period]

[(1) Subject to the provisions of this Part, a community treatment order shall cease to be in force on expiry of the period of six months beginning with the day on which it was made.

(2) That period is referred to in this Act as 'the community treatment period'.

(3) The community treatment period may, unless the order has previously ceased to be in force, be extended—

(a) from its expiration for a period of six months;

(b) from the expiration of any period of extension under paragraph (a) above for a further period of one year,

and so on for periods of one year at a time.

(4) Within the period of two months ending on the day on which the order would cease to be in force in default of an extension under this section, it shall be the duty of the responsible clinician—

(a) to examine the patient; and

(b) if it appears to him that the conditions set out in subsection (6) below are satisfied and if a statement under subsection (8) is made, to furnish to the managers of the responsible hospital a report to that effect in the prescribed form.

(5) Where such a report is furnished in respect of the patient, the managers shall, unless they discharge him under section 23 below, cause him to be informed.

(6) The conditions referred to in subsection (4) above are that—

(a) the patient is suffering from mental disorder of a nature or degree which makes it appropriate for him to receive medical treatment;

(b) it is necessary for his health or safety or for the protection of other persons that he should receive such treatment;

(c) subject to his continuing to be liable to be recalled as mentioned in paragraph (d) below, such treatment can be provided without his being detained in a hospital;

(d) it is necessary that the responsible clinician should continue to be able to exercise the power under section 17E(1) above to recall the patient to hospital; and

(e) appropriate medical treatment is available for him.

(7) In determining whether the criterion in subsection (6)(d) above is met, the responsible clinician shall, in particular, consider, having regard to the patient's history of mental disorder and any other relevant factors, what risk there would be of a deterioration of the patient's condition if he were to continue not to be detained in a hospital (as a result, for example, of his refusing or neglecting to receive the medical treatment he requires for his mental disorder).

(8) The statement referred to in subsection (4) above is a statement in writing by an approved mental health professional—

(a) that it appears to him that the conditions set out in subsection (6) above are satisfied; and

(b) that it is appropriate to extend the community treatment period.

(9) Before furnishing a report under subsection (4) above the responsible clinician shall consult one or more other persons who have been professionally concerned with the patient's medical treatment.

(10) Where a report is duly furnished under subsection (4) above, the community treatment period shall be thereby extended for the period prescribed in that case by subsection (3) above].

[*Section 20A inserted by section 32(3) of the 2007 Act.*]

[20B Effect of expiry of community treatment order]

[(1) A community patient shall be deemed to be discharged absolutely from liability to recall under this Part of this Act, and the application for admission for treatment cease to have effect, on expiry of the community treatment order, if the order has not previously ceased to be in force.

(2) For the purposes of subsection (1) above, a community treatment order expires on expiry of the community treatment period as extended under this Part of this Act, but this is subject to sections 21 and 22 below.]

[*Section 20B inserted by section 32(3) of the 2007 Act.*]

21 Special provisions as to patients absent without leave

(1) Where a patient is absent without leave—

    (a) on the day on which (apart from this section) he would cease to be liable to be detained or subject to guardianship under this Part of this Act [or, in the case of a community patient, the community treatment order would cease to be in force]; or

    (b) within the period of one week ending with that day,

he shall not cease to be so liable or subject[, or the order shall not cease to be in force,] until the relevant time.

(2) For the purposes of subsection (1) above the relevant time—

    (a) where the patient is taken into custody under section 18 above, is the end of the period of one week beginning with the day on which he is returned to the hospital or place where he ought to be;

    (b) where the patient returns himself to the hospital or place where he ought to be within the period during which he can be taken into custody under section 18 above, is the end of the period of one week beginning with the day on which he so returns himself; and

    (c) otherwise, is the end of the period during which he can be taken into custody under section 18 above.

[(3) Where a patient is absent without leave on the day on which (apart from this section) the managers would be required under section 68 below to refer the patient's case to a Mental Health Review Tribunal, that requirement shall not apply unless and until—

    (a) the patient is taken into custody under section 18 above and returned to the hospital where he ought to be; or

    (b) the patient returns himself to the hospital where he ought to be within the period during which he can be taken into custody under section 18 above.

(4) Where a community patient is absent without leave on the day on which (apart from this section) the 72-hour period mentioned in section 17F above would expire, that period shall not expire until the end of the period of 72 hours beginning with the time when—

    (a) the patient is taken into custody under section 18 above and returned to the hospital where he ought to be; or

    (b) the patient returns himself to the hospital where he ought to be within the period during which he can be taken into custody under section 18 above.

(5) Any reference in this section, or in sections 21A to 22 below, to the time when a community treatment order would cease, or would have ceased, to be in force shall be construed as a reference to the time when it would cease, or would have ceased, to be in force by reason only of the passage of time.]

[*Words in subsection (1) and subsections (4) & (5) inserted by paragraph 6(2) and (3) of Schedule 3 to the 2007 Act respectively. Subsection (3) inserted by section 37(2).*]

21A Patients who are taken into custody or return within 28 days

(1) This section applies where a patient who is absent without leave is taken into custody under section 18 above, or returns himself to the hospital or place where he ought to be, not later than the end of the period of 28 days beginning with the first day of his absence without leave.

(2) Where the period for which the patient is liable to be detained or subject to guardianship is extended by section 21 above, any examination and report to be made and furnished in respect of the patient under section 20(3) or (6) above may be made and furnished within the period as so extended.

326

(3) Where the authority for the detention or guardianship of the patient is renewed by virtue of subsection (2) above after the day on which (apart from section 21 above) that authority would have expired, the renewal shall take effect as from that day.

[(4) In the case of a community patient, where the period for which the community treatment order is in force is extended by section 21 above, any examination and report to be made and furnished in respect of the patient under section 20A(4) above may be made and furnished within the period as so extended.

(5) Where the community treatment period is extended by virtue of subsection (4) above after the day on which (apart from section 21 above) the order would have ceased to be in force, the extension shall take effect as from that day.]

[*Subsections (4) & (5) inserted by paragraph 7 of Schedule 3 to the 2007 Act.*]

21B Patients who are taken into custody or return after more than 28 days

(1) This section applies where a patient who is absent without leave is taken into custody under section 18 above, or returns himself to the hospital or place where he ought to be, later than the end of the period of 28 days beginning with the first day of his absence without leave.

(2) It shall be the duty of the *appropriate medical officer* [appropriate practitioner], within the period of one week beginning with the day on which the patient is returned or returns himself to the hospital or place where he ought to be [(his 'return day')]—

    (a) to examine the patient; and

    (b) if it appears to him that the relevant conditions are satisfied, to furnish to the appropriate body a report to that effect in the prescribed form;

and where such a report is furnished in respect of the patient the appropriate body shall cause him to be informed.

(3) Where the patient is liable to be detained [or is a community patient] (as opposed to subject to guardianship) the *appropriate medical officer* [appropriate practitioner] shall, before furnishing a report under subsection (2) above, consult—

    (a) one or more other persons who have been professionally concerned with the patient's medical treatment; and

    (b) an *approved social worker* [approved mental health professional].

(4) Where the patient would (apart from any renewal of the authority for his detention or guardianship on or after the day on which he is returned or returns himself to the hospital or place where he ought to be) be liable to be detained or subject to guardianship after the end of the period of one week beginning with that day, he shall cease to be so liable or subject at the end of that period unless a report is duly furnished in respect of him under subsection (2) above.

[(4) Where—

    (a) the patient would (apart from any renewal of the authority for his detention or guardianship on or after his return day) be liable to be detained or subject to guardianship after the end of the period of one week beginning with that day; or

    (b) in the case of a community patient, the community treatment order would (apart from any extension of the community treatment period on or after that day) be in force after the end of that period,

he shall cease to be so liable or subject, or the community treatment period shall be deemed to expire, at the end of that period unless a report is duly furnished in respect of him under subsection (2) above.

(4A) If, in the case of a community patient, the community treatment order is revoked under section 17F above during the period of one week beginning with his return day—
(a) subsections (2) and (4) above shall not apply; and
(b) any report already furnished in respect of him under subsection (2) above shall be of no effect.]

(5) Where the patient would (apart from section 21 above) have ceased to be liable to be detained or subject to guardianship on or before the day on which a report is duly furnished in respect of him under subsection (2) above, the report shall renew the authority for his detention or guardianship for the period prescribed in that case by section 20(2) above.

(6) Where the authority for the detention or guardianship of the patient is renewed by virtue of subsection (5) above—
(a) the renewal shall take effect as from the day on which (apart from section 21 above and that subsection) the authority would have expired; and
(b) if (apart from this paragraph) the renewed authority would expire on or before the day on which the report is furnished, the report shall further renew the authority, as from the day on which it would expire, for the period prescribed in that case by section 20(2) above.

[(6A) In the case of a community patient, where the community treatment order would (apart from section 21 above) have ceased to be in force on or before the day on which a report is duly furnished in respect of him under subsection (2) above, the report shall extend the community treatment period for the period prescribed in that case by section 20A(3) above.

(6B) Where the community treatment period is extended by virtue of subsection (6A) above—
(a) the extension shall take effect as from the day on which (apart from section 21 above and that subsection) the order would have ceased to be in force; and
(b) if (apart from this paragraph) the period as so extended would expire on or before the day on which the report is furnished, the report shall further extend that period, as from the day on which it would expire, for the period prescribed in that case by section 20A(3) above.]

(7) Where the authority for the detention or guardianship of the patient would expire within the period of two months beginning with the day on which a report is duly furnished in respect of him under subsection (2) above, the report shall, if it so provides, have effect also as a report duly furnished under section 20(3) or (6) above; and the reference in this subsection to authority includes any authority renewed under subsection (5) above by the report.

[(7A) In the case of a community patient, where the community treatment order would (taking account of any extension under subsection (6A) above) cease to be in force within the period of two months beginning with the day on which a report is duly furnished in respect of him under subsection (2) above, the report shall, if it so provides, have effect also as a report duly furnished under section 20A(4) above.]

(8) *Where the form of mental disorder specified in a report furnished under subsection (2) above is a form of disorder other than that specified in the application for admission for treatment or guardianship application concerned (and the report does not have effect as a report furnished under section 20(3) or (6) above), that application shall have effect as if that other form of mental disorder were specified in it.*

(9) *Where on any occasion a report specifying such a form of mental disorder is furnished under subsection (2) above the appropriate medical officer need not on that occasion furnish a report under section 16 above.*

(10) In this section—
'appropriate medical officer' has the same meaning as in section 16(5) above;

'the appropriate body' means—

(a) in relation to a patient who is liable to be detained in a hospital, the managers of the hospital; and

(b) in relation to a patient who is subject to guardianship, the responsible local social services authority; and

['the appropriate body' means—

(a) in relation to a patient who is liable to be detained in a hospital, the managers of the hospital;

(b) in relation to a patient who is subject to guardianship, the responsible local social services authority;

(c) in relation to a community patient, the managers of the responsible hospital; and]

'the relevant conditions' means—

(a) in relation to a patient who is liable to be detained in a hospital, the conditions set out in subsection (4) of section 20 above; and

(b) in relation to a patient who is subject to guardianship, the conditions set out in subsection (7) of that section.

['the relevant conditions' means—

(a) in relation to a patient who is liable to be detained in a hospital, the conditions set out in subsection (4) of section 20 above;

(b) in relation to a patient who is subject to guardianship, the conditions set out in subsection (7) of that section;

(c) in relation to a community patient, the conditions set out in section 20A(6) above.]

['Appropriate practitioner' substituted for 'appropriate medical officer' in subsections (2) and (3) by section 9(5)(a); '(his 'return day')' in subsection (2) and, 'or is a community patient' in subsection (3) inserted by paragraph 8(2) and (3) of Schedule 3 respectively; words in subsection (3)(b) substituted by paragraph 7(b) of Schedule 2; subsection (4) substituted by, and subsections (4A), (6A) & (6B) and (7A) inserted by paragraphs 8(4) to (7) of Schedule 3 respectively; subsections (8) and (9) omitted by Part 1 of Schedule 11; definition of 'appropriate medical officer' in subsection (10) omitted by section 9(5)(b) and the other definitions substituted by paragraph 8(8) of Schedule 3.]

22 Special provisions as to patients sentenced to imprisonment, etc

(1) Where a patient who is liable to be detained by virtue of an application for admission for treatment or is subject to guardianship by virtue of a guardianship application is detained in custody in pursuance of any sentence or order passed or made by a court in the United Kingdom (including an order committing or remanding him in custody), and is so detained for a period exceeding, or for successive periods exceeding in the aggregate, six months, the application shall cease to have effect at the expiration of that period.

(2) Where any such patient is so detained in custody but the application does not cease to have effect under subsection (1) above, then—

(a) if apart from this subsection the patient would have ceased to be liable to be so detained or subject to guardianship on or before the day on which he is discharged from custody, he shall not cease and shall be deemed not to have ceased to be so liable or subject until the end of that day; and

(b) in any case, sections 18, 21 and 21A above, shall apply in relation to the patient as if he had absented himself without leave on that day.

(3) In its application by virtue of subsection (2) above section 18(4) above shall have effect with the substitution of the words 'end of the period of 28 days beginning with the first day of his absence without leave.' for the words from 'later of' onwards.

[22 Special provisions as to patients sentenced to imprisonment, etc]

[(1) If—

(a) a qualifying patient is detained in custody in pursuance of any sentence or order passed or made by a court in the United Kingdom (including an order committing or remanding him in custody); and

(b) he is so detained for a period exceeding, or for successive periods exceeding in the aggregate, six months,

the relevant application shall cease to have effect on expiry of that period.

(2) A patient is a qualifying patient for the purposes of this section if—

(a) he is liable to be detained by virtue of an application for admission for treatment;

(b) he is subject to guardianship by virtue of a guardianship application; or

(c) he is a community patient.

(3) 'The relevant application', in relation to a qualifying patient, means—

(a) in the case of a patient who is subject to guardianship, the guardianship application in respect of him;

(b) in any other case, the application for admission for treatment in respect of him.

(4) The remaining subsections of this section shall apply if a qualifying patient is detained in custody as mentioned in subsection (1)(a) above but for a period not exceeding, or for successive periods not exceeding in the aggregate, six months.

(5) If apart from this subsection—

(a) the patient would have ceased to be liable to be detained or subject to guardianship by virtue of the relevant application on or before the day on which he is discharged from custody; or

(b) in the case of a community patient, the community treatment order would have ceased to be in force on or before that day,

he shall not cease and shall be deemed not to have ceased to be so liable or subject, or the order shall not cease and shall be deemed not to have ceased to be in force, until the end of that day.

(6) In any case (except as provided in subsection (8) below), sections 18, 21 and 21A above shall apply in relation to the patient as if he had absented himself without leave on that day.

(7) In its application by virtue of subsection (6) above section 18 shall have effect as if—

(a) in subsection (4) for the words from 'later of' to the end there were substituted 'end of the period of 28 days beginning with the first day of his absence without leave'; and

(b) subsections (4A) and (4B) were omitted.

(8) In relation to a community patient who was not recalled to hospital under section 17E above at the time when his detention in custody began—

(a) section 18 above shall not apply; but

(b) sections 21 and 21A above shall apply as if he had absented himself without leave on the day on which he is discharged from custody and had returned himself as provided in those sections on the last day of the period of 28 days beginning with that day.]

[*Section 22 substituted by paragraph 9 of Schedule 3 to the 2007 Act.*]

23 Discharge of patients

(1) Subject to the provisions of this section and section 25 below, a patient who is for the time being liable to be detained or subject to guardianship under this Part of this Act shall cease to be so liable or subject if an order in writing discharging him *from detention or guardianship (in this Act referred to as 'an order for discharge') is made in accordance with this section* [absolutely from detention or guardianship is made in accordance with this section].

[(1A) Subject to the provisions of this section and section 25 below, a community patient shall cease to be liable to recall under this Part of this Act, and the application for admission for treatment cease to have effect, if an order in writing discharging him from such liability is made in accordance with this section.

(1B) An order under subsection (1) or (1A) above shall be referred to in this Act as 'an order for discharge'.]

(2) An order for discharge may be made in respect of a patient—

    (a) where the patient is liable to be detained in a hospital in pursuance of an application for admission for assessment or for treatment by the *responsible medical officer* [responsible clinician], by the managers or by the nearest relative of the patient;

    (b) where the patient is subject to guardianship, by the *responsible medical officer* [responsible clinician], by the responsible local social services authority or by the nearest relative of the patient

    [(c) where the patient is a community patient, by the responsible clinician, by the managers of the responsible hospital or by the nearest relative of the patient.]

(3) Where the patient *is liable to be detained in a registered establishment in pursuance of an application for admission for assessment or for treatment* [falls within subsection (3A) below], an order for his discharge may, without prejudice to subsection (2) above, be made by the Secretary of State and, if *the patient is maintained* [arrangements have been made in respect of the patient] under a contract with a National Health Service trust, NHS foundation trust, Local Health Board, Special Health Authority or Primary Care Trust, by that National Health Service trust, NHS foundation trust, Local Health Board, Special Health Authority or Primary Care Trust.

[(3A) A patient falls within this subsection if—

    (a) he is liable to be detained in a registered establishment in pursuance of an application for admission for assessment or for treatment; or

    (b) he is a community patient and the responsible hospital is a registered establishment.]

(4) The powers conferred by this section on any authority, trust, board (other than an NHS foundation trust) or body of persons may be exercised subject to subsection (3) below by any three or more members of that authority, trust, board or body authorised by them in that behalf or by three or more members of a committee or sub-committee of that authority, trust, board or body which has been authorised by them in that behalf.

(5) The reference in subsection (4) above to the members of an authority, trust, board or body or the members of a committee or sub-committee of an authority, trust, board or body,—

    (a) in the case of a Local Health Board, Special Health Authority or Primary Care Trust or a committee or sub-committee of a Local Health Board, Special Health Authority or Primary Care Trust, is a reference only to the chairman of the authority, trust or board and such members (of the authority, trust, board, committee or sub-committee, as the case may be) as are not also officers of the authority, trust or board, within the meaning of the National Health Service Act 2006 or the National Health Service (Wales) Act 2006; and

    (b) in the case of a National Health Service trust or a committee or sub-committee of such a trust, is a reference only to the chairman of the trust and such directors or (in the case of a committee or sub-committee) members as are not also employees of the trust.

(6) The powers conferred by this section on any NHS foundation trust may be exercised by any three or more *non-executive directors of the board of the trust authorised by the board in that behalf.* [persons authorised by the board of the trust in that behalf each of whom is neither an executive director of the board nor an employee of the trust.]

[*Words in subsection (1) substituted by, and subsections (1A) & (1B) inserted by, paragraphs 10(2) and (3) respectively of Schedule 3 to the 2007 Act; words in subsections (2)(a) & (b) substituted by section 9(6); subsection (2)(c) and subsection (3A) inserted by paragraphs 10(4) and (6) of Schedule 3 respectively; words substituted in subsection (3) by paragraphs 10(5)(a)&(b) of that Schedule; and words substituted in subsection (6) by section 45(1).*]

24 Visiting and examination of patients

(1) For the purpose of advising as to the exercise by the nearest relative of a patient who is liable to be detained or subject to guardianship under this Part of this Act [, or who is a community patient,] of any power to order his discharge, any registered medical practitioner [or approved clinician] authorised by or on behalf of the nearest relative of the patient may, at any reasonable time, visit the patient and examine him in private.

(2) Any registered medical practitioner [or approved clinician] authorised for the purposes of subsection (1) above to visit and examine a patient may require the production of and inspect any records relating to the detention or treatment of the patient in any hospital or to any after-care services provided for the patient under section 117 below.

(3) Where application is made by the Secretary of State or a Local Health Board, Special Health Authority, Primary Care Trust, National Health Service trust or NHS foundation trust to exercise, *in respect of a patient liable to be detained in a registered establishment, any power to make an order for his discharge* [any power under section 23(3) above to make an order for a patient's discharge], the following persons, that is to say—

(a) any registered medical practitioner [or approved clinician] authorised by the Secretary of State or, as the case may be, that Local Health Board, Special Health Authority, Primary Care Trust, National Health Service trust or NHS foundation trust; and

(b) any other person (whether a registered medical practitioner [or approved clinician] or not) authorised under Part II of the Care Standards Act 2000 to inspect *the home* [the establishment in question];

may at any reasonable time visit the patient and interview him in private.

(4) Any person authorised for the purposes of subsection (3) above to visit a patient may require the production of and inspect any documents constituting or alleged to constitute the authority for the detention of the patient [, or (as the case may be) for his liability to recall,] under this Part of this Act; and any person so authorised, who is a registered medical practitioner [or approved clinician], may examine the patient in private, and may require the production of and inspect any other records relating to the treatment of the patient in *the home* [the establishment] or to any after-care services provided for the patient under section 117 below.

[*Words 'or who is a community patient' in subsection (1) inserted by paragraph 11(2) of Schedule 3 to the 2007 Act; 'or approved clinician' inserted in subsections (1), (2), (3) and (4) by section 9(7); words in opening part of subsection (3) substituted by paragraph 11(3)(a) of Schedule 3; words substituted in subsection (3)(b) by paragraph 11(3)(b) of that Schedule; words inserted in subsection (4) by paragraph 11(4)(a) and 'the establishment' substituted for 'the home' in the same subsection by paragraph 11(4)(b).*]

25 Restrictions on discharge by nearest relative

(1) An order for the discharge of a patient who is liable to be detained in a hospital shall not be made [under section 23 above] by his nearest relative except after giving not less than 72 hours' notice in writing to the managers of the hospital; and if, within 72 hours after such notice has been given, the *responsible medical officer* [responsible clinician] furnishes to the

managers a report certifying that in the opinion of *that officer* [that clinician] the patient, if discharged, would be likely to act in a manner dangerous to other persons or to himself—

   (a) any order for the discharge of the patient made by that relative in pursuance of the notice shall be of no effect; and

   (b) no further order for the discharge of the patient shall be made by that relative during the period of six months beginning with the date of the report.

[(1A) Subsection (1) above shall apply to an order for the discharge of a community patient as it applies to an order for the discharge of a patient who is liable to be detained in a hospital, but with the reference to the managers of the hospital being read as a reference to the managers of the responsible hospital.]

(2) In any case where a report under subsection (1) above is furnished in respect of a patient who is liable to be detained in pursuance of an application for admission for treatment[, or in respect of a community patient,] the managers shall cause the nearest relative of the patient to be informed.

[*Words 'under section 23 above' in subsection (1), whole of subsection (1A) and words in subsection (2) inserted by paragraphs 12(2) to (4) respectively of Schedule 3 to the 2007 Act; words in subsection (1) substituted by section 9(8)(a)&(b) respectively.*]

After-care under supervision

25A Application for supervision

(1) Where a patient—

   (a) is liable to be detained in a hospital in pursuance of an application for admission for treatment; and

   (b) has attained the age of 16 years,

an application may be made for him to be supervised after he leaves hospital, for the period allowed by the following provisions of this Act, with a view to securing that he receives the after-care services provided for him under section 117 below.

(2) In this Act an application for a patient to be so supervised is referred to as a 'supervision application'; and where a supervision application has been duly made and accepted under this Part of this Act in respect of a patient and he has left hospital, he is for the purposes of this Act 'subject to after-care under supervision' (until he ceases to be so subject in accordance with the provisions of this Act).

(3) A supervision application shall be made in accordance with this section and sections 25B and 25C below.

(4) A supervision application may be made in respect of a patient only on the grounds that—

   (a) he is suffering from mental disorder, being mental illness, severe mental impairment, psychopathic disorder or mental impairment;

   (b) there would be a substantial risk of serious harm to the health or safety of the patient or the safety of other persons, or of the patient being seriously exploited, if he were not to receive the after-care services to be provided for him under section 117 below after he leaves hospital; and

   (c) his being subject to after-care under supervision is likely to help to secure that he receives the after-care services to be so provided.

(5) A supervision application may be made only by the responsible medical officer.

(6) A supervision application in respect of a patient shall be addressed to the Primary Care Trust or Local Health Board which will have the duty under section 117 below to provide after-care services for the patient after he leaves hospital.

(7) Before accepting a supervision application in respect of a patient a Primary Care Trust or Local Health Board shall consult the local social services authority which will also have that duty.

(8) Where a Primary Care Trust or Local Health Board accept a supervision application in respect of a patient the Primary Care Trust or Local Health Board shall—

(a) inform the patient both orally and in writing—

(i) that the supervision application has been accepted; and

(ii) of the effect in his case of the provisions of this Act relating to a patient subject to after-care under supervision (including, in particular, what rights of applying to a Mental Health Review Tribunal are available);

(b) inform any person whose name is stated in the supervision application in accordance with sub-paragraph (i) of paragraph (e) of section 25B(5) below that the supervision application has been accepted; and

(c) inform in writing any person whose name is so stated in accordance with sub-paragraph (ii) of that paragraph that the supervision application has been accepted.

(9) Where a patient in respect of whom a supervision application is made is granted leave of absence from a hospital under section 17 above (whether before or after the supervision application is made), references in—

(a) this section and the following provisions of this Part of this Act; and

(b) Part V of this Act,

to his leaving hospital shall be construed as references to his period of leave expiring (otherwise than on his return to the hospital or transfer to another hospital).

[Section 25A omitted by section 36(2) of the 2007 Act.]

25B Making of supervision application

(1) The responsible medical officer shall not make a supervision application unless—

(a) subsection (2) below is complied with; and

(b) the responsible medical officer has considered the matters specified in subsection (4) below.

(2) This subsection is complied with if—

(a) the following persons have been consulted about the making of the supervision application—

(i) the patient;

(ii) one or more persons who have been professionally concerned with the patient's medical treatment in hospital;

(iii) one or more persons who will be professionally concerned with the after-care services to be provided for the patient under section 117 below; and

(iv) any person who the responsible medical officer believes will play a substantial part in the care of the patient after he leaves hospital but will not be professionally concerned with any of the after-care services to be so provided;

(b) such steps as are practicable have been taken to consult the person (if any) appearing to be the nearest relative of the patient about the making of the supervision application; and

(c) the responsible medical officer has taken into account any views expressed by the persons consulted.

(3) Where the patient has requested that paragraph (b) of subsection (2) above should not apply, that paragraph shall not apply unless—

(a) the patient has a propensity to violent or dangerous behaviour towards others; and

(b) the responsible medical officer considers that it is appropriate for steps such as are mentioned in that paragraph to be taken.

(4) The matters referred to in subsection (1)(b) above are—
  (a) the after-care services to be provided for the patient under section 117 below; and
  (b) any requirements to be imposed on him under section 25D below.
(5) A supervision application shall state—
  (a) that the patient is liable to be detained in a hospital in pursuance of an application for admission for treatment;
  (b) the age of the patient or, if his exact age is not known to the applicant, that the patient is believed to have attained the age of 16 years;
  (c) that in the opinion of the applicant (having regard in particular to the patient's history) all of the conditions set out in section 25A(4) above are complied with;
  (d) the name of the person who is to be the community responsible medical officer, and of the person who is to be the supervisor, in relation to the patient after he leaves hospital; and
  (e) the name of—
    (i) any person who has been consulted under paragraph (a)(iv) of subsection (2) above; and
    (ii) any person who has been consulted under paragraph (b) of that subsection.
(6) A supervision application shall be accompanied by—
  (a) the written recommendation in the prescribed form of a registered medical practitioner who will be professionally concerned with the patient's medical treatment after he leaves hospital or, if no such practitioner other than the responsible medical officer will be so concerned, of any registered medical practitioner; and
  (b) the written recommendation in the prescribed form of an approved social worker.
(7) A recommendation under subsection (6)(a) above shall include a statement that in the opinion of the medical practitioner (having regard in particular to the patient's history) all of the conditions set out in section 25A(4) above are complied with.
(8) A recommendation under subsection (6)(b) above shall include a statement that in the opinion of the social worker (having regard in particular to the patient's history) both of the conditions set out in section 25A(4)(b) and (c) above are complied with.
(9) A supervision application shall also be accompanied by—
  (a) a statement in writing by the person who is to be the community responsible medical officer in relation to the patient after he leaves hospital that he is to be in charge of the medical treatment provided for the patient as part of the after-care services provided for him under section 117 below;
  (b) a statement in writing by the person who is to be the supervisor in relation to the patient after he leaves hospital that he is to supervise the patient with a view to securing that he receives the after-care services so provided;
  (c) details of the after-care services to be provided for the patient under section 117 below; and
  (d) details of any requirements to be imposed on him under section 25D below.
(10) On making a supervision application in respect of a patient the responsible medical officer shall—
  (a) inform the patient both orally and in writing;
  (b) inform any person who has been consulted under paragraph (a)(iv) of subsection (2) above; and
  (c) inform in writing any person who has been consulted under paragraph (b) of that subsection of the matters specified in subsection (11) below.
(11) The matters referred to in subsection (10) above are—
  (a) that the application is being made;
  (b) the after-care services to be provided for the patient under section 117 below;
  (c) any requirements to be imposed on him under section 25D below; and

(d) the name of the person who is to be the community responsible medical officer, and of the person who is to be the supervisor, in relation to the patient after he leaves hospital.

[Section 25B omitted by section 36(2) of the 2007 Act.]

25C Supervision applications: supplementary

(1) Subject to subsection (2) below, a supervision application, and the recommendation under section 25B(6)(a) above accompanying it, may describe the patient as suffering from more than one of the following forms of mental disorder, namely, mental illness, severe mental impairment, psychopathic disorder and mental impairment.

(2) A supervision application shall be of no effect unless the patient is described in the application and the recommendation under section 25B(6)(a) above accompanying it as suffering from the same form of mental disorder, whether or not he is also described in the application or the recommendation as suffering from another form.

(3) A registered medical practitioner may at any reasonable time visit a patient and examine him in private for the purpose of deciding whether to make a recommendation under section 25B(6)(a) above.

(4) An approved social worker may at any reasonable time visit and interview a patient for the purpose of deciding whether to make a recommendation under section 25B(6)(b) above.

(5) For the purpose of deciding whether to make a recommendation under section 25B(6) above in respect of a patient, a registered medical practitioner or an approved social worker may require the production of and inspect any records relating to the detention or treatment of the patient in any hospital or to any after-care services provided for the patient under section 117 below.

(6) If, within the period of 14 days beginning with the day on which a supervision application has been accepted, the application, or any recommendation accompanying it, is found to be in any respect incorrect or defective, the application or recommendation may, within that period and with the consent of the Primary Care Trust or Local Health Board which accepted the application, be amended by the person by whom it was made or given.

(7) Where an application or recommendation is amended in accordance with subsection (6) above it shall have effect, and shall be deemed to have had effect, as if it had been originally made or given as so amended.

(8) A supervision application which appears to be duly made and to be accompanied by recommendations under section 25B(6) above may be acted upon without further proof of—

(a) the signature or qualification of the person by whom the application or any such recommendation was made or given; or

(b) any matter of fact or opinion stated in the application or recommendation.

(9) A recommendation under section 25B(6) above accompanying a supervision application in respect of a patient shall not be given by—

(a) the responsible medical officer;

(b) a person who receives or has an interest in the receipt of any payments made on account of the maintenance of the patient; or

(c) a close relative of the patient, of any person mentioned in paragraph (a) or (b) above or of a person by whom the other recommendation is given under section 25B(6) above for the purposes of the application.

(10) In subsection (9)(c) above 'close relative' means husband, wife, civil partner, father, father-in-law, mother, mother-in-law, son, son-in-law, daughter, daughter-in-law, brother, brother-in-law, sister or sister-in-law.

[Section 25C omitted by section 36(2) of the 2007 Act.]

25D Requirements to secure receipt of after-care under supervision

(1) Where a patient is subject to after-care under supervision (or, if he has not yet left hospital, is to be so subject after he leaves hospital), the responsible after-care bodies have power to impose any of the requirements specified in subsection (3) below for the purpose of securing that the patient receives the after-care services provided for him under section 117 below.

(2) In this Act 'the responsible after-care bodies', in relation to a patient, means the bodies which have (or will have) the duty under section 117 below to provide after-care services for the patient.

(3) The requirements referred to in subsection (1) above are—

(a) that the patient reside at a specified place;

(b) that the patient attend at specified places and times for the purpose of medical treatment, occupation, education or training; and

(c) that access to the patient be given, at any place where the patient is residing, to the supervisor, any registered medical practitioner or any approved social worker or to any other person authorised by the supervisor.

(4) A patient subject to after-care under supervision may be taken and conveyed by, or by any person authorised by, the supervisor to any place where the patient is required to reside or to attend for the purpose of medical treatment, occupation, education or training.

(5) A person who demands—

(a) to be given access to a patient in whose case a requirement has been imposed under subsection (3)(c) above; or

(b) to take and convey a patient in pursuance of subsection (4) above,

shall, if asked to do so, produce some duly authenticated document to show that he is a person entitled to be given access to, or to take and convey, the patient.

[Section 25D omitted by section 36(2) of the 2007 Act.]

25E Review of after-care under supervision etc

(1) The after-care services provided (or to be provided) under section 117 below for a patient who is (or is to be) subject to after-care under supervision, and any requirements imposed on him under section 25D above, shall be kept under review, and (where appropriate) modified, by the responsible after-care bodies.

(2) This subsection applies in relation to a patient who is subject to after-care under supervision where he refuses or neglects—

(a) to receive any or all of the after-care services provided for him under section 117 below; or

(b) to comply with any or all of any requirements imposed on him under section 25D above.

(3) Where subsection (2) above applies in relation to a patient, the responsible after-care bodies shall review, and (where appropriate) modify—

(a) the after-care services provided for him under section 117 below; and

(b) any requirements imposed on him under section 25D above.

(4) Where subsection (2) above applies in relation to a patient, the responsible after-care bodies shall also—

    (a) consider whether it might be appropriate for him to cease to be subject to after-care under supervision and, if they conclude that it might be, inform the community responsible medical officer; and

    (b) consider whether it might be appropriate for him to be admitted to a hospital for treatment and, if they conclude that it might be, inform an approved social worker.

(5) The responsible after-care bodies shall not modify—

    (a) the after-care services provided (or to be provided) under section 117 below for a patient who is (or is to be) subject to after-care under supervision; or

    (b) any requirements imposed on him under section 25D above,

    unless subsection (6) below is complied with.

(6) This subsection is complied with if—

    (a) the patient has been consulted about the modifications;

    (b) any person who the responsible after-care bodies believe plays (or will play) a substantial part in the care of the patient but is not (or will not be) professionally concerned with the after-care services provided for the patient under section 117 below has been consulted about the modifications;

    (c) such steps as are practicable have been taken to consult the person (if any) appearing to be the nearest relative of the patient about the modifications; and

    (d) the responsible after-care bodies have taken into account any views expressed by the persons consulted.

(7) Where the patient has requested that paragraph (c) of subsection (6) above should not apply, that paragraph shall not apply unless—

    (a) the patient has a propensity to violent or dangerous behaviour towards others; and

    (b) the community responsible medical officer (or the person who is to be the community responsible medical officer) considers that it is appropriate for steps such as are mentioned in that paragraph to be taken.

(8) Where the responsible after-care bodies modify the after-care services provided (or to be provided) for the patient under section 117 below or any requirements imposed on him under section 25D above, they shall—

    (a) inform the patient both orally and in writing;

    (b) inform any person who has been consulted under paragraph (b) of subsection (6) above; and

    (c) inform in writing any person who has been consulted under paragraph (c) of that subsection, that the modifications have been made.

(9) Where—

    (a) a person other than the person named in the supervision application becomes the community responsible medical officer when the patient leaves hospital; or

    (b) when the patient is subject to after-care under supervision, one person ceases to be, and another becomes, the community responsible medical officer,

    the responsible after-care bodies shall comply with subsection (11) below.

(10) Where—

    (a) a person other than the person named in the supervision application becomes the supervisor when the patient leaves hospital; or

    (b) when the patient is subject to after-care under supervision, one person ceases to be, and another becomes, the supervisor, the responsible after-care bodies shall comply with subsection (11) below.

(11) The responsible after-care bodies comply with this subsection if they—

    (a) inform the patient both orally and in writing;

    (b) inform any person who they believe plays a substantial part in the care of the patient but is not professionally concerned with the after-care services provided for the patient under section 117 below; and

    (c) unless the patient otherwise requests, take such steps as are practicable to inform in writing the person (if any) appearing to be the nearest relative of the patient,

of the name of the person who becomes the community responsible medical officer or the supervisor.

[Section 25E omitted by section 36(2) of the 2007 Act.]

25F Reclassification of patient subject to after-care under supervision

(1) If it appears to the community responsible medical officer that a patient subject to after-care under supervision is suffering from a form of mental disorder other than the form or forms specified in the supervision application made in respect of the patient, he may furnish a report to that effect to the Primary Care Trust or Local Health Board which have the duty under section 117 below to provide after-care services for the patient.

(2) Where a report is so furnished the supervision application shall have effect as if that other form of mental disorder were specified in it.

(3) Unless no-one other than the community responsible medical officer is professionally concerned with the patient's medical treatment, he shall consult one or more persons who are so concerned before furnishing a report under subsection (1) above.

(4) Where a report is furnished under subsection (1) above in respect of a patient, the responsible after-care bodies shall—

    (a) inform the patient both orally and in writing; and

    (b) unless the patient otherwise requests, take such steps as are practicable to inform in writing the person (if any) appearing to be the nearest relative of the patient, that the report has been furnished.

[Section 25F omitted by section 36(2) of the 2007 Act.]

25G Duration and renewal of after-care under supervision

(1) Subject to sections 25H and 25I below, a patient subject to after-care under supervision shall be so subject for the period—

    (a) beginning when he leaves hospital; and

    (b) ending with the period of six months beginning with the day on which the supervision application was accepted, but shall not be so subject for any longer period except in accordance with the following provisions of this section.

(2) A patient already subject to after-care under supervision may be made so subject—

    (a) from the end of the period referred to in subsection (1) above, for a further period of six months; and

    (b) from the end of any period of renewal under paragraph (a) above, for a further period of one year,

and so on for periods of one year at a time.

(3) Within the period of two months ending on the day on which a patient who is subject to after-care under supervision would (in default of the operation of subsection (7) below) cease to be so subject, it shall be the duty of the community responsible medical officer—

    (a) to examine the patient; and

  (b) if it appears to him that the conditions set out in subsection (4) below are complied with, to furnish to the responsible after-care bodies a report to that effect in the prescribed form.

(4) The conditions referred to in subsection (3) above are that—

  (a) the patient is suffering from mental disorder, being mental illness, severe mental impairment, psychopathic disorder or mental impairment;

  (b) there would be a substantial risk of serious harm to the health or safety of the patient or the safety of other persons, or of the patient being seriously exploited, if he were not to receive the after-care services provided for him under section 117 below;

  (c) his being subject to after-care under supervision is likely to help to secure that he receives the after-care services so provided.

(5) The community responsible medical officer shall not consider whether the conditions set out in subsection (4) above are complied with unless—

  (a) the following persons have been consulted—

    (i) the patient;

    (ii) the supervisor;

    (iii) unless no-one other than the community responsible medical officer is professionally concerned with the patient's medical treatment, one or more persons who are so concerned;

    (iv) one or more persons who are professionally concerned with the after-care services (other than medical treatment) provided for the patient under section 117 below; and

    (v) any person who the community responsible medical officer believes plays a substantial part in the care of the patient but is not professionally concerned with the after-care services so provided;

  (b) such steps as are practicable have been taken to consult the person (if any) appearing to be the nearest relative of the patient; and

  (c) the community responsible medical officer has taken into account any relevant views expressed by the persons consulted.

(6) Where the patient has requested that paragraph (b) of subsection (5) above should not apply, that paragraph shall not apply unless—

  (a) the patient has a propensity to violent or dangerous behaviour towards others; and

  (b) the community responsible medical officer considers that it is appropriate for steps such as are mentioned in that paragraph to be taken.

(7) Where a report is duly furnished under subsection (3) above, the patient shall be thereby made subject to after-care under supervision for the further period prescribed in that case by subsection (2) above.

(8) Where a report is furnished under subsection (3) above, the responsible after care bodies shall—

  (a) inform the patient both orally and in writing—

    (i) that the report has been furnished; and

    (ii) of the effect in his case of the provisions of this Act relating to making a patient subject to after-care under supervision for a further period (including, in particular, what rights of applying to a Mental Health Review Tribunal are available);

  (b) inform any person who has been consulted under paragraph (a)(v) of subsection (5) above that the report has been furnished; and

  (c) inform in writing any person who has been consulted under paragraph (b) of that subsection that the report has been furnished.

(9) Where the form of mental disorder specified in a report furnished under subsection (3) above is a form of disorder other than that specified in the supervision application, that application shall have effect as if that other form of mental disorder were specified in it.

(10) Where on any occasion a report specifying such a form of mental disorder is furnished under subsection (3) above the community responsible medical officer need not on that occasion furnish a report under section 25F above.

[*Section 25G omitted by section 36(2) of the 2007 Act.*]

25H Ending of after-care under supervision

(1) The community responsible medical officer may at any time direct that a patient subject to after-care under supervision shall cease to be so subject.

(2) The community responsible medical officer shall not give a direction under subsection (1) above unless subsection (3) below is complied with.

(3) This subsection is complied with if—

(a) the following persons have been consulted about the giving of the direction—

(i) the patient;

(ii) the supervisor;

(iii) unless no-one other than the community responsible medical officer is professionally concerned with the patient's medical treatment, one or more persons who are so concerned;

(iv) one or more persons who are professionally concerned with the after-care services (other than medical treatment) provided for the patient under section 117 below; and

(v) any person who the community responsible medical officer believes plays a substantial part in the care of the patient but is not professionally concerned with the after-care services so provided;

(b) such steps as are practicable have been taken to consult the person (if any) appearing to be the nearest relative of the patient about the giving of the direction; and

(c) the community responsible medical officer has taken into account any views expressed by the persons consulted.

(4) Where the patient has requested that paragraph (b) of subsection (3) above should not apply, that paragraph shall not apply unless—

(a) the patient has a propensity to violent or dangerous behaviour towards others; and

(b) the community responsible medical officer considers that it is appropriate for steps such as are mentioned in that paragraph to be taken.

(5) A patient subject to after-care under supervision shall cease to be so subject if he—

(a) is admitted to a hospital in pursuance of an application for admission for treatment; or

(b) is received into guardianship.

(6) Where a patient (for any reason) ceases to be subject to after-care under supervision the responsible after-care bodies shall—

(a) inform the patient both orally and in writing;

(b) inform any person who they believe plays a substantial part in the care of the patient but is not professionally concerned with the after-care services provided for the patient under section 117 below; and

(c) take such steps as are practicable to inform in writing the person (if any) appearing to be the nearest relative of the patient,

that the patient has ceased to be so subject.

(7) Where the patient has requested that paragraph (c) of subsection (6) above should not apply, that paragraph shall not apply unless subsection (3)(b) above applied in his case by virtue of subsection (4) above.

[*Section 25H omitted by section 36(2) of the 2007 Act.*]

25I Special provisions as to patients sentenced to imprisonment etc

(1) This section applies where a patient who is subject to after-care under supervision—
- *(a) is detained in custody in pursuance of any sentence or order passed or made by a court in the United Kingdom (including an order committing or remanding him in custody); or*
- *(b) is detained in hospital in pursuance of an application for admission for assessment.*

(2) At any time when the patient is detained as mentioned in subsection (1)(a) or (b) above he is not required—
- *(a) to receive any after-care services provided for him under section 117 below; or*
- *(b) to comply with any requirements imposed on him under section 25D above.*

(3) If the patient is detained as mentioned in paragraph (a) of subsection (1) above for a period of, or successive periods amounting in the aggregate to, six months or less, or is detained as mentioned in paragraph (b) of that subsection, and, apart from this subsection, he—
- *(a) would have ceased to be subject to after-care under supervision during the period for which he is so detained; or*
- *(b) would cease to be so subject during the period of 28 days beginning with the day on which he ceases to be so detained,*
  he shall be deemed not to have ceased, and shall not cease, to be so subject until the end of that period of 28 days.

(4) Where the period for which the patient is subject to after-care under supervision is extended by subsection (3) above, any examination and report to be made and furnished in respect of the patient under section 25G(3) above may be made and furnished within the period as so extended.

(5) Where, by virtue of subsection (4) above, the patient is made subject to after-care under supervision for a further period after the day on which (apart from subsection (3) above) he would have ceased to be so subject, the further period shall be deemed to have commenced with that day.

[Section 25I omitted by section 36(2) of the 2007 Act.]

25J Patients moving from Scotland to England and Wales

(2) Sections 25A to 25I above, section 117 below and any other provision of this Act relating to supervision applications or patients subject to after-care under supervision shall apply in relation to a patient in respect of whom a supervision application is or is to be made by virtue of this section subject to such modifications as the Secretary of State may by regulations prescribe.

[Section 25J omitted by section 36(2) of the 2007 Act.]

Functions of relatives of patients

26 Definition of 'relative' and 'nearest relative'

(1) In this Part of this Act 'relative' means any of the following persons:—
- (a) husband or wife [or civil partner];
- (b) son or daughter;
- (c) father or mother;
- (d) brother or sister;
- (e) grandparent;
- (f) grandchild;
- (g) uncle or aunt;
- (h) nephew or niece.

(2) In deducing relationships for the purposes of this section, any relationship of the half-blood shall be treated as a relationship of the whole blood, and an illegitimate person shall be treated as the legitimate child of

(a) his mother, and

(b) if his father has parental responsibility for him within the meaning of section 3 of the Children Act 1989, his father.

(3) In this Part of this Act, subject to the provisions of this section and to the following provisions of this Part of this Act, the 'nearest relative' means the person first described in subsection (1) above who is for the time being surviving, relatives of the whole blood being preferred to relatives of the same description of the half-blood and the elder or eldest of two or more relatives described in any paragraph of that subsection being preferred to the other or others of those relatives, regardless of sex.

(4) Subject to the provisions of this section and to the following provisions of this Part of this Act, where the patient ordinarily resides with or is cared for by one or more of his relatives (or, if he is for the time being an in-patient in a hospital, he last ordinarily resided with or was cared for by one or more of his relatives) his nearest relative shall be determined—

(a) by giving preference to that relative or those relatives over the other or others; and

(b) as between two or more such relatives, in accordance with subsection (3) above.

(5) Where the person who, under subsection (3) or (4) above, would be the nearest relative of a patient—

(a) in the case of a patient ordinarily resident in the United Kingdom, the Channel Islands or the Isle of Man, is not so resident; or

(b) is the husband or wife [or civil partner] of the patient, but is permanently separated from the patient, either by agreement or under an order of a court, or has deserted or has been deserted by the patient for a period which has come to an end; or

(c) is a person other than the husband, wife, [civil partner,] father or mother of the patient, and is for the time being under 18 years of age;

(d) the nearest relative of the patient shall be ascertained as if that person were dead.

(6) In this section 'husband' *and 'wife' include a person who is living with the patient as the patient's husband or wife*, ['wife' and 'civil partner' include a person who is living with the patient as the patient's husband or wife or as if they were civil partners], as the case may be (or, if the patient is for the time being an in-patient in a hospital, was so living until the patient was admitted), and has been or had been so living for a period of not less than six months; but a person shall not be treated by virtue of this subsection as the nearest relative of a married patient *unless the husband or wife* [or a patient in a civil partnership unless the husband, wife or civil partner] of the patient is disregarded by virtue of paragraph (b) of subsection (5) above.

(7) A person, other than a relative, with whom the patient ordinarily resides (or, if the patient is for the time being an in-patient in a hospital, last ordinarily resided before he was admitted), and with whom he has or had been ordinarily residing for a period of not less than five years, shall be treated for the purposes of this Part of this Act as if he were a relative but—

(a) shall be treated for the purposes of subsection (3) above as if mentioned last in sub-section (1) above; and

(b) shall not be treated by virtue of this subsection as the nearest relative of a married patient *unless the husband or wife* [or a patient in a civil partnership unless the husband, wife or civil partner] of the patient is disregarded by virtue of paragraph (b) of subsection (5) above.

[*Words inserted in subsection (1) by section 26(2) of the 2007 Act. Words inserted in subsection (5) by section 26(3)(a)&(b). Words substituted in subsection (6) by section 26(4)(a)&(b), and in subsection (7)(b) by section 26(5).*]

27 Children and young persons in care

Where—

    (a) a patient who is a child or young person is in the care of a local authority by virtue of a care order within the meaning of the Children Act 1989; or

    (b) the rights and powers of a parent of a patient who is a child or young person are vested in a local authority by virtue of section 16 of the Social Work (Scotland) Act 1968,

the authority shall be deemed to be the nearest relative of the patient in preference to any person except the patient's husband or wife [or civil partner] (if any).

[*Words inserted by section 26(6) of the 2007 Act.*]

28 Nearest relative of minor under guardianship, etc

(1) Where—

    (a) a guardian has been appointed for a person who has not attained the age of eighteen years; or

    (b) a residence order (as defined by section 8 of the Children Act 1989) is in force with respect to such a person,

the guardian (or guardians, where there is more than one) or the person named in the residence order shall, to the exclusion of any other person, be deemed to be his nearest relative.

(2) Subsection (5) of section 26 above shall apply in relation to a person who is, or who is one of the persons, deemed to be the nearest relative of a patient by virtue of this section as it applies in relation to a person who would be the nearest relative under subsection (3) of that section.

(3) In this section 'guardian' includes a special guardian (within the meaning of the Children Act 1989), but does not include a guardian under this Part of this Act.

(4) In this section 'court' includes a court in Scotland or Northern Ireland, and 'enactment' includes an enactment of the Parliament of Northern Ireland, a Measure of the Northern Ireland Assembly and an Order in Council under Schedule 1 of the Northern Ireland Act 1974.

29 Appointment by court of acting nearest relative

(1) The county court may, upon application made in accordance with the provisions of this section in respect of a patient, by order direct that the functions of the nearest relative of the patient under this Part of this Act and sections 66 and 69 below shall, during the continuance in force of the order, be exercisable by *the applicant, or by any other person specified in the application, being a person who, in the opinion of the court, is a proper person to act as the patient's nearest relative and is willing to do so.* [the person specified in the order].

[(1A) If the court decides to make an order on an application under subsection (1) above, the following rules have effect for the purposes of specifying a person in the order—

    (a) if a person is nominated in the application to act as the patient's nearest relative and that person is, in the opinion of the court, a suitable person to act as such and is willing to do so, the court shall specify that person (or, if there are two or more such persons, such one of them as the court thinks fit);

    (b) otherwise, the court shall specify such person as is, in its opinion, a suitable person to act as the patient's nearest relative and is willing to do so.]

(2) An order under this section may be made on the application of—

[(za) the patient;]

(a) any relative of the patient;

(b) any other person with whom the patient is residing (or, if the patient is then an in-patient in a hospital, was last residing before he was admitted); or

(c) *an approved social worker* [approved mental health professional];

but in relation to an application made by such a social worker, subsection (1) above shall have effect as if for the words 'the applicant' there were substituted the words 'the local social services authority'.

(3) An application for an order under this section may be made upon any of the following grounds, that is to say—

(a) that the patient has no nearest relative within the meaning of this Act, or that it is not reasonably practicable to ascertain whether he has such a relative, or who that relative is;

(b) that the nearest relative of the patient is incapable of acting as such by reason of mental disorder or other illness;

(c) that the nearest relative of the patient unreasonably objects to the making of an application for admission for treatment or a guardianship application in respect of the patient; *or*

(d) that the nearest relative of the patient has exercised without due regard to the welfare of the patient or the interests of the public his power to discharge the patient *from hospital or guardianship* under this Part of this Act, or is likely to do so; or

[(e) that the nearest relative of the patient is otherwise not a suitable person to act as such.]

(4) If, immediately before the expiration of the period for which a patient is liable to be detained by virtue of an application for admission for assessment, an application under this section, which is an application made on the ground specified in subsection (3)(c) or (d) above, is pending in respect of the patient, that period shall be extended—

(a) in any case, until the application under this section has been finally disposed of; and

(b) if an order is made in pursuance of the application under this section, for a further period of seven days;

and for the purposes of this subsection an application under this section shall be deemed to have been finally disposed of at the expiration of the time allowed for appealing from the decision of the court or, if notice of appeal has been given within that time, when the appeal has been heard or withdrawn, and 'pending' shall be construed accordingly.

(5) An order made on the ground specified in subsection *(3)(a) or (b)* [(3)(a), (b) or (e)] above may specify a period for which it is to continue in force unless previously discharged under section 30 below,

(6) While an order made under this section is in force, the provisions of this Part of this Act (other than this section and section 30 below) and sections 66, 69, 132(4) and 133 below shall apply in relation to the patient as if for any reference to the nearest relative of the patient there were substituted a reference to the person having the functions of that relative and (without prejudice to section 30 below) shall so apply notwithstanding that the person who was the patient's nearest relative when the order was made is no longer his nearest relative; but this subsection shall not apply to section 66 below in the case mentioned in paragraph (h) of subsection (1) of that section.

[*Words substituted in subsection (1)(a) by section 23(2) of the 2007 Act; subsection (1A) inserted by section 23(3); paragraph (za) inserted and words at the end of subsection (2) omitted by section 23(4); words in paragraph (c) of that subsection substituted by paragraph 7(c) of Schedule 2; 'or' omitted after paragraph (c) of subsection (3) and paragraph (e) (and the preceding 'or') inserted by section 23(5); words in paragraph (d) of that subsection omitted by paragraph 13 of Schedule 3; and words in subsection (5) substituted by section 23(6).*]

30 Discharge and variation of orders under s 29

(1) An order made under section 29 above in respect of a patient may be discharged by the county court upon application made—

(a) in any case, by [the patient or] the person having the functions of the nearest relative of the patient by virtue of the order;

(b) where the order was made on the ground specified in paragraph (a) *or paragraph (b)* [,(b) or (e)] of section 29(3) above, or where the person who was the nearest relative of the patient when the order was made has ceased to be his nearest relative, on the application of the nearest relative of the patient.

[(1A) But, in the case of an order made on the ground specified in paragraph (e) of section 29(3) above, an application may not be made under subsection (1)(b) above by the person who was the nearest relative of the patient when the order was made except with leave of the county court.]

(2) An order made under section 29 above in respect of a patient may be varied by the county court, on the application of the person having the functions of the nearest relative by virtue of the order or on the application of [the patient or of] *an approved social worker* [approved mental health professional], by substituting *for the first-mentioned person a local social services authority or any other person who in the opinion of the court is a proper person to exercise those functions, being an authority or person who is willing to do so* [another person for the person having those functions].

[(2A) If the court decides to vary an order on an application under subsection (2) above, the following rules have effect for the purposes of substituting another person—

(a) if a person is nominated in the application to act as the patient's nearest relative and that person is, in the opinion of the court, a suitable person to act as such and is willing to do so, the court shall specify that person (or, if there are two or more such persons, such one of them as the court thinks fit);

(b) otherwise, the court shall specify such person as is, in its opinion, a suitable person to act as the patient's nearest relative and is willing to do so.]

(3) If the person having the functions of the nearest relative of a patient by virtue of an order under section 29 above dies—

(a) subsections (1) and (2) above shall apply as if for any reference to that person there were substituted a reference to any relative of the patient, and

(b) until the order is discharged or varied under those provisions the functions of the nearest relative under this Part of this Act and sections 66 and 69 below shall not be exercisable by any person.

(4) *An order under section 29 above shall, unless previously discharged under subsection (1) above, cease to have effect at the expiration of the period, if any, specified under subsection (5) of that section or, where no such period is specified* [An order made on the ground specified in paragraph (c) or (d) of section 29(3) above shall, unless previously discharged under subsection (1) above, cease to have effect as follows]—

(a) *if the patient was on the date of the order liable to be detained in pursuance of an application for admission for treatment or by virtue of an order or direction under Part III of this Act (otherwise than under section 35, 36 or 38) or was subject to guardianship under this Part of this Act or by virtue of such an order or direction, or becomes so liable or subject within the period of three months beginning with that date, when he ceases to be so liable or subject (otherwise than on being transferred in pursuance of regulations under section 19 above);*

(b) if the patient was not on the date of the order, and has not within the said period become, so liable or subject, at the expiration of that period.

[(a) if—

> (i) on the date of the order the patient was liable to be detained or subject to guardianship by virtue of a relevant application, order or direction; or
>
> (ii) he becomes so liable or subject within the period of three months beginning with that date; or
>
> (iii) he was a community patient on the date of the order,

it shall cease to have effect when he is discharged under section 23 above or 72 below or the relevant application, order or direction otherwise ceases to have effect (except as a result of his being transferred in pursuance of regulations under section 19 above);

(b) otherwise, it shall cease to have effect at the end of the period of three months beginning with the date of the order.]

[(4A) In subsection (4) above, reference to a relevant application, order or direction is to any of the following—

(a) an application for admission for treatment;

(b) a guardianship application;

(c) an order or direction under Part 3 of this Act (other than under section 35, 36 or 38).

(4B) An order made on the ground specified in paragraph (a), (b) or (e) of section 29(3) above shall—

(a) if a period was specified under section 29(5) above, cease to have effect on expiry of that period, unless previously discharged under subsection (1) above;

(b) if no such period was specified, remain in force until it is discharged under subsection (1) above.]

(5) The discharge or variation under this section of an order made under section 29 above shall not affect the validity of anything previously done in pursuance of the order.

[*Words inserted and substituted in subsection (1) by section 24(2)(a)&(b) respectively of the 2007 Act; subsection (1A) inserted by section 24(3); 'approved mental health professional' substituted for 'approved social worker' in subsection (2) by paragraph 7(d) of Schedule 2; words inserted and other substitution in that subsection by section 24(4)(a)&(b) respectively; subsection (2A) inserted by section 24(5); words substituted at start of subsection (4) by section 24(6); paragraphs (a) and (b) of that subsection substituted, and subsection (4A) inserted by paragraphs 14(2) & (3) of Schedule 3 respectively; and subsection (4B) inserted by section 24(7).*]

Supplemental

31 Procedure on applications to county court

County court rules which relate to applications authorised by this Part of this Act to be made to a county court may make provision—

(a) for the hearing and determination of such applications otherwise than in open court;

(b) for the admission on the hearing of such applications of evidence of such descriptions as may be specified in the rules notwithstanding anything to the contrary in any enactment or rule of law relating to the admissibility of evidence;

(c) for the visiting and interviewing of patients in private by or under the directions of the court.

32 Regulations for purposes of Part II

(1) The Secretary of State may make regulations for prescribing anything which, under this Part of this Act, is required or authorised to be prescribed, and otherwise for carrying this Part of this Act into full effect.

(2) Regulations under this section may in particular make provision—

   (a) for prescribing the form of any application, recommendation, report, order, notice or other document to be made or given under this Part of this Act;

   (b) for prescribing the manner in which any such application, recommendation, report, order, notice or other document may be proved, and for regulating the service of any such application, report, order or notice;

   (c) for requiring such bodies as may be prescribed by the regulations to keep such registers or other records as may be so prescribed in respect of patients liable to be detained or subject to guardianship *or to after-care under supervision* under this Part of this Act [or community patients], and to furnish or make available to those patients, and their relatives, such written statements of their rights and powers under this Act as may be so prescribed;

   (d) for the determination in accordance with the regulations of the age of any person whose exact age cannot be ascertained by reference to the registers kept under the Births and Deaths Registration Act 1953; and

   (e) for enabling the functions under this Part of this Act of the nearest relative of a patient to be performed, in such circumstances and subject to such conditions (if any) as may be prescribed by the regulations, by any person authorised in that behalf by that relative;

   and for the purposes of this Part of this Act any application, report or notice the service of which is regulated under paragraph (b) above shall be deemed to have been received by or furnished to the authority or person to whom it is authorised or required to be furnished, addressed or given if it is duly served in accordance with the regulations.

(3) Without prejudice to subsections (1) and (2) above, but subject to section 23(4) [and (6)] above, regulations under this section may determine the manner in which functions under this Part of this Act of the managers of hospitals, local social services authorities, Local Health Board, Special Health Authorities, Primary Care Trusts, National Health Service trusts or NHS foundation trusts are to be exercised, and such regulations may in particular specify the circumstances in which, and the conditions subject to which, any such functions may be performed by officers of or other persons acting on behalf of those managers, boards, authorities and trusts.

[*Words deleted in subsection (2)(c) by Part 5 of Schedule 11 to the 2007 Act; words inserted into that same paragraph by paragraph 15 of Schedule 3. Words inserted in subsection (3) by section 45(2).*]

33 Special provisions as to wards of court

(1) An application for the admission to hospital of a minor who is a ward of court may be made under this Part of this Act with the leave of the court; and section 11(4) above shall not apply in relation to an application so made.

(2) Where a minor who is a ward of court is liable to be detained in a hospital by virtue of an application for admission under this Part of this Act [or is a community patient], any power exercisable under this Part of this Act or under section 66 below in relation to the patient by his nearest relative shall be exercisable by or with the leave of the court.

(3) Nothing in this Part of this Act shall be construed as authorising the making of a guardianship application in respect of a minor who is a ward of court, or the transfer into guardianship of any such minor.

(4) Where a supervision application has been made in respect of a minor who is a ward of court, the provisions of this Part of this Act relating to after-care under supervision have effect in relation to the minor subject to any order which the court may make in the exercise of its wardship jurisdiction.

[(4) Where a community treatment order has been made in respect of a minor who is a ward of court, the provisions of this Part of this Act relating to community treatment orders and community patients have effect in relation to the minor subject to any order which the court makes in the exercise of its wardship jurisdiction; but this does not apply as regards any period when the minor is recalled to hospital under section 17E above].

[Words in subsection (2) inserted by paragraph 16(2) of Schedule 3 to the 2007 Act; subsection (4) substituted by paragraph 16(3) of that Schedule].

34 Interpretation of Part II

(1) In this Part of this Act—

['the appropriate practitioner' means—

(a) in the case of a patient who is subject to the guardianship of a person other than a local social services authority, the nominated medical attendant of the patient; and

(b) in any other case, the responsible clinician;]

'the community responsible medical officer', in relation to a patient subject to after-care under supervision, means the person who, in accordance with section 117(2A)(a) below, is in charge of medical treatment provided for him;

'the nominated medical attendant', in relation to a patient who is subject to the guardianship of a person other than a local social services authority, means the person appointed in pursuance of regulations made under section 9(2) above to act as the medical attendant of the patient;

'registered establishment' means an establishment—

(a) which would not, apart from subsection (2) below, be a hospital for the purposes of this Part; and

(b) in respect of which a person is registered under Part II of the Care Standards Act 2000 as an independent hospital in which treatment or nursing (or both) are provided for persons liable to be detained under this Act;

'the responsible medical officer means (except in the phrase 'the community responsible medical officer')—

(a) in relation to a patient who is liable to be detained by virtue of an application for admission for assessment or an application for admission for treatment or who is to be subject to after-care under supervision after leaving hospital, the registered medical practitioner in charge of the treatment of the patient;

(b) in relation to a patient subject to guardianship, the medical officer authorised by the local social services authority to act (either generally or in any particular case or for any particular purpose) as the responsible medical officer.

['the responsible clinician' means—

(a) in relation to a patient liable to be detained by virtue of an application for admission for assessment or an application for admission for treatment, or a community patient, the approved clinician with overall responsibility for the patient's case;

(b) in relation to a patient subject to guardianship, the approved clinician authorised by the responsible local social services authority to act (either generally or in any particular case or for any particular purpose) as the responsible clinician;]

'the supervisor', in relation to a patient subject to after-care under supervision, means the person who, in accordance with section 117(2A)(b) below, is supervising him.

(1A) Nothing in this Act prevents the same person from acting as more than one of the following in relation to a patient, that is—

(a) the responsible medical officer;

(b) the community responsible medical officer; and

(c) the supervisor.

(2) Except where otherwise expressly provided, this Part of this Act applies in relation to a registered establishment, as it applies in relation to a hospital, and references in this Part of this Act to a hospital, and any reference in this Act to a hospital to which this Part of this Act applies, shall be construed accordingly.

(3) In relation to a patient who is subject to guardianship in pursuance of a guardianship application, any reference in this Part of this Act to the responsible local social services authority is a reference—

(a) where the patient is subject to the guardianship of a local social services authority, to that authority;

(b) where the patient is subject to the guardianship of a person other than a local social services authority, to the local social services authority for the area in which that person resides.

[*Definition of 'appropriate practitioner' inserted in subsection (1) by section 9(9) of the 2007 Act; definition of 'community responsible medical officer' repealed by Part 5 of Schedule 11; definition of 'responsible clinician' substituted for that of 'responsible medical officer' by section 9(10); definition of 'supervisor' and whole of subsection (1A) repealed by Part 5 of Schedule 11.*]

PART III
PATIENTS CONCERNED IN CRIMINAL PROCEEDINGS
OR UNDER SENTENCE

Remands to hospital

35 Remand to hospital for report on accused's mental condition

(1) Subject to the provisions of this section, the Crown Court or a magistrates' court may remand an accused person to a hospital specified by the court for a report on his mental condition.

(2) For the purposes of this section an accused person is—

(a) in relation to the Crown Court, any person who is awaiting trial before the court for an offence punishable with imprisonment or who has been arraigned before the court for such an offence and has not yet been sentenced or otherwise dealt with for the offence on which he has been arraigned;

(b) in relation to a magistrates' court, any person who has been convicted by the court of an offence punishable on summary conviction with imprisonment and any person charged with such an offence if the court is satisfied that he did the act or made the omission charged or he has consented to the exercise by the court of the powers conferred by this section.

(3) Subject to subsection (4) below, the powers conferred by this section may be exercised if—

(a) the court is satisfied, on the written or oral evidence of a registered medical practitioner, that there is reason to suspect that the accused person is suffering from *mental illness, psychopathic disorder, severe mental impairment or mental impairment* [mental disorder]; and

(b) the court is of the opinion that it would be impracticable for a report on his mental condition to be made if he were remanded on bail;

but those powers shall not be exercised by the Crown Court in respect of a person who has been convicted before the court if the sentence for the offence of which he has been convicted is fixed by law.

(4) The court shall not remand an accused person to a hospital under this section unless satisfied, on the written or oral evidence of the *registered medical practitioner* [approved clinician] who would be responsible for making the report or of some other person representing the managers of the hospital, that arrangements have been made for his admission to that hospital and for his admission to it within the period of seven days beginning with the date of the remand; and if the court is so satisfied it may, pending his admission, give directions for his conveyance to and detention in a place of safety.

(5) Where a court has remanded an accused person under this section it may further remand him if it appears to the court, on the written or oral evidence of the *registered medical practitioner* [approved clinician] responsible for making the report, that a further remand is necessary for completing the assessment of the accused person's mental condition.

(6) The power of further remanding an accused person under this section may be exercised by the court without his being brought before the court if he is represented by counsel or a solicitor and his counsel or solicitor is given an opportunity of being heard.

(7) An accused person shall not be remanded or further remanded under this section for more than 28 days at a time or for more than 12 weeks in all; and the court may at any time terminate the remand if it appears to the court that it is appropriate to do so.

(8) An accused person remanded to hospital under this section shall be entitled to obtain at his own expense an independent report on his mental condition from a registered medical practitioner [or approved clinician] chosen by him and to apply to the court on the basis of it for his remand to be terminated under subsection (7) above.

(9) Where an accused person is remanded under this section—

(a) a constable or any other person directed to do so by the court shall convey the accused person to the hospital specified by the court within the period mentioned in subsection (4) above; and

(b) the managers of the hospital shall admit him within that period and thereafter detain him in accordance with the provisions of this section.

(10) If an accused person absconds from a hospital to which he has been remanded under this section, or while being conveyed to or from that hospital, he may be arrested without warrant by any constable and shall, after being arrested, be brought as soon as practicable before the court that remanded him; and the court may thereupon terminate the remand and deal with him in any way in which it could have dealt with him if he had not been remanded under this section.

[*Words in subsection (3)(a) substituted by paragraph 5 of Schedule 1 to the 2007 Act; words substituted in subsections (4) & (5) by section 10(2)(a); and words inserted in subsection (8) by section 10(2)(b).*]

36 Remand of accused person to hospital for treatment

(1) Subject to the provisions of this section, the Crown Court may, instead of remanding an accused person in custody, remand him to a hospital specified by the court if satisfied, on the written or oral evidence of two registered medical practitioners, that *he is suffering from mental*

illness or severe mental impairment of a nature or degree which makes it appropriate for him to be detained in a hospital for medical treatment

[(a) he is suffering from mental disorder of a nature or degree which makes it appropriate for him to be detained in a hospital for medical treatment; and

(b) appropriate medical treatment is available for him.]

(2) For the purposes of this section an accused person is any person who is in custody awaiting trial before the Crown Court for an offence punishable with imprisonment (other than an offence the sentence for which is fixed by law) or who at any time before sentence is in custody in the course of a trial before that court for such an offence.

(3) The court shall not remand an accused person under this section to a hospital unless it is satisfied, on the written or oral evidence of the *registered medical practitioner who would be in charge of his treatment* [approved clinician who would have overall responsibility for his case] or of some other person representing the managers of the hospital, that arrangements have been made for his admission to that hospital and for his admission to it within the period of seven days beginning with the date of the remand; and if the court is so satisfied it may, pending his admission, give directions for his conveyance to and detention in a place of safety.

(4) Where a court has remanded an accused person under this section it may further remand him if it appears to the court, on the written or oral evidence of the *responsible medical officer* [responsible clinician], that a further remand is warranted.

(5) The power of further remanding an accused person under this section may be exercised by the court without his being brought before the court if he is represented by counsel or a solicitor and his counsel or solicitor is given an opportunity of being heard.

(6) An accused person shall not be remanded or further remanded under this section for more than 28 days at a time or for more than 12 weeks in all; and the court may at any time terminate the remand if it appears to the court that it is appropriate to do so.

(7) An accused person remanded to hospital under this section shall be entitled to obtain at his own expense an independent report on his mental condition from a registered medical practitioner [or approved clinician] chosen by him and to apply to the court on the basis of it for his remand to be terminated under subsection (6) above.

(8) Subsections (9) and (10) of section 35 above shall have effect in relation to a remand under this section as they have effect in relation to a remand under that section.

[Subsection (1)(a) substituted for words above it by paragraph 6 of Schedule 1 to the 2007 Act; paragraph (b) (and the word 'and' before it) inserted into subsection (1) by section 5(2). Words substituted in subsections (3) and (4) and words inserted in subsection (7) by section 10(3)(a) to (c) respectively.]

Hospital and guardianship orders

37 Powers of courts to order hospital admission or guardianship

(1) Where a person is convicted before the Crown Court of an offence punishable with imprisonment other than an offence the sentence for which is fixed by law, or is convicted by a magistrates' court of an offence punishable on summary conviction with imprisonment, and the conditions mentioned in subsection (2) below are satisfied, the court may by order authorise his admission to and detention in such hospital as may be specified in the order or, as the case may be, place him under the guardianship of a local social services authority or of such other person approved by a local social services authority as may be so specified.

(1A) In the case of an offence the sentence for which would otherwise fall to be imposed—
  (a) under section 51A(2) of the Firearms Act 1968,
  (b) under section 110(2) or 111(2) of the Powers of Criminal Courts (Sentencing) Act 2000
  (c) under any of sections 225 to 228 of the Criminal Justice Act 2003, or
  (d) under section 29(4) or (6) of the Violent Crime Reduction Act 2006 (minimum sentences in certain cases of using someone to mind a weapon),
nothing in those provisions shall prevent a court from making an order under subsection (1) above for the admission of the offender to a hospital.

(1B) References in subsection (1A) above to a sentence falling to be imposed under any of the provisions mentioned in that subsection are to be read in accordance with section 305(4) of the Criminal Justice Act 2003.

(2) The conditions referred to in subsection (1) above are that—
  (a) the court is satisfied, on the written or oral evidence of two registered medical practitioners, that the offender is suffering from *mental illness, psychopathic disorder, severe mental impairment or mental impairment* [mental disorder] and that either—
    (i) the mental disorder from which the offender is suffering is of a nature or degree which makes it appropriate for him to be detained in a hospital for medical treatment and, *in the case of psychopathic disorder or mental impairment, that such treatment is likely to alleviate or prevent a deterioration of his condition; or* [appropriate medical treatment is available for him; or]
    (ii) in the case of an offender who has attained the age of 16 years, the mental disorder is of a nature or degree which warrants his reception into guardianship under this Act; and
  (b) the court is of the opinion, having regard to all the circumstances including the nature of the offence and the character and antecedents of the offender, and to the other available methods of dealing with him, that the most suitable method of disposing of the case is by means of an order under this section.

(3) Where a person is charged before a magistrates' court with any act or omission as an offence and the court would have power, on convicting him of that offence, to make an order under subsection (1) above in his case *as being a person suffering from mental illness or severe mental impairment*, then, if the court is satisfied that the accused did the act or made the omission charged, the court may, if it thinks fit, make such an order without convicting him.

(4) An order for the admission of an offender to a hospital (in this Act referred to as 'a hospital order') shall not be made under this section unless the court is satisfied on the written or oral evidence of the *registered medical practitioner who would be in charge of his treatment* [approved clinician who would have overall responsibility for his case] or of some other person representing the managers of the hospital that arrangements have been made for his admission to that hospital, and for his admission to it within the period of 28 days beginning with the date of the making of such an order; and the court may, pending his admission within that period, give such directions as it thinks fit for his conveyance to and detention in a place of safety.

(5) If within the said period of 28 days it appears to the Secretary of State that by reason of an emergency or other special circumstances it is not practicable for the patient to be received into the hospital specified in the order, he may give directions for the admission of the patient to such other hospital as appears to be appropriate instead of the hospital so specified; and where such directions are given—
  (a) the Secretary of State shall cause the person having the custody of the patient to be informed, and

(b) the hospital order shall have effect as if the hospital specified in the directions were substituted for the hospital specified in the order.

(6) An order placing an offender under the guardianship of a local social services authority or of any other person (in this Act referred to as 'a guardianship order') shall not be made under this section unless the court is satisfied that that authority or person is willing to receive the offender into guardianship.

(7) *A hospital order or guardianship order shall specify the form or forms of mental disorder referred to in subsection (2)(a) above from which, upon the evidence taken into account under that subsection, the offender is found by the court to be suffering; and no such order shall be made unless the offender is described by each of the practitioners whose evidence is taken into account under that subsection as suffering from the same one of those forms of mental disorder, whether or not he is also described by either of them as suffering from another of them.*

(8) Where an order is made under this section, the court shall not—

(a) pass sentence of imprisonment or impose a fine or make a community order (within the meaning of Part 12 of the Criminal Justice Act 2003) in respect of the offence,

(b) if the order under this section is a hospital order, make a referral order (within the meaning of the Powers of Criminal Courts (Sentencing) Act 2000) in respect of the offence, or

(c) make in respect of the offender a supervision order (within the meaning of that Act) or an order under section 150 of that Act (binding over of parent or guardian),

but the court may make any other order which it has power to make apart from this section; and for the purposes of this subsection 'sentence of imprisonment' includes any sentence or order for detention.

[*Words in opening part of subsection 2(a) substituted by paragraph 7(a) of Schedule 1 to the 2007 Act; words in paragraph (i) of that subsection substituted by section 4(5); words omitted from subsection (3) by paragraph 7(b) of Schedule 1; words substituted in subsection (4) by section 10(4); subsection (7) repealed by Part 1 of Schedule 11.*]

38 Interim hospital orders

(1) Where a person is convicted before the Crown Court of an offence punishable with imprisonment (other than an offence the sentence for which is fixed by law) or is convicted by a magistrates' court of an offence punishable on summary conviction with imprisonment and the court before or by which he is convicted is satisfied, on the written or oral evidence of two registered medical practitioners—

(a) that the offender is suffering *from mental illness, psychopathic disorder, severe mental impairment or mental impairment* [mental disorder]; and

(b) that there is reason to suppose that the mental disorder from which the offender is suffering is such that it may be appropriate for a hospital order to be made in his case,

the court may, before making a hospital order or dealing with him in some other way, make an order (in this Act referred to as 'an interim hospital order') authorising his admission to such hospital as may be specified in the order and his detention there in accordance with this section.

(2) In the case of an offender who is subject to an interim hospital order the court may make a hospital order without his being brought before the court if he is represented by counsel or a solicitor and his counsel or solicitor is given an opportunity of being heard.

(3) At least one of the registered medical practitioners whose evidence is taken into account under subsection (1) above shall be employed at the hospital which is to be specified in the order.

(4) An interim hospital order shall not be made for the admission of an offender to a hospital unless the court is satisfied, on the written or oral evidence of the *registered medical practitioner*

who would be in charge of his treatment [approved clinician who would have overall responsibility for his case] or of some other person representing the managers of the hospital, that arrangements have been made for his admission to that hospital and for his admission to it within the period of 28 days beginning with the date of the order; and if the court is so satisfied the court may, pending his admission, give directions for his conveyance to and detention in a place of safety.

(5) An interim hospital order—

    (a) shall be in force for such period, not exceeding 12 weeks, as the court may specify when making the order; but

    (b) may be renewed for further periods of not more than 28 days at a time if it appears to the court, on the written or oral evidence of the *responsible medical officer* [responsible clinician], that the continuation of the order is warranted;

but no such order shall continue in force for more than twelve months in all and the court shall terminate the order if it makes a hospital order in respect of the offender or decides after considering the written or oral evidence of the *responsible medical officer* [responsible clinician], to deal with the offender in some other way.

(6) The power of renewing an interim hospital order may be exercised without the offender being brought before the court if he is represented by counsel or a solicitor and his counsel or solicitor is given an opportunity of being heard.

(7) If an offender absconds from a hospital in which he is detained in pursuance of an interim hospital order, or while being conveyed to or from such a hospital, he may be arrested without warrant by a constable and shall, after being arrested, be brought as soon as practicable before the court that made the order; and the court may thereupon terminate the order and deal with him in any way in which it could have dealt with him if no such order had been made.

[*Words in subsection (1)(a) substituted by paragraph 8 of Schedule 1 to the 2007 Act; and words in subsection (4) and (5) substituted by section 10(5)(a) and (b) respectively.*]

39 Information as to hospitals

(1) Where a court is minded to make a hospital order or interim hospital order in respect of any person it may request—

    (a) the Primary Care Trust or Local Health Board for the area in which that person resides or last resided; or

    (b) the National Assembly for Wales or any other Primary Care Trust or Local Health Board that appears to the court to be appropriate,

to furnish the court with such information as that Primary Care Trust or Local Health Board or National Assembly for Wales have or can reasonably obtain with respect to the hospital or hospitals (if any) in their area or elsewhere at which arrangements could be made for the admission of that person in pursuance of the order, and that Primary Care Trust or Local Health Board National Assembly for Wales shall comply with any such request.

[(1A) In relation to a person who has not attained the age of 18 years, subsection (1) above shall have effect as if the reference to the making of a hospital order included a reference to a remand under section 35 or 36 above or the making of an order under section 44 below.

(1B) Where the person concerned has not attained the age of 18 years, the information which may be requested under subsection (1) above includes, in particular, information about the availability of accommodation or facilities designed so as to be specially suitable for patients who have not attained the age of 18 years.]

[Subsections (1A) and (1B) inserted by section 31(2) of the 2007 Act.]

39A Information to facilitate guardianship orders

Where a court is minded to make a guardianship order in respect of any offender, it may request the local social services authority for the area in which the offender resides or last resided, or any other local social services authority that appears to the court to be appropriate—

(a) to inform the court whether it or any other person approved by it is willing to receive the offender into guardianship; and

(b) if so, to give such information as it reasonably can about how it or the other person could be expected to exercise in relation to the offender the powers conferred by section 40(2) below;

and that authority shall comply with any such request.

40 Effect of hospital orders, guardianship orders and interim hospital orders

(1) A hospital order shall be sufficient authority—

(a) for a constable, an *approved social worker* [approved mental health professional] or any other person directed to do so by the court to convey the patient to the hospital specified in the order within a period of 28 days; and

(b) for the managers of the hospital to admit him at any time within that period and thereafter detain him in accordance with the provisions of this Act.

(2) A guardianship order shall confer on the authority or person named in the order as guardian the same powers as a guardianship application made and accepted under Part II of this Act.

(3) Where an interim hospital order is made in respect of an offender—

(a) a constable or any other person directed to do so by the court shall convey the offender to the hospital specified in the order within the period mentioned in section 38(4) above; and

(b) the managers of the hospital shall admit him within that period and thereafter detain him in accordance with the provisions of section 38 above.

(4) A patient who is admitted to a hospital in pursuance of a hospital order, or placed under guardianship by a guardianship order, shall, subject to the provisions of this subsection, be treated for the purposes of the provisions of this Act mentioned in Part I of Schedule 1 to this Act as if he had been so admitted or placed on the date of the order in pursuance of an application for admission for treatment or a guardianship application, as the case may be, duly made under Part II of this Act, but subject to any modifications of those provisions specified in that Part of that Schedule.

(5) Where a patient is admitted to a hospital in pursuance of a hospital order, or placed under guardianship by a guardianship order, any previous application, hospital order or guardianship order by virtue of which he was liable to be detained in a hospital or subject to guardianship shall cease to have effect; but if the first-mentioned order, or the conviction on which it was made, is quashed on appeal, this subsection shall not apply and section 22 above shall have effect as if during any period for which the patient was liable to be detained or subject to guardianship under the order, he had been detained in custody as mentioned in that section.

(6) Where—

(a) a patient admitted to a hospital in pursuance of a hospital order is absent without leave;

(b) a warrant to arrest him has been issued under section 72 of the Criminal Justice Act 1967; and

(c) he is held pursuant to the warrant in any country or territory other than the United Kingdom, any of the Channel Islands and the Isle of Man,

he shall be treated as having been taken into custody under section 18 above on first being so held.

[*Words in subsection (1)(a) substituted by paragraph 7(e) of Schedule 2 to the 2007 Act.*]

Restriction orders

41 Power of higher courts to restrict discharge from hospital

(1) Where a hospital order is made in respect of an offender by the Crown Court, and it appears to the court, having regard to the nature of the offence, the antecedents of the offender and the risk of his committing further offences if set at large, that it is necessary for the protection of the public from serious harm so to do, the court may, subject to the provisions of this section, further order that the offender shall be subject to the special restrictions set out in this section, *either without limit of time or during such period as may be specified in the order,* and an order under this section shall be known as 'a restriction order'.

(2) A restriction order shall not be made in the case of any person unless at least one of the registered medical practitioners whose evidence is taken into account by the court under section 37(2)(a) above has given evidence orally before the court.

(3) The special restrictions applicable to a patient in respect of whom a restriction order is in force are as follows—

(a) none of the provisions of Part II of this Act relating to the duration, renewal and expiration of authority for the detention of patients shall apply, and the patient shall continue to be liable to be detained by virtue of the relevant hospital order until he is duly discharged under the said Part II or absolutely discharged under section 42, 73, 74 or 75 below;

(aa) none of the provisions of Part II of this Act relating to *after-care under supervision* [community treatment orders and community patients] shall apply;

(b) no application shall be made to a Mental Health Review Tribunal in respect of a patient under section 66 or 69(1) below;

(c) the following powers shall be exercisable only with the consent of the Secretary of State, namely—

(i) power to grant leave of absence to the patient under section 17 above;

(ii) power to transfer the patient in pursuance of regulations under section 19 above or in pursuance of subsection (3) of that section; and

(iii) power to order the discharge of the patient under section 23 above;

and if leave of absence is granted under the said section 17 power to recall the patient under that section shall vest in the Secretary of State as well as the *responsible medical officer* [responsible clinician]; and

(d) the power of the Secretary of State to recall the patient under the said section 17 and power to take the patient into custody and return him under section 18 above may be exercised at any time;

and in relation to any such patient section 40(4) above shall have effect as if it referred to Part II of Schedule 1 to this Act instead of Part I of that Schedule.

(4) A hospital order shall not cease to have effect under section 40(5) above if a restriction order in respect of the patient is in force at the material time.

(5) Where a restriction order in respect of a patient ceases to have effect while the relevant hospital order continues in force, the provisions of section 40 above and Part I of Schedule 1 to this Act shall apply to the patient as if he had been admitted to the hospital in pursuance of

a hospital order (without a restriction order) made on the date on which the restriction order ceased to have effect.

(6) While a person is subject to a restriction order the *responsible medical officer* [responsible clinician] shall at such intervals (not exceeding one year) as the Secretary of State may direct examine and report to the Secretary of State on that person; and every report shall contain such particulars as the Secretary of State may require.

[*Words in subsection (1) omitted by section 40(1) of the 2007 Act; words in subsection (3)(aa) substituted by paragraph 17 of Schedule 3; and words in subsection (3)(c) and (6) substituted by section 10(6).*]

42 Powers of Secretary of State in respect of patients subject to restriction orders

(1) If the Secretary of State is satisfied that in the case of any patient a restriction order is no longer required for the protection of the public from serious harm, he may direct that the patient cease to be subject to the special restrictions set out in section 41(3) above; and where the Secretary of State so directs, the restriction order shall cease to have effect, and section 41(5) above shall apply accordingly.

(2) At any time while a restriction order is in force in respect of a patient, the Secretary of State may, if he thinks fit, by warrant discharge the patient from hospital, either absolutely or subject to conditions; and where a person is absolutely discharged under this subsection, he shall thereupon cease to be liable to be detained by virtue of the relevant hospital order, and the restriction order shall cease to have effect accordingly.

(3) The Secretary of State may at any time during the continuance in force of a restriction order in respect of a patient who has been conditionally discharged under subsection (2) above by warrant recall the patient to such hospital as may be specified in the warrant.

(4) Where a patient is recalled as mentioned in subsection (3) above—

   (a) if the hospital specified in the warrant is not the hospital from which the patient was conditionally discharged, the hospital order and the restriction order shall have effect as if the hospital specified in the warrant were substituted for the hospital specified in the hospital order;

   (b) in any case, the patient shall be treated for the purposes of section 18 above as if he had absented himself without leave from the hospital specified in the warrant, *and, if the restriction order was made for a specified period, that period shall not in any event expire until the patient returns to the hospital or is returned to the hospital under that section.*

(5) If a restriction order in respect of a patient ceases to have effect after the patient has been conditionally discharged under this section, the patient shall, unless previously recalled under subsection (3) above, be deemed to be absolutely discharged on the date when the order ceases to have effect, and shall cease to be liable to be detained by virtue of the relevant hospital order accordingly.

(6) The Secretary of State may, if satisfied that the attendance at any place in Great Britain of a patient who is subject to a restriction order is desirable in the interests of justice or for the purposes of any public inquiry, direct him to be taken to that place; and where a patient is directed under this subsection to be taken to any place he shall, unless the Secretary of State otherwise directs, be kept in custody while being so taken, while at that place and while being taken back to the hospital in which he is liable to be detained.

[*Words in subsection (4)(b) omitted by section 40(2) of the 2007 Act.*]

43 Power of magistrates' courts to commit for restriction order

(1) If in the case of a person of or over the age of 14 years who is convicted by a magistrates' court of an offence punishable on summary conviction with imprisonment—

   (a) the conditions which under section 37(1) above are required to be satisfied for the making of a hospital order are satisfied in respect of the offender; but

   (b) it appears to the court, having regard to the nature of the offence, the antecedents of the offender and the risk of his committing further offences if set at large, that if a hospital order is made a restriction order should also be made,

   the court may, instead of making a hospital order or dealing with him in any other manner, commit him in custody to the Crown Court to be dealt with in respect of the offence.

(2) Where an offender is committed to the Crown Court under this section, the Crown Court shall inquire into the circumstances of the case and may—

   (a) if that court would have power so to do under the foregoing provisions of this Part of this Act upon the conviction of the offender before that court of such an offence as is described in section 37(1) above, make a hospital order in his case, with or without a restriction order;

   (b) if the court does not make such an order, deal with the offender in any other manner in which the magistrates' court might have dealt with him.

(3) The Crown Court shall have the same power to make orders under sections 35, 36 and 38 above in the case of a person committed to the court under this section as the Crown Court has under those sections in the case of an accused person within the meaning of section 35 or 36 above or of a person convicted before that court as mentioned in section 38 above.

(4) The powers of a magistrates' court under section 3 or 3B of the Powers of Criminal Courts (Sentencing) Act 2000 (which enable such a court to commit an offender to the Crown Court where the court is of the opinion, or it appears to the court, as mentioned in the section in question) shall also be exercisable by a magistrates' court where it is of that opinion (or it so appears to it) unless a hospital order is made in the offender's case with a restriction order.[1]

44 Committal to hospital under s 43

(1) Where an offender is committed under section 43(1) above and the magistrates' court by which he is committed is satisfied on written or oral evidence that arrangements have been made for the admission of the offender to a hospital in the event of an order being made under this section, the court may, instead of committing him in custody, by order direct him to be

---

[1] Subsection (4) is repealed and substituted by new subsections (4) and (5), by paragraph 55 of Schedule 2 to the Criminal Justice Act 2003. That substitution is not yet in force. When it is, subsections (4) and (5) will read:

   '(4) The power of a magistrates' court under section 3 of the Powers of Criminal Courts (Sentencing) Act 2000 (which enables such a court to commit an offender to the Crown Court where the court is of the opinion that greater punishment should be inflicted for the offence than the court has power to inflict) shall also be exercisable by a magistrates' court where it is of the opinion that greater punishment should be inflicted as aforesaid on the offender unless a hospital order is made in his case with a restriction order.

   (5) The power of the Crown Court to make a hospital order, with or without a restriction order, in the case of a person convicted before that court of an offence may, in the same circumstances and subject to the same conditions, be exercised by such a court in the case of a person committed to the court under section 5 of the Vagrancy Act 1824 (which provides for the committal to the Crown Court of persons who are incorrigible rogues within the meaning of that section).'

admitted to that hospital, specifying it, and to be detained there until the case is disposed of by the Crown Court, and may give such directions as it thinks fit for his production from the hospital to attend the Crown Court by which his case is to be dealt with.

(2) The evidence required by subsection (1) above shall be given by the *registered medical practitioner who would be in charge of the offender's treatment* [approved clinician who would have overall responsibility for the offender's case] or by some other person representing the managers of the hospital in question.

(3) The power to give directions under section 37(4) above, section 37(5) above and section 40(1) above shall apply in relation to an order under this section as they apply in relation to a hospital order, but as if references to the period of 28 days mentioned in section 40(1) above were omitted; and subject as aforesaid an order under this section shall, until the offender's case is disposed of by the Crown Court, have the same effect as a hospital order together with a restriction order, *made without limitation of time.*

[*Words in subsection (2) substituted by section 10(7) of the 2007 Act, and words omitted from subsection (3) by section 40(3)(a) (but see section 40(7) for saving provision in respect of that repeal.)*]

45 Appeals from magistrates' courts

(1) Where on the trial of an information charging a person with an offence a magistrates' court makes a hospital order or guardianship order in respect of him without convicting him, he shall have the same right of appeal against the order as if it had been made on his conviction; and on any such appeal the Crown Court shall have the same powers as if the appeal had been against both conviction and sentence.

(2) An appeal by a child or young person with respect to whom any such order has been made, whether the appeal is against the order or against the finding upon which the order was made, may be brought by him or by his parent or guardian on his behalf.

Hospital and limitation directions

45A Power of higher courts to direct hospital admission

(1) This section applies where, in the case of a person convicted before the Crown Court of an offence the sentence for which is not fixed by law—
  (a) the conditions mentioned in subsection (2) below are fulfilled; and
  (b) the court considers making a hospital order in respect of him before deciding to impose a sentence of imprisonment ('the relevant sentence') in respect of the offence.

(2) The conditions referred to in subsection (1) above are that the court is satisfied, on the written or oral evidence of two registered medical practitioners—
  (a) that the offender is suffering from *psychopathic disorder* [mental disorder];
  (b) that the mental disorder from which the offender is suffering is of a nature or degree which makes it appropriate for him to be detained in a hospital for medical treatment; and
  (c) *that such treatment is likely to alleviate or prevent a deterioration of his condition.*
  [(c) that appropriate medical treatment is available for him.]

(3) The court may give both of the following directions, namely—
  (a) a direction that, instead of being removed to and detained in a prison, the offender be removed to and detained in such hospital as may be specified in the direction (in this Act referred to as a 'hospital direction'); and

(b) a direction that the offender be subject to the special restrictions set out in section 41 above (in this Act referred to as a 'limitation direction').

(4) A hospital direction and a limitation direction shall not be given in relation to an offender unless at least one of the medical practitioners whose evidence is taken into account by the court under subsection (2) above has given evidence orally before the court.

(5) A hospital direction and a limitation direction shall not be given in relation to an offender unless the court is satisfied on the written or oral evidence of the *registered medical practitioner who would be in charge of his treatment* [approved clinician who would have overall responsibility for his case], or of some other person representing the managers of the hospital that arrangements have been made—

(a) for his admission to that hospital; and

(b) for his admission to it within the period of 28 days beginning with the day of the giving of such directions;

and the court may, pending his admission within that period, give such directions as it thinks fit for his conveyance to and detention in a place of safety.

(6) If within the said period of 28 days it appears to the Secretary of State that by reason of an emergency or other special circumstances it is not practicable for the patient to be received into the hospital specified in the hospital direction, he may give instructions for the admission of the patient to such other hospital as appears to be appropriate instead of the hospital so specified.

(7) Where such instructions are given—

(a) the Secretary of State shall cause the person having the custody of the patient to be informed, and

(b) the hospital direction shall have effect as if the hospital specified in the instructions were substituted for the hospital specified in the hospital direction.

(8) Section 38(1) and (5) and section 39 above shall have effect as if any reference to the making of a hospital order included a reference to the giving of a hospital direction and a limitation direction.

(9) A hospital direction and a limitation direction given in relation to an offender shall have effect not only as regards the relevant sentence but also (so far as applicable) as regards any other sentence of imprisonment imposed on the same or a previous occasion.

(10) The Secretary of State may by order provide that this section shall have effect as if the reference in subsection (2) above to psychopathic disorder included a reference to a mental disorder of such other description as may be specified in the order.

(11) An order made under this section may—

(a) apply generally, or in relation to such classes of offenders or offences as may be specified in the order;

(b) provide that any reference in this section to a sentence of imprisonment, or to a prison, shall include a reference to a custodial sentence, or to an institution, of such description as may be so specified; and

(c) include such supplementary, incidental or consequential provisions as appear to the Secretary of State to be necessary or expedient.

[*Words in subsection (2)(a) substituted by paragraph 9 of Schedule 1 to the 2007 Act; paragraph (c) of that subsection substituted by section 4(6); words in subsection (5) substituted by section 10(8); and subsections (10) and (11) repealed by Part 1 of Schedule 11.*]

45B Effect of hospital and limitation directions

(1) A hospital direction and a limitation direction shall be sufficient authority—

   (a) for a constable or any other person directed to do so by the court to convey the patient to the hospital specified in the hospital direction within a period of 28 days; and

   (b) for the managers of the hospital to admit him at any time within that period and thereafter detain him in accordance with the provisions of this Act.

(2) With respect to any person—

   (a) a hospital direction shall have effect as a transfer direction; and

   (b) a limitation direction shall have effect as a restriction direction.

(3) While a person is subject to a hospital direction and a limitation direction the *responsible medical officer* [responsible clinician] shall at such intervals (not exceeding one year) as the Secretary of State may direct examine and report to the Secretary of State on that person; and every report shall contain such particulars as the Secretary of State may require.

[*Words in subsection (3) substituted by section 10(9)(a) of the 2007 Act.*]

Transfer to hospital of prisoners etc

47 Removal to hospital of persons serving sentences of imprisonment, etc

(1) If in the case of a person serving a sentence of imprisonment the Secretary of State is satisfied, by reports from at least two registered medical practitioners—

   (a) that the said person is suffering from *mental illness, psychopathic disorder, severe mental impairment or mental impairment* [mental disorder]; and

   (b) that the mental disorder from which that person is suffering is of a nature or degree which makes it appropriate for him to be detained in a hospital for medical treatment *and, in the case of psychopathic disorder or mental impairment, that such treatment is likely to alleviate or prevent a deterioration of his condition* [; and

   (c) that appropriate medical treatment is available for him;]

   the Secretary of State may, if he is of the opinion having regard to the public interest and all the circumstances that it is expedient so to do, by warrant direct that that person be removed to and detained in such hospital as may be specified in the direction; and a direction under this section shall be known as 'a transfer direction'.

(2) A transfer direction shall cease to have effect at the expiration of the period of 14 days beginning with the date on which it is given unless within that period the person with respect to whom it was given has been received into the hospital specified in the direction.

(3) A transfer direction with respect to any person shall have the same effect as a hospital order made in his case.

(4) *A transfer direction shall specify the form or forms of mental disorder referred to in paragraph (a) of subsection (1) above from which, upon the reports taken into account under that subsection, the patient is found by the Secretary of State to be suffering; and no such direction shall be given unless the patient is described in each of those reports as suffering from the same form of disorder, whether or not he is also described in either of them as suffering from another form.*

(5) References in this Part of this Act to a person serving a sentence of imprisonment include references—

   (a) to a person detained in pursuance of any sentence or order for detention made by a court in criminal proceedings or service disciplinary proceedings (other than an order made in consequence of a finding of insanity or unfitness to stand trial or a sentence of service detention within the meaning of the Armed Forces Act 2006);[2]

(b) to a person committed to custody under section 115(3) of the Magistrates' Courts Act 1980 (which relates to persons who fail to comply with an order to enter into recognisances to keep the peace or be of good behaviour); and

(c) to a person committed by a court to a prison or other institution to which the Prison Act 1952 applies in default of payment of any sum adjudged to be paid on his conviction.

(6) In subsection (5)(a) 'service disciplinary proceedings' means proceedings in respect of a service offence within the meaning of the Armed Forces Act 2006.[3]

[*Words in subsection (1)(a) substituted by paragraph 10 of Schedule 1 to the 2007 Act; words omitted from paragraph (b), and paragraph (c) (and the word 'and' before it) inserted into that subsection by section 4(7); subsection (4) repealed by Part 1 of Schedule 11.*]

48 Removal to hospital of other prisoners

(1) If in the case of a person to whom this section applies the Secretary of State is satisfied by the same reports as are required for the purposes of section 47 above *that that person is suffering from mental illness or severe mental impairment of a nature or degree which makes it appropriate for him to be detained in a hospital for medical treatment and that he is in urgent need of such treatment,*

[(a) that person is suffering from mental disorder of a nature or degree which makes it appropriate for him to be detained in hospital for medical treatment; and

(b) he is in urgent need of such treatment; and

(c) appropriate medical treatment is available for him];

the Secretary of State shall have the same power of giving a transfer direction in respect of him under that section as if he were serving a sentence of imprisonment.

(2) This section applies to the following persons, that is to say—

(a) persons detained in a prison[4], not being person serving a sentence of imprisonment or persons falling within the following paragraphs of this subsection;

(b) persons remanded in custody by a magistrates' court;

(c) civil prisoners, that is to say, persons committed by a court to prison for a limited term, who are not persons falling to be dealt with under section 47 above;

(d) persons detained under the Immigration Act 1971 or under section 62 of the Nationality, Immigration and Asylum Act 2002 (detention by Secretary of State).

(3) Subsections (2) *to (4)* [and (3)] of section 47 above shall apply for the purposes of this section and of any transfer direction given by virtue of this section as they apply for the purposes of that section and of any transfer direction under that section.

[*Paragraphs (a) & (b) substituted for words omitted from subsection (1) by paragraph 11(a) of Schedule 1 to the 2007 Act; paragraph (c) (and the word 'and' before it) inserted into that subsection by section 5(3); and words substituted in subsection (3) by paragraph 11(b) of Schedule 1.*]

---

[2] Reference to service disciplinary hearings and sentences of service detention added by Schedule 16 to the Armed Forces Act 2006, but not yet in force.

[3] Subsection (6) inserted by Schedule 16 to the Armed Forces Act 2006, but not yet in force.

[4] Words 'or remand centre' omitted by paragraph 73 of Part 2of Schedule 7 to the Criminal Justice and Courts Service Act 2000, but that omission is not yet in force.

49 Restriction on discharge of prisoners removed to hospital

(1) Where a transfer direction is given in respect of any person, the Secretary of State, if he thinks fit, may by warrant further direct that that person shall be subject to the special restrictions set out in section 41 above; and where the Secretary of State gives a transfer direction in respect of any such person as is described in paragraph (a) or (b) of section 48(2) above, he shall also give a direction under this section applying those restrictions to him.

(2) A direction under this section shall have the same effect as a restriction order made under section 41 above and shall be known as 'a restriction direction'.

(3) While a person is subject to a restriction direction the *responsible medical officer* [responsible clinician] shall at such intervals (not exceeding one year) as the Secretary of State may direct examine and report to the Secretary of State on that person; and every report shall contain such particulars as the Secretary of State may require.

[*Words in subsection (3) substituted by section 10(9)(b).*]

50 Further provisions as to prisoners under sentence

(1) Where a transfer direction and a restriction direction have been given in respect of a person serving a sentence of imprisonment and before his release date the Secretary of State is notified by the *responsible medical officer* [responsible clinician], any other *registered medical practitioner* [approved clinician] or a Mental Health Review Tribunal that that person no longer requires treatment in hospital for mental disorder or that no effective treatment for his disorder can be given in the hospital to which he has been removed, the Secretary of State may—

    (a) by warrant direct that he be remitted to any prison or other institution in which he might have been detained if he had not been removed to hospital, there to be dealt with as if he had not been so removed; or

    (b) exercise any power of releasing him on licence or discharging him under supervision which could have been exercisable if he had been remitted to such a prison or institution as aforesaid,

and on his arrival in the prison or other institution or, as the case may be, his release or discharge as aforesaid, the transfer direction and the restriction direction shall cease to have effect.

(2) A restriction direction in the case of a person serving a sentence of imprisonment shall cease to have effect, if it has not previously done so, on his release date.

(3) In this section, references to a person's release date are to the day (if any) on which he would be entitled to be released (whether unconditionally or on licence) from any prison or other institution in which he might have been detained if the transfer direction had not been given; and in determining that day there shall be disregarded—

    (a) any powers that would be exercisable by the Parole Board if he were detained in such a prison or other institution, and

    (b) any practice of the Secretary of State in relation to the early release under discretionary powers of persons detained in such a prison or other institution.

(4) For the purposes of section 49(2) of the Prison Act 1952 (which provides for discounting from the sentences of certain prisoners periods while they are unlawfully at large) a patient who, having been transferred in pursuance of a transfer direction from any such institution as is referred to in that section, is at large in circumstances in which he is liable to be taken into custody under any provision of this Act, shall be treated as unlawfully at large and absent from that institution.

(5) The preceding provisions of this section shall have effect as if—

    (a) the reference in subsection (1) to a transfer direction and a restriction direction having been given in respect of a person serving a sentence of imprisonment included a reference to a hospital direction and a limitation direction having been given in respect of a person sentenced to imprisonment;

    (b) the reference in subsection (2) to a restriction direction included a reference to a limitation direction; and

    (c) references in subsections (3) and (4) to a transfer direction included references to a hospital direction.

[Substitutions in subsection (1) made by section 11(2)(a)&(b) respectively of the 2007 Act.]

51 Further provisions as to detained persons

(1) This section has effect where a transfer direction has been given in respect of any such person as is described in paragraph (a) of section 48(2) above and that person is in this section referred to as 'the detainee'.

(2) The transfer direction shall cease to have effect when the detainee's case is disposed of by the court having jurisdiction to try or otherwise deal with him, but without prejudice to any power of that court to make a hospital order or other order under this Part of this Act in his case.

(3) If the Secretary of State is notified by the *responsible medical officer* [responsible clinician], any other *registered medical practitioner* [approved clinician] or a Mental Health Review Tribunal at any time before the detainee's case is disposed of by that court—

    (a) that the detainee no longer requires treatment in hospital for mental disorder; or

    (b) that no effective treatment for his disorder can be given at the hospital to which he has been removed,

the Secretary of State may by warrant direct that he be remitted to any place where he might have been detained if he had not been removed to hospital, there to be dealt with as if he had not been so removed, and on his arrival at the place to which he is so remitted the transfer direction shall cease to have effect.

(4) If (no direction having been given under subsection (3) above) the court having jurisdiction to try or otherwise deal with the detainee is satisfied on the written or oral evidence of the *responsible medical officer* [responsible clinician]—

    (a) that the detainee no longer requires treatment in hospital for mental disorder; or

    (b) that no effective treatment for his disorder can be given at the hospital to which he has been removed,

the court may order him to be remitted to any such place as is mentioned in subsection (3) above or, subject to section 25 of the Criminal Justice and Public Order Act 1994, released on bail and on his arrival at that place or, as the case may be, his release on bail the transfer direction shall cease to have effect.

(5) If (no direction or order having been given or made under subsection (3) or (4) above) it appears to the court having jurisdiction to try or otherwise deal with the detainee—

    (a) that it is impracticable or inappropriate to bring the detainee before the court; and

    (b) that the conditions set out in subsection (6) below are satisfied,

the court may make a hospital order (with or without a restriction order) in his case in his absence and, in the case of a person awaiting trial, without convicting him.

(6) A hospital order may be made in respect of a person under subsection (5) above if the court—

    (a) is satisfied, on the written or oral evidence of at least two registered medical practitioners, that; *the detainee is suffering from mental illness or severe mental impairment of a nature or degree which makes it appropriate for the patient to be detained in a hospital for medical treatment; and*

        [(i) the detainee is suffering from mental disorder of a nature or degree which makes it appropriate for the patient to be detained in a hospital for medical treatment;] [and

        (ii) appropriate medical treatments is available for him; and]

    (b) is of the opinion, after considering any depositions or other documents required to be sent to the proper officer of the court, that it is proper to make such an order.

(7) Where a person committed to the Crown Court to be dealt with under section 43 above is admitted to a hospital in pursuance of an order under section 44 above, subsections (5) and (6) above shall apply as if he were a person subject to a transfer direction.

[*Substitutions in subsection (3) and (4) by section 11(3)(a)&(b) respectively of the 2007 Act; subsection (6)(a)(i) substituted for the words above it by paragraph 12 of Schedule 1; and sub-paragraph (ii) (and the word 'and' before it) inserted by section 5(4).*]

52 Further provisions as to persons remanded by magistrates' courts

(1) This section has effect where a transfer direction has been given in respect of any such person as is described in paragraph (b) of section 48(2) above; and that person is in this section referred to as 'the accused'.

(2) Subject to subsection (5) below, the transfer direction shall cease to have effect on the expiration of the period of remand unless the accused is sent in custody to the Crown Court for trial or to be otherwise dealt with.

(3) Subject to subsection (4) below, the power of further remanding the accused under section 128 of the Magistrates' Courts Act 1980 may be exercised by the court without his being brought before the court; and if the court further remands the accused in custody (whether or not he is brought before the court) the period of remand shall, for the purposes of this section, be deemed not to have expired.

(4) The court shall not under subsection (3) above further remand the accused in his absence unless he has appeared before the court within the previous six months.

(5) If the magistrates' court is satisfied, on the written or oral evidence of the *responsible medical officer* [responsible clinician]—

    (a) that the accused no longer requires treatment in hospital for mental disorder; or

    (b) that no effective treatment for his disorder can be given in the hospital to which he has been removed,

the court may direct that the transfer direction shall cease to have effect notwithstanding that the period of remand has not expired or that the accused is sent to the Crown Court as mentioned in subsection (2) above.

(6) If the accused is sent to the Crown Court as mentioned in subsection (2) above and the transfer direction has not ceased to have effect under subsection (5) above, section 51 above shall apply as if the transfer direction given in his case were a direction given in respect of a person falling within that section.

(7) The magistrates' court may, in the absence of the accused, send him to the Crown Court for trial under section 51 or 51A of the Crime and Disorder Act 1998 if—

    (a) the court is satisfied, on the written or oral evidence of the *responsible medical officer* [responsible clinician], that the accused is unfit to take part in the proceedings; and

(b) the accused is represented by counsel or a solicitor.

[*Words substituted in subsection (5) and 7(a) by section 11(4) of the 2007 Act.*]

53 Further provisions as to civil prisoners and persons detained under the Immigration Acts

(1) Subject to subsection (2) below, a transfer direction given in respect of any such person as is described in paragraph (c) or (d) of section 48(2) above shall cease to have effect on the expiration of the period during which he would, but for his removal to hospital, be liable to be detained in the place from which he was removed.

(2) Where a transfer direction and a restriction direction have been given in respect of any such person as is mentioned in subsection (1) above, then, if the Secretary of State is notified by the *responsible medical officer* [responsible clinician], any other *registered medical practitioner* [approved clinician] or a Mental Health Review Tribunal at any time before the expiration of the period there mentioned—

(a) that that person no longer requires treatment in hospital for mental disorder; or

(b) that no effective treatment for his disorder can be given in the hospital to which he has been removed,

the Secretary of State may by warrant direct that he be remitted to any place where he might have been detained if he had not been removed to hospital, and on his arrival at the place to which he is so remitted the transfer direction and the restriction direction shall cease to have effect.

[*Substitutions in subsection (2) made by section 11(5)(a)&(b) respectively of the 2007 Act.*]

Supplemental

54 Requirements as to medical evidence

(1) The registered medical practitioner whose evidence is taken into account under section 35(3)(a) above and at least one of the registered medical practitioners whose evidence is taken into account under sections 36(1), 37(2)(a), 38(1), 45A(2) and 51(6)(a) above and whose reports are taken into account under sections 47(1) and 48(1) above shall be a practitioner approved for the purposes of section 12 above by the Secretary of State as having special experience in the diagnosis or treatment of mental disorder.

(2) *For the purposes of any provision of this Part of this Act under which a court may act on the written evidence of—*

(a) *a registered medical practitioner or a registered medical practitioner of any description; or*

(b) *a person representing the managers of a hospital,*

a report in writing purporting to be signed by a registered medical practitioner or a registered medical practitioner of such a description by a person representing the managers of a hospital may, subject to the provisions of this section, be received in evidence without proof of the signature of the practitioner or that person and without proof that he has the requisite qualifications or authority or is of the requisite description; but the court may require the signatory of any such report to be called to give oral evidence.

[(2) For the purposes of any provision of this Part of this Act under which a court may act on the written evidence of any person, a report in writing purporting to be signed by that person may, subject to the provisions of this section, be received in evidence without proof of the following—

(a) the signature of the person; or

(b) his having the requisite qualifications or approval or authority or being of the requisite description to give the report.]

[(2A) But the court may require the signatory of any such report to be called to give oral evidence.]

(3) Where, in pursuance of a direction of the court, any such report is tendered in evidence otherwise than by or on behalf of the person who is the subject of the report, then—

(a) if that person is represented by counsel or a solicitor, a copy of the report shall be given to his counsel or solicitor;

(b) if that person is not so represented, the substance of the report shall be disclosed to him or, where he is a child or young person, to his parent or guardian if present in court; and

(c) except where the report relates only to arrangements for his admission to a hospital, that person may require the signatory of the report to be called to give oral evidence, and evidence to rebut the evidence contained in the report may be called by or on behalf of that person.

[*Subsections (2) and (2A) substituted for current subsection (2) by section 11(6) of the 2007 Act.*]

54A Reduction of period for making hospital orders

(1) The Secretary of State may by order reduce the length of the periods mentioned in sections 37(4) and (5) and 38(4) above.

(2) An order under subsection (1) above may make such consequential amendments of sections 40(1) and 44(3) above as appear to the Secretary of State to be necessary or expedient.

55 Interpretation of Part III

(1) In this Part of this Act—

'child' and 'young person' have the same meaning as in the Children and Young Persons Act 1933;

'civil prisoner' has the meaning given to it by section 48(2)(c) above;

'guardian', in relation to a child or young person, has the same meaning as in the Children and Young Persons Act 1933;

'place of safety', in relation to a person who is not a child or young person, means any police station, prison or remand centre, or any hospital the managers of which are willing temporarily to receive him, and in relation to a child or young person has the same meaning as in the Children and Young Persons Act 1933;

'responsible medical officer', in relation to a person liable to be detained in a hospital within the meaning of Part II of this Act, means the registered medical practitioner in charge of the treatment of the patient.

['responsible clinician', in relation to a person liable to be detained in a hospital within the meaning of Part 2 of this Act, means the approved clinician with overall responsibility for the patient's case].

(2) Any reference in this Part of this Act to an offence punishable on summary conviction with imprisonment shall be construed without regard to any prohibition or restriction imposed by or under any enactment relating to the imprisonment of young offenders.

(3) *Where a patient who is liable to be detained in a hospital in pursuance of an order or direction under this Part of this Act is treated by virtue of any provision of this Part of this Act as if he had been admitted to the hospital in pursuance of a subsequent order or direction under this Part of this Act or a subsequent application for admission for treatment under Part II of this Act, he shall be treated as if the subsequent order, direction or application had described him as suffering from the form or forms of mental disorder specified in the earlier order or direction or, where he is treated as*

if he had been so admitted by virtue of a direction under section 42(1) above, such form of mental disorder as may be specified in the direction under that section.

(4) Any reference to a hospital order, a guardianship order or a restriction order in section 40(2), (4) or (5), section 41(3) to (5), or section 42 above or section 69(1) below shall be construed as including a reference to any order or direction under this Part of this Act having the same effect as the first-mentioned order; and the exceptions and modifications set out in Schedule 1 to this Act in respect of the provisions of this Act described in that Schedule accordingly include those which are consequential on the provisions of this subsection.

(5) Section 34(2) above shall apply for the purposes of this Part of this Act as it applies for the purposes of Part II of this Act.

(6) References in this Part of this Act to persons serving a sentence of imprisonment shall be construed in accordance with section 47(5) above.

(7) Section 99 of the Children and Young Persons Act 1933 (which relates to the presumption and determination of age) shall apply for the purposes of this Part of this Act as it applies for the purposes of that Act.

[*Definition of 'responsible clinician' substituted for that of 'responsible medical officer' in subsection (1) by section 11(7) of the 2007 Act. Subsection (3) repealed by Part 1 of Schedule 11.*]

PART IV. CONSENT TO TREATMENT

56 *Patients to whom Part IV applies*

(1) This Part of this Act applies to any patient liable to be detained under this Act except—

  (a) a patient who is liable to be detained by virtue of an emergency application and in respect of whom the second medical recommendation referred to in section 4(4)(a) above has not been given and received;

  (b) a patient who is liable to be detained by virtue of section 5(2) or (4) or 35 above or section 135 or 136 below or by virtue of a direction under section 37(4) above; and

  (c) a patient who has been conditionally discharged under section 42(2) above or section 73 or 74 below and has not been recalled to hospital.

(2) Section 57 and, so far as relevant to that section, sections 59, 60 and 62 below, apply also to any patient who is not liable to be detained under this Act.

[56 **Patients to whom Part 4 applies**]

[(1) Section 57 and, so far as relevant to that section, sections 59 to 62 below apply to any patient.

(2) Subject to that and to subsection (5) below, this Part of this Act applies to a patient only if he falls within subsection (3) or (4) below.

(3) A patient falls within this subsection if he is liable to be detained under this Act but not if—

  (a) he is so liable by virtue of an emergency application and the second medical recommendation referred to in section 4(4)(a) above has not been given and received;

  (b) he is so liable by virtue of section 5(2) or (4) or 35 above or section 135 or 136 below or by virtue of a direction for his detention in a place of safety under section 37(4) or 45A(5) above; or

  (c) he has been conditionally discharged under section 42(2) above or section 73 or 74 below and he is not recalled to hospital.

(4) A patient falls within this subsection if
  (a) he is a community patient; and
  (b) he is recalled to hospital under section 17E above.
(5) Section 58A and, so far as relevant to that section, sections 59 to 62 below also apply to any patient who—
  (a) does not fall within subsection (3) above;
  (b) is not a community patient; and
  (c) has not attained the age of 18 years.]

[*Section 56 substituted by section 34(2) of the 2007 Act.*]

57 Treatment requiring consent and a second opinion

(1) This section applies to the following forms of medical treatment for mental disorder—
  (a) any surgical operation for destroying brain tissue or for destroying the· functioning of brain tissue; and
  (b) such other forms of treatment as may be specified for the purposes of this section by regulations made by the Secretary of State.
(2) Subject to section 62 below, a patient shall not be given any form of treatment to which this section applies unless he has consented to it and—
  (a) a registered medical practitioner appointed for the purposes of this Part of this Act by the Secretary of State (not being the *responsible medical officer* [responsible clinician (if there is one) or the] [person in charge of the treatment in question]) and two other persons appointed for the purposes of this paragraph by the Secretary of State (not being registered medical practitioners) have certified in writing that the patient is capable of understanding the nature, purpose and likely effects of the treatment in question and has consented to it; and
  (b) the registered medical practitioner referred to in paragraph (a) above has certified in writing that, *having regard to the likelihood of the treatment alleviating or preventing a deterioration of the patient's condition, the treatment should be given* [it is appropriate for the treatment to be given.]
(3) Before giving a certificate under subsection (2)(b) above the registered medical practitioner concerned shall consult two other persons who have been professionally concerned with the patient's medical treatment *and of those persons one shall be a nurse and the other shall be neither a nurse nor a registered medical practitioner* [but of those persons—
  (a) one shall be a nurse and the other shall be neither a nurse nor a registered medical practitioner; and
  (b) neither shall be the responsible clinician (if there is one) or the person in charge of the treatment in question].
(4) Before making any regulations for the purpose of this section the Secretary of State shall consult such bodies as appear to him to be concerned.

[*Words in subsection (2)(a) substituted by section 12(2)(a) of the 2007 Act; words in subsection (2)(b) substituted by section 6(2)(a); words in subsection (3) substituted by section 12(2)(b).*]

58 Treatment requiring consent or a second opinion

(1) This section applies to the following forms of medical treatment for mental disorder—
  (a) such forms of treatment as may be specified for the purposes of this section by regulations made by the Secretary of State;
  (b) the administration of medicine to a patient by any means (not being a form of treatment specified under paragraph (a) above or section 57 above [or section 58A(1)(b) below]) at

any time during a period for which he is liable to be detained as a patient to whom this Part of this Act applies if three months or more have elapsed since the first occasion in that period when medicine was administered to him by any means for his mental disorder.

(2) The Secretary of State may by order vary the length of the period mentioned in subsection (1)(b) above.

(3) Subject to section 62 below, a patient shall not be given any form of treatment to which this section applies unless—

    (a) he has consented to that treatment and either the *responsible medical officer* [approved clinician in charge of it] or a registered medical practitioner appointed for the purposes of this Part of this Act by the Secretary of State has certified in writing that the patient is capable of understanding its nature, purpose and likely effects and has consented to it;

    (b) a registered medical practitioner appointed as aforesaid (not being the *responsible medical officer* [responsible clinician or the approved clinician in charge of the treatment in question]) has certified in writing that the patient is not capable of understanding the nature, purpose and likely effects of that treatment or [being so capable] has not consented to it but that, *having regard to the likelihood of the treatment alleviating or preventing a deterioration of the patient's condition, the treatment should be given.* [it is appropriate for the treatment to be given.]

(4) Before giving a certificate under subsection (3)(b) above the registered medical practitioner concerned shall consult two other persons who have been professionally concerned with the patient's medical treatment, and of those persons one shall be a nurse *and the other shall be neither a nurse nor a registered medical practitioner* [but of those persons

    (a) one shall be a nurse and the other shall be neither a nurse nor a registered medical practitioner; and

    (b) neither shall be the responsible clinician or the person in charge of the treatment in question].

(5) Before making any regulations for the purposes of this section the Secretary of State shall consult such bodies as appear to him to be concerned.

[*Words inserted in subsection (1)(b) by section 28(2)(a) of the 2007 Act. The substitution in subsection (3)(a) and the first substitution in subsection (3)(b)made by section 12(3)(a); words 'being so capable' inserted in subsection 3(b) by section 28(2)(b); words substituted at end of subsection (3)(b) by section 6(2)(b); subsection (4) amended by section 12(3)(b).*]

[58A Electro-convulsive therapy, etc]

[(1) This section applies to the following forms of medical treatment for mental disorder—

    (a) electro-convulsive therapy; and

    (b) such other forms of treatment as may be specified for the purposes of this section by regulations made by the appropriate national authority.

(2) Subject to section 62 below, a patient shall be not be given any form of treatment to which this section applies unless he falls within subsection (3), (4) or (5) below.

(3) A patient falls within this subsection if—

    (a) he has attained the age of 18 years;

    (b) he has consented to the treatment in question; and

    (c) either the approved clinician in charge of it or a registered medical practitioner appointed as mentioned in section 58(3) above has certified in writing that the patient is capable of understanding the nature, purpose and likely effects of the treatment and has consented to it.

(4) A patient falls within this subsection if—
  (a) he has not attained the age of 18 years; but
  (b) he has consented to the treatment in question; and
  (c) a registered medical practitioner appointed as aforesaid (not being the approved clinician in charge of the treatment) has certified in writing—
    (i) that the patient is capable of understanding the nature, purpose and likely effects of the treatment and has consented to it; and
    (ii) that it is appropriate for the treatment to be given.
(5) A patient falls within this subsection if a registered medical practitioner appointed as aforesaid (not being the responsible clinician (if there is one) or the approved clinician in charge of the treatment in question) has certified in writing—
  (a) that the patient is not capable of understanding the nature, purpose and likely effects of the treatment; but
  (b) that it is appropriate for the treatment to be given; and
  (c) that giving him the treatment would not conflict with—
    (i) an advance decision which the registered medical practitioner concerned is satisfied is valid and applicable;
    (ii) a decision made by a donee or deputy or by the Court of Protection.
(6) Before giving a certificate under subsection (5) above the registered medical practitioner concerned shall consult two other persons who have been professionally concerned with the patient's medical treatment, but of those persons—
  (a) one shall be a nurse and the other shall be neither a nurse nor a registered medical practitioner; and
  (b) neither shall be the responsible clinician (if there is one) or the approved clinician in charge of the treatment in question.
(7) This section shall not by itself confer sufficient authority for a patient who falls within section 56(5) above to be given a form of treatment to which this section applies if he is not capable of understanding the nature, purpose and likely effects of the treatment (and cannot therefore consent to it).
(8) Before making any regulations for the purposes of this section, the appropriate national authority shall consult such bodies as appear to it to be concerned.
(9) In this section—
  (a) a reference to an advance decision is to an advance decision (within the meaning of the Mental Capacity Act 2005) made by the patient;
  (b) 'valid and applicable', in relation to such a decision, means valid and applicable to the treatment in question in accordance with section 25 of that Act;
  (c) a reference to a donee is to a donee of a lasting power of attorney (within the meaning of section 9 of that Act) created by the patient, where the donee is acting within the scope of his authority and in accordance with that Act; and
  (d) a reference to a deputy is to a deputy appointed for the patient by the Court of Protection under section 16 of that Act, where the deputy is acting within the scope of his authority and in accordance with that Act.
(10) In this section, 'the appropriate national authority' means—
  (a) in a case where the treatment in question would, if given, be given in England, the Secretary of State;
  (b) in a case where the treatment in question would, if given, be given in Wales, the Welsh Ministers.]

[*Section 58A inserted by section 27 of the 2007 Act.*]

59 Plans of treatment

Any consent or certificate under section 57 *or 58* [, 58 or 58A] above may relate to a plan of treatment under which the patient is to be given (whether within a specified period or otherwise) one or more of the forms of treatment to which that section applies.

[*Words substituted by section 28(3) of the 2007 Act.*]

60 Withdrawal of consent

(1) Where the consent of a patient to any treatment has been given for the purposes of section 57 *or 58* [, 58 or 58A] above, the patient may, subject to section 62 below, at any time before the completion of the treatment withdraw his consent, and those sections shall then apply as if the remainder of the treatment were a separate form of treatment.

[(1A) Subsection (1B) below applies where—
  (a) the consent of a patient to any treatment has been given for the purposes of section 57, 58 or 58A above; but
  (b) before the completion of the treatment, the patient ceases to be capable of understanding its nature, purpose and likely effects.

(1B) The patient shall, subject to section 62 below, be treated as having withdrawn his consent, and those sections shall then apply as if the remainder of the treatment were a separate form of treatment.

(1C) Subsection (1D) below applies where—
  (a) a certificate has been given under section 58 or 58A above that a patient is not capable of understanding the nature, purpose and likely effects of the treatment to which the certificate applies; but
  (b) before the completion of the treatment, the patient becomes capable of understanding its nature, purpose and likely effects.

(1D) The certificate shall, subject to section 62 below, cease to apply to the treatment and those sections shall then apply as if the remainder of the treatment were a separate form of treatment.]

(2) Without prejudice to the application of *subsection (1)* [subsections (1) to (1D)] above to any treatment given under the plan of treatment to which a patient has consented, a patient who has consented to such a plan may, subject to section 62 below, at any time withdraw his consent to further treatment, or to further treatment of any description, under the plan.

[*Words in subsection (1) substituted by section 28(4) of the 2007 Act. Subsections (1A) to (1D) inserted and words in subsection (2) substituted by section 29(2) & (3) respectively.*]

61 Review of treatment

(1) Where a patient is given treatment in accordance with section 57(2) *or 58(3)(b)* [, 58(3)(b) or 58A(4) or (5)] above[, or by virtue of section 62A below in accordance with a Part 4A certificate (within the meaning of that section),] a report on the treatment and the patient's condition shall be given *by the responsible medical officer* [by the approved clinician in charge of the treatment] to the Secretary of State—
  (a) on the next occasion on which the *responsible medical officer* [responsible clinician] furnishes a report under section 20(3) *or 21B(2) above renewing the authority for the detention* [, 20A(4) or 21B(2) above in respect] of the patient; and
  (b) at any other time if so required by the Secretary of State.

(2) In relation to a patient who is subject to a restriction order, limitation direction or restriction direction subsection (1) above shall have effect as if paragraph (a) required the report to be made—

(a) in the case of treatment in the period of six months beginning with the date of the order or direction, at the end of that period;

(b) in the case of treatment at any subsequent time, on the next occasion on which the *responsible medical officer* [responsible clinician] makes a report in respect of the patient under section 41(6), 45B(3) or 49(3) above.

(3) The Secretary of State may at any time give notice *to the responsible medical officer* directing that, subject to section 62 below, a certificate given in respect of a patient under section 57(2) *or 58 (3)(b)* [, or 58(3)(b) or 58A(4) or (5)] above shall not apply to treatment given to him after a date specified in the notice and sections 57 *and 58* [, 58 and 58A] above shall then apply to any such treatment as if that certificate had not been given.

[(3A) The notice under subsection (3) above shall be given to the approved clinician in charge of the treatment.]

[*Words substituted to insert references to section 58A in subsections (1) and (3) by section 28(5)(a)&(b) respectively of the 2007 Act; words 'or by virtue of section 62A . . . ' inserted into subsection (1) by section 34(3)(a); words substituted for phrases containing 'responsible medical officer' in subsections (1) & (2), and the words 'to the responsible medical officer' omitted from subsection (3) by section 12(4)(a) to (c) respectively; other substitution in paragraph (1)(b) made by section 34(3)(b). Subsection (3A) inserted by section 12(4)(d).*]

62 Urgent treatment

(1) Sections 57 and 58 above shall not apply to any treatment—

(a) which is immediately necessary to save the patient's life; or

(b) which (not being irreversible) is immediately necessary to prevent a serious deterioration of his condition; or

(c) which (not being irreversible or hazardous) is immediately necessary to alleviate serious suffering by the patient; or

(d) which (not being irreversible or hazardous) is immediately necessary and represents the minimum interference necessary to prevent the patient from behaving violently or being a danger to himself or to others.

[(1A) Section 58A above, in so far as it relates to electro-convulsive therapy by virtue of subsection (1)(a) of that section, shall not apply to any treatment which falls within paragraph (a) or (b) of subsection (1) above.

(1B) Section 58A above, in so far as it relates to a form of treatment specified by virtue of subsection (1)(b) of that section, shall not apply to any treatment which falls within such of paragraphs (a) to (d) of subsection (1) above as may be specified in regulations under that section.

(1C) For the purposes of subsection (1B) above, the regulations—

(a) may make different provision for different cases (and may, in particular, make different provision for different forms of treatment);

(b) may make provision which applies subject to specified exceptions; and

(c) may include transitional, consequential, incidental or supplemental provision.]

(2) Sections 60 and 61(3) above shall not preclude the continuation of any treatment or of treatment under any plan pending compliance with section 57 *and 58* [, 58 or 58A] above if the *responsible medical officer* [approved clinician in charge of the treatment] considers that the discontinuance of the treatment or of treatment under the plan would cause serious suffering to the patient.

(3) For the purposes of this section treatment is irreversible if it has unfavourable irreversible physical or psychological consequences and hazardous if it entails significant physical hazard.

[Subsections (1A) to (1C) inserted by section 28(6) of the 2007 Act. First substitution in subsection (2) made by section 28(7). Second substitution in subsection (2) made by section 12(5).]

[62A Treatment on recall of community patient or revocation of order]

[(1) This section applies where—
  (a) a community patient is recalled to hospital under section 17E above; or
  (b) a patient is liable to be detained under this Act following the revocation of a community treatment order under section 17F above in respect of him.

(2) For the purposes of section 58(1)(b) above, the patient is to be treated as if he had remained liable to be detained since the making of the community treatment order.

(3) But section 58 above does not apply to treatment given to the patient if—
  (a) the certificate requirement is met for the purposes of section 64C or 64E below; or
  (b) as a result of section 64B(4) or 64E(4) below, the certificate requirement would not apply (were the patient a community patient not recalled to hospital under section 17E above).

(4) Section 58A above does not apply to treatment given to the patient if there is authority to give the treatment, and the certificate requirement is met, for the purposes of section 64C or 64E below.

(5) In a case where this section applies, the certificate requirement is met only in so far as—
  (a) the Part 4A certificate expressly provides that it is appropriate for one or more specified forms of treatment to be given to the patient in that case (subject to such conditions as may be specified); or
  (b) a notice having been given under subsection (5) of section 64H below, treatment is authorised by virtue of subsection (8) of that section.

(6) Subsection (5)(a) above shall not preclude the continuation of any treatment, or of treatment under any plan, pending compliance with section 58 or 58A above if the approved clinician in charge of the treatment considers that the discontinuance of the treatment, or of the treatment under the plan, would cause serious suffering to the patient.

(7) In a case where subsection (1)(b) above applies, subsection (3) above only applies pending compliance with section 58 above.

(8) In subsection (5) above—
  'Part 4A certificate' has the meaning given in section 64H below; and
  'specified', in relation to a Part 4A certificate, means specified in the certificate.]

[Section 62A inserted by section 34(4) of the 2007 Act.]

63 Treatment not requiring consent

The consent of a patient shall not be required for any medical treatment given to him for the mental disorder from which he is suffering *not being treatment falling within ssection 57 of 58 above* [, not being a form of treatment to which section 57, 58 or 58A above applies,] if the treatment is given by or under the direction of *the responsible medical officer* [the approved clinician in charge of the treatment].

[First substitution made by section 28(8) of the 2007 Act. Second substitution made by section 12(6).]

64 Supplementary provisions for Part 4

(1) In this Part of this Act *'the responsible medical officer' means the registered medical practitioner in charge of the treatment* ['the responsible clinician' means the approved clinician with overall responsibility for the case] of the patient in question and 'hospital' includes a registered establishment.

[(1A) References in this Part of this Act to the approved clinician in charge of a patient's treatment shall, where the treatment in question is a form of treatment to which section 57 above applies, be construed as references to the person in charge of the treatment.

(1B) References in this Part of this Act to the approved clinician in charge of a patient's treatment shall, where the treatment in question is a form of treatment to which section 58A above applies and the patient falls within section 56(5) above, be construed as references to the person in charge of the treatment.

(1C) Regulations made by virtue of section 32(2)(d) above apply for the purposes of this Part as they apply for the purposes of Part 2 of this Act.]

(2) Any certificate for the purposes of this Part of this Act shall be in such form as may be prescribed by regulations made by the Secretary of State.

[(3) For the purposes of this Part of this Act, it is appropriate for treatment to be given to a patient if the treatment is appropriate in his case, taking into account the nature and degree of the mental disorder from which he is suffering and all other circumstances of his case.]

[*Words substituted in subsection (1) and subsection (1A) inserted by section 12(7)(a)&(b) respectively of the 2007 Act; subsections (1B) and (1C) inserted by section 28(9); and subsection (3) inserted by section 6(3).*]

[PART 4A
TREATMENT OF COMMUNITY PATIENTS NOT
RECALLED TO HOSPITAL]

[64A Meaning of 'relevant treatment']

[In this Part of this Act 'relevant treatment', in relation to a patient, means medical treatment which—

(a) is for the mental disorder from which the patient is suffering; and

(b) is not a form of treatment to which section 57 above applies.]

[*Section 64A inserted by section 35(1) of the 2007 Act.*]

[64B Adult community patients]

[(1) This section applies to the giving of relevant treatment to a community patient who—

(a) is not recalled to hospital under section 17E above; and

(b) has attained the age of 16 years.

(2) The treatment may not be given to the patient unless—

(a) there is authority to give it to him; and

(b) if it is section 58 type treatment or section 58A type treatment, the certificate requirement is met.

(3) But the certificate requirement does not apply if—

(a) giving the treatment to the patient is authorised in accordance with section 64G below; or

(b) the treatment is immediately necessary and—
    (i) the patient has capacity to consent to it and does consent to it; or
    (ii) a donee or deputy or the Court of Protection consents to the treatment on the patient's behalf.]

[(4) Nor does the certificate requirement apply in so far as the administration of medicine to the patient at any time during the period of one month beginning with the day on which the community treatment order is made is section 58 type treatment.

(5) The reference in subsection (4) above to the administration of medicine does not include any form of treatment specified under section 58(1)(a) above.

[*Section 64B inserted by section 35(1) of the 2007 Act.*]

[64C Section 64B: supplemental]

[(1) This section has effect for the purposes of section 64B above.

(2) There is authority to give treatment to a patient if—
    (a) he has capacity to consent to it and does consent to it;
    (b) a donee or deputy or the Court of Protection consents to it on his behalf; or
    (c) giving it to him is authorised in accordance with section 64D or 64G below.

(3) Relevant treatment is section 58 type treatment or section 58A type treatment if, at the time when it is given to the patient, section 58 or 58A (respectively) would have applied to it, had the patient remained liable to be detained at that time (rather than being a community patient).

(4) The certificate requirement is met in respect of treatment to be given to a patient if—
    (a) a registered medical practitioner appointed for the purposes of Part 4 of this Act (not being the responsible clinician or the person in charge of the treatment) has certified in writing that it is appropriate for the treatment to be given or for the treatment to be given subject to such conditions as may be specified in the certificate; and
    (b) if conditions are so specified, the conditions are satisfied.

(5) In a case where the treatment is section 58 type treatment, treatment is immediately necessary if—
    (a) it is immediately necessary to save the patient's life; or
    (b) it is immediately necessary to prevent a serious deterioration of the patient's condition and is not irreversible; or
    (c) it is immediately necessary to alleviate serious suffering by the patient and is not irreversible or hazardous; or
    (d) it is immediately necessary, represents the minimum interference necessary to prevent the patient from behaving violently or being a danger to himself or others and is not irreversible or hazardous.

(6) In a case where the treatment is section 58A type treatment by virtue of subsection (1)(a) of that section, treatment is immediately necessary if it falls within paragraph (a) or (b) of subsection (5) above.

(7) In a case where the treatment is section 58A type treatment by virtue of subsection (1)(b) of that section, treatment is immediately necessary if it falls within such of paragraphs (a) to (d) of subsection (5) above as may be specified in regulations under that section.

(8) For the purposes of subsection (7) above, the regulations—
    (a) may make different provision for different cases (and may, in particular, make different provision for different forms of treatment);
    (b) may make provision which applies subject to specified exceptions; and
    (c) may include transitional, consequential, incidental or supplemental provision.

(9) Subsection (3) of section 62 above applies for the purposes of this section as it applies for the purposes of that section.]

[Section 64C inserted by section 35(1) of the 2007 Act.]

[64D Adult community patients lacking capacity]

[(1) A person is authorised to give relevant treatment to a patient as mentioned in section 64C(2)(c) above if the conditions in subsections (2) to (6) below are met.

(2) The first condition is that, before giving the treatment, the person takes reasonable steps to establish whether the patient lacks capacity to consent to the treatment.

(3) The second condition is that, when giving the treatment, he reasonably believes that the patient lacks capacity to consent to it.

(4) The third condition is that—
  (a) he has no reason to believe that the patient objects to being given the treatment; or
  (b) he does have reason to believe that the patient so objects, but it is not necessary to use force against the patient in order to give the treatment.

(5) The fourth condition is that—
  (a) he is the person in charge of the treatment and an approved clinician;] [or
  (b) the treatment is given under the direction of that clinician.

(6) The fifth condition is that giving the treatment does not conflict with—
  (a) an advance decision which he is satisfied is valid and applicable; or
  (b) a decision made by a donee or deputy or the Court of Protection.

(7) In this section—
  (a) reference to an advance decision is to an advance decision (within the meaning of the Mental Capacity Act 2005) made by the patient; and
  (b) 'valid and applicable', in relation to such a decision, means valid and applicable to the treatment in question in accordance with section 25 of that Act.]

[Section 64D inserted by section 35(1) of the 2007 Act.]

[64E Child community patients]

[(1) This section applies to the giving of relevant treatment to a community patient who—
  (a) is not recalled to hospital under section 17E above; and
  (b) has not attained the age of 16 years.

(2) The treatment may not be given to the patient unless—
  (a) there is authority to give it to him; and
  (b) if it is section 58 type treatment or section 58A type treatment, the certificate requirement is met.

(3) But the certificate requirement does not apply if—
  (a) giving the treatment to the patient is authorised in accordance with section 64G below; or
  (b) in a case where the patient is competent to consent to the treatment and does consent to it, the treatment is immediately necessary.

(4) Nor does the certificate requirement apply in so far as the administration of medicine to the patient at any time during the period of one month beginning with the day on which the community treatment order is made is section 58 type treatment.

(5) The reference in subsection (4) above to the administration of medicine does not include any form of treatment specified under section 58(1)(a) above.

(6) For the purposes of subsection (2)(a) above, there is authority to give treatment to a patient if—

    (a) he is competent to consent to it and he does consent to it; or

    (b) giving it to him is authorised in accordance with section 64F or 64G below.

(7) Subsections (3) to (9) of section 64C above have effect for the purposes of this section as they have effect for the purposes of section 64B above.

(8) Regulations made by virtue of section 32(2)(d) above apply for the purposes of this section as they apply for the purposes of Part 2 of this Act.]

[Section 64E inserted by section 35(1) of the 2007 Act.]

[64F Child community patients lacking competence]

[(1) A person is authorised to give relevant treatment to a patient as mentioned in section 64E(6)(b) above if the conditions in subsections (2) to (5) below are met.

(2) The first condition is that, before giving the treatment, the person takes reasonable steps to establish whether the patient is competent to consent to the treatment.

(3) The second condition is that, when giving the treatment, he reasonably believes that the patient is not competent to consent to it.

(4) The third condition is that—

    (a) he has no reason to believe that the patient objects to being given the treatment; or

    (b) he does have reason to believe that the patient so objects, but it is not necessary to use force against the patient in order to give the treatment.

(5) The fourth condition is that—

    (a) he is the person in charge of the treatment and an approved clinician;] [or

    (b) the treatment is given under the direction of that clinician].

[Section 64F inserted by section 35(1) of the 2007 Act.]

[64G Emergency treatment for patients lacking capacity or competence]

[(1) A person is also authorised to give relevant treatment to a patient as mentioned in section 64C(2)(c) or 64E(6)(b) above if the conditions in subsections (2) to (4) below are met.

(2) The first condition is that, when giving the treatment, the person reasonably believes that the patient lacks capacity to consent to it or, as the case may be, is not competent to consent to it.

(3) The second condition is that the treatment is immediately necessary.

(4) The third condition is that if it is necessary to use force against the patient in order to give the treatment—

    (a) the treatment needs to be given in order to prevent harm to the patient; and

    (b) the use of such force is a proportionate response to the likelihood of the patient's suffering harm, and to the seriousness of that harm.

(5) Subject to subsections (6) to (8) below, treatment is immediately necessary if—

    (a) it is immediately necessary to save the patient's life; or

    (b) it is immediately necessary to prevent a serious deterioration of the patient's condition and is not irreversible; or

    (c) it is immediately necessary to alleviate serious suffering by the patient and is not irreversible or hazardous; or

    (d) it is immediately necessary, represents the minimum interference necessary to prevent the patient from behaving violently or being a danger to himself or others and is not irreversible or hazardous.

(6) Where the treatment is section 58A type treatment by virtue of subsection (1)(a) of that section, treatment is immediately necessary if it falls within paragraph (a) or (b) of subsection (5) above.

(7) Where the treatment is section 58A type treatment by virtue of subsection (1)(b) of that section, treatment is immediately necessary if it falls within such of paragraphs (a) to (d) of subsection (5) above as may be specified in regulations under section 58A above.

(8) For the purposes of subsection (7) above, the regulations—

(a) may make different provision for different cases (and may, in particular, make different provision for different forms of treatment);

(b) may make provision which applies subject to specified exceptions; and

(c) may include transitional, consequential, incidental or supplemental provision.

(9) Subsection (3) of section 62 above applies for the purposes of this section as it applies for the purposes of that section.]

[*Section 64G inserted by section 35(1) of the 2007 Act.*]

[64H Certificates: supplementary provisions]

[(1) A certificate under section 64B(2)(b) or 64E(2)(b) above (a 'Part 4A certificate') may relate to a plan of treatment under which the patient is to be given (whether within a specified period or otherwise) one or more forms of section 58 type treatment or section 58A type treatment.

(2) A Part 4A certificate shall be in such form as may be prescribed by regulations made by the appropriate national authority.

(3) Before giving a Part 4A certificate, the registered medical practitioner concerned shall consult two other persons who have been professionally concerned with the patient's medical treatment but, of those persons—

(a) at least one shall be a person who is not a registered medical practitioner; and

(b) neither shall be the patient's responsible clinician or the person in charge of the treatment in question.

(4) Where a patient is given treatment in accordance with a Part 4A certificate, a report on the treatment and the patient's condition shall be given by the person in charge of the treatment to the appropriate national authority if required by that authority.

(5) The appropriate national authority may at any time give notice directing that a Part 4A certificate shall not apply to treatment given to a patient after a date specified in the notice, and the relevant section shall then apply to any such treatment as if that certificate had not been given.

(6) The relevant section is—

(a) if the patient is not recalled to hospital in accordance with section 17E above, section 64B or 64E above;

(b) if the patient is so recalled or is liable to be detained under this Act following revocation of the community treatment order under section 17F above—

(i) section 58 above, in the case of section 58 type treatment;

(ii) section 58A above, in the case of section 58A type treatment;

(subject to section 62A(2) above).

(7) The notice under subsection (5) above shall be given to the person in charge of the treatment in question.

(8) Subsection (5) above shall not preclude the continuation of any treatment or of treatment under any plan pending compliance with the relevant section if the person in charge of the

treatment considers that the discontinuance of the treatment or of treatment under the plan would cause serious suffering to the patient.

(9) In this section, 'the appropriate national authority' means—

    (a) in relation to community patients in respect of whom the responsible hospital is in England, the Secretary of State;

    (b) in relation to community patients in respect of whom the responsible hospital is in Wales, the Welsh Ministers.]

[Section 64H inserted by section 35(1) of the 2007 Act.]

[64I Liability for negligence]

[Nothing in section 64D, 64F or 64G above excludes a person's civil liability for loss or damage, or his criminal liability, resulting from his negligence in doing anything authorised to be done by that section.]

[Section 64I inserted by section 35(1) of the 2007 Act.]

[64J Factors to be considered in determining whether patient objects to treatment]

[(1) In assessing for the purposes of this Part whether he has reason to believe that a patient objects to treatment, a person shall consider all the circumstances so far as they are reasonably ascertainable, including the patient's behaviour, wishes, feelings, views, beliefs and values.

(2) But circumstances from the past shall be considered only so far as it is still appropriate to consider them.]

[Section 64J inserted by section 35(1) of the 2007 Act.]

[64K Interpretation of Part 4A]

[(1) This Part of this Act is to be construed as follows.

(2) References to a patient who lacks capacity are to a patient who lacks capacity within the meaning of the Mental Capacity Act 2005.

(3) References to a patient who has capacity are to be read accordingly.

(4) References to a donee are to a donee of a lasting power of attorney (within the meaning of section 9 of the Mental Capacity Act 2005) created by the patient, where the donee is acting within the scope of his authority and in accordance with that Act.

(5) References to a deputy are to a deputy appointed for the patient by the Court of Protection under section 16 of the Mental Capacity Act 2005, where the deputy is acting within the scope of his authority and in accordance with that Act.

(6) Reference to the responsible clinician shall be construed as a reference to the responsible clinician within the meaning of Part 2 of this Act.

(7) References to a hospital include a registered establishment.

(8) Section 64(3) above applies for the purposes of this Part of this Act as it applies for the purposes of Part 4 of this Act.]

[Section 64K inserted by section 35(1) of the 2007 Act.]

PART V
MENTAL HEALTH REVIEW TRIBUNALS

Constitution etc

65 Mental Health Review Tribunals

(1) There shall be tribunals, known as Mental Health Review Tribunals, for the purpose of dealing with applications and references by and in respect of patients under the provisions of this Act.

(1A) There shall be—

(a) one tribunal for each region of England, and

(b) one tribunal for Wales.

(1B) The Secretary of State—

(a) shall by order determine regions for the purpose of subsection (1A)(a) above; and

(b) may by order vary a region determined for that purpose;

and the Secretary of State shall act under this subsection so as to secure that the regions together comprise the whole of England.

(1C) Any order made under subsection (1B) above may make such transitional, consequential, incidental or supplemental provision as the Secretary of State considers appropriate.

[(1) There shall be—

(a) a Mental Health Review Tribunal for England; and

(b) a Mental Health Review Tribunal for Wales.

(1A) The purpose of the Mental Health Review Tribunals is to deal with applications and references by and in respect of patients under the provisions of this Act.]

(2) The provisions of Schedule 2 to this Act shall have effect with respect to the constitution of Mental Health Review Tribunals.

(3) Subject to the provisions of Schedule 2 to this Act, and to rules made by the Lord Chancellor under this Act, the jurisdiction of a Mental Health Review Tribunal may be exercised by any three or more of its members, and references in this Act to a Mental Health Review Tribunal shall be construed accordingly.

(4) The Secretary of State may pay to the members of Mental Health Review Tribunals such remuneration and allowances as he may with the consent of the Treasury determine, and defray the expenses of such tribunals to such amount as he may with the consent of the Treasury determine, and may provide for each such tribunal such officers and servants, and such accommodation, as the tribunal may require.

[Subsections (1) & (1A) substituted for current subsections (1) to (1C) by section 37(2).]

Applications and references concerning Part II patients

66 Applications to tribunals

(1) Where—

(a) a patient is admitted to a hospital in pursuance of an application for admission for assessment; or

(b) a patient is admitted to a hospital in pursuance of an application for admission for treatment; or

(c) a patient is received into guardianship in pursuance of a guardianship application; or

[(ca) a community treatment order is made in respect of a patient; or (cb) a community treatment order is revoked under section 17F above in respect of a patient; or]

(d) a report is furnished under section 16 above in respect of a patient; or

(e) a patient is transferred from guardianship to a hospital in pursuance of regulations made under section 19 above; or

(f) a report is furnished under section 20 above in respect of a patient and the patient is not discharged [under section 23 above]; or

[(fza) a report is furnished under section 20A above in respect of a patient and the patient is not discharged under section 23 above; or]

(fa) a report is furnished under subsection (2) of section 21B above in respect of a patient and subsection (5) of that section applies (or subsections (5) and (6)(b) of that section apply) in the case of the report; or

[(faa) a report is furnished under subsection (2) of section 21B above in respect of a community patient and subsection (6A) of that section applies (or subsections (6A) and (6B)(b) of that section apply) in the case of the report; or]

(fb) a report is furnished under subsection (2) of section 21B above in respect of a patient and subsection (8) of that section applies in the case of the report; or

(g) a report is furnished under section 25 above in respect of a patient who is detained in pursuance of an application for admission for treatment [or a community patient]; or

(ga) a supervision application is accepted in respect of a patient; or

(gb) a report is furnished under section 25F above in respect of a patient; or

(gc) a report is furnished under section 25G above in respect of a patient; or

(h) an order is made under section 29 above [on the ground specified in paragraph (c) or (d) of subsection (3) of that section] in respect of a patient who is or subsequently becomes liable to be detained or subject to guardianship under Part II of this Act [or who is a community patient],

an application may be made to a Mental Health Review Tribunal within the relevant period—

(i) by the patient (except in the cases mentioned in paragraphs (g) and (h) above) *or, in the cases mentioned in paragraphs (d), (ga), (gb) and (gc), by his nearest relative if he has been (or was entitled to be) informed under this Act of the report or acceptance, and*

(ii) in the cases mentioned in paragraphs (g) and (h) above, by his nearest relative.

(2) In subsection (1) above 'the relevant period' means—

(a) in the case mentioned in paragraph (a) of that subsection, 14 days beginning with the day on which the patient is admitted as so mentioned;

(b) in the case mentioned in paragraph (b) of that subsection, six months beginning with the day on which the patient is admitted as so mentioned;

(c) *in the cases mentioned in paragraphs (c) and (ga)* [in the case mentioned in paragraph (c)] of that subsection, six months beginning with the day on which the application is accepted;

[(ca) in the case mentioned in paragraph (ca) of that subsection, six months beginning with the day on which the community treatment order is made;

(cb) in the case mentioned in paragraph (cb) of that subsection, six months beginning with the day on which the community treatment order is revoked;]

(d) *in the cases mentioned in paragraphs (d), (fb), (g)* [in the case mentioned in paragraph (g)] *and (gb)* of that subsection, 28 days beginning with the day on which the applicant is informed that the report has been furnished;

(e) in the case mentioned in paragraph (e) of that subsection, six months beginning with the day on which the patient is transferred;

(f) in the case mentioned in paragraph (f) or (fa) of that subsection, the period or periods for which authority for the patient's detention or guardianship is renewed by virtue of the report;

[(fza) in the cases mentioned in paragraphs (fza) and (faa) of that subsection, the period or periods for which the community treatment period is extended by virtue of the report;]

(fa) in the case mentioned in paragraph (gc) of that subsection, the further period for which the patient is made subject to after-care under supervision by virtue of the report;

(g) in the case mentioned in paragraph (h) of that subsection, 12 months beginning with the date of the order, and in any subsequent period of 12 months during which the order continues in force.

[(2A) Nothing in subsection (1)(b) above entitles a community patient to make an application by virtue of that provision even if he is admitted to a hospital on being recalled there under section 17E above.]

(3) Section 32 above shall apply for the purposes of this section as it applies for the purposes of Part II of this Act.

[Amendments in subsection (1) as follows:

• *paragraphs (ca) and (cb) inserted by paragraph 18(2)(a) of Schedule 3 to the 2007 Act*

• *paragraph (d) repealed by Part 1 of Schedule 11*

• *words inserted in paragraph (f) by paragraph 18(2)(b) of Schedule 3*

• *paragraph (fza) inserted by paragraph 18(2)(c) of Schedule 3*

• *paragraph (faa) inserted by paragraph 18(2)(d) of Schedule 3*

• *paragraph (fb) (and the word 'or' which follows) repealed by Part 1 of Schedule 11*

• *words inserted in paragraph (g) by paragraph 18(2)(e) of Schedule 3*

• *paragraphs (ga), (gb) & (gc) (and the 'or' following each) omitted by Part 5 of Schedule 11*

• *first insertion in paragraph (h) made by section 25*

• *second insertion in paragraph (h) made by paragraph 18(2)(f) of Schedule 3*

• *words omitted in paragraph (i) by Part 5 of Schedule 11.*

Amendments in subsection (2) as follows:

• *words substituted in paragraph (c) by section 36(3)*

• *paragraphs (ca) and (cb) inserted by paragraph 18(3)(a) of Schedule 3*

• *in paragraph (d), 'in the case mentioned in paragraph (g)' substituted for 'in the cases mentioned in paragraphs (d), (fb), (g)' by paragraph 13 of Schedule 1;*

• *words 'and (gb)' omitted from paragraph (d) by Part 5 of Schedule 11*

• *paragraph (fza) inserted by paragraph 18(3)(b) of Schedule 3*

• *paragraph (fa) omitted by Part 5 of Schedule 11*

Subsection (2A) inserted by paragraph 18(4) of Schedule 3.]

67 References to tribunals by Secretary of State concerning Part II patients

(1) The Secretary of State may, if he thinks fit, at any time refer to a Mental Health Review Tribunal the case of any patient who is liable to be detained or subject to guardianship or to *after-care under supervision* under Part II of this Act [or of any community patient].

(2) For the purpose of furnishing information for the purposes of a reference under subsection (1) above any registered medical practitioner [or approved clinician] authorised by or on behalf of the patient may, at any reasonable time, visit the patient and examine him in private and require the production of and inspect any records relating to the detention or treatment of the patient in any hospital or to any after-care services provided for the patient under section 117 below.

(3) Section 32 above shall apply for the purposes of this section as it applies for the purposes of Part II of this Act.

[*Words omitted from subsection (1) by Part 5 of Schedule 11 to the 2007 Act; words inserted in the same subsection by paragraph 19 of Schedule 3. Words inserted in subsection (2) by section 13(2)(a).*]

68 Duty of managers of hospitals to refer cases to tribunal

(1) Where a patient who is admitted to a hospital in pursuance of an application for admission for treatment or a patient who is transferred from guardianship to hospital does not exercise his right to apply to a Mental Health Review Tribunal under section 66(1) above by virtue of his case falling within paragraph (b) or, as the case may be, paragraph (e) of that section, the managers of the hospital shall at the expiration of the period for making such an application refer the patient's case to such a tribunal unless an application or reference in respect of the patient has then been made under section 66(1) above by virtue of his case falling within paragraph (d), (g) or (h) of that section or under section 67(1) above.

(2) If the authority for the detention of a patient in a hospital is renewed under section 20 or 21B above and a period of three years (or, if the patient has not attained the age of sixteen years, one year) has elapsed since his case was last considered by a Mental Health Review Tribunal, whether on his own application or otherwise, the managers of the hospital shall refer his case to such a tribunal.

(3) For the purpose of furnishing information for the purposes of any reference under this section, any registered medical practitioner authorised by or on behalf of the patient may at any reasonable time visit and examine the patient in private and require the production of and inspect any records relating to the detention or treatment of the patient in any hospital or to any after-care services provided for the patient under section 117 below.

(4) The Secretary of State may by order vary the length of the periods mentioned in subsection (2) above.

(5) For the purposes of subsection (1) above a person who applies to a tribunal but subsequently withdraws his application shall be treated as not having exercised his right to apply, and where a person withdraws his application on a date after the expiration of the period mentioned in that subsection, the managers shall refer the patient's case as soon as possible after that date.

[68 Duty of managers of hospitals to refer cases to tribunal]

[(1) This section applies in respect of the following patients—

(a) a patient who is admitted to a hospital in pursuance of an application for admission for assessment;

(b) a patient who is admitted to a hospital in pursuance of an application for admission for treatment;

(c) a community patient;

(d) a patient whose community treatment order is revoked under section 17F above;

(e) a patient who is transferred from guardianship to a hospital in pursuance of regulations made under section 19 above.

(2) On expiry of the period of six months beginning with the applicable day, the managers of the hospital shall refer the patient's case to a Mental Health Review Tribunal.

(3) But they shall not do so if during that period—

   (a) any right has been exercised by or in respect of the patient by virtue of any of paragraphs (b), (ca), (cb) (e), (g) and (h) of section 66(1) above;

   (b) a reference has been made in respect of the patient under section 67(1) above, not being a reference made while the patient is or was liable to be detained in pursuance of an application for admission for assessment; or

   (c) a reference has been made in respect of the patient under subsection (7) below.

(4) A person who applies to a tribunal but subsequently withdraws his application shall be treated for these purposes as not having exercised his right to apply, and if he withdraws his application on a date after expiry of the period mentioned in subsection (2) above, the managers shall refer the patient's case as soon as possible after that date.

(5) In subsection (2) above, 'the applicable day' means—

   (a) in the case of a patient who is admitted to a hospital in pursuance of an application for admission for assessment, the day on which the patient was so admitted;

   (b) in the case of a patient who is admitted to a hospital in pursuance of an application for admission for treatment—

      (i) the day on which the patient was so admitted; or

      (ii) if, when he was so admitted, he was already liable to be detained in pursuance of an application for admission for assessment, the day on which he was originally admitted in pursuance of the application for admission for assessment;

   (c) in the case of a community patient or a patient whose community treatment order is revoked under section 17F above, the day mentioned in sub-paragraph (i) or (ii), as the case may be, of paragraph (b) above;

   (d) in the case of a patient who is transferred from guardianship to a hospital, the day on which he was so transferred.

(6) The managers of the hospital shall also refer the patient's case to a Mental Health Review Tribunal if a period of more than three years (or, if the patient has not attained the age of 18 years, one year) has elapsed since his case was last considered by such a tribunal, whether on his own application or otherwise.

(7) If, in the case of a community patient, the community treatment order is revoked under section 17F above, the managers of the hospital shall also refer the patient's case to a Mental Health Review Tribunal as soon as possible after the order is revoked.

(8) For the purposes of furnishing information for the purposes of a reference under this section, a registered medical practitioner or approved clinician authorised by or on behalf of the patient may at any reasonable time—

   (a) visit and examine the patient in private; and

   (b) require the production of and inspect any records relating to the detention or treatment of the patient in any hospital or any after-care services provided for him under section 117 below.

(9) Reference in this section to the managers of the hospital—

   (a) in relation to a community patient, is to the managers of the responsible hospital;

   (b) in relation to any other patient, is to the managers of the hospital in which he is liable to be detained.]

[*Section 68 substituted by section 37(3) of the 2007 Act.*]

[68A Power to reduce periods under section 68]

[(1) The appropriate national authority may from time to time by order amend subsections (2) or (6) of section 68 above so as to substitute for a period mentioned there such shorter period as is specified in the order.

(2) The order may include such transitional, consequential, incidental or supplemental provision as the appropriate national authority thinks fit.

(3) The order may, in particular, make provision for a case where—

(a) a patient in respect of whom subsection (1) of section 68 above applies is, or is about to be, transferred from England to Wales or from Wales to England; and

(b) the period by reference to which subsection (2) or (6) of that section operates for the purposes of the patient's case is not the same in one territory as it is in the other.

(4) A patient is transferred from one territory to the other if—

(a) he is transferred from a hospital, or from guardianship, in one territory to a hospital in the other in pursuance of regulations made under section 19 above;

(b) he is removed under subsection (3) of that section from a hospital or accommodation in one territory to a hospital or accommodation in the other;

(c) he is a community patient responsibility for whom is assigned from a hospital in one territory to a hospital in the other in pursuance of regulations made under section 19A above;

(d) on the revocation of a community treatment order in respect of him under section 17F above he is detained in a hospital in the territory other than the one in which the responsible hospital was situated; or

(e) he is transferred or removed under section 123 below from a hospital in one territory to a hospital in the other.

(5) Provision made by virtue of subsection (3) above may require or authorise the managers of a hospital determined in accordance with the order to refer the patient's case to a Mental Health Review Tribunal.

(6) In so far as making provision by virtue of subsection (3) above, the order—

(a) may make different provision for different cases;

(b) may make provision which applies subject to specified exceptions.

(7) Where the appropriate national authority for one territory makes an order under subsection (1) above, the appropriate national authority for the other territory may by order make such provision in consequence of the order as it thinks fit.

(8) An order made under subsection (7) above may, in particular, make provision for a case within subsection (3) above (and subsections (4) to (6) above shall apply accordingly).

(9) In this section, 'the appropriate national authority' means—

(a) in relation to the managers of a hospital in England, the Secretary of State;

(b) in relation to the managers of a hospital in Wales, the Welsh Ministers.]

[*Section 68A substituted (with new section 68) for current section 68 section 37(3) of the 2007 Act.*]

Applications and references concerning Part III patients

69 Applications to tribunals concerning patients subject to hospital and guardianship orders

(1) Without prejudice to any provision of section 66(1) above as applied by section 40(4) above, an application to a Mental Health Review Tribunal may also be made—

(a) *in respect of a patient admitted to a hospital in pursuance of a hospital order, by the nearest relative of the patient in the period between the expiration of six months and the expiration of*

12 months beginning with the date of the order and in any subsequent period of 12 months; and

[(a) in respect of a patient liable to be detained in pursuance of a hospital order or a community patient who was so liable immediately before he became a community patient, by the nearest relative of the patient in any period in which an application may be made by the patient under any such provision as so applied;]

(b) in respect of a patient placed under guardianship by a guardianship order—

    (i) by the patient, within the period of six months beginning with the date of the order;

    (ii) by the nearest relative of the patient, within the period of 12 months beginning with the date of the order and in any subsequent period of 12 months.

(2) Where a person detained in a hospital—

(a) is treated as subject to a hospital order[, hospital direction] or transfer direction by virtue of section 41(5) above, *82(2) or 85(2) below, or article 2(2) of the Mental Health (Care and Treatment) (Scotland) Act 2003 (Consequential Provisions) Order 2005* [or section 80B(2), 82(2) or 85(2) below]; or

(b) is subject to a direction having the same effect as a hospital order by virtue of section *45B(2), 46(3)*, 47(3) or 48(3) above,

then, without prejudice to any provision of Part II of this Act as applied by section 40 above, that person may make an application to a Mental Health Review Tribunal in the period of six months beginning with the date of the order or direction mentioned in paragraph (a) above or, as the case may be, the date of the direction mentioned in paragraph (b) above.

[(3) The provisions of section 66 above as applied by section 40(4) above are subject to subsection (4) below.

(4) If the initial detention period has not elapsed when the relevant application period begins, the right of a hospital order patient to make an application by virtue of paragraph (ca) or (cb) of section 66(1) above shall be exercisable only during whatever remains of the relevant application period after the initial detention period has elapsed.

(5) In subsection (4) above—

(a) 'hospital order patient' means a patient who is subject to a hospital order, excluding a patient of a kind mentioned in paragraph (a) or (b) of subsection (2) above;

(b) 'the initial detention period', in relation to a hospital order patient, means the period of six months beginning with the date of the hospital order; and

(c) 'the relevant application period' means the relevant period mentioned in paragraph (ca) or (cb), as the case may be, of section 66(2) above.]

[*Subsection (1)(a) substituted by paragraph 20(a) of Schedule 3 to the 2007 Act; words inserted and substituted in subsection 2(a) by paragraph 18(a)&(b) respectively of Schedule 5; words omitted in subsection 2(b), and subsections (3) to (5) inserted, by paragraph 20(b)&(c) respectively of Schedule 3.*]

70 Applications to tribunals concerning restricted patients

A patient who is a restricted patient within the meaning of section 79 below and is detained in a hospital may apply to a Mental Health Review Tribunal—

(a) in the period between the expiration of six months and the expiration of 12 months beginning with the date of the relevant hospital order, hospital direction or transfer direction; and

(b) in any subsequent period of 12 months.

71 **References by Secretary of State concerning restricted patients**

(1) The Secretary of State may at any time refer the case of a restricted patient to a Mental Health Review Tribunal.

(2) The Secretary of State shall refer to a Mental Health Review Tribunal the case of any restricted patient detained in a hospital whose case has not been considered by such a tribunal, whether on his own application or otherwise, within the last three years.

(3) The Secretary of State may by order vary the length of the period mentioned in subsection (2) above.

[(3A) An order under subsection (3) above may include such transitional, consequential, incidental or supplemental provision as the Secretary of State thinks fit.]

(4) Any reference under subsection (1) above in respect of a patient who has been conditionally discharged and not recalled to hospital shall be made to the tribunal for the area in which the patient resides.

[*Subsection (3A) inserted by section 37(4) of the 2007 Act.*]

Discharge of patients

72 **Powers of tribunals**

(1) Where application is made to a Mental Health Review Tribunal by or in respect of a patient who is liable to be detained under this Act [or is a community patient], the tribunal may in any case direct that the patient be discharged, and—

(a) the tribunal shall direct the discharge of a patient liable to be detained under section 2 above if they are not satisfied—

    (i) that he is then suffering from mental disorder or from mental disorder of a nature or degree which warrants his detention in a hospital for assessment (or for assessment followed by medical treatment) for at least a limited period; or

    (ii) that his detention as aforesaid is justified in the interests of his own health or safety or with a view to the protection of other persons;

(b) the tribunal shall direct the discharge of a patient liable to be detained otherwise than under section 2 above if they are not satisfied—

    (i) that he is then suffering from *mental illness, psychopathic disorder, severe mental impairment or mental impairment or from any of those forms of disorder* [mental disorder or from mental disorder] of a nature or degree which makes it appropriate for him to be liable to be detained in a hospital for medical treatment; or

    (ii) that it is necessary for the health of safety of the patient or for the protection of other persons that he should receive such treatment; or

    [(iia) that appropriate medical treatment is available for him; or]

    (iii) in the case of an application by virtue of paragraph (g) of section 66(1) above, that the patient, if released, would be likely to act in a manner dangerous to other persons or to himself.

[(c) the tribunal shall direct the discharge of a community patient if they are not satisfied—

    (i) that he is then suffering from mental disorder or mental disorder of a nature or degree which makes it appropriate for him to receive medical treatment; or

    (ii) that it is necessary for his health or safety or for the protection of other persons that he should receive such treatment; or

    (iii) that it is necessary that the responsible clinician should be able to exercise the power under section 17E(1) to recall the patient to hospital; or

(iv) that appropriate medical treatment is available for him; or

(v) in the case of an application by virtue of paragraph (g) of section 66(1) above, that the patient, if discharged, would be likely to act in a manner dangerous to other persons or to himself.]

[(1A) In determining whether the criterion in subsection (1)(c)(iii) above is met, the responsible clinician shall, in particular, consider, having regard to the patient's history of mental disorder and any other relevant factors, what risk there would be of a deterioration of the patient's condition if he were to continue not to be detained in a hospital (as a result, for example, of his refusing or neglecting to receive the medical treatment he requires for his mental disorder).]

(2) *In determining whether to direct the discharge of a patient detained otherwise than under section 2 above in a case not falling within paragraph (b) of subsection (1) above, the tribunal shall have regard—*

(a) *to the likelihood of medical treatment alleviating or preventing a deterioration of the patient's condition; and*

(b) *in the case of a patient suffering from mental illness or severe mental impairment, to the likelihood of the patient, if discharged, being able to care for himself, to obtain the care he needs or to guard himself against serious exploitation.*

(3) A tribunal may under subsection (1) above direct the discharge of a patient on a future date specified in the direction; and where a tribunal do not direct the discharge of a patient under that subsection the tribunal may—

(a) with a view to facilitating his discharge on a future date, recommend that he be granted leave of absence or transferred to another hospital or into guardianship; and

(b) further consider his case in the event of any such recommendation not being complied with.

(3A) *Where, in the case of an application to a tribunal by or in respect of a patient who is liable to be detained in pursuance of an application for admission for treatment or by virtue of an order or direction for his admission or removal to hospital under Part III of this Act, the tribunal do not direct the discharge of the patient under subsection (1) above, the tribunal may—*

(a) *recommend that the responsible medical officer consider whether to make a supervision application in respect of the patient; and*

(b) *further consider his case in the event of no such application being made.*

[(3A) Subsection (1) above does not require a tribunal to direct the discharge of a patient just because they think it might be appropriate for the patient to be discharged (subject to the possibility of recall) under a community treatment order; and a tribunal—

(a) may recommend that the responsible clinician consider whether to make a community treatment order; and

(b) may (but need not) further consider the patient's case if the responsible clinician does not make an order].

(4) Where application is made to a Mental Health Review Tribunal by or in respect of a patient who is subject to guardianship under this Act, the tribunal may in any case direct that the patient be discharged, and shall so direct if they are satisfied—

(a) that he is not then suffering from *mental illness, psychopathic disorder, severe mental impairment or mental impairment* [mental disorder]; or

(b) that it is not necessary in the interests of the welfare of the patient, or for the protection of other persons, that the patient should remain under such guardianship.

(4A) Where application is made to a Mental Health Review Tribunal by or in respect of a patient who is subject to after-care under supervision (or, if he has not yet left hospital, is to be so subject after he leaves hospital), the tribunal may in any case direct that the patient shall cease to be so subject (or not become so subject), and shall so direct if they are satisfied—

(a) in a case where the patient has not yet left hospital, that the conditions set out in section 25A(4) above are not complied with; or

(b) in any other case, that the conditions set out in section 25G(4) above are not complied with.

(5) Where application is made to a Mental Health Review Tribunal under any provision of this Act by or in respect of a patient and the tribunal do not direct that the patient be discharged or, if he is (or is to be) subject to after-care under supervision, that he cease to be so subject (or not become so subject), the tribunal may, if satisfied that the patient is suffering from a form of mental disorder other than the form specified in the application, order or direction relating to him, direct that that application, order or direction be amended by substituting for the form of mental disorder specified in it such other form of mental disorder as appears to the tribunal to be appropriate.

(6) Subsections (1) to *(5)* ([4]) above apply in relation to references to a Mental Health Review Tribunal as they apply in relation to applications made to such a tribunal by or in respect of a patient.

(7) Subsection (1) above shall not apply in the case of a restricted patient except as provided in sections 73 and 74 below.

[Words 'or is a community patient', and paragraph (c) inserted into subsection (1) by paragraphs 21(2)(a) & (b) respectively of Schedule 3 to the 2007 Act; words substituted in paragraph (b)(i) of that subsection by paragraphs 14(a) of Schedule 1; sub-paragraph (b)(ii)(a) inserted into that subsection by section 4(8)(a); subsection (1A) inserted by paragraph 21(3) of Schedule 3; subsection (2) omitted by section 4(8)(b); subsection (3A) substituted by paragraph 21(4) of Schedule 3; words substituted in subsection (4) by paragraph 14(b) of Schedule 1; subsection (4A) repealed by Part 5 of Schedule 11; subsection (5) repealed by Part 1 of Schedule 11; and words in subsection (6) substituted by paragraph 14(c) of Schedule 1.]

73 Power to discharge restricted patients

(1) Where an application to a Mental Health Review Tribunal is made by a restricted patient who is subject to a restriction order, or where the case of such a patient is referred to such a tribunal, the tribunal shall direct the absolute discharge of the patient if—

(a) the tribunal are not satisfied as to the matters mentioned in paragraph (b)(i) *or (ii)* [,(ii) or (iia)] of section 72(1) above;

(b) the tribunal are satisfied that it is not appropriate for the patient to remain liable to be recalled to hospital for further treatment.

(2) Where in the case of any such patient as is mentioned in subsection (1) above—

(a) paragraph (a) of that subsection applies; but

(b) paragraph (b) of that subsection does not apply,

the tribunal shall direct the conditional discharge of the patient.

(3) Where a patient is absolutely discharged under this section he shall thereupon cease to be liable to be detained by virtue of the relevant hospital order, and the restriction order shall cease to have effect accordingly.

(4) Where a patient is conditionally discharged under this section—

(a) he may be recalled by the Secretary of State under subsection (3) of section 42 above as if he had been conditionally discharged under subsection (2) of that section; and

(b) the patient shall comply with such conditions (if any) as may be imposed at the time of discharge by the tribunal or at any subsequent time by the Secretary of State.

(5) The Secretary of State may from time to time vary any condition imposed (whether by the tribunal or by him) under subsection (4) above.

(6) Where a restriction order in respect of a patient ceases to have effect after he has been conditionally discharged under this section the patient shall, unless previously recalled, be deemed to be absolutely discharged on the date when the order ceases to have effect and shall cease to be liable to be detained by virtue of the relevant hospital order.

(7) A tribunal may defer a direction for the conditional discharge of a patient until such arrangements as appear to the tribunal to be necessary for that purpose have been made to their satisfaction; and where by virtue of any such deferment no direction has been given on an application or reference before the time when the patient's case comes before the tribunal on a subsequent application or reference, the previous application or reference shall be treated as one on which no direction under this section can be given.

(8) This section is without prejudice to section 42 above.

[*Words in subsection (1)(a) substituted by section 4(9) of the 2007 Act.*]

74 Restricted patients subject to restriction directions

(1) Where an application to a Mental Health Review Tribunal is made by a restricted patient who is subject to a limitation direction or restriction direction, or where the case of such a patient is referred to such a tribunal the tribunal—

    (a) shall notify the Secretary of State whether, in their opinion, the patient would, if subject to a restriction order, be entitled to be absolutely or conditionally discharged under section 73 above; and

    (b) if they notify him that the patient would be entitled to be conditionally discharged, may recommend that in the event of his not being discharged under this section he should continue to be detained in hospital.

(2) If in the case of a patient not falling within subsection (4) below—

    (a) the tribunal notify the Secretary of State that the patient would be entitled to be absolutely or conditionally discharged; and

    (b) within the period of 90 days beginning with the date of that notification the Secretary of State gives notice to the tribunal that the patient may be so discharged,

the tribunal shall direct the absolute or, as the case may be, the conditional discharge of the patient.

(3) Where a patient continues to be liable to be detained in a hospital at the end of the period referred to in subsection (2)(b) above because the Secretary of State has not given the notice there mentioned, the managers of the hospital shall, unless the tribunal have made a recommendation under subsection (1)(b) above, transfer the patient to a prison or other institution in which he might have been detained if he had not been removed to hospital, there to be dealt with as if he had not been so removed.

(4) If, in the case of a patient who is subject to a transfer direction under section 48 above, the tribunal notify the Secretary of State that the patient would be entitled to be absolutely or conditionally discharged, the Secretary of State shall, unless the tribunal have made a recommendation under subsection (1)(b) above, by warrant direct that the patient be remitted to a prison or other institution in which he might have been detained if he had not been removed to hospital, there to be dealt with as if he had not been so removed.

(5) Where a patient is transferred or remitted under subsection (3) or (4) above the relevant hospital direction and the limitation direction or, as the case may be, the relevant transfer direction and the restriction direction shall cease to have effect on his arrival in the prison or other institution.

(5A) Where the tribunal have made a recommendation under subsection (1)(b) above in the case of a patient who is subject to a restriction direction or a limitation direction—

(a) the fact that the restriction direction or limitation direction remains in force does not prevent the making of any application or reference to the Parole Board by or in respect of him or the exercise by him of any power to require the Secretary of State to refer his case to the Parole Board, and

(b) if the Parole Board make a direction or recommendation by virtue of which the patient would become entitled to be released (whether unconditionally or on licence) from any prison or other institution in which he might have been detained if he had not been removed to hospital, the restriction direction or limitation direction shall cease to have effect at the time when he would become entitled to be so released.

(6) Subsections (3) to (8) of section 73 above shall have effect in relation to this section as they have effect in relation to that section, taking references to the relevant hospital order and the restriction order as references to the hospital direction and the limitation direction or, as the case may be, to the transfer direction and the restriction direction.

(7) This section is without prejudice to sections 50 to 53 above in their application to patients who are not discharged under this section.

75 Applications and references concerning conditionally discharged restricted patients

(1) Where a restricted patient has been conditionally discharged under section 42(2), 73 or 74 above and is subsequently recalled to hospital—

(a) the Secretary of State shall, within one month of the day on which the patient returns or is returned to hospital, refer his case to a Mental Health Review Tribunal; and

(b) section 70 above shall apply to the patient as if the relevant hospital order, hospital direction or transfer direction had been made on that day.

(2) Where a restricted patient has been conditionally discharged as aforesaid but has not been recalled to hospital he may apply to a Mental Health Review Tribunal—

(a) in the period between the expiration of 12 months and the expiration of two years beginning with the date on which he was conditionally discharged; and

(b) in any subsequent period of two years.

(3) Sections 73 and 74 above shall not apply to an application under subsection (2) above but on any such application the tribunal may—

(a) vary any condition to which the patient is subject in connection with his discharge or impose any condition which might have been imposed in connection therewith; or

(b) direct that the restriction order[, limitation direction] or restriction direction to which he is subject shall cease to have effect;

and if the tribunal give a direction under paragraph (b) above the patient shall cease to be liable to be detained by virtue of the relevant hospital order[, hospital direction] or transfer direction.

[*Words inserted in subsection (3) by section 41(a)&(b) respectively of the 2007 Act.*]

General

76 Visiting and examination of patients

(1) For the purpose of advising whether an application to a Mental Health Review Tribunal should be made by or in respect of a patient who is liable to be detained or subject to guardianship *or to after-care under supervision (or, if he has not yet left hospital, is to be subject to*

after-care under supervision after he leaves hospital) under Part II of this Act [or a community patient,] or of furnishing information as to the condition of a patient for the purposes of such an application, any registered medical practitioner [or approved clinician] authorised by or on behalf of the patient or other person who is entitled to make or has made the application—

(a) may at any reasonable time visit the patient and examine him in private, and

(b) may require the production of and inspect any records relating to the detention or treatment of the patient in any hospital or to any after-care services provided for the patient under section 117 below.

(2) Section 32 above shall apply for the purposes of this section as it applies for the purposes of Part II of this Act.

[*Words omitted from subsection (1) by Part 5 of Schedule 11 to the 2007 Act; words 'or a community patient' inserted in that subsection by paragraph 22 of Schedule 3 and 'or approved clinician' by section 13(2)(b).*]

77 General provisions concerning tribunal applications

(1) No application shall be made to a Mental Health Review Tribunal by or in respect of a patient except in such cases and at such times as are expressly provided by this Act.

(2) Where under this Act any person is authorised to make an application to a Mental Health Review Tribunal within a specified period, not more than one such application shall be made by that person within that period but for that purpose there shall be disregarded any application which is withdrawn in accordance with rules made under section 78 below.

(3) Subject to subsection (4) below an application to a Mental Health Review Tribunal authorised to be made by or in respect of a patient under this Act shall be made by notice in writing addressed *to the tribunal for the area in which the hospital in which the patient is detained is situated or in which the patient is residing under guardianship or when subject to after-care under supervision (or in which he is to reside on becoming so subject after leaving hospital) as the case may be.*

[(a) in the case of a patient who is liable to be detained in a hospital, to the tribunal for the area in which that hospital is situated;

(b) in the case of a community patient, to the tribunal for the area in which the responsible hospital is situated;

(c) in the case of a patient subject to guardianship, to the tribunal for the area in which the patient is residing.]

(4) Any application under section 75(2) above shall be made to the tribunal for the area in which the patient resides.

[*Paragraphs (3)(a) to (c) substituted for words above them by paragraph 23 of Schedule 3 to the 2007 Act.*]

78 Procedure of tribunals

(1) The Lord Chancellor may make rules with respect to the making of applications to Mental Health Review Tribunals and with respect to the proceedings of such tribunals and matters incidental to or consequential on such proceedings.

(2) Rules made under this section may in particular make provision—

(a) for enabling a tribunal, or the *chairman* [President] of a tribunal, to postpone the consideration of any application by or in respect of a patient, or of any such application of any specified class, until the expiration of such period (not exceeding 12 months) as may be specified in the rules from the date on which an application by or in respect of the same patient was last considered and determined by that or *any other* [the other] tribunal under this Act;

(b) for the transfer of proceedings from one tribunal to *another* [the other] in any case where, after the making of the application, the patient is removed out of the area of the tribunal to which it was made;

(c) for restricting the persons qualified to serve as members of a tribunal for the consideration of any application, or of an application of any specified class;

(d) for enabling a tribunal to dispose of an application without a formal hearing where such a hearing is not requested by the applicant or it appears to the tribunal that such a hearing would be detrimental to the health of the patient;

(e) for enabling a tribunal to exclude members of the public, or any specified class of members of the public, from any proceedings of the tribunal, or to prohibit the publication of reports of any such proceedings or the names of any persons concerned in such proceedings;

(f) for regulating the circumstances in which, and the persons by whom, applicants and patients in respect of whom applications are made to a tribunal may, if not desiring to conduct their own case, be represented for the purposes of those applications;

(g) for regulating the methods by which information relevant to an application may be obtained by or furnished to the tribunal, and in particular for authorising the members of a tribunal, or any one or more of them, to visit and interview in private any patient by or in respect of whom an application has been made;

(h) for making available to any applicant, and to any patient in respect of whom an application is made to a tribunal, copies of any documents obtained by or furnished to the tribunal in connection with the application, and a statement of the substance of any oral information so obtained or furnished except where the tribunal considers it undesirable in the interests of the patient or for other special reasons;

(i) for requiring a tribunal, if so requested in accordance with the rules, to furnish such statements of the reasons for any decision given by the tribunal as may be prescribed by the rules, subject to any provision made by the rules for withholding such a statement from a patient or any other person in cases where the tribunal considers that furnishing it would be undesirable in the interests of the patient or for other special reasons;

(j) for conferring on the tribunals such ancillary powers as the Lord Chancellor thinks necessary for the purposes of the exercise of their functions under this Act;

(k) for enabling any functions of a tribunal which relate to matters preliminary or incidental to an application to be performed by the *chairman* [President] of the tribunal.

(3) Subsections (1) and (2) above apply in relation to references to Mental Health Review Tribunals as they apply in relation to applications to such tribunals by or in respect of patients.

(4) Rules under this section may make provision as to the procedure to be adopted in cases concerning restricted patients and, in particular—

(a) for restricting the persons qualified to serve as *president* [chairman] of a tribunal for the consideration of an application or reference relating to a restricted patient;

(b) for the transfer of proceedings from one tribunal to *another* [the other] in any case where, after the making of a reference or application in accordance with section 71(4) or 77(4) above, the patient ceases to reside in the area of the tribunal to which the reference or application was made.

(5) Rules under this section may be so framed as to apply to all applications or references or to applications or references of any specified class and may make different provision in relation to different cases.

(6) Any functions conferred on the *chairman* [President] of a Mental Health Review Tribunal by rules under this section may, *if for any reason he is unable to act,* be exercised by another member of that tribunal appointed by him for the purpose.

(7) A Mental Health Review Tribunal may pay allowances in respect of travelling expenses, subsistence and loss of earnings to any person attending the tribunal as an applicant or witness, to the patient who is the subject of the proceedings if he attends otherwise than as the applicant or a witness and to any person (other than counsel or a solicitor) who attends as the representative of an applicant.

(8) A Mental Health Review Tribunal may, and if so required by the High Court shall, state in the form of a special case for determination by the High Court any question of law which may arise before them. ·

(9) Part I of the Arbitration Act 1996 shall not apply to any proceedings before a Mental Health Review Tribunal except so far as any provisions of that Act may be applied, with or without modifications, by rules made under this section.

[In subsections (2)(a) & (k) and subsection (6) 'President' substituted for 'chairman' by section 38(3)(a) of the 2007 Act In subsection (2)(a) 'the other' substituted for 'any other' by section 38(3)(b). Substitutions in subsection (2)(b) and 4(b) made by section 38(3)(c). Word substituted in subsection (4)(a) by section 38(3)(d). Words omitted in subsection (6) by section 38(3)(e).]

79 Interpretation of Part V

(1) In this Part of this Act 'restricted patient' means a patient who is subject to a restriction order, limitation direction or restriction direction and this Part of this Act shall, subject to the provisions of this section, have effect in relation to any person who—

    (a) is treated by virtue of any enactment as subject to a hospital order and a restriction order; or

    (c) is treated as subject to a hospital order and a restriction order or to a transfer direction and a restriction direction by virtue of section 82(2) or 85(2) below or article 2(2) of the Mental Health (Care and Treatment) (Scotland) Act 2003 (Consequential Provisions) Order 2005,

    [(c) is treated as subject to a hospital order and a restriction order, or to a hospital direction and a limitation direction, or to a transfer direction and a restriction direction, by virtue of any provision of Part 6 of this Act (except section 80D(3), 82A(2) or 85A(2) below),]

    as it has effect in relation to a restricted patient.

(2) Subject to the following provisions of this section, in this Part of this Act 'the relevant hospital order', 'the relevant hospital direction' and 'the relevant transfer direction', in relation to a restricted patient, mean the hospital order, the hospital direction or transfer direction by virtue of which he is liable to be detained in a hospital.

(3) In the case of a person within paragraph (a) of subsection (1) above, references in this Part of this Act to the relevant hospital order or restriction order shall be construed as references to the direction referred to in that paragraph.

(4) In the case of a person within paragraph (b) of subsection (1) above, references in this Part of this Act to the relevant hospital order or restriction order shall be construed as references to the order under the provisions mentioned in that paragraph.

(5) In the case of a person within paragraph (c) of subsection (1) above, references in this Part of this Act to the relevant hospital order, [the relevant hospital direction,] the relevant transfer direction, the restriction order [, limitation direction] or the restriction direction or to a transfer direction under section 48 above shall be construed as references to the hospital order, [hospital direction,] transfer direction, restriction order, [limitation direction,] restriction

direction or transfer direction under that section to which that person is treated as subject by virtue of the provisions mentioned in that paragraph.

[(5A) Section 75 above shall, subject to the modifications in subsection (5C) below, have effect in relation to a qualifying patient as it has effect in relation to a restricted patient who is conditionally discharged under section 42(2), 73 or 74 above.

(5B) A patient is a qualifying patient if he is treated by virtue of section 80D(3), 82A(2) or 85A(2) below as if he had been conditionally discharged and were subject to a hospital order and a restriction order, or to a hospital direction and a limitation direction, or to a transfer direction and a restriction direction.

(5C) The modifications mentioned in subsection (5A) above are—

(a) references to the relevant hospital order, hospital direction or transfer direction, or to the restriction order, limitation direction or restriction direction to which the patient is subject, shall be construed as references to the hospital order, hospital direction or transfer direction, or restriction order, limitation direction or restriction direction, to which the patient is treated as subject by virtue of section 80D(3), 82A(2) or 85A(2) below; and

(b) the reference to the date on which the patient was conditionally discharged shall be construed as a reference to the date on which he was treated as conditionally discharged by virtue of a provision mentioned in paragraph (a) above.]

(6) In this Part of this Act, unless the context otherwise requires, 'hospital' means a hospital, *and 'the responsible medical officer' means the responsible medical officer* [, and 'the responsible clinician' means the responsible clinician], within the meaning of Part II of this Act.

(7) In this Part of this Act any reference to the area of a tribunal is—

(a) in relation to a tribunal for a region of England, a reference to that region; and

(b) in relation to the tribunal for Wales, a reference to Wales.

[(7) For the purposes of this Part of this Act—

(a) the area of the Mental Health Review Tribunal for England is England; and

(b) the area of the Mental Health Review Tribunal for Wales is Wales.]

[*Subsection (1)(c) substituted by paragraph 19(2) of Schedule 5 to the 2007 Act; words inserted in subsection (5) by paragraphs 19(3)(a) to (d) respectively of Schedule 5; subsections (5A) to (5C) inserted by paragraph 19(4) of Schedule 5; words substituted in subsection (6) by section 13(3); and subsection (7) substituted by section 38(4).*]

PART VI
REMOVAL AND RETURN OF PATIENTS WITHIN UNITED KINGDOM, ETC

Removal to [and from] *Scotland*

80 Removal of patients to Scotland

(1) If it appears to the Secretary of State, in the case of a patient who is for the time being liable to be detained *or subject to guardianship* under this Act (otherwise than by virtue of section 35, 36 or 38 above), that it is in the interests of the patient to remove him to Scotland, and that arrangements have been made for admitting him to a hospital *or, as the case may be, for receiving him into guardianship there,* or, where he is not to be admitted to a hospital, for his detention in hospital to be authorised by virtue of the Mental Health (Care and Treatment) (Scotland) Act 2003 or the Criminal Procedure (Scotland) Act 1995 the Secretary of State may authorise his removal to Scotland and may give any necessary directions for his conveyance to his destination.

(7) In this section 'hospital' has the same meaning as in the Mental Health (Care and Treatment) (Scotland) Act 2003.

(8) Reference in this section to a patient's detention in hospital being authorised by virtue of the Mental Health (Care and Treatment) (Scotland) Act 2003 or the Criminal Procedure (Scotland) Act 1995 shall be read as including references to a patient in respect of whom a certificate under one of the provisions listed in section 290(7)(a) of the Act of 2003 is in operation.

[*Cross-head above section 80 amended, and words omitted in subsection (1) by paragraph 2 of Schedule 5 to the 2007 Act.*]

[80ZA Transfer of responsibility for community patients to Scotland

[(1) If it appears to the appropriate national authority, in the case of a community patient, that the conditions mentioned in subsection (2) below are met, the authority may authorise the transfer of responsibility for him to Scotland.

(2) The conditions are—
  (a) a transfer under this section is in the patient's interests; and
  (b) arrangements have been made for dealing with him under enactments in force in Scotland corresponding or similar to those relating to community patients in this Act.

(3) The appropriate national authority may not act under subsection (1) above while the patient is recalled to hospital under section 17E above.

(4) In this section, 'the appropriate national authority' means—
  (a) in relation to a community patient in respect of whom the responsible hospital is in England, the Secretary of State;
  (b) in relation to a community patient in respect of whom the responsible hospital is in Wales, the Welsh Ministers.]

[*Section 80ZA inserted by paragraph 3(1) of Schedule 5 to the 2007 Act. Note: this amendment does not extend to Scotland.*]

80A Transfer of responsibility for [conditionally discharged] patients to Scotland

(1) If it appears to the Secretary of State, in the case of a patient who—
  (a) is subject to a restriction order under section 41 above; and
  (b) has been conditionally discharged under section 42 or 73 above,
that a transfer under this section would be in the interests of the patient, the Secretary of State may, with the consent of the Minister exercising corresponding functions in Scotland, transfer responsibility for the patient to that Minister.

[*Title of section 80A amended by paragraph 4(1) of Schedule 5 to the 2007 Act.*]

[80B Removal of detained patients from Scotland]

[(1) This section applies to a patient if—
  (a) he is removed to England and Wales under regulations made under section 290(1)(a) of the Mental Health (Care and Treatment) (Scotland) Act 2003 ('the 2003 Act');
  (b) immediately before his removal, his detention in hospital was authorised by virtue of that Act or the Criminal Procedure (Scotland) Act 1995; and
  (c) on his removal, he is admitted to a hospital in England or Wales.

(2) He shall be treated as if, on the date of his admission to the hospital, he had been so admitted in pursuance of an application made, or an order or direction made or given, on that date under the enactment in force in England and Wales which most closely corresponds to the

enactment by virtue of which his detention in hospital was authorised immediately before his removal.

(3) If, immediately before his removal, he was subject to a measure under any enactment in force in Scotland restricting his discharge, he shall be treated as if he were subject to an order or direction under the enactment in force in England and Wales which most closely corresponds to that enactment.

(4) If, immediately before his removal, the patient was liable to be detained under the 2003 Act by virtue of a transfer for treatment direction, given while he was serving a sentence of imprisonment (within the meaning of section 136(9) of that Act) imposed by a court in Scotland, he shall be treated as if the sentence had been imposed by a court in England and Wales.

(5) If, immediately before his removal, the patient was subject to a hospital direction or transfer for treatment direction, the restriction direction to which he is subject by virtue of subsection (3) above shall expire on the date on which that hospital direction or transfer for treatment direction (as the case may be) would have expired if he had not been so removed.

(6) If, immediately before his removal, the patient was liable to be detained under the 2003 Act by virtue of a hospital direction, he shall be treated as if any sentence of imprisonment passed at the time when that hospital direction was made had been imposed by a court in England and Wales.

(7) Any directions given by the Scottish Ministers under regulations made under section 290 of the 2003 Act as to the removal of a patient to which this section applies shall have effect as if they were given under this Act.

(8) Subsection (8) of section 80 above applies to a reference in this section as it applies to one in that section.

(9) In this section—

'hospital direction' means a direction made under section 59A of the Criminal Procedure (Scotland) Act 1995; and

'transfer for treatment direction' has the meaning given by section 136 of the 2003 Act.]

[*Section 80B inserted by paragraph 4(1) of Schedule 5 to the 2007 Act.*]

[80C Removal of patients subject to compulsion in the community from Scotland]

[(1) This section applies to a patient if—

    (a) he is subject to an enactment in force in Scotland by virtue of which regulations under section 289(1) of the Mental Health (Care and Treatment) (Scotland) Act 2003 apply to him; and

    (b) he is removed to England and Wales under those regulations.

(2) He shall be treated as if on the date of his arrival at the place where he is to reside in England or Wales—

    (a) he had been admitted to a hospital in England or Wales in pursuance of an application or order made on that date under the corresponding enactment; and

    (b) a community treatment order had then been made discharging him from the hospital.

(3) For these purposes—

    (a) if the enactment to which the patient was subject in Scotland was an enactment contained in the Mental Health (Care and Treatment) (Scotland) Act 2003, the corresponding enactment is section 3 of this Act;

(b) if the enactment to which he was subject in Scotland was an enactment contained in the Criminal Procedure (Scotland) Act 1995, the corresponding enactment is section 37 of this Act.

(4) 'The responsible hospital', in the case of a patient in respect of whom a community treatment order is in force by virtue of subsection (2) above, means the hospital to which he is treated as having been admitted by virtue of that subsection, subject to section 19A above.

(5) As soon as practicable after the patient's arrival at the place where he is to reside in England or Wales, the responsible clinician shall specify the conditions to which he is to be subject for the purposes of section 17B(1) above, and the conditions shall be deemed to be specified in the community treatment order.

(6) But the responsible clinician may only specify conditions under subsection (5) above which an approved mental health professional agrees should be specified.]

[Section 80C inserted by paragraph 4(1) of Schedule 5 to the 2007 Act.]

[80D Transfer of conditionally discharged patients from Scotland]

[(1) This section applies to a patient who is subject to—
   (a) a restriction order under section 59 of the Criminal Procedure (Scotland) Act 1995; and
   (b) a conditional discharge under section 193(7) of the Mental Health (Care and Treatment) (Scotland) Act 2003 ('the 2003 Act').

(2) A transfer of the patient to England and Wales under regulations made under section 290 of the 2003 Act shall have effect only if the Secretary of State has consented to the transfer.

(3) If a transfer under those regulations has effect, the patient shall be treated as if—
   (a) on the date of the transfer he had been conditionally discharged under section 42 or 73 above; and
   (b) he were subject to a hospital order under section 37 above and a restriction order under section 41 above.

(4) If the restriction order to which the patient was subject immediately before the transfer was of limited duration, the restriction order to which he is subject by virtue of subsection (3) above shall expire on the date on which the first-mentioned order would have expired if the transfer had not been made.]

[Section 80D inserted by paragraph 4(1) of Schedule 5 to the 2007 Act. Note: this amendment does not extend to Scotland.]

Removal to and from Northern Ireland

81 Removal of patients to Northern Ireland

(1) If it appears to the Secretary of State, in the case of a patient who is for the time being liable to be detained or subject to guardianship under this Act (otherwise than by virtue of section 35, 36 or 38 above), that it is in the interests of the patient to remove him to Northern Ireland, and that arrangements have been made for admitting him to a hospital or, as the case may be, for receiving him into guardianship there, the Secretary of State may authorise his removal to Northern Ireland and may give any necessary directions for his conveyance to his destination.

(2) Subject to the provisions of subsections (4) and (5) below, where a patient liable to be detained under this Act by virtue of an application, order or direction under any enactment in force in England and Wales is removed under this section and admitted to a hospital in Northern Ireland, he shall be treated as if on the date of his admission he had been so admitted in

pursuance of an application made, or an order or direction made or given, on that date under the corresponding enactment in force in Northern Ireland, and, *where he is subject to a restriction order or restriction direction under any enactment in this Act, as if he were subject to a restriction order or a restriction direction under the corresponding enactment* [where he is subject to a hospital order and a restriction order or a transfer direction and a restriction direction under any enactment in this Act, as if he were subject to a hospital order and a restriction order or a transfer direction and a restriction direction under the corresponding enactment] in force in Northern Ireland.

(3) Where a patient subject to guardianship under this Act by virtue of an application, order or direction under any enactment in force in England and Wales is removed under this section and received into guardianship in Northern Ireland, he shall be treated as if on the date on which he arrives at the place where he is to reside he had been so received in pursuance of an application, order or direction under the corresponding enactment in force in Northern Ireland, and as if the application had been accepted or, as the case may be, the order or direction had been made or given on that date.

(4) Where a person removed under this section was immediately before his removal liable to be detained by virtue of an application for admission for assessment under this Act, he shall, on his admission to a hospital in Northern Ireland, be treated as if he had been admitted to the hospital in pursuance of an application for assessment under Article 4 of the Mental Health (Northern Ireland) Order 1986 made on the date of his admission.

(5) Where a person removed under this section was immediately before his removal liable to be detained by virtue of an application for admission for treatment under this Act, he shall, on his admission to a hospital in Northern Ireland, be treated as if he were detained for treatment under Part II of the Mental Health (Northern Ireland) Order 1986 by virtue of a report under Article 12(1) of that Order made on the date of his admission.

(6) Where a patient removed under this section was immediately before his removal liable to be detained under this Act by virtue of a transfer direction given while he was serving a sentence of imprisonment (within the meaning of section 47(5) above) imposed by a court in England and Wales, he shall be treated as if the sentence had been imposed by a court in Northern Ireland.

(7) Where a person removed under this section was immediately before his removal subject to a *restriction order or* restriction direction of limited duration, the *restriction order or* restriction direction to which he is subject by virtue of subsection (2) above shall expire on the date on which the first-mentioned *restriction order or* restricted direction would have expired if he had not been so removed.

(8) In this section 'hospital' has the same meaning as in the (Northern Ireland) Order 1986.

[*Words in subsection (2) substituted by paragraph 5 of Schedule 5 to the 2007 Act. Words in subsection (7) omitted by section 40(4)— but see subsection (7) of that section for saving provision.*]

[81ZA Removal of community patients to Northern Ireland]

[(1) Section 81 above shall apply in the case of a community patient as it applies in the case of a patient who is for the time being liable to be detained under this Act, as if the community patient were so liable.

(2) Any reference in that section to the application, order or direction by virtue of which a patient is liable to be detained under this Act shall be construed, for these purposes, as a reference to the application, order or direction under this Act in respect of the patient.]

[*Section 81ZA inserted by paragraph 6 of Schedule 5 to the 2007 Act.*]

81A Transfer of responsibility for patients to Northern Ireland

(1) If it appears to the Secretary of State, in the case of a patient who—

    (a) is subject to a restriction order or restriction direction under section 41 or 49 above;

    [(a) is subject to a hospital order under section 37 above and a restriction order under section 41 above or to a transfer direction under section 47 above and a restriction direction under section 49 above;] and

    (b) has been conditionally discharged under section 42 or 73 above,

that a transfer under this section would be in the interests of the patient, the Secretary of State may, with the consent of the Minister exercising corresponding functions in Northern Ireland, transfer responsibility for the patient to that Minister.

(2) Where responsibility for such a patient is transferred under this section, the patient shall be treated—

    (a) as if on the date of the transfer he had been conditionally discharged under the corresponding enactment in force in Northern Ireland; and

    (b) as if he were subject to a *restriction order or restriction direction* [a hospital order and a restriction order, or to a transfer direction and a restriction direction,] under the corresponding enactment in force in Northern Ireland.

(3) Where a patient responsibility for whom is transferred under this section was immediately before the transfer subject to a *restriction order* or restriction direction of limited duration, the *restriction order or* restriction direction to which he is subject by virtue of subsection (2) above shall expire on the date on which the first-mentioned *order or* direction would have expired if the transfer had not been made.

[Subsection 1(a) and words in subsection (2)(b) substituted by paragraph 7(2) & (3) respectively of Schedule 5 to the 2007 Act; words omitted in subsection (3) by section 40(5)—but see subsection (7) of that section for saving provision.]

82 Removal to England and Wales of patients from Northern Ireland

(1) If it appears to the responsible authority, in the case of a patient who is for the time being liable to be detained or subject to guardianship under the (Northern Ireland) Order 1986 (otherwise than by virtue of Article 42, 43 or 45 of that Order), that it is in the interests of the patient to remove him to England and Wales, and that arrangements have been made for admitting him to a hospital or, as the case may be, for receiving him into guardianship there, the responsible authority may authorise his removal to England and Wales and may give any necessary directions for his conveyance to his destination.

(2) Subject to the provisions of subsections (4) and (4A) below, where a patient who is liable to be detained under the Mental Health (Northern Ireland) Order 1986 by virtue of an application, order or direction under any enactment in force in Northern Ireland is removed under this section and admitted to a hospital in England and Wales, he shall be treated as if on the date of his admission he had been so admitted in pursuance of an application made, or an order or direction made or given, on that date under the corresponding enactment in force in England and Wales and, *where he is subject to a restriction order or restriction direction under any enactment in that Order, as if he were subject to a restriction order or restriction direction under the corresponding enactment* [where he is subject to a hospital order and a restriction order or a transfer direction and a restriction direction under any enactment in that Order, as if he were subject to a hospital order and a restriction order or a transfer direction and a restriction direction under the corresponding enactment] in force in England and Wales.

(3) Where a patient subject to guardianship under the Mental Health (Northern Ireland) Order 1986 by virtue of an application, order or direction under any enactment in force in Northern Ireland is removed under this section and received into guardianship in England and Wales, he shall be treated as if on the date on which he arrives at the place where he is to reside he had been so received in pursuance of an application, order or direction under the corresponding enactment in force in England and Wales and as if the application had been accepted or, as the case may be, the order or direction had been made or given on that date.

(4) Where a person removed under this section was immediately before his removal liable to be detained for treatment by virtue of a report under Article 12(1) or 13 of the Mental Health (Northern Ireland) Order 1986, he shall be treated, on his admission to a hospital in England and Wales, as if he had been admitted to the hospital in pursuance of an application for admission for treatment made on the date of his admission.

(4A) Where a person removed under this section was immediately before his removal liable to be detained by virtue of an application for assessment under Article 4 of the Mental Health (Northern Ireland) Order 1986, he shall be treated, on his admission to a hospital in England and Wales, as if he had been admitted to the hospital in pursuance of an application for admission for assessment made on the date of his admission.

(5) Where a patient removed under this section was immediately before his removal liable to be detained under the Mental Health (Northern Ireland) Order 1986 by virtue of a transfer direction given while he was serving a sentence of imprisonment (within the meaning of Article 53(5) of that Order) imposed by a court in Northern Ireland, he shall be treated as if the sentence had been imposed by a court in England and Wales.

(6) Where a person removed under this section was immediately before his removal subject to a restriction order or restriction direction of limited duration, the restriction order or restriction direction to which he is subject by virtue of subsection (2) above shall expire on the date on which the first-mentioned restriction order or restriction direction would have expired if he had not been so removed.

(7) In this section 'the responsible authority' means the Department of Health and Social Services for Northern Ireland or, in relation to a patient who is subject to a restriction order or restriction direction, the Secretary of State.

[*Words in subsection (2) substituted by paragraph 8 of Schedule 5 to the 2007 Act.*]

82A Transfer of responsibility for [conditionally discharged] patients to England and Wales from Northern Ireland

(1) If it appears to the relevant Minister, in the case of a patient who—

(a) is subject to a restriction order or restriction direction under Article 47(1) or 55(1) of the Mental Health (Northern Ireland) Order 1986; and

(b) has been conditionally discharged under Article 48(2) or 78(2) of that Order,

that a transfer under this section would be in the interests of the patient, that Minister may, with the consent of the Secretary of State, transfer responsibility for the patient to the Secretary of State.

(2) Where responsibility for such a patient is transferred under this section, the patient shall be treated—

(a) as if on the date of the transfer he had been conditionally discharged under section 42 or 73 above; and

(b) as if he were subject to a restriction order or restriction direction under section 41 or 49 above.

[(b) as if he were subject to a hospital order under section 37 above and a restriction order under section 41 above or to a transfer direction under section 47 above and a restriction direction under section 49 above.]

(3) Where a patient responsibility for whom is transferred under this section was immediately before the transfer subject to a restriction order or restriction direction of limited duration, the restriction order or restriction direction to which he is subject by virtue of subsection (2) above shall expire on the date on which the first-mentioned order or direction would have expired if the transfer had not been made.

(4) In this section 'the relevant Minister' means the Minister exercising in Northern Ireland functions corresponding to those of the Secretary of State.

[*Title of section 82A amended and subsection (2)(b) substituted by paragraph 9 of Schedule 5 to the 2007 Act.*]

Removal to and from Channel Islands and Isle of Man

83 Removal of patients to Channel Islands or Isle of Man

If it appears to the Secretary of State, in the case of a patient who is for the time being liable to be detained or subject to guardianship under this Act (otherwise than by virtue of section 35, 36 or 38 above), that it is in the interests of the patient to remove him to any of the Channel Islands or to the Isle of Man, and that arrangements have been made for admitting him to a hospital or, as the case may be, for receiving him into guardianship there, the Secretary of State may authorise his removal to the island in question and may give any necessary directions for his conveyance to his destination.

[83ZA Removal or transfer of community patients to Channel Islands or Isle of Man]

[(1) Section 83 above shall apply in the case of a community patient as it applies in the case of a patient who is for the time being liable to be detained under this Act, as if the community patient were so liable.

(2) But if there are in force in any of the Channel Islands or the Isle of Man enactments ('relevant enactments') corresponding or similar to those relating to community patients in this Act—
(a) subsection (1) above shall not apply as regards that island; and
(b) subsections (3) to (6) below shall apply instead.

(3) If it appears to the appropriate national authority, in the case of a community patient, that the conditions mentioned in subsection (4) below are met, the authority may authorise the transfer of responsibility for him to the island in question.

(4) The conditions are—
(a) a transfer under subsection (3) above is in the patient's interests; and
(b) arrangements have been made for dealing with him under the relevant enactments.

(5) But the authority may not act under subsection (3) above while the patient is recalled to hospital under section 17E above.

(6) In this section, 'the appropriate national authority' means—
(a) in relation to a community patient in respect of whom the responsible hospital is in England, the Secretary of State;
(b) in relation to a community patient in respect of whom the responsible hospital is in Wales, the Welsh Ministers.]

[*Section 83ZA inserted by paragraph 10 of Schedule 5 to the 2007 Act.*]

83A Transfer of responsibility for [conditionally discharged] patients to Channel Islands or Isle of Man

If it appears to the Secretary of State, in the case of a patient who—

(a) is subject to a restriction order or restriction direction under section 41 or 49 above; and

(b) has been conditionally discharged under section 42 or 73 above,

that a transfer under this section would be in the interests of the patient, the Secretary of State may, with the consent of the authority exercising corresponding functions in any of the Channel Islands or in the Isle of Man, transfer responsibility for the patient to that authority.

[*Title of section 83A amended by paragraph 10 of Schedule 5 to the 2007 Act.*]

84 Removal to England and Wales of offenders found insane in Channel Islands and Isle of Man

(1) The Secretary of State may by warrant direct that any offender found by a court in any of the Channel Islands or in the Isle of Man to be insane or to have been insane at the time of the alleged offence, and ordered to be detained during Her Majesty's pleasure, be removed to a hospital in England and Wales.

(2) A patient removed under subsection (1) above shall, on his reception into the hospital in England and Wales, be treated as if he were subject to a hospital order together with a restriction order, *made without limitation of time.*

(3) The Secretary of State may by warrant direct that any patient removed under this section from any of the Channel Islands or from the Isle of Man be returned to the island from which he was so removed, there to be dealt with according to law in all respects as if he had not been removed under this section.

[*Words omitted in subsection (2) by section 40(3)(b)of the 2007 Act—but see subsection (7) of that section for saving provision.*]

85 Patients removed from Channel Islands or Isle of Man

(1) This section applies to any patient who is removed to England and Wales from any of the Channel Islands or the Isle of Man under a provision corresponding to section 83 above and who immediately before his removal was liable to be detained or subject to guardianship in the island in question under a provision corresponding to an enactment contained in this Act (other than section 35, 36 or 38 above).

(2) Where the patient is admitted to a hospital in England and Wales he shall be treated as if on the date of his admission he had been so admitted in pursuance of an application made, or an order or direction made or given, on that date under the corresponding enactment contained in this Act and, where he is subject to an order or direction restricting his discharge, as if he were subject *to a restriction order or restriction direction* [to a hospital order and a restriction order or to a hospital direction and a limitation direction or to a transfer direction and a restriction direction].

(3) Where the patient is received into guardianship in England and Wales, he shall be treated as if on the date on which he arrives at the place where he is to reside he had been so received in pursuance of an application, order or direction under the corresponding enactment contained in this Act and as if the application had been accepted or, as the case may be, the order or direction had been made or given on that date.

(4) Where the patient was immediately before his removal liable to be detained by virtue of a transfer direction given while he was serving a sentence of imprisonment imposed by a court

in the island in question, he shall be treated as if the sentence had been imposed by a court in England and Wales.

(5) Where the patient was immediately before his removal subject to an order or direction restricting his discharge, being an order or direction of limited duration, the restriction order or restriction direction to which he is subject by virtue of subsection (2) above shall expire on the date on which the first-mentioned order or direction would have expired if he had not been removed.

(6) While being conveyed to the hospital referred to in subsection (2) or, as the case may be, the place referred to in subsection (3) above, the patient shall be deemed to be in legal custody, and section 138 below shall apply to him as if he were in legal custody by virtue of section 137 below.

(7) In the case of a patient removed from the Isle of Man the reference in subsection (4) above to a person serving a sentence of imprisonment includes a reference to a person detained as mentioned in section 60(6)(a) of the Mental Health Act 1974 (an Act of Tynwald).

[*Words in subsection (2) substituted by paragraph 11 of Schedule 5 to the 2007 Act.*]

[85ZA Responsibility for community patients transferred from Channel Islands or Isle of Man]

[(1) This section shall have effect if there are in force in any of the Channel Islands or the Isle of Man enactments ('relevant enactments') corresponding or similar to those relating to community patients in this Act.

(2) If responsibility for a patient is transferred to England or Wales under a provision corresponding to section 83ZA(3) above, he shall be treated as if on the date of his arrival at the place where he is to reside in England or Wales—

    (a) he had been admitted to the hospital in pursuance of an application made, or an order or direction made or given, on that date under the enactment in force in England and Wales which most closely corresponds to the relevant enactments; and

    (b) a community treatment order had then been made discharging him from the hospital.

(3) 'The responsible hospital', in his case, means the hospital to which he is treated as having been admitted by virtue of subsection (2), subject to section 19A above.

(4) As soon as practicable after the patient's arrival at the place where he is to reside in England or Wales, the responsible clinician shall specify the conditions to which he is to be subject for the purposes of section 17B(1) above, and the conditions shall be deemed to be specified in the community treatment order.

(5) But the responsible clinician may only specify conditions under subsection (4) above which an approved mental health professional agrees should be specified.]

[*Section 85ZA inserted by paragraph 12 of Schedule 5 to the 2007 Act.*]

85A Responsibility for [conditionally discharged] patients transferred from Channel Islands or Isle of Man

(1) This section applies to any patient responsibility for whom is transferred to the Secretary of State by the authority exercising corresponding functions in any of the Channel Islands or the Isle of Man under a provision corresponding to section 83A above.

(2) The patient shall be treated—

    (a) as if on the date of the transfer he had been conditionally discharged under section 42 or 73 above; and

(b) as if he were subject to a restriction order or restriction direction under section 41 or 49 above.

[(b) as if he were subject to a hospital order under section 37 above and a restriction order under section 41 above, or to a hospital direction and a limitation direction under section 45A above, or to a transfer direction under section 47 above and a restriction direction under section 49 above.]

(3) Where the patient was immediately before the transfer subject to an order or direction restricting his discharge, being an order or direction of limited duration, the restriction order[, limitation direction] or restriction direction to which he is subject by virtue of subsection (2) above shall expire on the date on which the first-mentioned order or direction would have expired if the transfer had not been made.

[*Title of section 85A amended by paragraph 12 of Schedule 5 to the 2007 Act. Subsection (2)(b) substituted by paragraph 13(2) and words inserted in subsection (3) by paragraph 13(3) of that Schedule.*]

Removal of aliens

86 Removal of alien patients

(1) This section applies to any patient who is neither a British citizen nor a Commonwealth citizen having the right of abode in the United Kingdom by virtue of section 2(1)(b) of the Immigration Act 1971, being a patient who is receiving treatment for *mental illness* [mental disorder] as an in-patient in a hospital in England and Wales or a hospital within the meaning of the Mental Health (Northern Ireland) Order 1986 and is detained pursuant to—

(a) an application for admission for treatment or a report under Article 12(1) or 13 of that Order;

(b) a hospital order under section 37 above or Article 44 of that Order; or

(c) an order or direction under this Act (other than under section 35, 36 or 38 above) or under that Order (other than under Article 42, 43 or 45 of that Order) having the same effect as such a hospital order.

(2) If it appears to the Secretary of State that proper arrangements have been made for the removal of a patient to whom this section applies to a country or territory outside the United Kingdom, the Isle of Man and the Channel Islands and for his care or treatment there and that it is in the interests of the patient to remove him, the Secretary of State may, subject to subsection (3) below—

(a) by warrant authorise the removal of the patient from the place where he is receiving treatment as mentioned in subsection (1) above, and

(b) give such directions as the Secretary of State thinks fit for the conveyance of the patient to his destination in that country or territory and for his detention in any place or on board any ship or aircraft until his arrival at any specified port or place in any such country or territory.

(3) The Secretary of State shall not exercise his powers under subsection (2) above in the case of any patient except with the approval of a Mental Health Review Tribunal or, as the case may be, of the Mental Health Review Tribunal for Northern Ireland.

[(4) In relation to a patient receiving treatment in a hospital within the meaning of the Mental Health (Northern Ireland) Order 1986, the reference in subsection (1) above to mental disorder shall be construed in accordance with that Order].

[*Words substituted in subsection (1) and subsection (4) inserted by paragraphs 15(2) and (3) respectively of Schedule 1 to the 2007.*]

Return of patients absent without leave

87 Patients absent from hospitals in Northern Ireland

(1) Any person who—

    (a) under Article 29 or 132 of the Mental Health (Northern Ireland) Order 1986 (which provide, respectively, for the retaking of patients absent without leave and for the retaking of patients escaping from custody); or

    (b) under the said Article 29 as applied by Article 31 of the said Order (which makes special provision as to persons sentenced to imprisonment);

may be taken into custody in Northern Ireland, may be taken into custody in, and returned to Northern Ireland from, England and Wales by an *approved social worker* [approved mental health professional], by any constable or by any person authorised by or by virtue of the said Order to take him into custody.

(2) This section does not apply to any person who is subject to guardianship.

[*Words in subsection (1) substituted by paragraph 7(f) of Schedule 2 to the 2007 Act.*]

88 Patients absent from hospitals in England and Wales

(1) Subject to the provisions of this section, any person who, under section 18 above or section 138 below or under the said section 18 as applied by section 22 above, may be taken into custody in England and Wales may be taken into custody in, and returned to England and Wales from, *any other part of the United Kingdom or the Channel Islands or the Isle of Man* [Northern Ireland].

(2) *For the purposes of the enactments referred to in subsection (1) above, in their application by virtue of this section to Scotland, Northern Ireland, the Channel Islands or the Isle of Man, the expression 'constable' includes a Scottish constable, an officer or constable of the Police Service of Northern Ireland, a member of the police in Jersey, an officer of police within the meaning of section 43 of the Larceny (Guernsey) Law 1958 or any corresponding law for the time being in force, or a constable in the Isle of Man, as the case may be.*

[(2) For the purposes of the enactments referred to in subsection (1) above in their application by virtue of this section, the expression 'constable' includes an officer or constable of the Police Service of Northern Ireland.]

(3) For the purposes of the said enactments in their application by virtue of this section *to Scotland or Northern Ireland,* any reference to an *approved social worker* [approved mental health professional] shall be construed as including a reference—

    (a) *in Scotland, to any mental health officer within the meaning of the Mental Health (Care and Treatment) (Scotland) Act 2003;*

    (b) *in Northern Ireland,* to any approved social worker within the meaning of the Mental Health (Northern Ireland) Order 1986.

(4) This section does not apply to any person who is subject to guardianship.

[*Words in subsection (1) and whole of subsection (2) substituted by paragraphs 14(2) & (3) respectively of Schedule 5 to the 2007 Act; words omitted from subsection (3) by paragraph 14(4)(a) to (c) of that Schedule; and words substituted in that subsection by paragraph 7(g) of Schedule 2.*]

89 Patients absent from hospitals in the Channel Islands or Isle of Man

(1) Any person who under any provision corresponding to section 18 above or 138 below may be taken into custody in any of the Channel Islands or the Isle of Man may be taken into custody in, and returned to the island in question from, England and Wales by an *approved social worker* [approved mental health professional] or a constable.

(2) This section does not apply to any person who is subject to guardianship.

[*Words substituted in subsection (1) by paragraph 7(h) of Schedule 2 to the 2007 Act.*]

General

90 Regulations for purposes of Part VI

Section 32 above shall have effect as if references in that section to Part II of this Act included references to this Part of this Act *and to regulations made under section 290 of the Mental Health (Care and Treatment) (Scotland) Act 2003 and articles 2, 3 and 10 of the Mental Health (Care and Treatment) (Scotland) Act 2003 (Consequential Provisions) Order 2005, so far as that Part or those regulations or articles apply to patients removed to England and Wales thereunder* [so far as this Part of this Act applies to patients removed to England and Wales or for whom responsibility is transferred to England and Wales].

[*Words substituted by paragraph 15 of Schedule 5 to the 2007 Act.*]

91 General provisions as to patients removed from England and Wales

(1) Subject to subsection (2) below, where a patient liable to be detained or subject to guardianship by virtue of an application, order or direction under Part II or III of this Act (other than section 35, 36 or 38 above) is removed from England and Wales in pursuance of arrangements under this Part of this Act, the application, order or direction shall cease to have effect when he is duly received into a hospital or other institution, or placed under guardianship or, where he is not received into a hospital but his detention in hospital is authorised by virtue of the Mental Health (Care and Treatment) (Scotland) Act 2003 or the Criminal Procedure (Scotland) Act 1995, in pursuance of those arrangements.

(2) Where the Secretary of State exercises his powers under section 86(2) above in respect of a patient who is detained pursuant to a hospital order under section 37 above and in respect of whom a restriction order is in force, those orders shall continue in force so as to apply to the patient if he returns to England and Wales *at any time before the end of the period for which those orders would have continued in force.*

[(2A) Where responsibility for a community patient is transferred to a jurisdiction outside England and Wales (or such a patient is removed outside England and Wales) in pursuance of arrangements under this Part of this Act, the application, order or direction mentioned in subsection (1) above in force in respect of him shall cease to have effect on the date on which responsibility is so transferred (or he is so removed) in pursuance of those arrangements.]

(3) Reference in this section to a patient's detention in hospital being authorised by virtue of the Mental Health (Care and Treatment) (Scotland) Act 2003 or the Criminal Procedure (Scotland) Act 1995 shall be read as including references to a patient in respect of whom a certificate under one of the provisions listed in section 290(7)(a) of the Act of 2003 is in operation.

[*Words omitted from subsection (2) by section 40(6) of the 2007 Act— but see subsection (7) of that section for saving provision. Subsection (2A) inserted by paragraph 16 of Schedule 5.*]

92 Interpretation of Part VI

(1) References in this Part of this Act to a hospital, being a hospital in England and Wales, shall be construed as references to a hospital within the meaning of Part II of this Act.

[(1A) References in this Part of this Act to the responsible clinician shall be construed as references to the responsible clinician within the meaning of Part 2 of this Act.]

(2) Where a patient is treated by virtue of this Part of this Act as if he had been removed to a hospital in England and Wales in pursuance of a direction under Part III of this Act, that direction shall be deemed to have been given on the date of his reception into the hospital.

(3) *A patient removed to England and Wales under this Part of this Act or the Mental Health (Care and Treatment) (Scotland) Act 2003 (Consequential Provisions) Order 2005 and regulations made under section 290 of the Mental Health (Care and Treatment) (Scotland) Act 2003 shall be treated for the purposes of this Act as suffering from such form of mental disorder as may be recorded in his case in pursuance of regulations made by virtue of section 90 above, and references in this Act to the form or forms of mental disorder specified in the relevant application, order or direction shall be construed as including references to the form or forms of mental disorder so recorded.*

(4) Sections 80 to 85A above shall have effect as if—

(a) any hospital direction under section 45A above were a transfer direction under section 47 above; and

(b) any limitation direction under section 45A above were a restriction direction under section 49 above.

(5) Sections 80(5), 81(6) and 85(4) above shall have effect as if any reference to a transfer direction given while a patient was serving a sentence of imprisonment imposed by a court included a reference to a hospital direction given by a court after imposing a sentence of imprisonment on a patient.

[*Subsection (1A) inserted by paragraph 17 of Schedule 5 to the 2007 Act. Subsection (3) repealed by Part 1 of Schedule 11.*]

PART VIII
MISCELLANEOUS FUNCTIONS OF LOCAL AUTHORITIES AND THE SECRETARY OF STATE

Approved social workers

114 *Appointment of approved social workers*

(1) *A local social services authority shall appoint a sufficient number of approved social workers for the purpose of discharging the functions conferred on them by this Act.*

(2) *No person shall be appointed by a local social services authority as an approved social worker unless he is approved by the authority as having appropriate competence in dealing with persons who are suffering from mental disorder.*

(3) *In approving a person for appointment as an approved social worker a local social services authority shall have regard to such matters as the Secretary of State may direct.*

[Approved mental health professionals]

[114 Approval by local social services authority]

[(1) A local social services authority may approve a person to act as an approved mental health professional for the purposes of this Act.

(2) But a local social services authority may not approve a registered medical practitioner to act as an approved mental health professional.

(3) Before approving a person under subsection (1) above, a local social service authority shall be satisfied that he has appropriate competence in dealing with persons who are suffering from mental disorder.

(4) The appropriate national authority may by regulations make provision in connection with the giving of approvals under subsection (1) above.

(5) The provision which may be made by regulations under subsection (4) above includes, in particular, provision as to—
   (a) the period for which approvals under subsection (1) above have effect;
   (b) the courses to be undertaken by persons before such approvals are to be given and during the period for which such approvals have effect;
   (c) the conditions subject to which such approvals are to be given; and
   (d) the factors to be taken into account in determining whether persons have appropriate competence as mentioned in subsection (3) above.

(6) Provision made by virtue of subsection (5)(b) above may relate to courses approved or provided by such person as may be specified in the regulations (as well as to courses approved under section 114A below).

(7) An approval by virtue of subsection (6) above may be in respect of a course in general or in respect of a course in relation to a particular person.

(8) The power to make regulations under subsection (4) above includes power to make different provision for different cases or areas.

(9) In this section 'the appropriate national authority' means—
   (a) in relation to persons who are or wish to become approved to act as approved mental health professionals by a local social services authority whose area is in England, the Secretary of State;
   (b) in relation to persons who are or wish to become approved to act as approved mental health professionals by a local social services authority whose area is in Wales, the Welsh Ministers.

(10) In this Act 'approved mental health professional' means—
   (a) in relation to acting on behalf of a local social services authority whose area is in England, a person approved under subsection (1) above by any local social services authority whose area is in England, and
   (b) in relation to acting on behalf of a local social services authority whose area is in Wales, a person approved under that subsection by any local social services authority whose area is in Wales.]

[Section 114 (and cross heading above it) substituted by section 18 of the 2007 Act.]

[114A Approval of courses etc for approved mental health professionals]

[(1) The relevant Council may, in accordance with rules made by it, approve courses for persons who are or wish to become approved mental health professionals.

(2) For that purpose—

    (a) subsections (2) to (4)(a) and (7) of section 63 of the Care Standards Act 2000 apply as they apply to approvals given, rules made and courses approved under that section; and

    (b) sections 66 and 71 of that Act apply accordingly.

(3) In subsection (1), 'the relevant Council' means—

    (a) in relation to persons who are or wish to become approved to act as approved mental health professionals by a local social services authority whose area is in England, the General Social Care Council;

    (b) in relation to persons who are or wish to become approved to act as approved mental health professionals by a local social services authority whose area is in Wales, the Care Council for Wales.

(4) The functions of an approved mental health professional shall not be considered to be relevant social work for the purposes of Part 4 of the Care Standards Act 2000.

(5) The General Social Care Council and the Care Council for Wales may also carry out, or assist other persons in carrying out, research into matters relevant to training for approved mental health professionals.]

[*Section 114A inserted by section 19 of the 2007 Act.*]

115 Powers of entry and inspection

An approved social worker of a local social services authority may at all reasonable times after producing, if asked to do so, some duly authenticated document showing that he is such a social worker, enter and inspect any premises (not being a hospital) in the area of that authority in which a mentally disordered patient is living, if he has reasonable cause to believe that the patient is not under proper care.

[115 Powers of entry and inspection]

[(1) An approved mental health professional may at all reasonable times enter and inspect any premises (other than a hospital) in which a mentally disordered patient is living, if he has reasonable cause to believe that the patient is not under proper care.

(2) The power under subsection (1) above shall be exercisable only after the professional has produced, if asked to do so, some duly authenticated document showing that he is an approved mental health professional.]

[*Section 115 substituted by paragraph 8 of Schedule 2 to the 2007 Act.*]

Visiting patients

116 Welfare of certain hospital patients

(1) Where a patient to whom this section applies is admitted to a hospital, independent hospital or care home in England and Wales (whether for treatment for mental disorder or for any other reason) then, without prejudice to their duties in relation to the patient apart from the provisions of this section, the authority shall arrange for visits to be made to him on behalf of the authority, and shall take such other steps in relation to the patient while in the hospital, independent hospital or care home as would be expected to be taken by his parents.

(2) This section applies to—

    (a) a child or young person—

        (i) who is in the care of a local authority by virtue of a care order within the meaning of the Children Act 1989, or

(ii) in respect of whom the rights and powers of a parent are vested in a local authority by virtue of section 16 of the Social Work (Scotland) Act 1968;

(b) a person who is subject to the guardianship of a local social services authority under the provisions of this Act; or

(c) a person the functions of whose nearest relative under this Act are for the time being transferred to a local social services authority.

After-care

117 After-care

(1) This section applies to persons who are detained under section 3 above, or admitted to a hospital in pursuance of a hospital order made under section 37 above, or transferred to a hospital in pursuance of a hospital direction made under section 45A above or a transfer direction made under section 47 or 48 above, and then cease to be detained and (whether or not immediately after so ceasing) leave hospital.

(2) It shall be the duty of the Primary Care Trust or Local Health Board and of the local social services authority to provide, in co-operation with relevant voluntary agencies, after-care services for any person to whom this section applies until such time as the Primary Care Trust or Local Health Board and the local social services authority are satisfied that the person concerned is no longer in need of such services; but they shall not be so satisfied in the case of a *patient who is subject to after-care under supervision at any time while he remains so subject* [community patient while he remains such a patient].

(2A) *It shall be the duty of the Primary Care Trust or Local Health Board to secure that at all times while a patient is subject to after-care under supervision—*

(a) *a person who is a registered medical practitioner approved for the purposes of section 12 above by the Secretary of State as having special experience in the diagnosis or treatment of mental disorder is in charge of the medical treatment provided for the patient as part of the after-care services provided for him under this section; and*

(b) *a person professionally concerned with any of the after-care services so provided is supervising him with a view to securing that he receives the after-care services so provided.*

(2B) Section 32 above shall apply for the purposes of this section as it applies for the purposes of Part II of this Act.

(3) In this section 'the Primary Care Trust or Local Health Board' means the Primary Care Trust or Local Health Board, and 'the local social services authority' means the local social services authority, for the area in which the person concerned is resident or to which he is sent on discharge by the hospital in which he was detained.

[*Words in subsection (2) substituted by paragraph 24 of Schedule 3 to the 2007 Act. Subsection (2A) omitted by Part 5 of Schedule 11.*]

Functions of the Secretary of State

118 Code of practice

(1) The Secretary of State shall prepare, and from time to time revise, a code of practice—

(a) for the guidance of registered medical practitioners[, approved clinicians], managers and staff of hospitals, independent hospitals and care homes and *approved social workers* [approved mental health professionals] in relation to the admission of patients to hospitals and registered establishments under this Act and to guardianship and *after-care under supervision* [community patients] under this Act; and

(b) for the guidance of registered medical practitioners and members of other professions in relation to the medical treatment of patients suffering from mental disorder.

(2) The code shall, in particular, specify forms of medical treatment in addition to any specified by regulations made for the purposes of section 57 above which in the opinion of the Secretary of State give rise to special concern and which should accordingly not be given by a registered medical practitioner unless the patient has consented to the treatment (or to a plan of treatment including that treatment) and a certificate in writing as to the matters mentioned in subsection (2)(a) and (b) of that section has been given by another registered medical practitioner, being a practitioner appointed for the purposes of this section by the Secretary of State.

[(2A) The code shall include a statement of the principles which the Secretary of State thinks should inform decisions under this Act.

(2B) In preparing the statement of principles the Secretary of State shall, in particular, ensure that each of the following matters is addressed—

(a) respect for patients' past and present wishes and feelings,

(b) respect for diversity generally including, in particular, diversity of religion, culture and sexual orientation (within the meaning of section 35 of the Equality Act 2006),

(c) minimising restrictions on liberty,

(d) involvement of patients in planning, developing and delivering care and treatment appropriate to them,

(e) avoidance of unlawful discrimination,

(f) effectiveness of treatment,

(g) views of carers and other interested parties,

(h) patient wellbeing and safety, and

(i) public safety.

(2C) The Secretary of State shall also have regard to the desirability of ensuring—

(a) the efficient use of resources, and

(b) the equitable distribution of services.

(2D) In performing functions under this Act persons mentioned in subsection (1)(a) or (b) shall have regard to the code.]

(3) Before preparing the code or making any alteration in it the Secretary of State shall consult such bodies as appear to him to be concerned.

(4) The Secretary of State shall lay copies of the code and of any alteration in the code before Parliament; and if either House of Parliament passes a resolution requiring the code or any alteration in it to be withdrawn the Secretary of State shall withdraw the code or alteration and, where he withdraws the code, shall prepare a code in substitution for the one which is withdrawn.

(5) No resolution shall be passed by either House of Parliament under subsection (4) above in respect of a code or alteration after the expiration of the period of 40 days beginning with the day on which a copy of the code or alteration was laid before that House; but for the purposes of this subsection no account shall be taken of any time during which Parliament is dissolved or prorogued or during which both Houses are adjourned for more than four days.

(6) The Secretary of State shall publish the code as for the time being in force.

[*In subsection (1)(a): 'approved clinicians' inserted by section 14(2) of the 2007 Act; 'approved mental health professional' substituted for 'approved social workers' by paragraph 9 of Schedule 2; and 'community patients' substituted for 'after-care under supervision' by paragraph 25 of Schedule 3. Subsections (2A) to (2D) inserted by section 8.*]

119 Practitioners approved for Part IV and s 118

(1) The Secretary of State may make such provision as he may with the approval of the Treasury determine for the payment of remuneration, allowances, pensions or gratuities to or in respect of registered medical practitioners appointed by him for the purposes of Part IV of this Act and section 118 above and to or in respect of other persons appointed for the purposes of section 57(2)(a) above.

(2) A registered medical practitioner or other person appointed by the Secretary of State for the purposes of the provisions mentioned in subsection (1) above may, for the purpose of exercising his functions under those provisions [or under Part 4A of this Act], at any reasonable time—

  (a) visit and interview and, in the case of a registered medical practitioner, examine in private any patient detained *in a registered establishment* [in a hospital or registered establishment or any community patient in a hospital or establishment of any description or (if access is granted) other place]; and

  (b) require the production of and inspect any records relating to the treatment of the patient *in that home* [there].

[(3) In this section, 'establishment of any description' shall be construed in accordance with section 4(8) of the Care Standards Act 2000.]

[*Words inserted and substituted in subsection (2) by section 35(2)(a) of the 2007 Act. Subsection (3) inserted by section 35(2)(b).*]

120 General protection of detained patients

(1) The Secretary of State shall keep under review the exercise of the powers and the discharge of the duties conferred or imposed by this Act so far as relating to the detention of patients or to patients liable to be detained under this Act [or to community patients] and shall make arrangements for persons authorised by him in that behalf—

  (a) to visit and interview in private patients detained under this Act in hospitals and registered establishments [and community patients in hospitals and establishments of any description and (if access is granted) other places]; and

  (b) to investigate—

    (i) any complaint made by a person in respect of a matter that occurred while he was detained under this Act in [, or recalled under section 17E above to,] a hospital or registered establishment and which he considers has not been satisfactorily dealt with by the managers of that hospital or registered establishment; and

    (ii) any other complaint as to the exercise of the powers or the discharge of the duties conferred or imposed by this Act in respect of a person who is or has been so detained [or is or has been a community patient].

(2) The arrangements made under this section in respect of the investigation of complaints may exclude matters from investigation in specified circumstances and shall not require any person exercising functions under the arrangements to undertake or continue with any investigation where he does not consider it appropriate to do so.

(3) Where any such complaint as is mentioned in subsection (1)(b)(ii) above is made by a Member of Parliament and investigated under the arrangements made under this section the results of the investigation shall be reported to him.

(4) For the purpose of any such review as is mentioned in subsection (1) above or of carrying out his functions under arrangements made under this section any person authorised in that behalf by the Secretary of State may at any reasonable time—

(a) visit and interview and, if he is a registered medical practitioner [or approved clinician], examine in private any patient in a *registered establishment* [hospital or establishment of any description]; and

(b) require the production of and inspect any records relating to the detention or treatment of any person who is or has been detained *in a registered establishment* [under this Act or who is or has been a community patient].

(6) The Secretary of State may make such provision as he may with the approval of the Treasury determine for the payment of remuneration, allowances, pensions or gratuities to or in respect of persons exercising functions in relation to any such review as is mentioned in subsection (1) above or functions under arrangements made under this section.

(7) The powers and duties referred to in subsection (1) above do not include any power or duty conferred or imposed by Part VII of this Act.

[(8) In this section, 'establishment of any description' has the same meaning as in section 119 above.]

[*Words inserted in subsection (1) by paragraph 26(2) of Schedule 3 to the 2007 Act. Words inserted in subsection (4)(a) by section 14(3)(a). Words substituted in that same paragraph (a) and words inserted in paragraph (b) by paragraph 26(3)(a)&(b) respectively of Schedule 3. Subsection (8) inserted by paragraph 26(4) of that Schedule.*]

121 Mental Health Act Commission

(1) Without prejudice to section 273(1) of the National Health Service Act 2006, or section 204(1) of the National Health Service (Wales) Act 2006 (power to vary or revoke orders or directions) there shall continue to be a Special Health Authority known as the Mental Health Act Commission established under section 11 of that Act.

(2) Without prejudice to the generality of his powers under section 13 of that Act, the Secretary of State shall direct the Commission to perform on his behalf—

(a) the function of appointing registered medical practitioners for the purposes of Part IV of this Act and section 118 above and of appointing other persons for the purposes of section 57(2)(a) above; and

(b) the functions of the Secretary of State under sections 61[, 64H(5)] and 120(1) and (4) above.

(3) The registered medical practitioners and other persons appointed for the purposes mentioned in subsection (2)(a) above may include members of the Commission.

(4) The Secretary of State may, at the request of or after consultation with the Commission and after consulting such other bodies as appear to him to be concerned, direct the Commission to keep under review the care and treatment, or any aspect of the care and treatment, in hospitals, independent hospitals and care homes of patients who are *not liable to be detained under this Act* [neither liable to be detained under this Act nor community patients].

(5) For the purpose of any such review as is mentioned in subsection (4) above any person authorised in that behalf by the Commission may at any reasonable time—

(a) visit and interview and, if he is a registered medical practitioner [or approved clinician], examine in private any patient in an independent hospital or a care home; and

(b) require the production of and inspect any records relating to the treatment of any person who is or has been a patient in an independent hospital or a care home.

(6) The Secretary of State may make such provision as he may with the approval of the Treasury determine for the payment of remuneration, allowances, pensions or gratuities to or in respect of persons exercising functions in relation to any such review as is mentioned in subsection (4) above.

(7) The Commission shall review any decision to withhold a postal packet (or anything contained in it) under subsection (1)(b) or (2) of section 134 below if any application in that behalf is made—

(a) in a case under subsection (1)(b), by the patient; or

(b) in a case under subsection (2), either by the patient or by the person by whom the postal packet was sent;

and any such application shall be made within six months of the receipt by the applicant of the notice referred to in subsection (6) of that section.

(8) On an application under subsection (7) above the Commission may direct that the postal packet which is the subject of the application (or anything contained in it) shall not be withheld and the managers in question shall comply with any such direction.

(9) The Secretary of State may by regulations make provision with respect to the making and determination of applications under subsection (7) above, including provision for the production to the Commission of any postal packet which is the subject of such an application.

(10) The Commission shall in the second year after its establishment and subsequently in every second year publish a report on its activities; and copies of every such report shall be sent by the Commission to the Secretary of State who shall lay a copy before each House of Parliament.

(11) Paragraph 2 of Schedule 6 to the National Health Service Act 2006, and paragraph 2 of Schedule 5 to the National Health Service (Wales) Act 2006 (pay and allowances for chairmen and members of Special Health Authorities) shall have effect in relation to the Mental Health Act Commission as if references in sub-paragraphs (1) and (2) to the chairman included references to any member and as if the reference to a member in sub-paragraph (4) included a reference to the chairman.

[*'64H(5)' inserted in subsection (2) by Section 32(3). Words substituted in subsection (4) by paragraph 27 of Schedule 3. Words inserted in subsection (5)(a) by section 14(3)(b).*]

122 Provision of pocket money for in-patients in hospital

(1) The Secretary of State may pay to persons who are receiving treatment as in-patients (whether liable to be detained or not) in hospitals wholly or mainly used for the treatment of persons suffering from mental disorder, such amounts as he thinks fit in respect of their occasional personal expenses where it appears to him that they would otherwise be without resources to meet those expenses.

(2) For the purposes of the National Health Service Act 2006 and the National Health Service (Wales) Act 2006, the making of payments under this section to persons for whom hospital services are provided under either of those Acts shall be treated as included among those services.

123 Transfers to and from special hospitals

(1) Without prejudice to any other provisions of this Act with respect to the transfer of patients, any patient who is for the time being liable to be detained under this Act (other than under section 35, 36 or 38 above) in a hospital at which high security psychiatric services are provided

may, upon the directions of the Secretary of State, at any time be removed into any other hospital at which those services are provided.

(2) Without prejudice to any such provision, the Secretary of State may give directions for the transfer of any patient who is for the time being liable to be so detained into a hospital at which those services are not provided.

(3) Subsections (2) and (4) of section 19 above shall apply in relation to the transfer or removal of a patient under this section as they apply in relation to the transfer or removal of a patient from one hospital to another under that section.

PART IX
OFFENCES

126 Forgery, false statements, etc

(1) Any person who without lawful authority or excuse has in his custody or under his control any document to which this subsection applies, which is, and which he knows or believes to be, false within the meaning of Part I of the Forgery and Counterfeiting Act 1981, shall be guilty of an offence.

(2) Any person who without lawful authority or excuse makes, or has in his custody or under his control, any document so closely resembling a document to which subsection (1) above applies as to be calculated to deceive shall be guilty of an offence.

(3) The documents to which subsection (1) above applies are any documents purporting to be—
   (a) an application under Part II of this Act;
   (b) a medical or other recommendation or report under this Act; and
   (c) any other document required or authorised to be made for any of the purposes of this Act.

(4) Any person who—
   (a) wilfully makes a false entry or statement in any application, recommendation, report, record or other document required or authorised to be made for any of the purposes of this Act; or
   (b) with intent to deceive, makes use of any such entry or statement which he knows to be false,
   shall be guilty of an offence.

(5) Any person guilty of an offence under this section shall be liable—
   (a) on summary conviction, to imprisonment for a term not exceeding six months or to a fine not exceeding the statutory maximum, or to both;
   (b) on conviction on indictment, to imprisonment for a term not exceeding two years or to a fine of any amount, or to both.

127 Ill-treatment of patients

(1) It shall be an offence for any person who is an officer on the staff of or otherwise employed in, or who is one of the managers of, a hospital, independent hospital or care home—
   (a) to ill-treat or wilfully to neglect a patient for the time being receiving treatment for mental disorder as an in-patient in that hospital or home; or
   (b) to ill-treat or wilfully to neglect, on the premises of which the hospital or home forms part, a patient for the time being receiving such treatment there as an out-patient.

(2) It shall be an offence for any individual to ill-treat or wilfully to neglect a mentally disordered patient who is for the time being subject to his guardianship under this Act or otherwise in his custody or care (whether by virtue of any legal or moral obligation or otherwise).

(2A) It shall be an offence for any individual to ill-treat or wilfully to neglect a mentally disordered patient who is for the time being subject to after-care under supervision.

(3) Any person guilty of an offence under this section shall be liable—

    (a) on summary conviction, to imprisonment for a term not exceeding six months or to a fine not exceeding the statutory maximum, or to both;

    (b) on conviction on indictment, to imprisonment for a term not exceeding *two years* [five years] or to a fine of any amount, or to both.

(4) No proceedings shall be instituted for an offence under this section except by or with the consent of the Director of Public Prosecutions.

[Subsection (2A) omitted by Part 5 of Schedule 11 to the 2007 Act. Substitution in subsection (3) made by section 42.]

128 Assisting patients to absent themselves without leave, etc

(1) Where any person induces or knowingly assists another person who is liable to be detained in a hospital within the meaning of Part II of this Act or is subject to guardianship under this Act [or is a community patient] to absent himself without leave he shall be guilty of an offence.

(2) Where any person induces or knowingly assists another person who is in legal custody by virtue of section 137 below to escape from such custody he shall be guilty of an offence.

(3) Where any person knowingly harbours a patient who is absent without leave or is otherwise at large and liable to be retaken under this Act or gives him any assistance with intent to prevent, hinder or interfere with his being taken into custody or returned to the hospital or other place where he ought to be he shall be guilty of an offence.

(4) Any person guilty of an offence under this section shall be liable—

    (a) on summary conviction, to imprisonment for a term not exceeding six months or to a fine not exceeding the statutory maximum, or to both;

    (b) on conviction on indictment, to imprisonment for a term not exceeding two years or to a fine of any amount, or to both.

[Words inserted in subsection (1) by paragraph 28 of Schedule 3 to the 2007 Act.]

129 Obstruction

(1) Any person who without reasonable cause—

    (a) refuses to allow the inspection of any premises; or

    (b) refuses to allow the visiting, interviewing or examination of any person by a person authorised in that behalf by or under this Act or to give access to any person to a person so authorised; or

    (c) refuses to produce for the inspection of any person so authorised any document or record the production of which is duly required by him; or

    (d) otherwise obstructs any such person in the exercise of his functions,

shall be guilty of an offence.

(2) Without prejudice to the generality of subsection (1) above, any person who insists on being present when required to withdraw by a person authorised by or under this Act to interview or examine a person in private shall be guilty of an offence.

(3) Any person guilty of an offence under this section shall be liable on summary conviction[5] to imprisonment for a term not exceeding three months or to a fine not exceeding level 4 on the standard scale or to both.

130 Prosecutions by local authorities

A local social services authority may institute proceedings for any offence under this Part of this Act, but without prejudice to any provision of this Part of this Act requiring the consent of the Director of Public Prosecutions for the institution of such proceedings.

PART X
MISCELLANEOUS AND SUPPLEMENTARY

Miscellaneous provisions

[130A Independent mental health advocates]

[(1) The appropriate national authority shall make such arrangements as it considers reasonable to enable persons ('independent mental health advocates') to be available to help qualifying patients.

(2) The appropriate national authority may by regulations make provision as to the appointment of persons as independent mental health advocates.

(3) The regulations may, in particular, provide—
   (a) that a person may act as an independent mental health advocate only in such circumstances, or only subject to such conditions, as may be specified in the regulations;
   (b) for the appointment of a person as an independent mental health advocate to be subject to approval in accordance with the regulations.

(4) In making arrangements under this section, the appropriate national authority shall have regard to the principle that any help available to a patient under the arrangements should, so far as practicable, be provided by a person who is independent of any person who is professionally concerned with the patient's medical treatment.

(5) For the purposes of subsection (4) above, a person is not to be regarded as professionally concerned with a patient's medical treatment merely because he is representing him in accordance with arrangements—
   (a) under section 35 of the Mental Capacity Act 2005; or
   (b) of a description specified in regulations under this section.

(6) Arrangements under this section may include provision for payments to be made to, or in relation to, persons carrying out functions in accordance with the arrangements.

(7) Regulations under this section—
   (a) may make different provision for different cases;
   (b) may make provision which applies subject to specified exceptions;
   (c) may include transitional, consequential, incidental or supplemental provision.]

[*Section 130A inserted by section 30(2) of the 2007 Act.*]

---

[5] Words 'to imprisonment for a term not exceeding three months or' omitted by Part 9 of Schedule 37 to the Criminal Justice Act 2007, but that amendment is not yet in force.

[130B Arrangements under section 130A]

[(1) The help available to a qualifying patient under arrangements under section 130A above shall include help in obtaining information about and understanding—

(a) the provisions of this Act by virtue of which he is a qualifying patient;

(b) any conditions or restrictions to which he is subject by virtue of this Act;

(c) what (if any) medical treatment is given to him or is proposed or discussed in his case;

(d) why it is given, proposed or discussed;

(e) the authority under which it is, or would be, given; and

(f) the requirements of this Act which apply, or would apply, in connection with the giving of the treatment to him.

(2) The help available under the arrangements to a qualifying patient shall also include—

(a) help in obtaining information about and understanding any rights which may be exercised under this Act by or in relation to him; and

(b) help (by way of representation or otherwise) in exercising those rights.

(3) For the purpose of providing help to a patient in accordance with the arrangements, an independent mental health advocate may—

(a) visit and interview the patient in private;

(b) visit and interview any person who is professionally concerned with his medical treatment;

(c) require the production of and inspect any records relating to his detention or treatment in any hospital or registered establishment or to any after-care services provided for him under section 117 above;

(d) require the production of and inspect any records of, or held by, a local social services authority which relate to him.

(4) But an independent mental health advocate is not entitled to the production of, or to inspect, records in reliance on subsection (3)(c) or (d) above unless—

(a) in a case where the patient has capacity or is competent to consent, he does consent; or

(b) in any other case, the production or inspection would not conflict with a decision made by a donee or deputy or the Court of Protection and the person holding the records, having regard to such matters as may be prescribed in regulations under section 130A above, considers that—

(i) the records may be relevant to the help to be provided by the advocate; and

(ii) the production or inspection is appropriate.

(5) For the purpose of providing help to a patient in accordance with the arrangements, an independent mental health advocate shall comply with any reasonable request made to him by any of the following for him to visit and interview the patient—

(a) the person (if any) appearing to the advocate to be the patient's nearest relative;

(b) the responsible clinician for the purposes of this Act;

(c) an approved mental health professional.

(6) But nothing in this Act prevents the patient from declining to be provided with help under the arrangements.

(7) In subsection (4) above—

(a) the reference to a patient who has capacity is to be read in accordance with the Mental Capacity Act 2005;

(b) the reference to a donee is to a donee of a lasting power of attorney (within the meaning of section 9 of that Act) created by the patient, where the donee is acting within the scope of his authority and in accordance with that Act;

(c) the reference to a deputy is to a deputy appointed for the patient by the Court of Protection under section 16 of that Act, where the deputy is acting within the scope of his authority and in accordance with that Act.]

[*Section 130B inserted by section 30(2) of the 2007 Act.*]

[130C Section 130A: supplemental]

[(1) This section applies for the purposes of section 130A above.

(2) A patient is a qualifying patient if he is—
  (a) liable to be detained under this Act (otherwise than by virtue of section 4 or 5(2) or (4) above or section 135 or 136 below);
  (b) subject to guardianship under this Act; or
  (c) a community patient.

(3) A patient is also a qualifying patient if—
  (a) not being a qualifying patient falling within subsection (2) above, he discusses with a registered medical practitioner or approved clinician the possibility of being given a form of treatment to which section 57 above applies; or
  (b) not having attained the age of 18 years and not being a qualifying patient falling within subsection (2) above, he discusses with a registered medical practitioner or approved clinician the possibility of being given a form of treatment to which section 58A above applies.

(4) Where a patient who is a qualifying patient falling within subsection (3) above is informed that the treatment concerned is proposed in his case, he remains a qualifying patient falling within that subsection until—
  (a) the proposal is withdrawn; or
  (b) the treatment is completed or discontinued.

(5) References to the appropriate national authority are—
  (a) in relation to a qualifying patient in England, to the Secretary of State;
  (b) in relation to a qualifying patient in Wales, to the Welsh Ministers.

(6) For the purposes of subsection (5) above—
  (a) a qualifying patient falling within subsection (2)(a) above is to be regarded as being in the territory in which the hospital or registered establishment in which he is liable to be detained is situated;
  (b) a qualifying patient falling within subsection (2)(b) above is to be regarded as being in the territory in which the area of the responsible local social services authority within the meaning of section 34(3) above is situated;
  (c) a qualifying patient falling within subsection (2)(c) above is to be regarded as being in the territory in which the responsible hospital is situated;
  (d) a qualifying patient falling within subsection (3) above is to be regarded as being in the territory determined in accordance with arrangements made for the purposes of this paragraph, and published, by the Secretary of State and the Welsh Ministers.]

[*Section 130C inserted by section 30(2) of the 2007 Act.*]

[130D Duty to give information about independent mental health advocates]

[(1) The responsible person in relation to a qualifying patient (within the meaning given by section 130C above) shall take such steps as are practicable to ensure that the patient understands—
  (a) that help is available to him from an independent mental health advocate; and
  (b) how he can obtain that help.

(2) In subsection (1) above, 'the responsible person' means—

    (a) in relation to a qualifying patient falling within section 130C(2)(a) above (other than one also falling within paragraph (b) below), the managers of the hospital or registered establishment in which he is liable to be detained;

    (b) in relation to a qualifying patient falling within section 130C(2)(a) above and conditionally discharged by virtue of section 42(2), 73 or 74 above, the responsible clinician;

    (c) in relation to a qualifying patient falling within section 130C(2)(b) above, the responsible local social services authority within the meaning of section 34(3) above;

    (d) in relation to a qualifying patient falling within section 130C(2)(c) above, the managers of the responsible hospital;

    (e) in relation to a qualifying patient falling within section 130C(3) above, the registered medical practitioner or approved clinician with whom the patient first discusses the possibility of being given the treatment concerned.

(3) The steps to be taken under subsection (1) above shall be taken—

    (a) where the responsible person falls within subsection (2)(a) above, as soon as practicable after the patient becomes liable to be detained;

    (b) where the responsible person falls within subsection (2)(b) above, as soon as practicable after the conditional discharge;

    (c) where the responsible person falls within subsection (2)(c) above, as soon as practicable after the patient becomes subject to guardianship;

    (d) where the responsible person falls within subsection (2)(d) above, as soon as practicable after the patient becomes a community patient;

    (e) where the responsible person falls within subsection (2)(e) above, while the discussion with the patient is taking place or as soon as practicable thereafter.

(4) The steps to be taken under subsection (1) above shall include giving the requisite information both orally and in writing.

(5) The responsible person in relation to a qualifying patient falling within section 130C(2) above (other than a patient liable to be detained by virtue of Part 3 of this Act) shall, except where the patient otherwise requests, take such steps as are practicable to furnish the person (if any) appearing to the responsible person to be the patient's nearest relative with a copy of any information given to the patient in writing under subsection (1) above.

(6) The steps to be taken under subsection (5) above shall be taken when the information concerned is given to the patient or within a reasonable time thereafter.]

[*Section 130D inserted by section 30(2) of the 2007 Act.*]

131 Informal admission of patients

(1) Nothing in this Act shall be construed as preventing a patient who requires treatment for mental disorder from being admitted to any hospital or registered establishment in pursuance of arrangements made in that behalf and without any application, order or direction rendering him liable to be detained under this Act, or from remaining in any hospital or registered establishment in pursuance of such arrangements after he has ceased to be so liable to be detained.

(2) *In the case of a minor who has attained the age of 16 years and is capable of expressing his own wishes, any such arrangements as are mentioned in subsection (1) above may be made, carried out and determined even though there are one or more persons who have parental responsibility for him (within the meaning of the Children Act 1989).*

[(2) Subsections (3) and (4) below apply in the case of a patient aged 16 or 17 years who has capacity to consent to the making of such arrangements as are mentioned in subsection (1) above.

(3) If the patient consents to the making of the arrangements, they may be made, carried out and determined on the basis of that consent even though there are one or more persons who have parental responsibility for him.

(4) If the patient does not consent to the making of the arrangements, they may not be made, carried out or determined on the basis of the consent of a person who has parental responsibility for him.

(5) In this section—

    (a) the reference to a patient who has capacity is to be read in accordance with the Mental Capacity Act 2005; and

    (b) 'parental responsibility' has the same meaning as in the Children Act 1989.]

[*Subsections (2) to (5) substituted for subsection (2) by section 43 of the 2007 Act.*]

[131A Accommodation, etc for children]

[(1) This section applies in respect of any patient who has not attained the age of 18 years and who—

    (a) is liable to be detained in a hospital under this Act; or

    (b) is admitted to, or remains in, a hospital in pursuance of such arrangements as are mentioned in section 131(1) above.

(2) The managers of the hospital shall ensure that the patient's environment in the hospital is suitable having regard to his age (subject to his needs).

(3) For the purpose of deciding how to fulfil the duty under subsection (2) above, the managers shall consult a person who appears to them to have knowledge or experience of cases involving patients who have not attained the age of 18 years which makes him suitable to be consulted.

(4) In this section, 'hospital' includes a registered establishment.]

[*Section 131A inserted by section 31(3) of the 2007 Act.*]

132 Duty of managers of hospitals to give information to detained patients

(1) The managers of a hospital or registered establishment in which a patient is detained under this Act shall take such steps as are practicable to ensure that the patient understands—

    (a) under which of the provisions of this Act he is for the time being detained and the effect of that provision; and

    (b) what rights of applying to a Mental Health Review Tribunal are available to him in respect of his detention under that provision;

and those steps shall be taken as soon as practicable after the commencement of the patient's detention under the provision in question.

(2) The managers of a hospital or registered establishment in which a patient is detained as aforesaid shall also take such steps as are practicable to ensure that the patient understands the effect, so far as relevant in his case, of sections 23, 25, 56 to 64, 66(1)(g), 118 and 120 above and section 134 below; and those steps shall be taken as soon as practicable after the commencement of the patient's detention in the hospital or *nursing home* [establishment].

(3) The steps to be taken under subsections (1) and (2) above shall include giving the requisite information both orally and in writing.

(4) The managers of a hospital or registered establishment in which a patient is detained as aforesaid shall, except where the patient otherwise requests, take such steps as are practicable to furnish the person (if any) appearing to them to be his nearest relative with a copy of any information given to him in writing under subsections (1) and (2) above; and those steps shall be taken when the information is given to the patient or within a reasonable time thereafter.

[*Words substituted in subsection (2) by paragraph 29 of Schedule 3 to the 2007 Act.*]

[132A Duty of managers of hospitals to give information to community patients]

[(1) The managers of the responsible hospital shall take such steps as are practicable to ensure that a community patient understands—

(a) the effect of the provisions of this Act applying to community patients; and

(b) what rights of applying to a Mental Health Review Tribunal are available to him in that capacity;

and those steps shall be taken as soon as practicable after the patient becomes a community patient.

(2) The steps to be taken under subsection (1) above shall include giving the requisite information both orally and in writing.

(3) The managers of the responsible hospital shall, except where the community patient otherwise requests, take such steps as are practicable to furnish the person (if any) appearing to them to be his nearest relative with a copy of any information given to him in writing under subsection (1) above; and those steps shall be taken when the information is given to the patient or within a reasonable time thereafter.]

[*Section 132A inserted by paragraph 30 of Schedule 3 to the 2007 Act.*]

133 Duty of managers of hospitals to inform nearest relatives of discharge

(1) Where a patient liable to be detained under this Act in a hospital or registered establishment is to be discharged otherwise than by virtue of an order for discharge made by his nearest relative, the managers of the hospital or registered establishment shall, subject to subsection (2) below, take such steps as are practicable to inform the person (if any) appearing to them to be the nearest relative of the patient; and that information shall, if practicable, be given at least seven days before the date of discharge.

[(1A) The reference in subsection (1) above to a patient who is to be discharged includes a patient who is to be discharged from hospital under section 17A above.

(1B) Subsection (1) above shall also apply in a case where a community patient is discharged under section 23 or 72 above (otherwise than by virtue of an order for discharge made by his nearest relative), but with the reference in that subsection to the managers of the hospital or registered establishment being read as a reference to the managers of the responsible hospital.]

(2) Subsection (1) above shall not apply if the patient or his nearest relative has requested that information about the patient's discharge should not be given under this section.

[*Subsections (1A) and (1B) inserted by paragraph 31 of Schedule 3 to the 2007 Act.*]

134 Correspondence of patients

(1) A postal packet addressed to any person by a patient detained in a hospital under this Act and delivered by the patient for dispatch may be withheld from the postal operator concerned—

(a) if that person has requested that communications addressed to him by the patient should be withheld; or

(b) subject to subsection (3) below, if the hospital is one at which high security psychiatric services are provided and the managers of the hospital consider that the postal packet is likely—

(i) to cause distress to the person to whom it is addressed or to any other person (not being a person on the staff of the hospital); or

(ii) to cause danger to any person;

and any request for the purposes of paragraph (a) above shall be made by a notice in writing given to the managers of the hospital, the *registered medical practitioner in charge of the treatment of the patient* [approved clinician with overall responsibility for the patient's case] or the Secretary of State.

(2) Subject to subsection (3) below, a postal packet addressed to a patient detained under this Act in a hospital at which high security psychiatric services are provided may be withheld from the patient if, in the opinion of the managers of the hospital, it is necessary to do so in the interests of the safety of the patient or for the protection of other persons.

(3) Subsections (1)(b) and (2) above do not apply to any postal packet addressed by a patient to, or sent to a patient by or on behalf of—

(a) any Minister of the Crown or the Scottish Ministers or Member of either House of Parliament or member of the Scottish Parliament or of the Northern Ireland Assembly;

(b) any judge or officer of the Court of Protection, any of the Court of Protection Visitors or any person asked by that Court for a report under section 49 of the Mental Capacity Act 2005 concerning the patient;

(c) the Parliamentary Commissioner for Administration, the Scottish Public Services Ombudsman, the Public Services Ombudsman for Wales, the Health Service Commissioner for England or a Local Commissioner within the meaning of Part III of the Local Government Act 1974;

(d) a Mental Health Review Tribunal;

(e) a Strategic Health Authority, Local Health Board, Special Health Authority or Primary Care Trust, a local social services authority, a Community Health Council, a Patients' Forum or a local probation board established under section 4 of the Criminal Justice and Court Services Act 2000;

(ea) a provider of a patient advocacy and liaison service for the assistance of patients at the hospital and their families and carers;

(eb) a provider of independent advocacy services for the patient;

(f) the managers of the hospital in which the patient is detained;

(g) any legally qualified person instructed by the patient to act as his legal adviser; or

(h) the European Commission of Human Rights or the European Court of Human Rights.

(3A) In subsection (3) above—

(a) 'patient advocacy and liaison service' means a service of a description prescribed by regulations made by the Secretary of State, and

(b) *'independent advocacy services' means services provided under arrangements under section 248 of the National Health Service Act 2006 or section 187 of the National Health Service (Wales) Act 2006.*

[(b) 'independent advocacy services' means services provided under—

(i) arrangements under section 130A above;

(ii) arrangements under section 248 of the National Health Service Act 2006 or section 187 of the National Health Service (Wales) Act 2006; or

(iii) arrangements of a description prescribed as mentioned in paragraph (a) above.]

(4) The managers of a hospital may inspect and open any postal packet for the purposes of determining—

(a) whether it is one to which subsection (1) or (2) applies, and

(b) in the case of a postal packet to which subsection (1) or (2) above applies, whether or not it should be withheld under that subsection;

and the power to withhold a postal packet under either of those subsections includes power to withhold anything contained in it.

(5) Where a postal packet or anything contained in it is withheld under subsection (1) or (2) above the managers of the hospital shall record that fact in writing.

(6) Where a postal packet or anything contained in it is withheld under subsection (1)(b) or (2) above the managers of the hospital shall within seven days give notice of that fact to the patient and, in the case of a packet withheld under subsection (2) above, to the person (if known) by whom the postal packet was sent; and any such notice shall be given in writing and shall contain a statement of the effect of section 121(7) and (8) above.

(7) The functions of the managers of a hospital under this section shall be discharged on their behalf by a person on the staff of the hospital appointed by them for that purpose and different persons may be appointed to discharge different functions.

(8) The Secretary of State may make regulations with respect to the exercise of the powers conferred by this section.

(9) In this section 'hospital' has the same meaning as in Part II of this Act and 'postal operator' and 'postal packet' have the same meaning as in the Postal Services Act 2000.

[*Words substituted in subsection (1) by section 14(4) of the 2007 Act. Subsection (3A)(b) substituted by section 30(3).*]

135 Warrant to search for and remove patients

(1) If it appears to a justice of the peace, on information on oath laid by an *approved social worker* [approved mental health professional], that there is reasonable cause to suspect that a person believed to be suffering from mental disorder—

    (a) has been, or is being, ill-treated, neglected or kept otherwise than under proper control, in any place within the jurisdiction of the justice, or

    (b) being unable to care for himself, is living alone in any such place,

the justice may issue a warrant authorising any constable to enter, if need be by force, any premises specified in the warrant in which that person is believed to be, and, if thought fit, to remove him to a place of safety with a view to the making of an application in respect of him under Part II of this Act, or of other arrangements for his treatment or care.

(2) If it appears to a justice of the peace, on information on oath laid by any constable or other person who is authorised by or under this Act or under article 8 of the Mental Health (Care and Treatment) (Scotland) Act 2003 (Consequential Provisions) Order 2005 to take a patient to any place, or to take into custody or retake a patient who is liable under this Act or under the said article 8 to be so taken or retaken—

    (a) that there is reasonable cause to believe that the patient is to be found on premises within the jurisdiction of the justice; and

    (b) that admission to the premises has been refused or that a refusal of such admission is apprehended,

the justice may issue a warrant authorising any constable to enter the premises, if need be by force, and remove the patient.

(3) A patient who is removed to a place of safety in the execution of a warrant issued under this section may be detained there for a period not exceeding 72 hours.

[(3A) A constable, an approved mental health professional or a person authorised by either of them for the purposes of this subsection may, before the end of the period of 72 hours mentioned in subsection (3) above, take a person detained in a place of safety under that subsection to one or more other places of safety.

(3B) A person taken to a place of safety under subsection (3A) above may be detained there for a period ending no later than the end of the period of 72 hours mentioned in subsection (3) above.]

(4) In the execution of a warrant issued under subsection (1) above, a constable shall be accompanied by an *approved social worker* [approved mental health professional] and by a registered medical practitioner, and in the execution of a warrant issued under subsection (2) above a constable may be accompanied—

   (a) by a registered medical practitioner;

   (b) by any person authorised by or under this Act or under article 8 of the Mental Health (Care and Treatment) (Scotland) Act 2003 (Consequential Provisions) Order 2005 to take or retake the patient.

(5) It shall not be necessary in any information or warrant under subsection (1) above to name the patient concerned.

(6) In this section 'place of safety' means residential accommodation provided by a local social services authority under Part III of the National Assistance Act 1948, a hospital as defined by this Act, a police station, an independent hospital or care home for mentally disordered persons or any other suitable place the occupier of which is willing temporarily to receive the patient.

[*Words substituted in subsections (1) & (4) by paragraph 10(a) of Schedule 2 to the 2007 Act. Subsections (3A) and (3B) inserted by section 44(2).*]

136 Mentally disordered persons found in public places

(1) If a constable finds in a place to which the public have access a person who appears to him to be suffering from mental disorder and to be in immediate need of care or control, the constable may, if he thinks it necessary to do so in the interests of that person or for the protection of other persons, remove that person to a place of safety within the meaning of section 135 above.

(2) A person removed to a place of safety under this section may be detained there for a period not exceeding 72 hours for the purpose of enabling him to be examined by a registered medical practitioner and to be interviewed by an *approved social worker* [approved mental health professional] and of making any necessary arrangements for his treatment or care.

[(3) A constable, an approved mental health professional or a person authorised by either of them for the purposes of this subsection may, before the end of the period of 72 hours mentioned in subsection (2) above, take a person detained in a place of safety under that subsection to one or more other places of safety.

(4) A person taken to a place of a safety under subsection (3) above may be detained there for a purpose mentioned in subsection (2) above for a period ending no later than the end of the period of 72 hours mentioned in that subsection.]

[*Words substituted in subsection (2) by paragraph 10(b) of Schedule 2 to the 2007 Act. Subsections (3) and (4) inserted by section 44(3).*]

137 Provisions as to custody, conveyance and detention

(1) Any person required or authorised by or by virtue of this Act to be conveyed to any place or to be kept in custody or detained in a place of safety or at any place to which he is taken under section 42(6) above shall, while being so conveyed, detained or kept, as the case may be, be deemed to be in legal custody.

(2) A constable or any other person required or authorised by or by virtue of this Act to take any person into custody, or to convey or detain any person shall, for the purposes of taking him into custody or conveying or detaining him, have all the powers, authorities, protection and privileges which a constable has within the area for which he acts as constable.

(3) In this section 'convey' includes any other expression denoting removal from one place to another.

138 Retaking of patients escaping from custody

(1) If any person who is in legal custody by virtue of section 137 above escapes, he may, subject to the provisions of this section, be retaken—

   (a) in any case, by the person who had his custody immediately before the escape, or by any constable or *approved social worker* [approved mental health professional];

   (b) if at the time of the escape he was liable to be detained in a hospital within the meaning of Part II of this Act, or subject to guardianship under this Act, [or a community patient who was recalled to hospital under section 17E above,] by any other person who could take him into custody under section 18 above if he had absented himself without leave.

(2) A person to whom paragraph (b) of subsection (1) above applies shall not be retaken under this section after the expiration of the period within which he could be retaken under section 18 above if he had absented himself without leave on the day of the escape unless he is subject to a restriction order under Part III of this Act or an order or direction having the same effect as such an order; and subsection (4) of the said section 18 shall apply with the necessary modifications accordingly.

(3) A person who escapes while being taken to or detained in a place of safety under section 135 or 136 above shall not be retaken under this section after the expiration of the period of 72 hours beginning with the time when he escapes or the period during which he is liable to be so detained, whichever expires first.

(4) This section, so far as it relates to the escape of a person liable to be detained in a hospital within the meaning of Part II of this Act, shall apply in relation to a person who escapes—

   (a) while being taken to or from such a hospital in pursuance of regulations under section 19 above, or of any order, direction or authorisation under Part III or VI of this Act (other than under section 35, 36, 38, 53, 83 or 85) or under section 123 above; or

   (b) while being taken to or detained in a place of safety in pursuance of an order under Part III of this Act (other than under section 35, 36 or 38 above) pending his admission to such a hospital,

as if he were liable to be detained in that hospital and, if he had not previously been received in that hospital, as if he had been so received.

(5) In computing for the purposes of the power to give directions under section 37(4) above and for the purposes of sections 37(5) and 40(1) above the period of 28 days mentioned in those sections, no account shall be taken of any time during which the patient is at large and liable to be retaken by virtue of this section.

(6) Section 21 above shall, with any necessary modifications, apply in relation to a patient who is at large and liable to be retaken by virtue of this section as it applies in relation to a patient who is absent without leave and references in that section to section 18 above shall be construed accordingly.

[*Words in subsection (1)(a) substituted by paragraph 10(c) of Schedule 2 to the 2007 Act. Words in subsection 1(b) inserted by paragraph 32 of Schedule 3.*]

139 Protection for acts done in pursuance of this Act

(1) No person shall be liable, whether on the ground of want of jurisdiction or on any other ground, to any civil or criminal proceedings to which he would have been liable apart from this section in respect of any act purporting to be done in pursuance of this Act or any regulations or rules made under this Act, unless the act was done in bad faith or without reasonable care.

(2) No civil proceedings shall be brought against any person in any court in respect of any such act without the leave of the High Court; and no criminal proceedings shall be brought against any person in any court in respect of any such act except by or with the consent of the Director of Public Prosecutions.

(3) This section does not apply to proceedings for an offence under this Act, being proceedings which, under any other provision of this Act, can be instituted only by or with the consent of the Director of Public Prosecutions.

(4) This section does not apply to proceedings against the Secretary of State or against a Strategic Health Authority, Local Health Board, Special Health Authority or Primary Care Trust or against a National Health Service trust established under the National Health Service Act 2006 or the National Health Service (Wales) Act 2006 or NHS foundation trust.

(5) In relation to Northern Ireland the reference in this section to the Director of Public Prosecutions shall be construed as a reference to the Director of Public Prosecutions for Northern Ireland.

140 Notification of hospitals having arrangements for *reception of urgent* [special] cases

It shall be the duty of every Primary Care Trust and of every Local Health Board to give notice to every local social services authority for an area wholly or partly comprised within the area of the Primary Care Trust or Local Health Board specifying the hospital or hospitals administered by or otherwise available to the Primary Care Trust or Local Health Board in which arrangements are from time to time in force *for the reception, in case of special urgency, of patients requiring treatment for mental disorder*

    [(a) for the reception of patients in cases of special urgency;

    (b) for the provision of accommodation or facilities designed so as to be specially suitable for patients who have not attained the age of 18 years].

[Section 140 (and title) amended by section 31(4) of the 2007 Act.]

141 Members of Parliament suffering from mental illness

(1) Where a member of the House of Commons is authorised to be detained [under a relevant enactment] on the ground (however formulated) that he is suffering from *mental illness* [mental disorder], it shall be the duty of the court, authority or person on whose order or application, and of any registered medical practitioner upon whose recommendation or certificate, the detention was authorised, and of the person in charge of the hospital or other place in which the member is authorised to be detained, to notify the Speaker of the House of Commons that the detention has been authorised.

(2) Where the Speaker receives a notification under subsection (1) above, or is notified by two members of the House of Commons that they are credibly informed that such an authorisation has been given, the Speaker shall cause the member to whom the notification relates to be visited and examined by two registered medical practitioners appointed in accordance with subsection (3) below.

(3) The registered medical practitioners to be appointed for the purposes of subsection (2) above shall be appointed by the President of the Royal College of Psychiatrists and shall be practitioners appearing to the President to have special experience in the diagnosis or treatment of mental disorders.

(4) The registered medical practitioners appointed in accordance with subsection (3) above shall report to the Speaker whether the member is suffering from *mental illness* [mental disorder] and is authorised to be detained [under a relevant enactment] as such.

(5) If the report is to the effect that the member is suffering from *mental illness* [mental disorder] and authorised to be detained as aforesaid, the Speaker shall at the expiration of six months from the date of the report, if the House is then sitting, and otherwise as soon as may be after the House next sits, again cause the member to be visited and examined by two such registered medical practitioners as aforesaid, and the registered medical practitioners shall report as aforesaid.

(6) If the second report is that the member is suffering from *mental illness* [mental disorder] and authorised to be detained as mentioned in subsection (4) above, the Speaker shall forthwith lay both reports before the House of Commons, and thereupon the seat of the member shall become vacant.

[(6A) For the purposes of this section, the following are relevant enactments—
  (a) this Act;
  (b) the Criminal Procedure (Scotland) Act 1995 and the Mental Health (Care and Treatment) (Scotland) Act 2003 ('the Scottish enactments'); and
  (c) the Mental Health (Northern Ireland) Order 1986 ('the 1986 Order').

(6B) In relation to an authorisation for detention under the Scottish enactments or the 1986 Order, the references in this section to mental disorder shall be construed in accordance with those enactments or that Order (as the case may be).

(6C) References in this section to a member who is authorised to be detained shall not include a member who is a community patient (whether or not he is recalled to hospital under section 17E above).]

(7) Any sums required for the payment of fees and expenses to registered medical practitioners acting in relation to a member of the House of Commons under this section shall be defrayed out of moneys provided by Parliament.

(8) This section also has effect in relation to members of the Scottish Parliament but as if—
  (a) any references to the House of Commons or the Speaker were references to the Scottish Parliament or (as the case may be) the Presiding Officer, and
  (b) subsection (7) were omitted.

(9) This section also has effect in relation to members of the National Assembly for Wales but as if—
  (a) references to the House of Commons were to the Assembly and references to the Speaker were to the presiding officer, and
  (b) in subsection (7), for 'defrayed out of moneys provided by Parliament' there were substituted 'paid by the National Assembly for Wales Commission'.

(10) This section also has effect in relation to members of the Northern Ireland Assembly but as if—
  (a) references to the House of Commons were to the Assembly and references to the Speaker were to the Presiding Officer; and
  (b) in subsection (7), for 'provided by Parliament' there were substituted 'appropriated by Act of the Assembly'.

[*Words inserted and substituted in subsection (1) by paragraphs 16(2)(a)&(b) respectively of Schedule 1 to the 2007 Act. Words substituted and inserted in subsection (4) by paragraphs 16(3)(a)&(b) respectively of that Schedule. Words substituted in subsection (5) and (6), and subsections (6A) and (6B) inserted by paragraphs 16(4) and (5) respectively of that Schedule. Subsection (6C) inserted by paragraph 33 of Schedule 3.*]

[142A Regulations as to approvals in relation to England and Wales]

[The Secretary of State jointly with the Welsh Ministers may by regulations make provision as to the circumstances in which—

(a) a practitioner approved for the purposes of section 12 above, or

(b) a person approved to act as an approved clinician for the purposes of this Act,

approved in relation to England is to be treated, by virtue of his approval, as approved in relation to Wales too, and vice versa.]

[*Section 142A inserted by section 17 of the 2007 Act.*]

[142B Delegation of powers of managers of NHS foundation trusts]

[(1) The constitution of an NHS foundation trust may not provide for a function under this Act to be delegated otherwise than in accordance with provision made by or under this Act.

(2) Paragraph 15(3) of Schedule 7 to the National Health Service Act 2006 (which provides that the powers of a public benefit corporation may be delegated to a committee of directors or to an executive director) shall have effect subject to this section.]

[*Section 142B Inserted by section 45(3) of the 2007 Act.*]

Supplemental

143 General provisions as to regulations, orders and rules

(1) Any power of the Secretary of State or the Lord Chancellor to make regulations, orders or rules under this Act shall be exercisable by statutory instrument.

(2) Any Order in Council under this Act or any order made [by the Secretary of State] under section 54A [or 68A(7)] *or 65* above and any statutory instrument containing regulations *or rules made* [made by the Secretary of State, or rules made,] under this Act shall be subject to annulment in pursuance of a resolution of either House of Parliament.

(3) No order shall be made [by the Secretary of State] under section 45A(10), *68(4)* [68A(1)] or 71(3) above unless a draft of it has been approved by a resolution of each House of Parliament.

[(3A) Subsections (3B) to (3D) apply where power to make regulations or an order under this Act is conferred on the Welsh Ministers (other than by or by virtue of the Government of Wales Act 2006).

(3B) Any power of the Welsh Ministers to make regulations or an order shall be exercisable by statutory instrument.

(3C) Any statutory instrument containing regulations made by the Welsh Ministers, or an order under section 68A(7) above, made by the Welsh Ministers shall be subject to annulment in pursuance of a resolution of the National Assembly for Wales.

(3D) No order shall be made under section 68A(1) above by the Welsh Ministers unless a draft of it has been approved by a resolution of the National Assembly for Wales.

(3E) In this section—

(a) references to the Secretary of State include the Secretary of State and the Welsh Ministers acting jointly; and

(b) references to the Welsh Ministers include the Welsh Ministers and the Secretary of State acting jointly.]

(4) This section does not apply to rules which are, by virtue of section 108 of this Act, to be made in accordance with Part 1 of Schedule 1 to the Constitutional Reform Act 2005.

[First 'by the Secretary of State' and 'or 68A(7)' inserted in subsection (2) by section 38(5)(a) of the 2007 Act. 'or 65' omitted from that same subsection by Part 6 of Schedule 11; words from 'made by the Secretary of State . . . ' substituted by section 47(2). Words inserted and substituted in subsection (3) by section 38(5)(b). Subsections (3A) to (3E) inserted by section 47(3).]

144 Power to amend local Acts

Her Majesty may by Order in Council repeal or amend any local enactment so far as appears to Her Majesty to be necessary in consequence of this Act.

145 Interpretation

(1) In this Act, unless the context otherwise requires—

'absent without leave' has the meaning given to it by section 18 above and related expressions [(including expressions relating to a patient's liability to be returned to a hospital or other place)] shall be construed accordingly;

'application for admission for assessment' has the meaning given in section 2 above;

'application for admission for treatment' has the meaning given in section 3 above;

['approved clinician' means a person approved by the Secretary of State (in relation to England) or by the Welsh Ministers (in relation to Wales) to act as an approved clinician for the purposes of this Act;]

'approved social worker' means an officer of a local social services authority appointed to act as an approved social worker for the purposes of this Act;

['approved mental health professional' has the meaning given in section 114 above;]

'care home' has the same meaning as in the Care Standards Act 2000;

['community patient' has the meaning given in section 17A above;

'community treatment order' and 'the community treatment order' have the meanings given in section 17A above;

'the community treatment period' has the meaning given in section 20A above;]

'high security psychiatric services' has the same meaning as in section 4 of the National Health Service Act 2006 or section 4 of the National Health Service (Wales) Act 2006;

'hospital' means—

(a) any health service hospital within the meaning of the National Health Service Act 2006 or the National Health Service (Wales) Act 2006; and

(b) any accommodation provided by a local authority and used as a hospital by or on behalf of the Secretary of State under that Act; [and

(c) any hospital as defined by section 206 of the National Health Service (Wales) Act 2006 which is vested in a Local Health Board;]

and 'hospital within the meaning of Part II of this Act' has the meaning given in section 34 above;

'hospital direction' has the meaning given in section 45A(3)(a) above;

'hospital order' and 'guardianship order' have the meanings respectively given in section 37 above;

'independent hospital' has the same meaning as in the Care Standards Act 2000;

'interim hospital order' has the meaning given in section 38 above;

'limitation direction' has the meaning given in section 45A(3)(b) above;

'Local Health Board' means a Local Health Board established under section 11 of the National Health Services (Wales) Act 2006.

'local social services authority' means a council which is a local authority for the purpose of the Local Authority Social Services Act 1970;

'the managers' means—

(a) in relation to a hospital vested in the Secretary of State for the purposes of his functions under the National Health Service Act 2006, or in the Welsh Ministers for the purposes of their functions under the National Health Service (Wales) Act 2006, and in relation to any accommodation provided by a local authority and used as a hospital by or on behalf of the Secretary of State under the National Health Service Act 2006, or of the Welsh Ministers under the National Health Service (Wales) Act 2006, the Primary Care Trust, Strategic Health Authority, Local Health Board or Special Health Authority responsible for the administration of the hospital;

(bb) in relation to a hospital vested in a Primary Care Trust or a National Health Service trust, the trust;

(bc) in relation to a hospital vested in an NHS foundation trust, the trust;

[(bd) in relation to a hospital vested in a Local Health Board, the Board;]

(c) in relation to a registered establishment, the person or persons registered in respect of the establishment;

and in this definition 'hospital' means a hospital within the meaning of Part II of this Act;

'medical treatment' includes nursing, *and also includes care, habilitation and rehabilitation under medical supervision*; [psychological intervention and specialist mental health habilitation, rehabilitation and care (but see also subsection (4) below);]

'mental disorder', 'severe mental impairment', 'mental impairment' and 'psychopathic disorder' have the meanings given in section 1 above;

['mental disorder' has the meaning given in section 1 above (subject to sections 86(4) and 141(6B));]

'nearest relative', in relation to a patient, has the meaning given in Part II of this Act;

'patient' means a person suffering or appearing to be suffering from mental disorder;

'Primary Care Trust' means a Primary Care Trust established under section 18 of the National Health Service Act 2006;

'registered establishment' has the meaning given in section 34 above;

'the responsible after-care bodies' has the meaning given in section 25D above;

['the responsible hospital' has the meaning given in section 17A above;]

'restriction direction' has the meaning given to it by section 49 above;

'restriction order' has the meaning given to it by section 41 above;

'special Health Authority' means a Special Health Authority established under section 28 of the National Health Service Act 2006, or section 22 of the National Health Service (Wales) Act 2006;

'strategic Health Authority' means a Strategic Health Authority established under section 13 of the National Health Service Act 2006;

'supervision application' has the meaning given in section 25A above;

'transfer direction' has the meaning given to it by section 47 above.

(1A) *References in this Act to a patient being subject to after-care under supervision (or to after-care under supervision) shall be construed in accordance with section 25A above.*

(1AA) Where high security psychiatric services and other services are provided at a hospital, the part of the hospital at which high security psychiatric services are provided and the other part shall be treated as separate hospitals for the purposes of this Act.

[(1AB) References in this Act to appropriate medical treatment shall be construed in accordance with section 3(4) above.

(1AC) References in this Act to an approved mental health professional shall be construed as references to an approved mental health professional acting on behalf of a local social services authority, unless the context otherwise requires.]

(3) In relation to a person who is liable to be detained or subject to guardianship [or a community patient] by virtue of an order or direction under Part III of this Act (other than under section 35, 36 or 38), any reference in this Act to any enactment contained in Part II of this Act or in section 66 or 67 above shall be construed as a reference to that enactment as it applies to that person by virtue of Part III of this Act.

[(4) Any reference in this Act to medical treatment, in relation to mental disorder, shall be construed as a reference to medical treatment the purpose of which is to alleviate, or prevent a worsening of, the disorder or one or more of its symptoms or manifestations.]

[*In subsection (1), definitions amended as follows:*

- *'absent without leave', words inserted by paragraph 34(2) of Schedule 3 to the 2007 Act*

- *'approved clinician' inserted by section 14(5)*

- *'approved mental health professional' substituted for 'approved social worker' by paragraph 11(2) of Schedule 2*

- *'community patient', 'community treatment order' (etc), 'community treatment period' inserted by paragraph 34(3) of Schedule 3*

- *'hospital'— sub-paragraph (c) (and preceding 'and') inserted by section 46(3)(a)*

- *'the managers'— sub-paragraph (bd) inserted by section 46(3)(b)*

- *'medical treatment'— words substituted by section 7(2).*

- *'mental disorder' (etc) substituted by paragraph 17 of Schedule 1*

- *'the responsible after-care bodies' omitted by Part 5 of Schedule 11*

- *'the responsible hospital' inserted by paragraph 34 of Schedule 3*

- *'supervision application' omitted by Part 5 of Schedule 11.*

Subsection (1A) omitted by Part 5 of Schedule 11, subsection (1AB) inserted by section 4(10), subsection (1AC) inserted by paragraph 11(3) of Schedule 2, and words inserted in subsection 3 by paragraph 34(4) of Schedule 3. Subsection (4) inserted by section 7(3).]

146 Application to Scotland

Sections 42(6), 80, *88 (and so far as applied by that section sections 18, 22 and 138)* 116, 122, 128 (except so far as it relates to patients subject to guardianship), 137, 139(1), 141, 142, 143 (so far as applicable to any Order in Council extending to Scotland) and 144 above shall extend to Scotland together with any amendment or repeal by this Act of or any provision of Schedule 5 to this Act relating to any enactment which so extends; but, except as aforesaid and except so far as it relates to the interpretation or commencement of the said provisions, this Act shall not extend to Scotland.

[*First set of words omitted by paragraph 20 of Schedule 5 to the 2007 Act. Second set of words omitted by paragraph 35 of Schedule 3. Note: the amendments themselves do not extend to Scotland.*]

147 Application to Northern Ireland

Sections 81, 82, 86, 87, 88 (and so far as applied by that section sections 18, 22 and 138), section 128 (except so far as it relates to patients subject to guardianship), 137, 139, 141, 142, 143 (so far as applicable to any Order in Council extending to Northern Ireland) and 144 above shall extend to Northern Ireland together with any amendment or repeal by this Act of or any provision of Schedule 5 to this Act relating to any enactment which so extends; but except as aforesaid and except so far as it relates to the interpretation or commencement of the said provisions, this Act shall not extend to Northern Ireland.

148 Consequential and transitional provisions and repeals

(1) Schedule 4 (consequential amendments) and Schedule 5 (transitional and saving provisions) to this Act shall have effect but without prejudice to the operation of sections 15 to 17 of the Interpretation Act 1978 (which relate to the effect of repeals).
(2) Where any amendment in Schedule 4 to this Act affects an enactment amended by the Mental Health (Amendment) Act 1982 the amendment in Schedule 4 shall come into force immediately after the provision of the Act of 1982 amending that enactment.
(3) The enactments specified in Schedule 6 to this Act are hereby repealed to the extent mentioned in the third column of that Schedule.

149 Short title, commencement and application to Scilly Isles

(1) This Act may be cited as the Mental Health Act 1983.
(2) Subject to subsection (3) below and Schedule 5 to this Act, this Act shall come into force on 30th September 1983.
(4) Section 130(4) of the National Health Service Act 1977 (which provides for the extension of that Act to the Isles of Scilly) shall have effect as if the references to that Act included references to this Act.

SCHEDULE 1

APPLICATION OF CERTAIN PROVISIONS TO PATIENTS SUBJECT
TO HOSPITAL AND GUARDIANSHIP ORDERS

Sections 40(4), 41(3), (5), 55(4)

Part I Patients not subject to special restrictions

1   Sections 9, 10, 17 [to 17C, 17E, 17F, 20A], 21 to 21B, 24(3) and (4), *25C* [26] to 28, 31, 32, 34, 67 and 76 shall apply in relation to the patient without modification.

[*Words inserted by paragraph 36(2) of Schedule 3 to the 2007 Act. '26' substituted for '25C' by section 36(4).*]

2   Sections *16, 18, 19, 20* [17D, 17G, 18 to 20, 20B], 22, 23, *25A, 25B and 66* [, 66 and 68] shall apply in relation to the patient with the modifications specified in *paragraphs 3* [paragraphs 2A] *to 9* [to10] below.

['*16' repealed by Part 1 of Schedule 11 to the 2007 Act; '17D, 17G, 18 to 20, 20B' substituted for '18, 19, 20' by paragraph 36(3)(a) of Schedule 3; ',25A, 25B' omitted by Part 5 of Schedule 11; ',66 and 68' substituted for 'and 66' by section 37(6)(a)(i); 'paragraphs 2A' substituted for 'paragraphs 3' by paragraph 36(3)(b) of Schedule 3; and 'to 10' substituted for 'to 9' by section 37(6)(a)(ii).*]

[2A In section 17D(2)(a) for the reference to section 6(2) above there shall be substituted a reference to section 40(1) (b) below.]

[Paragraph 2A inserted by paragraph 36(4) of Schedule 3 to the 2007 Act.]

[2B In section 17G—

(a) in subsection (2) for the reference to section 6(2) above there shall be substituted a reference to section 40(1)(b) below;

(b) in subsection (4) for paragraphs (a) and (b) there shall be substituted the words 'the order or direction under Part 3 of this Act in respect of him were an order or direction for his admission or removal to that other hospital'; and

(c) in subsection (5) for the words from 'the patient' to the end there shall be substituted the words 'the date of the relevant order or direction under Part 3 of this Part were the date on which the community treatment order is revoked'.]

[Paragraph 2B inserted by paragraph 36(4) of Schedule 3 to the 2007 Act.]

3   *In section 16(1) for references to an application for admission or a guardianship application there shall be substituted references to the order or direction under Part III of this Act by virtue of which the patient is liable to be detained or subject to guardianship.*

[Paragraph 3 repealed by Part 1 of Schedule 11 to the 2007 Act.]

4   In section 18 subsection (5) shall be omitted.

5   In section 19(2) for the words from 'as follows' to the end of the subsection there shall be substituted the words 'as if the order or direction under Part III of this Act by virtue of which he was liable to be detained or subject to guardianship before being transferred were an order or direction for his admission or removal to the hospital to which he is transferred, or placing him under the guardianship of the authority or person into whose guardianship he is transferred, as the case may be'.

[5A In section 19A(2), paragraph (b) shall be omitted.]

[Paragraph 5A inserted by paragraph 36(5) of Schedule 3 to the 2007 Act.]

6   In section 20—

(a) in subsection (1) for the words from 'day on which he was' to 'as the case may be' there shall be substituted the words 'date of the relevant order or direction under Part III of this Act'; *and*

(b) *in subsection (9) for the words 'the application for admission for treatment or, as the case may be, in the guardianship application, that application' there shall be substituted the words 'the relevant order or direction under Part III of this Act, that order or direction'.*

[Sub-paragraph (b) (and preceding 'and') omitted by Part 1 of Schedule 11 to the 2007 Act.]

[6A In section 20B(1), for the reference to the application for admission for treatment there shall be substituted a reference to the order or direction under Part 3 of this Act by virtue of which the patient is liable to be detained.]

[Paragraph 6B inserted by paragraph 36(6) of Schedule 3 to the 2007 Act.]

7   In section 22 for references to an application for admission or a guardianship application there shall be substituted references to the order or direction under Part III of this Act by virtue of which the patient is liable to be detained or subject to guardianship.

8   In section 23(2)—

(a) in paragraph (a) the words 'for assessment or' shall be omitted; and

(b) in paragraphs (a) *and (b)* [to (c)] the references to the nearest relative shall be omitted.

[Words substituted by paragraph 36(7) of Schedule 3 to the 2007 Act.]

8A In sections 25A(1)(a) and 25B(5)(a) for the words 'in pursuance of an application for admission for treatment' there shall be substituted the words 'by virtue of an order or direction for his admission or removal to hospital under Part III of this Act'.

[*Paragraph 8A omitted by Part 5 of Schedule 11 to the 2007 Act.*]

9 In section 66—

    (a) in subsection (1), paragraphs (a), (b), (c), (g) and (h), the words in parenthesis in paragraph (i) and paragraph (ii) shall be omitted; and

    (b) in subsection (2), paragraphs (a), (b), (c) and (g), and in paragraph (d) ', (g)', shall be omitted.

[10 In section 68—

    (a) in subsection (1) paragraph (a) shall be omitted; and

    (b) subsections (2) to (5) shall apply if the patient falls within paragraph (e) of subsection (1), but not otherwise.]

[*Paragraph 10 inserted by section 37(6)(b) of the 2007 Act.*]

Part II Patients subject to special restrictions

1 Sections 24(3) and (4), 32 and 76 shall apply in relation to the patient without modification.

2 Sections *17 to 19* [17, 18, 19], 22, 23 and 34 shall apply in relation to the patient with the modifications specified in paragraphs 3 to 8 below.

[*Words substituted by paragraph 37(2) of Schedule 3 to the 2007 Act.*]

3 In section 17—

    (a) in subsection (1) after the word 'may' there shall be inserted the words 'with the consent of the Secretary of State';

    [(aa) subsections (2A) and (2B) shall be omitted;]

    (b) in subsection (4) after the words *'the responsible medical officer' and after the words 'that officer'* ['the responsible clinician' and after the words 'that clinician'] there shall be inserted the words 'or the Secretary of State'; and

    (c) in subsection (5) after the word 'recalled' there shall be inserted the words *'by the responsible medical officer'* ['by the responsible clinician'], and for the words from 'he has ceased' to the end of the subsection there shall be substituted the words 'the expiration of the period of twelve months beginning with the first day of his absence on leave'.

[*Sub-paragraph (aa) inserted by section 33(3) of the 2007 Act. Words substituted in sub-paragraphs (b) and (c) by section 11(8)(a)&(b) respectively.*]

4 In section 18 there shall be omitted—

    (a) in subsection (1) the words 'subject to the provisions of this section'; and

    (b) subsections (3), (4) and (5).

5 In section 19—

    (a) in subsection (1) after the word 'may' in paragraph (a) there shall be inserted the words 'with the consent of the Secretary of State', and the words from 'or into' to the end of the subsection shall be omitted;

    (b) in subsection (2) for the words from 'as follows' to the end of the subsection there shall be substituted the words 'as if the order or direction under Part III of this Act by virtue of which he was liable to be detained before being transferred were an order or direction for his admission or removal to the hospital to which he is transferred'; and

    (c) in subsection (3) after the words 'may at any time' there shall be inserted the words ', with the consent of the Secretary of State,'.

6 *In section 22 subsection (1) and paragraph (a) of subsection (2) shall not apply.*

[6 In section 22, subsections (1) and (5) shall not apply.]

[Paragraph 6 substituted by paragraph 37(3) of Schedule 3 to the 2007 Act.]

7 In section 23—
   (a) in subsection (1) references to guardianship shall be omitted and after the word 'made' there shall be inserted the words 'with the consent of the Secretary of State and'; and
   (b) in subsection (2)—
        (i) in paragraph (a) to the words 'for assessment or' and 'or by the nearest relative of the patient' shall be omitted; and
        (ii) paragraph (b) shall be omitted.

8 In section 34, in subsection (1) the definition of 'the nominated medical attendant' and subsection (3) shall be omitted.

SCHEDULE 2
MENTAL HEALTH REVIEW TRIBUNALS

Section 65(2)

1 Each of the Mental Health Review Tribunals shall consist of—
   (a) a number of persons (referred to in this Schedule as 'the legal members') appointed by the Lord Chancellor and having such legal experience as the Lord Chancellor considers suitable;
   (b) a number of persons (referred to in this Schedule as 'the medical members') being registered medical practitioners appointed by the Lord Chancellor; and
   (c) a number of persons appointed by the Lord Chancellor having such experience in administration, such knowledge of social services or such other qualifications or experience as the Lord Chancellor considers suitable.

1A As part of the selection process for an appointment under paragraph 1(b) or (c) the Judicial Appointments Commission shall consult the Secretary of State.

2 Subject to paragraph 2A below the members of Mental Health Review Tribunals shall hold and vacate office under the terms of the instrument under which they are appointed, but may resign office by notice in writing to the Lord Chancellor; and any such member who ceases to hold office shall be eligible for re-appointment.

2A A member of a Mental Health Review Tribunal shall vacate office on the day on which he attains the age of 70 years; but this paragraph is subject to section 26(4) to (6) of the Judicial Pensions and Retirement Act 1993 (power to authorise continuance in office up to the age of 75 years).

3 *One of the legal members of each Mental Health Review Tribunal shall be appointed by the Lord Chancellor as chairman of the Tribunal.*

[3 (1) The Lord Chancellor shall appoint one of the legal members of the Mental Health Review Tribunal for England to be the President of that tribunal.

(2) The Lord Chancellor shall appoint one of the legal members of the Mental Health Review Tribunal for Wales to be the President of that tribunal.]

[Paragraph 3 substituted by section 38(6) of the 2007 Act.]

4 Subject to rules made by the Lord Chancellor under section 78(2)(c) above, the members who are to constitute a Mental Health Review Tribunal for the purposes of any proceedings or class or group of proceedings under this Act shall be appointed by the *chairman* [President] of the

tribunal or, *if for any reason he is unable to act*, by another member of the tribunal appointed for the purpose by the *chairman* [President]; and of the members so appointed—

(a) one or more shall be appointed from the legal members;

(b) one or more shall be appointed from the medical members; and

(c) one or more shall be appointed from the members who are neither legal nor medical members.

[*Words substituted by section 38(7)(a)of the 2007 Act and words omitted by section 38(7)(b).*]

5   A member of a Mental Health Review Tribunal for *any area* [one area] may be appointed under paragraph 4 above as one of the persons to constitute a Mental Health Review Tribunal for *any other* [the other] area for the purposes of any proceedings or class or group of proceedings; and for the purposes of this Act, a person so appointed shall, in relation to the proceedings for which he was appointed, be deemed to be a member of that other tribunal.

[*Words substituted by section 38(8)(a) and (b) respectively of the 2007 Act.*]

6   Subject to any rules made by the Lord Chancellor under section 78(4)(a) above, where the *chairman* [President] of the tribunal is included among the persons appointed under paragraph 4 above, he shall be *president* [chairman] of the tribunal; and in any other case the *president* [chairman] of the tribunal shall be such one of the members so appointed (being one of the legal members) as the *chairman* [President] may nominate.

[*'President' substituted for 'chairman' by section 38(9)(a) of the 2007 Act and 'chairman' for 'president' by section 38(9)(b).*]

SCHEDULE 5
TRANSITIONAL AND SAVING PROVISIONS

[NOT REPRODUCED]

SCHEDULE 6
REPEALS

[NOT REPRODUCED]

APPENDIX 2

Mental Capacity Act 2005

AS IT IS TO BE AMENDED BY THE MENTAL HEALTH ACT 2007

KEY

Material to be deleted by the 2007 Act is in italics, eg *omitted material looks like this.*
Material to be added by the 2007 Act is in square brackets, eg [added material looks like this].
Existing sections and schedules to be amended by the Act are marked '##'

ANNOTATIONS

At the end of each section (or paragraph of a Schedule) the relevant provision of the 2007 Act is in italics, square brackets, and also in smaller type.

MENTAL CAPACITY ACT 2005

CONTENTS

PART 1
PERSONS WHO LACK CAPACITY

The principles

1   The principles

Preliminary

2   People who lack capacity
3   Inability to make decisions
4   Best interests
[4A] [Restriction on deprivation of liberty]
[4B] [Deprivation of liberty necessary for life-sustaining treatment etc]
5   Acts in connection with care or treatment
6   Section 5 acts: limitations ##
7   Payment for necessary goods and services
8   Expenditure

Lasting powers of attorney

9 Lasting powers of attorney
10 Appointment of donees
11 Lasting powers of attorney: restrictions ##
12 Scope of lasting powers of attorney: gifts
13 Revocation of lasting powers of attorney etc.
14 Protection of donee and others if no power created or power revoked

General powers of the court and appointment of deputies

15 Power to make declarations
16 Powers to make decisions and appoint deputies: general
[16A] [Section 16 powers: Mental Health Act patients etc]
17 Section 16 powers: personal welfare
18 Section 16 powers: property and affairs
19 Appointment of deputies
20 Restrictions on deputies ##
21 Transfer of proceedings relating to people under 18

[Powers of the court in relation to Schedule A1]

[21A] [Powers of court in relation to Schedule A1]

Powers of the court in relation to lasting powers of attorney

22 Powers of court in relation to validity of lasting powers of attorney
23 Powers of court in relation to operation of lasting powers of attorney

Advance decisions to refuse treatment

24 Advance decisions to refuse treatment: general
25 Validity and applicability of advance decisions
26 Effect of advance decisions

Excluded decisions

27 Family relationships etc.
28 Mental Health Act matters ##
29 Voting rights

Research

30 Research
31 Requirements for approval
32 Consulting carers etc.
33 Additional safeguards
34 Loss of capacity during research project

Independent Medical Capacity Advocates

35 Appointment of independent mental capacity advocates ##
36 Functions of independent mental capacity advocates
37 Provision of serious medical treatment by NHS body ##
38 Provision of accommodation by NHS body ##
39 Provision of accommodation by local authority ##
[39A] [Person becomes subject to Schedule A1]
[39A] [Section 39A: supplementary provision]
[39C] [Person unrepresented whilst subject to Schedule A1]
[39D] [Person subject to Schedule A1 without paid representative]
[39E] [Limitation on duty to instruct advocate under section 39D]
40 Exceptions ##
41 Power to adjust role of independent mental capacity advocate

Miscellaneous and supplementary

42 Codes of practice ##
43 Codes of practice: procedure
44 Ill-treatment or neglect

PART 2
THE COURT OF PROTECTION AND THE PUBLIC GUARDIAN

The Court of Protection

45 The Court of Protection
46 The judges of the Court of Protection

Supplementary powers

47 General powers and effect of orders etc.
48 Interim orders and directions
49 Power to call for reports

Practice and procedure

50 Applications to the Court of Protection ##
51 Court of Protection Rules
52 Practice directions
53 Rights of appeal

Fees and costs

54 Fees
55 Costs
56 Fees and costs: supplementary

The Public Guardian

57   The Public Guardian
58   Functions of the Public Guardian
59   Public Guardian Board
60   Annual report

Court of Protection Visitors

61   Court of Protection Visitors

PART 3
MISCELLANEOUS AND GENERAL

Declaratory provision

62   Scope of the Act

Private international law

63   International protection of adults

General

64   Interpretation ##
65   Rules, regulations and orders ##
66   Existing receivers and enduring powers of attorney etc.
67   Minor and consequential amendments and repeals
68   Commencement and extent
69   Short title

Schedules

[Schedule A1   Hospital and care Home Residents: Deprivation of Liberty]

     [Part 1   Authorisation To Deprive Residents Of Liberty Etc]
     [Part 2   Interpretation: Main Terms]
     [Part 3   The Qualifying Requirements]
     [Part 4   Standard Authorisations]
     [Part 5   Urgent Authorisations]
     [Part 6   Eligibility Requirement Not Met: Suspension Of Standard Authorisation]
     [Part 7   Standard Authorisations: Change In Supervisory Responsibility]
     [Part 8   Standard Authorisations: Review]
     [Part 9   Assessments Under This Schedule]
     [Part 10 Relevant Person's Representative]

[Part 11 IMCAs]
[Part 12 Miscellaneous]
[Part 13 Interpretation]

Schedule 1 Lasting Powers of Attorney: Formalities

Part 1 Making Instruments
Part 2 Registration
Part 3 Cancellation Of Registration And Notification Of Severance
Part 4 Records Of Alterations In Registered Powers

[Schedule 1A Persons Ineligible to be Deprived of Liberty by this Act]

[Part 1 Ineligible Persons]
[Part 2 Interpretation]

Schedule 2 Property and Affairs: Supplementary Provision

Schedule 3 International Protection of Adults

Part 1 Preliminary
Part 2 Jurisdiction Of Competent Authority
Part 3 Applicable Law
Part 4 Recognition And Enforcement
Part 5 Co-operation
Part 6 General

Schedule 4 Provisions Applying to Existing Enduring Powers of Attorney ##

Part 1 Enduring Powers Of Attorney
Part 2 Action On Actual Or Impending Incapacity Of Donor
Part 3 Notification Prior To Registration
Part 4 Registration
Part 5 Legal Position After Registration
Part 6 Protection Of Attorney And Third Parties
Part 7 Joint And Joint And Several Attorneys
Part 8 Interpretation ##

Schedule 5 Transitional Provisions and Savings

Part 1 Repeal of Part 7 of The Mental Health Act 1983
Part 2 Repeal of The Enduring Powers of Attorney Act 1985

Schedule 6 Minor and Consequential Amendments

Schedule 7 Repeals

MENTAL CAPACITY ACT 2005

2005 CHAPTER 9

An Act to make new provision relating to persons who lack capacity; to establish a superior court of record called the Court of Protection in place of the office of the Supreme Court called by that name; to make provision in connection with the Convention on the International Protection of Adults signed at the Hague on 13th January 2000; and for connected purposes. [7th April 2005]

BE IT ENACTED by the Queen's most Excellent Majesty, by and with the advice and consent of the Lords Spiritual and Temporal, and Commons, in this present
Parliament assembled, and by the authority of the same, as follows:—

PART 1
PERSONS WHO LACK CAPACITY

The principles

1 The principles

(1) The following principles apply for the purposes of this Act.

(2) A person must be assumed to have capacity unless it is established that he lacks capacity.

(3) A person is not to be treated as unable to make a decision unless all practicable steps to help him to do so have been taken without success.

(4) A person is not to be treated as unable to make a decision merely because he makes an unwise decision.

(5) An act done, or decision made, under this Act for or on behalf of a person who lacks capacity must be done, or made, in his best interests.

(6) Before the act is done, or the decision is made, regard must be had to whether the purpose for which it is needed can be as effectively achieved in a way that is less restrictive of the person's rights and freedom of action.

Preliminary

2 People who lack capacity

(1) For the purposes of this Act, a person lacks capacity in relation to a matter if at the material time he is unable to make a decision for himself in relation to the matter because of an impairment of, or a disturbance in the functioning of, the mind or brain.

(2) It does not matter whether the impairment or disturbance is permanent or temporary.

(3) A lack of capacity cannot be established merely by reference to—

(a) a person's age or appearance, or

(b) a condition of his, or an aspect of his behaviour, which might lead others to make unjustified assumptions about his capacity.

(4) In proceedings under this Act or any other enactment, any question whether a person lacks capacity within the meaning of this Act must be decided on the balance of probabilities.

(5) No power which a person ('D') may exercise under this Act—

(a) in relation to a person who lacks capacity, or

(b) where D reasonably thinks that a person lacks capacity,

is exercisable in relation to a person under 16.

(6) Subsection (5) is subject to section 18(3).

3 Inability to make decisions

(1) For the purposes of section 2, a person is unable to make a decision for himself if he is unable—

(a) to understand the information relevant to the decision,

(b) to retain that information,

(c) to use or weigh that information as part of the process of making the decision, or

(d) to communicate his decision (whether by talking, using sign language or any other means).

(2) A person is not to be regarded as unable to understand the information relevant to a decision if he is able to understand an explanation of it given to him in a way that is appropriate to his circumstances (using simple language, visual aids or any other means).

(3) The fact that a person is able to retain the information relevant to a decision for a short period only does not prevent him from being regarded as able to make the decision.

(4) The information relevant to a decision includes information about the reasonably foreseeable consequences of—

(a) deciding one way or another, or

(b) failing to make the decision.

4 Best interests

(1) In determining for the purposes of this Act what is in a person's best interests, the person making the determination must not make it merely on the basis of—

(a) the person's age or appearance, or

(b) a condition of his, or an aspect of his behaviour, which might lead others to make unjustified assumptions about what might be in his best interests.

(2) The person making the determination must consider all the relevant circumstances and, in particular, take the following steps.

(3) He must consider—

(a) whether it is likely that the person will at some time have capacity in relation to the matter in question, and

(b) if it appears likely that he will, when that is likely to be.

(4) He must, so far as reasonably practicable, permit and encourage the person to participate, or to improve his ability to participate, as fully as possible in any act done for him and any decision affecting him.

(5) Where the determination relates to life-sustaining treatment he must not, in considering whether the treatment is in the best interests of the person concerned, be motivated by a desire to bring about his death.

(6) He must consider, so far as is reasonably ascertainable—

    (a) the person's past and present wishes and feelings (and, in particular, any relevant written statement made by him when he had capacity),

    (b) the beliefs and values that would be likely to influence his decision if he had capacity, and

    (c) the other factors that he would be likely to consider if he were able to do so.

(7) He must take into account, if it is practicable and appropriate to consult them, the views of—

    (a) anyone named by the person as someone to be consulted on the matter in question or on matters of that kind,

    (b) anyone engaged in caring for the person or interested in his welfare,

    (c) any donee of a lasting power of attorney granted by the person, and

    (d) any deputy appointed for the person by the court,as to what would be in the person's best interests and, in particular, as to the matters mentioned in subsection (6).

(8) The duties imposed by subsections (1) to (7) also apply in relation to the exercise of any powers which—

    (a) are exercisable under a lasting power of attorney, or

    (b) are exercisable by a person under this Act where he reasonably believes that another person lacks capacity.

(9) In the case of an act done, or a decision made, by a person other than the court, there is sufficient compliance with this section if (having complied with the requirements of subsections (1) to (7)) he reasonably believes that what he does or decides is in the best interests of the person concerned.

(10) 'Life-sustaining treatment' means treatment which in the view of a person providing health care for the person concerned is necessary to sustain life.

(11) 'Relevant circumstances' are those—

    (a) of which the person making the determination is aware, and

    (b) which it would be reasonable to regard as relevant.

[4A Restriction on deprivation of liberty]

[(1) This Act does not authorise any person ('D') to deprive any other person ('P') of his liberty.

(2) But that is subject to—

    (a) the following provisions of this section, and

    (b) section 4B.

(3) D may deprive P of his liberty if, by doing so, D is giving effect to a relevant decision of the court.

(4) A relevant decision of the court is a decision made by an order under section 16(2)(a) in relation to a matter concerning P's personal welfare.

(5) D may deprive P of his liberty if the deprivation is authorised by Schedule A1 (hospital and care home residents: deprivation of liberty).]

[*Section 4A inserted by section 50(2) of the 2007 Act.*]

[4B Deprivation of liberty necessary for life-sustaining treatment etc]

[(1) If the following conditions are met, D is authorised to deprive P of his liberty while a decision as respects any relevant issue is sought from the court.

(2) The first condition is that there is a question about whether D is authorised to deprive P of his liberty under section 4A.

(3) The second condition is that the deprivation of liberty—
    (a) is wholly or partly for the purpose of—
        (i) giving P life-sustaining treatment, or
        (ii) doing any vital act, or
    (b) consists wholly or partly of—
        (i) giving P life-sustaining treatment, or
        (ii) doing any vital act.

(4) The third condition is that the deprivation of liberty is necessary in order to—
    (a) give the life-sustaining treatment, or
    (b) do the vital act.

(5) A vital act is any act which the person doing it reasonably believes to be necessary to prevent a serious deterioration in P's condition.]

[Section 4B inserted by section 50(2) of the 2007 Act.]

5 Acts in connection with care or treatment

(1) If a person ('D') does an act in connection with the care or treatment of another person ('P'), the act is one to which this section applies if—
    (a) before doing the act, D takes reasonable steps to establish whether P lacks capacity in relation to the matter in question, and
    (b) when doing the act, D reasonably believes—
        (i) that P lacks capacity in relation to the matter, and
        (ii) that it will be in P's best interests for the act to be done.

(2) D does not incur any liability in relation to the act that he would not have incurred if P—
    (a) had had capacity to consent in relation to the matter, and
    (b) had consented to D's doing the act.

(3) Nothing in this section excludes a person's civil liability for loss or damage, or his criminal liability, resulting from his negligence in doing the act.

(4) Nothing in this section affects the operation of sections 24 to 26 (advance decisions to refuse treatment).

6 Section 5 acts: limitations

(1) If D does an act that is intended to restrain P, it is not an act to which section 5 applies unless two further conditions are satisfied.

(2) The first condition is that D reasonably believes that it is necessary to do the act in order to prevent harm to P.

(3) The second is that the act is a proportionate response to—
    (a) the likelihood of P's suffering harm, and
    (b) the seriousness of that harm.

(4) For the purposes of this section D restrains P if he—
    (a) uses, or threatens to use, force to secure the doing of an act which P resists, or
    (b) restricts P's liberty of movement, whether or not P resists.

(5) But D does more than merely restrain P if he deprives P of his liberty within the meaning of Article 5(1) of the Human Rights Convention (whether or not D is a public authority).

(6) Section 5 does not authorise a person to do an act which conflicts with a decision made, within the scope of his authority and in accordance with this Part, by—
   (a) a donee of a lasting power of attorney granted by P, or
   (b) a deputy appointed for P by the court.

(7) But nothing in subsection (6) stops a person—
   (a) providing life-sustaining treatment, or
   (b) doing any act which he reasonably believes to be necessary to prevent a serious deterioration in P's condition, while a decision as respects any relevant issue is sought from the court.

[Subsection (5) omitted by section 50(4)(a) of the 2007 Act.]

7 Payment for necessary goods and services

(1) If necessary goods or services are supplied to a person who lacks capacity to contract for the supply, he must pay a reasonable price for them.

(2) 'Necessary' means suitable to a person's condition in life and to his actual requirements at the time when the goods or services are supplied.

8 Expenditure

(1) If an act to which section 5 applies involves expenditure, it is lawful for D—
   (a) to pledge P's credit for the purpose of the expenditure, and
   (b) to apply money in P's possession for meeting the expenditure.

(2) If the expenditure is borne for P by D, it is lawful for D—
   (a) to reimburse himself out of money in P's possession, or
   (b) to be otherwise indemnified by P.

(3) Subsections (1) and (2) do not affect any power under which (apart from those subsections) a person—
   (a) has lawful control of P's money or other property, and
   (b) has power to spend money for P's benefit.

Lasting powers of attorney

9 Lasting powers of attorney

(1) A lasting power of attorney is a power of attorney under which the donor ('P') confers on the donee (or donees) authority to make decisions about all or any of the following—
   (a) P's personal welfare or specified matters concerning P's personal welfare, and
   (b) P's property and affairs or specified matters concerning P's property and affairs, and which includes authority to make such decisions in circumstances where P no longer has capacity.

(2) A lasting power of attorney is not created unless—
   (a) section 10 is complied with,
   (b) an instrument conferring authority of the kind mentioned in subsection (1) is made and registered in accordance with Schedule 1, and
   (c) at the time when P executes the instrument, P has reached 18 and has capacity to execute it.

(3) An instrument which—
   (a) purports to create a lasting power of attorney, but

(b) does not comply with this section, section 10 or Schedule 1, confers no authority.

(4) The authority conferred by a lasting power of attorney is subject to—

    (a) the provisions of this Act and, in particular, sections 1 (the principles) and 4 (best interests), and

    (b) any conditions or restrictions specified in the instrument.

10 Appointment of donees

(1) A donee of a lasting power of attorney must be—

    (a) an individual who has reached 18, or

    (b) if the power relates only to P's property and affairs, either such an individual or a trust corporation.

(2) An individual who is bankrupt may not be appointed as donee of a lasting power of attorney in relation to P's property and affairs.

(3) Subsections (4) to (7) apply in relation to an instrument under which two or more persons are to act as donees of a lasting power of attorney.

(4) The instrument may appoint them to act—

    (a) jointly,

    (b) jointly and severally, or

    (c) jointly in respect of some matters and jointly and severally in respect of others.

(5) To the extent to which it does not specify whether they are to act jointly or jointly and severally, the instrument is to be assumed to appoint them to act jointly.

(6) If they are to act jointly, a failure, as respects one of them, to comply with the requirements of subsection (1) or (2) or Part 1 or 2 of Schedule 1 prevents a lasting power of attorney from being created.

(7) If they are to act jointly and severally, a failure, as respects one of them, to comply with the requirements of subsection (1) or (2) or Part 1 or 2 of Schedule 1—

    (a) prevents the appointment taking effect in his case, but

    (b) does not prevent a lasting power of attorney from being created in the case of the other or others.

(8) An instrument used to create a lasting power of attorney—

    (a) cannot give the donee (or, if more than one, any of them) power to appoint a substitute or successor, but

    (b) may itself appoint a person to replace the donee (or, if more than one, any of them) on the occurrence of an event mentioned in section 13(6)(a) to (d) which has the effect of terminating the donee's appointment.

11 Lasting powers of attorney: restrictions

(1) A lasting power of attorney does not authorise the donee (or, if more than one, any of them) to do an act that is intended to restrain P, unless three conditions are satisfied.

(2) The first condition is that P lacks, or the donee reasonably believes that P lacks capacity in relation to the matter in question.

(3) The second is that the donee reasonably believes that it is necessary to do the act in order to prevent harm to P.

(4) The third is that the act is a proportionate response to—

    (a) the likelihood of P's suffering harm, and

    (b) the seriousness of that harm.

(5) For the purposes of this section, the donee restrains P if he—
  (a) uses, or threatens to use, force to secure the doing of an act which P resists, or
  (b) restricts P's liberty of movement, whether or not P resists,
  or if he authorises another person to do any of those things.
(6) But the donee does more than merely restrain P if he deprives P of his liberty within the meaning of Article 5(1) of the Human Rights Convention.
(7) Where a lasting power of attorney authorises the donee (or, if more than one, any of them) to make decisions about P's personal welfare, the authority—
  (a) does not extend to making such decisions in circumstances other than those where P lacks, or the donee reasonably believes that P lacks, capacity,
  (b) is subject to sections 24 to 26 (advance decisions to refuse treatment), and
  (c) extends to giving or refusing consent to the carrying out or continuation of a treatment by a person providing health care for P.
(8) But subsection (7)(c)—
  (a) does not authorise the giving or refusing of consent to the carrying out or continuation of life-sustaining treatment, unless the instrument contains express provision to that effect, and
  (b) is subject to any conditions or restrictions in the instrument.
[Subsection (6) omitted by section 50(4)(b) of the 2007 Act.]

12 Scope of lasting powers of attorney: gifts

(1) Where a lasting power of attorney confers authority to make decisions about P's property and affairs, it does not authorise a donee (or, if more than one, any of them) to dispose of the donor's property by making gifts except to the extent permitted by subsection (2).
(2) The donee may make gifts—
  (a) on customary occasions to persons (including himself) who are related to or connected with the donor, or
  (b) to any charity to whom the donor made or might have been expected to make gifts, if the value of each such gift is not unreasonable having regard to all the circumstances and, in particular, the size of the donor's estate.
(3) 'Customary occasion' means—
  (a) the occasion or anniversary of a birth, a marriage or the formation of a civil partnership, or
  (b) any other occasion on which presents are customarily given within families or among friends or associates.
(4) Subsection (2) is subject to any conditions or restrictions in the instrument.

13 Revocation of lasting powers of attorney etc

(1) This section applies if—
  (a) P has executed an instrument with a view to creating a lasting power of attorney, or
  (b) a lasting power of attorney is registered as having been conferred by P,
  and in this section references to revoking the power include revoking the instrument.
(2) P may, at any time when he has capacity to do so, revoke the power.
(3) P's bankruptcy revokes the power so far as it relates to P's property and affairs.
(4) But where P is bankrupt merely because an interim bankruptcy restrictions order has effect in respect of him, the power is suspended, so far as it relates to P's property and affairs, for so long as the order has effect.

(5) The occurrence in relation to a donee of an event mentioned in subsection (6)—
  (a) terminates his appointment, and
  (b) except in the cases given in subsection (7), revokes the power.
(6) The events are—
  (a) the disclaimer of the appointment by the donee in accordance with such requirements as may be prescribed for the purposes of this section in regulations made by the Lord Chancellor,
  (b) subject to subsections (8) and (9), the death or bankruptcy of the donee or, if the donee is a trust corporation, its winding-up or dissolution,
  (c) subject to subsection (11), the dissolution or annulment of a marriage or civil partnership between the donor and the donee,
  (d) the lack of capacity of the donee.
(7) The cases are—
  (a) the donee is replaced under the terms of the instrument,
  (b) he is one of two or more persons appointed to act as donees jointly and severally in respect of any matter and, after the event, there is at least one remaining donee.
(8) The bankruptcy of a donee does not terminate his appointment, or revoke the power, in so far as his authority relates to P's personal welfare.
(9) Where the donee is bankrupt merely because an interim bankruptcy restrictions order has effect in respect of him, his appointment and the power are suspended, so far as they relate to P's property and affairs, for so long as the order has effect.
(10) Where the donee is one of two or more appointed to act jointly and severally under the power in respect of any matter, the reference in subsection (9) to the suspension of the power is to its suspension in so far as it relates to that donee.
(11) The dissolution or annulment of a marriage or civil partnership does not terminate the appointment of a donee, or revoke the power, if the instrument provided that it was not to do so.

14 Protection of donee and others if no power created or power revoked

(1) Subsections (2) and (3) apply if—
  (a) an instrument has been registered under Schedule 1 as a lasting power of attorney, but
  (b) a lasting power of attorney was not created, whether or not the registration has been cancelled at the time of the act or transaction in question.
(2) A donee who acts in purported exercise of the power does not incur any liability (to P or any other person) because of the non-existence of the power unless at the time of acting he—
  (a) knows that a lasting power of attorney was not created, or
  (b) is aware of circumstances which, if a lasting power of attorney had been created, would have terminated his authority to act as a donee.
(3) Any transaction between the donee and another person is, in favour of that person, as valid as if the power had been in existence, unless at the time of the transaction that person has knowledge of a matter referred to in subsection (2).
(4) If the interest of a purchaser depends on whether a transaction between the donee and the other person was valid by virtue of subsection (3), it is conclusively presumed in favour of the purchaser that the transaction was valid if—
  (a) the transaction was completed within 12 months of the date on which the instrument was registered, or

(b) the other person makes a statutory declaration, before or within 3 months after the completion of the purchase, that he had no reason at the time of the transaction to doubt that the donee had authority to dispose of the property which was the subject of the transaction.

(5) In its application to a lasting power of attorney which relates to matters in addition to P's property and affairs, section 5 of the Powers of Attorney Act 1971 (c. 27) (protection where power is revoked) has effect as if references to revocation included the cessation of the power in relation to P's property and affairs.

(6) Where two or more donees are appointed under a lasting power of attorney, this section applies as if references to the donee were to all or any of them.

General powers of the court and appointment of deputies

15 Power to make declarations

(1) The court may make declarations as to—
    (a) whether a person has or lacks capacity to make a decision specified in the declaration;
    (b) whether a person has or lacks capacity to make decisions on such matters as are described in the declaration;
    (c) the lawfulness or otherwise of any act done, or yet to be done, in relation to that person.

(2) 'Act' includes an omission and a course of conduct.

16 Powers to make decisions and appoint deputies: general

(1) This section applies if a person ('P') lacks capacity in relation to a matter or matters concerning—
    (a) P's personal welfare, or
    (b) P's property and affairs.

(2) The court may—
    (a) by making an order, make the decision or decisions on P's behalf in relation to the matter or matters, or
    (b) appoint a person (a 'deputy') to make decisions on P's behalf in relation to the matter or matters.

(3) The powers of the court under this section are subject to the provisions of this Act and, in particular, to sections 1 (the principles) and 4 (best interests).

(4) When deciding whether it is in P's best interests to appoint a deputy, the court must have regard (in addition to the matters mentioned in section 4) to the principles that—
    (a) a decision by the court is to be preferred to the appointment of a deputy to make a decision, and
    (b) the powers conferred on a deputy should be as limited in scope and duration as is reasonably practicable in the circumstances.

(5) The court may make such further orders or give such directions, and confer on a deputy such powers or impose on him such duties, as it thinks necessary or expedient for giving effect to, or otherwise in connection with, an order or appointment made by it under subsection (2).

(6) Without prejudice to section 4, the court may make the order, give the directions or make the appointment on such terms as it considers are in P's best interests, even though no application is before the court for an order, directions or an appointment on those terms.

(7) An order of the court may be varied or discharged by a subsequent order.

(8) The court may, in particular, revoke the appointment of a deputy or vary the powers conferred on him if it is satisfied that the deputy—

    (a) has behaved, or is behaving, in a way that contravenes the authority conferred on him by the court or is not in P's best interests, or

    (b) proposes to behave in a way that would contravene that authority or would not be in P's best interests.

[16A Section 16 powers: Mental Health Act patients etc]

[(1) If a person is ineligible to be deprived of liberty by this Act, the court may not include in a welfare order provision which authorises the person to be deprived of his liberty.

(2) If—

    (a) a welfare order includes provision which authorises a person to be deprived of his liberty, and

    (b) that person becomes ineligible to be deprived of liberty by this Act,

the provision ceases to have effect for as long as the person remains ineligible.

(3) Nothing in subsection (2) affects the power of tshe court under section 16(7) to vary or discharge the welfare order.

(4) For the purposes of this section—

    (a) Schedule 1A applies for determining whether or not P is ineligible to be deprived of liberty by this Act;

    (b) 'welfare order' means an order under section 16(2)(a).]

[Section 16A inserted by section 50(3) of the 2007 Act.]

17 Section 16 powers: personal welfare

(1) The powers under section 16 as respects P's personal welfare extend in particular to—

    (a) deciding where P is to live;

    (b) deciding what contact, if any, P is to have with any specified persons;

    (c) making an order prohibiting a named person from having contact with P;

    (d) giving or refusing consent to the carrying out or continuation of a treatment by a person providing health care for P;

    (e) giving a direction that a person responsible for P's health care allow a different person to take over that responsibility.

(2) Subsection (1) is subject to section 20 (restrictions on deputies).

18 Section 16 powers: property and affairs

(1) The powers under section 16 as respects P's property and affairs extend in particular to—

    (a) the control and management of P's property;

    (b) the sale, exchange, charging, gift or other disposition of P's property;

    (c) the acquisition of property in P's name or on P's behalf;

    (d) the carrying on, on P's behalf, of any profession, trade or business;

    (e) the taking of a decision which will have the effect of dissolving a partnership of which P is a member;

    (f) the carrying out of any contract entered into by P;

    (g) the discharge of P's debts and of any of P's obligations, whether legally enforceable or not;

    (h) the settlement of any of P's property, whether for P's benefit or for the benefit of others;

    (i) the execution for P of a will;

(j) the exercise of any power (including a power to consent) vested in P whether beneficially or as trustee or otherwise;

(k) the conduct of legal proceedings in P's name or on P's behalf.

(2) No will may be made under subsection (1)(i) at a time when P has not reached 18.

(3) The powers under section 16 as respects any other matter relating to P's property and affairs may be exercised even though P has not reached 16, if the court considers it likely that P will still lack capacity to make decisions in respect of that matter when he reaches 18.

(4) Schedule 2 supplements the provisions of this section.

(5) Section 16(7) (variation and discharge of court orders) is subject to paragraph 6 of Schedule 2.

(6) Subsection (1) is subject to section 20 (restrictions on deputies).

19 Appointment of deputies

(1) A deputy appointed by the court must be—
   (a) an individual who has reached 18, or
   (b) as respects powers in relation to property and affairs, an individual who has reached 18 or a trust corporation.

(2) The court may appoint an individual by appointing the holder for the time being of a specified office or position.

(3) A person may not be appointed as a deputy without his consent.

(4) The court may appoint two or more deputies to act—
   (a) jointly,
   (b) jointly and severally, or
   (c) jointly in respect of some matters and jointly and severally in respect of others.

(5) When appointing a deputy or deputies, the court may at the same time appoint one or more other persons to succeed the existing deputy or those deputies—
   (a) in such circumstances, or on the happening of such events, as may be specified by the court;
   (b) for such period as may be so specified.

(6) A deputy is to be treated as P's agent in relation to anything done or decided by him within the scope of his appointment and in accordance with this Part.

(7) The deputy is entitled—
   (a) to be reimbursed out of P's property for his reasonable expenses in discharging his functions, and
   (b) if the court so directs when appointing him, to remuneration out of P's property for discharging them.

(8) The court may confer on a deputy powers to—
   (a) take possession or control of all or any specified part of P's property;
   (b) exercise all or any specified powers in respect of it, including such powers of investment as the court may determine.

(9) The court may require a deputy—
   (a) to give to the Public Guardian such security as the court thinks fit for the due discharge of his functions, and
   (b) to submit to the Public Guardian such reports at such times or at such intervals as the court may direct.

20 Restrictions on deputies

(1) A deputy does not have power to make a decision on behalf of P in relation to a matter if he knows or has reasonable grounds for believing that P has capacity in relation to the matter.

(2) Nothing in section 16(5) or 17 permits a deputy to be given power—

(a) to prohibit a named person from having contact with P;

(b) to direct a person responsible for P's health care to allow a different person to take over that responsibility.

(3) A deputy may not be given powers with respect to—

(a) the settlement of any of P's property, whether for P's benefit or for the benefit of others,

(b) the execution for P of a will, or

(c) the exercise of any power (including a power to consent) vested in P whether beneficially or as trustee or otherwise.

(4) A deputy may not be given power to make a decision on behalf of P which is inconsistent with a decision made, within the scope of his authority and in accordance with this Act, by the donee of a lasting power of attorney granted by P (or, if there is more than one donee, by any of them).

(5) A deputy may not refuse consent to the carrying out or continuation of life sustaining treatment in relation to P.

(6) The authority conferred on a deputy is subject to the provisions of this Act and, in particular, sections 1 (the principles) and 4 (best interests).

(7) A deputy may not do an act that is intended to restrain P unless four conditions are satisfied.

(8) The first condition is that, in doing the act, the deputy is acting within the scope of an authority expressly conferred on him by the court.

(9) The second is that P lacks, or the deputy reasonably believes that P lacks, capacity in relation to the matter in question.

(10) The third is that the deputy reasonably believes that it is necessary to do the act in order to prevent harm to P.

(11) The fourth is that the act is a proportionate response to—

(a) the likelihood of P's suffering harm, *or* [and]

(b) the seriousness of that harm.

(12) For the purposes of this section, a deputy restrains P if he—

(a) uses, or threatens to use, force to secure the doing of an act which P resists, or

(b) restricts P's liberty of movement, whether or not P resists,

or if he authorises another person to do any of those things.

(13) *But a deputy does more than merely restrain P if he deprives P of his liberty within the meaning of Article 5(1) of the Human Rights Convention (whether or not the deputy is a public authority).*

[*Subsection (11) amended by section 51 of the 2007 Act. Subsection (13) omitted by section 50(4)(c).*]

21 Transfer of proceedings relating to people under 18

(1) The Lord Chief Justice, with the concurrence of the Lord Chancellor, may by order make provision as to the transfer of proceedings relating to a person under 18, in such circumstances as are specified in the order—

(a) from the Court of Protection to a court having jurisdiction under the Children Act 1989 (c. 41), or

(b) from a court having jurisdiction under that Act to the Court of Protection.

(2) The Lord Chief Justice may nominate any of the following to exercise his functions under this section-

(a) the President of the Court of Protection;

(b) a judicial officer holder (as defined in section 109(4) of the Constitutional Reform Act 2005).

[Powers of court in relation to Schedule A1]

[21A Powers of court in relation to Schedule A1]

[(1) This section applies if either of the following has been given under Schedule A1—

(a) a standard authorisation;

(b) an urgent authorisation.

(2) Where a standard authorisation has been given, the court may determine any question relating to any of the following matters—

(a) whether the relevant person meets one or more of the qualifying requirements;

(b) the period during which the standard authorisation is to be in force;

(c) the purpose for which the standard authorisation is given;

(d) the conditions subject to which the standard authorisation is given.

(3) If the court determines any question under subsection (2), the court may make an order—

(a) varying or terminating the standard authorisation, or

(b) directing the supervisory body to vary or terminate the standard authorisation.

(4) Where an urgent authorisation has been given, the court may determine any question relating to any of the following matters—

(a) whether the urgent authorisation should have been given;

(b) the period during which the urgent authorisation is to be in force;

(c) the purpose for which the urgent authorisation is given.

(5) Where the court determines any question under subsection (4), the court may make an order—

(a) varying or terminating the urgent authorisation, or

(b) directing the managing authority of the relevant hospital or care home to vary or terminate the urgent authorisation.

(6) Where the court makes an order under subsection (3) or (5), the court may make an order about a person's liability for any act done in connection with the standard or urgent authorisation before its variation or termination.

(7) An order under subsection (6) may, in particular, exclude a person from liability.]

[Section 21A inserted by paragraph 2 of Schedule 9 to the 2007 Act.]

Powers of the court in relation to lasting powers of attorney

22 Powers of court in relation to validity of lasting powers of attorney

(1) This section and section 23 apply if—

(a) a person ('P') has executed or purported to execute an instrument with a view to creating a lasting power of attorney, or

(b) an instrument has been registered as a lasting power of attorney conferred by P.

(2) The court may determine any question relating to—

(a) whether one or more of the requirements for the creation of a lasting power of attorney have been met;

    (b) whether the power has been revoked or has otherwise come to an end.

(3) Subsection (4) applies if the court is satisfied—

    (a) that fraud or undue pressure was used to induce P—

        (i) to execute an instrument for the purpose of creating a lasting power of attorney, or

        (ii) to create a lasting power of attorney, or

    (b) that the donee (or, if more than one, any of them) of a lasting power of attorney—

        (i) has behaved, or is behaving, in a way that contravenes his authority or is not in P's best interests, or

        (ii) proposes to behave in a way that would contravene his authority or would not be in P's best interests.

(4) The court may—

    (a) direct that an instrument purporting to create the lasting power of attorney is not to be registered, or

    (b) if P lacks capacity to do so, revoke the instrument or the lasting power of attorney.

(5) If there is more than one donee, the court may under subsection (4)(b) revoke the instrument or the lasting power of attorney so far as it relates to any of them.

(6) 'Donee' includes an intended donee.

23 Powers of court in relation to operation of lasting powers of attorney

(1) The court may determine any question as to the meaning or effect of a lasting power of attorney or an instrument purporting to create one.

(2) The court may—

    (a) give directions with respect to decisions—

        (i) which the donee of a lasting power of attorney has authority to make, and

        (ii) which P lacks capacity to make;

    (b) give any consent or authorisation to act which the donee would have to obtain from P if P had capacity to give it.

(3) The court may, if P lacks capacity to do so—

    (a) give directions to the donee with respect to the rendering by him of reports or accounts and the production of records kept by him for that purpose;

    (b) require the donee to supply information or produce documents or things in his possession as donee;

    (c) give directions with respect to the remuneration or expenses of the donee;

    (d) relieve the donee wholly or partly from any liability which he has or may have incurred on account of a breach of his duties as donee.

(4) The court may authorise the making of gifts which are not within section 12(2) (permitted gifts).

(5) Where two or more donees are appointed under a lasting power of attorney, this section applies as if references to the donee were to all or any of them.

Advance decisions to refuse treatment

24 Advance decisions to refuse treatment: general

(1) 'Advance decision' means a decision made by a person ('P'), after he has reached 18 and when he has capacity to do so, that if—

    (a) at a later time and in such circumstances as he may specify, a specified treatment is proposed to be carried out or continued by a person providing health care for him, and

(b) at that time he lacks capacity to consent to the carrying out or continuation of the treatment, the specified treatment is not to be carried out or continued.

(2) For the purposes of subsection (1)(a), a decision may be regarded as specifying a treatment or circumstances even though expressed in layman's terms.

(3) P may withdraw or alter an advance decision at any time when he has capacity to do so.

(4) A withdrawal (including a partial withdrawal) need not be in writing.

(5) An alteration of an advance decision need not be in writing (unless section 25(5) applies in relation to the decision resulting from the alteration).

25 Validity and applicability of advance decisions

(1) An advance decision does not affect the liability which a person may incur for carrying out or continuing a treatment in relation to P unless the decision is at the material time—
  (a) valid, and
  (b) applicable to the treatment.

(2) An advance decision is not valid if P—
  (a) has withdrawn the decision at a time when he had capacity to do so,
  (b) has, under a lasting power of attorney created after the advance decision was made, conferred authority on the donee (or, if more than one, any of them) to give or refuse consent to the treatment to which the advance decision relates, or
  (c) has done anything else clearly inconsistent with the advance decision remaining his fixed decision.

(3) An advance decision is not applicable to the treatment in question if at the material time P has capacity to give or refuse consent to it.

(4) An advance decision is not applicable to the treatment in question if—
  (a) that treatment is not the treatment specified in the advance decision,
  (b) any circumstances specified in the advance decision are absent, or
  (c) there are reasonable grounds for believing that circumstances exist which P did not anticipate at the time of the advance decision and which would have affected his decision had he anticipated them.

(5) An advance decision is not applicable to life-sustaining treatment unless—
  (a) the decision is verified by a statement by P to the effect that it is to apply to that treatment even if life is at risk, and
  (b) the decision and statement comply with subsection (6).

(6) A decision or statement complies with this subsection only if—
  (a) it is in writing,
  (b) it is signed by P or by another person in P's presence and by P's direction,
  (c) the signature is made or acknowledged by P in the presence of a witness, and
  (d) the witness signs it, or acknowledges his signature, in P's presence.

(7) The existence of any lasting power of attorney other than one of a description mentioned in subsection (2)(b) does not prevent the advance decision from being regarded as valid and applicable.

26 Effect of advance decisions

(1) If P has made an advance decision which is—
  (a) valid, and
  (b) applicable to a treatment,
  the decision has effect as if he had made it, and had had capacity to make it, at the time when the question arises whether the treatment should be carried out or continued.

(2) A person does not incur liability for carrying out or continuing the treatment unless, at the time, he is satisfied that an advance decision exists which is valid and applicable to the treatment.

(3) A person does not incur liability for the consequences of withholding or withdrawing a treatment from P if, at the time, he reasonably believes that an advance decision exists which is valid and applicable to the treatment.

(4) The court may make a declaration as to whether an advance decision—

    (a) exists;

    (b) is valid;

    (c) is applicable to a treatment.

(5) Nothing in an apparent advance decision stops a person—

    (a) providing life-sustaining treatment, or

    (b) doing any act he reasonably believes to be necessary to prevent a serious deterioration in P's condition,

while a decision as respects any relevant issue is sought from the court.

Excluded decisions

27 Family relationships etc.

(1) Nothing in this Act permits a decision on any of the following matters to be made on behalf of a person—

    (a) consenting to marriage or a civil partnership,

    (b) consenting to have sexual relations,

    (c) consenting to a decree of divorce being granted on the basis of two years' separation,

    (d) consenting to a dissolution order being made in relation to a civil partnership on the basis of two years' separation,

    (e) consenting to a child's being placed for adoption by an adoption agency,

    (f) consenting to the making of an adoption order,

    (g) discharging parental responsibilities in matters not relating to a child's property,

    (h) giving a consent under the Human Fertilisation and Embryology Act 1990 (c. 37).

(2) 'Adoption order' means—

    (a) an adoption order within the meaning of the Adoption and Children Act 2002 (c. 38) (including a future adoption order), and

    (b) an order under section 84 of that Act (parental responsibility prior to adoption abroad).

28 Mental Health Act matters

(1) Nothing in this Act authorises anyone—

    (a) to give a patient medical treatment for mental disorder, or

    (b) to consent to a patient's being given medical treatment for mental disorder,

if, at the time when it is proposed to treat the patient, his treatment is regulated by Part 4 of the Mental Health Act.

[(1A)Subsection (1) does not apply in relation to any form of treatment to which section 58A of that Act (electro-convulsive therapy, etc.) applies if the patient comes within subsection (7) of that section (informal patient under 18 who cannot give consent).

(1B) Section 5 does not apply to an act to which section 64B of the Mental Health Act applies (treatment of community patients not recalled to hospital).]

(2) 'Medical treatment', 'mental disorder' and 'patient' have the same meaning as in that Act.

[Subsection (1A) inserted by section 28(10) of the 2007 Act. Subsection (1B) inserted by section 35(5).]

29 Voting rights

(1) Nothing in this Act permits a decision on voting at an election for any public office, or at a referendum, to be made on behalf of a person.

(2) 'Referendum' has the same meaning as in section 101 of the Political Parties, Elections and Referendums Act 2000 (c. 41).

Research

30 Research

(1) Intrusive research carried out on, or in relation to, a person who lacks capacity to consent to it is unlawful unless it is carried out—
  (a) as part of a research project which is for the time being approved by the appropriate body for the purposes of this Act in accordance with section 31, and
  (b) in accordance with sections 32 and 33.

(2) Research is intrusive if it is of a kind that would be unlawful if it was carried out—
  (a) on or in relation to a person who had capacity to consent to it, but
  (b) without his consent.

(3) A clinical trial which is subject to the provisions of clinical trials regulations is not to be treated as research for the purposes of this section.

(4) 'Appropriate body', in relation to a research project, means the person, committee or other body specified in regulations made by the appropriate authority as the appropriate body in relation to a project of the kind in question.

(5) 'Clinical trials regulations' means—
  (a) the Medicines for Human Use (Clinical Trials) Regulations 2004 (S.I. 2004/1031) and any other regulations replacing those regulations or amending them, and
  (b) any other regulations relating to clinical trials and designated by the Secretary of State as clinical trials regulations for the purposes of this section.

(6) In this section, section 32 and section 34, 'appropriate authority' means—
  (a) in relation to the carrying out of research in England, the Secretary of State, and
  (b) in relation to the carrying out of research in Wales, the National Assembly for Wales.

31 Requirements for approval

(1) The appropriate body may not approve a research project for the purposes of this Act unless satisfied that the following requirements will be met in relation to research carried out as part of the project on, or in relation to, a person who lacks capacity to consent to taking part in the project ('P').

(2) The research must be connected with—
  (a) an impairing condition affecting P, or
  (b) its treatment.

(3) 'Impairing condition' means a condition which is (or may be) attributable to, or which causes or contributes to (or may cause or contribute to), the impairment of, or disturbance in the functioning of, the mind or brain.

(4) There must be reasonable grounds for believing that research of comparable effectiveness cannot be carried out if the project has to be confined to, or relate only to, persons who have capacity to consent to taking part in it.

(5) The research must—

(a) have the potential to benefit P without imposing on P a burden that is disproportionate to the potential benefit to P, or

(b) be intended to provide knowledge of the causes or treatment of, or of the care of persons affected by, the same or a similar condition.

(6) If the research falls within paragraph (b) of subsection (5) but not within paragraph (a), there must be reasonable grounds for believing—

(a) that the risk to P from taking part in the project is likely to be negligible, and

(b) that anything done to, or in relation to, P will not—

(i) interfere with P's freedom of action or privacy in a significant way, or

(ii) be unduly invasive or restrictive.

(7) There must be reasonable arrangements in place for ensuring that the requirements of sections 32 and 33 will be met.

32 Consulting carers etc

(1) This section applies if a person ('R')—

(a) is conducting an approved research project, and

(b) wishes to carry out research, as part of the project, on or in relation to a person ('P') who lacks capacity to consent to taking part in the project.

(2) R must take reasonable steps to identify a person who—

(a) otherwise than in a professional capacity or for remuneration, is engaged in caring for P or is interested in P's welfare, and

(b) is prepared to be consulted by R under this section.

(3) If R is unable to identify such a person he must, in accordance with guidance issued by the appropriate authority, nominate a person who—

(a) is prepared to be consulted by R under this section, but

(b) has no connection with the project.

(4) R must provide the person identified under subsection (2), or nominated under subsection (3), with information about the project and ask him—

(a) for advice as to whether P should take part in the project, and

(b) what, in his opinion, P's wishes and feelings about taking part in the project would be likely to be if P had capacity in relation to the matter.

(5) If, at any time, the person consulted advises R that in his opinion P's wishes and feelings would be likely to lead him to decline to take part in the project (or to wish to withdraw from it) if he had capacity in relation to the matter, R must ensure—

(a) if P is not already taking part in the project, that he does not take part in it;

(b) if P is taking part in the project, that he is withdrawn from it.

(6) But subsection (5)(b) does not require treatment that P has been receiving as part of the project to be discontinued if R has reasonable grounds for believing that there would be a significant risk to P's health if it were discontinued.

(7) The fact that a person is the donee of a lasting power of attorney given by P, or is P's deputy, does not prevent him from being the person consulted under this section.

(8) Subsection (9) applies if treatment is being, or is about to be, provided for P as a matter of urgency and R considers that, having regard to the nature of the research and of the particular circumstances of the case—

    (a) it is also necessary to take action for the purposes of the research as a matter of urgency, but

    (b) it is not reasonably practicable to consult under the previous provisions of this section.

(9) R may take the action if—

    (a) he has the agreement of a registered medical practitioner who is not involved in the organisation or conduct of the research project, or

    (b) where it is not reasonably practicable in the time available to obtain that agreement, he acts in accordance with a procedure approved by the appropriate body at the time when the research project was approved under section 31.

(10) But R may not continue to act in reliance on subsection (9) if he has reasonable grounds for believing that it is no longer necessary to take the action as a matter of urgency.

33 Additional safeguards

(1) This section applies in relation to a person who is taking part in an approved research project even though he lacks capacity to consent to taking part.

(2) Nothing may be done to, or in relation to, him in the course of the research—

    (a) to which he appears to object (whether by showing signs of resistance or otherwise) except where what is being done is intended to protect him from harm or to reduce or prevent pain or discomfort, or

    (b) which would be contrary to—

        (i) an advance decision of his which has effect, or

        (ii) any other form of statement made by him and not subsequently withdrawn,

    of which R is aware.

(3) The interests of the person must be assumed to outweigh those of science and society.

(4) If he indicates (in any way) that he wishes to be withdrawn from the project he must be withdrawn without delay.

(5) P must be withdrawn from the project, without delay, if at any time the person conducting the research has reasonable grounds for believing that one or more of the requirements set out in section 31(2) to (7) is no longer met in relation to research being carried out on, or in relation to, P.

(6) But neither subsection (4) nor subsection (5) requires treatment that P has been receiving as part of the project to be discontinued if R has reasonable grounds for believing that there would be a significant risk to P's health if it were discontinued.

34 Loss of capacity during research project

(1) This section applies where a person ('P')—

    (a) has consented to take part in a research project begun before the commencement of section 30, but

    (b) before the conclusion of the project, loses capacity to consent to continue to take part in it.

(2) The appropriate authority may by regulations provide that, despite P's loss of capacity, research of a prescribed kind may be carried out on, or in relation to, P if—

    (a) the project satisfies prescribed requirements,

    (b) any information or material relating to P which is used in the research is of a prescribed description and was obtained before P's loss of capacity, and

    (c) the person conducting the project takes in relation to P such steps as may be prescribed for the purpose of protecting him.

(3) The regulations may, in particular,—

 (a) make provision about when, for the purposes of the regulations, a project is to be treated as having begun;

 (b) include provision similar to any made by section 31, 32 or 33.

Independent Medical Capacity Advocates

35 Appointment of independent mental capacity advocates

(1) The appropriate authority must make such arrangements as it considers reasonable to enable persons ('independent mental capacity advocates') to be available to represent and support persons to whom acts or decisions proposed under sections 37, 38 and 39 relate [or persons who fall within section 39A, 39C or 39D].

(2) The appropriate authority may make regulations as to the appointment of independent mental capacity advocates.

(3) The regulations may, in particular, provide—

 (a) that a person may act as an independent mental capacity advocate only in such circumstances, or only subject to such conditions, as may be prescribed;

 (b) for the appointment of a person as an independent mental capacity advocate to be subject to approval in accordance with the regulations.

(4) In making arrangements under subsection (1), the appropriate authority must have regard to the principle that a person to whom a proposed act or decision relates should, so far as practicable, be represented and supported by a person who is independent of any person who will be responsible for the act or decision.

(5) The arrangements may include provision for payments to be made to, or in relation to, persons carrying out functions in accordance with the arrangements.

(6) For the purpose of enabling him to carry out his functions, an independent mental capacity advocate—

 (a) may interview in private the person whom he has been instructed to represent, and

 (b) may, at all reasonable times, examine and take copies of—

  (i) any health record,

  (ii) any record of, or held by, a local authority and compiled in connection with a social services function, and

  (iii) any record held by a person registered under Part 2 of the Care Standards Act 2000 (c. 14),

which the person holding the record considers may be relevant to the independent mental capacity advocate's investigation.

(7) In this section, section 36 and section 37, 'the appropriate authority' means—

 (a) in relation to the provision of the services of independent mental capacity advocates in England, the Secretary of State, and

 (b) in relation to the provision of the services of independent mental capacity advocates in Wales, the National Assembly for Wales.

[*Subsection (1) amended by paragraph 3 of Schedule 9 to the 2007 Act.*]

36 Functions of independent mental capacity advocates

(1) The appropriate authority may make regulations as to the functions of independent mental capacity advocates.

(2) The regulations may, in particular, make provision requiring an advocate to take such steps as may be prescribed for the purpose of—

(a) providing support to the person whom he has been instructed to represent ('P') so that P may participate as fully as possible in any relevant decision;

(b) obtaining and evaluating relevant information;

(c) ascertaining what P's wishes and feelings would be likely to be, and the beliefs and values that would be likely to influence P, if he had capacity;

(d) ascertaining what alternative courses of action are available in relation to P;

(e) obtaining a further medical opinion where treatment is proposed and the advocate thinks that one should be obtained.

(3) The regulations may also make provision as to circumstances in which the advocate may challenge, or provide assistance for the purpose of challenging, any relevant decision.

37 Provision of serious medical treatment by NHS body

(1) This section applies if an NHS body—

(a) is proposing to provide, or secure the provision of, serious medical treatment for a person ('P') who lacks capacity to consent to the treatment, and

(b) is satisfied that there is no person, other than one engaged in providing care or treatment for P in a professional capacity or for remuneration, whom it would be appropriate to consult in determining what would be in P's best interests.

(2) But this section does not apply if P's treatment is regulated by Part 4 [or 4A] of the Mental Health Act.

(3) Before the treatment is provided, the NHS body must instruct an independent mental capacity advocate to represent P.

(4) If the treatment needs to be provided as a matter of urgency, it may be provided even though the NHS body has not been able to comply with subsection (3).

(5) The NHS body must, in providing or securing the provision of treatment for P, take into account any information given, or submissions made, by the independent mental capacity advocate.

(6) 'Serious medical treatment' means treatment which involves providing, withholding or withdrawing treatment of a kind prescribed by regulations made by the appropriate authority.

(7) 'NHS body' has such meaning as may be prescribed by regulations made for the purposes of this section by—

(a) the Secretary of State, in relation to bodies in England, or

(b) the National Assembly for Wales, in relation to bodies in Wales.

[*Words 'or 4A' inserted in subsection (2) by section 35(6) of the 2007 Act.*]

38 Provision of accommodation by NHS body

(1) This section applies if an NHS body proposes to make arrangements—

(a) for the provision of accommodation in a hospital or care home for a person ('P') who lacks capacity to agree to the arrangements, or

(b) for a change in P's accommodation to another hospital or care home, and is satisfied that there is no person, other than one engaged in providing care or treatment for P in a professional capacity or for remuneration, whom it would be appropriate for it to consult in determining what would be in P's best interests.

(2) But this section does not apply if P is accommodated as a result of an obligation imposed on him under the Mental Health Act.

[(2A) And this section does not apply if—

    (a) an independent mental capacity advocate must be appointed under section 39A or 39C (whether or not by the NHS body) to represent P, and

    (b) the hospital or care home in which P is to be accommodated under the arrangements referred to in this section is the relevant hospital or care home under the authorisation referred to in that section.]

(3) Before making the arrangements, the NHS body must instruct an independent mental capacity advocate to represent P unless it is satisfied that—

    (a) the accommodation is likely to be provided for a continuous period which is less than the applicable period, or

    (b) the arrangements need to be made as a matter of urgency.

(4) If the NHS body—

    (a) did not instruct an independent mental capacity advocate to represent P before making the arrangements because it was satisfied that subsection (3)(a) or (b) applied, but

    (b) subsequently has reason to believe that the accommodation is likely to be provided for a continuous period—

        (i) beginning with the day on which accommodation was first provided in accordance with the arrangements, and

        (ii) ending on or after the expiry of the applicable period,

    it must instruct an independent mental capacity advocate to represent P.

(5) The NHS body must, in deciding what arrangements to make for P, take into account any information given, or submissions made, by the independent mental capacity advocate.

(6) 'Care home' has the meaning given in section 3 of the Care Standards Act 2000 (c. 14).

(7) 'Hospital' means—

    (a) a health service hospital as defined by section 275 of the National Health Service Act 2006 or section 206 of the National Health Service (Wales) Act 2006, or

    (b) an independent hospital as defined by section 2 of the Care Standards Act 2000.

(8) 'NHS body' has such meaning as may be prescribed by regulations made for the purposes of this section by—

    (a) the Secretary of State, in relation to bodies in England, or

    (b) the National Assembly for Wales, in relation to bodies in Wales.

(9) 'Applicable period' means—

    (a) in relation to accommodation in a hospital, 28 days, and

    (b) in relation to accommodation in a care home, 8 weeks.

[(10) For the purposes of subsection (1), a person appointed under Part 10 of Schedule A1 to be P's representative is not, by virtue of that appointment, engaged in providing care or treatment for P in a professional capacity or for remuneration.]

[*Subsections (2A) and (10) inserted by paragraphs 4(2) and 4(3) respectively of Schedule 9 to the 2007 Act.*]

39 Provision of accommodation by local authority

(1) This section applies if a local authority propose to make arrangements—

    (a) for the provision of residential accommodation for a person ('P') who lacks capacity to agree to the arrangements, or

    (b) for a change in P's residential accommodation, and are satisfied that there is no person, other than one engaged in providing care or treatment for P in a professional capacity or for remuneration, whom it would be appropriate for them to consult in determining what would be in P's best interests.

(2) But this section applies only if the accommodation is to be provided in accordance with—
   (a) section 21 or 29 of the National Assistance Act 1948 (c. 29), or
   (b) section 117 of the Mental Health Act,
   as the result of a decision taken by the local authority under section 47 of the National Health Service and Community Care Act 1990 (c. 19).

(3) This section does not apply if P is accommodated as a result of an obligation imposed on him under the Mental Health Act.

[(3A) And this section does not apply if—
   (a) an independent mental capacity advocate must be appointed under section 39A or 39C (whether or not by the local authority) to represent P, and
   (b) the place in which P is to be accommodated under the arrangements referred to in this section is the relevant hospital or care home under the authorisation referred to in that section.]

(4) Before making the arrangements, the local authority must instruct an independent mental capacity advocate to represent P unless they are satisfied that—
   (a) the accommodation is likely to be provided for a continuous period of less than 8 weeks, or
   (b) the arrangements need to be made as a matter of urgency.

(5) If the local authority—
   (a) did not instruct an independent mental capacity advocate to represent P before making the arrangements because they were satisfied that subsection (4)(a) or (b) applied, but
   (b) subsequently have reason to believe that the accommodation is likely to be provided for a continuous period that will end 8 weeks or more after the day on which accommodation was first provided in accordance with the arrangements, they must instruct an independent mental capacity advocate to represent P.

(6) The local authority must, in deciding what arrangements to make for P, take into account any information given, or submissions made, by the independent mental capacity advocate.

[(7) For the purposes of subsection (1), a person appointed under Part 10 of Schedule A1 to be P's representative is not, by virtue of that appointment, engaged in providing care or treatment for P in a professional capacity or for remuneration.]

[*Subsections (3A) and (7) inserted by paragraphs 5(2) and (3) respectively of Schedule 9 to the 2007 Act.*]

[39A Person becomes subject to Schedule A1]

[(1) This section applies if—
   (a) a person ('P') becomes subject to Schedule A1, and
   (b) the managing authority of the relevant hospital or care home are satisfied that there is no person, other than one engaged in providing care or treatment for P in a professional capacity or for remuneration, whom it would be appropriate to consult in determining what would be in P's best interests.

(2) The managing authority must notify the supervisory body that this section applies.

(3) The supervisory body must instruct an independent mental capacity advocate to represent P.

(4) Schedule A1 makes provision about the role of an independent mental capacity advocate appointed under this section.

(5) This section is subject to paragraph 161 of Schedule A1.

(6) For the purposes of subsection (1), a person appointed under Part 10 of Schedule A1 to be P's representative is not, by virtue of that appointment, engaged in providing care or treatment for P in a professional capacity or for remuneration.]

[*Section 39A inserted by paragraph 6 of Schedule 9 to the 2007 Act.*]

[39B Section 39A: supplementary provision]

[(1) This section applies for the purposes of section 39A.

(2) P becomes subject to Schedule A1 in any of the following cases.

(3) The first case is where an urgent authorisation is given in relation to P under paragraph 76(2) of Schedule A1 (urgent authorisation given before request made for standard authorisation).

(4) The second case is where the following conditions are met.

(5) The first condition is that a request is made under Schedule A1 for a standard authorisation to be given in relation to P ('the requested authorisation').

(6) The second condition is that no urgent authorisation was given under paragraph 76(2) of Schedule A1 before that request was made.

(7) The third condition is that the requested authorisation will not be in force on or before, or immediately after, the expiry of an existing standard authorisation.

(8) The expiry of a standard authorisation is the date when the authorisation is expected to cease to be in force.

(9) The third case is where, under paragraph 69 of Schedule 6, the supervisory body select a person to carry out an assessment of whether or not the relevant person is a detained resident.]

[Section 39B inserted by paragraph 6 of Schedule 9 to the 2007 Act.]

[39C Person unrepresented whilst subject to Schedule A1]

[(1) This section applies if—

    (a) an authorisation under Schedule A1 is in force in relation to a person ('P'),

    (b) the appointment of a person as P's representative ends in accordance with regulations made under Part 10 of Schedule A1, and

    (c) the managing authority of the relevant hospital or care home are satisfied that there is no person, other than one engaged in providing care or treatment for P in a professional capacity or for remuneration, whom it would be appropriate to consult in determining what would be in P's best interests.

(2) The managing authority must notify the supervisory body that this section applies.

(3) The supervisory body must instruct an independent mental capacity advocate to represent P.

(4) Paragraph 159 of Schedule A1 makes provision about the role of an independent mental capacity advocate appointed under this section.

(5) The appointment of an independent mental capacity advocate under this section ends when a new appointment of a person as P's representative is made in accordance with Part 10 of Schedule A1.

(6) For the purposes of subsection (1), a person appointed under Part 10 of Schedule A1 to be P's representative is not, by virtue of that appointment, engaged in providing care or treatment for P in a professional capacity or for remuneration.]

[Section 39C inserted by paragraph 6 of Schedule 9 to the 2007 Act.]

[39D Person subject to Schedule A1 without paid representative]

[(1) This section applies if—

    (a) an authorisation under Schedule A1 is in force in relation to a person ('P'),

    (b) P has a representative ('R') appointed under Part 10 of Schedule A1, and

    (c) R is not being paid under regulations under Part 10 of Schedule A1 for acting as P's representative.

(2) The supervisory body must instruct an independent mental capacity advocate to represent P in any of the following cases.

(3) The first case is where P makes a request to the supervisory body to instruct an advocate.

(4) The second case is where R makes a request to the supervisory body to instruct an advocate.

(5) The third case is where the supervisory body have reason to believe one or more of the following—

(a) that, without the help of an advocate, P and R would be unable to exercise one or both of the relevant rights;

(b) that P and R have each failed to exercise a relevant right when it would have been reasonable to exercise it;

(c) that P and R are each unlikely to exercise a relevant right when it would be reasonable to exercise it.

(6) The duty in subsection (2) is subject to section 39E.

(7) If an advocate is appointed under this section, the advocate is, in particular, to take such steps as are practicable to help P and R to understand the following matters—

(a) the effect of the authorisation;

(b) the purpose of the authorisation;

(c) the duration of the authorisation;

(d) any conditions to which the authorisation is subject;

(e) the reasons why each assessor who carried out an assessment in connection with the request for the authorisation, or in connection with a review of the authorisation, decided that P met the qualifying requirement in question;

(f) the relevant rights;

(g) how to exercise the relevant rights.

(8) The advocate is, in particular, to take such steps as are practicable to help P or R—

(a) to exercise the right to apply to court, if it appears to the advocate that P or R wishes to exercise that right, or

(b) to exercise the right of review, if it appears to the advocate that P or R wishes to exercise that right.

(9) If the advocate helps P or R to exercise the right of review—

(a) the advocate may make submissions to the supervisory body on the question of whether a qualifying requirement is reviewable;

(b) the advocate may give information, or make submissions, to any assessor carrying out a review assessment.

(10) In this section—

'relevant rights' means—

(a) the right to apply to court, and

(b) the right of review;

'right to apply to court' means the right to make an application to the court to exercise its jurisdiction under section 21A;

'right of review' means the right under Part 8 of Schedule A1 to request a review.]

[*Section 39D inserted by paragraph 6 of Schedule 9 to the 2007 Act.*]

[39E Limitation on duty to instruct advocate under section 39D]

[(1) This section applies if an advocate is already representing P in accordance with an instruction under section 39D.

(2) Section 39D(2) does not require another advocate to be instructed, unless the following conditions are met.

(3) The first condition is that the existing advocate was instructed—

   (a) because of a request by R, or

   (b) because the supervisory body had reason to believe one or more of the things in section 39D(5).

(4) The second condition is that the other advocate would be instructed because of a request by P.]

[Section 39E inserted by paragraph 6 of Schedule 9 to the 2007 Act.]

40 Exceptions

Sections 37(3), 38(3) and (4), and 39(4) and (5) do not apply if there is—

   (a) a person nominated by P (in whatever manner) as a person to be consulted in matters affecting his interests,

   (b) a donee of a lasting power of attorney created by P,

   (c) a deputy appointed by the court for P, or

   (d) a donee of an enduring power of attorney (within the meaning of Schedule 4) created by P.

[(1)] The duty imposed by section 37(3), 38(3) or (4), *or 39(4) or (5)* [39(4) or 39(5), [39A(3), 39C(3) or 39D(2)]] does not apply where there is—

   (a) a person nominated by P (in whatever manner) as a person to be consulted on matters to which that duty relates,

   (b) a donee of a lasting power of attorney created by P who is authorised to make decisions in relation to those matters, or

   (c) a deputy appointed by the court for P with power to make decisions in relation to those matters.

[(2) A person appointed under Part 10 of Schedule A1 to be P's representative is not, by virtue of that appointment, a person nominated by P as a person to be consulted in matters to which a duty mentioned in subsection (1) relates.]

[New subsection (1) inserted (unnumbered) by section 49 of the 2007 Act, which came into force on 1 October 2007 replacing existing s 40. The words 'or 39(4) or (5)' are deleted and the words 'or 39(4) or 39(5), 39A(3), 39C(3) or 39D(2)' substituted by paragraphs 7(2)&(3) respectively of Schedule 9, which also adds the paragraph number (1). Subsection (2) inserted by paragraph 7(4) of Schedule 9. These amendments will not take effect until the 'deprivation of liberty' safeguards come into force, in April 2009.]

41 Power to adjust role of independent mental capacity advocate

(1) The appropriate authority may make regulations—

   (a) expanding the role of independent mental capacity advocates in relation to persons who lack capacity, and

   (b) adjusting the obligation to make arrangements imposed by section 35.

(2) The regulations may, in particular—

   (a) prescribe circumstances (different to those set out in sections 37, 38 and 39) in which an independent mental capacity advocate must, or circumstances in which one may, be instructed by a person of a prescribed description to represent a person who lacks capacity, and

   (b) include provision similar to any made by section 37, 38, 39 or 40.

(3) 'Appropriate authority' has the same meaning as in section 35.

Miscellaneous and supplementary

42 Codes of practice

(1) The Lord Chancellor must prepare and issue one or more codes of practice—

    (a) for the guidance of persons assessing whether a person has capacity in relation to any matter,

    (b) for the guidance of persons acting in connection with the care or treatment of another person (see section 5),

    (c) for the guidance of donees of lasting powers of attorney,

    (d) for the guidance of deputies appointed by the court,

    (e) for the guidance of persons carrying out research in reliance on any provision made by or under this Act (and otherwise with respect to sections 30 to 34),

    (f) for the guidance of independent mental capacity advocates,

    [(fa) for the guidance of persons exercising functions under Schedule A1,

    (fb) for the guidance of representatives appointed under Part 10 of Schedule A1,]

    (g) with respect to the provisions of sections 24 to 26 (advance decisions and apparent advance decisions), and

    (h) with respect to such other matters concerned with this Act as he thinks fit.

(2) The Lord Chancellor may from time to time revise a code.

(3) The Lord Chancellor may delegate the preparation or revision of the whole or any part of a code so far as he considers expedient.

(4) It is the duty of a person to have regard to any relevant code if he is acting in relation to a person who lacks capacity and is doing so in one or more of the following ways—

    (a) as the donee of a lasting power of attorney,

    (b) as a deputy appointed by the court,

    (c) as a person carrying out research in reliance on any provision made by or under this Act (see sections 30 to 34),

    (d) as an independent mental capacity advocate,

    [(da) in the exercise of functions under Schedule A1,

    (db) as a representative appointed under Part 10 of Schedule A1,]

    (e) in a professional capacity,

    (f) for remuneration.

(5) If it appears to a court or tribunal conducting any criminal or civil proceedings that—

    (a) a provision of a code, or

    (b) a failure to comply with a code,

is relevant to a question arising in the proceedings, the provision or failure must be taken into account in deciding the question.

(6) A code under subsection (1)(d) may contain separate guidance for deputies appointed by virtue of paragraph 1(2) of Schedule 5 (functions of deputy conferred on receiver appointed under the Mental Health Act).

(7) In this section and in section 43, 'code' means a code prepared or revised under this section.

[Sub-paragraphs (fa) and (fb) inserted into subsection (2) and sub-paragraphs (da) and (db) inserted into subsection (4) by paragraphs 8(2) and (3) respectively of Schedule 9 to the 2007 Act.]

43 Codes of practice: procedure

(1) Before preparing or revising a code, the Lord Chancellor must consult—

    (a) the National Assembly for Wales, and

    (b) such other persons as he considers appropriate.

(2) The Lord Chancellor may not issue a code unless—

    (a) a draft of the code has been laid by him before both Houses of Parliament, and

    (b) the 40 day period has elapsed without either House resolving not to approve the draft.

(3) The Lord Chancellor must arrange for any code that he has issued to be published in such a way as he considers appropriate for bringing it to the attention of persons likely to be concerned with its provisions.

(4) '40 day period', in relation to the draft of a proposed code, means—

    (a) if the draft is laid before one House on a day later than the day on which it is laid before the other House, the period of 40 days beginning with the later of the two days;

    (b) in any other case, the period of 40 days beginning with the day on which it is laid before each House.

(5) In calculating the period of 40 days, no account is to be taken of any period during which Parliament is dissolved or prorogued or during which both Houses are adjourned for more than 4 days.

44 Ill-treatment or neglect

(1) Subsection (2) applies if a person ('D')—

    (a) has the care of a person ('P') who lacks, or whom D reasonably believes to lack, capacity,

    (b) is the donee of a lasting power of attorney, or an enduring power of attorney (within the meaning of Schedule 4), created by P, or

    (c) is a deputy appointed by the court for P.

(2) D is guilty of an offence if he ill-treats or wilfully neglects P.

(3) A person guilty of an offence under this section is liable—

    (a) on summary conviction, to imprisonment for a term not exceeding 12 months or a fine not exceeding the statutory maximum or both;

    (b) on conviction on indictment, to imprisonment for a term not exceeding 5 years or a fine or both.

PART 2
THE COURT OF PROTECTION AND THE PUBLIC GUARDIAN

The Court of Protection

45 The Court of Protection

(1) There is to be a superior court of record known as the Court of Protection.

(2) The court is to have an official seal.

(3) The court may sit at any place in England and Wales, on any day and at any time.

(4) The court is to have a central office and registry at a place appointed by the Lord Chancellor, after consulting the Lord Chief Justice.

(5) The Lord Chancellor may, after consulting the Lord Chief Justice, designate as additional registries of the court any district registry of the High Court and any county court office.

(5A) The Lord Chief Justice may nominate any of the following to exercise his functions under this section-

    (a) the President of the Court of Protection;

    (b) a judicial officer holder (as defined in section 109(4) of the Constitutional Reform Act 2005).

(6) The office of the Supreme Court called the Court of Protection ceases to exist.

46 The judges of the Court of Protection

(1) Subject to Court of Protection Rules under section 51(2)(d), the jurisdiction of the court is exercisable by a judge nominated for that purpose by—

    (a) the Lord Chief Justice, or

    (b) where nominated by the Lord Chief Justice to act on his behalf under this subsection-

        (i) the President of the Court of Protection;

        (ii) a judicial officer holder (as defined in section 109(4) of the Constitutional Reform Act 2005).

(2) To be nominated, a judge must be—

    (a) the President of the Family Division,

    (b) the Vice-Chancellor,

    (c) a puisne judge of the High Court,

    (d) a circuit judge, or

    (e) a district judge.

(3) The Lord Chief Justice, after consulting the Lord Chancellor, must—

    (a) appoint one of the judges nominated by virtue of subsection (2)(a) to (c) to be President of the Court of Protection, and

    (b) appoint another of those judges to be Vice-President of the Court of Protection.

(4) The Chief Justice, after consulting the Lord Chancellor, must appoint one of the judges nominated by virtue of subsection (2)(d) or (e) to be Senior Judge of the Court of Protection, having such administrative functions in relation to the court as the Lord Chancellor, after consulting the Lord Chief Justice, may direct.

Supplementary powers

47 General powers and effect of orders etc

(1) The court has in connection with its jurisdiction the same powers, rights, privileges and authority as the High Court.

(2) Section 204 of the Law of Property Act 1925 (c. 20) (orders of High Court conclusive in favour of purchasers) applies in relation to orders and directions of the court as it applies to orders of the High Court.

(3) Office copies of orders made, directions given or other instruments issued by the court and sealed with its official seal are admissible in all legal proceedings as evidence of the originals without any further proof.

48 Interim orders and directions

The court may, pending the determination of an application to it in relation to a person ('P'), make an order or give directions in respect of any matter if—

    (a) there is reason to believe that P lacks capacity in relation to the matter,

    (b) the matter is one to which its powers under this Act extend, and

    (c) it is in P's best interests to make the order, or give the directions, without delay.

49 Power to call for reports

(1) This section applies where, in proceedings brought in respect of a person ('P') under Part 1, the court is considering a question relating to P.

(2) The court may require a report to be made to it by the Public Guardian or by a Court of Protection Visitor.

(3) The court may require a local authority, or an NHS body, to arrange for a report to be made—

(a) by one of its officers or employees, or

(b) by such other person (other than the Public Guardian or a Court of Protection Visitor) as the authority, or the NHS body, considers appropriate.

(4) The report must deal with such matters relating to P as the court may direct.

(5) Court of Protection Rules may specify matters which, unless the court directs otherwise, must also be dealt with in the report.

(6) The report may be made in writing or orally, as the court may direct.

(7) In complying with a requirement, the Public Guardian or a Court of Protection Visitor may, at all reasonable times, examine and take copies of—

(a) any health record,

(b) any record of, or held by, a local authority and compiled in connection with a social services function, and

(c) any record held by a person registered under Part 2 of the Care Standards Act 2000 (c. 14), so far as the record relates to P.

(8) If the Public Guardian or a Court of Protection Visitor is making a visit in the course of complying with a requirement, he may interview P in private.

(9) If a Court of Protection Visitor who is a Special Visitor is making a visit in the course of complying with a requirement, he may if the court so directs carry out in private a medical, psychiatric or psychological examination of P's capacity and condition.

(10) 'NHS body' has the meaning given in section 148 of the Health and Social Care (Community Health and Standards) Act 2003 (c. 43).

(11) 'Requirement' means a requirement imposed under subsection (2) or (3).

Practice and procedure

50 Applications to the Court of Protection

(1) No permission is required for an application to the court for the exercise of any of its powers under this Act—

(a) by a person who lacks, or is alleged to lack, capacity,

(b) if such a person has not reached 18, by anyone with parental responsibility for him,

(c) by the donor or a donee of a lasting power of attorney to which the application relates,

(d) by a deputy appointed by the court for a person to whom the application relates, or

(e) by a person named in an existing order of the court, if the application relates to the order.

[(1A) Nor is permission required for an application to the court under section 21A by the relevant person's representative.]

(2) But, subject to Court of Protection Rules and to paragraph 20(2) of Schedule 3 (declarations relating to private international law), permission is required for any other application to the court.

(3) In deciding whether to grant permission the court must, in particular, have regard to—

(a) the applicant's connection with the person to whom the application relates,

(b) the reasons for the application,

(c) the benefit to the person to whom the application relates of a proposed order or directions, and

(d) whether the benefit can be achieved in any other way.

(4) 'Parental responsibility' has the same meaning as in the Children Act 1989 (c. 41).
[*Subsection (1A) inserted by paragraph 9 of Schedule 9 to the 2007 Act.*]

51 Court of Protection Rules

(1) Rules of court with respect to the practice and procedure of the court (to be called 'Court of Protection Rules') may be made in accordance with Part 1 of Schedule 1 to the Constitutional Reform Act 2005.

(2) Court of Protection Rules may, in particular, make provision—

(a) as to the manner and form in which proceedings are to be commenced;

(b) as to the persons entitled to be notified of, and be made parties to, the proceedings;

(c) for the allocation, in such circumstances as may be specified, of any specified description of proceedings to a specified judge or to specified descriptions of judges;

(d) for the exercise of the jurisdiction of the court, in such circumstances as may be specified, by its officers or other staff;

(e) for enabling the court to appoint a suitable person (who may, with his consent, be the Official Solicitor) to act in the name of, or on behalf of, or to represent the person to whom the proceedings relate;

(f) for enabling an application to the court to be disposed of without a hearing;

(g) for enabling the court to proceed with, or with any part of, a hearing in the absence of the person to whom the proceedings relate;

(h) for enabling or requiring the proceedings or any part of them to be conducted in private and for enabling the court to determine who is to be admitted when the court sits in private and to exclude specified persons when it sits in public;

(i) as to what may be received as evidence (whether or not admissible apart from the rules) and the manner in which it is to be presented;

(j) for the enforcement of orders made and directions given in the proceedings.

(3) Court of Protection Rules may, instead of providing for any matter, refer to provision made or to be made about that matter by directions.

(4) Court of Protection Rules may make different provision for different areas.

52 Practice directions

(1) Directions as to the practice and procedure of the court may be given in accordance with Part 1 of Schedule 2 to the Constitutional Reform Act 2005.

(2) Practice directions given otherwise than under subsection (1) may not be given without the approval of—

(a) the Lord Chancellor, and

(b) the Lord Chief Justice.

(3) The Lord Chief Justice may nominate any of the following to exercise his functions under this section—

(a) the President of the Court of Protection;

(b) a judicial office holder (as defined in section 109(4) of the Constitutional Reform Act 2005).

53 Rights of appeal

(1) Subject to the provisions of this section, an appeal lies to the Court of Appeal from any decision of the court.

(2) Court of Protection Rules may provide that where a decision of the court is made by—

    (a) a person exercising the jurisdiction of the court by virtue of rules made under section 51(2)(d),

    (b) a district judge, or

    (c) a circuit judge,

an appeal from that decision lies to a prescribed higher judge of the court and not to the Court of Appeal.

(3) For the purposes of this section the higher judges of the court are—

    (a) in relation to a person mentioned in subsection (2)(a), a circuit judge or a district judge;

    (b) in relation to a person mentioned in subsection (2)(b), a circuit judge;

    (c) in relation to any person mentioned in subsection (2), one of the judges nominated by virtue of section 46(2)(a) to (c).

(4) Court of Protection Rules may make provision—

    (a) that, in such cases as may be specified, an appeal from a decision of the court may not be made without permission;

    (b) as to the person or persons entitled to grant permission to appeal;

    (c) as to any requirements to be satisfied before permission is granted;

    (d) that where a higher judge of the court makes a decision on an appeal, no appeal may be made to the Court of Appeal from that decision unless the Court of Appeal considers that—

        (i) the appeal would raise an important point of principle or practice, or

        (ii) there is some other compelling reason for the Court of Appeal to hear it;

    (e) as to any considerations to be taken into account in relation to granting or refusing permission to appeal.

Fees and costs

54 Fees

(1) The Lord Chancellor may with the consent of the Treasury by order prescribe fees payable in respect of anything dealt with by the court.

(2) An order under this section may in particular contain provision as to—

    (a) scales or rates of fees;

    (b) exemptions from and reductions in fees;

    (c) remission of fees in whole or in part.

(3) Before making an order under this section, the Lord Chancellor must consult—

    (a) the President of the Court of Protection,

    (b) the Vice-President of the Court of Protection, and

    (c) the Senior Judge of the Court of Protection.

(4) The Lord Chancellor must take such steps as are reasonably practicable to bring information about fees to the attention of persons likely to have to pay them.

(5) Fees payable under this section are recoverable summarily as a civil debt.

55 Costs

(1) Subject to Court of Protection Rules, the costs of and incidental to all proceedings in the court are in its discretion.

(2) The rules may in particular make provision for regulating matters relating to the costs of those proceedings, including prescribing scales of costs to be paid to legal or other representatives.

(3) The court has full power to determine by whom and to what extent the costs are to be paid.

(4) The court may, in any proceedings—
    (a) disallow, or
    (b) order the legal or other representatives concerned to meet,
  the whole of any wasted costs or such part of them as may be determined in accordance with the rules.

(5) 'Legal or other representative', in relation to a party to proceedings, means any person exercising a right of audience or right to conduct litigation on his behalf.

(6) 'Wasted costs' means any costs incurred by a party—
    (a) as a result of any improper, unreasonable or negligent act or omission on the part of any legal or other representative or any employee of such a representative, or
    (b) which, in the light of any such act or omission occurring after they were incurred, the court considers it is unreasonable to expect that party to pay.

56 Fees and costs: supplementary

(1) Court of Protection Rules may make provision—
    (a) as to the way in which, and funds from which, fees and costs are to be paid;
    (b) for charging fees and costs upon the estate of the person to whom the proceedings relate;
    (c) for the payment of fees and costs within a specified time of the death of the person to whom the proceedings relate or the conclusion of the proceedings.

(2) A charge on the estate of a person created by virtue of subsection (1)(b) does not cause any interest of the person in any property to fail or determine or to be prevented from recommencing.

The Public Guardian

57 The Public Guardian

(1) For the purposes of this Act, there is to be an officer, to be known as the Public Guardian.

(2) The Public Guardian is to be appointed by the Lord Chancellor.

(3) There is to be paid to the Public Guardian out of money provided by Parliament such salary as the Lord Chancellor may determine.

(4) The Lord Chancellor may, after consulting the Public Guardian—
    (a) provide him with such officers and staff, or
    (b) enter into such contracts with other persons for the provision (by them or their sub-contractors) of officers, staff or services,
  as the Lord Chancellor thinks necessary for the proper discharge of the Public Guardian's functions.

(5) Any functions of the Public Guardian may, to the extent authorised by him, be performed by any of his officers.

58 Functions of the Public Guardian

(1) The Public Guardian has the following functions—
    (a) establishing and maintaining a register of lasting powers of attorney,
    (b) establishing and maintaining a register of orders appointing deputies,
    (c) supervising deputies appointed by the court,
    (d) directing a Court of Protection Visitor to visit—
        (i) a donee of a lasting power of attorney,
        (ii) a deputy appointed by the court, or

(iii) the person granting the power of attorney or for whom the deputy is appointed ('P'),

and to make a report to the Public Guardian on such matters as he may direct,

(e) receiving security which the court requires a person to give for the discharge of his functions,

(f) receiving reports from donees of lasting powers of attorney and deputies appointed by the court,

(g) reporting to the court on such matters relating to proceedings under this Act as the court requires,

(h) dealing with representations (including complaints) about the way in which a donee of a lasting power of attorney or a deputy appointed by the court is exercising his powers,

(i) publishing, in any manner the Public Guardian thinks appropriate, any information he thinks appropriate about the discharge of his functions.

(2) The functions conferred by subsection (1)(c) and (h) may be discharged in cooperation with any other person who has functions in relation to the care or treatment of P.

(3) The Lord Chancellor may by regulations make provision—

(a) conferring on the Public Guardian other functions in connection with this Act;

(b) in connection with the discharge by the Public Guardian of his functions.

(4) Regulations made under subsection (3)(b) may in particular make provision as to—

(a) the giving of security by deputies appointed by the court and the enforcement and discharge of security so given;

(b) the fees which may be charged by the Public Guardian;

(c) the way in which, and funds from which, such fees are to be paid;

(d) exemptions from and reductions in such fees;

(e) remission of such fees in whole or in part;

(f) the making of reports to the Public Guardian by deputies appointed by the court and others who are directed by the court to carry out any transaction for a person who lacks capacity.

(5) For the purpose of enabling him to carry out his functions, the Public Guardian may, at all reasonable times, examine and take copies of—

(a) any health record,

(b) any record of, or held by, a local authority and compiled in connection with a social services function, and

(c) any record held by a person registered under Part 2 of the Care Standards Act 2000 (c. 14),

so far as the record relates to P.

(6) The Public Guardian may also for that purpose interview P in private.

59 Public Guardian Board

(1) There is to be a body, to be known as the Public Guardian Board.

(2) The Board's duty is to scrutinise and review the way in which the Public Guardian discharges his functions and to make such recommendations to the Lord Chancellor about that matter as it thinks appropriate.

(3) The Lord Chancellor must, in discharging his functions under sections 57 and 58, give due consideration to recommendations made by the Board.

(5) The Board must have—

(a) at least one member who is a judge of the court, and

(b) at least four members who are persons appearing to the Lord Chancellor to have appropriate knowledge or experience of the work of the Public Guardian.

(5A) Where a person to be appointed as a member of the Board is a judge of the court, the appointment is to be made by the Lord Chief Justice after consulting the Lord Chancellor.

(5B) In any other case, the appointment of a person as a member of the Board is to be made by the Lord Chancellor.

(6) The Lord Chancellor may by regulations make provision as to—

(a) the appointment of members of the Board (and, in particular, the procedures to be followed in connection with appointments);

(b) the selection of one of the members to be the chairman;

(c) the term of office of the chairman and members;

(d) their resignation, suspension or removal;

(e) the procedure of the Board (including quorum);

(f) the validation of proceedings in the event of a vacancy among the members or a defect in the appointment of a member.

(7) Subject to any provision made in reliance on subsection (6)(c) or (d), a person is to hold and vacate office as a member of the Board in accordance with the terms of the instrument appointing him.

(8) The Lord Chancellor may make such payments to or in respect of members of the Board by way of reimbursement of expenses, allowances and remuneration as he may determine.

(9) The Board must make an annual report to the Lord Chancellor about the discharge of its functions.

(10) The Lord Chief Justice may nominate any of the following to exercise his functions under this section-

(a) the President of the Court of Protection

(b) a judicial office holder (as defined in section 109(4) of the Constitutional Reform Act 2005.)

60 Annual report

(1) The Public Guardian must make an annual report to the Lord Chancellor about the discharge of his functions.

(2) The Lord Chancellor must, within one month of receiving the report, lay a copy of it before Parliament.

Court of Protection Visitors

61 Court of Protection Visitors

(1) A Court of Protection Visitor is a person who is appointed by the Lord Chancellor to—

(a) a panel of Special Visitors, or

(b) a panel of General Visitors.

(2) A person is not qualified to be a Special Visitor unless he—

(a) Is a registered medical practitioner or appears to the Lord Chancellor to have other suitable qualifications or training, and

(b) appears to the Lord Chancellor to have special knowledge of and experience in cases of impairment of or disturbance in the functioning of the mind or brain.

(3) A General Visitor need not have a medical qualification.

(4) A Court of Protection Visitor—

(a) may be appointed for such term and subject to such conditions, and

(b) may be paid such remuneration and allowances,

as the Lord Chancellor may determine.

(5) For the purpose of carrying out his functions under this Act in relation to a person who lacks capacity ('P'), a Court of Protection Visitor may, at all reasonable times, examine and take copies of—

    (a) any health record,

    (b) any record of, or held by, a local authority and compiled in connection with a social services function, and

    (c) any record held by a person registered under Part 2 of the Care Standards Act 2000 (c. 14), so far as the record relates to P.

(6) A Court of Protection Visitor may also for that purpose interview P in private.

PART 3
MISCELLANEOUS AND GENERAL

Declaratory provision

62 Scope of the Act

For the avoidance of doubt, it is hereby declared that nothing in this Act is to be taken to affect the law relating to murder or manslaughter or the operation of section 2 of the Suicide Act 1961 (c. 60) (assisting suicide).

Private international law

63 International protection of adults

Schedule 3—

    (a) gives effect in England and Wales to the Convention on the International Protection of Adults signed at the Hague on 13th January 2000 (Cm. 5881) (in so far as this Act does not otherwise do so), and

    (b) makes related provision as to the private international law of England and Wales.

General

64 Interpretation

(1) In this Act—

    'the 1985 Act' means the Enduring Powers of Attorney Act 1985 (c. 29),

    'advance decision' has the meaning given in section 24(1),

    ['authorisation under Schedule A1' means either—

        (a)   a standard authorisation under that Schedule, or

        (b)   an urgent authorisation under that Schedule.]

    'the court' means the Court of Protection established by section 45,

    'Court of Protection Rules' has the meaning given in section 51(1),

    'Court of Protection Visitor' has the meaning given in section 61,

    'deputy' has the meaning given in section 16(2)(b),

    'enactment' includes a provision of subordinate legislation (within the meaning of the Interpretation Act 1978 (c. 30)),

    'health record' has the meaning given in section 68 of the Data Protection Act 1998 (c. 29) (as read with section 69 of that Act), 'the Human Rights Convention' has the same meaning as 'the Convention' in the Human Rights Act 1998 (c. 42),

'independent mental capacity advocate' has the meaning given in section 35(1),

'lasting power of attorney' has the meaning given in section 9,

'life-sustaining treatment' has the meaning given in section 4(10),

'local authority' [, except in Schedule A1,] means—

    (a)   the council of a county in England in which there are no district councils,

    (b)   the council of a district in England,

    (c)   the council of a county or county borough in Wales,

    (d)   the council of a London borough,

    (e)   the Common Council of the City of London, or

    (f)   the Council of the Isles of Scilly,

'Mental Health Act' means the Mental Health Act 1983 (c. 20),

'prescribed', in relation to regulations made under this Act, means prescribed by those regulations,

'property' includes any thing in action and any interest in real or personal property,

'public authority' has the same meaning as in the Human Rights Act 1998,

'Public Guardian' has the meaning given in section 57,

'purchaser' and 'purchase' have the meaning given in section 205(1) of the Law of Property Act 1925 (c. 20),

'social services function' has the meaning given in section 1A of the Local Authority Social Services Act 1970 (c. 42),

'treatment' includes a diagnostic or other procedure

'trust corporation' has the meaning given in section 68(1) of the Trustee Act 1925 (c. 19), and

'will' includes codicil.

(2) In this Act, references to making decisions, in relation to a donee of a lasting power of attorney or a deputy appointed by the court, include, where appropriate, acting on decisions made.

(3) In this Act, references to the bankruptcy of an individual include a case where a bankruptcy restrictions order under the Insolvency Act 1986 (c. 45) has effect in respect of him.

(4) 'Bankruptcy restrictions order' includes an interim bankruptcy restrictions order.

[(5) In this Act, references to deprivation of a person's liberty have the same meaning as in Article 5(1) of the Human Rights Convention.

(6) For the purposes of such references, it does not matter whether a person is deprived of his liberty by a public authority or not.]

[*Definition of 'authorisation under Schedule A1', additional words in definition of 'local authority' and new subsections (5) & (6) inserted by paragraphs 10(2), (3) and (4) respectively of Schedule 9 to the 2007 Act.*]

65 Rules, regulations and orders

(1) Any power to make rules, regulations or orders under this Act, other than the power in section 21—

    (a)   is exercisable by statutory instrument;

    (b)   includes power to make supplementary, incidental, consequential, transitional or saving provision;

    (c)   includes power to make different provision for different cases.

(2) Any statutory instrument containing rules, regulations or orders made by the Lord Chancellor or the Secretary of State under this Act, other than—

    (a)   regulations under section 34 (loss of capacity during research project),

    (b)   regulations under section 41 (adjusting role of independent mental capacity advocacy service),

   (c) regulations under paragraph 32(1)(b) of Schedule 3 (private international law relating to the protection of adults),

   (d) an order of the kind mentioned in section 67(6) (consequential amendments of primary legislation), or

   (e) an order under section 68 (commencement),

is subject to annulment in pursuance of a resolution of either House of Parliament.

(3) A statutory instrument containing an Order in Council under paragraph 31 of Schedule 3 (provision to give further effect to Hague Convention) is subject to annulment in pursuance of a resolution of either House of Parliament.

(4) A statutory instrument containing regulations made by the Secretary of State under section 34 or 41, or by the Lord Chancellor under paragraph 32(1)(b) of Schedule 3 may not be made unless a draft has been laid before and approved by resolution of each House of Parliament.

[(4A) Subsection (2) does not apply to a statutory instrument containing regulations made by the Secretary of State under Schedule A1.

(4B) If such a statutory instrument contains regulations under paragraph 42(2)(b), 129, 162 or 164 of Schedule A1 (whether or not it also contains other regulations), the instrument may not be made unless a draft has been laid before and approved by resolution of each House of Parliament.

(4C) Subject to that, such a statutory instrument is subject to annulment in pursuance of a resolution of either House of Parliament.]

(5) An order under section 21—

   (a) may include supplementary, incidental, consequential, transitional or saving provision;

   (b) may make different provision for different cases;

   (c) is to be made in the form of a statutory instrument to which the Statutory Instruments Act 1946 applies as if the order were made by a Minister of the Crown; and

   (d) is subject to annulment in pursuance of a resolution of either House of Parliament.

[Subsections (4A) to (4C) inserted by paragraph 11(2) of Schedule 9 to the 2007 Act.]

66 Existing receivers and enduring powers of attorney etc.

(1) The following provisions cease to have effect—

   (a) Part 7 of the Mental Health Act,

   (b) the Enduring Powers of Attorney Act 1985 (c. 29).

(2) No enduring power of attorney within the meaning of the 1985 Act is to be created after the commencement of subsection (1)(b).

(3) Schedule 4 has effect in place of the 1985 Act in relation to any enduring power of attorney created before the commencement of subsection (1)(b).

(4) Schedule 5 contains transitional provisions and savings in relation to Part 7 of the Mental Health Act and the 1985 Act.

67 Minor and consequential amendments and repeals

(1) Schedule 6 contains minor and consequential amendments.

(2) Schedule 7 contains repeals.

(3) The Lord Chancellor may by order make supplementary, incidental, consequential, transitional or saving provision for the purposes of, in consequence of, or for giving full effect to a provision of this Act.

(4) An order under subsection (3) may, in particular—

    (a) provide for a provision of this Act which comes into force before another provision of this Act has come into force to have effect, until the other provision has come into force, with specified modifications;

    (b) amend, repeal or revoke an enactment, other than one contained in an Act or Measure passed in a Session after the one in which this Act is passed.

(5) The amendments that may be made under subsection (4)(b) are in addition to those made by or under any other provision of this Act.

(6) An order under subsection (3) which amends or repeals a provision of an Act or Measure may not be made unless a draft has been laid before and approved by resolution of each House of Parliament.

68 Commencement and extent

(1) This Act, other than sections 30 to 41, comes into force in accordance with provision made by order by the Lord Chancellor.

(2) Sections 30 to 41 come into force in accordance with provision made by order by—

    (a) the Secretary of State, in relation to England, and

    (b) the National Assembly for Wales, in relation to Wales.

(3) An order under this section may appoint different days for different provisions and different purposes.

(4) Subject to subsections (5) and (6), this Act extends to England and Wales only.

(5) The following provisions extend to the United Kingdom—

    (a) paragraph 16(1) of Schedule 1 (evidence of instruments and of registration of lasting powers of attorney),

    (b) paragraph 15(3) of Schedule 4 (evidence of instruments and of registration of enduring powers of attorney).

(6) Subject to any provision made in Schedule 6, the amendments and repeals made by Schedules 6 and 7 have the same extent as the enactments to which they relate.

69 Short title

This Act may be cited as the Mental Capacity Act 2005.

SCHEDULES

[SCHEDULE A1

HOSPITAL AND CARE HOME RESIDENTS:
DEPRIVATION OF LIBERTY

PART 1
AUTHORISATION TO DEPRIVE RESIDENTS OF LIBERTY ETC

Application of Part

1 (1) This Part applies if the following conditions are met.

(2) The first condition is that a person ('P') is detained in a hospital or care home—for the purpose of being given care or treatment—in circumstances which amount to deprivation of the person's liberty.

(3) The second condition is that a standard or urgent authorisation is in force.

(4) The third condition is that the standard or urgent authorisation relates—
   (a) to P, and
   (b) to the hospital or care home in which P is detained.

Authorisation to deprive P of liberty

2 The managing authority of the hospital or care home may deprive P of his liberty by detaining him as mentioned in paragraph 1(2).

No liability for acts done for purpose of depriving P of liberty

3 (1) This paragraph applies to any act which a person ('D') does for the purpose of detaining P as mentioned in paragraph 1(2).

(2) D does not incur any liability in relation to the act that he would not have incurred if P—
   (a) had had capacity to consent in relation to D's doing the act, and
   (b) had consented to D's doing the act.

No protection for negligent acts etc

4(1) Paragraphs 2 and 3 do not exclude a person's civil liability for loss or damage, or his criminal liability, resulting from his negligence in doing any thing.

(2) Paragraphs 2 and 3 do not authorise a person to do anything otherwise than for the purpose of the standard or urgent authorisation that is in force.

(3) In a case where a standard authorisation is in force, paragraphs 2 and 3 do not authorise a person to do anything which does not comply with the conditions (if any) included in the authorisation.

PART 2
INTERPRETATION: MAIN TERMS

Introduction

5 This Part applies for the purposes of this Schedule.

Detained resident

6 'Detained resident' means a person detained in a hospital or care home—for the purpose of being given care or treatment—in circumstances which amount to deprivation of the person's liberty.

Relevant person etc

7 In relation to a person who is, or is to be, a detained resident—
   'relevant person' means the person in question;
   'relevant hospital or care home' means the hospital or care home in question;
   'relevant care or treatment' means the care or treatment in question.

Authorisations

8 'Standard authorisation' means an authorisation given under Part 4.

9 'Urgent authorisation' means an authorisation given under Part 5.

10 'Authorisation under this Schedule' means either of the following—

(a) a standard authorisation;

(b) an urgent authorisation.

11 (1) The purpose of a standard authorisation is the purpose which is stated in the authorisation in accordance with paragraph 55(1)(d).

(2) The purpose of an urgent authorisation is the purpose which is stated in the authorisation in accordance with paragraph 80(d).

PART 3
THE QUALIFYING REQUIREMENTS

The qualifying requirements

12 (1) These are the qualifying requirements referred to in this Schedule—

(a) the age requirement;

(b) the mental health requirement;

(c) the mental capacity requirement;

(d) the best interests requirement;

(e) the eligibility requirement;

(f) the no refusals requirement.

(2) Any question of whether a person who is, or is to be, a detained resident meets the qualifying requirements is to be determined in accordance with this Part.

(3) In a case where—

(a) the question of whether a person meets a particular qualifying requirement arises in relation to the giving of a standard authorisation, and

(b) any circumstances relevant to determining that question are expected to change between the time when the determination is made and the time when the authorisation is expected to come into force,

those circumstances are to be taken into account as they are expected to be at the later time.

The age requirement

13 The relevant person meets the age requirement if he has reached 18.

The mental health requirement

14 (1) The relevant person meets the mental health requirement if he is suffering from mental disorder (within the meaning of the Mental Health Act, but disregarding any exclusion for persons with learning disability).

(2) An exclusion for persons with learning disability is any provision of the Mental Health Act which provides for a person with learning disability not to be regarded as suffering from mental disorder for one or more purposes of that Act.

The mental capacity requirement

15 The relevant person meets the mental capacity requirement if he lacks capacity in relation to the question whether or not he should be accommodated in the relevant hospital or care home for the purpose of being given the relevant care or treatment.

The best interests requirement

16(1) The relevant person meets the best interests requirement if all of the following conditions are met.

(2) The first condition is that the relevant person is, or is to be, a detained resident.

(3) The second condition is that it is in the best interests of the relevant person for him to be a detained resident.

(4) The third condition is that, in order to prevent harm to the relevant person, it is necessary for him to be a detained resident.

(5) The fourth condition is that it is a proportionate response to—

    (a) the likelihood of the relevant person suffering harm, and

    (b) the seriousness of that harm,

for him to be a detained resident.

The eligibility requirement

17(1) The relevant person meets the eligibility requirement unless he is ineligible to be deprived of liberty by this Act.

(2) Schedule 1A applies for the purpose of determining whether or not P is ineligible to be deprived of liberty by this Act.

The no refusals requirement

18 The relevant person meets the no refusals requirement unless there is a refusal within the meaning of paragraph 19 or 20.

19(1) There is a refusal if these conditions are met—

    (a) the relevant person has made an advance decision;

    (b) the advance decision is valid;

    (c) the advance decision is applicable to some or all of the relevant treatment.

(2) Expressions used in this paragraph and any of sections 24, 25 or 26 have the same meaning in this paragraph as in that section.

20(1) There is a refusal if it would be in conflict with a valid decision of a donee or deputy for the relevant person to be accommodated in the relevant hospital or care home for the purpose of receiving some or all of the relevant care or treatment—

    (a) in circumstances which amount to deprivation of the person's liberty, or

    (b) at all.

(2) A donee is a donee of a lasting power of attorney granted by the relevant person.

(3) A decision of a donee or deputy is valid if it is made—

    (a) within the scope of his authority as donee or deputy, and

    (b) in accordance with Part 1 of this Act.

PART 4

STANDARD AUTHORISATIONS

Supervisory body to give authorisation

21 Only the supervisory body may give a standard authorisation.

22 The supervisory body may not give a standard authorisation unless—

(a) the managing authority of the relevant hospital or care home have requested it, or

(b) paragraph 71 applies (right of third party to require consideration of whether authorisation needed).

23 The managing authority may not make a request for a standard authorisation unless—

(a) they are required to do so by paragraph 24 (as read with paragraphs 27 to 29),

(b) they are required to do so by paragraph 25 (as read with paragraph 28), or

(c) they are permitted to do so by paragraph 30.

Duty to request authorisation: basic cases

24(1) The managing authority must request a standard authorisation in any of the following cases.

(2) The first case is where it appears to the managing authority that the relevant person—

(a) is not yet accommodated in the relevant hospital or care home,

(b) is likely—at some time within the next 28 days—to be a detained resident in the relevant hospital or care home, and

(c) is likely—

(i) at that time, or

(ii) at some later time within the next 28 days,

to meet all of the qualifying requirements.

(3) The second case is where it appears to the managing authority that the relevant person—

(a) is already accommodated in the relevant hospital or care home,

(b) is likely—at some time within the next 28 days—to be a detained resident in the relevant hospital or care home, and

(c) is likely—

(i) at that time, or

(ii) at some later time within the next 28 days,

to meet all of the qualifying requirements.

(4) The third case is where it appears to the managing authority that the relevant person—

(a) is a detained resident in the relevant hospital or care home, and

(b) meets all of the qualifying requirements, or is likely to do so at some time within the next 28 days.

(5) This paragraph is subject to paragraphs 27 to 29.

Duty to request authorisation: change in place of detention

25(1) The relevant managing authority must request a standard authorisation if it appears to them that these conditions are met.

(2) The first condition is that a standard authorisation—

(a) has been given, and

(b) has not ceased to be in force.

(3) The second condition is that there is, or is to be, a change in the place of detention.

(4) This paragraph is subject to paragraph 28.

26(1) This paragraph applies for the purposes of paragraph 25.

(2) There is a change in the place of detention if the relevant person—

    (a) ceases to be a detained resident in the stated hospital or care home, and

    (b) becomes a detained resident in a different hospital or care home ('the new hospital or care home').

(3) The stated hospital or care home is the hospital or care home to which the standard authorisation relates.

(4) The relevant managing authority are the managing authority of the new hospital or care home.

Other authority for detention: request for authorisation

27(1) This paragraph applies if, by virtue of section 4A(3), a decision of the court authorises the relevant person to be a detained resident.

(2) Paragraph 24 does not require a request for a standard authorisation to be made in relation to that detention unless these conditions are met.

(3) The first condition is that the standard authorisation would be in force at a time immediately after the expiry of the other authority.

(4) The second condition is that the standard authorisation would not be in force at any time on or before the expiry of the other authority.

(5) The third condition is that it would, in the managing authority's view, be unreasonable to delay making the request until a time nearer the expiry of the other authority.

(6) In this paragraph—

    (a) the other authority is—

        (i) the decision mentioned in sub-paragraph (1), or

        (ii) any further decision of the court which, by virtue of section 4A(3), authorises, or is expected to authorise, the relevant person to be a detained resident;

    (b) the expiry of the other authority is the time when the other authority is expected to cease to authorise the relevant person to be a detained resident.

Request refused: no further request unless change of circumstances

28(1) This paragraph applies if—

    (a) a managing authority request a standard authorisation under paragraph 24 or 25, and

    (b) the supervisory body are prohibited by paragraph 50(2) from giving the authorisation.

(2) Paragraph 24 or 25 does not require that managing authority to make a new request for a standard authorisation unless it appears to the managing authority that—

    (a) there has been a change in the relevant person's case, and

    (b) because of that change, the supervisory body are likely to give a standard authorisation if requested.

Authorisation given: request for further authorisation

29(1) This paragraph applies if a standard authorisation—

    (a) has been given in relation to the detention of the relevant person, and

    (b) that authorisation ('the existing authorisation') has not ceased to be in force.

(2) Paragraph 24 does not require a new request for a standard authorisation ('the new authorisation') to be made unless these conditions are met.

(3) The first condition is that the new authorisation would be in force at a time immediately after the expiry of the existing authorisation.

(4) The second condition is that the new authorisation would not be in force at any time on or before the expiry of the existing authorisation.

(5) The third condition is that it would, in the managing authority's view, be unreasonable to delay making the request until a time nearer the expiry of the existing authorisation.

(6) The expiry of the existing authorisation is the time when it is expected to cease to be in force.

Power to request authorisation

30(1) This paragraph applies if—

    (a) a standard authorisation has been given in relation to the detention of the relevant person,

    (b) that authorisation ('the existing authorisation') has not ceased to be in force,

    (c) the requirement under paragraph 24 to make a request for a new standard authorisation does not apply, because of paragraph 29, and

    (d) a review of the existing authorisation has been requested, or is being carried out, in accordance with Part 8.

(2) The managing authority may request a new standard authorisation which would be in force on or before the expiry of the existing authorisation; but only if it would also be in force immediately after that expiry.

(3) The expiry of the existing authorisation is the time when it is expected to cease to be in force.

(4) Further provision relating to cases where a request is made under this paragraph can be found in—

    (a) paragraph 62 (effect of decision about request), and

    (b) paragraph 134 (effect of request on Part 8 review).

Information included in request

31 A request for a standard authorisation must include the information (if any) required by regulations.

Records of requests

32 (1) The managing authority of a hospital or care home must keep a written record of—

    (a) each request that they make for a standard authorisation, and

    (b) the reasons for making each request.

(2) A supervisory body must keep a written record of each request for a standard authorisation that is made to them.

Relevant person must be assessed

33 (1) This paragraph applies if the supervisory body are requested to give a standard authorisation.

(2) The supervisory body must secure that all of these assessments are carried out in relation to the relevant person—

    (a) an age assessment;

    (b) a mental health assessment;

    (c) a mental capacity assessment;

    (d) a best interests assessment;

    (e) an eligibility assessment;

    (f) a no refusals assessment.

(3) The person who carries out any such assessment is referred to as the assessor.

(4) Regulations may be made about the period (or periods) within which assessors must carry out assessments.

(5) This paragraph is subject to paragraphs 49 and 133.

Age assessment

34 An age assessment is an assessment of whether the relevant person meets the age requirement.

Mental health assessment

35 A mental health assessment is an assessment of whether the relevant person meets the mental health requirement.

36 When carrying out a mental health assessment, the assessor must also—

(a) consider how (if at all) the relevant person's mental health is likely to be affected by his being a detained resident, and

(b) notify the best interests assessor of his conclusions.

Mental capacity assessment

37 A mental capacity assessment is an assessment of whether the relevant person meets the mental capacity requirement.

Best interests assessment

38 A best interests assessment is an assessment of whether the relevant person meets the best interests requirement.

39(1) In carrying out a best interests assessment, the assessor must comply with the duties in sub-paragraphs (2) and (3).

(2) The assessor must consult the managing authority of the relevant hospital or care home.

(3) The assessor must have regard to all of the following—

(a) the conclusions which the mental health assessor has notified to the best interests assessor in accordance with paragraph 36(b);

(b) any relevant needs assessment;

(c) any relevant care plan.

(4) A relevant needs assessment is an assessment of the relevant person's needs which—

(a) was carried out in connection with the relevant person being accommodated in the relevant hospital or care home, and

(b) was carried out by or on behalf of—

(i) the managing authority of the relevant hospital or care home, or

(ii) the supervisory body.

(5) A relevant care plan is a care plan which—

(a) sets out how the relevant person's needs are to be met whilst he is accommodated in the relevant hospital or care home, and

(b) was drawn up by or on behalf of—

(i) the managing authority of the relevant hospital or care home, or

(ii) the supervisory body.

(6) The managing authority must give the assessor a copy of—

(a) any relevant needs assessment carried out by them or on their behalf, or

(b) any relevant care plan drawn up by them or on their behalf.

(7) The supervisory body must give the assessor a copy of—
  (a) any relevant needs assessment carried out by them or on their behalf, or
  (b) any relevant care plan drawn up by them or on their behalf.

(8) The duties in sub-paragraphs (2) and (3) do not affect any other duty to consult or to take the views of others into account.

40(1) This paragraph applies whatever conclusion the best interests assessment comes to.

(2) The assessor must state in the best interests assessment the name and address of every interested person whom he has consulted in carrying out the assessment.

41 Paragraphs 42 and 43 apply if the best interests assessment comes to the conclusion that the relevant person meets the best interests requirement.

42(1) The assessor must state in the assessment the maximum authorisation period.

(2) The maximum authorisation period is the shorter of these periods—
  (a) the period which, in the assessor's opinion, would be the appropriate maximum period for the relevant person to be a detained resident under the standard authorisation that has been requested;
  (b) 1 year, or such shorter period as may be prescribed in regulations.

(3) Regulations under sub-paragraph (2)(b)—
  (a) need not provide for a shorter period to apply in relation to all standard authorisations;
  (b) may provide for different periods to apply in relation to different kinds of standard authorisations.

(4) Before making regulations under sub-paragraph (2)(b) the Secretary of State must consult all of the following—
  (a) each body required by regulations under paragraph 162 to monitor and report on the operation of this Schedule in relation to England;
  (b) such other persons as the Secretary of State considers it appropriate to consult.

(5) Before making regulations under sub-paragraph (2)(b) the National Assembly for Wales must consult all of the following—
  (a) each person or body directed under paragraph 163(2) to carry out any function of the Assembly of monitoring and reporting on the operation of this Schedule in relation to Wales;
  (b) such other persons as the Assembly considers it appropriate to consult.

43 The assessor may include in the assessment recommendations about conditions to which the standard authorisation is, or is not, to be subject in accordance with paragraph 53.

44(1) This paragraph applies if the best interests assessment comes to the conclusion that the relevant person does not meet the best interests requirement.

(2) If, on the basis of the information taken into account in carrying out the assessment, it appears to the assessor that there is an unauthorised deprivation of liberty, he must include a statement to that effect in the assessment.

(3) There is an unauthorised deprivation of liberty if the managing authority of the relevant hospital or care home are already depriving the relevant person of his liberty without authority of the kind mentioned in section 4A.

45 The duties with which the best interests assessor must comply are subject to the provision included in appointment regulations under Part 10 (in particular, provision made under paragraph 146).

Eligibility assessment

46 An eligibility assessment is an assessment of whether the relevant person meets the eligibility requirement.

47(1) Regulations may—

    (a) require an eligibility assessor to request a best interests assessor to provide relevant eligibility information, and

    (b) require the best interests assessor, if such a request is made, to provide such relevant eligibility information as he may have.

(2) In this paragraph—

    'best interests assessor' means any person who is carrying out, or has carried out, a best interests assessment in relation to the relevant person;

    'eligibility assessor' means a person carrying out an eligibility assessment in relation to the relevant person;

    'relevant eligibility information' is information relevant to assessing whether or not the relevant person is ineligible by virtue of paragraph 5 of Schedule 1A.

No refusals assessment

48 A no refusals assessment is an assessment of whether the relevant person meets the no refusals requirement.

Equivalent assessment already carried out

49(1) The supervisory body are not required by paragraph 33 to secure that a particular kind of assessment ('the required assessment') is carried out in relation to the relevant person if the following conditions are met.

(2) The first condition is that the supervisory body have a written copy of an assessment of the relevant person ('the existing assessment') that has already been carried out.

(3) The second condition is that the existing assessment complies with all requirements under this Schedule with which the required assessment would have to comply (if it were carried out).

(4) The third condition is that the existing assessment was carried out within the previous 12 months; but this condition need not be met if the required assessment is an age assessment.

(5) The fourth condition is that the supervisory body are satisfied that there is no reason why the existing assessment may no longer be accurate.

(6) If the required assessment is a best interests assessment, in satisfying themselves as mentioned in sub-paragraph (5), the supervisory body must take into account any information given, or submissions made, by—

    (a) the relevant person's representative,

    (b) any section 39C IMCA or

    (c) any section 39D IMCA.

(7) It does not matter whether the existing assessment was carried out in connection with a request for a standard authorisation or for some other purpose.

(8) If, because of this paragraph, the supervisory body are not required by paragraph 33 to secure that the required assessment is carried out, the existing assessment is to be treated for the purposes of this Schedule—

    (a) as an assessment of the same kind as the required assessment, and

    (b) as having been carried out under paragraph 33 in connection with the request for the standard authorisation.

Duty to give authorisation

50 (1) The supervisory body must give a standard authorisation if—

    (a) all assessments are positive, and

    (b) the supervisory body have written copies of all those assessments.

(2) The supervisory body must not give a standard authorisation except in accordance with sub-paragraph (1).

(3) All assessments are positive if each assessment carried out under paragraph 33 has come to the conclusion that the relevant person meets the qualifying requirement to which the assessment relates.

Terms of authorisation

51(1) If the supervisory body are required to give a standard authorisation, they must decide the period during which the authorisation is to be in force.

(2) That period must not exceed the maximum authorisation period stated in the best interests assessment.

52 A standard authorisation may provide for the authorisation to come into force at a time after it is given.

53(1) A standard authorisation may be given subject to conditions.

(2) Before deciding whether to give the authorisation subject to conditions, the supervisory body must have regard to any recommendations in the best interests assessment about such conditions.

(3) The managing authority of the relevant hospital or care home must ensure that any conditions are complied with.

Form of authorisation

54 A standard authorisation must be in writing.

55(1) A standard authorisation must state the following things—
- (a) the name of the relevant person;
- (b) the name of the relevant hospital or care home;
- (c) the period during which the authorisation is to be in force;
- (d) the purpose for which the authorisation is given;
- (e) any conditions subject to which the authorisation is given;
- (f) the reason why each qualifying requirement is met.

(2) The statement of the reason why the eligibility requirement is met must be framed by reference to the cases in the table in paragraph 2 of Schedule 1A.

56 (1) If the name of the relevant hospital or care home changes, the standard authorisation is to be read as if it stated the current name of the hospital or care home.

(2) But sub-paragraph (1) is subject to any provision relating to the change of name which is made in any enactment or in any instrument made under an enactment.

Duty to give information about decision

57(1) This paragraph applies if—
- (a) a request is made for a standard authorisation, and
- (b) the supervisory body are required by paragraph 50(1) to give the standard authorisation.

(2) The supervisory body must give a copy of the authorisation to each of the following—
- (a) the relevant person's representative;
- (b) the managing authority of the relevant hospital or care home;
- (c) the relevant person;
- (d) any section 39A IMCA;
- (e) every interested person consulted by the best interests assessor.

(3) The supervisory body must comply with this paragraph as soon as practicable after they give the standard authorisation.

58(1) This paragraph applies if—

    (a) a request is made for a standard authorisation, and

    (b) the supervisory body are prohibited by paragraph 50(2) from giving the standard authorisation.

(2) The supervisory body must give notice, stating that they are prohibited from giving the authorisation, to each of the following—

    (a) the managing authority of the relevant hospital or care home;

    (b) the relevant person;

    (c) any section 39A IMCA;

    (d) every interested person consulted by the best interests assessor.

(3) The supervisory body must comply with this paragraph as soon as practicable after it becomes apparent to them that they are prohibited from giving the authorisation.

Duty to give information about effect of authorisation

59(1) This paragraph applies if a standard authorisation is given.

(2) The managing authority of the relevant hospital or care home must take such steps as are practicable to ensure that the relevant person understands all of the following—

    (a) the effect of the authorisation;

    (b) the right to make an application to the court to exercise its jurisdiction under section 21A;

    (c) the right under Part 8 to request a review

    (d) the right to have a section 39D IMCA appointed;

    (e) how to have a section 39D IMCA appointed.

(3) Those steps must be taken as soon as is practicable after the authorisation is given.

(4) Those steps must include the giving of appropriate information both orally and in writing.

(5) Any written information given to the relevant person must also be given by the managing authority to the relevant person's representative.

(6) They must give the information to the representative as soon as is practicable after it is given to the relevant person.

(7) Sub-paragraph (8) applies if the managing authority is notified that a section 39D IMCA has been appointed.

(8) As soon as is practicable after being notified, the managing authority must give the section 39D IMCA a copy of the written information given in accordance with sub-paragraph (4).

Records of authorisations

60 A supervisory body must keep a written record of all of the following information—

    (a) the standard authorisations that they have given;

    (b) the requests for standard authorisations in response to which they have not given an authorisation;

    (c) in relation to each standard authorisation given: the matters stated in the authorisation in accordance with paragraph 55.

Variation of an authorisation

61(1) A standard authorisation may not be varied except in accordance with Part 7 or 8.

(2) This paragraph does not affect the powers of the Court of Protection or of any other court.

Effect of decision about request made under paragraph 25 or 30

62(1) This paragraph applies where the managing authority request a new standard authorisation under either of the following—

(a) paragraph 25 (change in place of detention);

(b) paragraph 30 (existing authorisation subject to review).

(2) If the supervisory body are required by paragraph 50(1) to give the new authorisation, the existing authorisation terminates at the time when the new authorisation comes into force.

(3) If the supervisory body are prohibited by paragraph 50(2) from giving the new authorisation, there is no effect on the existing authorisation's continuation in force.

When an authorisation is in force

63(1) A standard authorisation comes into force when it is given.

(2) But if the authorisation provides for it to come into force at a later time, it comes into force at that time.

64(1) A standard authorisation ceases to be in force at the end of the period stated in the authorisation in accordance with paragraph 55(1)(c).

(2) But if the authorisation terminates before then in accordance with paragraph 62(2) or any other provision of this Schedule, it ceases to be in force when the termination takes effect.

(3) This paragraph does not affect the powers of the Court of Protection or of any other court.

65(1) This paragraph applies if a standard authorisation ceases to be in force.

(2) The supervisory body must give notice that the authorisation has ceased to be in force.

(3) The supervisory body must give that notice to all of the following—

(a) the managing authority of the relevant hospital or care home;

(b) the relevant person;

(c) the relevant person's representative;

(d) every interested person consulted by the best interests assessor.

(4) The supervisory body must give that notice as soon as practicable after the authorisation ceases to be in force.

When a request for a standard authorisation is 'disposed of'

66 A request for a standard authorisation is to be regarded for the purposes of this Schedule as disposed of if the supervisory body have given—

(a) a copy of the authorisation in accordance with paragraph 57, or

(b) notice in accordance with paragraph 58.

Right of third party to require consideration of whether authorisation needed

67 For the purposes of paragraphs 68 to 73 there is an unauthorised deprivation of liberty if—

(a) a person is already a detained resident in a hospital or care home, and

(b) the detention of the person is not authorised as mentioned in section 4A

68(1) If the following conditions are met, an eligible person may request the supervisory body to decide whether or not there is an unauthorised deprivation of liberty.

(2) The first condition is that the eligible person has notified the managing authority of the relevant hospital or care home that it appears to the eligible person that there is an unauthorised deprivation of liberty.

(3) The second condition is that the eligible person has asked the managing authority to request a standard authorisation in relation to the detention of the relevant person.

(4) The third condition is that the managing authority has not requested a standard authorisation within a reasonable period after the eligible person asks it to do so.

(5) In this paragraph 'eligible person' means any person other than the managing authority of the relevant hospital or care home.

69(1) This paragraph applies if an eligible person requests the supervisory body to decide whether or not there is an unauthorised deprivation of liberty.

(2) The supervisory body must select and appoint a person to carry out an assessment of whether or not the relevant person is a detained resident.

(3) But the supervisory body need not select and appoint a person to carry out such an assessment in either of these cases.

(4) The first case is where it appears to the supervisory body that the request by the eligible person is frivolous or vexatious.

(5) The second case is where it appears to the supervisory body that—

(a) the question of whether or not there is an unauthorised deprivation of liberty has already been decided, and

(b) since that decision, there has been no change of circumstances which would merit the question being decided again.

(6) The supervisory body must not select and appoint a person to carry out an assessment under this paragraph unless it appears to the supervisory body that the person would be—

(a) suitable to carry out a best interests assessment (if one were obtained in connection with a request for a standard authorisation relating to the relevant person), and

(b) eligible to carry out such a best interests assessment.

(7) The supervisory body must notify the persons specified in sub-paragraph (8)—

(a) that the supervisory body have been requested to decide whether or not there is an unauthorised deprivation of liberty;

(b) of their decision whether or not to select and appoint a person to carry out an assessment under this paragraph;

(c) if their decision is to select and appoint a person, of the person appointed.

(8) The persons referred to in sub-paragraph (7) are—

(a) the eligible person who made the request under paragraph 68;

(b) the person to whom the request relates;

(c) the managing authority of the relevant hospital or care home;

(d) any section 39A IMCA.

70(1) Regulations may be made about the period within which an assessment under paragraph 69 must be carried out.

(2) Regulations made under paragraph 129(3) apply in relation to the selection and appointment of a person under paragraph 69 as they apply to the selection of a person under paragraph 129 to carry out a best interests assessment.

(3) The following provisions apply to an assessment under paragraph 69 as they apply to an assessment carried out in connection with a request for a standard authorisation—

(a) paragraph 131 (examination and copying of records);

(b) paragraph 132 (representations);

(c) paragraphs 134 and 135(1) and (2) (duty to keep records and give copies).

(4) The copies of the assessment which the supervisory body are required to give under paragraph 135(2) must be given as soon as practicable after the supervisory body are themselves given a copy of the assessment.

71(1) This paragraph applies if—

(a) the supervisory body obtain an assessment under paragraph 69,

(b) the assessment comes to the conclusion that the relevant person is a detained resident, and

(c) it appears to the supervisory body that the detention of the person is not authorised as mentioned in section 4A.

(2) This Schedule (including Part 5) applies as if the managing authority of the relevant hospital or care home had, in accordance with Part 4, requested the supervisory body to give a standard authorisation in relation to the relevant person.

(3) The managing authority of the relevant hospital or care home must supply the supervisory body with the information (if any) which the managing authority would, by virtue of paragraph 31, have had to include in a request for a standard authorisation.

(4) The supervisory body must notify the persons specified in paragraph 69(8)—

(a) of the outcome of the assessment obtained under paragraph 69, and

(b) that this Schedule applies as mentioned in sub-paragraph (2).

72(1) This paragraph applies if—

(a) the supervisory body obtain an assessment under paragraph 69, and

(b) the assessment comes to the conclusion that the relevant person is not a detained resident.

(2) The supervisory body must notify the persons specified in paragraph 69(8) of the outcome of the assessment.

73(1) This paragraph applies if—

(a) the supervisory body obtain an assessment under paragraph 69,

(b) the assessment comes to the conclusion that the relevant person is a detained resident, and

(c) it appears to the supervisory body that the detention of the person is authorised as mentioned in section 4A.

(2) The supervisory body must notify the persons specified in paragraph 69(8)—

(a) of the outcome of the assessment, and

(b) that it appears to the supervisory body that the detention is authorised.

PART 5
URGENT AUTHORISATIONS

Managing authority to give authorisation

74 Only the managing authority of the relevant hospital or care home may give an urgent authorisation.

75 The managing authority may give an urgent authorisation only if they are required to do so by paragraph 76 (as read with paragraph 77).

Duty to give authorisation

76(1) The managing authority must give an urgent authorisation in either of the following cases.

(2) The first case is where—

(a) the managing authority are required to make a request under paragraph 24 or 25 for a standard authorisation, and

(b) they believe that the need for the relevant person to be a detained resident is so urgent that it is appropriate for the detention to begin before they make the request.

(3) The second case is where—

(a) the managing authority have made a request under paragraph 24 or 25 for a standard authorisation, and

(b) they believe that the need for the relevant person to be a detained resident is so urgent that it is appropriate for the detention to begin before the request is disposed of.

(4) References in this paragraph to the detention of the relevant person are references to the detention to which paragraph 24 or 25 relates.

(5) This paragraph is subject to paragraph 77.

77(1) This paragraph applies where the managing authority have given an urgent authorisation ('the original authorisation') in connection with a case where a person is, or is to be, a detained resident ('the existing detention').

(2) No new urgent authorisation is to be given under paragraph 76 in connection with the existing detention.

(3) But the managing authority may request the supervisory body to extend the duration of the original authorisation.

(4) Only one request under sub-paragraph (3) may be made in relation to the original authorisation.

(5) Paragraphs 84 to 86 apply to any request made under subparagraph (3).

Terms of authorisation

78 (1) If the managing authority decide to give an urgent authorisation, they must decide the period during which the authorisation is to be in force.

(2) That period must not exceed 7 days.

Form of authorisation

79 An urgent authorisation must be in writing.

80 An urgent authorisation must state the following things—
   (a) the name of the relevant person;
   (b) the name of the relevant hospital or care home;
   (c) the period during which the authorisation is to be in force;
   (d) the purpose for which the authorisation is given.

81(1) If the name of the relevant hospital or care home changes, the urgent authorisation is to be read as if it stated the current name of the hospital or care home.

(2) But sub-paragraph (1) is subject to any provision relating to the change of name which is made in any enactment or in any instrument made under an enactment.

Duty to keep records and give copies

82(1) This paragraph applies if an urgent authorisation is given.

(2) The managing authority must keep a written record of why they have given the urgent authorisation.

(3) As soon as practicable after giving the authorisation, the managing authority must give a copy of the authorisation to all of the following—
   (a) the relevant person;
   (b) any section 39A IMCA.

Duty to give information about authorisation

83(1) This paragraph applies if an urgent authorisation is given.

(2) The managing authority of the relevant hospital or care home must take such steps as are practicable to ensure that the relevant person understands all of the following—
   (a) the effect of the authorisation;
   (b) the right to make an application to the court to exercise its jurisdiction under section 21A.

(3) Those steps must be taken as soon as is practicable after the authorisation is given.

(4) Those steps must include the giving of appropriate information both orally and in writing.

Request for extension of duration

84(1) This paragraph applies if the managing authority make a request under paragraph 77 for the supervisory body to extend the duration of the original authorisation.

(2) The managing authority must keep a written record of why they have made the request.

(3) The managing authority must give the relevant person notice that they have made the request.

(4) The supervisory body may extend the duration of the original authorisation if it appears to them that—

    (a) the managing authority have made the required request for a standard authorisation,

    (b) there are exceptional reasons why it has not yet been possible for that request to be disposed of, and

    (c) it is essential for the existing detention to continue until the request is disposed of.

(5) The supervisory body must keep a written record that the request has been made to them.

(6) In this paragraph and paragraphs 85 and 86—

    (a) 'original authorisation' and 'existing detention' have the same meaning as in paragraph 77;

    (b) the required request for a standard authorisation is the request that is referred to in paragraph 76(2) or (3).

85(1) This paragraph applies if, under paragraph 84, the supervisory body decide to extend the duration of the original authorisation.

(2) The supervisory body must decide the period of the extension.

(3) That period must not exceed 7 days.

(4) The supervisory body must give the managing authority notice stating the period of the extension.

(5) The managing authority must then vary the original authorisation so that it states the extended duration.

(6) Paragraphs 82(3) and 83 apply (with the necessary modifications) to the variation of the original authorisation as they apply to the giving of an urgent authorisation.

(7) The supervisory body must keep a written record of—

    (a) the outcome of the request, and

    (b) the period of the extension.

86(1) This paragraph applies if, under paragraph 84, the supervisory body decide not to extend the duration of the original authorisation.

(2) The supervisory body must give the managing authority notice stating—

    (a) the decision, and

    (b) their reasons for making it.

(3) The managing authority must give a copy of that notice to all of the following—

    (a) the relevant person;

    (b) any section 39A IMCA.

(4) The supervisory body must keep a written record of the outcome of the request.

No variation

87(1) An urgent authorisation may not be varied except in accordance with paragraph 85.

(2) This paragraph does not affect the powers of the Court of Protection or of any other court.

When an authorisation is in force

88 An urgent authorisation comes into force when it is given.

89(1) An urgent authorisation ceases to be in force at the end of the period stated in the authorisation in accordance with paragraph 80(c) (subject to any variation in accordance with paragraph 85).

(2) But if the required request is disposed of before the end of that period, the urgent authorisation ceases to be in force as follows.

(3) If the supervisory body are required by paragraph 50(1) to give the requested authorisation, the urgent authorisation ceases to be in force when the requested authorisation comes into force.

(4) If the supervisory body are prohibited by paragraph 50(2) from giving the requested authorisation, the urgent authorisation ceases to be in force when the managing authority receive notice under paragraph 58.

(5) In this paragraph—

'required request' means the request referred to in paragraph 76(2) or (3);

'requested authorisation' means the standard authorisation to which the required request relates.

(6) This paragraph does not affect the powers of the Court of Protection or of any other court.

90(1) This paragraph applies if an urgent authorisation ceases to be in force.

(2) The supervisory body must give notice that the authorisation has ceased to be in force.

(3) The supervisory body must give that notice to all of the following—

(a) the relevant person;

(b) any section 39A IMCA.

(4) The supervisory body must give that notice as soon as practicable after the authorisation ceases to be in force.

PART 6

ELIGIBILITY REQUIREMENT NOT MET: SUSPENSION
OF STANDARD AUTHORISATION

91(1) This Part applies if the following conditions are met.

(2) The first condition is that a standard authorisation—

(a) has been given, and

(b) has not ceased to be in force.

(3) The second condition is that the managing authority of the relevant hospital or care home are satisfied that the relevant person has ceased to meet the eligibility requirement.

(4) But this Part does not apply if the relevant person is ineligible by virtue of paragraph 5 of Schedule 1A (in which case see Part 8).

92 The managing authority of the relevant hospital or care home must give the supervisory body notice that the relevant person has ceased to meet the eligibility requirement.

93(1) This paragraph applies if the managing authority give the supervisory body notice under paragraph 92.

(2) The standard authorisation is suspended from the time when the notice is given.

(3) The supervisory body must give notice that the standard authorisation has been suspended to the following persons—

(a) the relevant person;

(b) the relevant person's representative;

(c) the managing authority of the relevant hospital or care home.

94(1) This paragraph applies if, whilst the standard authorisation is suspended, the managing authority are satisfied that the relevant person meets the eligibility requirement again.

(2) The managing authority must give the supervisory body notice that the relevant person meets the eligibility requirement again.

95(1) This paragraph applies if the managing authority give the supervisory body notice under paragraph 94.

(2) The standard authorisation ceases to be suspended from the time when the notice is given.

(3) The supervisory body must give notice that the standard authorisation has ceased to be suspended to the following persons—

(a) the relevant person;

(b) the relevant person's representative;

(c) any section 39D IMCA;

(d) the managing authority of the relevant hospital or care home.

(4) The supervisory body must give notice under this paragraph as soon as practicable after they are given notice under paragraph 94.

96(1) This paragraph applies if no notice is given under paragraph 94 before the end of the relevant 28 day period.

(2) The standard authorisation ceases to have effect at the end of the relevant 28 day period.

(3) The relevant 28 day period is the period of 28 days beginning with the day on which the standard authorisation is suspended under paragraph 93.

97 The effect of suspending the standard authorisation is that Part 1 ceases to apply for as long as the authorisation is suspended.

PART 7
STANDARD AUTHORISATIONS: CHANGE
IN SUPERVISORY RESPONSIBILITY

Application of this Part

98(1) This Part applies if these conditions are met.

(2) The first condition is that a standard authorisation—

(a) has been given, and

(b) has not ceased to be in force.

(3) The second condition is that there is a change in supervisory responsibility.

(4) The third condition is that there is not a change in the place of detention (within the meaning of paragraph 25).

99 For the purposes of this Part there is a change in supervisory responsibility if—

(a) one body ('the old supervisory body') have ceased to be supervisory body in relation to the standard authorisation, and

(b) a different body ('the new supervisory body') have become supervisory body in relation to the standard authorisation.

Effect of change in supervisory responsibility

100 (1) The new supervisory body becomes the supervisory body in relation to the authorisation.

(2) Anything done by or in relation to the old supervisory body in connection with the authorisation has effect, so far as is necessary for continuing its effect after the change, as if done by or in relation to the new supervisory body.

(3) Anything which relates to the authorisation and which is in the process of being done by or in relation to the old supervisory body at the time of the change may be continued by or in relation to the new supervisory body.

(4) But—

    (a) the old supervisory body do not, by virtue of this paragraph, cease to be liable for anything done by them in connection with the authorisation before the change; and

    (b) the new supervisory body do not, by virtue of this paragraph, become liable for any such thing.

PART 8
STANDARD AUTHORISATIONS: REVIEW

Application of this Part

101(1) This Part applies if a standard authorisation—

    (a) has been given, and

    (b) has not ceased to be in force.

(2) Paragraphs 102 to 122 are subject to paragraphs 123 to 125.

Review by supervisory body

102(1) The supervisory body may at any time carry out a review of the standard authorisation in accordance with this Part.

(2) The supervisory body must carry out such a review if they are requested to do so by an eligible person.

(3) Each of the following is an eligible person—

    (a) the relevant person;

    (b) the relevant person's representative;

    (c) the managing authority of the relevant hospital or care home.

Request for review

103(1) An eligible person may, at any time, request the supervisory body to carry out a review of the standard authorisation in accordance with this Part.

(2) The managing authority of the relevant hospital or care home must make such a request if one or more of the qualifying requirements appear to them to be reviewable.

Grounds for review

104(1) Paragraphs 105 to 107 set out the grounds on which the qualifying requirements are reviewable.

(2) A qualifying requirement is not reviewable on any other ground.

Non-qualification ground

105(1) Any of the following qualifying requirements is reviewable on the ground that the relevant person does not meet the requirement—

    (a) the age requirement;

    (b) the mental health requirement;

    (c) the mental capacity requirement;

    (d) the best interests requirement;

(e) the no refusals requirement.

(2) The eligibility requirement is reviewable on the ground that the relevant person is ineligible by virtue of paragraph 5 of Schedule 1A.

(3) The ground in sub-paragraph (1) and the ground in sub-paragraph (2) are referred to as the non-qualification ground.

Change of reason ground

106(1) Any of the following qualifying requirements is reviewable on the ground set out in sub-paragraph (2)—

(a) the mental health requirement;

(b) the mental capacity requirement;

(c) the best interests requirement;

(d) the eligibility requirement;

(e) the no refusals requirement.

(2) The ground is that the reason why the relevant person meets the requirement is not the reason stated in the standard authorisation.

(3) This ground is referred to as the change of reason ground.

Variation of conditions ground

107(1) The best interests requirement is reviewable on the ground that—

(a) there has been a change in the relevant person's case, and

(b) because of that change, it would be appropriate to vary the conditions to which the standard authorisation is subject.

(2) This ground is referred to as the variation of conditions ground.

(3) A reference to varying the conditions to which the standard authorisation is subject is a reference to—

(a) amendment of an existing condition,

(b) omission of an existing condition, or

(c) inclusion of a new condition (whether or not there are already any existing conditions).

Notice that review to be carried out

108(1) If the supervisory body are to carry out a review of the standard authorisation, they must give notice of the review to the following persons—

(a) the relevant person;

(b) the relevant person's representative;

(c) the managing authority of the relevant hospital or care home.

(2) The supervisory body must give the notice—

(a) before they begin the review, or

(b) if that is not practicable, as soon as practicable after they have begun it.

(3) This paragraph does not require the supervisory body to give notice to any person who has requested the review.

Starting a review

109 To start a review of the standard authorisation, the supervisory body must decide which, if any, of the qualifying requirements appear to be reviewable.

No reviewable qualifying requirements

110(1) This paragraph applies if no qualifying requirements appear to be reviewable.

(2) This Part does not require the supervisory body to take any action in respect of the standard authorisation.

One or more reviewable qualifying requirements

111(1) This paragraph applies if one or more qualifying requirements appear to be reviewable.

(2) The supervisory body must secure that a separate review assessment is carried out in relation to each qualifying requirement which appears to be reviewable.

(3) But sub-paragraph (2) does not require the supervisory body to secure that a best interests review assessment is carried out in a case where the best interests requirement appears to the supervisory body to be non-assessable.

(4) The best interests requirement is non-assessable if—

  (a) the requirement is reviewable only on the variation of conditions ground, and

  (b) the change in the relevant person's case is not significant.

(5) In making any decision whether the change in the relevant person's case is significant, regard must be had to—

  (a) the nature of the change, and

  (b) the period that the change is likely to last for.

Review assessments

112(1) A review assessment is an assessment of whether the relevant person meets a qualifying requirement.

(2) In relation to a review assessment—

  (a) a negative conclusion is a conclusion that the relevant person does not meet the qualifying requirement to which the assessment relates;

  (b) a positive conclusion is a conclusion that the relevant person meets the qualifying requirement to which the assessment relates.

(3) An age review assessment is a review assessment carried out in relation to the age requirement.

(4) A mental health review assessment is a review assessment carried out in relation to the mental health requirement.

(5) A mental capacity review assessment is a review assessment carried out in relation to the mental capacity requirement.

(6) A best interests review assessment is a review assessment carried out in relation to the best interests requirement.

(7) An eligibility review assessment is a review assessment carried out in relation to the eligibility requirement.

(8) A no refusals review assessment is a review assessment carried out in relation to the no refusals requirement.

113(1) In carrying out a review assessment, the assessor must comply with any duties which would be imposed upon him under Part 4 if the assessment were being carried out in connection with a request for a standard authorisation.

(2) But in the case of a best interests review assessment, paragraphs 43 and 44 do not apply.

(3) Instead of what is required by paragraph 43, the best interests review assessment must include recommendations about whether—and, if so, how—it would be appropriate to vary the conditions to which the standard authorisation is subject.

Best interests requirement reviewable but non-assessable

114(1) This paragraph applies in a case where—
- (a) the best interests requirement appears to be reviewable, but
- (b) in accordance with paragraph 111(3), the supervisory body are not required to secure that a best interests review assessment is carried out.

(2) The supervisory body may vary the conditions to which the standard authorisation is subject in such ways (if any) as the supervisory body think are appropriate in the circumstances.

Best interests review assessment positive

115(1) This paragraph applies in a case where—
- (a) a best interests review assessment is carried out, and
- (b) the assessment comes to a positive conclusion.

(2) The supervisory body must decide the following questions—
- (a) whether or not the best interests requirement is reviewable on the change of reason ground;
- (b) whether or not the best interests requirement is reviewable on the variation of conditions ground;
- (c) if so, whether or not the change in the person's case is significant.

(3) If the supervisory body decide that the best interests requirement is reviewable on the change of reason ground, they must vary the standard authorisation so that it states the reason why the relevant person now meets that requirement

(4) If the supervisory body decide that—
- (a) the best interests requirement is reviewable on the variation of conditions ground, and
- (b) the change in the relevant person's case is not significant,

they may vary the conditions to which the standard authorisation is subject in such ways (if any) as they think are appropriate in the circumstances.

(5) If the supervisory body decide that—
- (a) the best interests requirement is reviewable on the variation of conditions ground, and
- (b) the change in the relevant person's case is significant,

they must vary the conditions to which the standard authorisation is subject in such ways as they think are appropriate in the circumstances.

(6) If the supervisory body decide that the best interests requirement is not reviewable on—
- (a) the change of reason ground, or
- (b) the variation of conditions ground,

this Part does not require the supervisory body to take any action in respect of the standard authorisation so far as the best interests requirement relates to it.

Mental health, mental capacity, eligibility or no refusals review assessment positive

116(1) This paragraph applies if the following conditions are met.

(2) The first condition is that one or more of the following are carried out—
- (a) a mental health review assessment;
- (b) a mental capacity review assessment;
- (c) an eligibility review assessment;
- (d) a no refusals review assessment.

(3) The second condition is that each assessment carried out comes to a positive conclusion.

(4) The supervisory body must decide whether or not each of the assessed qualifying requirements is reviewable on the change of reason ground.

(5) If the supervisory body decide that any of the assessed qualifying requirements is reviewable on the change of reason ground, they must vary the standard authorisation so that it states the reason why the relevant person now meets the requirement or requirements in question.

(6) If the supervisory body decide that none of the assessed qualifying requirements are reviewable on the change of reason ground, this Part does not require the supervisory body to take any action in respect of the standard authorisation so far as those requirements relate to it.

(7) An assessed qualifying requirement is a qualifying requirement in relation to which a review assessment is carried out.

One or more review assessments negative

117(1) This paragraph applies if one or more of the review assessments carried out comes to a negative conclusion.

(2) The supervisory body must terminate the standard authorisation with immediate effect.

Completion of a review

118(1) The review of the standard authorisation is complete in any of the following cases.

(2) The first case is where paragraph 110 applies.

(3) The second case is where—
  (a) paragraph 111 applies, and
  (b) paragraph 117 requires the supervisory body to terminate the standard authorisation.

(4) In such a case, the supervisory body need not comply with any of the other provisions of paragraphs 114 to 116 which would be applicable to the review (were it not for this sub-paragraph).

(5) The third case is where—
  (a) paragraph 111 applies,
  (b) paragraph 117 does not require the supervisory body to terminate the standard authorisation, and
  (c) the supervisory body comply with all of the provisions of paragraphs 114 to 116 (so far as they are applicable to the review).

Variations under this Part

119 Any variation of the standard authorisation made under this Part must be in writing.

Notice of outcome of review

120(1) When the review of the standard authorisation is complete, the supervisory body must give notice to all of the following—
  (a) the managing authority of the relevant hospital or care home;
  (b) the relevant person;
  (c) the relevant person's representative;
  (d) any section 39D IMCA.

(2) That notice must state—
  (a) the outcome of the review, and
  (b) what variation (if any) has been made to the authorisation under this Part.

Records

121 A supervisory body must keep a written record of the following information—
  (a) each request for a review that is made to them;
  (b) the outcome of each request;
  (c) each review which they carry out;
  (d) the outcome of each review which they carry out;
  (e) any variation of an authorisation made in consequence of a review.

Relationship between review and suspension under Part 6

122(1) This paragraph applies if a standard authorisation is suspended in accordance with Part 6.
(2) No review may be requested under this Part whilst the standard authorisation is suspended.
(3) If a review has already been requested, or is being carried out, when the standard authorisation is suspended, no steps are to be taken in connection with that review whilst the authorisation is suspended.

Relationship between review and request for new authorisation

123(1) This paragraph applies if, in accordance with paragraph 24 (as read with paragraph 29), the managing authority of the relevant hospital or care home make a request for a new standard authorisation which would be in force after the expiry of the existing authorisation.
(2) No review may be requested under this Part until the request for the new standard authorisation has been disposed of.
(3) If a review has already been requested, or is being carried out, when the new standard authorisation is requested, no steps are to be taken in connection with that review until the request for the new standard authorisation has been disposed of.

124(1) This paragraph applies if—
  (a) a review under this Part has been requested, or is being carried out, and
  (b) the managing authority of the relevant hospital or care home make a request under paragraph 30 for a new standard authorisation which would be in force on or before, and after, the expiry of the existing authorisation.
(2) No steps are to be taken in connection with the review under this Part until the request for the new standard authorisation has been disposed of.

125 In paragraphs 123 and 124—
  (a) the existing authorisation is the authorisation referred to in paragraph 101;
  (b) the expiry of the existing authorisation is the time when it is expected to cease to be in force.

PART 9
ASSESSMENTS UNDER THIS SCHEDULE

Introduction

126 This Part contains provision about assessments under this Schedule.
127 An assessment under this Schedule is either of the following—
  (a) an assessment carried out in connection with a request for a standard authorisation under Part 4;
  (b) a review assessment carried out in connection with a review of a standard authorisation under Part 8.

128 In this Part, in relation to an assessment under this Schedule—

'assessor' means the person carrying out the assessment;

'relevant procedure' means—

(a) the request for the standard authorisation, or

(b) the review of the standard authorisation;

'supervisory body' means the supervisory body responsible for securing that the assessment is carried out.

Supervisory body to select assessor

129(1) It is for the supervisory body to select a person to carry out an assessment under this Schedule.

(2) The supervisory body must not select a person to carry out an assessment unless the person—

(a) appears to the supervisory body to be suitable to carry out the assessment (having regard, in particular, to the type of assessment and the person to be assessed), and

(b) is eligible to carry out the assessment.

(3) Regulations may make provision about the selection, and eligibility, of persons to carry out assessments under this Schedule.

(4) Sub-paragraphs (5) and (6) apply if two or more assessments are to be obtained for the purposes of the relevant procedure.

(5) In a case where the assessments to be obtained include a mental health assessment and a best interests assessment, the supervisory body must not select the same person to carry out both assessments.

(6) Except as prohibited by sub-paragraph (5), the supervisory body may select the same person to carry out any number of the assessments which the person appears to be suitable, and is eligible, to carry out.

130(1) This paragraph applies to regulations under paragraph 129(3).

(2) The regulations may make provision relating to a person's—

(a) qualifications,

(b) skills,

(c) training,

(d) experience,

(e) relationship to, or connection with, the relevant person or any other person,

(f) involvement in the care or treatment of the relevant person,

(g) connection with the supervisory body, or

(h) connection with the relevant hospital or care home, or with any other establishment or undertaking.

(3) The provision that the regulations may make in relation to a person's training may provide for particular training to be specified by the appropriate authority otherwise than in the regulations.

(4) In sub-paragraph (3) the 'appropriate authority' means—

(a) in relation to England: the Secretary of State;

(b) in relation to Wales: the National Assembly for Wales.

(5) The regulations may make provision requiring a person to be insured in respect of liabilities that may arise in connection with the carrying out of an assessment.

(6) In relation to cases where two or more assessments are to be obtained for the purposes of the relevant procedure, the regulations may limit the number, kind or combination of assessments which a particular person is eligible to carry out.

(7) Sub-paragraphs (2) to (6) do not limit the generality of the provision that may be made in the regulations.

Examination and copying of records

131 An assessor may, at all reasonable times, examine and take copies of—
  (a) any health record,
  (b) any record of, or held by, a local authority and compiled in accordance with a social services function, and
  (c) any record held by a person registered under Part 2 of the Care Standards Act 2000,
  which the assessor considers may be relevant to the assessment which is being carried out.

Representations

132 In carrying out an assessment under this Schedule, the assessor must take into account any information given, or submissions made, by any of the following—
  (a) the relevant person's representative;
  (b) any section 39A IMCA;
  (c) any section 39C IMCA
  (d) any section 39D IMCA.

Assessments to stop if any comes to negative conclusion

133(1) This paragraph applies if an assessment under this Schedule comes to the conclusion that the relevant person does not meet one of the qualifying requirements.
(2) This Schedule does not require the supervisory body to secure that any other assessments under this Schedule are carried out in relation to the relevant procedure.
(3) The supervisory body must give notice to any assessor who is carrying out another assessment in connection with the relevant procedure that they are to cease carrying out that assessment.
(4) If an assessor receives such notice, this Schedule does not require the assessor to continue carrying out that assessment.

Duty to keep records and give copies

134(1) This paragraph applies if an assessor has carried out an assessment under this Schedule (whatever conclusions the assessment has come to).
(2) The assessor must keep a written record of the assessment.
(3) As soon as practicable after carrying out the assessment, the assessor must give copies of the assessment to the supervisory body.
135(1) This paragraph applies to the supervisory body if they are given a copy of an assessment under this Schedule.
(2) The supervisory body must give copies of the assessment to all of the following—
  (a) the managing authority of the relevant hospital or care home;
  (b) the relevant person;
  (c) any section 39A IMCA;
  (d) the relevant person's representative.
(3) If—
  (a) the assessment is obtained in relation to a request for a standard authorisation, and
  (b) the supervisory body are required by paragraph 50(1) to give the standard authorisation,
  the supervisory body must give the copies of the assessment when they give copies of the authorisation in accordance with paragraph 57.

(4) If—
- (a) the assessment is obtained in relation to a request for a standard authorisation, and
- (b) the supervisory body are prohibited by paragraph 50(2) from giving the standard authorisation,

the supervisory body must give the copies of the assessment when they give notice in accordance with paragraph 58.

(5) If the assessment is obtained in connection with the review of a standard authorisation, the supervisory body must give the copies of the assessment when they give notice in accordance with paragraph 120.

136(1) This paragraph applies to the supervisory body if—
- (a) they are given a copy of a best interests assessment, and
- (b) the assessment includes, in accordance with paragraph 44(2), a statement that it appears to the assessor that there is an unauthorised deprivation of liberty.

(2) The supervisory body must notify all of the persons listed in sub-paragraph (3) that the assessment includes such a statement.

(3) Those persons are—
- (a) the managing authority of the relevant hospital or care home;
- (b) the relevant parties;
- (c) any section 39A IMCA
- (d) any interested person consulted by the best interests assessor.

(4) The supervisory body must comply with this paragraph when (or at some time before) they comply with paragraph 135.

PART 10
RELEVANT PERSON'S REPRESENTATIVE

The representative

137 In this Schedule the relevant person's representative is the person appointed as such in accordance with this Part.

138(1) Regulations may make provision about the selection and appointment of representatives.

(2) In this Part such regulations are referred to as 'appointment regulations'.

Supervisory body to appoint representative

139(1) The supervisory body must appoint a person to be the relevant person's representative as soon as practicable after a standard authorisation is given.

(2) The supervisory body must appoint a person to be the relevant person's representative if a vacancy arises whilst a standard authorisation is in force.

(3) Where a vacancy arises, the appointment under sub-paragraph (2) is to be made as soon as practicable after the supervisory body becomes aware of the vacancy.

140(1) The selection of a person for appointment under paragraph 139 must not be made unless it appears to the person making the selection that the prospective representative would, if appointed—
- (a) maintain contact with the relevant person,
- (b) represent the relevant person in matters relating to or connected with this Schedule, and
- (c) support the relevant person in matters relating to or connected with this Schedule.

141(1) Any appointment of a representative for a relevant person is in addition to, and does not affect, any appointment of a donee or deputy.

(2) The functions of any representative are in addition to, and do not affect—

    (a) the authority of any donee,

    (b) the powers of any deputy, or

    (c) any powers of the court.

Appointment regulations

142 Appointment regulations may provide that the procedure for appointing a representative may begin at any time after a request for a standard authorisation is made (including a time before the request has been disposed of).

143(1) Appointment regulations may make provision about who is to select a person for appointment as a representative.

    (2) But regulations under this paragraph may only provide for the following to make a selection—

        (a) the relevant person, if he has capacity in relation to the question of which person should be his representative;

        (b) a donee of a lasting power of attorney granted by the relevant person, if it is within the scope of his authority to select a person;

        (c) a deputy, if it is within the scope of his authority to select a person;

        (d) a best interests assessor;

        (e) the supervisory body.

    (3) Regulations under this paragraph may provide that a selection by the relevant person, a donee or a deputy is subject to approval by a best interests assessor or the supervisory body.

    (4) Regulations under this paragraph may provide that, if more than one selection is necessary in connection with the appointment of a particular representative—

        (a) the same person may make more than one selection;

        (b) different persons may make different selections.

    (5) For the purposes of this paragraph a best interests assessor is a person carrying out a best interests assessment in connection with the standard authorisation in question (including the giving of that authorisation).

144(1) Appointment regulations may make provision about who may, or may not, be—

    (a) selected for appointment as a representative, or

    (b) appointed as a representative.

    (2) Regulations under this paragraph may relate to any of the following matters—

        (a) a person's age;

        (b) a person's suitability;

        (c) a person's independence;

        (d) a person's willingness;

        (e) a person's qualifications.

145 Appointment regulations may make provision about the formalities of appointing a person as a representative.

146 In a case where a best interests assessor is to select a person to be appointed as a representative, appointment regulations may provide for the variation of the assessor's duties in relation to the assessment which he is carrying out.

Monitoring of representatives

147 Regulations may make provision requiring the managing authority of the relevant hospital or care home to—

    (a) monitor, and

(b) report to the supervisory body on,

the extent to which a representative is maintaining contact with the relevant person.

Termination

148 Regulations may make provision about the circumstances in which the appointment of a person as the relevant person's representative ends or may be ended.

149 Regulations may make provision about the formalities of ending the appointment of a person as a representative.

Suspension of representative's functions

150(1) Regulations may make provision about the circumstances in which functions exercisable by, or in relation to, the relevant person's representative (whether under this Schedule or not) may be—
(a) suspended, and
(b) if suspended, revived.
(2) The regulations may make provision about the formalities for giving effect to the suspension or revival of a function.
(3) The regulations may make provision about the effect of the suspension or revival of a function.

Payment of representative

151 Regulations may make provision for payments to be made to, or in relation to, persons exercising functions as the relevant person's representative.

Regulations under this Part

152 The provisions of this Part which specify provision that may be made in regulations under this Part do not affect the generality of the power to make such regulations.

Effect of appointment of section 39C IMCA

153 Paragraphs 159 and 160 make provision about the exercise of functions by, or towards, the relevant person's representative during periods when—
(a) no person is appointed as the relevant person's representative, but
(b) a person is appointed as a section 39C IMCA.

PART 11
IMCAS

Application of Part

154 This Part applies for the purposes of this Schedule.

The IMCAs

155 A section 39A IMCA is an independent mental capacity advocate appointed under section 39A.

156 A section 39C IMCA is an independent mental capacity advocate appointed under section 39C.

157 A section 39D IMCA is an independent mental capacity advocate appointed under section 39D.

158 An IMCA is a section 39A IMCA or a section 39C IMCA or a section 39D IMCA.

Section 39C IMCA: functions

159(1) This paragraph applies if, and for as long as, there is a section 39C IMCA.

(2) In the application of the relevant provisions, references to the relevant person's representative are to be read as references to the section 39C IMCA.

(3) But sub-paragraph (2) does not apply to any function under the relevant provisions for as long as the function is suspended in accordance with provision made under Part 10.

(4) In this paragraph and paragraph 160 the relevant provisions are—

(a) paragraph 102(3)(b) (request for review under Part 8);

(b) paragraph 108(1)(b) (notice of review under Part 8);

(c) paragraph 120(1)(c) (notice of outcome of review under Part 8).

160(1) This paragraph applies if—

(a) a person is appointed as the relevant person's representative, and

(b) a person accordingly ceases to hold an appointment as a section 39C IMCA.

(2) Where a function under a relevant provision has been exercised by, or towards, the section 39C IMCA, there is no requirement for that function to be exercised again by, or towards, the relevant person's representative.

Section 39A IMCA: restriction of functions

161(1) This paragraph applies if—

(a) there is a section 39A IMCA, and

(b) a person is appointed under Part 10 to be the relevant person's representative (whether or not that person, or any person subsequently appointed, is currently the relevant person's representative).

(2) The duties imposed on, and the powers exercisable by, the section 39A IMCA do not apply.

(3) The duties imposed on, and the powers exercisable by, any other person do not apply, so far as they fall to be performed or exercised towards the section 39A IMCA.

(4) But sub-paragraph (2) does not apply to any power of challenge exercisable by the section 39A IMCA.

(5) And sub-paragraph (3) does not apply to any duty or power of any other person so far as it relates to any power of challenge exercisable by the section 39A IMCA.

(6) Before exercising any power of challenge, the section 39A IMCA must take the views of the relevant person's representative into account.

(7) A power of challenge is a power to make an application to the court to exercise its jurisdiction under section 21A in connection with the giving of the standard authorisation.

PART 12

MISCELLANEOUS

Monitoring of operation of Schedule

162(1) Regulations may make provision for, and in connection with, requiring one or more prescribed bodies to monitor, and report on, the operation of this Schedule in relation to England.

(2) The regulations may, in particular, give a prescribed body authority to do one or more of the following things—

(a) to visit hospitals and care homes;

(b) to visit and interview persons accommodated in hospitals and care homes;

(c) to require the production of, and to inspect, records relating to the care or treatment of persons.

(3) 'Prescribed' means prescribed in regulations under this paragraph.

163(1) Regulations may make provision for, and in connection with, enabling the National Assembly for Wales to monitor, and report on, the operation of this Schedule in relation to Wales.

(2) The National Assembly may direct one or more persons or bodies to carry out the Assembly's functions under regulations under this paragraph.

Disclosure of information

164(1) Regulations may require either or both of the following to disclose prescribed information to prescribed bodies—

(a) supervisory bodies;

(b) managing authorities of hospitals or care homes.

(2) 'Prescribed' means prescribed in regulations under this paragraph.

(3) Regulations under this paragraph may only prescribe information relating to matters with which this Schedule is concerned.

Directions by National Assembly in relation to supervisory functions

165(1) The National Assembly for Wales may direct a Local Health Board to exercise in relation to its area any supervisory functions which are specified in the direction.

(2) Directions under this paragraph must not preclude the National Assembly from exercising the functions specified in the directions.

(3) In this paragraph 'supervisory functions' means functions which the National Assembly have as supervisory body, so far as they are exercisable in relation to hospitals (whether NHS or independent hospitals, and whether in Wales or England).

166(1) This paragraph applies where, under paragraph 165, a Local Health Board ('the specified LHB') is directed to exercise supervisory functions ('delegated functions').

(2) The National Assembly for Wales may give directions to the specified LHB about the Board's exercise of delegated functions.

(3) The National Assembly may give directions for any delegated functions to be exercised, on behalf of the specified LHB, by a committee, sub-committee or officer of that Board.

(4) The National Assembly may give directions providing for any delegated functions to be exercised by the specified LHB jointly with one or more other Local Health Boards.

(5) Where, under sub-paragraph (4), delegated functions are exercisable jointly, the National Assembly may give directions providing for the functions to be exercised, on behalf of the Local Health Boards in question, by a joint committee or joint subcommittee.

167(1) Directions under paragraph 165 must be given in regulations.

(2) Directions under paragraph 166 may be given—

(a) in regulations, or

(b) by instrument in writing.

168 The power under paragraph 165 or paragraph 166 to give directions includes power to vary or revoke directions given under that paragraph.

Notices

169 Any notice under this Schedule must be in writing.

Regulations

170(1) This paragraph applies to all regulations under this Schedule, except regulations under paragraph 162, 163, 167 or 183.

(2) It is for the Secretary of State to make such regulations in relation to authorisations under this Schedule which relate to hospitals and care homes situated in England.

(3) It is for the National Assembly for Wales to make such regulations in relation to authorisations under this Schedule which relate to hospitals and care homes situated in Wales.

171 It is for the Secretary of State to make regulations under paragraph 162.

172 It is for the National Assembly for Wales to make regulations under paragraph 163 or 167.

173(1) This paragraph applies to regulations under paragraph 183.

(2) It is for the Secretary of State to make such regulations in relation to cases where a question as to the ordinary residence of a person is to be determined by the Secretary of State.

(3) It is for the National Assembly for Wales to make such regulations in relation to cases where a question as to the ordinary residence of a person is to be determined by the National Assembly.

PART 13
INTERPRETATION

Introduction

174 This Part applies for the purposes of this Schedule.

Hospitals and their managing authorities

175(1) 'Hospital' means—
  (a) an NHS hospital, or
  (b) an independent hospital.

(2) 'NHS hospital' means—
  (a) a health service hospital as defined by section 275 of the National Health Service Act 2006 or section 206 of the National Health Service (Wales) Act 2006, or
  (b) a hospital as defined by section 206 of the National Health Service (Wales) Act 2006 vested in a Local Health Board.

(3) 'Independent hospital' means a hospital as defined by section 2 of the Care Standards Act 2000 which is not an NHS hospital.

176(1) 'Managing authority', in relation to an NHS hospital, means—
  (a) if the hospital—
    (i) is vested in the appropriate national authority for the purposes of its functions under the National Health Service Act 2006 or of the National Health Service (Wales) Act 2006, or
    (ii) consists of any accommodation provided by a local authority and used as a hospital by or on behalf of the appropriate national authority under either of those Acts,
    the Primary Care Trust, Strategic Health Authority, Local Health Board or Special Health Authority responsible for the administration of the hospital;

(b) if the hospital is vested in a Primary Care Trust, National Health Service trust or NHS foundation trust, that trust;

(c) if the hospital is vested in a Local Health Board, that Board.

(2) For this purpose the appropriate national authority is—

(a) in relation to England: the Secretary of State;

(b) in relation to Wales: the National Assembly for Wales;

(c) in relation to England and Wales: the Secretary of State and the National Assembly acting jointly.

177 'Managing authority', in relation to an independent hospital, means the person registered, or required to be registered, under Part 2 of the Care Standards Act 2000 in respect of the hospital.

Care homes and their managing authorities

178 'Care home' has the meaning given by section 3 of the Care Standards Act 2000.

179 'Managing authority', in relation to a care home, means the person registered, or required to be registered, under Part 2 of the Care Standards Act 2000 in respect of the care home.

Supervisory bodies: hospitals

180(1) The identity of the supervisory body is determined under this paragraph in cases where the relevant hospital is situated in England.

(2) If a Primary Care Trust commissions the relevant care or treatment, that Trust is the supervisory body.

(3) If the National Assembly for Wales or a Local Health Board commission the relevant care or treatment, the National Assembly are the supervisory body.

(4) In any other case, the supervisory body are the Primary Care Trust for the area in which the relevant hospital is situated.

(5) If a hospital is situated in the areas of two (or more) Primary Care Trusts, it is to be regarded for the purposes of sub-paragraph (4) as situated in whichever of the areas the greater (or greatest) part of the hospital is situated.

181(1) The identity of the supervisory body is determined under this paragraph in cases where the relevant hospital is situated in Wales.

(2) The National Assembly for Wales are the supervisory body.

(3) But if a Primary Care Trust commissions the relevant care or treatment, that Trust is the supervisory body.

Supervisory bodies: care homes

182(1) The identity of the supervisory body is determined under this paragraph in cases where the relevant care home is situated in England or in Wales.

(2) The supervisory body are the local authority for the area in which the relevant person is ordinarily resident.

(3) But if the relevant person is not ordinarily resident in the area of a local authority, the supervisory body are the local authority for the area in which the care home is situated.

(4) In relation to England 'local authority' means—

(a) the council of a county;

(b) the council of a district for which there is no county council;

(c) the council of a London borough;

(d) the Common Council of the City of London;

(e) the Council of the Isles of Scilly.

(5) In relation to Wales 'local authority' means the council of a county or county borough.

(6) If a care home is situated in the areas of two (or more) local authorities, it is to be regarded for the purposes of sub-paragraph (3) as situated in whichever of the areas the greater (or greatest) part of the care home is situated.

183(1) Subsections (5) and (6) of section 24 of the National Assistance Act 1948 (deemed place of ordinary residence) apply to any determination of where a person is ordinarily resident for the purposes of paragraph 182 as those subsections apply to such a determination for the purposes specified in those subsections.

(2) In the application of section 24(6) of the 1948 Act by virtue of subparagraph (1), section 24(6) is to be read as if it referred to a hospital vested in a Local Health Board as well as to hospitals vested in the Secretary of State and the other bodies mentioned in section 24(6).

(3) Any question arising as to the ordinary residence of a person is to be determined by the Secretary of State or by the National Assembly for Wales.

(4) The Secretary of State and the National Assembly must make and publish arrangements for determining which cases are to be dealt with by the Secretary of State and which are to be dealt with by the National Assembly.

(5) Those arrangements may include provision for the Secretary of State and the National Assembly to agree, in relation to any question that has arisen, which of them is to deal with the case.

(6) Regulations may make provision about arrangements that are to have effect before, upon, or after the determination of any question as to the ordinary residence of a person.

(7) The regulations may, in particular, authorise or require a local authority to do any or all of the following things—

(a) to act as supervisory body even though it may wish to dispute that it is the supervisory body;

(b) to become the supervisory body in place of another local authority;

(c) to recover from another local authority expenditure incurred in exercising functions as the supervisory body.

Same body managing authority and supervisory body

184(1) This paragraph applies if, in connection with a particular person's detention as a resident in a hospital or care home, the same body are both—

(a) the managing authority of the relevant hospital or care home, and

(b) the supervisory body.

(2) The fact that a single body are acting in both capacities does not prevent the body from carrying out functions under this Schedule in each capacity.

(3) But, in such a case, this Schedule has effect subject to any modifications contained in regulations that may be made for this purpose.

Interested persons

185 Each of the following is an interested person—

(a) the relevant person's spouse or civil partner;

(b) where the relevant person and another person of the opposite sex are not married to each other but are living together as husband and wife: the other person;

(c) where the relevant person and another person of the same sex are not civil partners of each other but are living together as if they were civil partners: the other person;

(d) the relevant person's children and step-children;

(e) the relevant person's parents and step-parents;

(f) the relevant person's brothers and sisters, half-brothers and half-sisters, and stepbrothers and stepsisters;

(g) the relevant person's grandparents;

(h) a deputy appointed for the relevant person by the court;

(i) a donee of a lasting power of attorney granted by the relevant person.

186(1) An interested person consulted by the best interests assessor is any person whose name is stated in the relevant best interests assessment in accordance with paragraph 40 (interested persons whom the assessor consulted in carrying out the assessment).

(2) The relevant best interests assessment is the most recent best interests assessment carried out in connection with the standard authorisation in question (whether the assessment was carried out under Part 4 or Part 8).

186 Where this Schedule imposes on a person a duty towards an interested person, the duty does not apply if the person on whom the duty is imposed—

(a) is not aware of the interested person's identity or of a way of contacting him, and

(b) cannot reasonably ascertain it.

187 The following table contains an index of provisions defining or otherwise explaining expressions used in this Schedule—

age assessment	paragraph 34
age requirement	paragraph 13
age review assessment	paragraph 112(3)
appointment regulations	paragraph 138
assessment under this Schedule	paragraph 127
assessor (except in Part 9)	paragraph 33
assessor (in Part 9)	paragraphs 33 and 128
authorisation under this Schedule	paragraph 10
best interests (determination of)	section 4
best interests assessment	paragraph 38
best interests requirement	paragraph 16
best interests review assessment	paragraph 112(6)
care home	paragraph 178
change of reason ground	paragraph 106
complete (in relation to a review of a standard authorisation)	paragraph 118
deprivation of a person's liberty	section 64(5) and (6)
deputy	section 16(2)(b)
detained resident	paragraph 6
disposed of (in relation to a request for a standard authorisation)	paragraph 66
eligibility assessment	paragraph 46
eligibility requirement	paragraph 17
eligibility review assessment	paragraph 112(7)
eligible person (in relation to paragraphs 68 to 73)	paragraph 68
eligible person (in relation to Part 8)	paragraph 102(3)
expiry (in relation to an existing authorisation)	paragraph 125(b)
existing authorisation (in Part 8)	paragraph 125(a)
hospital	paragraph 175
IMCA	paragraph 158
in force (in relation to a standard authorisation)	paragraphs 63 and 64

in force (in relation to an urgent authorisation)	paragraphs 88 and 89
ineligible (in relation to the eligibility requirement)	Schedule 1A
interested person	paragraph 185
interested person consulted by the best interests assessor	paragraph 186
lack of capacity	section 2
lasting power of attorney	section 9
managing authority (in relation to a care home)	paragraph 179
managing authority (in relation to a hospital)	paragraph 176 or 177
maximum authorisation period	paragraph 42
mental capacity assessment	paragraph 37
mental capacity requirement	paragraph 15
mental capacity review assessment	paragraph 112(5)
mental health assessment	paragraph 35
mental health requirement	paragraph 14
mental health review assessment	paragraph 112(4)
negative conclusion	paragraph 112(2)(a)
new supervisory body	paragraph 99(b)
no refusals assessment	paragraph 48
no refusals requirement	paragraph 18
no refusals review assessment	paragraph 112(8)
non-qualification ground	paragraph 105
old supervisory body	paragraph 99(a)
positive conclusion	paragraph 112(2)(b)
purpose of a standard authorisation	paragraph 11(1)
purpose of an urgent authorisation	paragraph 11(2)
qualifying requirements	paragraph 12
refusal (for the purposes of the no refusals requirement)	paragraphs 19 and 20
relevant care or treatment	paragraph 7
relevant hospital or care home	paragraph 7
relevant managing authority	paragraph 26(4)
relevant person	paragraph 7
relevant person's representative	paragraph 137
relevant procedure	paragraph 128
review assessment	paragraph 112(1)
reviewable	paragraph 104
section 39A IMCA	paragraph 155
section 39C IMCA	paragraph 156
section 39D IMCA	paragraph 157
standard authorisation	paragraph 8
supervisory body (except in Part 9)	paragraph 180, 181 or 182
supervisory body (in Part 9)	paragraph 128 and paragraph 180, 181 or 182
unauthorised deprivation of liberty (in relation to paragraphs 68 to 73)	paragraph 67
urgent authorisation	paragraph 9
variation of conditions ground	paragraph 107]

[*Schedule A1 inserted by section 50(5) and Schedule 7 to the 2007 Act.*]

SCHEDULE 1
LASTING POWERS OF ATTORNEY: FORMALITIES

Section 9

PART 1
MAKING INSTRUMENTS

General requirements as to making instruments

1(1) An instrument is not made in accordance with this Schedule unless—

(a) it is in the prescribed form,

(b) it complies with paragraph 2, and

(c) any prescribed requirements in connection with its execution are satisfied.

(2) Regulations may make different provision according to whether—

(a) the instrument relates to personal welfare or to property and affairs (or to both);

(b) only one or more than one donee is to be appointed (and if more than one, whether jointly or jointly and severally).

(3) In this Schedule—

(a) 'prescribed' means prescribed by regulations, and

(b) 'regulations' means regulations made for the purposes of this Schedule by the Lord Chancellor.

Requirements as to content of instruments

2(1) The instrument must include—

(a) the prescribed information about the purpose of the instrument and the effect of a lasting power of attorney,

(b) a statement by the donor to the effect that he—

(i) has read the prescribed information or a prescribed part of it (or has had it read to him), and

(ii) intends the authority conferred under the instrument to include authority to make decisions on his behalf in circumstances where he no longer has capacity,

(c) a statement by the donor—

(i) naming a person or persons whom the donor wishes to be notified of any application for the registration of the instrument, or

(ii) stating that there are no persons whom he wishes to be notified of any such application,

(d) a statement by the donee (or, if more than one, each of them) to the effect that he—

(i) has read the prescribed information or a prescribed part of it (or has had it read to him), and

(ii) understands the duties imposed on a donee of a lasting power of attorney under sections 1 (the principles) and 4 (best interests), and

(e) a certificate by a person of a prescribed description that, in his opinion, at the time when the donor executes the instrument—

(i) the donor understands the purpose of the instrument and the scope of the authority conferred under it,

(ii) no fraud or undue pressure is being used to induce the donor to create a lasting power of attorney, and

(iii) there is nothing else which would prevent a lasting power of attorney from being created by the instrument.

(2) Regulations may—
  (a) prescribe a maximum number of named persons;
  (b) provide that, where the instrument includes a statement under subparagraph (1)(c)(ii), two persons of a prescribed description must each give a certificate under sub-paragraph (1)(e).

(3) The persons who may be named persons do not include a person who is appointed as donee under the instrument.

(4) In this Schedule, 'named person' means a person named under subparagraph (1)(c).

(5) A certificate under sub-paragraph (1)(e)—
  (a) must be made in the prescribed form, and
  (b) must include any prescribed information.

(6) The certificate may not be given by a person appointed as donee under the instrument.

Failure to comply with prescribed form

3(1) If an instrument differs in an immaterial respect in form or mode of expression from the prescribed form, it is to be treated by the Public Guardian as sufficient in point of form and expression.

(2) The court may declare that an instrument which is not in the prescribed form is to be treated as if it were, if it is satisfied that the persons executing the instrument intended it to create a lasting power of attorney.

PART 2
REGISTRATION

Applications and procedure for registration

4(1) An application to the Public Guardian for the registration of an instrument intended to create a lasting power of attorney—
  (a) must be made in the prescribed form, and
  (b) must include any prescribed information.

(2) The application may be made—
  (a) by the donor,
  (b) by the donee or donees, or
  (c) if the instrument appoints two or more donees to act jointly and severally in respect of any matter, by any of the donees.

(3) The application must be accompanied by—
  (a) the instrument, and
  (b) any fee provided for under section 58(4)(b).

(4) A person who, in an application for registration, makes a statement which he knows to be false in a material particular is guilty of an offence and is liable—
  (a) on summary conviction, to imprisonment for a term not exceeding 12 months or a fine not exceeding the statutory maximum or both;
  (b) on conviction on indictment, to imprisonment for a term not exceeding 2 years or a fine or both.

5 Subject to paragraphs 11 to 14, the Public Guardian must register the instrument as a lasting power of attorney at the end of the prescribed period.

Notification requirements

6(1) A donor about to make an application under paragraph 4(2)(a) must notify any named persons that he is about to do so.

(2) The donee (or donees) about to make an application under paragraph 4(2)(b) or (c) must notify any named persons that he is (or they are) about to do so.

7   As soon as is practicable after receiving an application by the donor under paragraph 4(2)(a), the Public Guardian must notify the donee (or donees) that the application has been received.

8(1) As soon as is practicable after receiving an application by a donee (or donees) under paragraph 4(2)(b), the Public Guardian must notify the donor that the application has been received.

(2) As soon as is practicable after receiving an application by a donee under paragraph 4(2)(c), the Public Guardian must notify—

(a) the donor, and

(b) the donee or donees who did not join in making the application,

that the application has been received.

9(1) A notice under paragraph 6 must be made in the prescribed form.

(2) A notice under paragraph 6, 7 or 8 must include such information, if any, as may be prescribed.

Power to dispense with notification requirements

10 The court may—

(a) on the application of the donor, dispense with the requirement to notify under paragraph 6(1), or

(b) on the application of the donee or donees concerned, dispense with the requirement to notify under paragraph 6(2),

if satisfied that no useful purpose would be served by giving the notice.

Instrument not made properly or containing ineffective provision

11(1) If it appears to the Public Guardian that an instrument accompanying an application under paragraph 4 is not made in accordance with this Schedule, he must not register the instrument unless the court directs him to do so.

(2) Sub-paragraph (3) applies if it appears to the Public Guardian that the instrument contains a provision which—

(a) would be ineffective as part of a lasting power of attorney, or

(b) would prevent the instrument from operating as a valid lasting power of attorney.

(3) The Public Guardian—

(a) must apply to the court for it to determine the matter under section 23(1), and

(b) pending the determination by the court, must not register the instrument.

(4) Sub-paragraph (5) applies if the court determines under section 23(1) (whether or not on an application by the Public Guardian) that the instrument contains a provision which—

(a) would be ineffective as part of a lasting power of attorney, or

(b) would prevent the instrument from operating as a valid lasting power of attorney.

(5) The court must—

(a) notify the Public Guardian that it has severed the provision, or

(b) direct him not to register the instrument.

(6) Where the court notifies the Public Guardian that it has severed a provision, he must register the instrument with a note to that effect attached to it.

Deputy already appointed

12(1) Sub-paragraph (2) applies if it appears to the Public Guardian that—
  (a) there is a deputy appointed by the court for the donor, and
  (b) the powers conferred on the deputy would, if the instrument were registered, to any extent conflict with the powers conferred on the attorney.
(2) The Public Guardian must not register the instrument unless the court directs him to do so.

Objection by donee or named person

13(1) Sub-paragraph (2) applies if a donee or a named person—
  (a) receives a notice under paragraph 6, 7 or 8 of an application for the registration of an instrument, and
  (b) before the end of the prescribed period, gives notice to the Public Guardian of an objection to the registration on the ground that an event mentioned in section 13(3) or (6)(a) to (d) has occurred which has revoked the instrument.
(2) If the Public Guardian is satisfied that the ground for making the objection is established, he must not register the instrument unless the court, on the application of the person applying for the registration—
  (a) is satisfied that the ground is not established, and
  (b) directs the Public Guardian to register the instrument.
(3) Sub-paragraph (4) applies if a donee or a named person—
  (a) receives a notice under paragraph 6, 7 or 8 of an application for the registration of an instrument, and
  (b) before the end of the prescribed period—
     (i) makes an application to the court objecting to the registration on a prescribed ground, and
     (ii) notifies the Public Guardian of the application.
(4) The Public Guardian must not register the instrument unless the court directs him to do so.

Objection by donor

14(1) This paragraph applies if the donor—
  (a) receives a notice under paragraph 8 of an application for the registration of an instrument, and
  (b) before the end of the prescribed period, gives notice to the Public Guardian of an objection to the registration.
(2) The Public Guardian must not register the instrument unless the court, on the application of the donee or, if more than one, any of them—
  (a) is satisfied that the donor lacks capacity to object to the registration, and
  (b) directs the Public Guardian to register the instrument.

Notification of registration

15 Where an instrument is registered under this Schedule, the Public Guardian must give notice of the fact in the prescribed form to—

(a) the donor, and

(b) the donee or, if more than one, each of them.

Evidence of registration

16(1) A document purporting to be an office copy of an instrument registered under this Schedule is, in any part of the United Kingdom, evidence of—

(a) the contents of the instrument, and

(b) the fact that it has been registered.

(2) Sub-paragraph (1) is without prejudice to—

(a) section 3 of the Powers of Attorney Act 1971 (c. 27) (proof by certified copy), and

(b) any other method of proof authorised by law.

PART 3
CANCELLATION OF REGISTRATION AND NOTIFICATION OF SEVERANCE

17(1) The Public Guardian must cancel the registration of an instrument as a lasting power of attorney on being satisfied that the power has been revoked—

(a) as a result of the donor's bankruptcy, or

(b) on the occurrence of an event mentioned in section 13(6)(a) to (d).

(2) If the Public Guardian cancels the registration of an instrument he must notify—

(a) the donor, and

(b) the donee or, if more than one, each of them.

18 The court must direct the Public Guardian to cancel the registration of an instrument as a lasting power of attorney if it—

(a) determines under section 22(2)(a) that a requirement for creating the power was not met,

(b) determines under section 22(2)(b) that the power has been revoked or has otherwise come to an end, or

(c) revokes the power under section 22(4)(b) (fraud etc.).

19(1) Sub-paragraph (2) applies if the court determines under section 23(1) that a lasting power of attorney contains a provision which—

(a) is ineffective as part of a lasting power of attorney, or

(b) prevents the instrument from operating as a valid lasting power of attorney.

(2) The court must—

(a) notify the Public Guardian that it has severed the provision, or

(b) direct him to cancel the registration of the instrument as a lasting power of attorney.

20 On the cancellation of the registration of an instrument, the instrument and any office copies of it must be delivered up to the Public Guardian to be cancelled.

PART 4
RECORDS OF ALTERATIONS IN REGISTERED POWERS

Partial revocation or suspension of power as a result of bankruptcy

21 If in the case of a registered instrument it appears to the Public Guardian that under section 13 a lasting power of attorney is revoked, or suspended, in relation to the donor's property and affairs (but not in relation to other matters), the Public Guardian must attach to the instrument a note to that effect.

Termination of appointment of donee which does not revoke power

22 If in the case of a registered instrument it appears to the Public Guardian that an event has occurred—
(a) which has terminated the appointment of the donee, but
(b) which has not revoked the instrument,
the Public Guardian must attach to the instrument a note to that effect.

Replacement of donee

23 If in the case of a registered instrument it appears to the Public Guardian that the donee has been replaced under the terms of the instrument the Public Guardian must attach to the instrument a note to that effect.

Severance of ineffective provisions

24 If in the case of a registered instrument the court notifies the Public Guardian under paragraph 19(2)(a) that it has severed a provision of the instrument, the Public Guardian must attach to it a note to that effect.

Notification of alterations

25 If the Public Guardian attaches a note to an instrument under paragraph 21, 22, 23 or 24 he must give notice of the note to the donee or donees of the power (or, as the case may be, to the other donee or donees of the power).

[SCHEDULE 1A
PERSONS INELIGIBLE TO BE DEPRIVED OF LIBERTY BY THIS ACT

PART 1
INELIGIBLE PERSONS

Application

1 This Schedule applies for the purposes of—
(a) section 16A, and
(b) paragraph 17 of Schedule A1.

Determining ineligibility

2 A person ('P') is ineligible to be deprived of liberty by this Act ('ineligible') if—

    (a) P falls within one of the cases set out in the second column of the following table, and

    (b) the corresponding entry in the third column of the table — or the provision, or one of the provisions, referred to in that entry — provides that he is ineligible.

	Status of P	*Determination of ineligibility*
Case A	P is— (a) subject to the hospital treatment regime, and (b) detained in a hospital under that regime.	P is ineligible.
Case B	P is— (a) subject to the hospital treatment regime, but (b) not detained in a hospital under that regime.	See paragraphs 3 and 4.
Case C	P is subject to the community treatment regime.	See paragraphs 3 and 4.
Case D	P is subject to the guardianship regime.	See paragraphs 3 and 5.
Case E	P is— (a) within the scope of the Mental Health Act, but (b) not subject to any of the mental health regimes.	See paragraph 5.

Authorised course of action not in accordance with regime

3(1) This paragraph applies in cases B, C and D in the table in paragraph 2.

(2) P is ineligible if the authorised course of action is not in accordance with a requirement which the relevant regime imposes.

(3) That includes any requirement as to where P is, or is not, to reside.

(4) The relevant regime is the mental health regime to which P is subject.

Treatment for mental disorder in a hospital

4(1) This paragraph applies in cases B and C in the table in paragraph.

(2) P is ineligible if the relevant care or treatment consists in whole or in part of medical treatment for mental disorder in a hospital.

P objects to being a mental health patient etc

5(1) This paragraph applies in cases D and E in the table in paragraph 2.

(2) P is ineligible if the following conditions are met.

(3) The first condition is that the relevant instrument authorises P to be a mental health patient.

(4) The second condition is that P objects—

    (a) to being a mental health patient, or

    (b) to being given some or all of the mental health treatment.

(5) The third condition is that a donee or deputy has not made a valid decision to consent to each matter to which P objects.

(6) In determining whether or not P objects to something, regard must be had to all the circumstances (so far as they are reasonably ascertainable), including the following—

    (a) P's behaviour;

    (b) P's wishes and feelings;

    (c) P's views, beliefs and values.

(7) But regard is to be had to circumstances from the past only so far as it is still appropriate to have regard to them.

PART 2

INTERPRETATION

Application

6 This Part applies for the purposes of this Schedule.

Mental health regimes

7 The mental health regimes are—
- (a) the hospital treatment regime,
- (b) the community treatment regime, and
- (c) the guardianship regime.

Hospital treatment regime

8(1) P is subject to the hospital treatment regime if he is subject to—
- (a) a hospital treatment obligation under the relevant enactment, or
- (b) an obligation under another England and Wales enactment which has the same effect as a hospital treatment obligation.

(2) But where P is subject to any such obligation, he is to be regarded as not subject to the hospital treatment regime during any period when he is subject to the community treatment regime.

(3) A hospital treatment obligation is an application, order or direction of a kind listed in the first column of the following table.

(4) In relation to a hospital treatment obligation, the relevant enactment is the enactment in the Mental Health Act which is referred to in the corresponding entry in the second column of the following table.

Hospital treatment obligation	Relevant enactment
Application for admission for assessment	Section 2
Application for admission for assessment	Section 4
Application for admission for treatment	Section 3
Order for remand to hospital	Section 35
Order for remand to hospital	Section 36
Hospital order	Section 37
Interim hospital order	Section 38
Order for detention in hospital	Section 44
Hospital direction	Section 45A
Transfer direction	Section 47
Transfer direction	Section 48
Hospital order	Section 51

Community treatment regime

9 P is subject to the community treatment regime if he is subject to—
- (a) a community treatment order under section 17A of the Mental Health Act, or
- (b) an obligation under another England and Wales enactment which has the same effect as a community treatment order.

Guardianship regime

10 P is subject to the guardianship regime if he is subject to—
- (a) a guardianship application under section 7 of the Mental Health Act,

(b) a guardianship order under section 37 of the Mental Health Act, or

(c) an obligation under another England and Wales enactment which has the same effect as a guardianship application or guardianship order.

England and Wales enactments

11(1) An England and Wales enactment is an enactment which extends to England and Wales (whether or not it also extends elsewhere).

(2) It does not matter if the enactment is in the Mental Health Act or not.

P within scope of Mental Health Act

12(1) P is within the scope of the Mental Health Act if—

(a) an application in respect of P could be made under section 2 or 3 of the Mental Health Act, and

(b) P could be detained in a hospital in pursuance of such an application, were one made.

(2) The following provisions of this paragraph apply when determining whether an application in respect of P could be made under section 2 or 3 of the Mental Health Act.

(3) If the grounds in section 2(2) of the Mental Health Act are met in P's case, it is to be assumed that the recommendations referred to in section 2(3) of that Act have been given.

(4) If the grounds in section 3(2) of the Mental Health Act are met in P's case, it is to be assumed that the recommendations referred to in section 3(3) of that Act have been given.

(5) In determining whether the ground in section 3(2)(c) of the Mental Health Act is met in P's case, it is to be assumed that the treatment referred to in section 3(2)(c) cannot be provided under this Act.

Authorised course of action, relevant care or treatment & relevant instrument

13 In a case where this Schedule applies for the purposes of section 16A—

'authorised course of action' means any course of action amounting to deprivation of liberty which the order under section 16(2)(a) authorises;

'relevant care or treatment' means any care or treatment which—

(a) comprises, or forms part of, the authorised course of action, or

(b) is to be given in connection with the authorised course of action;

'relevant instrument' means the order under section 16(2)(a).

14 In a case where this Schedule applies for the purposes of paragraph 17 of Schedule A1—

'authorised course of action' means the accommodation of the relevant person in the relevant hospital or care home for the purpose of being given the relevant care or treatment;

'relevant care or treatment' has the same meaning as in Schedule A1;

'relevant instrument' means the standard authorisation under Schedule A1.

15 (1) This paragraph applies where the question whether a person is ineligible to be deprived of liberty by this Act is relevant to either of these decisions—

(a) whether or not to include particular provision ('the proposed provision') in an order under section 16(2)(a);

(b) whether or not to give a standard authorisation under Schedule A1.

(2) A reference in this Schedule to the authorised course of action or the relevant care or treatment is to be read as a reference to that thing as it would be if—

(a) the proposed provision were included in the order, or

(b) the standard authorisation were given.

(3) A reference in this Schedule to the relevant instrument is to be read as follows—

(a) where the relevant instrument is an order under section 16(2)(a): as a reference to the order as it would be if the proposed provision were included in it;

(b) where the relevant instrument is a standard authorisation: as a reference to the standard authorisation as it would be if it were given.

Expressions used in paragraph 5

16(1) These expressions have the meanings given—

'donee' means a donee of a lasting power of attorney granted by P;

'mental health patient' means a person accommodated in a hospital for the purpose of being given medical treatment for mental disorder;

'mental health treatment' means the medical treatment for mental disorder referred to in the definition of 'mental health patient'.

(2) A decision of a donee or deputy is valid if it is made—

(a) within the scope of his authority as donee or deputy, and

(b) in accordance with Part 1 of this Act.

Expressions with same meaning as in Mental Health Act

17(1) 'Hospital' has the same meaning as in Part 2 of the Mental Health Act.

(2) 'Medical treatment' has the same meaning as in the Mental Health Act.

(3) 'Mental disorder' has the same meaning as in Schedule A1 (see paragraph 14).]

[*Schedule 1A inserted by section 50(6) and Schedule 8 to the 2007 Act.*]

SCHEDULE 2
PROPERTY AND AFFAIRS: SUPPLEMENTARY PROVISIONS

Section 18(4)

[NOT REPRODUCED]

SCHEDULE 3
INTERNATIONAL PROTECTION OF ADULTS

Section 63

PART 1
PRELIMINARY

Introduction

1 This Part applies for the purposes of this Schedule.

The Convention

2(1) 'Convention' means the Convention referred to in section 63.

(2) 'Convention country' means a country in which the Convention is in force.

(3) A reference to an Article or Chapter is to an Article or Chapter of the Convention.

(4) An expression which appears in this Schedule and in the Convention is to be construed in accordance with the Convention.

Countries, territories and nationals

3(1) 'Country' includes a territory which has its own system of law.

(2) Where a country has more than one territory with its own system of law, a reference to the country, in relation to one of its nationals, is to the territory with which the national has the closer, or the closest, connection.

Adults with incapacity

4   'Adult' means a person who—
  (a) as a result of an impairment or insufficiency of his personal faculties, cannot protect his interests, and
  (b) has reached 16.

Protective measures

5(1) 'Protective measure' means a measure directed to the protection of the person or property of an adult; and it may deal in particular with any of the following—
  (a) the determination of incapacity and the institution of a protective regime,
  (b) placing the adult under the protection of an appropriate authority,
  (c) guardianship, curatorship or any corresponding system,
  (d) the designation and functions of a person having charge of the adult's person or property, or representing or otherwise helping him,
  (e) placing the adult in a place where protection can be provided,
  (f) administering, conserving or disposing of the adult's property,
  (g) authorising a specific intervention for the protection of the person or property of the adult.

(2) Where a measure of like effect to a protective measure has been taken in relation to a person before he reaches 16, this Schedule applies to the measure in so far as it has effect in relation to him once he has reached 16.

Central Authority

6(1) Any function under the Convention of a Central Authority is exercisable in England and Wales by the Lord Chancellor.

(2) A communication may be sent to the Central Authority in relation to England and Wales by sending it to the Lord Chancellor.

PART 2
JURISDICTION OF COMPETENT AUTHORITY

Scope of jurisdiction

7(1) The court may exercise its functions under this Act (in so far as it cannot otherwise do so) in relation to—
  (a) an adult habitually resident in England and Wales,
  (b) an adult's property in England and Wales,

(c) an adult present in England and Wales or who has property there, if the matter is urgent, or

(d) an adult present in England and Wales, if a protective measure which is temporary and limited in its effect to England and Wales is proposed in relation to him.

(2) An adult present in England and Wales is to be treated for the purposes of this paragraph as habitually resident there if—

(a) his habitual residence cannot be ascertained,

(b) he is a refugee, or

(c) he has been displaced as a result of disturbance in the country of his habitual residence.

8(1) The court may also exercise its functions under this Act (in so far as it cannot otherwise do so) in relation to an adult if sub-paragraph (2) or (3) applies in relation to him.

(2) This sub-paragraph applies in relation to an adult if—

(a) he is a British citizen,

(b) he has a closer connection with England and Wales than with Scotland or Northern Ireland, and

(c) Article 7 has, in relation to the matter concerned, been complied with.

(3) This sub-paragraph applies in relation to an adult if the Lord Chancellor, having consulted such persons as he considers appropriate, agrees to a request under Article 8 in relation to the adult.

Exercise of jurisdiction

9(1) This paragraph applies where jurisdiction is exercisable under this Schedule in connection with a matter which involves a Convention country other than England and Wales.

(2) Any Article on which the jurisdiction is based applies in relation to the matter in so far as it involves the other country (and the court must, accordingly, comply with any duty conferred on it as a result).

(3) Article 12 also applies, so far as its provisions allow, in relation to the matter in so far as it involves the other country.

10 A reference in this Schedule to the exercise of jurisdiction under this Schedule is to the exercise of functions under this Act as a result of this Part of this Schedule.

PART 3
APPLICABLE LAW

Applicable law

11 In exercising jurisdiction under this Schedule, the court may, if it thinks that the matter has a substantial connection with a country other than England and Wales, apply the law of that other country.

12 Where a protective measure is taken in one country but implemented in another, the conditions of implementation are governed by the law of the other country.

Lasting powers of attorney, etc.

13(1) If the donor of a lasting power is habitually resident in England and Wales at the time of granting the power, the law applicable to the existence, extent, modification or extinction of the power is—

(a) the law of England and Wales, or

    (b) if he specifies in writing the law of a connected country for the purpose, that law.

(2) If he is habitually resident in another country at that time, but England and Wales is a connected country, the law applicable in that respect is—

    (a) the law of the other country, or

    (b) if he specifies in writing the law of England and Wales for the purpose, that law.

(3) A country is connected, in relation to the donor, if it is a country—

    (a) of which he is a national,

    (b) in which he was habitually resident, or

    (c) in which he has property.

(4) Where this paragraph applies as a result of sub-paragraph (3)(c), it applies only in relation to the property which the donor has in the connected country.

(5) The law applicable to the manner of the exercise of a lasting power is the law of the country where it is exercised.

(6) In this Part of this Schedule, 'lasting power' means—

    (a) a lasting power of attorney (see section 9),

    (b) an enduring power of attorney within the meaning of Schedule 4, or

    (c) any other power of like effect.

14(1) Where a lasting power is not exercised in a manner sufficient to guarantee the protection of the person or property of the donor, the court, in exercising jurisdiction under this Schedule, may disapply or modify the power.

(2) Where, in accordance with this Part of this Schedule, the law applicable to the power is, in one or more respects, that of a country other than England and Wales, the court must, so far as possible, have regard to the law of the other country in that respect (or those respects).

15 Regulations may provide for Schedule 1 (lasting powers of attorney: formalities) to apply with modifications in relation to a lasting power which comes within paragraph 13(6)(c) above.

Protection of third parties

16(1) This paragraph applies where a person (a 'representative') in purported exercise of an authority to act on behalf of an adult enters into a transaction with a third party.

(2) The validity of the transaction may not be questioned in proceedings, nor may the third party be held liable, merely because—

    (a) where the representative and third party are in England and Wales when entering into the transaction, sub-paragraph (3) applies;

    (b) here they are in another country at that time, sub-paragraph (4) applies.

(3) This sub-paragraph applies if—

    (a) the law applicable to the authority in one or more respects is, as a result of this Schedule, the law of a country other than England and Wales, and

    (b) the representative is not entitled to exercise the authority in that respect (or those respects) under the law of that other country.

(4) This sub-paragraph applies if—

    (a) the law applicable to the authority in one or more respects is, as a result of this Part of this Schedule, the law of England and Wales, and

    (b) the representative is not entitled to exercise the authority in that respect (or those respects) under that law.

(5) This paragraph does not apply if the third party knew or ought to have known that the applicable law was—

    (a) in a case within sub-paragraph (3), the law of the other country;

(b) in a case within sub-paragraph (4), the law of England and Wales.

Mandatory rules

17 Where the court is entitled to exercise jurisdiction under this Schedule, the mandatory provisions of the law of England and Wales apply, regardless of any system of law which would otherwise apply in relation to the matter.

Public policy

18 Nothing in this Part of this Schedule requires or enables the application in England and Wales of a provision of the law of another country if its application would be manifestly contrary to public policy.

PART 4
RECOGNITION AND ENFORCEMENT

Recognition

19(1) A protective measure taken in relation to an adult under the law of a country other than England and Wales is to be recognised in England and Wales if it was taken on the ground that the adult is habitually resident in the other country.

(2) A protective measure taken in relation to an adult under the law of a Convention country other than England and Wales is to be recognised in England and Wales if it was taken on a ground mentioned in Chapter 2 (jurisdiction).

(3) But the court may disapply this paragraph in relation to a measure if it thinks that—

(a) the case in which the measure was taken was not urgent,

(b) the adult was not given an opportunity to be heard, and

(c) that omission amounted to a breach of natural justice.

(4) It may also disapply this paragraph in relation to a measure if it thinks that—

(a) recognition of the measure would be manifestly contrary to public policy,

(b) the measure would be inconsistent with a mandatory provision of the law of England and Wales, or

(c) the measure is inconsistent with one subsequently taken, or recognised, in England and Wales in relation to the adult.

(5) And the court may disapply this paragraph in relation to a measure taken under the law of a Convention country in a matter to which Article 33 applies, if the court thinks that that Article has not been complied with in connection with that matter.

20(1) An interested person may apply to the court for a declaration as to whether a protective measure taken under the law of a country other than England and Wales is to be recognised in England and Wales.

(2) No permission is required for an application to the court under this paragraph.

21 For the purposes of paragraphs 19 and 20, any finding of fact relied on when the measure was taken is conclusive.

Enforcement

22(1) An interested person may apply to the court for a declaration as to whether a protective measure taken under the law of, and enforceable in, a country other than England and Wales is enforceable, or to be registered, in England and Wales in accordance with Court of Protection Rules.

(2) The court must make the declaration if—

    (a) the measure comes within sub-paragraph (1) or (2) of paragraph 19, and

    (b) the paragraph is not disapplied in relation to it as a result of subparagraph (3), (4) or (5).

(3) A measure to which a declaration under this paragraph relates is enforceable in England and Wales as if it were a measure of like effect taken by the court.

Measures taken in relation to those aged under 16

23(1) This paragraph applies where—

    (a) provision giving effect to, or otherwise deriving from, the Convention in a country other than England and Wales applies in relation to a person who has not reached 16, and

    (b) a measure is taken in relation to that person in reliance on that provision.

(2) This Part of this Schedule applies in relation to that measure as it applies in relation to a protective measure taken in relation to an adult under the law of a Convention country other than England and Wales.

Supplementary

24 The court may not review the merits of a measure taken outside England and Wales except to establish whether the measure complies with this Schedule in so far as it is, as a result of this Schedule, required to do so.

25 Court of Protection Rules may make provision about an application under paragraph 20 or 22.

PART 5
CO-OPERATION

Proposal for cross-border placement

26(1) This paragraph applies where a public authority proposes to place an adult in an establishment in a Convention country other than England and Wales.

(2) The public authority must consult an appropriate authority in that other country about the proposed placement and, for that purpose, must send it—

    (a) a report on the adult, and

    (b) a statement of its reasons for the proposed placement.

(3) If the appropriate authority in the other country opposes the proposed placement within a reasonable time, the public authority may not proceed with it.

27 A proposal received by a public authority under Article 33 in relation to an adult is to proceed unless the authority opposes it within a reasonable time.

Adult in danger etc

28(1) This paragraph applies if a public authority is told that an adult—

    (a) who is in serious danger, and

    (b) in relation to whom the public authority has taken, or is considering taking, protective measures

is, or has become resident, in a Convention country other than England and Wales.

(2) The public authority must tell an appropriate authority in that other country about—

    (a) the danger, and

    (b) the measures taken or under consideration.

29 A public authority may not request from, or send to, an appropriate authority in a Convention country information in accordance with Chapter 5 (co-operation) in relation to an adult if it thinks that doing so—

    (a) would be likely to endanger the adult or his property, or

    (b) would amount to a serious threat to the liberty or life of a member of the adult's family.

PART 6
GENERAL

Certificates

30 A certificate given under Article 38 by an authority in a Convention country other than England and Wales is, unless the contrary is shown, proof of the matters contained in it.

Powers to make further provision as to private international law

31 Her Majesty may by Order in Council confer on the Lord Chancellor, the court or another public authority functions for enabling the Convention to be given effect in England and Wales.

32(1) Regulations may make provision—

    (a) giving further effect to the Convention, or

    (b) otherwise about the private international law of England and Wales in relation to the protection of adults.

(2) The regulations may—

    (a) confer functions on the court or another public authority;

    (b) amend this Schedule;

    (c) provide for this Schedule to apply with specified modifications;

    (d) make provision about countries other than Convention countries.

Exceptions

33 Nothing in this Schedule applies, and no provision made under paragraph 32 is to apply, to any matter to which the Convention, as a result of Article 4, does not apply.

Regulations and orders

34 A reference in this Schedule to regulations or an order (other than an Order in Council) is to regulations or an order made for the purposes of this Schedule by the Lord Chancellor.

Commencement

35 The following provisions of this Schedule have effect only if the Convention is in force in accordance with Article 57—

    (a) paragraph 8,

    (b) paragraph 9,

    (c) paragraph 19(2) and (5),

(d) Part 5,
(e) paragraph 30.

SCHEDULE 4
PROVISIONS APPLYING TO EXISTING ENDURING POWERS
OF ATTORNEY ##

[NOT REPRODUCED]

SCHEDULE 5
TRANSITIONAL PROVISIONS AND SAVINGS

[NOT REPRODUCED]

SCHEDULE 6
MINOR AND CONSEQUENTIAL AMENDMENTS

[NOT REPRODUCED]

SCHEDULE 7
REPEALS

[NOT REPRODUCED]

APPENDIX 3

Mental Health Act 2007

CHAPTER 12

CONTENTS

PART 1
AMENDMENTS TO MENTAL HEALTH ACT 1983

Chapter 1. Changes to key provisions

Mental disorder

Section
1 Removal of categories of mental disorder
2 Learning disability
3 Changes to exclusions from operation of 1983 Act

Tests for detention etc

4 Replacement of 'treatability' and 'care' tests with appropriate treatment test
5 Further cases in which appropriate treatment test is to apply

Medical treatment

6 Appropriate treatment test in Part 4 of 1983 Act
7 Change in definition of 'medical treatment'

Fundamental principles

8 The fundamental principles

Chapter 2. Professional roles

Approved clinicians and responsible clinicians

9 Amendments to Part 2 of 1983 Act
10 Amendments to Part 3 of 1983 Act
11 Further amendments to Part 3 of 1983 Act
12 Amendments to Part 4 of 1983 Act

13 Amendments to Part 5 of 1983 Act
14 Amendments to other provisions of 1983 Act
15 Amendments to other Acts
16 Certain registered medical practitioners to be treated as approved under section 12 of 1983 Act
17 Regulations as to approvals in relation to England and Wales

Approved mental health professionals

18 Approved mental health professionals
19 Approval of courses etc for approved mental health professionals
20 Amendment to section 62 of Care Standards Act 2000
21 Approved mental health professionals: further amendments

Conflicts of interest in professional roles

22 Conflicts of interest

Chapter 3. Safeguards for patients

Patient's nearest relative

23 Extension of power to appoint acting nearest relative
24 Discharge and variation of orders appointing nearest relative
25 Restriction of nearest relative's right to apply to tribunal
26 Civil partners

Consent to treatment

27 Electro-convulsive therapy, etc
28 Section 27: supplemental
29 Withdrawal of consent

Advocacy

30 Independent mental health advocates

Accommodation, etc

31 Accommodation, etc

Chapter 4. Supervised community treatment

32 Community treatment orders, etc
33 Relationship with leave of absence
34 Consent to treatment

35 Authority to treat
36 Repeal of provisions for after-care under supervision

Chapter 5. Mental health review tribunals

37 References
38 Organisation

Chapter 6. Cross-border patients

39 Cross-border arrangements

Chapter 7. Restricted patients

40 Restriction orders
41 Conditionally discharged patients subject to limitation directions

Chapter 8. Miscellaneous

42 Offence of ill-treatment: increase in maximum penalty on conviction on indictment
43 Informal admission of patients aged 16 or 17
44 Places of safety
45 Delegation of powers of managers of NHS foundation trusts
46 Local Health Boards
47 Welsh Ministers: procedure for instruments

PART 2
AMENDMENTS TO OTHER ACTS

Chapter 1. Amendments to Domestic Violence, Crime and Victims Act 2004

48 Victims' rights

Chapter 2. Amendments to Mental Capacity Act 2005

49 Independent mental capacity advocacy service: exceptions
50 Mental Capacity Act 2005: deprivation of liberty
51 Amendment to section 20(11) of Mental Capacity Act 2005

PART 3
GENERAL

52 Meaning of '1983 Act'
53 Transitional provisions and savings

54 Consequential provisions
55 Repeals and revocations
56 Commencement
57 Commencement of section 36
58 Extent
59 Short title
   Schedule 1—Categories of mental disorder: further amendments etc
   Part 1—Amendments to 1983 Act
   Part 2—Amendments to other Acts
   Schedule 2—Approved mental health professionals: further amendments to 1983 Act
   Schedule 3—Supervised community treatment: further amendments to 1983 Act
   Schedule 4—Supervised community treatment: amendments to other Acts
   Schedule 5—Cross-border arrangements
   Part 1—Amendments to Part 6 of 1983 Act
   Part 2—Related amendments
   Schedule 6—Victims' rights
   Schedule 7—Mental Capacity Act 2005: new Schedule A1
   Schedule 8—Mental Capacity Act 2005: new Schedule 1A
   Schedule 9—Amendments relating to new section 4A of, & Schedule A1 to, Mental Capacity
      Act 2005
   Part 1—Other amendments to Mental Capacity Act 2005
   Part 2—Amendments to other Acts
   Schedule 10—Transitional provisions and savings
   Schedule 11—Repeals and revocations
   Part 1—Removal of categories of mental disorder
   Part 2—Replacement of 'treatability' and 'care' tests
   Part 3—Approved clinicians and responsible clinicians
   Part 4—Safeguards for patients
   Part 5—Supervised community treatment
   Part 6—Organisation of tribunals
   Part 7—Cross-border arrangements
   Part 8—Restricted patients
   Part 9—Miscellaneous
   Part 10—Deprivation of liberty

MENTAL HEALTH ACT 2007

2007 CHAPTER 12

An Act to amend the Mental Health Act 1983, the Domestic Violence, Crime and Victims Act 2004 and the Mental Capacity Act 2005 in relation to mentally disordered persons; to amend section 40 of the Mental Capacity Act 2005; and for connected purposes.

[19th July 2007]

Be it enacted by the Queen's most Excellent Majesty, by and with the advice and consent of the Lords Spiritual and Temporal, and Commons, in this present Parliament assembled, and by the authority of the same, as follows:—

PART 1
AMENDMENTS TO MENTAL HEALTH ACT 1983

[SECTIONS 1–47 NOT REPRODUCED HERE BUT IN APPENDIX 1]

PART 2
AMENDMENTS TO OTHER ACTS

Chapter 1. Amendments to Domestic Violence, Crime and Victims Act 2004

48 Victims' rights

Schedule 6 (which makes amendments to Chapter 2 of Part 3 of the Domestic Violence, Crime and Victims Act 2004 (c 28)) has effect.

Chapter 2. Amendments to Mental Capacity Act 2005

[SECTIONS 49–51 NOT REPRODUCED HERE BUT IN APPENDIX 2]

PART 3
GENERAL

52 Meaning of '1983 Act'

In this Act 'the 1983 Act' means the Mental Health Act 1983 (c 20).

53 Transitional provisions and savings

Schedule 10 (which contains transitional provisions and savings) has effect.

54 Consequential provisions

(1) The Secretary of State may by order made by statutory instrument make supplementary, incidental or consequential provision for the purposes of, in consequence of, or for giving full effect to a provision of this Act.

(2) An order under subsection (1) may, in particular—

    (a) amend or repeal any provision of an Act passed before, or in the same Session as, this Act;

    (b) amend or revoke any provision of subordinate legislation made before the passing of this Act;

    (c) include transitional or saving provision in connection with the coming into force of provision made by the order.

(3) In relation to provision which deals with matters with respect to which functions are exercisable by the Welsh Ministers—

    (a) the power under subsection (1) is exercisable by the Secretary of State only with agreement of the Welsh Ministers, and

(b) the power under that subsection is also exercisable by the Welsh Ministers except that provision may not be made by virtue of subsection (2)(a).

(4) The amendments that may be made by virtue of subsection (2) are in addition to those made by or by virtue of any other provision of this Act.

(5) A statutory instrument containing an order under subsection (1) which makes provision by virtue of subsection (2)(a) may not be made unless a draft of the instrument has been laid before and approved by a resolution of each House of Parliament.

(6) A statutory instrument containing any other order under subsection (1) made by the Secretary of State is subject to annulment in pursuance of a resolution of either House of Parliament.

(7) A statutory instrument containing an order under subsection (1) made by the Welsh Ministers is subject to annulment in pursuance of a resolution of the National Assembly for Wales.

(8) In subsection (2), 'subordinate legislation' has the same meaning as in the Interpretation Act 1978 (c 30).

55 Repeals and revocations

The enactments mentioned in Schedule 11 are repealed or revoked to the extent specified.

56 Commencement

(1) This Act (other than sections 51 to 53 (and Schedule 10), this section and sections 57 to 59) comes into force in accordance with provision made by the Secretary of State by order made by statutory instrument.

(2) In relation to provision which deals with matters with respect to which functions are exercisable by the Welsh Ministers, the power under subsection (1) is exercisable only with their agreement.

(3) Section 51 comes into force in accordance with provision made by the Lord Chancellor by order made by statutory instrument.

(4) An order under this section may—
   (a) make different provision for different purposes (including different provision for different areas and different provision for different descriptions of patient);
   (b) include transitional or saving provision.

(5) The provision which may be made by virtue of subsection (4)(b) includes provision modifying the application of a provision of this Act pending the commencement of a provision of another enactment.

(6) A statutory instrument containing an order under this section which makes provision by virtue of subsection (4)(b) (including provision within section 57) is subject to annulment in pursuance of a resolution of either House of Parliament.

57 Commencement of section 36

(1) An order under section 56 providing for the commencement of section 36 may, in particular, provide—
   (a) for that section not to apply to or affect a patient who is subject to after-care under supervision immediately before that commencement, and
   (b) for the patient to cease to be subject to after-care under supervision, and for his case to be dealt with, in accordance with provision made by the order.

(2) The order may require—

    (a) a Primary Care Trust or Local Health Board to secure that the patient is examined by a registered medical practitioner of a description specified in the order;

    (b) the registered medical practitioner to examine the patient with a view to making a decision about his case by reference to criteria specified in the order.

(3) The order may require the registered medical practitioner, having complied with provision made by virtue of subsection (2)(b)—

    (a) to discharge the patient,

    (b) to recommend that he be detained in hospital,

    (c) to recommend that he be received into guardianship, or

    (d) to make a community treatment order in respect of him.

(4) The order may, in respect of a recommendation made by virtue of subsection (3)(b) or (c)—

    (a) provide that the recommendation is to be made to a local social services authority determined in accordance with the order;

    (b) provide that the recommendation is to be made in accordance with any other requirements specified in the order;

    (c) require the local social services authority determined in accordance with paragraph (a), in response to the recommendation, to make arrangements for an approved mental health professional to consider the patient's case on their behalf.

(5) The order may provide that a registered medical practitioner shall not make a community treatment order in respect of a patient unless an approved mental health professional states in writing—

    (a) that he agrees with the decision made by the practitioner about the patient's case, and

    (b) that it is appropriate to make the order.

(6) An order requiring a registered medical practitioner to make a community treatment order in respect of a patient shall include provision about—

    (a) the effect of the community treatment order (in particular, replacing after-care under supervision with a contingent requirement to attend, and be detained at, a hospital), and

    (b) the effect of its revocation (including, in particular, provision for detention under section 3 of the 1983 Act).

(7) The order may modify a provision of the 1983 Act in its application in relation to a patient who is subject to after-care under supervision immediately before the commencement of section 36.

(8) Provision made by virtue of subsection (7) may, in particular—

    (a) modify any of sections 25A to 25J of the 1983 Act in their application in relation to a patient for so long as he is, by virtue of subsection (1)(a), subject to after-care under supervision after the commencement of section 36;

    (b) modify any of sections 17A to 17G, 20A and 20B of that Act (inserted by section 32 of this Act) in their application in relation to a patient in respect of whom a community treatment order is made by virtue of subsection (3)(d).

(9) A reference in this section to section 36 includes the amendments and repeals in Schedules 3 and 11 consequential on that section.

(10) An expression used in this section and in the 1983 Act has the same meaning in this section as it has in that Act.

58 Extent

(1) The provisions of this Act which amend other enactments have the same extent as the enactments which they amend.

(2) But subsection (1) is subject to—
   (a) paragraph 35 of Schedule 3,
   (b) paragraphs 3, 4 and 20 of Schedule 5, and
   (c) paragraph 12 of Schedule 9.
(3) Section 54 extends to the United Kingdom.

59 Short title

This Act may be cited as the Mental Health Act 2007.

SCHEDULES

SCHEDULE 1
CATEGORIES OF MENTAL DISORDER:
FURTHER AMENDMENTS ETC

Section 1

PART 1
AMENDMENTS TO 1983 ACT

[PARAS 1–17 NOT REPRODUCED HERE BUT IN APPENDIX 1]

PART 2
AMENDMENTS TO OTHER ACTS

Juries Act 1974

18

(1) Part 1 of Schedule 1 to the Juries Act 1974 (c 23) (mentally disordered persons) is amended as follows.
(2) In paragraph 1, for 'mental illness, psychopathic disorder, mental handicap or severe mental handicap' substitute 'mental disorder within the meaning of the Mental Health Act 1983'.
(3) Omit paragraph 4(1).

Contempt of Court Act 1981

19

In section 14 of the Contempt of Court Act 1981 (c 49) (proceedings in England and Wales), in subsection (4) and the first subsection (4A), for 'mental illness or severe mental impairment' substitute 'mental disorder within the meaning of that Act'.

Family Law Act 1996

20

(1) The Family Law Act 1996 (c 27) is amended as follows.

(2) In section 48 (remand for medical examination and report), in subsection (4)—

    (a) for 'mental illness or severe mental impairment' substitute 'mental disorder within the meaning of the Mental Health Act 1983',

    (b) for 'the Mental Health Act 1983' substitute 'that Act', and

    (c) for 'section 35 of the Act of 1983' substitute 'that section'.

(3) In section 51 (power of magistrates' court to order hospital admission or guardianship), in subsection (1), for 'mental illness or severe mental impairment' substitute 'mental disorder within the meaning of that Act'.

Housing Act 1996

21

In section 156 of the Housing Act 1996 (c 52) (remand for medical examination and report), in subsection (4)—

    (a) for 'mental illness or severe mental impairment' substitute 'mental disorder within the meaning of the Mental Health Act 1983',

    (b) for 'the Mental Health Act 1983' substitute 'that Act', and

    (c) for 'section 35 of that Act' substitute 'that section'.

Care Standards Act 2000

22

In section 121 of the Care Standards Act 2000 (c 14) (general interpretation), in subsection (1), for the definition of 'mental disorder' substitute—

    'mental disorder' has the same meaning as in the Mental Health Act 1983;'.

Mental Capacity Act 2005

23

(1) In Schedule 4 to the Mental Capacity Act 2005 (c 9) (provisions applying to existing enduring powers of attorney), paragraph 23 is amended as follows.

(2) In sub-paragraph (1), omit the words '(within the meaning of the Mental Health Act)'.

(3) After sub-paragraph (1) insert—

    '(1A) In sub-paragraph (1), 'mental disorder' has the same meaning as in the Mental Health Act but disregarding the amendments made to that Act by the Mental Health Act 2007.'

National Health Service Act 2006

24

In section 275 of the National Health Service Act 2006 (c 41) (interpretation), in the definition of 'illness' in subsection (1), for 'mental disorder within the meaning of the Mental Health Act 1983' substitute 'any disorder or disability of the mind'.

National Health Service (Wales) Act 2006

25

In section 206 of the National Health Service (Wales) Act 2006 (c 42) (interpretation), in the definition of 'illness' in subsection (1), for 'mental disorder within the meaning of the Mental Health Act 1983' substitute 'any disorder or disability of the mind'.

Police and Justice Act 2006

26

In section 27 of the Police and Justice Act 2006 (c 48) (anti-social behaviour injunctions: power of arrest and remand), in subsection (11)—

(a) for 'mental illness or severe mental impairment' substitute 'mental disorder within the meaning of the Mental Health Act 1983', and

(b) for 'the Mental Health Act 1983 (c 20)' substitute 'that Act'.

SCHEDULE 2
APPROVED MENTAL HEALTH PROFESSIONALS: FURTHER AMENDMENTS TO 1983 ACT

[SCH 2 NOT REPRODUCED HERE BUT IN APPENDIX 1]

Section 21

SCHEDULE 3
SUPERVISED COMMUNITY TREATMENT: FURTHER AMENDMENTS TO 1983 ACT

[SCH 3 NOT REPRODUCED HERE BUT IN APPENDIX 1]

Section 32

SCHEDULE 4
SUPERVISED COMMUNITY TREATMENT: AMENDMENTS TO OTHER ACTS

Section 32

Administration of Justice Act 1960

1

After section 5 of the Administration of Justice Act 1960 (c 65) insert—

'5A Power to order continuation of community treatment order

(1) Where the defendant in any proceedings from which an appeal lies under section 1 of this Act would, but for the decision of the court below, be liable to recall, and immediately after that decision the prosecutor is granted, or gives notice that he intends to apply for, leave to appeal, the court may make an order under this section.

(2) For the purposes of this section, a person is liable to recall if he is subject to a community treatment order (within the meaning of the Mental Health Act 1983) and, when that order was made, he was liable to be detained in pursuance of an order or direction under Part 3 of that Act.

(3) An order under this section is an order providing for the continuation of the community treatment order and the order or direction under Part 3 of that Act so long as any appeal under section 1 of this Act is pending.

(4) Where the court makes an order under this section, the provisions of the Mental Health Act 1983 with respect to persons liable to recall (including provisions as to the extension of the community treatment period, the removal or discharge of community patients, the revocation of community treatment orders and the re-detention of patients following revocation) shall apply accordingly.

(5) An order under this section shall (unless the appeal has previously been disposed of) cease to have effect at the expiration of the period for which the defendant would, but for the decision of the court below, have been—

(a) liable to recall; or

(b) where the community treatment order is revoked, liable to be detained in pursuance of the order or direction under Part 3 of the Mental Health Act 1983.

(6) Where the court below has power to make an order under this section, and either no such order is made or the defendant is discharged by virtue of subsection (4) or (5) of this section before the appeal is disposed of, the defendant shall not be liable to be again detained as the result of the decision of the Supreme Court on the appeal.'

Criminal Appeal Act 1968

2

(1) The Criminal Appeal Act 1968 (c 19) is amended as follows.

(2) In section 8 (supplementary provisions as to retrial), after subsection (3A) insert—

'(3B) If the person ordered to be retried—

(a) was liable to be detained in pursuance of an order or direction under Part 3 of the Mental Health Act 1983;

(b) was then made subject to a community treatment order (within the meaning of that Act); and

(c) was subject to that community treatment order immediately before the determination of his appeal,

the order or direction under Part 3 of that Act and the community treatment order shall continue in force pending the retrial as if the appeal had not been allowed, and any order made by the Court of Appeal under this section for his release on bail shall have effect subject to the community treatment order.'

(3) After section 37 insert—

'37A Continuation of community treatment order on appeal by the Crown

(1) The following provisions apply where, immediately after a decision of the Court of Appeal from which an appeal lies to the Supreme Court, the prosecutor is granted, or gives notice that he intends to apply for, leave to appeal.

(2) If, but for the decision of the Court of Appeal, the defendant would be liable to recall, the Court of Appeal may make an order under this section.

(3) For the purposes of this section, a person is liable to recall if he is subject to a community treatment order (within the meaning of the Mental Health Act 1983) and, when that order was made, he was liable to be detained in pursuance of an order or direction under Part 3 of that Act.

(4) An order under this section is an order providing for the continuation of the community treatment order and the order or direction under Part 3 of that Act so long as an appeal to the Supreme Court is pending.

(5) Where an order is made under this section the provisions of the Mental Health Act 1983 with respect to persons liable to recall (including provisions as to the extension of the community treatment period, the removal or discharge of community patients, the revocation of community treatment orders and the re-detention of patients following revocation) shall apply accordingly.

(6) An order under this section shall (unless the appeal has previously been disposed of) cease to have effect at the expiration of the period for which the defendant would, but for the decision of the Court of Appeal, have been—
   (a) liable to recall; or
   (b) where the community treatment order is revoked, liable to be detained in pursuance of the order or direction under Part 3 of the Mental Health Act 1983.

(7) Where the Court of Appeal have power to make an order under this section, and either no such order is made or the defendant is discharged, by virtue of subsection (5) or (6) of this section, before the appeal is disposed of, the defendant shall not be liable to be again detained as the result of the decision of the Supreme Court on the appeal.'

Courts-Martial (Appeals) Act 1968

3

(1) The Courts-Martial (Appeals) Act 1968 (c 20) is amended as follows.

(2) In section 20 (implementation of authority for retrial etc), after subsection (4) insert—

'(4A) Where retrial is authorised in the case of a person who—
   (a) was liable to be detained in pursuance of an order or direction under Part 3 of the Mental Health Act 1983;
   (b) was then made subject to a community treatment order (within the meaning of that Act); and
   (c) was subject to that community treatment order immediately before the date of the authorisation,
the order or direction under Part 3 of that Act and the community treatment order shall continue in force until the relevant time (as defined in subsection (3A)) as if his conviction had not been quashed.

(4B) An order under subsection (1E)(a) is of no effect in relation to a person for so long as he is subject to a community treatment order.'

(3) In section 43 (detention of accused), after subsection (3) insert—

'(3A) The relevant provisions of the Mental Health Act 1983 with respect to community treatment orders (within the meaning of that Act) shall also apply for the purposes of subsection (3).'

549

(4) After that section insert—

'43A Continuation of community treatment order

(1) The Appeal Court may make an order under this section where—
  (a) but for the decision of the Appeal Court, the accused would be liable to recall; and
  (b) immediately after that decision, the Director of Service Prosecutions is granted leave to appeal or gives notice that he intends to apply for leave to appeal.
(2) For the purposes of this section, a person is liable to recall if he is subject to a community treatment order (within the meaning of the Mental Health Act 1983) and, when that order was made, he was liable to be detained in pursuance of an order or direction under Part 3 of that Act.
(3) An order under this section is an order providing for the continuation of the community treatment order and the order or direction under Part 3 of that Act so long as any appeal to the Supreme Court is pending.
(4) Where the Appeal Court makes an order under this section, the relevant provisions of the Mental Health Act 1983 with respect to persons liable to recall (including provisions as to the extension of the community treatment period, the removal or discharge of community patients, the revocation of community treatment orders and the re-detention of patients following revocation) shall apply accordingly.
(5) An order under this section shall (unless the appeal has been previously disposed of) cease to have effect at the end of the period for which the accused would, but for the decision of the Appeal Court, have been—
  (a) liable to recall; or
  (b) where the community treatment order is revoked, liable to be detained in pursuance of the order or direction under Part 3 of the Mental Health Act 1983.
(6) Where the Appeal Court has power to make an order under this section and either no such order is made or the accused is discharged by virtue of subsection (4) or (5) above before the appeal is disposed of, the accused shall not be liable to be again detained as a result of the decision of the Supreme Court on the appeal.'

Juries Act 1974

4

In Schedule 1 to the Juries Act 1974 (c 23) (mentally disordered persons and persons disqualified from serving), at the end of paragraph 2 insert 'or subject to a community treatment order under section 17A of that Act'.

SCHEDULE 5
CROSS-BORDER ARRANGEMENTS

Section 39

PART 1
AMENDMENTS TO PART 6 OF 1983 ACT

[PART 1 NOT REPRODUCED HERE BUT IN APPENDIX 1]

PART 2
RELATED AMENDMENTS

The 1983 Act

[PART 2 NOT REPRODUCED HERE BUT IN APPENDIX 1]

Mental Health (Care and Treatment) (Scotland) Act 2003 (Consequential Provisions)
Order 2005 (SI 2005/2078)

21

(1) The Mental Health (Care and Treatment) (Scotland) Act 2003 (Consequential Provisions) Order 2005 is amended as follows.

(2) Omit the following provisions—
   (a) article 1(5),
   (b) article 2, and
   (c) article 3.

(3) In article 8 (the title to which becomes 'Patients absent from hospitals or other places in Scotland'), in paragraph (1)(b), for '290' substitute '289, 290, 309, 309A'.

(4) In article 12(2), for '2 to 11' substitute '4 to 11'.

SCHEDULE 6
VICTIMS' RIGHTS

Section 48

Introduction

1

Chapter 2 of Part 3 of the Domestic Violence, Crime and Victims Act 2004 (c 28) (provision of information to victims of restricted patients under the 1983 Act, etc) is amended as set out in this Schedule.

Hospital orders (with or without restriction orders)

2

(1) Section 36 (victims' rights: preliminary) is amended as follows.

(2) In subsection (3), for 'with a restriction order' substitute ', whether with or without a restriction order,'.

(3) In subsection (5)—

    (a) in paragraph (a), after 'discharge from hospital' insert 'while a restriction order is in force in respect of him', and

    (b) after paragraph (b) insert

';

'(c) what conditions he should be subject to in the event of his discharge from hospital under a community treatment order'.

3

After section 36 insert—

'36A Supplemental provision for case where no restriction order made

(1) This section applies if, in a case where section 36 applies, the hospital order in respect of the patient was made without a restriction order.

(2) Subsection (3) applies if a person who appears to the local probation board mentioned in section 36(4) to be the victim of the offence or to act for the victim of the offence, when his wishes are ascertained under section 36(4), expresses a wish—

    (a) to make representations about a matter specified in section 36(5), or

    (b) to receive the information specified in section 36(6).

(3) The local probation board must—

    (a) notify the managers of the hospital in which the patient is detained of that person's wish and of that person's name and address, and

    (b) notify that person of the name and address of the hospital.

(4) Subsection (5) applies if a person who appears to the local probation board mentioned in section 36(4) to be the victim of the offence or to act for the victim of the offence, subsequently to his wishes being ascertained under section 36(4), expresses a wish to do something specified in subsection (2)(a) or (b).

(5) The local probation board mentioned in section 36(4) must take all reasonable steps—

    (a) to ascertain whether the hospital order made in respect of the patient continues in force and whether a community treatment order is in force in respect of him, and

    (b) if the board ascertains that the hospital order does continue in force—

        (i) to notify the managers of the relevant hospital of that person's wish, and

        (ii) to notify that person of the name and address of the hospital.

(6) The relevant hospital is—

    (a) the hospital in which the patient is detained, or

    (b) if a community treatment order is in force in respect of the patient, the responsible hospital.'

4

In section 37 (the title to which becomes 'Representations where restriction order made'), in subsection (1), for 'if section 36 applies' substitute 'if, in a case where section 36 applies, the hospital order in respect of the patient was made with a restriction order'.

5

After section 37 insert—

'37A Representations where restriction order not made

(1) This section applies if, in a case where section 36 applies, the hospital order in respect of the patient was made without a restriction order.

(2) Subsection (3) applies if—

   (a) a person makes representations about a matter specified in section 36(5) to the managers of the relevant hospital, and

   (b) it appears to the managers that the person is the victim of the offence or acts for the victim of the offence.

(3) The managers must forward the representations to the persons responsible for determining the matter.

(4) The responsible clinician must inform the managers of the relevant hospital if he is considering making—

   (a) an order for discharge in respect of the patient under section 23(2) of the Mental Health Act 1983,

   (b) a community treatment order in respect of the patient, or

   (c) an order under section 17B(4) of the Mental Health Act 1983 to vary the conditions specified in a community treatment order in force in respect of the patient.

(5) Any person who has the power to make an order for discharge in respect of the patient under section 23(3) of the Mental Health Act 1983 must inform the managers of the relevant hospital if he is considering making that order.

(6) A Mental Health Review Tribunal must inform the managers of the relevant hospital if—

   (a) an application is made to the tribunal under section 66 or 69 of the Mental Health Act 1983, or

   (b) the patient's case is referred to the tribunal under section 67 of that Act.

(7) Subsection (8) applies if—

   (a) the managers of the relevant hospital receive information under subsection (4), (5) or (6), and

   (b) a person who appears to the managers to be the victim of the offence or to act for the victim of the offence—

      (i) when his wishes were ascertained under section 36(4), expressed a wish to make representations about a matter specified in section 36(5), or

      (ii) has made representations about such a matter to the managers of the hospital in which the patient was, at the time in question, detained.

(8) The managers of the relevant hospital must provide the information to the person.

(9) The relevant hospital has the meaning given in section 36A(6).'

6

In section 38 (the title to which becomes 'Information where restriction order made'), in subsection (1) for 'if section 36 applies' substitute 'if, in a case where section 36 applies, the hospital order in respect of the patient was made with a restriction order'.

7

After section 38 insert—

'38A Information where restriction order not made

(1) This section applies if, in a case where section 36 applies, the hospital order in respect of the patient was made without a restriction order.

(2) The responsible clinician must inform the managers of the relevant hospital—

    (a) whether he is to make an order for discharge in respect of the patient under section 23(2) of the Mental Health Act 1983;

    (b) whether he is to make a community treatment order in respect of the patient;

    (c) if a community treatment order is to be made in respect of the patient, what conditions are to be specified in the order;

    (d) if a community treatment order is in force in respect of the patient, of any variation to be made under section 17B(4) of the Mental Health Act 1983 of the conditions specified in the order;

    (e) if a community treatment order in respect of the patient is to cease to be in force, of the date on which it is to cease to be in force;

    (f) if, following the examination of the patient under section 20 of the Mental Health Act 1983, it does not appear to the responsible clinician that the conditions set out in subsection (4) of that section are satisfied, of the date on which the authority for the patient's detention is to expire.

(3) Any person who has the power to make an order for discharge in respect of the patient under section 23(3) of the Mental Health Act 1983 must inform the managers of the relevant hospital if he is to make that order.

(4) Subsection (5) applies if—

    (a) an application is made to a Mental Health Review Tribunal under section 66 or 69 of the Mental Health Act 1983,

    (b) the patient's case is referred to a Mental Health Review Tribunal under section 67 of that Act, or

    (c) the managers of the relevant hospital refer the patient's case to a Mental Health Review Tribunal under section 68 of that Act.

(5) The tribunal must inform the managers of the relevant hospital if it directs that the patient is to be discharged.

(6) Subsection (7) applies if a person who appears to the managers of the relevant hospital to be the victim of the offence or to act for the victim of the offence—

    (a) when his wishes were ascertained under section 36(4), expressed a wish to receive the information specified in section 36(6), or

    (b) has subsequently informed the managers of the relevant hospital that he wishes to receive that information.

(7) The managers of the relevant hospital order must take all reasonable steps—

    (a) to inform that person whether the patient is to be discharged under section 23 or 72 of the Mental Health Act 1983;

    (b) to inform that person whether a community treatment order is to be made in respect of the patient;

    (c) if a community treatment order is to be made in respect of the patient and is to specify conditions which relate to contact with the victim or his family, to provide that person with details of those conditions;

    (d) if a community treatment order is in force in respect of the patient and the conditions specified in the order are to be varied under section 17B(4) of the Mental Health Act 1983, to provide that person with details of any variation which relates to contact with the victim or his family;

(e) if a community treatment order in respect of the patient is to cease to be in force, to inform that person of the date on which it is to cease to be in force;

(f) if, following the examination of the patient under section 20 of the Mental Health Act 1983, the authority for the patient's detention is not to be renewed, to inform that person of the date on which the authority is to expire;

(g) to provide that person with such other information as the managers of the relevant hospital consider appropriate in all the circumstances of the case.

(8) The relevant hospital has the meaning given by section 36A(6).

38B Removal of restriction

(1) This section applies if, in a case where section 36 applies—
   (a) the hospital order in respect of the patient was made with a restriction order, and
   (b) the restriction order ceases to have effect while the hospital order continues in force.

(2) Subsection (3) applies if a person who appears to the relevant local probation board to be the victim of the offence or to act for the victim of the offence—
   (a) when his wishes were ascertained under section 36(4), expressed a wish to make representations about a matter specified in section 36(5) or to receive the information specified in section 36(6), or
   (b) has subsequently informed the relevant local probation board that he wishes to make representations about such a matter or to receive that information.

(3) The relevant local probation board must take all reasonable steps—
   (a) to notify the managers of the relevant hospital of an address at which that person may be contacted;
   (b) to notify that person of the name and address of the hospital.

(4) While the hospital order continues in force, the patient is to be regarded as a patient in respect of whom a hospital order was made without a restriction order; and sections 37A and 38A are to apply in relation to him accordingly.

(5) The relevant hospital has the meaning given in section 36A(6).

(6) The relevant local probation board has the meaning given in section 37(8).'

Hospital directions and limitation directions

8

In section 39 (victims' rights: preliminary), in subsection (3)—
   (a) in paragraph (a), after 'discharge from hospital' insert 'while he is subject to a limitation direction', and
   (b) after that paragraph insert—
   '(aa) what conditions he should be subject to in the event of his discharge from hospital under a community treatment order;'.

9

After section 41 insert—

'41A Removal of restriction

(1) This section applies if, in a case where section 39 applies—
   (a) the limitation direction in respect of the offender ceases to be in force, and

(b) he is treated for the purposes of the Mental Health Act 1983 as a patient in respect of whom a hospital order has effect.

(2) Subsection (3) applies if a person who appears to the relevant local probation board to be the victim of the offence or to act for the victim of the offence—

(a) when his wishes were ascertained under section 39(2), expressed a wish to make representations about a matter specified in section 39(3) or to receive the information specified in section 39(4), or

(b) has subsequently informed the relevant local probation board that he wishes to make representations about such a matter or to receive that information.

(3) The relevant local probation board must take all reasonable steps—

(a) to notify the managers of the relevant hospital of an address at which that person may be contacted;

(b) to notify that person of the address of the hospital.

(4) The offender is to be regarded as a patient in respect of whom a hospital order was made without a restriction order; and sections 37A and 38A are to apply in relation to him accordingly.

(5) The relevant hospital has the meaning given in section 36A(6).

(6) The relevant local probation board has the meaning given in section 40(8).'

Transfer directions (with or without restriction directions)

10

(1) Section 42 (victims' rights: preliminary) is amended as follows.

(2) In subsection (1)(c), for 'and a restriction direction in respect of him' substitute 'in respect of the offender (whether or not he also gives a restriction direction in respect of the offender)'.

(3) In subsection (3)—

(a) in paragraph (a), after 'discharge from hospital' insert 'at a time when a restriction direction is in force in respect of him', and

(b) after paragraph (b) insert

';

'(c) what conditions he should be subject to in the event of his discharge from hospital under a community treatment order'.

11

After section 42 insert—

'42A Supplemental provision for case where no restriction direction given

(1) This section applies if, in a case where section 42 applies, the transfer direction in respect of the patient was given without a restriction direction.

(2) Subsection (3) applies if a person who appears to the local probation board mentioned in section 42(2) to be the victim of the offence or to act for the victim of the offence, when his wishes are ascertained under section 42(2), expresses a wish—

(a) to make representations about a matter specified in section 42(3), or

(b) to receive the information specified in section 42(4).

(3) The local probation board must—

(a) notify the managers of the hospital in which the patient is detained of that person's wish and of that person's name and address, and

(b) notify that person of the name and address of the hospital.

(4) Subsection (5) applies if a person who appears to the local probation board mentioned in section 42(2) to be the victim of the offence or to act for the victim of the offence, subsequently to his wishes being ascertained under section 42(2), expressed a wish to do something specified in subsection (2)(a) or (b).

(5) The local probation board mentioned in section 42(2) must take all reasonable steps—

   (a) to ascertain whether the transfer direction given in respect of the patient continues in force and whether a community treatment order is in force in respect of him, and

   (b) if the board ascertains that the transfer direction does continue in force—

      (i) to notify the managers of the relevant hospital of that person's wish, and

      (ii) to notify that person of the name and address of the hospital.

(6) The relevant hospital has the meaning given in section 36A(6).'

12

In section 43 (the title to which becomes 'Representations where restriction direction made'), in subsection (1), for 'if section 42 applies' substitute 'if, in a case where section 42 applies, the transfer direction in respect of the patient was given with a restriction direction'.

13

After section 43 insert—

'43A Representations where restriction direction not given

(1) This section applies if, in a case where section 42 applies, the transfer direction in respect of the patient was given without a restriction direction.

(2) Subsection (3) applies if—

   (a) a person makes representations about a matter specified in section 42(3) to the managers of the relevant hospital, and

   (b) it appears to the managers that the person is the victim of the offence or acts for the victim of the offence.

(3) The managers must forward the representations to the persons responsible for determining the matter.

(4) The responsible clinician must inform the managers of the relevant hospital if he is considering making—

   (a) an order for discharge in respect of the patient under section 23(2) of the Mental Health Act 1983,

   (b) a community treatment order in respect of him, or

   (c) an order under section 17B(4) of the Mental Health Act 1983 to vary the conditions specified in a community treatment order in force in respect of the patient.

(5) Any person who has power to make an order for discharge in respect of the patient under section 23(3) of the Mental Health Act 1983 must inform the managers of the relevant hospital if he is considering making that order.

(6) A Mental Health Review Tribunal must inform the managers of the relevant hospital if—

   (a) an application is made to the tribunal under section 66 or 69 of the Mental Health Act 1983, or

   (b) the patient's case is referred to the tribunal under section 67 of that Act.

(7) Subsection (8) applies if—

   (a) the managers of the relevant hospital receive information under subsection (4), (5) or (6), and

(b) a person who appears to the managers to be the victim of the offence or to act for the victim of the offence—

    (i) when his wishes were ascertained under section 42(2), expressed a wish to make representations about a matter specified in section 42(3), or

    (ii) has made representations about such a matter to the managers of the hospital in which the patient was, at the time in question, detained.

(8) The managers of the relevant hospital must provide the information to the person.

(9) The relevant hospital has the meaning given in section 36A(6).'

14

In section 44 (the title to which becomes 'Information where restriction direction made'), in subsection (1), for 'if section 42 applies' substitute 'if, in a case where section 42 applies, the transfer direction in respect of the patient was given with a restriction direction'.

15

After section 44 insert—

'44A Information where restriction direction not given

(1) This section applies if, in a case where section 42 applies, the transfer direction in respect of the patient was given without a restriction direction.

(2) The responsible clinician must inform the managers of the relevant hospital—

    (a) whether he is to make an order for discharge in respect of the patient under section 23(2) of the Mental Health Act 1983;

    (b) whether he is to make a community treatment order in respect of the patient;

    (c) if a community treatment order is to be made in respect of the patient, what conditions are to be specified in the order;

    (d) if a community treatment order is in force in respect of the patient, of any variation to be made under section 17B(4) of the Mental Health Act 1983 of the conditions specified in the order;

    (e) if a community treatment order in respect of the patient is to cease to be in force, of the date on which it is to cease to be in force;

    (f) if, following the examination of the patient under section 20 of the Mental Health Act 1983, it does not appear to the responsible clinician that the conditions set out in subsection (4) of that section are satisfied, of the date on which the authority for the patient's detention is to expire.

(3) Any person who has power to make an order for discharge in respect of the patient under section 23(3) of the Mental Health Act 1983 must inform the managers of the relevant hospital if he is to make that order.

(4) Subsection (5) applies if—

    (a) an application is made to a Mental Health Review Tribunal under section 66 or 69 of the Mental Health Act 1983,

    (b) the patient's case is referred to a Mental Health Review Tribunal under section 67 of that Act, or

    (c) the managers of the relevant hospital refer the patient's case to a Mental Health Review Tribunal under section 68 of that Act.

(5) The tribunal must inform the managers of the relevant hospital if it directs that the patient be discharged.

(6) Subsection (7) applies if a person who appears to the managers of the relevant hospital to be the victim of the offence or to act for the victim of the offence—

(a) when his wishes were ascertained under section 42(2), expressed a wish to receive the information specified in section 42(4), or

(b) has subsequently informed the managers of the relevant hospital that he wishes to receive that information.

(7) The managers of the relevant hospital order must take all reasonable steps—

(a) to inform that person whether the patient is to be discharged under section 23 or 72 of the Mental Health Act 1983;

(b) to inform that person whether a community treatment order is to be made in respect of the patient;

(c) if a community treatment order is to be made in respect of the patient and is to specify conditions which relate to contact with the victim or his family, to provide that person with details of those conditions;

(d) if a community treatment order is in force in respect of the patient and the conditions specified in the order are to be varied under section 17B(4) of the Mental Health Act 1983, to provide that person with details of any variation which relates to contact with the victim or his family;

(e) if a community treatment order in respect of the patient is to cease to be in force, to inform that person of the date on which it is to cease to be in force;

(f) if, following the examination of the patient under section 20 of the Mental Health Act 1983, the authority for the patient's detention is not to be renewed, to inform that person of the date on which the authority is to expire;

(g) to provide that person with such other information as the managers of the relevant hospital consider appropriate in all the circumstances of the case.

(8) The relevant hospital has the meaning given by section 36A(6).

44B Removal of restriction

(1) This section applies if, in a case where section 42 applies—

(a) the transfer direction in respect of the patient was given with a restriction direction, and

(b) the restriction direction ceases to be in force while the transfer direction continues in force.

(2) Subsection (3) applies if a person who appears to the relevant local probation board to be the victim of the offence or to act for the victim of the offence—

(a) when his wishes were ascertained under section 42(2), expressed a wish to make representations about a matter specified in section 42(3) or to receive the information specified in section 42(4), or

(b) has subsequently informed the relevant local probation board that he wishes to make representations about such a matter or to receive that information.

(3) The relevant local probation board must take all reasonable steps—

(a) to notify the managers of the relevant hospital of an address at which that person may be contacted;

(b) to notify that person of the name and address of the hospital.

(4) While the transfer direction continues in force, the patient is to be regarded as a patient in respect of whom a transfer direction was given without a restriction direction; and sections 43A and 44A are to apply in relation to him accordingly.

(5) The relevant hospital has the meaning given in section 36A(6).

(6) The relevant local probation board has the meaning given in section 43(8).'

Interpretation

16

(1) Section 45 (the title to which becomes 'Interpretation: sections 35 to 44B') is amended as follows.

(2) In subsection (1)—

    (a) for '44' substitute '44B', and

    (b) at the appropriate places insert—

        "community treatment order" has the meaning given in section 17A of the Mental Health Act 1983;',

        "the managers" has the meaning given in section 145 of the Mental Health Act 1983;',

        "responsible clinician" means the responsible clinician for the purposes of Part 3 of the Mental Health Act 1983;', and

        "responsible hospital" has the meaning given in section 17A of the Mental Health Act 1983;'.

(3) In subsection (2), for '44' substitute '44B'.

(4) After subsection (2) insert—

'(3) A reference in sections 35 to 44B to a place in which a person is detained includes a reference to a place in which he is liable to be detained under the Mental Health Act 1983.

(4) For the purposes of section 32(3) of that Act (regulations as to delegation of managers' functions, etc) as applied by Parts 1 and 2 of Schedule 1 to that Act, a function conferred on the managers of a hospital under sections 35 to 44B of this Act is to be treated as a function of theirs under Part 3 of that Act.'

SCHEDULE 7
MENTAL CAPACITY ACT 2005: NEW SCHEDULE A1

[SCH 7 NOT REPRODUCED HERE BUT IN APPENDIX 2]

Section 50

SCHEDULE 8
MENTAL CAPACITY ACT 2005: NEW SCHEDULE 1A

[SCH 8 NOT REPRODUCED HERE BUT IN APPENDIX 2]

Section 50

SCHEDULE 9
AMENDMENTS RELATING TO NEW SECTION 4A OF, & SCHEDULE A1
TO MENTAL CAPACITY ACT 2005

[SCH 9 NOT REPRODUCED HERE BUT IN APPENDIX 2]

Section 50

PART 2

AMENDMENTS TO OTHER ACTS

National Assistance Act 1948 (c 29)

12

(1) Section 47 of the National Assistance Act 1948 (removal to suitable premises of persons in need of care and attention) is amended as follows.

(2) After subsection (1) insert—

'(1A) But this section does not apply to a person ('P') in either of the following cases.

(1B) The first case is where an order of the Court of Protection authorises the managing authority of a hospital or care home (within the meaning of Schedule A1 to the Mental Capacity Act 2005) to provide P with proper care and attention.

(1C) The second case is where—

(a) an authorisation under Schedule A1 to the Mental Capacity Act 2005 is in force, or

(b) the managing authority of a hospital or care home are under a duty under paragraph 24 of that Schedule to request a standard authorisation, and

P is, or would be, the relevant person in relation to the authorisation.'

(3) This paragraph does not extend to Scotland.

Local Authority Social Services Act 1970 (c 42)

13

(1) Schedule 1 to the Local Authority Social Services Act 1970 (Social Services functions of local authorities) is amended as follows.

(2) In the entry relating to the Mental Capacity Act 2005 (c 9), insert the following entries at the appropriate places—

'Section 39A	Instructing independent mental capacity advocate when giving an urgent authorisation, or making a request for a standard authorisation, under Schedule A1 to the Act.'
'Section 39C	Instructing independent mental capacity advocate when no representative for relevant person under Part 10 of Schedule A1 to the Act.'
'Section 39D	Instructing independent mental capacity advocate when representative for relevant person under Part 10 of Schedule A1 to the Act is not being paid.'
'Schedule A1	Any functions.'

SCHEDULE 10
TRANSITIONAL PROVISIONS AND SAVINGS

Section 53

Interpretation

1

(1) This Schedule is to be read as follows.

(2) Reference to an enactment is to an enactment contained in this Act, unless otherwise stated.

(3) Reference to an enactment contained in the 1983 Act includes reference to that enactment as applied by section 40(4) of that Act (patients concerned in criminal proceedings or under sentence).

Authority to detain etc

2

(1) The provisions mentioned in sub-paragraph (4) do not affect—

    (a) the authority for the detention or guardianship of a person who is liable to be detained or subject to guardianship under the 1983 Act immediately before the date on which those provisions come into force,

    (b) the 1983 Act in relation to any application, order or direction for admission or removal to a hospital, or any guardianship application or order, made under that Act before that date or the exercise, before that date, of any power to remand,

    (c) the power to make on or after that date an application for the admission of a person to a hospital, or a guardianship application, where all the recommendations on which the application is to be founded are signed before that date, or

    (d) the authority for the detention or guardianship of a person in pursuance of such an application.

(2) But those provisions do apply to the following events occurring on or after that date—

    (a) any renewal of the authority for the person's detention or guardianship,

    (b) any consideration of his case by a Mental Health Review Tribunal, and

    (c) any decision about the exercise of any power to discharge him from detention or guardianship.

(3) Sub-paragraph (2)(b) is subject to paragraph 4.

(4) The provisions are—

    (a) section 1 and Schedule 1 (removal of categories of mental disorder),

    (b) section 2 (special provision for persons with learning disability),

    (c) section 3 (exclusions),

    (d) section 4 (replacement of 'treatability' and 'care' tests with appropriate treatment test),

    (e) section 5 (addition of appropriate treatment test),

    (f) section 7 (definition of 'medical treatment'), and

    (g) the repeals in Schedule 11 which are consequential on any of those sections or that Schedule.

Consent to treatment

3

(1) The amendments made by section 6 (appropriate treatment test in Part 4 of the 1983 Act) do not affect the application of a certificate under section 57(2)(b) or 58(3)(b) of the 1983 Act given before the date on which the amendments come into force.

(2) The amendments made by sections 27 and 28 (electro-convulsive therapy, etc) do not affect the application of a certificate under subsection (3) of section 58 of the 1983 Act which—

   (a) relates to electro-convulsive therapy (by virtue of regulations under subsection (1)(a) of that section), and

   (b) is given before the date on which those amendments come into force.

(3) But any certificate under section 58(3)(b) of the 1983 Act that the patient has not consented to electro-convulsive therapy ceases to apply when those amendments come into force.

Reclassification of patients

4

The amendment made by paragraph 13 of Schedule 1 and the repeal in Schedule 11 of section 66(1)(d) and (fb) of the 1983 Act (which concern a patient's right to apply to a Mental Health Review Tribunal following a report about the form of his mental disorder) do not affect any right to apply in consequence of a report furnished before the date on which the amendment and repeal come into force.

Supervised community treatment

5

Section 32 and the amendments and repeals in Schedules 3 and 11 which are consequential on that section apply to a patient who is liable to be detained under the 1983 Act immediately before the date on which that section and those amendments and repeals come into force, as they apply to a patient who becomes so liable on or after that date.

Nearest relative

6

(1) Subsections (2), (3) and (4)(b) of section 23 (extension of power to appoint acting nearest relative) do not apply to the making of an order under section 29 of the 1983 Act on or after the date on which those provisions come into force, if the application for the order was made before that date.

(2) Subsections (6) and (7) of section 24 (duration of orders appointing nearest relative) do not affect—

   (a) any order made under section 29 of the 1983 Act before the date on which those subsections come into force, or

   (b) any order made under that section on or after that date if the application for it was made before that date.

(3) But subsections (2)(a), (4) and (5) of section 24 (applications for discharge and variation) do apply in relation to an order mentioned in sub-paragraph (2)(a) or (b).

(4) Section 25 (restriction of nearest relative's right to apply to tribunal) does not apply in relation to an order mentioned in sub-paragraph (2)(a) or (b).

7

(1) If, by virtue of section 26 (civil partners) coming into force, a person ceases to be a patient's nearest relative, this does not affect—

    (a) any application to a Mental Health Review Tribunal under the 1983 Act made by that person, but not determined or withdrawn, before the date on which that section comes into force,

    (b) any notice under section 25 of that Act given by that person before that date, or

    (c) any application to a county court under section 30(1) of that Act made by that person, but not determined or withdrawn, before that date.

(2) But section 26 does apply to the determination on or after that date of any application under section 29 or 30 of the 1983 Act made before that date.

Independent mental health advocates

8

(1) Section 30—

    (a) applies to a patient who is liable to be detained under the 1983 Act immediately before the commencement date as it applies to a patient who becomes so liable on or after that date;

    (b) applies to a patient who is subject to guardianship under that Act immediately before the commencement date as it applies to a patient who becomes so subject on or after that date;

    (c) applies to a patient who is a community patient under that Act immediately before the commencement date as it applies to a patient who becomes a community patient on or after that date.

(2) For the purposes of the provisions inserted by that section, a patient is to be treated as a qualifying patient within section 130C(3) of the 1983 Act if—

    (a) not being a formal patient, he discussed before the commencement date with a registered medical practitioner or approved clinician the possibility of being given a form of treatment to which section 57 of that Act applies, and

    (b) sub-paragraph (4) or (5) applies in relation to him.

(3) A patient is also to be treated for those purposes as a qualifying patient within section 130C(3) of the 1983 Act if—

    (a) not having attained the age of 18 years and not being a formal patient, he discussed before the commencement date with a registered medical practitioner or approved clinician the possibility of being given a form of treatment to which section 58A of that Act applies, and

    (b) sub-paragraph (4) or (5) applies in relation to him.

(4) This sub-paragraph applies in relation to the patient if, immediately before the commencement date, he has yet to be informed whether or not the treatment is proposed in his case.

(5) This sub-paragraph applies in relation to the patient if, immediately before the commencement date—

    (a) he has been informed that the treatment is proposed in his case,

    (b) the proposal has not been withdrawn, and

    (c) the treatment has not been completed or discontinued.

(6) A qualifying patient in relation to whom sub-paragraph (4) applies and who is informed on or after the commencement date that the treatment is proposed in his case, or in relation to whom sub-paragraph (5) applies, remains a qualifying patient until—

    (a) the proposal is withdrawn, or

    (b) the treatment is completed or discontinued.

(7) In relation to a patient who is a qualifying patient within section 130C(3) of the 1983 Act by virtue of this paragraph, the responsible person under section 130D of that Act is to be the person with overall responsibility for the patient's case (and subsection (2)(e) of that section is to be read accordingly).

(8) Sub-paragraph (9) applies in relation to a patient—

    (a) who is a qualifying patient within section 130C(2) of the 1983 Act by virtue of being a formal patient immediately before the commencement date, or

    (b) who is a qualifying patient within section 130C(3) of that Act by virtue of this paragraph.

(9) The steps to be taken under subsection (1) of section 130D of that Act are to be taken on, or as soon as practicable after, the commencement date (and subsection (3) of that section is to be read accordingly).

(10) In this paragraph—

'approved clinician' has the same meaning as in the 1983 Act,

'the commencement date' means the date on which section 30 comes into force, and

'formal patient' means a patient who is—

    (a) liable to be detained under the 1983 Act (otherwise than by virtue of section 4, 5(2) or (4), 135 or 136 of that Act),

    (b) subject to guardianship under that Act, or

    (c) a community patient under that Act.

Applications and references to Mental Health Review Tribunal

9

(1) The amendments made by section 37 apply in relation to a patient who is liable to be detained under the 1983 Act immediately before the date on which the amendments come into force as they apply in relation to one who becomes so liable on or after that date.

(2) The repeal in paragraph 20(b) of Schedule 3 of the reference in section 69(2)(b) of the 1983 Act to section 45B(2) of that Act (which concerns the right of a patient subject to a hospital direction to apply to a Mental Health Review Tribunal in the period of six months beginning with the date of the direction) does not affect any right to apply by virtue of a hospital direction dated before the date on which the repeal comes into force.

SCHEDULE 11
REPEALS AND REVOCATIONS

Section 55

PART 1
REMOVAL OF CATEGORIES OF MENTAL DISORDER

Reference	Extent of repeal or revocation
Juries Act 1974 (c 23)	In Schedule 1, paragraph 4(1).
Mental Health Act 1983 (c 20)	In section 1(2), the definitions of--
	(a) 'severe mental impairment' and 'severely mentally impaired',
	(b) 'mental impairment' and 'mentally impaired', and
	(c) 'psychopathic disorder'.
	In section 7(2)(a), the words ', being mental illness, severe mental impairment, psychopathic disorder or mental impairment and his mental disorder is'.
	Section 11(6).
	In section 15(3), the words from '; but this subsection' to the end.
	Section 16.
	Section 20(9).
	Section 21B(8) and (9).
	In section 37--
	(a) in subsection (3), the words 'as being a person suffering from mental illness or severe mental impairment', and
	(b) subsection (7).
	In section 45A, subsections (10) and (11).
	Section 47(4).
	Section 55(3).
	In section 66(1), paragraphs (d) and (fb) (and the word 'or' at the end of those paragraphs).
	Section 72(5).
	Section 92(3).
	In Part 1 of Schedule 1--
	(a) in paragraph 2, the word '16,',
	(b) paragraph 3, and
	(c) in paragraph 6, paragraph (b) (and the word 'and' immediately preceding it).
	In Schedule 5--
	(a) in paragraph 37(5), the words from ', and he shall be so treated' to the end, and
	(b) paragraph 39.
Mental Health (Patients in the Community) Act 1995 (c 52)	In Schedule 1, paragraph 10(4).
Mental Capacity Act 2005 (c 9)	In Schedule 4, in paragraph 23(1), the words '(within the meaning of the Mental Health Act)'.
Mental Health (Care and Treatment) (Scotland) Act 2003 (Consequential (Provisions) Order 2005 (SI 2005/2078)	In Schedule 1, paragraph 2(8).

PART 2
REPLACEMENT OF 'TREATABILITY' AND 'CARE' TESTS

Reference	Extent of repeal or revocation
Mental Health Act 1983 (c 20)	In section 3(2), paragraph (b) (and the word 'and' at the end of that paragraph).
	In section 20(4)--
	(a) paragraph (b) (and the word 'and' at the end of that paragraph), and
	(b) the words from 'but, in the case of mental illness' to the end.
	Section 72(2).

PART 3
APPROVED CLINICIANS AND RESPONSIBLE CLINICIANS

Reference	Extent of repeal or revocation
Mental Health Act 1983 (c 20)	Section 20(10).
	In section 21B(10), the definition of 'appropriate medical officer'.
	In section 61(3), the words 'to the responsible medical officer'.
Health and Social Care (Community Health and Standards) Act 2003 (c 43)	In Schedule 4, paragraph 51.
Civil Partnership Act 2004 (c 33)	In Schedule 27, paragraph 86(a).
National Health Service (Consequential Provisions) Act 2006 (c 43)	In Schedule 1, paragraph 63.

PART 4
SAFEGUARDS FOR PATIENTS

Reference	Extent of repeal or revocation
Mental Health Act 1983	In section 29--
	(a) in subsection (2), the words from 'but in relation to' to the end, and
	(b) in subsection (3), the word 'or' at the end of paragraph (c).

PART 5
SUPERVISED COMMUNITY TREATMENT

Reference	Extent of repeal or revocation
Mental Health Act 1983	In section 18(4), the words from 'and, in determining' to the end.
Sections 25A to 25J.	In section 29(3)(d), the words 'from hospital or guardianship'.
	In section 32(2)(c), the words 'or to after-care under supervision'.
	In section 34--
	(a) in subsection (1), the definitions of 'the community responsible medical officer' and 'the supervisor', and

	(b) subsection (1A).
	In section 66(1)--
	(a) paragraphs (ga), (gb) and (gc) (and the word 'or' at the end of each of those paragraphs), and
	(b) in sub-paragraph (i), the words from 'or, in the cases' to the end.
	In section 66(2)--
	(a) in paragraph (d), the words 'and (gb)', and
	(b) paragraph (fa).
	In section 67(1), the words 'or to after-care under supervision'.
	In section 69(2)(b), the words '45B(2), 46(3),'.
	Section 72(4A).
	In section 76(1), the words from 'or to after-care' to 'leaves hospital'.
	Section 117(2A).
	Section 127(2A).
	In section 145--
	(a) in subsection (1), the definitions of 'the responsible after-care bodies' and 'supervision application', and
	(b) subsection (1A).
	In section 146, the words from '128' to 'guardianship'.
	In Part 1 of Schedule 1--
	(a) in paragraph 2, the words ', 25A, 25B', and
	(b) paragraph 8A.
Mental Health (Patients in the Community) Act 1995 (c 52)	Section 1(1).
	In Schedule 1--
	(a) in paragraph 2, paragraph (c) (and the word 'and' immediately preceding it),
	(b) in paragraph 11, paragraph (a) (and the word 'and' at the end of that paragraph), and
	(c) paragraphs 3, 4, 6, 7, 8(2), 10(1) to (3), 12, 13, 18 and 20.
Crime (Sentences) Act 1997 (c 43)	In Schedule 4, paragraph 12(8).
National Health Service Reform and Health Care Professions Act 2002 (c 17)	In Schedule 2, paragraphs 43 to 45.
Civil Partnership Act 2004 (c 33)	In Schedule 27, in paragraph 86, paragraph (b) (and the word 'and' immediately preceding it).

PART 6
ORGANISATION OF TRIBUNALS

Reference	Extent of repeal or revocation
Mental Health Act 1983 (c 20)	In section 78(6), the words ', if for any reason he is unable to act,'.
In section 143(2), the words 'or 65'.	In paragraph 4 of Schedule 2, the words ', if for any reason he is unable to act,'.
Health Authorities Act 1995 (c 17)	In Schedule 1, paragraph 107(13).

PART 7
CROSS-BORDER ARRANGEMENTS

Reference	Extent of repeal or revocation
Mental Health Act 1983	In section 80(1), the words 'or subject to guardianship' and the words 'or, as the case may be, for receiving him into guardianship'. In section 88(3)-- (a) the words 'to Scotland or Northern Ireland', (b) paragraph (a), and (c) in paragraph (b), the words 'in Northern Ireland,'. In section 146, the words from '88' to '138)'.
Mental Health (Care and Treatment) (Scotland) Act 2003 (Consequential Provisions) Order 2005 (SI 2005/2078)	Articles 1(5), 2 and 3. In Schedule 1, paragraph 2(5).

PART 8
RESTRICTED PATIENTS

Reference	Extent of repeal or revocation
Colonial Prisoners Removal Act 1884 (c 31)	In section 10(3)(a), the words ', made without limitation of time'.
Mental Health Act 1983	In section 41(1), the words ', either without limit of time or during such period as may be specified in the order'. In section 42(4)(b), the words from ', and, if the restriction order was made for a specified period,' to the end. In section 44(3), the words ', made without limitation of time'. In section 81(7), the words 'restriction order or' in each place, In section 81A(3)-- (a) the words 'restriction order or' in each place, and (b) the words 'order or'. In section 84(2), the words ', made without limitation of time'. In section 91(2), the words 'at any time before the end of the period for which those orders would have continued in force'.

PART 9
MISCELLANEOUS

Reference	Extent of repeal or revocation
Children Act 1989 (c 41)	In Schedule 13, paragraph 48(5).

PART 10
DEPRIVATION OF LIBERTY

Reference	Extent of repeal or revocation
Mental Capacity Act 2005 (c 9)	Section 6(5).
	Section 11(6).
	Section 20(13).

APPENDIX 4

THE STANDARD AUTHORISATION PROCEDURE
UNDER SCHDULE A1 OF THE 2005 ACT

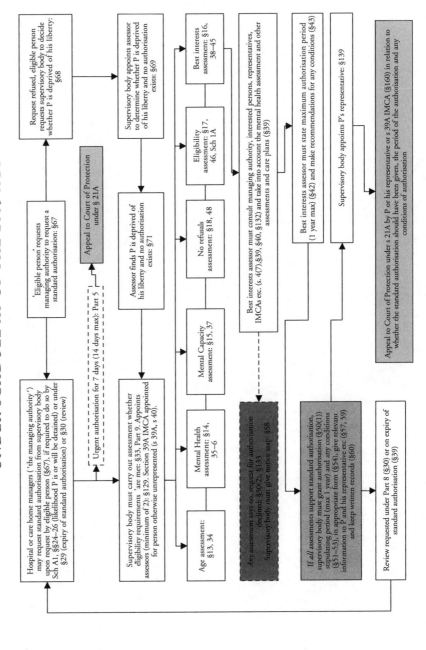

Index

Admission
  children 4.43–4.53
  codes of practice 4.01–4.11
  Commission 4.54
  fundamental principles 4.12–4.15
  IMHAs 4.33–4.42
  Mental Health Review Tribunal 4.24–4.32
  nearest relatives 4.16–4.23
'Advance decisions' to refuse treatment
  applicable treatment 10.29
  competence 10.20
  dispute resolution 10.34
  life-sustaining treatment 10.30–10.31
  nature and effect 10.21–10.26
  treatment under MHA 1983 6.51, 6.109,
    10.32–10.33
  validity 10.27–10.28
Advocates *see* **Independent Mental Capacity**
    Advocates; Independent Mental Health
    Advocates
Aftercare
  overview 2.20–2.21
  SCTs 5.79–5.81
Abnormally aggressive or seriously irresponsible
    behaviour 3.44–3.46
Appeals
  authorizations
    standard authorizations 12.89–12.90
    urgent authorizations 12.91–12.92
  jurisdiction of Court of Protection 14.11
'Appropriate treatment' test
  current criteria for guardianship and
    detention 3.14–3.18
  defined 3.71
  implications of amendments 3.93–3.100
  parliamentary opposition 3.74
  replacement of 'treatability' test 3.66–3.70
'Approved social workers' 7.18–7.21
Assessors
  appointment 12.44
  functions 12.45–12.47
  powers and duties 12.48–12.49
Authorizations
  appeals 12.89–12.90
  assessment process 12.41–12.57
  conflicts of interest 12.13
  detention for care and treatment under MCA
    2005 11.41
  human rights 12.93–12.94
  'managing authorities' 12.01–12.04, 12.12
  'qualifying requirements' 12.14–12.38

  standard authorizations
    appropriate circumstances 12.30–12.40
    grant 12.61
    procedure 12.29
    refusal 12.58–12.60
    renewal 12.81
    review 12.62–12.77
    suspension 12.79–12.80
    termination 12.78
  'supervisory bodies' 12.04–12.12
  urgent authorizations
    appointment of IMCA 12.87
    duration 12.85–12.86
    formalities 12.88
    required conditions 12.82–12.84
Autonomy
  care and treatment at common law 9.03–9.05
  children aged 16 and 17 9.36–9.39, 10.05
  children under 16 9.27–9.30

'Best interests'
  assessment process 12.51–12.55
  care and treatment without detention under
    MCA 2005
  children 9.25
  at common law 9.13–9.18
  standard and urgent authorizations under MCA
    2005 12.20–12.24
Bodily integrity 9.03–9.05
***Bournewood* patients**
  application before ECtHR
    Art.5(4) 11.19–11.20
    'deprivation of liberty' 11.14
    procedural defects 11.15–11.18
  facts of case 11.04–11.07
  history
    jurisprudence 8.17–8.21
    Schedule A1 amendments 8.22
  House of Lords decision 11.09–11.12
  judicial review and *habeas corpus* 11.08
  overview of case 11.01–11.03

Capacity
  care and treatment without detention 10.11–10.14
  at common law 9.06–9.09
  litigation friends 14.67–14.72
  standard and urgent authorizations 12.18
Care and treatment
  at common law
    'best interests' 9.13–9.18
    bodily integrity and autonomy 9.03–9.05

Care and treatment (*cont.*)
at common law (*cont.*)
Bournewood patients 11.01–11.12
capacity and incapacity 9.06–9.09
children 9.25–9.39
importance 9.01–9.02
inherent jurisdiction 9.19–9.24
necessity 9.10–9.12
detention for care and treatment under MCA 2005
amendments under MHA 2007 11.38–11.39
children 11.49–11.57
Court of Protection role 11.45–11.48
'deprivation of liberty' 11.21–11.34
emergency treatment 11.58–11.61
life-sustaining treatment 11.42–11.44
prior to statutory amendment 11.35–11.37
standard and urgent
authorizations 11.40–11.41
without detention under MCA 2005
'advance decisions' to refuse
treatment 10.20–10.34
applicability 10.01
'best interests' 10.15–10.17
capacity 10.11–10.14
children aged 16 or 17 10.03–10.06
children under 16 10.07–10.09
codes of practice 10.89–10.93
court-appointed deputies 10.57–10.58
deprivations of liberty 10.69
excluded decisions 10.70–10.75
hierarchy of decision-making 10.18–10.19
ill-treatment or neglect 10.76–10.77
independent mental health advocates
(IMHAs) 10.78–10.88
lasting powers of attorney 10.35–10.53
life-sustaining treatment 10.61–10.65
necessity 10.59–10.60
personal welfare decisions by Court of
Protection 10.54–10.56
restraint and use of force 10.66–10.68
statutory principles 10.10
Children
additional safeguards for ECT 6.53–6.56
additional safeguards under MHA 1953
consent 4.44
referrals to MHRT 4.53
specialist facilities 4.50–4.52
suitable environment 4.45–4.49
care and treatment at common law
aged 16 and 17 9.36–9.38
under 16 9.25–9.35
care and treatment without detention under
MCA 2005
aged 16 or 17 10.03–10.06
under 16 10.07–10.09
detention for care and treatment under MCA 2005
aged 16 or 17 11.50–11.54
overview 11.49

under 16 11.55–11.57
High Court jurisdiction 9.31–9.35
interface between legislation and common law
aged 16 or 17 15.58–15.73
under 16 15.74–15.76
litigation friends 14.71–14.72
overview 2.25–2.28
Codes of practice
care and treatment without detention under
MCA 2005
duty to have regard for 10.92
duty to prepare 10.89–10.91
relevance to proceedings 10.93
Mental Health Act 1983
additional safeguards for admission and
detention 4.01–4.11
overview 2.22–2.23
Commission, Mental Health Act
additional safeguards under MHA 1953 4.54
overview 2.24
Common law
Bournewood patients 11.01–11.12
care and treatment
'best interests' 9.13–9.18
bodily integrity and autonomy 9.03–9.05
capacity and incapacity 9.06–9.09
children 9.25–9.39
importance 9.01–9.02
inherent jurisdiction 9.19–9.24
necessity 9.10–9.12
interface with legislation
children aged 16 or 17 15.58–15.73
children under 16 15.74–15.76
detention 15.02–15.24
overview 15.01
physical disorders 15.47–15.49
treatment 15.26–15.46
urgent authorizations 15.50–15.57
Community treatment orders (CTOs)
admission for treatment ceasing to have
effect 5.55–5.58
aftercare 5.79–5.81
background 5.01–5.06
conditions under s 17B 5.33–5.37
discharge by clinician 5.45–5.46
discharge by Tribunal 5.47–5.54
duration 5.42–5.44
effects under s 17D 5.38–5.41
effects under s 20B(1) 5.59
existing forms compared 5.07–5.22
human rights 5.83–5.93
'medical treatment' for recalled
patients 6.108–6.116
'medical treatment' under Pt 4A MHA
1983 6.58–6.107
orders under s 17A 5.23–5.32
overview 2.06–2.07
recall of patients 5.60–5.65

Community treatment orders (CTOs) (*cont.*)
  return of patients absent without leave 5.70–5.78
  revocation 5.66–5.69
Conditional discharge of patients 4.32
Conflicts of interest
  authorizations under MCA 2005 12.13
  extension of professional
     responsibilities 7.22–7.23
Consent
  admission and detention of children 4.44
  amendments to Pt 4 6.40
  summary of existing legal framework 6.19
Consultees
  appointment 13.37
  functions 13.38
  statutory provisions 13.35–13.38
Costs
  public funding 14.21–14.24
Court of Protection
  authorization appeals 12.89–12.90
  court-appointed deputies 10.57–10.58
  detention for care and treatment 11.45–11.48
  jurisdiction
     advance decisions 14.07
     appeals 14.11
     appointment of deputies 14.10
     declarations 14.05–14.06
     interim orders and directions 14.12–14.13
     lasting powers of attorney 14.08
     overview 14.02–14.04
     personal welfare decisions 14.09
     restrictions and limitations 14.14–14.19
  lasting powers of attorney 10.50–10.53
  new status 14.01
  personal welfare decisions
     jurisdiction 10.54–10.55
     limitations 10.56
  procedure
     applications 14.25–14.66
     litigation friends 14.67–14.72
     public funding 14.21–14.24
  Public Guardian 14.73–14.74
  Visitors 14.75
Criminal proceedings 7.25–7.29

'Deprivation of liberty' under Art 5(1)
  and the MCA 2005 11.21–11.22
  Bournewood case 11.14
  interface between legislation and common
     law 15.06–15.24
  jurisdiction of Court of Protection 14.14
  necessary elements 11.23–11.27
  private care homes 11.33–11.34
  relevant factors 11.28–11.32
Detention
  additional safeguards under MHA 1953
     codes of practice 4.01–4.11
     Commission 4.54

  fundamental principles 4.12–4.15
  IMHAs 4.33–4.42
  Mental Health Review Tribunal 4.24–4.32
  nearest relatives 4.16–4.23
  Bournewood patients 11.01–11.12
  care and treatment under MCA 2005
     amendments under MHA 2007 11.38–11.39
     children 11.49–11.57
     Court of Protection role 11.45–11.48
     'deprivation of liberty' 11.21–11.34
     emergency treatment 11.58–11.61
     life-sustaining treatment 11.42–11.44
     prior to statutory amendment 11.35–11.37
     standard and urgent
        authorizations 11.40–11.41
  care and treatment without detention under
     MCA 2005 10.69
  current criteria under MHA 1983 3.01–3.3–28
  current definition of 'mental disorder' 3.29–3.48
  current 'treatability' requirement 3.49–3.57
  extension of professional
     responsibilities 7.06–7.17
  human rights 1.39
  implications of amendments
     charter for preventive detention 3.105–3.108
     failure to adopt 'impaired judgment'
        test 3.109–3.112
     global effects 3.101–3.104
     learning disabilities 3.92
     'mental disorder' test 3.77–3.87
     public concern 3.75–3.76
     removal of sexual deviancy 3.88–3.91
     'treatability' and 'appropriate treatment'
        tests 3.93–3.100
  interface between legislation and common law
     physical disorders 15.47–15.49
     treatment for mental disorder 15.02–15.24
  new 'appropriate treatment' test 3.66–3.71
  new definition of 'mental disorder' 3.58–3.61
  new 'treatability' test 3.72
  origins of mental health law 1.20–1.22
  overview 2.04–2.05
  persons with 'learning disabilities' 3.63–3.65
  in place of safety 7.33
  representation under MCA 2005
     consultees 13.35–13.38
     donees and deputies 13.29–13.34
     provisions under s 39A 13.01–13.07
     provisions under s 39C 13.20–13.23
     provisions under s 39D 13.24–13.28
     Pt 10 representatives 13.07–13.19
Discharge of patients
  CTOs
     by clinician 5.45–5.46
     by Tribunal 5.47–5.54
  hospital managers 7.22–7.23
  overview 2.15–2.16
  supervised discharge 5.12–5.17

Electro-convulsive therapy (ECT) 6.12–6.15
    additional safeguards 6.42–6.57
Emergency treatment
    additional safeguards for ECT 6.57
    detention for care and treatment under MCA
        2005 11.58–11.61
    summary of existing legal framework 6.16–6.17
Exploitation
    current criteria for guardianship and
        detention 3.27–3.28

Family *see* Relatives
Force *see* Use of force

Guardianship
    current criteria under MHA 1983 3.01–3.3–28
    current definition of 'mental disorder' 3.29–3.48
    current 'treatability' requirement 3.49–3.57
    MHA 1983
        overview 2.11–2.12
    new 'appropriate treatment' test 3.66–3.71
    new definition of 'mental disorder' 3.58–3.61
    new 'treatability' test 3.72
    persons with 'learning disabilities' 3.63–3.65
    SCT compared 5.19–5.22

Hospital managers
    child referrals to MHRT 4.53
    discharge powers 7.22–7.23
    referrals to MHRT 4.28–4.31
    withholding correspondence 4.42
Human rights
    Bournewood case
        Art.5(4) 11.19–11.20
        'deprivation of liberty' 11.14
        procedural defects 11.15–11.18
    compatibility of MHA 2007 1.48
    Convention rights 1.38–1.39
    domestic incorporation 1.44
    implied procedural obligations 1.41
    international standards 1.42
    Joint Parliamentary Committee 1.45–1.47
    'medical treatment' under MHA 1983
        6.120–6.140
    positive and negative obligations 1.40
    Recommendation No Rec (2004) 10 1.43
    SCTs 5.83–5.93
    standard and urgent authorizations 12.93
    swing in favour of legalism 1.27–1.29

Ill-treatment of patients
    care and treatment without detention under
        MCA 2005 10.76–10.77
    MHA 1983 7.31
Immoral conduct *see* Promiscuity or immoral
        conduct
Impairment
    current definition of mental disorder
        3.38–3.39

'impaired judgment' test 3.109–3.112
Imprisonment
    admission for treatment ceasing to have effect
        5.56–5.57
Incapacity *see* Capacity
Independent Mental Capacity Advocates (IMCAs)
    generally s 39A IMCAs 13.01–13.06
    provisions under s 39C IMCAs 13.20–13.23
    provisions under s 39D IMCAs 13.24–13.28
    urgent authorizations 12.87
Independent mental health advocates (IMHAs)
    appointment 4.34–4.36
    background 4.33
    duties 4.37
    functions 4.38–4.41, 10.86–10.88
    statutory rights 10.78
    withholding correspondence 4.42
Informal admission, generally 2.03
    children 4.44, 11.50
Inherent jurisdiction 9.19–9.24
Interface between MHA 1983, MCA 2005, and
        common law
    children aged 16 15.74–15.76
    children aged 16 or 17 15.58–15.73
    detention 15.02–15.24
    medical treatment for mental
        disorder 15.26–15.46
    physical disorders 15.47–15.49
    urgent cases 15.50–15.57
Interim orders and directions 14.12–14.13
Irresponsible behaviour *see* Aggressive or
        irresponsible behaviour
Irreversible treatment 6.10–6.11

Lasting powers of attorney
    donee's powers 10.38–10.42
    formalities 10.44–10.47
    jurisdiction of Court of Protection
        10.50–10.53, 14.08
    limitations 10.43
    nature and effect 10.35–10.37
    representation of Sch A1 detainees under
        MCA 2005 13.29–13.34
    revocation 10.48–10.49
Learning disabilities
    implications of amendments 3.92
    new exceptions 3.63–3.64
Legal aid 14.21–14.24
Legalism
    human rights influence 1.27–1.29
    Lunacy Act 1890 1.23–1.25
Life-sustaining treatment
    acts intended to end life 10.62–10.65
    'advance directives' to refuse
        treatment 10.30–10.33
    detention for care and treatment under MCA
        2005 11.42–11.44
    special status 10.61
Litigation friends 14.67–14.72

Managers *see* **Hospital managers**
'**Managing authorities**' 12.01–12.04, 12.12
'**Medical treatment**' **for mental disorder**
  additional safeguards for ECT 6.42–6.57
  'advance directives' to refuse
    treatment 10.32–10.33
  amendments to Pt 4 1983 Act 6.21–6.41
  common law, at 9.01–9.36
  community patients under Pt 4A MHA
    1983 6.58–6.90
    'authority to treat' 6.71–6.89
    background 6.58–6.63
    Certificate requirements 6.90–6.107
    children 6.67–6.69
    conditions 6.66
    overview of new procedure 6.64–6.65
    relevant treatment 6.70
  human rights 6.120–6.140
  interface with MCA 2005 6.117–6.119
  new test 3.72–3.73
  recalled community patients 6.108–6.116
  existing framework under Pt 4 1983
    Act 6.01–6.20
Mental Capacity Act 2005
  authorizations
    appeals 12.89–12.92
    assessment process 12.41–12.57
    conflicts of interest 12.13
    grant of standard authorization 12.61
    human rights 12.93–12.94
    'managing authorities' 12.01–12.04, 12.12
    'qualifying requirements' 12.14–12.38
    refusal of standard authorization 12.58–12.60
    renewal of standard authorization 12.81
    review of standard authorization 12.62–12.77
    standard authorizations 12.29–12.40
    'supervisory bodies' 12.04–12.12
    suspension of standard
      authorization 12.79–12.80
    termination of standard authorization 12.78
    urgent authorizations 12.82–12.88
  care and treatment without detention
    'advance decisions' to refuse
      treatment 10.20–10.34
    applicability 10.01
    'best interests' 10.15–10.17
    capacity 10.11–10.14
    children aged 16 or 17 10.03–10.06
    children under 16 10.07–10.09
    codes of practice 10.89–10.93
    court-appointed deputies 10.57–10.58
    deprivations of liberty 10.69
    excluded decisions 10.70–10.75
    hierarchy of decision-making 10.18–10.19
    ill-treatment or neglect 10.76–10.77
    independent mental health advocates
      (IMHAs) 10.78–10.88
    lasting powers of attorney 10.35–10.53
    life-sustaining treatment 10.61–10.65

    necessity 10.59–10.60
    personal welfare decisions by Court of
      Protection 10.54–10.56
    restraint and use of force 10.66–10.68
    statutory principles 10.10
  detention for care and treatment
    amendments under MHA 2007 11.38–11.39
    children 11.49–11.57
    Court of Protection role 11.45–11.48
    'deprivation of liberty' 11.21–11.34
    emergency treatment 11.58–11.61
    life-sustaining treatment 11.42–11.44
    prior to statutory amendment 11.35–11.37
    standard and urgent authorizations
      11.40–11.41
  full text App 2
  history
    Bournewood patients 8.17–8.21
    earlier legislation 8.05–8.09
    government proposals 8.14
    need for reform 8.10–8.13
    Schedule A1 amendments 8.22
  interface with MHA 1983 6.117–6.119, 8.23
  interface with other legislation and common law
    children aged 16 or 17 15.58–15.73
    children under 16 15.74–15.76
    detention 15.02–15.24
    medical treatment for mental
      disorder 15.26–15.46
    overview 15.01
    physical disorders 15.47–15.49
    urgent authorizations 15.50–15.57
  overview 1.03, 8.01–8.04
  structure of Act 8.15–8.16
'**Mental disorder**'
  current definition
    aggressive or irresponsible
      behaviour 3.44–3.46
    exclusions 3.47–3.48
    four classifications 3.30–3.37
    impairment 3.38–3.39
    psychopathic disorder 3.38–3.39
  current test 3.06–3.13
  implications of amendments 3.77–3.87
  interface between legislation and common law
    detention 15.02–15.24
    treatment 15.26–15.46
  new definition
    removal of classifications 3.61
    removal of promiscuity provisions 3.62
    wider definition 3.59–3.60
  overview 2.10
Mental Health Act 1983
  additional safeguards for admission and detention
    children 4.43–4.53
    codes of practice 4.01–4.11
    Commission 4.54
    fundamental principles 4.12–4.15
    IMHAs 4.33–4.42

Mental Health Act 1983 (*cont.*)
additional safeguards for admission and detention
(*cont.*)
Mental Health Review Tribunal 4.24–4.32
nearest relatives 4.16–4.23
current criteria for guardianship and
detention 3.01–3.28
current definition of 'mental disorder' 3.29–3.48
current 'treatability' requirement 3.49–3.57
detention in place of safety 7.33
extension of professional responsibilities
'approved social workers' 7.18–7.21
conflicts of interest 7.22–7.23
discharge by hospital managers 7.24
key policy objective 7.01
recommendations for detention 7.06–7.17
'responsible clinicians' 7.023–7.025
full text App 1
ill-treatment of patients 7.31
implications of amendments
charter for preventive detention 3.105–3.108
failure to adopt 'impaired judgment'
test 3.109–3.112
global effects 3.101–3.104
learning disabilities 3.92
'mental disorder' test 3.77–3.87
public concern 3.75–3.76
removal of sexual deviancy 3.88–3.91
'treatability' and 'appropriate treatment'
tests 3.93–3.100
interface with MCA 2005 8.23
interface with other legislation and common law
children aged 16 or 17 15.58–15.73
children under 16 15.74–15.76
detention 15.02–15.24
overview 15.01
physical disorders 15.47–15.49
medical treatment for mental
disorder 15.26–15.46
urgent authorizations 15.50–15.57
medical treatment for mental disorder
additional safeguards for ECT 6.42–6.57
amendments to Pt 4 6.21–6.41
community patients under Pt 4A 1983
Act 6.58–6.107
human rights 6.120–6.140
interface with MCA 2005 6.117–6.119
recalled community patients 6.108–6.116
summary of existing legal
framework 6.01–6.20
new 'appropriate treatment' test 3.66–3.71
new definition of 'mental disorder' 3.58–3.61
new 'treatability' test 3.72
overview of the 1983 Act and its
amendments 1.02
aftercare 2.20–2.21
children 2.25–2.28
codes of practice 2.22–2.23

Commission, Mental Health Act 2.24
community patients 2.06–2.07
detention 2.04–2.05
discharge of patients 2.15–2.16
framework 2.01–2.02
guardianship 2.11–2.12
informal admission 2.03
mental disorder 2.10
Mental Health Review Tribunal 2.17–2.19
nearest relatives 2.08–2.09
treatment 2.13–2.14
patients facing imprisonment 7.25–7.30
persons with 'learning disabilities' 3.63–3.65
supervised community treatment
admission for treatment ceasing to have
effect 5.55–5.58
aftercare 5.79–5.81
background 5.01–5.06
conditions under s 17B 5.33–5.37
discharge by clinician 5.45–5.46
discharge by Tribunal 5.47–5.54
duration 5.42–5.44
effects under s 17D 5.38–5.41
effects under s 20B(1) 5.59
existing forms compared 5.07–5.22
human rights 5.83–5.93
orders under s 17A 5.23–5.32
recall of patients 5.60–5.65
return of patients absent without
leave 5.70–5.78
revocation 5.66–5.69
transfer of patients to and from Scotland 7.32
victims rights 7.34–7.39
Mental Health Act 2007
background 1.04–1.16
commencement and transnational
provisions 1.49–1.51
compatability with human rights 1.48
full text App 3
interface with other legislation and
common law
children aged 16 or 17 15.58–15.73
children under 16 15.74–15.76
detention 15.02–15.24
overview 15.01
physical disorders 15.47–15.49
treatment 15.26–15.46
overview of amendments to 2005 Act 1.03
urgent authorizations 15.50–15.57
overview of amendments to 1983 Act 1.02
overview of amendments to 2005 Act 1.03
swing towards informalism 1.34–1.37
territorial extent 1.52
Mental Health Review Tribunal
conditional discharges and limited detentions 4.32
discharge of CTOs 5.47–5.54
Mental Health Act 1983
overview 2.17–2.19

Mental Health Review Tribunal (*cont.*)
referrals from hospital managers 4.28–4.31
reorganization 4.27
statutory provisions 4.24–4.26
Nearest relatives
amendments in MHA 2007 4.20–4.23
flaws in current law 4.17–4.19
overview 2.08–2.09
role 4.16
Necessity
care and treatment without detention under
MCA 2005 10.59–10.60
at common law 9.10–9.12
Neglect
care and treatment without detention under
MCA 2005 10.76–10.77

Personal welfare decisions
care and treatment without detention under
MCA 2005 10.54–10.56
jurisdiction of Court of Protection 14.09
limitations 10.56
Powers of attorney *see* **Lasting
powers of attorney**
Promiscuity or immoral conduct
current exclusion from mental
disorder 3.47–3.48
implications of amendments 3.88–3.91
removal from new definition of mental
disorder 3.62
'Psychopathic disorder'
current definition of mental disorder 3.38–3.39
Pt 4A 1983 Act 6.58–6.111
Pt 10 representatives 13.07–13.19
Public funding 14.21–14.24
Public Guardian 14.73–14.74

Recalled community patients
admission for treatment ceasing to have
effect 5.58
criteria 5.60–5.62
effect 5.63–5.65
'medical treatment' under MHA
1983 6.108–6.116
return of patients absent without
leave 5.70–5.78
Representation of Sch A1 detainees
consultees 13.35–13.38
donees and deputies 13.29–13.34
IMCAs
s 39A IMCAs 13.01–13.07
s 39C IMCAs 13.20–13.23
s 39D IMCAs 13.24–13.28
Pt 10 representatives 13.07–13.19
Research studies 10.75
'Responsible clinicians'
extension of professional
responsibilities 7.023–7.025

'medical treatment' 6.34–6.36
Restraint
MCA 2005 10.66–10.68
'Safety' test
current criteria for guardianship and
detention 3.22–3.26
Sch A1 'deprivation of liberty' safeguards
11.38–11.41, 12.93
Scotland
transfer of patients to and from 7.32
Self-neglect
current criteria for guardianship and
detention 3.27–3.28
Sexual deviancy
current exclusion from mental
disorder 3.47–3.48
implications of amendments 3.88–3.91
removal from new definition of mental
disorder 3.62
Social workers *see* **Approved social workers**
Standard authorizations
appeals 12.89–12.90
appropriate circumstances 12.30–12.40
assessment process 12.41–12.57
conflicts of interest 12.13
detention for care and treatment under MCA
2005 11.40
grant 12.61
'managing authorities' 12.01–12.04, 12.12
procedure 12.29
'qualifying requirements' 12.14–12.38
refusal 12.58–12.60
renewal 12.81
review 12.62–12.77
'supervisory bodies' 12.04–12.12
suspension 12.79–12.80
termination 12.78
Supervised community treatment (SCT)
admission for treatment ceasing to have
effect 5.55–5.58
aftercare 5.79–5.81
background 5.01–5.06
conditions under s 17B 5.33–5.37
discharge by clinician 5.45–5.46
discharge by Tribunal 5.47–5.54
duration 5.42–5.44
effects under s 17D 5.38–5.41
effects under s 20B(1) 5.59
existing forms of community treatment
compared 5.07–5.22
human rights 5.83–5.93
'medical treatment' under Pt 4A MHA 1983
'authority to treat' 6.71–6.89
background 6.58–6.63
Certificate requirements 6.90–6.107
children 6.67–6.69
conditions 6.66
overview of new procedure 6.64–6.65

Supervised community treatment (SCT) (*cont.*)
'medical treatment' under Pt 4A MHA
1983 (*cont.*)
recalled patients 6.108–6.116
relevant treatment 6.70
orders under s 17A 5.23–5.32
recall of patients 5.60–5.65
return of patients absent without leave 5.70–5.78
revocation 5.66–5.69
Supervised discharge 5.12–5.17
'Supervisory bodies' 12.04–12.12

'Treatability' test
amendments to Pt 4 6.21–6.33
current criteria for guardianship and
detention 3.19–3.21
current requirements
background 3.51–3.52
definitions 3.54–3.56
impetus for change 3.57
importation into test for discharge 3.53
overview 3.49–3.50
implications of amendments 3.93–3.100
replacement with 'appropriate treatment'
test 3.66–3.70

summary of existing legal framework 6.01–6.20
Tribunals *see* **Mental Health Review Tribunal**

Urgent authorizations
appeals 12.91–12.92
appointment of IMCA 12.87
assessment process 12.41–12.57
conflicts of interest 12.13
detention for care and treatment under MCA
2005 11.41
duration 12.85–12.86
interface between legislation and common law
15.50–15.57
'managing authorities' 12.01–12.04 12.12
'qualifying requirements' 12.14–12.38
required conditions 12.82–12.84
'supervisory bodies' 12.04–12.12
Use of force
MCA 2005 10.66

Victims rights 7.34–7.39
Voting 10.74